Human Rights and Corporations

The International Library of Essays on Rights

Series Editor: Tom Campbell

Titles in the Series:

Human Rights and Corporations

Edited by

David Kinley

Professor of Human Rights Law, Faculty of Law,
University of Sydney, Australia

ASHGATE

Published by
Ashgate Publishing Ltd
Wey Court East
Union Road
Farnham
Surrey GU9 7PT
England

Ashgate Publishing Company
Suite 420
101 Cherry Street
Burlington, VT 05401-4405
USA

Ashgate website: http://www.ashgate.com

British Library Cataloguing in Publication Data
Human rights and corporations. – (The international library
     of essays on rights)
     1. Human rights. 2. Social responsibility of business
     3. International business enterprises – law and legislation
     I. Kinley, David, lecturer in law
     342'.085

Library of Congress Cataloging-in-Publication Data
Human rights and corporations / edited by David Kinley.
     p. cm. – (International library of essays on rights)
     Includes index.
     1. Human rights. 2. Social responsibility of business. 3. International business enterprises–Law and legislation. I. Kinley, David, lecturer in law. II. Series.

K3240.H8483 2008
341.4'8–dc22

                                                                      2008003791

ISBN: 978-0-7546-2742-5

Mixed Sources
Product group from well-managed
forests and other controlled sources
www.fsc.org Cert no. SGS-COC-2482
© 1996 Forest Stewardship Council
FSC

Printed and bound in Great Britain by
TJ International Ltd, Padstow, Cornwall.

Contents

Acknowledgements

For assistance in the preparation of this volume, their comments, suggestions and identification of editorial infelicities, I would like to thank Odette Murray, Justine Nolan and Vanessa Zimmerman.

The editor and publishers wish to thank the following for permission to use copyright material.

Blackwell Publishing for the essay: Peter T. Muchlinski (2001), 'Human Rights and Multinationals: Is There a Problem?', *International Affairs*, **77**, pp. 31–47. Copyright © 2001 Blackwell publishing Ltd;

Boston College Law School for the essay: Dinah Shelton (2002), 'Protecting Human Rights in a Globalized World', *Boston College International & Comparative Law Review*, **25**, pp. 273–322. Copyright © 2002 Boston College Law School.

Cambridge University Press for the essay: Christine Parker (2007) 'Meta-Regulation: Legal Accountability for Corporate Social Responsibility', in Doreen McBarnet, Aurora Voiculescu and Tom Campbell (eds), *The New Corporate Accountability: Corporate Social Responsibility and the Law*, Cambridge: Cambridge University Press, pp. 207–37. Copyright © 2007 Cambridge University Press.

Surya Deva (2004), 'The *Sangam* of Foreign Investment, Multinational Corporations and Human Rights: An Indian Perspective for a Developing Asia', *Singapore Journal of Legal Studies*, pp. 305–27. Copyright © 2004 Surya Deva, originally published by The Singapore Journal of Legal Studies.

The Johns Hopkins University Press for the essay: Mahmood Monshipouri, Claude E. Welch, Jr and Evan T. Kennedy (2003), 'Multinational Corporations and the Ethics of Global Responsibility: Problems and Possibilities', *Human Rights Quarterly*, **25**, pp. 965–89. Copyright © 2003 The Johns Hopkins University Press.

Oxford University Press for the essays: Christopher McCrudden (1999), 'Human Rights Codes for Transnational Corporations: What Can the Sullivan and MacBride Principles Tell Us?', *Oxford Journal of Legal Studies*, **19**, pp. 167–201. Copyright © 1999 Oxford University Press; David Kinley and Rachel Chambers (2006), 'The UN Human Rights Norms for Corporations: The Private Implications of Public International Law', *Human Rights Law Review*, **6**, pp. 447–97. Copyright © 2006 David Kinley and Rachel Chambers, published by Oxford University Press; Harold Hongju Koh (2004), 'Separating Myth From Reality About Corporate Responsibility Litigation', *Journal of International Economic Law*, 7, pp. 263–74. Copyright © 2004 Oxford University Press.

Series Preface

Much of contemporary moral, political and legal discourse is conducted in terms of rights and increasingly in terms of human rights. Yet there is considerable disagreement about the nature of rights, their foundations and their practical implications and more concrete controversies as to the content, scope and force and particular rights. Consequently the discourse of rights calls for extensive analysis in its general meaning and significance, particularly in relation to the nature, location of content of the duties and responsibilities that correlate with rights. Equally important is the determination of the forms of argument that are appropriate to establish whether or not someone or some group has or has not a particular right, and what that might entail in practice.

This series brings together essays that exhibit careful analysis of the concept of rights and detailed knowledge of specific rights and the variety of systems of rights articulation, interpretation, protection and enforcement. Volumes deal with general philosophical and practical issues about different sorts of rights, taking account of international human rights, regional rights conventions and regimes, and domestic bills of rights, as well as the moral and political literature concerning the articulation and implementation of rights.

The volumes are intended to assist those engaged in scholarly research by making available the most important and enduring essays on particular topics. Essays are reproduced in full with the original pagination for ease of reference and citation.

The editors are selected for their eminence in the study of law, politics and philosophy. Each volume represents the editor's selection of the most seminal recent essays in English on an aspect of rights or on rights in a particular field. An introduction presents an overview of the issues in that particular area of rights together with comments on the background and significance of the selected essays.

TOM CAMPBELL
Series Editor
Professorial Fellow, The Centre for Applied Philosophy and Public Ethics (CAPPE),
Charles Sturt University, Canberra

Introduction

The relationship between corporations and human rights that is portrayed in the essays in this collection is essentially one concerned with the social implications of commercial enterprise. How best can we harness the undoubted benefits that flow from a vibrant and bountiful economy, while at the same time regulating such vibrancy when it forgets or dismisses the plight of the human beings its enterprise affects, and insisting on some degree of justice in the sharing of the bounty? This is not a new idea. For as long as there have been entities that trade and do business, whether incorporated or not, societal demands have been variously made of them to give as well as take. The key question is, and always has been, how to define and delimit the balance between giving and taking, both in economic and social terms.

One answer to this question is that, within the prevailing world of a free-market economy, in which corporations are 'kings', the market will itself provide, and interfering (or at least interfering too much) with the market for social ends will probably kill the free-range goose that lays the golden economic egg. According to Adam Smith, untrammelled self-interest in commerce will deliver satisfaction not only to the merchant and to those with whom he trades, but also, thereby, through a multiplicity of such transactions, to society at large:

> It is not from the benevolence of the butcher, the brewer, or the baker, that we expect our dinner, but from their regard to their own interest. We address ourselves, not to their humanity but to their self-love, and never talk to them of our own necessities but of their advantages. ([1776] 1976, pp. 26–27; I.ii.2)

No less famously, and somewhat more pithily, Milton Friedman argued the same point when he proclaimed that:

> . . . there is only one social responsibility of business – to use its resources to engage in activities designed to increase its profits so long as it stays within the rules of the game, which is to say, engages in open and free competition, without deception or fraud. (1970, p. 32)

But, of course, not everyone believes in the power of the market to deliver what it promises. The answer, then, for such sceptics is not to reject or deny the market altogether, but rather to build on Friedman's important qualification, by, in effect, asking what other rules of the game should there be beyond anti-trust and anti-corruption laws? Should there not also be anti-discrimination, and anti-pollution laws, as well as laws that protect people from infringements of privacy, bodily integrity, free association, movement or speech, or from degradations of their standards of living, health and education? In short, should the rules of the game not also protect certain basic standards of human existence, certain human rights that would, could and are sometimes compromised by corporations in their pursuit of profits?

The concern to dull the sharper corners of capitalism by insisting upon recognition by corporations of their social – and increasingly human rights – responsibilities has grown especially quickly over the last 30 years.[1] There are a host of interrelated reasons for this, all of which, to some degree or other, revolve around the capacity and impact of globalization in the broadest sense of the term – encompassing not only (i) the rapid expansion over this period of the global economy and the multiplication of trade and commercial relations, but also growth in the instance, importance, impact and appeal of universal human rights standards, especially in the form of international law, as well as the extraordinary capacity for information exchange, personal and professional interconnection, and coalition-building on a global scale that is facilitated by the Internet. The combination of these three dimensions of globalization has produced a potent mix of conspicuous corporate success alongside the setting of international human rights standards, which has resulted, very largely through the efforts of civil society, in the elevated expectations that corporations, as well as states, have some level of responsibility to meet those standards.

The essays in this volume are all, in their diversity of approaches taken and arguments made, concerned with stipulating what is, should be, and might yet be the nature of the relationship between corporations and human rights. By the very character of such a project as this *International Library of Essays* – with its necessarily limited space, unavoidably biased single-editorship and the (understandable) stipulation that the essays should be drawn almost exclusively from journal publications (rather than edited books or even chapters in monographs) – the yield will inevitably strike some as incomplete, eclectic or even wrong-headed, and others as simply 'rudely stamp'd'.[2] I am not seeking to be spared such criticisms, but wish to make it plain that I was, throughout the selection process, intensely aware of my predicament and took what I considered to be the most prudent course of action to minimize such distortions in the final product.

Thus, let me explain my approach. At the broadest level my guiding principle in choosing the essays has been to opt for good-quality pieces that together provide coverage of all the major issues, initiatives and debates that this topic encompasses. I have sought such coverage while paying heed to the authors' temporal, geographical, professional and institutional perspectives, trying to assemble different, and sometimes opposing, positions, as well as non-legal as well as legal angles; and also to give preference to those essays whose treatment of issues will most likely have ongoing significance, rather than those – even if significant – that deal only or largely with specific and time-bound matters (for example, the many essays that focus on litigation under the Alien Torts Claims Act or on *forum non conveniens*).[3] And, in any case, it should be noted that these particular matters are in fact liberally addressed in a number of the essays selected (for example, in those by Stephens, Ratner, Kinley and Chambers, Koh and Ward). Some preference has also been given to more recent pieces (that is, relatively speaking, in what is still a very youthful genre),[4] not only for the reason of their currency,

---

[1]   As evidenced, for example, by the exponential growth of the *Business and Human Rights Resource Centre*, a comprehensive and contemporaneous web-based compendium of all matters pertaining to the interrelations between business and human rights, available at: http://www.business-humanrights.org/Home. See also the collected essays in Dine and Fagan (2006).

[2]   As Shakespeare had Richard III declaim on his own deformities (*Richard III*, Act I, Scene I, Line 16).

[3]   And beyond essays, whole books; see for example: Joseph (2004).

[4]   Though in its 'second wave', as Olivier de Schutter puts it, in 'The Challenge of Imposing Human Rights Norms on Corporate Actors' in de Schutter (2006, p. 9). The charting of the origins of the

but also because of their reliable capture and citation of earlier seminal works for their own purposes and thereby to the benefit of the readership.

In terms of organization of the volume, I grouped the essays in three parts reflecting three broad themes: Part I – Framing the relationship between human rights and corporations; Part II – Conceptual perspectives of the relationship; Part III – The practice, problems and potential of the relationship.

Framing the relationship

Together, the six pieces in Part I establish the nature and parameters of the perceived problem of corporations and human rights, analyse the problem from an edifying array of angles, and place the problem within the context of possible 'solutions'. In the light of what he sees as the mounting pressure for greater corporate accountability, Peter Muchlinski (Chapter 1) quite properly poses the twin basal questions of whether there is indeed a major problem of human rights abuse by corporations on the international stage and, if so, how, legally, is it to be addressed. While cautioning against tarring all multinational corporations with the same brush, Muchlinski concludes that abuses do indeed occur and that although states may and should remain the primary bearers of responsibility for reining in abusive corporations at international law, there should be soft and hard law mechanisms which address corporations directly. Importantly, his perspective as a corporate law specialist, such legal regulation is technically possible. The devil is, however, as he concludes, in the deficiency of political will rather than the detail of legal technicalities.

Beth Stephens (Chapter 2) delves deeper into the nature of abuse by corporations in her analysis of the political, moral legal, dimensions of corporate transgressions of human rights. In particular, she focuses on the thorny problem of whether the depiction of a corporation's central endeavour to maximize profits as amoral – 'not necessarily immoral, but morally neutral' (p. 22) – is to any significant degree a protection against charges that corporations should be more responsible for the consequences of their actions, whether direct or indirect, intended or not. Using the involvement of corporations in the Holocaust as an initial case-study, she argues that decisions made by corporations in circumstances of moral, social and/or human rights outrage cannot be taken on economic grounds alone – that is, as if the commercial concerns can be hermetically sealed from non-economic realities. Like Muchlinski, Stephens is concerned to build her argument for the imposition of human rights responsibilities on corporations on the solid ground of what is possible in corporate law, but she is also insistent on what the existence and expectations of international and domestic human rights standards can add to such legal measures of regulation and accountability, especially in respect of the persistent problem of effective enforcement, be it through civil suit or criminal prosecution.

Christopher McCrudden and David Weissbrodt tell the tales of initiatives that were designed to address the expected roles and responsibilities of corporations in human rights terms. Chris McCrudden (Chapter 3) examines the provenance and operation of, and lessons learnt from, the foundational Sullivan and MacBride Principles, which were US-based initiatives aimed at American corporations with commercial interests in the then intractable

---

movement and its development into a 'second wave' can be found in a number of seminal collections of essays, including: Fatouros (1994); Addo (1999); and Bottomley and Kinley (2002).

political and social circumstances of apartheid South Africa and sectarian Northern Ireland, respectively. These private initiatives operating in the internationally public sphere have long been held up as beacons of what can be done where a coalition of civil society, states and international regulators is willing – especially as they were both able to secure some degree of legal enforceability, accompanied by political and economic leverage. The importance of such coalitions of institutions and interests, as well as the adaptability of initiatives themselves, are, argues McCrudden, the key lessons to be learnt by those who concern themselves with the many and various codes of conduct that festoon the corporate and human rights landscape of today.

The much more ambitious (because they were globally focused and legally framed) UN Human Rights Norms for Corporations are the focus of the essay by David Weissbrodt (Chapter 4), who was a principal architect of the Norms. The lessons to be learnt from this initiative can be drawn as much from what has not been achieved and why not, as from what has been achieved and might yet be. Weissbrodt's overview of the concept, content and context of the Norms[5] – which are as yet 'unfinished business'[6] – helps frame the whole topic for us, precisely because of the nature of the Norms project and because of its prominence within the current debate (a prominence that is reflected in many of the other selected essays) concerning how international law should deal with the category of corporations within the broader phenomenon of non-state actors on the international stage.

The final two essays in Part I pick up two defining themes of the corporations and human rights debate: first, the human rights implications of corporate enterprise, especially in its globalized form, for developing countries as they strive to harness the economic benefits of globalization (Monshipouri, Welch and Kennedy); and second, the place of human rights within the vast and nebulous phenomenon of corporate social responsibility (CSR) (Dickerson). In stressing the responsibility of the rich and powerful actors, both private and public, in the global economy not to ignore the social justice needs of less rich and powerful states, Mahmood Monshipouri, Claude Welch and Evan Kennedy (Chapter 5) advocate the adoption of a rights-based approach to the regulation of global corporate activities which emphasizes the sharing of responsibilities between states and TNCs. Claire Dickerson's study of US corporations' CSR behaviour (Chapter 6) underlines what she sees as the evolution of the concept from one that was originally defined by corporations themselves to a position now where the inputs from all (or at least many) stakeholders – employees, local communities and civil society, as well as shareholders and governments – are not only expected but increasingly mandated by law and/or commercial prudence. What is more, Dickerson argues, this opening up has permitted more focused and direct consideration of the types of human rights obligations that are being, and can be, made of corporations under the rubric of CSR.

---

5   A more detailed account of the content and form of the Norms is provided by Kinley and Chambers in Chapter 11 of this volume; see also Nolan (2005).

6   Professor John Ruggie, the UN Secretary-General's Special Representative on Business and Human Rights, has argued that future directions to be taken in the field generally (and in respect of the Norms specifically) must be sure (i): to bolster the capacity of states to regulate corporate activities that affect human rights; (ii) to focus as much on policy options that address systemic human rights infractions by corporations collective as on individual corporate liability; and (iii) not to overlook the importance of soft-law and non-law responses by too great a reliance on (hard) law approaches (see Ruggie, 2007).

Conceptual Perspectives

The essays in Part II provide three different conceptual perspectives of the interaction between corporations and human rights. At the broadest level, Dinah Shelton (Chapter 7) provides us with an understanding of the new situation of human rights within the context of economic globalization generally, and, more specifically, the resultant shifting loci of power and responsibility between states and non-state actors. Her analysis is by no means focused on corporations alone, though the fact that they feature conspicuously in her essay fairly represents their importance. Shelton analyses both the impact of economic globalization on human rights and the impact of human rights on economic globalization, paying particular attention to the agents of each – namely, the WTO, the Bretton Woods institutions and TNCs themselves on one side, and UN organs, the ILO and civil society organizations on the other. She concludes that the pivotal role that non-state actors have always played in developing human rights law is now, in the welter of globalization, even more obvious and the implications even more demanding.

Steven Ratner's essay (Chapter 8) is perhaps the most prodigious contribution to the canon, as well as being seminal to such essays as those by David Kinley and Junko Tadaki (2004) and Larry Catá Backer (2006), who further developed and extended Ratner's thesis. His intention is to map out a theory of how corporations can be held responsible for their human rights transgressions at the level of international law. His thesis is that corporate duties in this regard can be established in at least four main ways: a corporation's ties with governments; its nexus with affected communities; the fact that certain rights (regarding labour, non-discrimination and security of the person) are directly translatable into corporate duties; and, finally, that while the often complex nature of corporate structure and control (especially of TNCs) can clearly inhibit the attribution of responsibility, it does not absolve the corporation from its duties. He supports these propositions with meticulously constructed arguments as to the patent need for such regulation, the established existence of at least some 'private sphere' human rights responsibilities in certain international forms (including in treaties, practice and jurisprudence), and the political as well as legal imperatives that are driving the tides of the debate. Ratner concludes his piece with a candid and persuasive rebuttal of anticipated objections to his theory – including, in principle, that it illegitimately transgresses the public/private divide and, in practice, that the absence of political will on the part of states (and corporations) renders the exercise futile. Ultimately, he proclaims that the strongest defence of his theory of legal responsibility lies in its potential to provide 'a framework and rationality to the dialogue of the deaf' (p. 332), which dialogue still characterizes so much of the debate between the various stakeholders.

Christine Parker's essay (Chapter 9) shifts the spotlight away from globalization and international law to the question of regulatory theory; specifically, how to make corporations accountable for their responsibilities. Her concern is with the array of responsibilities that fall under the general tag of CSR, including human rights concerns. Parker builds her argument for the 'meta-regulation' of corporations upon the foundation that such an initiative should operate as a sort of 'corporate conscience', such that it works best when it makes companies '*want* to do what they *should* do' (p. 336). She is insistent that while the accountability and enforcement mechanisms that facilitate such an outcome might be highly plural (encompassing legal and non-legal, formal and informal), they must be both external to the corporation and outcome-oriented. Parker is critical of the all-too-common approach within CSR today of instituting internally referenced, process-oriented mechanisms (for example, corporate codes of conduct), which allow corporations to manufacture the outcomes that suit them best, rather than those that flow from effective, external regulation. She is careful not to be misinterpreted as courting conflict, but rather as a critic keen to point out the dangers of allowing the development of initiatives within the field of corporate responsibility that simply mask or mollify conflict, rather than deal with its root causes. This is especially important with such an inflammatory matter as concerns over human rights abuses.

Practice, Problems and Potential

The challenge of moving from concept to practice in this field has been characterized by Upendra Baxi (2005, p. 17) as a question of 'how best to craft normativity that centimetre by centimetre paves the way to real life achievement in a zodiac of globalization that profits by the theory of competitive advantage'. The essays in Part III are all variously oriented towards ideas and initiatives that seek to answer this question.

In Chapter 10 Surya Deva reminds us of the particularities of the developing world, to which arena so much of the corporations and human rights debate is directed. Taking Asia, and specifically India, as his medium, Deva considers the challenges that the tense confluence of the expectations of foreign direct investment (FDI), the activities of TNCs and the demands of human rights standards pose for developing states. At base, he sees a battle for primacy between the forces of desperately desired economic development, on the one hand, and the concerns for rights of the individual and social welfare on the other. Here he echoes Amartya Sen (1999) not only in the characterization of the problem, but also in the approach to its solution – namely, pursuing a course of engagement and reconciliation between the two camps (in terms of ideas and institutions). For Deva, foreign investment is necessary, but not sufficient, for developing states to reach the goals of increased economic prosperity and better human rights protection. The spectacle of increased FDI, corporate activity and aggregate economic growth can, of course, hide immense distributive inequities. So, to ensure that benefits are shared more fairly, and specifically in terms of human rights standards, Deva advocates the institution of means by which 'direction and flow' of the benefits can be better managed. These would include attending to the manner and form in which developing countries 'bargain' with TNCs over terms of investment and return, and the enhancement of regional cooperation between, or 'diversified integration' of, developing countries in terms of their interests and competencies, as well as, more generally, the adoption of universal human rights standards as a regulating factor in these interrelations and dealings.

David Kinley and Rachel Chambers (Chapter 11) analyse the verities, virtues and shibboleths of the UN's Human Rights Norms for Corporations as an instrument that might be tailor-made for the purpose Deva intends. As distinct from the Weissbrodt essay in Part I, the Kinley and Chambers essay not only presents a more detailed account of the structure and substance of the Norms and the controversies they excited, but also separates out the essential legal, and indeed political, values that the Norms have bequeathed, whatever the infelicities of their packaging.[7] The authors draw on the enduring reasons why the Norms were conceived in the first place, on the practice to which they have already been put, and on the lessons learnt by all sides to the Norms debate, to build an argument for how and why international human rights standards for corporations will indeed become a fixture of the legal landscape, whether or not in the form of the 'Norms II' or some similar derivation. In that way, the implications of public international law – even in the form of an initiative as yet still in draft – will be brought to bear on private legal relations such as those that frame the operations and activities of corporations. And despite the sidelining of any UN-based international initiative in this regard by the SRSG in preference of a combination of domestic regulation and corporate self-regulation, the debate continues.[8]

The importance of the essay by John Conley and Cynthia Williams (Chapter 12) lies in the salutary messages it conveys about the capacity of CSR to deliver all that is expected of it, including in terms of corporations' protection of human rights. They do not doubt the ascendancy of CSR within the field of corporate governance, nor its coherence and even impact. Rather, the results of their empirical research – which focuses on the UK and the US (though also encompasses reference to Continental European experiences as well) – leads them to be 'sceptical' (though 'still hopeful') about the prospects for CSR (p. 482). At bottom, they do not see the many reporting and accountability mechanisms now embraced by big business (in particular) under the CSR rubric as exacting the sort of meaningful accountability that civil society organizations and others invest in them. Very often, they argue, the corporations are able to dictate the nature and terms of their interaction with stakeholders and thereby ensure that the outcomes fall comfortably within their zones of tolerance, or are, indeed, to their advantage. Echoing the concerns raised by Christine Parker (Chapter 9) above, Conley and Williams lament the paucity or absence of independent, enforceable review of corporate behaviour that flows directly from the disaggregated sites of power and responsibility that characterize the post-regulatory world of so-called 'new corporate governance'. The blurring of the public/private divide in terms of authority and capacity is allowing well-organized, well-resourced and self-interested corporations stealthily to divide and conquer those who seek to bring them to account for the social consequences of their actions. 'Foucault himself could not have conjured up a better example of the exercise of power through subtle and distributed disciplinary practices', the authors declare ruefully (p. 478).

The timing ('post-honeymoon') and significance of Conley's and Williams' caveats cannot be underestimated, since better human rights protection by corporations depends, to a considerable degree, on the success of CSR, in theory and in practice. But the final two essays highlight the particular roles that lawyers can play in the development of the relationship between corporations and human rights. Harold Koh's short but powerful polemic (Chapter 13) is concerned with busting myths about the pursuit of human rights litigation against corporations by way of the very particular tool of the Alien Torts Claims Act (ATCA). The main thrust of the piece is to offer a persuasive refutation of claims (made specifically by the Bush administration and certain corporate lobby groups) that the statute is spawning a flood of spurious, unjustifiable and impracticable domestic claims against corporations in the US in respect of their conduct overseas. Beyond that, Koh'sessay sits well in this volume by

---

[7] The SRSG, John Ruggie, argues that these are both conceptual and factual (Ruggie, 2007, pp. 822–38).

[8] See SRSG's 2008 Report to the Human Rights Council (Ruggie 2008).

serving three additional ends – namely, it provides: (i) an overview of ATCA jurisprudence;[9] (ii) an appraisal of the statute's limitations as a general tool to bring corporations to book;[10] and (iii), the previous point notwithstanding, a consideration of the specific role the Act has to play in providing a litigation option where none other might be available. Koh, who acted for plaintiffs in a number of these cases, stresses the point, however, that litigation should not be seen as *the* option when a dispute occurs, but rather as *an* option. Socially responsible corporations, he concludes, have little to fear from such litigation, and those that do not act responsibly overseas should rightly be concerned.

The final essay by Halina Ward (Chapter 14) broaches a most important, yet still somewhat puzzling, question about paucity of legal practice in the area of corporations and human rights – beyond the obvious, if relatively limited, avenue of litigation (as noted by Koh above). This is puzzling because, as mentions, one might otherwise expect lawyers – especially those in commercial practice – to be more interested in, if not proactive about, CSR generally and human rights standards in particular. Such standards are, after all, now widely expressed in both hard and soft law terms, and so it would be reasonable to assume that corporations are in need of legal advice on such matter. In practice, however, such advice has come from in-house, corporate counsel rather than from private practice. Ward charts these developments through the lens of legal ethics, asking why it is that so little attention has been paid to the consequences for legal ethics of the burgeoning CSR agenda, when so much attention has been paid to the consequences for legal ethics of the not unrelated phenomenon of economic globalization. Ward concludes that there is not only an important ethical dimension to the reasons why lawyers and law firms ought to be more concerned with matters of social responsibility performance, both in respect of themselves and their clients, but also, crucially, a strong business case for being so concerned. This is so, despite the 'natural' ethical inclinations of lawyers to focus on questions of liability, confidentiality and cautious defensiveness, as opposed to CSR's mandate of pursuing responsibility, transparency and the building of bridges (p. 511).

In conclusion, let me say that, despite the acknowledged limitations and compromises inherent in producing a selection of essays such as this, I nonetheless believe that the result provides a *dégustation* of what the vast (and getting vaster) menu of literature on human rights

---

[9]   That is up to 2004. For a valuable account of significant developments since that date, see (2005); and for an assessment of the impact of the US Supreme Court's decision in *Sosa* v. *Alvarez-Machain*, 542 US 692 (2004), see Dhooge (2006).

[10]   It was only in July 2007 that the first claim under the Alien Tort Claims Act (ATCA) went to trial: *The Estate of Valmore Lacarno Rodriquez* v. *Drummond Company, Inc.*, in an Alabama District Court. On 26 July 2007 the jury delivered its verdict, finding that the company was not liable for alleged complicity in the murder of three trade union leaders by Colombian paramilitary units: see Stier (2007).

N.B. On 12 October 2007, the United States Court of Appeals for the Second Circuit ruled that the plaintiffs in *Khulumani* v. *Barclays* (the apartheid litigation) could plead a theory of aiding and abetting liability under the ATCA, relating to the conduct of certain multinational companies operating in South Africa under the apartheid regime. The Second Circuit thereby overruled (in part) the decision of Justice Sprizzo of the District Court for the Southern District of New York, who had dismissed the plaintiffs' claims under the ATCA and the Torture Victim Protection Act. See *Khulumani* v. *Barclay National Bank Ltd*, 504 F. 3d 254 (2d Cir. 2007).

and corporations has to offer. I hope you agree. Even more so, I hope you get what you want from this volume.

References

Addo, Michael K (ed.) (1999), *Human Rights Standards and the Responsibility of Transnational Corporations*, The Hague: Kluwer.

Backer, Larry Catá (2006), 'Multinational Corporations, Transnational Law: The United Nations' Norms on the Responsibilities of Transnational Corporations as a Harbinger of Corporate Social Responsibility in International Law', *Columbia Human Rights Law Review*, 37, pp. 287–390.

Baxi, Upendra (2005), 'Market Fundamentalisms: Business Ethics at the Altar of Human Rights', *Human Rights Law Review*, 5(1), pp. 1–26.

Bottomley, Stephen and Kinley, David (eds) (2002), *Commercial Law and Human Rights*, Aldershot: Ashgate.

Chambers, Rachel (2005), 'The *Unocal* Settlement: Implications for the Developing Law on Corporate Complicity in Human Rights Abuses', *Human Rights Brief*, 13(1), pp. 14–16, 36.

de Schutter, Olivier (2006), 'The Challenge of Imposing Human Rights Norms on Corporate Actors', in O. de Schutter (ed.), *Transnational Corporations and Human Rights*, Oxford: Hart.

Dhooge, Lucien J. (2006), 'Lohengrin Revealed: The Implications of *Sosa* v. *Alvarez-Machain* for Human Rights Litigation Pursuant to the Alien Tort Claims Act', *Loyola of Los Angeles International and Comparative Law Review*, 28, pp. 393–496.

Dine, Janet and Fagan, Andrew (eds) (2006), *Capitalism and Human Rights*, Cheltenham: Edward Elgar.

Fatouros, A.A. (ed.) (1994), *Transnational Corporations: The International Legal Framework*, London: Routledge.

Friedman, Milton (1970), 'The Social Responsibility of Business is to Increase Profits', *New York Times Magazine*, 13 September.

Joseph, Sarah (2004), *Corporations and Transnational Human Rights Litigation*, Oxford: Hart.

Kinley, David and Tadaki, Junko (2004), 'From Talk to Walk: The Emergence of Human Rights Responsibilities for Corporations at International Law', *Virginia Journal of International Law*, 44, pp. 931–1024.

Nolan, Justine (2005), 'With Power Comes Responsibility: Human Rights and Corporate Accountability', *University of New South Wales Law Journal*, 28(3), pp. 581–613.

Ruggie, John (2007), 'Business and Human Rights: The Evolving International Agenda', *American Journal of International Law*, 101(4), pp. 838–40.

Ruggie, John (2008), 'Protect, Respect and Remedy: A Framework for Business and Human Rights: Report of the Special Representative of the Secretary-General on the Issue of Human Rights and Transnational Corporations and Other Business Enterprises, *Human Rights Council*, A/HRC/8/5, 7 April 2008.

Sen, Amartya (1999), *Development as Freedom*, New York, Oxford: Oxford University Press.

Smith, Adam ([1776] 1976), *An Inquiry into the Nature and Causes of the Wealth of Nations*, ed. R.H. Campbell, A.S. Skinner and W.B. Todd, Oxford: Clarendon Press.

Stier, Ken (2007), 'Suing Multinationals Over Murder', *Time*, 1 August, at: http://www.time.com/time/world/article/0,8599,1648903,00.html.

Part I
Framing the Relationship

[1]

Human rights and multinationals:

is there a problem?

PETER T. MUCHLINSKI

In recent years there has been an upsurge of concern over human rights and multinational enterprises (MNEs). A number of significant cases have been documented of apparent collusion between MNEs and host governments in major violations of human rights. These have been brought to public attention in the media through the actions of concerned individuals and groups, most notably by non-governmental organizations (NGOs) concerned with human rights. Among the most publicized cases have been the operations of Shell in Ogoniland,[1] BP in Colombia,[2] and Unocal in Burma (Myanmar), the last of these having led to landmark litigation in the United States.[3] Thus, *prima facie*, there is a problem: multinationals can take part in alleged violations of human rights. Such allegations are not really new: concerns about the complicity of corporate and/or commercial actors in human rights violations can be traced back through the era of apartheid in southern Africa, to the use of slave labour by the Nazis in the Second World War, which has itself generated recent legal action, to the exploitation of workers on colonial plantations and to the movement for the abolition of slavery in the eighteenth century. What is new is the context in which these more recent cases are being discussed. The traditional notion that only states and state agents can be held accountable for violations of human rights is being challenged as the economic and social power of MNEs appears to rise in the wake of the increasing integration of the global economy that they have helped to bring about.

This article is based on an inaugural lecture of the same title given by the author on the occasion of his appointment to the Drapers' Chair of Law at Queen Mary and Westfield College, University of London, on 14 November 2000.

[1] See Human Rights Watch, *Nigeria, the Ogoni crisis: a case study of military repression in south east Nigeria* (New York: Human Rights Watch, 1995); Ben Naanen, 'Oil producing minorities and the restructuring of Nigerian federalism: the case of the Ogoni people', *Journal of Commonwealth and Comparative Politics* 33, 1995, p. 45; Eghosa Osaghae, 'The Ogoni uprising: oil, politics, minority agitation and the future of the Nigerian state', *African Affairs* 94, 1991, p. 325; S. Skogly, 'Complexities in human rights protection: actors and rights involved in the Ogoni conflict in Nigeria', *NQHR* 15: 52, 1997; Heike Fabig, 'The Body Shop and the Ogoni', in Michael Addo, ed., *Human rights standards and the responsibility of transnational corporations* (The Hague: Kluwer Law International, 1999), pp. 309–21.

[2] 'BP accused of funding Colombian death squads', *Observer*, 20 Oct. 1996, pp. 1, 18.

[3] See further note 45 below.

Peter T. Muchlinski

Furthermore, the increased vigilance and sophistication of NGOs, with their global networks of information, cooperation through the Internet and skilful use of the mass media, is making ignorance of, and indifference to, the suffering of workers and others who come into contact with unscrupulous MNEs less easy to sustain. On the other hand, the vast majority of MNEs do not engage in practices or relations with states that may lead to human rights abuses. Indeed, they are becoming more sensitive to the risk of becoming parties to such actions. Thus a mood is developing which sees the subjection of MNEs to human rights scrutiny as perfectly acceptable. It is the purpose of this article to look behind this situation and to examine more closely the arguments used both to deny and to uphold an extension of human rights responsibilities to MNEs. This is necessary because if MNEs are to be subjected to direct and legally enforceable obligations to observe fundamental human rights, the grounds for doing so must be strong and conceptually unassailable.

The extension of human rights into what Andrew Clapham has called 'the private sphere' presumes a change in legal, political and social relations which, in turn, changes the very foundations of human rights thinking.[4] Hitherto, the only relationship between MNEs and human rights has been that of victim and beneficiary: the corporation can be protected from intrusions into its private rights on the part of the state by reference to human rights standards.[5] Leaving the conceptual difficulty surrounding the notion of 'corporate human rights' to one side, what is now expected is that corporations—not unlike states—can be holders of duties to observe human rights. This goes well beyond the furthest limits of responsibility hitherto imposed by human rights law in response to violations committed by private actors. Thus far such actors could not be held directly responsible for violations of human rights. Rather, they could cause the state to be held responsible on the basis that it had neglected to control the activities of the non-state actor which have led to the violation of the human rights of another private party.[6]

Against this background the article will address the resulting issues, first, by looking more closely at the intellectual context in which the debate is developing; second, it will deal in more detail with the principal arguments for and against the extension of human rights responsibilities to MNEs; and finally, it will consider what conclusions can be drawn, in particular, as to the relationship between states and corporations for the observance of human rights. The ensuing discussion should not be read as being necessarily confined to MNEs alone. They are, for the purposes of this paper, the main object of analysis. However, if the applicability of human rights in the private sphere is to be accepted, then these norms must extend to all forms of non-governmental human association, whether foreign or domestic, business or non-business, unincorporated or incorporated.

4 Andrew Clapham, *Human rights in the private sphere* (Oxford: Clarendon Press, 1993).
5 On which see further Michael Addo, 'The corporation as victim of human rights violations', in Addo, ed., *Human rights standards*, pp. 187–97.
6 See further text at notes 49–51.

Human rights and multinationals

The context of the debate

Modern human rights doctrine emerged historically from the struggle of the individual property holder against the autocratic monarchic state. It is, in essence, a market-based theory of rights.[7] Thus the first human right to emerge clearly is the right to private property. This in turn gives rise, by the nineteenth century, to a conception of human rights that distinguishes different classes of actors as to the extent of their rights. It is an exclusionary theory. As Upendra Baxi has pointed out, 'The "Rights of Man" were human rights of all *men* capable of autonomous reason and will. While by no means the prerogative of "modernity", the large number of human beings were excluded by this peculiar ontological construction.' It has, in his view, led to the exclusion, at various times, of slaves, heathens, barbarians, colonized peoples, indigenous populations, women, children, the impoverished and the insane from being bearers of human rights.[8] At the same time, this conception of human rights has also led to the extension of its protection to private accumulations of capital. Thus Article 1 of the First Protocol to the European Convention on Human Rights (ECHR) makes clear that both natural and legal persons have the right to the peaceful enjoyment of their possessions. Equally, cases have been heard by the European Court of Human Rights involving alleged violations of human rights against corporations. Corporations have been held to possess, apart from the right to property in Article 1 Protocol 1, rights to free speech under Article 10, to a fair trial under Article 6 and to privacy under Article 8.[9] Similar rights have been recognized in other jurisdictions.[10] It is not the purpose of this article to argue that corporations should not have the equal protection of the law. However, the traditional conception of human rights accepts *only* this protective approach to the relationship between corporations and human rights. It is therefore a conceptual barrier to the extension of human rights *obligations* to private corporations.

A second contextual factor to be considered is the partial disembodiment of human rights theory from its liberal, possessive individualist origins in the wake of the Nazi atrocities in occupied Europe, which led directly to the adoption of the Universal Declaration of Human Rights in 1948 and the ECHR in 1950.[11] Although maintaining a liberal catalogue of civil and political rights, the Universal Declaration also extends to economic social and cultural rights, recognizing the indivisibility of such welfare values from the more traditional liberal conceptions

---

[7] See C. B. Macpherson, *The political theory of possessive individualism* (Oxford: Oxford University Press, 1962).

[8] Upendra Baxi, 'Voices of suffering and the future of human rights', *Transnational Law and Contemporary Problems* 8, 1998, pp. 126–175 at p. 135.

[9] See Addo, 'The corporation as victim of human rights violations', note 5.

[10] Ibid. See too the discussion by Phillip Blumberg of the extension of US constitutional rights to corporations in his *The multinational challenge to corporation law* (Oxford: Oxford University Press, 1993), pp. 30–45.

[11] See D. J. Harris, M. O'Boyle and C. Warbrick, *The law of the European Convention on Human Rights* (London: Butterworths, 1995), pp. 1–3.

Peter T. Muchlinski

of earlier ages. This reflects the concerns of the 1940s that societies should never return to the cruelty that accompanied traditional liberal capitalist models of economic and social organization, as witnessed particularly in the Great Depression of the 1930s. Thus, in the early postwar period, at the national level economic planning and state intervention remained central to policy-making. On the other hand, in relation to the organization of international trade and commerce, the liberal approach was adopted, with the progressive liberalization of trade and, more recently, investment being at the heart of policy-making.[12]

However, as the Cold War developed, a stratification of human rights emerged based on ideological preferences. Thus Western powers emphasized the individualistic civil and political rights agenda, as shown for example by the exclusive concentration of the ECHR on such rights, while the Soviet bloc states and their allies emphasized economic, social and cultural rights as pre-requisites which justified, where necessary, even the curtailment of civil and political rights for the improvement of the welfare of the people. The resulting sense of cultural and political relativism in human rights was furthered by the rise of anti-imperialist decolonization movements in Asia and Africa. Their prime opponents were the liberal Western powers. The latter had to live with the paradox of the observance of human rights at home and their denial in overseas colonial possessions.

This disintegration of human rights theory continues to this day, despite influential voices being raised to the contrary, claiming that human rights are once again indivisible.[13] It has the effect of redefining the contemporary participants in the debate on MNEs and human rights as 'pro-' or 'anti-'capitalists, thereby making them harder to hear by the other side of the debate. The main difference from the Cold War is that the antagonists cannot be identified with specific geopolitical blocs but have taken on a transnational group character. Furthermore, the selective stratification of human rights is still possible. The Cold War rules our discourse from its grave, as does a residual consciousness of imperial supremacy. It is this that in part underlies arguments opposed to the extension of human rights responsibilities to MNEs.

A third contextual current is the rise, since the 1960s, of identity and lifestyle politics.[14] This has had the effect of supplementing traditional economic/political debates with (indeed, possibly subordinating them to) those of race, gender, sexual orientation, youth culture, the 'third age' politics of the elderly, consumerism and environmentalism.[15] This has led to an awareness of the need for individual space for self-identification and a growing impetus for individuals

[12] See Mark Mazower, *Dark continent: Europe's twentieth century* (London: Penguin Books, 1999), pp. 206–9.
[13] See e.g. Clare Short, Secretary of State for International Development, 'All human rights for all', speech to the Law Society, London, 3 Dec. 1998.
[14] See Mazower, *Dark continent*, pp. 356–63; Eric Hobsbawm, *Age of extremes: the short history of the twentieth century* (London: Abacus Books, 1995), ch. 11, 'Cultural revolution'.
[15] See further Leslie Sklair, *Sociology of the global system*, 2nd edn (London: Harvester Wheatsheaf, 1995); Yannis Gabriel and Tim Lang, *The unmanageable consumer* (London: Sage, 1995); P. T. Muchlinski, *Multinational enterprises and the law*, rev. pb edn (Oxford: Blackwell, 1999), pp. 99–101.

Human rights and multinationals

to detach themselves from mass movements, mass ideologies, mass religion and mass production. The impact of these trends on the debate under discussion has been considerable. The expectation that MNEs should observe human rights can itself been seen as an identity and lifestyle statement. MNEs are purveyors of lifestyles and identities through their products, services and marketing. Consumers select their lifestyles and identities through their patterns of consumption. The 'ethical consumer' has become a target customer for the 'ethical corporation'. Through this discourse a new sense of what corporations and markets should be about appears to be emerging. We are rediscovering a need to control what an earlier generation would have referred to as 'the unacceptable face of capitalism'.

Arguments for and against the extension of human rights obligations to MNEs

Working within the context outlined above, this section will now critically assess the main arguments against and in favour of extending responsibilities for human rights observance to MNEs. Some may think it almost inconceivable to argue against such a self-evidently 'good' idea as the extension of human rights responsibilities to MNEs. Yet there are a number of strong arguments against it. First, MNEs are in business. Their only social responsibility is to make profits for their shareholders. It is not for them to act as moral arbiters in relation to the wider issues arising in the communities in which they operate. Indeed, to do so may be seen as unwarranted interference in the internal affairs of those communities, something that MNEs have, in the past, been urged not to commit.[16] Second, private non-state actors, such as MNEs, do not have any positive duty to observe human rights. Their only duty is to obey the law. Thus it is for the state to regulate on matters of social importance and for MNEs to observe the law. It follows also that, as pointed out above, MNEs, as private actors, can be only beneficiaries of human rights protection, not human rights protectors themselves. Third, which human rights are MNEs to observe? They may have some influence over social and economic matters, as for example by ensuring the proper treatment of their workers; but they can do nothing to protect civil and political rights. Only states have the power and the ability to do that. Fourth, the extension of human rights obligations to MNEs will create a 'free rider' problem.[17] It is predictable that not all states and not all MNEs will take the same care to observe fundamental human rights. Thus the more conscientious corporations that invest time and money in observing human rights, and in making themselves accountable for their record in this field, will be at a competitive disadvantage in relation to more unscrupulous corporations that do

---

[16] See e.g. the UN Draft Code of Conduct for Transnational Corporations, paras 15–16, in UNCTAD, *International investment agreements: a compendium* (New York and Geneva: United Nations, 1996), vol. 1, p. 165.

[17] See Ray Vernon in *Business and human rights* (Cambridge, MA: Harvard Law School Human Rights Program, 1999), p. 49.

Peter T. Muchlinski

not undertake such responsibilities.] They may also lose business opportunities in countries with poor human rights records, where the host governments may not wish to do business with ethically driven MNEs and they may not want to do business with these regimes. Fifth, unfairness may be exacerbated by the selective and politically driven activities of NGOs, whose principal concern may be to maintain a high profile for their particular campaigns and not to ensure that all corporations are held equally to account.

Such arguments assume that MNEs are no different from private persons engaging in lawful private activities; that they have no wider social responsibilities; that there are risks of unfair treatment of individual corporations; and that MNEs themselves need protection from such unfairness. Do they stand up to scrutiny? This depends, of course, on one's ideological predilections and personal prejudices. However, a significant reason for being sceptical about these 'anti' arguments lies in recent changes, first, in the perception of the corporation and its functions, which sees it as a social organization with real social responsibilities to workers and others,[18] and, second, in the wider political reaction to global economic integration, with its emphasis on the 'democratic deficit' behind global business regulation;[19] both of these shifts render many of the underlying assumptions behind those arguments hard to sustain, as will be shown below. On the other hand, the 'anti' arguments predate the arguments in favour of extending human rights to private non-state actors and they are based, as suggested above, on a remarkably resilient model of a liberal market society characterized by a clear distinction between the public and private spheres.[20] Thus their continued endurance can be expected. Against this backdrop, the principal arguments in favour of extending human rights obligations to MNEs will now be considered in turn.

The social responsibility of MNEs

The arguments for extending social responsibility standards to corporations are well known.[21] Suffice it to say, for present purposes, that MNEs have for a long time been expected to observe socially responsible standards of behaviour, as expressed in numerous codes of conduct drawn up by intergovernmental organizations, of which the most significant have been the ILO Tripartite Declaration of Principles Concerning Multinational Enterprises and Social Policy of 1977,[22]

---

[18] See further J. E. Parkinson, *Corporate power and responsibility* (Oxford: Clarendon Press, 1993); J. Dine, *The governance of corporate groups* (Cambridge: Cambridge University Press, 2000).

[19] See further John Braithwaite and Peter Drahos, *Global business regulation* (Cambridge: Cambridge University Press, 2000).

[20] On which see further Clapham, *Human rights in the private sphere.*

[21] See Parkinson, *Corporate power and responsibility*; Dine, *The governance of corporate groups*; Muchlinski, *Multinational enterprises and the law*, pp. 93–5; UNCTAD, *The social responsibility of transnational corporations* (New York and Geneva: United Nations, 1999); UNCTAD, *World Investment Report 1999* (New York and Geneva: United Nations, 1999), ch. XII.

[22] ILO, *Official Bulletin* (Geneva, 1978), vol. LXI, series A, no. 1, pp. 49–56, reproduced in UNCTAD, *International investment agreements: a compendium*, pp. 89–102. See also ILO, Declaration on Fundamental Principles and Rights at Work (Geneva: ILO, 18 June 1998).

Human rights and multinationals

and the OECD Guidelines for Multinational Enterprises of 1976, which have recently been revised.[23] However, too much should not be read into these instruments. They are non-binding, and so create no legal duties to observe the standards contained therein. On the other hand, they do create an expectation that MNEs will observe such minimum standards in the conduct of their operations, and they provide concerned NGOs with a benchmark against which to compare corporate behaviour.[24]

Furthermore, MNEs themselves appear to be rejecting a purely non-social role for themselves through the adoption of corporate and industry-based codes of conduct.[25] At the very least, these create a moral expectation that the codes will be observed. They can also gain legal force through their incorporation into contracts, as where, for example, a retailer includes ethical supplier standards in its contracts with its suppliers.[26] In addition, national laws continue to display a concern for corporate social responsibility, whether through the development of protective standards, as exemplified by the social dimension of EU law, or through the extension of public law standards of accountability to privatized industries. Indeed, in certain Commonwealth countries, notably Namibia and Uganda, privatization has been accompanied by an extension of the jurisdiction of their respective national Ombudsman's Office and Human Rights Commission to the activities of the privatized entities.[27] Even at the multilateral level, liberalization is not the dominant value that it was, as exemplified by the rejection of the Multilateral Agreement on Investment on the basis that it constituted an unwarranted interference with state sovereignty, thereby jeopardizing legitimate regulation in the public interest in such fields as environmental protection and labour standards.[28] Furthermore, as the most recent revision of the OECD Guidelines for Multinational Enterprises asserts: 'Enterprises should…2. Respect the human rights of those affected by their activities consistent with the host government's international obligations and commitments.' In relation to issues of employment and industrial relations the Guidelines expect MNEs to respect the rights of their employees to be represented by trade unions, to contribute to the effective abolition of child labour and to the

[23] OECD Guidelines for Multinational Enterprises, 27 June 2000 (Paris: OECD, 2000) and on *www.oecd.org/daf/investment/guidelines/mnetext.htm*

[24] See further Sol Picciotto and Ruth Mayne, eds, *Regulating international business* (London: Macmillan/ Oxfam, 1999).

[25] For examples see UNCTAD, *World Investment Report 1994* (New York and Geneva: United Nations, 1994), ch. VIII; UNCTAD, *The Social Responsibility of Transnational Corporations* (New York and Geneva: United Nations, 1999), pp. 31–42.

[26] See e.g. the Sainsbury's Code of Practice for Socially Responsible Trading, in Picciotto and Mayne, eds, *Regulating international business*, pp. 228–34; analysis by Petrina Fridd and Jessica Sainsbury, ibid., pp. 221–8. Sainsbury's is prepared to stop using suppliers who do not live up to the standards contained in its code. It is unlikely that such suppliers could sue for breach of contract, given their notice of the code.

[27] See John Hatchard, 'Privatisation and accountability: developing appropriate institutions in Commonwealth Africa', in Addo, ed., *Human rights standards*, pp. 289–305.

[28] See further Sol Picciotto, 'Linkages and international investment regulation: the antinomies of the Draft Multilateral Agreement on Investment', *University of Pennsylvania Journal of International Economic Law* 19, 1998, pp. 731–68; P. T. Muchlinski, 'The rise and fall of the Multilateral Agreement on Investment: where now?', *International Lawyer* 34, Fall 2000.

Peter T. Muchlinski

elimination of all forms of forced or compulsory labour, and not to discriminate against their employees with respect to employment or occupation on such grounds as race, colour, sex, religion, political opinion, national extraction or social origin, save where this furthers established government policies of greater equality of employment opportunity or relates to the inherent requirements of the job.[29] Thus, the trend appears to be turning towards a social dimension to the activities of MNEs, one in which an active duty to observe fundamental human rights standards can be included.

Human rights are good for business

Writing in 1998 the UN Human Rights Commissioner, Mary Robinson, asked: 'Why should business care about human rights?' Her answer was that, 'business needs human rights and human rights needs business'.[30] She suggested that the rationale behind this assertion was twofold: first, business cannot flourish in an environment where fundamental human rights are not respected—what firm would be happy with the disappearance or imprisonment without trial of employees for their political opinions?—and, second, corporations that do not themselves observe the fundamental human rights of their employees, or of the individuals or communities among which they operate, will be monitored and their reputations will suffer. Such sentiments have also been echoed in the recent UN Global Compact initiative, which calls upon major MNEs to observe fundamental workers' rights, human rights and environmental standards,[31] and in relation to the current moves towards the adoption of a human rights code of conduct for companies by the UN Sub-Commission on the Promotion and Protection of Human Rights.[32]

Businesses themselves may justify the adoption of human rights policies by reference to good reputation.[33] The benefit to be reaped from espousing a stance supportive of human rights is seen as outweighing any 'free rider' problem. Indeed, this problem may be an exaggerated one. It supposes that, say, the employment of child or slave labour is actually more profitable than employing adults at reasonable wages. A firm that needs to compete at such marginal cost levels is likely to be on the brink of insolvency. Furthermore, it is likely to be in an industry where there is little, if any, investment in new technology or where such investment would make little difference to overall profitability. Very few MNEs are in such a marginal position. Generally, they can afford to be model employers. Indeed, in developing countries they are likely to be among the

---

[29] OECD Guidelines, pp. 19, 21.

[30] Mary Robinson, 'The business case for human rights', in Financial Times Management, *Visions of ethical business* (London: Financial Times Professional, 1998), p. 14.

[31] See further UNCTAD, *Social Responsibility*, pp. 15–18; *www.unglobalcompact.org*; Carola Hoyos, 'Principled partnership with world business', *Financial Times*, 6 Sept. 2000, p. 14.

[32] see *http://www.unhchr.ch*.

[33] See e.g. Simon Williams, 'How principles benefit the bottom line: the experience of the Co-operative Bank', in Addo, ed., *Human rights standards*, pp. 63–8. See also Harvard Law School, *Human Rights and Business*, pp. 19–22.

Human rights and multinationals

best, offering superior wages and conditions of work as compared with local employers.[34] Thus MNEs are more likely to pull conditions up than to pull them down.

On the other hand, failure to pursue a human rights strategy may not affect all firms in the same way. The firms with the most to lose appear to be those in high-profile, branded goods industries in which productive efficiency gains are crucial to profitability, due to the essentially mature nature of their products and productive technologies. Thus firms in the apparel industry, a relatively labour-intensive sector with strong incentives to cut labour costs, have been among the most prominent to suffer from a bad record on fundamental workers' rights. Similarly, firms with a very high market profile due to their size or centrality in their home-country markets may be more sensitive to criticism over human rights abuses. By comparison, firms operating far from the public gaze may have little to fear. Furthermore, even if a firm is identified as having a poor human rights record, and even where it is the object of a consumer boycott, the financial markets are unlikely to react. According to one study, while Shell, Nestlé, Monsanto and Nike were being subjected to very public boycotts, there appeared to be no demonstrable effect on their share prices or dividends. Even where, as in the case of Nike, chief executives have claimed an adverse effect on share prices, the empirical evidence does not back this up.[35] Thus, where firms are concerned about human rights, it appears that this is not because they will definitely go out of business otherwise, but because they feel that their public place on the market, and/or their brand image, require it. What is interesting is whether, in due course, financial markets will become more sensitive to the publicly perceived stance of a company on human rights and social responsibility when taking account of its likely future value.

The private legal status of MNEs is irrelevant

Central to the arguments in favour of extending responsibilities for human rights to MNEs is the view that their status as private legal persons is no longer a bar to such a development. This position involves both theoretical issues and technical legal issues. As to the theoretical perspective, this rests on an acceptance that there has been a significant change in the context in which MNEs operate which makes them liable to responsibilities in this field. Thus, Andrew Clapham has identified three trends which have forced a reconsideration of the boundaries between the private and the public spheres with the consequence that non-state actors, including MNEs, may in principle be subjected to human rights obligations.[36] The first of these is the emergence of fragmented centres of power—including MNEs—which extend the individual's perception of

---

[34] UNCTAD, *World Investment Report 1994*, pp. 197–203.

[35] See Simon Zadek and Maya Forstater, 'Making civil regulation work', in Addo, ed., *Human rights standards*, pp. 69–70.

[36] See Clapham, *Human rights in the private sphere*, pp. 137–8, on which this paragraph draws.

Peter T. Muchlinski

authority, repression and alienation beyond the apparatus of the state. Second, the definition of the private sphere has undergone a transformation, due to the emergence of *inter alia* the kinds of identity politics mentioned earlier in this article. Thus the notion of a 'private' sphere, based on a paternalistic model of the domestic space, has been replaced by a more regulated sphere of private behaviour. This, in turn, has brought into question other divisions of 'private' and 'public' including the notion of the corporation as a private enterprise with no social or public obligations. Third, the supranational dimension has created new institutional centres of power which allow MNEs, among others, to bypass the state machinery and to exercise direct influence on these institutions which, in turn, directly exercise power over the individual. Thus bodies such as the EU or the WTO are perceived as being involved in a direct relationship with transnational capital, without a clear system of democratic accountability being in place to represent other, equally valid, interests. These changes, in turn, create the perception of MNEs as entities capable of exerting power over public policy and individuals without being held accountable. This coincides with the fear that such powerful entities may disregard human rights and, thereby, violate human dignity. It follows that MNEs must be subjected to human rights responsibilities, notwithstanding their status as creatures of private law, because human dignity must be protected in every circumstance.[37]

The abovementioned theoretical position is reinforced by certain technical legal developments which recognize an emergent, albeit as yet incomplete, responsibility for human rights violations on the part of non-state actors. These start with the Universal Declaration of Human Rights, in which the obligation to promote respect for human rights and to secure their universal and effective recognition and observance is addressed not only to states but also to 'every individual and every organ of society', a formulation wide enough to encompass private corporations.[38] Furthermore, as established by the Nuremberg Tribunal,[39] corporate responsibility for war crimes and crimes against humanity may be possible, given that the Tribunal declared the Gestapo and 55 other Nazi organizations to be criminal in nature. However, it may be said that such bodies are not directly analogous to private corporations, representing as they did the Nazi state, and that therefore the Nuremberg Tribunal decision does not take us very far. It does not assert that private corporations can be responsible under international law for human rights violations, although the Tribunal made quite clear that individuals could be so responsible, a fact reaffirmed in Article IV of the UN Convention on the Prevention and Punishment of the Crime of Genocide 1948, which asserts that individuals shall be punished for this crime.

---

[37] See ibid., p. 147.
[38] Ibid., Preamble. See further Amnesty International Dutch Section and Pax Christi International, *Multinational enterprises and human rights* (Utrecht, November 1998), pp. 33–4.
[39] *AJIL* 41, 1947, p. 172.

Human rights and multinationals

It has been argued that MNEs should not be regarded as addressees of international human rights obligations, as this would grant them a measure of international personality.[40] This view has, in turn, been questioned in more recent academic writings on the basis that various non-state actors, including MNEs, are *participants* in the evolution of international law.[41] Thus their formal legal status is said not to be relevant when determining the extent of their legal rights and duties, a matter that can only be decided in relation to the issue at hand. Consequently, any formal objection to the extension of human rights responsibilities to MNEs can be avoided by an appeal to pragmatism. In strictly legal terms this may be achieved by introducing positive legal duties to observe fundamental human rights into international agreements which are directly addressed to MNEs.

There are, in addition, early signs at the level of national law that a degree of direct responsibility for human rights violations on the part of MNEs is being recognized. Thus in the recent United States District Court case of *Doe* v. *Unocal* it was held, for the first time,[42] that MNEs could, in principle, be directly liable for violations of human rights under the Alien Tort Claims Act.[43] However, on 31 August 2000 the US District Court awarded a summary judgment to Unocal on the ground that although there was evidence that Unocal knew about, and benefited from, forced labour on the pipeline project in Burma in which it was a joint venture partner, it was not directly involved in the alleged abuses. These were the responsibility of the Burmese authorities alone. Giving the court's judgment, Judge Ronald Lew followed a series of decisions by US military tribunals after the Second World War, involving the prosecution of German industrialists for their participation in the Third Reich's slave labour policies.[44] These established that, in order to be liable, the defendant industrialists had to take active steps in cooperating or participating in the forced labour practices. Mere knowledge that someone else would commit abuses was insufficient. By analogy with these cases, Unocal could not be held liable as a matter of international law and so the claim under the Alien Tort Claims Act failed.[45] Therefore, the case has failed on the facts and is subject to an appeal. However, the principle that a private non-state actor can be sued

[40] See A. Cassese, *International law in a divided world* (1986), p. 103.

[41] See Menno T. Kamminga, 'Holding multinational corporations accountable for human rights abuses: a challenge for the EC', in Philip Alston, ed., *The EU and human rights* (Oxford: Oxford University Press, 1999), p. 558; Amnesty International Dutch Section and Pax Christi Internatiônal, *Multinational enterprises and human rights*, pp. 23–5; Rosalyn Higgins, *Problems and process: international law and how we use it* (Oxford: Oxford University Press, 1993), pp. 49–50.

[42] 963 F.Supp. 880 US Dist Ct, C.D.Cal, 25 March 1997, noted in *AJIL* 92, 1998, pp. 309–14. See also *Wiwa* v. *Royal Dutch Petroleum Company* 96 Civ 8389 (SDNY).

[43] 28 USC s.1350.

[44] *US* v. *Flick*, 6 Trials of War Criminals Before the Nuremberg Military Tribunals Under Control Council Law No. 10 (1952); *US* v. *Carl Krauch*, ibid., vol. 8; *US* v. *Alfred Krupp*, ibid., vol. 9; *Flick* v. *Johnson*, 85 US App. DC 70, 174 F.2d 983 (DC Cir 1949).

[45] *Doe* v. *Unocal*, US Dist Ct, C.D.Cal. 31 August 2000, 2000 U.S.Dist. LEXIS 13327. See also William Branigin, 'Claim against Unocal rejected: judge cites evidence of abuses in Burma but no jurisdiction', *Washington Post*, 8 Sept. 2000, p. E10.

ـ٦ski

ﻟ courts for alleged violations of human rights was not quest-
ﺍrthermore, in the recent case of *Wiwa* v. *Royal Dutch Petroleum*
ﻟ*y and Shell Transport and Trading Company PLC*[47] the US Court of
ﻟﻣal held that the US interest in pursuing claims for torture under the Alien
ﻟort Claims Act and the more recent Torture Victim Prevention Act[48] was a
significant factor to be taken into account when determining whether an action
brought on such grounds before a US court against a foreign MNE should be
removed to a foreign jurisdiction on the basis that it was a more suitable forum
for the litigation. Thus on the facts the USCA held that an action brought
against the defendant corporation for allegedly supporting the Nigerian state in
its repression of the Ogoni people through *inter alia* the supply of money,
weapons and logistical support to the Nigerian military which carried out the
alleged abuses, could be heard in the United States. In effect, then, the US
courts have set themselves up as a forum in which allegations of complicity in
torture made against private corporations can be heard. However, this case was
brought by US resident plaintiffs. It is not certain that US jurisdiction will be so
readily accepted where the plaintiffs are from outside the United States.

Although a finding of direct responsibility for human rights violations is as
yet unprecedented, there is, as noted at the beginning of this article, some
support for establishing the indirect responsibility of MNEs for human rights
violations. Here the state may be held liable for the conduct of non-state actors
that amounts to a violation of the human rights of a third person. Such a
responsibility could be established by international convention.[49] No such
responsibility has ever been expressly provided for. Instead, there is some
evidence from the case law under the ECHR that the state may be under an
obligation to 'secure' the rights of third persons against interference by a non-
state actor. Failure to do so may result in a violation of the Convention.[50]
However, this case law is uncertain in its scope and too much cannot be read
into it. At most, it is clear that the state cannot absolve itself of its direct human
rights responsibilities by hiving them off to a privatized entity.[51]

From the above discussion it can be seen that, while there are compelling
theoretical reasons for extending direct responsibility for human rights
violations to MNEs, the legal reality is still that such responsibility remains to be
achieved. None the less, in the light of the *Unocal* and *Wiwa* litigation, there are

---

[46] In this regard see also *Kadic* v. *Karadzic*, 70 F.3d 232 (2d Cir. 1995), where it was held that the Alien Tort Claims Act reaches the conduct of private parties provided that their conduct is undertaken under the colour of state authority or violates a norm of international law that is recognized as extending to the conduct of private parties.

[47] USCA 2d Cir.,14 Sept. 2000: 2000 US App. LEXIS 23274.

[48] 28 USC s.1350 App (1991).

[49] See Kamminga, 'Holding multinational corporations accountable', pp. 559, 569.

[50] See e.g. *Young James and Webster* v. *UK* (1981) E.Ct.HR Series A vol. 44; *X and Y* v. *The Netherlands* (1985) E.Ct.HR Series A vol. 91; *Arzte für das Leben* (1988) E. Ct.HR Series A, vol. 139. See further Harris, O'Boyle and Warbrick, *The law of the European Convention on Human Rights*, pp. 19–22; A. Drzemczewski, *European Human Rights Convention in domestic law* (Oxford: Oxford University Press, 1983), ch. 8; Clapham, *Human rights in the private sphere*, ch. 7.

[51] *Costello-Roberts* v. *UK*, E.Ct.HR (1993) Series A vol. 247.

Human rights and multinationals

some signs that an emergent direct liability of this kind may be accepted, provided that it can be shown that the firm in question has taken a direct part in the alleged violation of fundamental human rights.

MNEs can observe fundamental human rights

In response to the view that MNEs cannot be subjected to human rights responsibilities because they are incapable of observing human rights designed to direct state action, it may be said that, to the contrary, MNEs can affect the economic welfare of the communities in which they operate and, given the indivisibility of human rights, this means that they have a direct impact on the extent that economic and social rights, especially labour rights in the workplace, can be enjoyed. Furthermore, although it is true that MNEs may not have direct control over matters arising outside the workplace they may none the less exercise important influence in this regard. Thus, MNEs may seek to defend the human rights of their employees outside the workplace, to set standards for their subcontractors and to refuse to accept the benefits of governmental measures that seek to improve the business climate at the expense of fundamental human rights.[52] Furthermore, where firms operate in unstable environments they should ensure that their security arrangements comply with fundamental human rights standards.[53] Moreover, where companies have no direct means of influence they should avoid, at the very least, making statements or engaging in actions that appear to condone human rights violations. These may include silence in the face of such violations.[54] Finally, all firms should develop an internal human rights policy which ensures that such concerns are taken into account in management decision-making, and which may find expression in a corporate code of conduct.[55]

NGOs are not the problem

Finally, the argument that MNEs may be subjected to arbitrary and selective targeting by NGOs should not be overstated. While it is true that such behaviour can arise out of what Upendra Baxi has termed 'the market for human rights',[56] in which NGOs strive for support from a consuming public in a manner not dissimilar to that of a service industry, MNEs are big enough to take care of themselves. In any case the activities of campaigning NGOs depend, in part, for their success on complicity from the mass media, which

[52] See Amnesty International Dutch Section and Pax Christi International, *Multinational enterprises and human rights*, pp. 50–1.

[53] See Amnesty International UK Business Group, *Human rights guidelines for companies* (London: Amnesty International, 1998), pp. 8–11.

[54] Amnesty International Dutch Section and Pax Christi International, *Multinational enterprises and human rights*, pp. 52–4.

[55] Ibid., ch. 5.

[56] Baxi, 'Voices of suffering', pp. 161–9.

Peter T. Muchlinski

must be prepared to publicize the unacceptable behaviour of targeted MNEs. Thus the NGOs depend on one set of MNEs—the media corporations—to raise consciousness about the wrongdoing of other MNEs. As a result they may not be in full control of the process of consciousness raising, notwithstanding the claims made about the strength of direct contact between activists and concerned individuals through the Internet. However, as NGOs become more prominent as representatives of a critical approach to transnational business, calls for their regulation and increased accountability may be expected.[57]

A proper balance: state and MNE responsibility for human rights compared

What, then, is the proper role of MNEs in the attribution of responsibility for human rights violations? The first thing to stress again is that, in general, corporations are unlikely to act in a manner that deliberately seeks to violate fundamental human rights. They are business organizations and on the whole they will not espouse such policies.[58] States, by contrast, are far more prone to act in a manner that violates fundamental human rights, whether due to an inadvertent and isolated abuse of power by officials or as a result of a concerted state policy. Indeed, it may be said that the extension of human rights responsibilities to corporations makes them appear more important than they should be. It appears to treat corporations as quasi-governmental public institutions. That is to give them a constitutional status that they neither deserve nor need in order to be useful social actors. They can be regulated to act in a socially responsible manner without an alteration of their status as private law entities. The whole point of the argument here is that private entities can themselves violate human rights, and can be made accountable for this through the normal operation of the law. There is no need to alter their status to do so, and it is not part of the position being taken by advocates of this extension of human rights responsibilities. Furthermore, in treating corporations as if they were quasi-public institutions there is a risk that the continuing responsibility of states, as the prime movers behind violations of human rights, will be down-played. In all the major cases of reported corporate abuses of human rights, the host state was prominently and actively involved. It should not escape full blame for situations that it has primarily created and human rights activists must not settle for holding the corporation alone responsible.

Moreover, appeals to corporate responsibilities for human rights violations must not absolve states from the responsibility for putting into place effective regulatory systems for the protection and promotion of the social and political goals implicit in appeals to human rights. It is the duty of the socially responsible

[57] See Michael Edwardes, 'Make the protesters accountable', *Financial Times*, 20 June 2000, p. 27; The Foreign Policy Centre, 'NGO rights and responsibilities: a new deal for global governance' (2000) at *www.fpc.org.uk*.
[58] See 'Doing business in difficult places', *The Economist*, 20 May 2000, p. 127.

Human rights and multinationals

state to adopt policies that help to foster the well-being of its citizens. A proper system of regulation which demands that corporations observe fundamental rights at work, and in their relations with the wider community, is one way of achieving this goal. It entails the adoption of detailed and specialized regulatory laws. These will give effect to the aspirations behind human rights standards through the establishment of wider regulatory regimes in areas such as labour rights, health and safety or environmental protection, to name but a few. Thus the overall content of the host country's legal system, both substantive and procedural, may be more significant than the institution of wide and general exhortations for firms to observe human rights.

However, such appeals may be useful where the host state lacks an effective legal order for the regulation of socially responsible corporate behaviour. In this sense, the movement towards binding corporate obligations to observe human rights is, in reality, a method for the extraterritorial extension, through the transnational management network of the MNE, of high regulatory standards to be found in democratic market economies to host countries that fail to acknowledge such standards in their national laws and practices.[59] It is this aspect of the issue that has encouraged some states to express concerns about the importation of higher regulatory standards as a form of protectionism and cultural imperialism. That in turn raises the question of the relativity of human rights, which, as noted above, has been a major problem throughout the history of human rights discourse. All that needs to be said here is that, if one accepts the indivisibility and universality of human rights, such arguments carry little weight and may be dismissed as little more than justifications for an unwillingness to espouse human rights based policies on the part of the objecting state.

Thus the argument put here insists on keeping the state at the heart of responsibilities for the protection and promotion of human rights, and on seeing the responsibility of corporations for violations of human rights as a subordinate concern, given the general unlikelihood that MNEs will deliberately and knowingly violate such rights.

However, it has also been accepted that, in certain extreme cases, the direct involvement of an MNE with the host country in violations of fundamental human rights can be shown to exist. Here, legal doctrine can develop to ensure a proper sharing of responsibility between the state and the corporation. Of particular value is the notion of the 'joint enterprise' or 'joint venture' between the state and firm. If it can be shown that an MNE obtains a material economic benefit from operating in an environment where it knows that the business venture in which it is engaged involves state-sponsored violations of human rights, or where, in extreme cases, the firm itself engages in such violations in the course of operating the venture, that firm will be directly liable for those violations on a joint and several basis with the host state. This will be so

---

[59] For a developed application of this argument to fundamental labour rights see Bob Hepple, 'A race to the top? International investment guidelines and corporate codes of conduct', *Comparative Labour Law and Policy Journal* 20, 1999, pp. 347–63.

Peter T. Muchlinski

irrespective of the private legal status of the firm, or of the formal legal relationship between the host state and the firm, so long as it can be shown that the two were collaborating in the conduct of the venture.[60] That much can be gleaned from the decisions of the US District Court in *Unocal*. The remaining question arising in the light of *Unocal* is whether the threshold for liability should remain with proof of direct involvement in the violations under review, or whether indirect involvement and benefit to the corporation should be enough to ground liability. The choice depends on the extent to which the legal order sees fit to make the firm responsible. In this regard the deterrent effect of a liability based on knowledge of violations coupled with proof of a tangible benefit therefrom may be important. In addition, there is the question of where MNE liability for alleged abuses of human rights ultimately falls. Should the entire group enterprise of the MNE including, especially, the ultimate parent be liable, or only the local affiliate most directly involved in the alleged abuses? This raises complex questions of enterprise liability. Again, if a deterrent effect is sought then the entire managerial network of the MNE should be responsible for violations of human rights. The parent should not be allowed to hide behind the corporate veil that separates it from its affiliates, nor to escape liability by way of 'forum shopping' for a jurisdiction in which its defence is more likely to prevail.[61] In this connection the USCA decision in the *Wiwa* case is a welcome precedent, although it is confined to the particular public policy environment of US law relating to torture claims.

Furthermore, a climate of expectation as to proper corporate conduct should be built up through both 'soft law' and 'hard law' options. Developments in 'soft law' through corporate and NGO codes of conduct are already creating a climate in which it may be expected that the management of MNEs includes a conscious assessment of the human rights implications of an investment, particularly in host countries known to have a poor human rights record. Such analysis can be expected as part of the risk assessment associated with an investment decision. If such an input is missing from the corporation's decision-making, or where the corporation deliberately accepts that it will be complicit in human rights violations, then at least moral corporate responsibility for violations of human rights will follow. This may be highlighted by concerned NGOs to the detriment of the firm's public image and social standing. Whether or not that results in financial loss is not really the issue—loss of corporate reputation is in itself the loss of a valuable asset.

Turning to 'hard law' approaches, it remains to be seen whether national laws and international instruments will develop positive duties on the part of corporations to observe fundamental human rights. Apart from the nascent

---

[60] See further Anita Ramasastry, 'Secrets and lies? Swiss banks and international human rights', *Vanderbilt Journal of Transnational Law* 31, 1998, pp. 325–456.
[61] See Kamminga, 'Holding multinational corporations accountable', pp. 562–3; Muchlinski, *Multinational enterprises and the law*, ch. 9; P. T. Muchlinski, 'Corporations in international litigation: problems of jurisdiction and the United Kingdom asbestos cases', *International and Comparative Law Quarterly* 50, 2001, pp. 1–25.

Human rights and multinationals

'joint enterprise' doctrine mentioned above, it may become common practice for national company laws to include a legally binding commitment to the observance of human rights as part of the directors' duties, supplemented by reporting obligations on corporate social policy. Furthermore, specialized laws may be passed to ensure the observance of minimum standards of human rights and social responsibility by national corporations while operating abroad. A bill to this effect is currently before the Australian parliament.[62] Finally, provisions in international investment agreements addressed both to states and to corporations, requiring the observance of fundamental human rights in the course of their economic operations, may be included.[63] Thus, it is not difficult to create technical legal solutions to the question of corporate responsibility for human rights violations. The real issue is whether the political will exists to put them in place. Although the problem of violations of human rights by corporations can be overstated, in those exceptional cases where a MNE is implicated in such activities the law must not remain silent. It must be able to meet the problem head-on and to control and to deter such behaviour.

---

[62] Corporate Code of Conduct Bill 2000, The Parliament of the Commonwealth of Australia, draft of 28 August 2000.
[63] See Kamminga, 'Holding multinational corporations accountable'.

[2]

The Amorality of Profit: Transnational Corporations and Human Rights

By
Beth Stephens*

I.
INTRODUCTION

On the plane to California in March 2001, on my way to present a paper on corporate accountability and the Holocaust, I discovered a remarkably pertinent book review in that day's New York Times.[1] The review addressed a recently published book on the role of IBM in Nazi Germany, *IBM and the Holocaust,* by Edwin Black.[2] In his book, Black condemns IBM and its management for selling a revolutionary data management system to the Nazis. Black concludes that this system enabled Nazi Germany to organize information about the tens of millions of people under their control, a key tool without which they would not have been able to implement their brutally efficient extermination program. The reviewer, Richard Bernstein, challenges the conclusion that Germany needed IBM's technology.[3] Even if Black's assertions were true, however, Bernstein offers a pointed critique of Black's underlying moral assumptions. IBM's conduct, according to Bernstein, merely demonstrated "the utter amorality of the profit motive and its indifference to consequences."[4] "[M]any American companies did what I.B.M. did," Bernstein writes.[5] That is, "they refused to walk

---

*   Associate Professor of Law, Rutgers-Camden Law School. My thanks to several generations of Rutgers-Camden research assistants: Christine Park, Mellany Alio, Danielle Buckley, Evelyn Cox, Kelly Lenahan, and Mark Morgan, as well as to the staff of the Rutgers-Camden law library. I should note that as a cooperating attorney with the Center for Constitutional Rights, I have assisted the plaintiffs in several of the human rights lawsuits against corporations discussed in this article.
1.   Richard Bernstein, *I.B.M.'s Sales to the Nazis: Assessing the Culpability,* N.Y. TIMES, March 7, 2001, at E8.
2.   EDWIN BLACK, IBM AND THE HOLOCAUST: THE STRATEGIC ALLIANCE BETWEEN NAZI GERMANY AND AMERICA'S MOST POWERFUL CORPORATION (2001).
3.   Bernstein questions whether the Nazis in fact required IBM technology:

> Is Mr. Black really correct in his assumption that without I.B.M.'s technology, which consisted mainly of punch cards and the machines to tabulate them, the Germans wouldn't have figured out a way to do what they did anyway? Would the country that devised the Messerschmitt and the V-2 missile have been unable to devise the necessary means to slaughter millions of victims without I.B.M. at its disposal?

Bernstein, *supra* note 1, at E8.
4.   *Id.*
5.   *Id.*

46	*BERKELEY JOURNAL OF INTERNATIONAL LAW*	[Vol. 20:45

away from the extraordinary profits obtainable from trading with a pariah state such as Nazi Germany."[6] Such business decisions, he concludes, were reasonable, morally neutral choices.

Over the past decade, new revelations about corporate involvement in the Holocaust have sharpened our understanding of the extent to which even businesses that remained neutral towards Nazi Germany were able to profit from the Holocaust. Bernstein's perspective makes clear one ethical evaluation of such conduct: business as usual. At the same time, however, litigation against those corporations has demonstrated that the law takes a very different approach. Morally defensible or not, business as usual or not, if corporations are complicit in human rights violations, the victims of the abuses have a legal right to compensation from those corporations.

It is appropriate that the Holocaust serve as the trigger for a reassessment of corporations, morality and legal accountability. The horrors of World War II triggered the transformation of international human rights law. Over the fifty years since the Holocaust, the international community has recognized that governments can be held liable for abuses directed at both their own citizens and foreigners, during war and when at peace—and that individuals can be held accountable as well. Today, the abuses of the Holocaust are contributing to the development of new approaches to human rights accountability, this time focusing on corporate human rights violations and the line between the legally acceptable pursuit of profit and criminal or tortious behavior.

Profit-maximization, if not the *only* goal of all business activity, is certainly central to the endeavor. And the pursuit of profit is, by definition, an amoral goal—not necessarily immoral, but rather morally neutral.[7] An individual or business will achieve the highest level of profit by weighing all decisions according to a self-serving economic scale. Large corporations magnify the consequences of the amoral profit motive. Multiple layers of control and ownership insulate individuals from a sense of responsibility for corporate actions. The enormous power of multinational corporations enables them to inflict greater harms, while their economic and political clout renders them difficult to regulate.

Corporate involvement in the Holocaust illustrates each of these points. Decisions as to whether to conduct business with the Nazi regime were often made in purely economic, amoral terms. Shareholders and managers were able to enjoy the profits generated from such business without directly confronting the human consequences of their business operations. Hundreds of thousands of people were harmed by corporate activities that spanned national borders and thus escaped regulation.

The role of corporations in the Holocaust also highlights an additional observation: Allowing corporate misdeeds to go unresolved compounds the problem dramatically. Fifty years later, attempts to compensate those harmed raise

6. *Id.* (quoting BLACK, *supra* note 2, at 232).
7. Unless, of course, one believes either that the pursuit of economic gain is by definition immoral or, at the other extreme, that making money is by itself a moral good.

thorny questions, even beyond the factual issues generally present when attempting to determine the details of events that took place half a century ago. The use of slave labor by the Ford Motor Company, for example, arguably contributed to the vast expansion of that company over the following decades.[8] But our modern judicial systems have difficulty calculating the value of that input to the company or to the millions of individual shareholders who might be asked to disgorge profits based in part on that labor. One of the many painful lessons we can draw from the Holocaust, then, is the need to settle corporate accounts in a timely fashion.[9] By providing prompt compensation to those injured, we both offer justice to the victims of abuse and also prevent ill-gotten profits from becoming the foundation for future corporate growth.

With corporate abuses during the Holocaust as a background, I discuss in this article the development of corporate human rights law, looking both at the norms to which corporations must now conform and at the still weak efforts to enforce those norms. Corporate accountability for human rights abuses has received much attention over the past few years from governments, human rights organizations, business groups, and even the United Nations. Little has been written, however, about the relationship between corporate human rights norms and the legal structure of business organizations. My first goal in this essay is to strengthen the foundation of corporate human rights regulation by situating it within the extensive literature on the nature of the corporate entity and government power to impose limits on that entity.

My second goal is to propose an assertive approach to interpreting corporate human rights responsibilities. Both domestic governments and international organizations have danced around this topic, urging voluntary codes of conduct rather than seeking to impose binding rules of law. I argue that such circumspection is unfounded. Corporations are already bound by many core human rights norms. So-called voluntary codes that ask business entities to refrain from committing genocide or to avoid profiting from slave labor are weak concessions to the enormous economic and political power of multinational corporations.

Before beginning, a definitional parenthesis: I define the multinational corporation as any firm which "owns (in whole or in part), controls and manages income generating assets in more than one country."[10] As Muchlinski explains, control is central to this definition—multinational corporations do not merely have a financial stake in foreign ventures but also exercise managerial control.[11] This control enables a level of coordination among the various subparts that

---

8. *See, e.g.,* Iwanowa v. Ford Motor Co., 67 F. Supp. 2d 424, 432-34 (D.N.J. 1999) (discussing allegations about Ford's use of slave labor and the impact of that labor on the company's profitability).

9. Current demands for compensation for slavery raise similar issues, over an even longer time period.

10. *See* Peter Muchlinski, Multinational Enterprises and the Law 12 (1995).

11. *Id.*

transforms the multinational corporation from a mere network of independent entities into an entirely new business structure.[12]

I begin in part II with an overview of the human rights problems presented by multinational corporations, looking at modern human rights abuses as well as the Holocaust. Part III explains the regulatory challenge posed by transnational corporations, examining the historical development of the corporate structure and the disjuncture between modern multinational entities and the still largely independent domestic legal systems. Despite these challenges, governments clearly have the legal authority to regulate corporations, either through national or international legal regimes.

I discuss in part IV the foundation of this governmental power to regulate and demonstrate that such regulation is well-accepted in domestic legal systems around the world. In part V, I analyze the current state of the international law governing corporate human rights practices, concluding that core human rights norms apply to corporations as well as to states and individuals. Enforcement of these norms, however, remains "the Achilles' heel" of the system, as it does generally in the human rights arena.[13] In part VI, I discuss this weakness and argue that international norms enforced through international mechanisms or co-ordinated domestic approaches are essential to the effective regulation of corporate human rights abuses.

A final caveat: My purpose in this article is not to enter the debate about whether multinational corporations have, as a whole, been good or bad for humanity. I do not address the benefits that this economic structure may or may not offer. My goal is to address the largely uncontrolled human rights danger posed by multinationals, and I do not pretend to offer a balanced assessment of multinational corporations. I do not accept that human rights abuses are the unavoidable price of economic development. To the contrary: our international and domestic legal systems have available the legal tools necessary to regulate multinational corporations and to deter and punish their human rights abuses.

---

12. International commentary uses various combinations of two sets of terms to refer to this entity: transnational/multinational and corporation/enterprise. The various combinations of these four terms are then abbreviated as MNCs, MNEs, TNCs and TNEs. A spirited literature ascribes content to the debate. *See* MUCHLINSKI, *supra* note 10, at 12-15 (explaining history and content of the disagreements); Menno T. Kamminga & Saman Zia-Zarifi, *Liability of Multinational Corporations Under International Law: An Introduction, in* LIABILITY OF MULTINATIONAL CORPORATIONS UNDER INTERNATIONAL LAW 1, 2-4 (Menno T. Kamminga & Saman Zia-Zarifi eds., 2000) (comparing varying usages of multinational, transnational, corporation and enterprise) [hereinafter LIABILITY OF MULTINATIONAL CORPORATIONS].

"Multinational corporation" has a somewhat wider use and I will give it preference, while taking an expansive view of each of its terms. Thus, I include all cross-border corporate activities, whether they be "trans-" or "multi-" national. My use of the term "corporation" is similarly broad. In the interest of flexibility and readability, and in quotations from other works, I occasionally use the terms transnational and enterprise interchangeably with multinational and corporation.

13. *See* Beth Stephens, *Book Review and Note: Remedies in International Human Rights Law, by Dinah Shelton,* 95 AM. J. INT'L L. 257, 257 (2001) (discussing the absence of an effective enforcement system).

II.

THE CORPORATE HUMAN RIGHTS PROBLEM

Corporate human rights abuses, of course, did not begin with World War II and the Holocaust. The earliest corporate-style multinational enterprises, the British and Dutch East India Companies, abused their extraordinary powers in Asia, Africa and the Americas to undermine local governments and exploit both human and natural resources.[14] These abuses also triggered early consumer human rights protests, including seventeenth century British protests against the slave trade and boycotts in Massachusetts during the eighteenth and nineteenth centuries.[15]

In this section, I discuss the harsh reality that corporations often profit from abusive behavior. From oppressive working conditions to slavery and even genocide, from pollution to environmental destruction, corporations are capable of extracting economic gain from harms inflicted on people and on the environment in which we live. I focus first on the Holocaust, during which thousands of corporations profited in varied ways, and then offer some modern examples. These extreme cases expose the degree to which the corporate pursuit of profit can lead to human rights abuses.

A. The Holocaust

Almost sixty years after World War II, the full extent to which corporations profited from the Holocaust is only now receiving widespread attention. The delayed investigations reflect both the power of corporations to mask their dealings and the difficulties created when justice is so long denied.

Most directly, financial corporations profited by retaining the assets of those killed by the Nazis. Banks and insurance companies pocketed the deposits of families who were exterminated or whose heirs were unaware of their relatives' accounts, as well as those who were unable to supply documentation to support their claims.[16] In addition, banks profited from the mere fact that they

---

14. *See, e.g.,* Teemu Ruskola, *Conceptualizing Corporations and Kinship: Comparative Law and Development Theory in a Chinese Perspective,* 52 STAN. L. REV. 1599, 1677 (2000) (describing the British East India Company as "one of the most notorious corporations of all time," with a bitter legacy in China); Antony Anghie, *Finding the Peripheries: Sovereignty and Colonialism in Nineteenth-century International Law,* 40 HARV. INT'L L.J. 1, 37 (1999) (describing problems in the administration of colonies by corporate bodies as the "unsurprising" result of the fact that "the territories were administered simply for profit."); Bruce P. Frohnen & Charles J. Reid, Jr., *Diversity in Western Constitutionalism: Chartered Rights, Federated Structure, and Natural-law Reasoning in Burke's Theory of Empire,* 29 McGEORGE L. REV. 27, 34-46 (1997) (describing East India Company's rule in India as one of tyranny, despotism, corruption and bribery).

15. *See* Donald C. Dowling, Jr., *The Multinational's Manifesto on Sweatshops, Trade/Labor Linkage, and Codes of Conduct,* 8 TULSA J. COMP. & INT'L L. 27, 52 (2000) ("As far back as the seventeenth century, Britons were outraged at the East India Company's ventures in the slave trade."); Akhil Reed Amar, *A State's Right, a Government's Wrong,* WASH. POST, Mar. 19, 2000, at B1 (Massachusetts citizens boycotted tea from the morally unattractive East India Company in the 18th century.).

16. See Michael J. Bazyler, *Nuremberg in America: Litigating the Holocaust in United States Courts,* 34 U. RICH. L. REV. 1, 31-39 (2000), for discussion of Holocaust claims against Swiss banks; *id.* at 93-136, for claims against European insurance companies; *id.* at 237-249, for claims

were able to handle large accounts from Germany, investing the profits from assets stolen from Nazi victims as well as from goods produced by slave labor.

At the same time, companies exploited slave labor supplied to them by the German army. Recent investigations estimate that hundreds or even thousands of German companies benefited from the slave labor of eight to ten million people.[17] In addition to paying little or nothing to the workers, the companies were often literally permitted to work their laborers to death.[18] Major companies accused of profiting from slave labor include Ford, Siemens, Volkswagen, Daimler-Benz and BMW.[19] According to claims filed against Ford, for example, the Ford affiliate in Germany operated with as much as half of its labor force composed of forced laborers. The company grew rapidly during the war years, emerging from the war as a powerful economic entity.[20] Plaintiffs in the lawsuit sought disgorgement of profits accrued over more than fifty years, alleging that the U.S.-based Ford parent company profited from the rapid growth of its German subsidiary.

Thousands of corporations also did business with the German war industry. Deutsche Bank financed the construction of the Auschwitz concentration camp.[21] Allianz, the second largest insurance company in the world, insured buildings and other facilities in the camp.[22] Pharmaceutical companies supplied medication and other chemicals used in Nazi medical experiments.[23] IBM supplied punch cards for Nazi record-keeping.[24] Profits from these activities enriched successor corporations and have been distributed to investors throughout much of the Western world.

---

against non-Swiss banks. More than a dozen insurance companies have been accused of failing to honor policies issued before World War II. *Id.* at 101.

17. *Id.* at 191-92.

18. The Nazi system included distinctions among workers of different "classes," regulating the amount of food and degree of abuse to which they would be subjected. *Id.* at 191 n.784. Some were intentionally worked to death:

> The Jewish concentration camp workers were less than slaves. Slavemasters care for their human property and try to preserve it; it was the Nazi plan and intention that the Jews would be used up and then burned. The term "slave" is used in this [book] only because our vocabulary has no precise word to describe the lowly status of unpaid workers who are earmarked for destruction.

BENJAMIN B. FERENCZ, LESS THAN SLAVES: JEWISH FORCED LABOR AND THE QUEST FOR COMPENSATION at xvii (1979), quoted in Bazyler, *supra* note 16, at 191 n.784.

19. *Companies and the Holocaust: Industrial Actions,* ECONOMIST, Nov. 14, 1998, at 75, *available in* 1998 WL 11700614.

20. Iwanowa v. Ford Motor Co., 67 F. Supp.2d 424, 432-33 (D.N.J. 1999).

21. *See Deutsche Bank Admits Auschwitz Role,* IRISH TIMES, Feb. 5, 1999, at 51, *cited in* Bazyler, *supra* note 16, at 237-38 n.1030.

22. *See* John Marks & Jack Egan, *Insuring Nazi Death Camps: History Catches Up with Another German Corporation,* U.S. NEWS & WORLD REP., Feb. 22, 1999, at 52, *cited in* Bazyler, *supra* note 16, at 99 n.400.

23. Bazyler, *supra* note 16, at 207 n.843, 249-55.

24. *See* BLACK, *supra* note 2.

B. Modern Day Abuses

Corporate human rights abuses during the Holocaust raised issues unique in human history, as businesses profited from the systematic extermination of millions of people. Similar concerns, on a lesser scale, have been raised by corporate abuses during the past fifty years. Particularly egregious examples include the involvement of the United Fruit Company and ITT in overthrowing elected governments in Guatemala and Chile.[25] Corporations have also participated on a massive scale in the exploitation of natural resources and corruption of national governments.[26]

Such conduct is not a relic of the past: corporate abuses today raise identical issues. In the pursuit of profit and often in partnership with repressive governments, corporations violate the rights to life, to health, to gainful employment, and to political participation. In offering a few examples, I focus on corporate abuses that have generated widely acknowledged violations over the past decade: security measures; sweatshops and other labor rights violations; and environmental harm.

When a business invests in a region with a repressive government and political unrest, it is often impossible to operate without becoming complicit in human rights abuses. Corporations, of course, have legitimate security concerns and a right to protect their employees and property. However, in some situations, it may be impossible to do so without participating in human rights abuses. At one extreme, corporate involvement may include paying such forces to suppress opposition to corporate activities. The Enron Corporation, for example, has been accused of collaborating with the Indian police to violently repress local residents opposed to a massive energy project.[27] Royal Dutch Shell has been sued for alleged complicity in the executions of activists protesting the

---

25. *See* Stephen C. Schlesinger & Stephen Kinzer, Bitter Fruit: The Untold Story of the American Coup in Guatemala (1982) (detailing role of United Fruit in overthrow of government of Guatemala); Multinational Corporations and United States Foreign Policy: Hearings before the Subcomm. on Multinational Corporations of the Senate Comm. on Foreign Relations, 94th Cong., 1st Sess. 381-86 (1975) (describing role of ITT in overthrow of Chilean government).

26. See, for example, Theodore Panayotou, *Counting the Cost: Resource Degradation in the Developing World,* in The Fletcher Forum of World Affairs 270, 271, 272 (1990), for discussions of the environmental impact of multinational activities; Louis Turner, Multinational Companies and the Third World 11-12 (1973), for description of the impact of a 1968 corruption scandal on the government of Peru. Saman Zia-Zarifi explains why "resource extraction" corporations are "particularly prone to associate with egregious violators of human rights":

> [R]esource extraction MNCs . . . have to dig for resources where they find them, typically in the developing world, and where the resource is one of the main sources of income for the government; all this in addition to the massive physical presence demanded for resource extraction work, including construction of large-scale infrastructure and intensive use of labor. . . . [W]ithout slandering the character and image of these corporations, their officers, shareholders, and employees, it is safe to say that sometimes resource extraction MNCs, like other MNCs, follow the path to profit around the world through rough moral terrain and get some of the dirt—if not blood—on their hands.

Saman Zia-Zarifi, *Suing Multinational Corporations in the U.S. for Violating International Law,* 4 UCLA J. Int'l L. & Foreign Aff. 81, 82-83 (1999) (footnotes omitted).

27. *See* Human Rights Watch, The Enron Corporation: Corporate Complicity in Human Rights Violations (1999); Amnesty International, *India: The "Enron Project" in*

company's environmental and development policies in Nigeria.[28] Human rights groups have also criticized British Petroleum for contracting with the Colombian armed forces despite reports of military human rights abuses from many sources, including the U.S. State Department.[29] British Petroleum has acknowledged paying millions of dollars to the government to protect oil operations and has been criticized for taking no steps to ensure that human rights will be respected.[30]

A hotly contested lawsuit has charged the Unocal Corporation with complicity in human rights violations committed by the Burmese military government. A district court last year found that Unocal should not be held liable because it had not been actively involved in the abuses, a holding that is currently on appeal, but nevertheless found credible evidence of substantial corporate knowledge of the abuses:

> Plaintiffs present[ed] evidence demonstrating that before joining the Project, Unocal knew that the [Burmese] military had a record of committing human rights abuses; that the Project hired the military to provide security for the Project, a military that forced villagers to work and entire villages to relocate for the benefit of the Project; that the military, while forcing villagers to work and relocate, committed numerous acts of violence; and that Unocal knew or should have known that the military did commit, was committing and would continue to commit these tortious acts.[31]

These examples highlight the problems raised not only when corporations directly commit human rights abuses, but also when they enter situations in which their activities foster or contribute to such abuses.

Such issues are also presented in the area of labor rights. Certain core labor rights have been recognized as entitled to international protection, including the rights to organize and to collective bargaining and the prohibitions of forced labor and certain kinds of child labor.[32] Transnational corporations search out inexpensive locations to manufacture their products, often choosing countries with low wages and weak protection of labor rights. These practices often lead to denials of these basic rights. Investigations of working conditions in factories supplying goods to well-known brands such as Disney, Nike, and Levi Strauss have drawn attention to abuses including unpaid overtime, child labor, illegally low wages and dangerous working conditions.[33]

Maharashtra: Protests Suppressed in the Name of Development, AMNESTY INTERNATIONAL INDEX: ASA 20/31/97 (July 1997).

28. See summary of allegations in Wiwa v. Royal Dutch Petroleum Co., 226 F.3d 88 (2d Cir. 2000), *cert. denied,* 121 S.Ct. 1402 (2001).

29. Human Rights Watch, *Columbia: Human Rights Concerns Raised by the Security Arrangements of Transnational Oil Companies* (April 1998), *at* http://www.hrw.org/advocacy/corporations/columbia/Oilpat.htm.

30. *Id.*

31. Doe I v. Unocal Corp., 110 F. Supp. 2d 1294, 1306 (C.D. Cal. 2000).

32. *See* International Labor Organization, *Declaration of Fundamental Principles and Rights at Work,* June 18, 1998, ¶ 2(a),(b),(c).

33. *See generally* NO SWEAT: FASHION, FREE TRADE, AND THE RIGHTS OF GARMENT WORKERS (Andrew Ross ed., 1997); Clean Clothes Campaign, *at* www.cleanclothes.org.

Several lawsuits illustrate the environmental harm that transnationals can inflict when freed from the environmental regulations that apply in their home countries. Texaco in Ecuador, Freeport-McMaron in Indonesia, and Shell in Nigeria have all been accused of using devastating practices long banned in Europe and the United States.[34] In Ecuador, for example, Texaco oil operations have reportedly spilled million gallons of oil and dumped billions of gallons of untreated toxic brine into the water and soil.[35] One commentator has described Texaco as using "antiquated, pre-Love Canal technology" in Ecuador.[36] In Indonesia, investigators have accused Freeport-McMaron of dumping hundreds of thousands of tons of toxic mine tailings into local waterways, destroying the local river, flooding surrounding forests, and polluting lakes and ground water.[37] Shell's operations in Nigeria are reported to have devastated large tracts of land, producing fires that burn around the clock and soaking the groundwater with oil.[38]

Current economic incentives are insufficient to trigger voluntary compliance with international human rights standards in the areas of physical integrity, labor rights or the environment. The legal system, however, is also at a disadvantage when regulating multinational actors, particularly those with the economic and political clout of multinational corporations. I look next at the difficulties of regulating multinational corporations, before turning to the options open to both national governments and the international community.

---

34. *See, e.g.,* Wiwa v. Royal Dutch Petroleum Co., 226 F.3d 88 (2d Cir. 2000), *cert. denied,* 121 S.Ct. 1402 (2001) (Shell/Nigeria); Beanal v. Freeport-McMoran, Inc., 197 F.3d 161 (5th Cir. 1999) (Freeport-McMoran/Indonesia); Jota v. Texaco, Inc., 157 F.3d 153 (2d Cir. 1998) (Texaco/Ecuador).

35. *See* Judith Kimerling, *Disregarding Environmental Law: Petroleum Development in Protected Natural Areas and Indigenous Homelands in the Ecuadorian Amazon,* 14 HASTINGS INT'L & COMP. L. REV. 849, 864-72 (1991) (summarizing environmental abuses in Ecuador); Richard L. Herz, *Litigating Environmental Abuses under the Alien Tort Claims Act: A Practical Assessment,* 40 VA. J. INT'L L. 545, 547-48 (2000) (same).

36. Zia-Zarifi, *supra* note 26, at 99.

37. *See* PROJECT UNDERGROUND, RISKY BUSINESS: THE GRASBERG GOLD MINE 10, 14-18 (1998); Herz, *supra* note 35, at 548.

38. *See* Ariadne K. Sacharoff, Note, *Multinationals in Host Countries: Can They Be Held Liable Under the Alien Tort Claims Act for Human Rights Violations?,* 23 BROOK. J. INT'L L. 927, 958-63 (1998) (describing of allegations of violations of environmental norms in Nigeria); *see also* Joshua P. Eaton, Note, *The Nigerian Tragedy, Environmental Regulation of Transnational Corporations, and the Human Right to a Healthy Environment,* 15 B.U. INT'L L.J. 261 (1997) (same).

See also Sudhir K. Chopra, *Multinational Corporations in the Aftermath of Bhopal: The Need for a New Comprehensive Global Regime for Transnational Corporate Activity,* 29 VAL. U. L. REV. 235 (1994) (detailing multinational corporate responsibility for a series of industrial disasters); Hari M. Osofsky, Note, *Environmental Human Rights Under the Alien Tort Statute: Redress for Indigenous Victims of Multinational Corporations,* 20 SUFFOLK TRANSNAT'L L. REV. 335 (1997) (allegations of corporate abuses in Indonesia and Ecuador); William A. Wines, Mark A. Buchanan & Donald J. Smith, *The Critical Need for Law Reform to Regulate the Abusive Practices of Transnational Corporations: The Illustrative Case of Boise Cascade Corporation in Mexico's Costa Grande and Elsewhere,* 26 DENV. J. INT'L L. & POL'Y 453 (1998) (alleging abuses by a logging company in Mexico, including environmental degradation and harassment of protestors).

54   *BERKELEY JOURNAL OF INTERNATIONAL LAW*   [Vol. 20:45

III.

THE REGULATORY CHALLENGE

The modern multinational corporation has evolved over centuries, reaching its current form over the course of the past hundred years. The legal structures governing this modern entity, however, still reflect, to a large degree, the outmoded single-nation structure of the nineteenth century corporation. Corporations are multinational while legal systems are still largely national, creating a disconnect between international corporate structures and the law. A review of the history and focus of the transnational enterprise demonstrates that the multilayered, multinational division of labor and responsibility of the modern corporation, its singled-minded focus on economic gain, and its economic and political power all render multinational corporations a difficult regulatory target. Multinational corporations have long outgrown the legal structures that govern them, reaching a level of transnationality and economic power that exceeds domestic law's ability to impose basic human rights norms.

A. *The Rise of the Transnational Corporation*

The key characteristics of modern transnational business corporations developed piecemeal over the course of hundreds of years. This disjointed history explains the gap between the economic reality and the legal tools available to hold corporate groups accountable for their actions.

The concept of a corporation as a legal unit distinct from its owners traces back to Roman law.[39] The first *business* corporations were chartered by the British Crown in the fifteenth century. These early business corporations followed the already settled corporate model of "a legal unit with its own legal rights and responsibilities, distinct from those of the individuals who constituted its members or shareholders . . . ."[40] The core attributes of a corporation, present in these early models, included the right to sue and be sued, to contract, and to acquire and dispose of property. Shares in the corporation were transferable, and the corporation maintained a continuing existence regardless of its membership.[41] Limited liability, now generally viewed as an additional core element of

---

39. See PHILLIP I. BLUMBERG, THE MULTINATIONAL CHALLENGE TO CORPORATION LAW: THE SEARCH FOR A NEW CORPORATE PERSONALITY 3-7 (1993), for a general history of the corporation. Blackstone credits Numa Pompilius (715-672 B.C.) with the development of the corporation as a means to dilute the power of two warring Roman factions by dividing them into smaller trade and professional groups. 1 WILLIAM BLACKSTONE, COMMENTARIES ON THE LAWS OF ENGLAND 468-69, *cited in* Mark B. Baker, *Private Codes of Corporate Conduct: Should the Fox Guard the Henhouse?*, 24 U. MIAMI INTER-AM. L. REV. 399, 406 n.41 (1993). Baker locates the earliest corporate structures in Rome, in approximately 700 B.C., then traces the development of the modern multinational corporation from fifteenth century merchant families with businesses throughout Europe, through seventeenth and eighteenth century merchant companies with royal charters and monopolies, to nineteenth century industries seeking raw materials from nations around the globe. *Id.* at 401-02.

40. BLUMBERG, *supra* note 39, at 4.

41. *Id.* Additional attributes of the corporation at that time have not survived: a public purpose and monopoly powers. *Id.* at 5-7.

the corporate form, became widespread only in the early nineteenth century in the U.S. and some fifty years later in England.[42]

Until well into the nineteenth century, corporations could be formed only by an act of the government—the king or Parliament in England, or the state legislatures in the United States. General statutes permitting incorporation through registration were not widespread until after the Civil War.[43] The articles of incorporation approved by the government limited the corporation to a specific task. As one means to restrict the scope of activity of any one corporation, ownership of stock in another corporation was generally prohibited. This restriction persisted until the late nineteenth century: the generally accepted rule was that corporations could not own stock in other corporations. This limitation reflected in part a "deep suspicion and hostility" towards corporations and fear of corporate monopoly power.[44] In the words of a Georgia court, "It has ever been considered the very highest public policy to keep a strict watch upon corporations, to confine them within their appointed bounds and especially to guard against the accumulation of large interests under their control."[45]

Despite these restrictions, large multinational enterprises began to develop in the second half of the nineteenth century, as individual corporations expanded their operations.[46] U.S. firms quickly expanded their manufacturing and distribution networks around the world. Muchlinski describes the growth of the American Singer Sewing Company as "the first true manufacturing" multinational enterprise.[47] Over the course of the second half of the nineteenth century, the Singer Company sold finished machines in Europe; it began to assemble sewing machines in Europe from parts manufactured in the United States; and in 1882, it built a factory in Glasgow to manufacture machines from local parts.[48] During the same time period, during the last years of the nineteenth century, corporations based in England, Germany and other European countries began to expand their direct investments in foreign nations.[49]

The rise of the modern transnational corporation in the United States traces to the late 1880s. The legislature of New Jersey, in an effort to attract corporate licensing fees, liberalized corporate regulatory statutes, authorizing businesses incorporated in New Jersey to own stock in any other corporation.[50] This New Jersey statute represented a major turning point in the history of U.S. business. As the other states followed suit, "Corporate groups soon grew to occupy a

---

42. *Id.* at 7-19. Moreover, exceptions to limited liability continued well into the twentieth century, including provisions for double and triple indemnity, and pro rata liability in California. *Id.*

43. *Id.* at 22. The Constitutional Convention overwhelmingly rejected a proposal to grant the power of incorporation to the new Congress. *Id.* at 31.

44. *Id.* at 52-54. "United States colonists were suspicious of corporations, viewing them as representing 'the privileged society against which the settlers were rebelling.'" Baker, *supra* note 39, at 407, *citing* I. MAURICE WORMSER, FRANKENSTEIN, INCORPORATED 28 (1931).

45. Central R.R. v. Collins, 40 Ga. 582, 625, 630 (1869).

46. MUCHLINSKI, *supra* note 10, at 20-21.

47. *Id.* at 21.

48. *Id.*

49. *Id.* at 21-22.

50. BLUMBERG, *supra* note 39, at 56.

56   *BERKELEY JOURNAL OF INTERNATIONAL LAW*   [Vol. 20:45

commanding role in American industry and eventually in the world economy as well."[51]

The protections of limited liability were transferred immediately to these new corporate groups—without any recognition of the distinction between the limited liability of individual shareholders and that of a collective enterprise composed of parent and subsidiary companies engaged in a common enterprise.[52] Blumberg has pointed out the illogic of this extension of limited liability protections to the components of a corporate group:

> It overlooked the fact that the parent corporation and its subsidiaries were collectively conducting a common enterprise, that the business had been fragmented among the component companies of the group, and that limited liability—a doctrine designed to protect investors in an enterprise, not the enterprise itself—would be extended to protect each fragment of the business from liability for the obligations of all the other fragments.[53]

Nevertheless, limited liability within the corporate group remains the norm today.

With this new authority to own stock in other corporations, multinational corporate groups grew rapidly during the years leading up to the first World War, followed by a slow period between the two World Wars, and resumption of rapid expansion after World War II.[54] Post-World War II multinational growth followed a new style. Pre-World War I, international trade had been dominated by imports of raw materials and agricultural products from the developing countries of the South to meet the needs of manufacturers and consumers in the industrialized North.[55] After World War II, the truly modern multinational corporation came to dominate, with integrated production across borders, and goods and services flowing in multiple directions.[56] This modern model has proven difficult to regulate with the legal tools available to the governments of sovereign states.

B. The Difficulty of Regulating Transnational Corporations: Corporate Economic, Political and Legal Power

Multinational corporations have proven to be remarkably efficient economic entities, "formidably effective and swift machine[s]," capable through their coordinated operations of far outperforming smaller scale, national business models.[57] The multinationals exploit to great effect their ability to coordinate operations and to trade and invest internally, seeking the greatest return for

---

51. *Id.* at 58.

52. *Id.* at 58-59.

53. *Id.* at 59.

54. U.S. companies dominated this expansion until the 1960s, when the economies of Europe and Japan recovered from the devastation of the war. The past decade has seen the entry of both the former Socialist nations and developing countries onto the international trade and investment stage. MUCHLINSKI, *supra* note 10, at 26-32.

55. *Id.* at 22.

56. *Id.* at 26.

57. Detlev F. Vagts, *The Multinational Enterprise: A New Challenge for Transnational Law*, 83 HARV. L. REV. 739, 756 (1970).

the group as a whole. In short, "multinational groups pursue a policy of group profit maximization in which the interests of the individual constituent members of the group are subordinated to the interests of the parent, that is, the group as a whole."[58]

The tremendous growth of multinational corporations has raised new accountability dilemmas. Corporations have grown to a level of economic power that dwarfs most nation-states. General Motors, for example, is larger than the national economies of all but seven countries.[59] The largest fifteen corporations have revenues greater than all but thirteen nations.[60] And the trend is toward greater corporate dominance: a comparison of figures from 1991 and 2000 shows a dramatic change over nine years. In 1991, nineteen countries had revenues greater than General Motors, compared to only seven today; similarly, in 1991, three corporations were among the top twenty-eight economic entities, compared to fifteen today.[61]

Concerns about corporate economic power are not new: analysts have decried growing corporate power as far back as the Dutch East India Corporation.[62] President Lincoln expressed concern about the growth of corporate power following the Civil War.[63] On the international stage, corporate dominance over the economy became an issue of global concern in the 1960s.[64] This pattern has accelerated over the past decade, as the socialist economies collapsed

---

58. BLUMBERG, *supra,* note 39, at 139. Vagts cautions against exaggeration of the internal consistency of corporate decision-making, noting that corporate "structures house considerable tensions between different levels of management, between home offices and branches abroad, between line and staff," so that "one must consider MNE activities as the end-product of a coalition of individuals pursuing somewhat different goals and coordinated only to a limited degree toward the achievement of a common purpose." Vagts, *supra* note 57, at 753. Despite this caution, however, he concludes that the multinational corporation is "basically a coherent organization with a narrow range of economic motivations," capable of efficient, coordinated economic activity. *Id.* at 756.

59. Only the economies of the United States, Germany, Italy, the United Kingdom, Japan, France and the Netherlands are larger than General Motors. *See* Global Policy Forum, *Comparison of Revenues Among States and TNCs, at* http://www.globalpolicy.org/socecon/tncstat2.htm (last visited May 23, 2001).

60. *Id.*

61. Compare *id.* with *Nations v. Corporations, at* http://www.ratical.com/corporations/NvC.html (last visited May 23, 2001).

62. *See* sources cited *supra,* note 14 (noting contemporary concerns about Dutch East India Company and its powers).

63. Lincoln wrote in a letter in 1864:

> I see in the near future a crisis approaching that unnerves me and causes me to tremble for the safety of my country. As a result of the war, corporations have been enthroned and an era of corruption in high places will follow, and the money power of the country will endeavor to prolong its reign by working upon the prejudices of the people until all wealth is aggregated in a few hands and the Republic is destroyed. I feel at this moment more anxiety for the safety of my country than ever before, even in the midst of war. God grant that my suspicions may prove groundless.

Letter from Lincoln to Col. William F. Elkins, Nov. 21, 1864, *in* THE LINCOLN ENCYCLOPEDIA 40 (Archer H. Shaw ed., 1950) (quoting EMANUEL HERTZ, 2 ABRAHAM LINCOLN: A NEW PORTRAIT 954 (1931)).

64. "That the world's largest multinational corporations . . . are more powerful and influential than many States has been a cliché since the 1960s." Menno T. Kamminga, *Holding Multinational Corporations Accountable for Human Rights Abuses: A Challenge for the EC, in* THE EU AND HUMAN RIGHTS 553, 553 (Philip Alston ed., 1999).

and opened up to capitalist investment, and as developed nations reduced regulation of international trade and investment, and pressured developing nations to do the same. "No longer is the control of the potentially negative impacts of TNCs the major issue; rather it is how best to reintegrate developing countries into the global economy in a manner that ensures inflows of new investment capital."[65] With the fall of the Soviet bloc, economic deregulation has become the mantra of the new millennium. International trade agreements have pushed the free trade model upon even the more reluctant national governments. "States once critical of TNCs now find themselves competing for the benefits of foreign direct investment from multinational companies."[66]

As both cause and effect of growing corporate economic power, the international and domestic political systems have increasingly relinquished their control over business. Economic power carries with it a growing political clout. Corporations play influential direct and indirect roles in negotiations over issues ranging from trade agreements to international patent protections to national and international economic policy.[67] This political power is in part a recognition of the economic advantages of the multinational corporate model. But it also reflects corporate power advantages that put governments at a disadvantage. Governments themselves are coalitions, representing varying interests, and may have difficulty submerging those differences into a common policy.[68] "MNE's [Multi-National Enterprises] in the past often have used their bargaining skills, their clearly conceived purposes and their overall experience to outdo naive and divided governments."[69]

The very strengths of transnationals render them difficult regulatory targets. As corporate power becomes increasingly international and increasingly disassociated from the nation-state, regulation becomes more difficult. "The fact that they have multiple production facilities means that TNCs can evade state power and the constraints of national regulatory schemes by moving their operations between their different facilities around the world."[70] Regulatory schemes are largely domestic, based upon national laws, administrative bodies and judicial systems, while transnationals operate across borders.[71] Over thirty years ago, Professor Vagts pointed out that "the present legal framework has no comfortable, tidy receptacle for such an institution," producing a tension between the legal theory of independent corporate units, each "operating as a native within the country of its incorporation," and the reality of the "economic interdepen-

---

65. MUCHLINSKI, *supra* note 10, at 596.

66. Barbara A. Frey, *The Legal and Ethical Responsibilities of Transnational Corporations in the Protection of International Human Rights*, 6 MINN. J. GLOBAL TRADE 153, 160 (1997).

67. *See generally* Vivien A. Schmidt, *The New World Order, Incorporated: The Rise of Business and the Decline of the Nation State, in* 124 DAEDALUS 75 (1995).

68. Vagts, *supra* note 57, at 757.

69. *Id.* at 780.

70. Claudio Grossman & Daniel D. Bradlow, *Are We Being Propelled Towards a People-Centered Transnational Legal Order?*, 9 AM. U. J. INT'L L. & POL'Y 1, 8 (1993).

71. "In the modern world of transnational corporations, the economic actor is typically the corporate group; however, the law continues to focus on each component company, rather than on the group, as the legal actor." BLUMBERG, *supra* note 39, at 205.

dence" of the multinational corporation.[72] More recently, even George Soros has decried the lack of a global system capable of regulating global capitalism.[73]

In addition, the recent trend toward decreasing government control over international commerce has led to the weakening of ties between transnational corporations and particular states. The state of incorporation may be nothing more than a convenient location chosen for tax and other regulatory advantages.[74] "One important effect of these developments is that TNCs have become 'de-nationalized' in the sense that they view the world, rather than their home or host states, as their base of operations."[75] With multinational sources of financing, operations, and international joint ventures, "corporations are part of a 'global web' that increasingly defies categorization by national origin."[76] The dispersed corporate form permits corporations to establish legally independent entities around the world, a multinationality that transforms into statelessness.

However, states cannot regulate transnational corporations effectively without addressing all aspects of the operation. "From the viewpoint of effective economic regulation, it is not merely appropriate, it is essential that the legal structure match the economic structure of the enterprise subject to the regulatory system."[77] Otherwise, multinationals shift capital and goods to avoid regulation, taxation, capital repatriation rules, and currency exchange controls, and to resist union demands.[78] Prevention of corporate evasion of regulatory standards requires international consensus on the norms applicable to corporations. Enforcement of regulations requires coordinated enforcement mechanisms, whether through international systems or through coordinated domestic structures. I lay the foundation for my discussion of international norms and coordinated enforcement mechanisms by examining the state's power to regulate transnational corporations.

---

72. Vagts, *supra* note 57, at 740, 743.

73. George Soros, *Towards a Global Open Society,* 1/1/98 ATLANTIC MONTHLY 20 (1998) ("[T]he capacity of the state to look after the welfare of its citizens has been severely impaired by the globalization of the capitalist system . . . .").

74. Fleur Johns, *The Invisibility of the Transnational Corporation: An Analysis of International Law and Legal Theory,* 19 MELBOURNE UNIV. L. REV. 893, 895-96 (1994). ("[S]election of a state of incorporation may be a matter of mere convenience—a decision made at a particular time for tax or other reasons. The fact that this decision may have lasting significance at international law seems therefore ludicrous.").

75. Grossman & Bradlow, *supra* note 70, at 8.

76. Schmidt, *supra* note 67, at 79, *citing* ROBERT REICH, THE WORK OF NATIONS (Knopf 1991).

77. BLUMBERG, *supra* note 39, at 201. "The reality of the matter is that effective regulation of corporate groups or their activities inevitably requires control of all the components participating in the enterprise." *Id.* at 200-01. "While the economic forms of enterprise organization have evolved in the direction of multicorporate structures, the legal forms of its organization have remained stuck to a statutory model designed and conceived exclusively for the case of single corporate enterprises." Jose Engracia Antunes, *The Liability of Polycorporate Enterprises,* 13 CONN. J. INT'L L. 197, 207 (1999).

78. BLUMBERG, *supra* note 39, at 139-40.

IV.
THE STATE'S POWER TO REGULATE

Despite centuries of development, and the fact that corporations support the world economy, economists, lawyers, political theorists and philosophers continue to debate the essential definition of the corporation. Under any of the myriad of conflicting views, however, a government has the right and power to regulate corporate firms. Moreover, governments of every variety have done so, holding corporations accountable for their actions through some combination of criminal, civil or administrative sanctions. This section will first demonstrate that whatever their nature and whatever their inherent social responsibilities, governments have the legal authority to hold corporations liable for harms their operations inflict. Next, a comparative review of disparate legal systems will demonstrate that states assert that right through varied legal procedures.

A.   The Inherent Nature of the Corporation: Whatever It Is, It Can Be Held Accountable

Academics and practitioners from several disciplines have produced a vast literature debating the nature of the corporation. The fault lines of this debate reflect several heated disputes about the nature of the corporation, its formation, and its social obligations. Under any of these views, however, government has the right and power to restrict corporate behavior. Without a doubt, states can forbid corporate conduct constituting human rights abuses, such as physical harm, denials of basic labor rights, and harm to the environment, and can hold corporations liable for violations of these basic rights.

1.   The Corporate Nature Debate and Accountability for Human Rights Violations

Debate over the nature of the corporation as a legal and economic institution has continued for centuries. Ninety years ago, the literature on the controversy was described as of "appalling size,"[79] and it has grown apace during the ensuing decades.[80] One product of this multitude of analyses is disagreement even about how to classify the varied theories. Bratton lists three sets of "recurring questions" that are the subject of the inquiry.[81] The first set of questions examines the corporation's "being"—is the corporation a construct of people's minds or a real thing with a separate existence? A second and related line of questions examines the distinction between the corporate being, whatever it is, and "the aggregate of separate individuals and transactions in and around it,"[82] the "entity" or "aggregate" debate. Third is what Bratton terms a "political ver-

---

79.   Arthur W. Machen, Jr., *Corporate Personality,* 24 HARV. L. REV. 253, 254 n.3 (1911).

80.   See William W. Bratton, *The New Economic Theory of the Firm: Critical Perspectives From History,* 41 STAN. L. REV. 1471 (1989), for a thorough analysis and history of the debates.

81.   *Id.* at 1474-75.

82.   *Id.* at 1475.

sion" of these questions, which asks whether the corporation is a creature formed by the state or rather the sum of contractual arrangements by individuals.

Working within a similar framework, Blumberg summarizes three historical answers to these questions.[83] The earliest view of corporate nature, reflecting a time when corporations could only be formed through a special legislative decree, saw the corporation as an artificial person, created by the legislature, not by individuals. Chief Justice Marshall articulated this view of the firm as the artificial creation of law, existing only by virtue of government's permission:

> A corporation is an artificial being, invisible, intangible, and existing only in contemplation of law. Being the mere creature of law, it possesses only those properties which the charter of its creation confers upon it, either expressly, or as incidental to its very existence.[84]

Under this view, the corporation has only those rights and obligations attributed to it by the enacting legislation.[85]

A second view of the corporation describes it as primarily an association of individuals contracting with each other to form the corporation. The Supreme Court employed this view as a means to explain the attribution of constitutional rights to corporations:

> Private corporations are, it is true, artificial persons, but . . . they consist of aggregations of individuals united for some legitimate business . . . . It would be a most singular result if a constitutional provision intended for the protection of every person against partial and discriminating legislation by the states, should cease to exert such protection the moment the person becomes a member of a corporation.[86]

The corporation thus claims certain rights to protect the rights of the individuals of whom it is composed.[87]

A third view, which Professor Blumberg describes as a "strong" version of the entity theory, defines the corporation as an organic being, with independent legal rights that go beyond both those of its shareholders and those granted by the government.[88]

Whether the corporation is a creature created by law, one arising out of a web of individual contractual agreements, or a distinct legal being, it is subject to state regulation. Indeed, as John Dewey pointed out many decades ago, the debate about the inherent nature of the corporation is essentially no different than a debate about what rights and obligations society will choose to impose upon it.[89] " 'The corporation is . . . a right-and-duty-bearing unit,' " with those

---

83. Phillip I. Blumberg, *The Corporate Entity in an Era of Multinational Corporations*, 15 DEL. J. CORP. L. 283, 291-99 (1990).

84. Trustees of Dartmouth College v. Woodward, 17 U.S. (4 Wheat.) 518, 636 (1819).

85. Blumberg, *The Corporate Entity*, supra note 83, at 293.

86. The Railroad Tax Cases, 13 F. 722, 743-44 (C.C.D. Cal. 1882), *writ of error dismissed as moot sub nom. See also* San Mateo County v. Southern Pac. R.R., 116 U.S. 138 (1885); Santa Clara v. Southern Pac. R.R., 18 F. 385 (C.C.D. Cal. 1883), *aff'd*, 118 U.S. 394 (1886).

87. Blumberg, *The Corporate Entity*, supra note 83, at 293-95.

88. *Id.* at 295.

89. *See* John Dewey, *The Historic Background of Corporate Legal Personality*, 35 YALE L.J. 655 (1926).

rights and duties which the law ascribes to it.[90] The imposition of duties upon the corporate unit applies either to the corporation as an entity or to the individuals who contract to establish the corporation. Either way, the state can impose limits on corporate behavior, including accountability for harms caused to others.

To be sure, proponents of the view that the corporation is no more than a set of contractual relations have argued against government regulation, asserting that individuals left to negotiate contracts will better achieve their own and society's goals. "Since their firm 'is contract,' and since private actors do a better job at making contracts than do government officials, they see little constructive role for public policy."[91] This policy argument, however, does not challenge the underlying governmental authority to regulate the corporation. The contracts that form the basis of a corporation under this theory are no more immune from government oversight than individual agreements. Government can impose civil and criminal liability on those who contract to violate the law, regardless of whether or not the contract is formed in a corporate context. The state may prohibit individuals from committing physical abuses, labor law violations, and environmental harm; under any of these corporate theories, the state may also prohibit corporations from committing these offenses.

2. Corporate Amorality

Are multinational corporations amoral by definition? In the vast literature on this issue, vigorous calls for corporate social responsibility are countered by equally spirited cries that business enterprises are, by definition, created only to make a profit.[92] Neither view, however, challenges government's authority to impose regulations on corporations.

In a now-famous essay, Milton Friedman insisted that "the social responsibility of business is to increase its profits."[93] William Safire picked up the refrain decades later, railing against "new socialists" who sought to impose social responsibilities on corporations.[94] Safire argues that his model of unregulated business operations need not entail disregard for the social consequences of business decisions. He insists that corporate executives inevitably adopt socially responsible policies out of self interest:

> Capitalism's defenders know that only stupidly shortsighted executives overlook the need for a loyal, motivated work force; we also know that good community relations help attract the best managers and innovators to a company. And easing the shock of necessary belt-tightening on workers who are not producing is "good P.R.," which makes business sense—provided it does not squander assets on ego-

---

90. *Id.* at 656 (quoting 3 MAITLAND, COLLECTED PAPERS 307 (1911)).
91. Bratton, *supra* note 80, at 1482 (footnote omitted).
92. See ETHICAL THEORY AND BUSINESS (Tom L. Beauchamp & Norman E. Bowie eds., 5th ed. 1997), for a collection of essays giving an overview of the issues.
93. Milton Friedman, *The Social Responsibility of Business is to Increase Its Profits*, N.Y. TIMES MAGAZINE, Sept. 13, 1970, *reprinted in* ETHICAL THEORY AND BUSINESS, *supra* note 92, at 56.
94. William Safire, *The New Socialism*, N.Y. TIMES, Feb. 26, 1996, p. A13.

satisfying do-gooding or becoming the new delivery system for politicians' largesse.

What are the primary "social" responsibilities of a corporation? To serve its owners by returning a profit and its community by paying taxes; to earn the allegiance of customers by delivering value, and to provide a secure future for employees who help it succeed in the marketplace.[95]

However, Safire's premise is questionable even within the United States, with its democratic political system and active media. As Safire describes the motivations leading to socially responsible behavior, profit-based incentives only deter abusive corporate behavior if such behavior leads to "bad P.R." The various interest groups Safire identifies—shareholders, management, employees—have multiple goals, but their self interest is not necessarily advanced by adopting protections against corporate human rights violations.

Moreover, these business-based motives are of no relevance in repressive societies. If the media are unable to report on abusive behavior, there will be no public relations consequences of corporate bad acts. If government leaders share in the inflated profits generated by abusive behavior, they will have no incentive to enforce even the most basic norms. As Douglas Cassel suggests, theories of self-regulating corporate structures work, if at all, only in democratic systems.[96] "In most countries, governments have limited power or resources to do good."[97] The profit motive will inevitably exert pressure against responsibility, creating incentives to cut corners, and to commit abuses. If this is the case even in a democratic society, it is much more the case in a repressive system, where the citizenry has no means by which to force corporate accountability.

The issue of whether businesses are defined as purely profit-seeking or as obligated to respond to certain societal needs is, fundamentally, a question to be decided by society as a whole. Debates about the social obligations of the corporation are "hopelessly circular" because "[o]ur beliefs about what are proper concerns of the business community are themselves social constructs, and have evolved significantly over time in tandem with broader changes in the social and political environment."[98] As proponents of the amorality of profit disengage corporate policy from social concerns, they merely emphasize the role of government in setting the boundaries of acceptable corporate behavior:

> [T]o the extent that this argument asserts that it is the role of government to fashion and implement policy—in this case human rights policy—it also necessarily concedes to government the right to further specific policies by, inter alia, regulating the practices of U.S. corporations. Examples of such regulation, from legislation restricting companies' ability to discriminate or pollute at home, to laws prohibiting corrupt practices by corporations abroad, are too numerous to leave any room for doubting the legitimacy of government efforts to advance social policies in part by regulating corporate behavior.[99]

---

95. *Id.*

96. Douglas Cassel, *Corporate Initiatives: A Second Human Rights Revolution?*, 19 Fordham Int'l L. J. 1963, 1978-80 (1996).

97. *Id.* at 1980.

98. Diane F. Orentlicher & Timothy A. Gelatt, *Public Law, Private Actors: The Impact of Human Rights on Business Investors in China*, 14 Nw. J. Int'l L. & Bus. 66, 96 n.83 (1993).

99. *Id.*

64   *BERKELEY JOURNAL OF INTERNATIONAL LAW*   [Vol. 20:45

Society has the authority to regulate corporate behavior, by defining the terms of the corporate entity and its relationship with the surrounding society. Such has been the conclusion of domestic legal and political systems around the world, a comparative perspective to which I now turn.

B. A Comparative View: Corporate Accountability Across Legal Systems

All domestic legal systems recognize that corporations can be held accountable for harm they cause to others. Part of the core definition of the corporation is that it can both sue and *be sued*. In all legal systems, corporations are held accountable in some way, be it through criminal or civil procedures or through administrative regulations. The collective enterprise, not just the individuals who compose it, is the legal unit for purposes of both claims and obligations.

1. Criminal Liability and Equivalent Sanctions

Legal accountability includes a range of possible procedures and sanctions, including criminal, civil and administrative. In most legal systems, corporate accountability includes criminal liability.[100]

Corporate criminal liability was common in continental Europe in the seventeenth and eighteenth centuries, imposed in great detail, for example, in the French Criminal Code of 1670.[101] The concept fell into disfavor after the French Revolution, however, when corporate-style associations were disbanded and individualism dominated.[102] With the rise of industrialization over the course of the nineteenth and early twentieth century came a corresponding interest in holding businesses liable for injuries inflicted by their operations. In England and Canada as well as the U.S., legislatures and courts gradually expanded the notion of corporate criminal accountability. Starting with liability for breaches of statutory duties, by the mid-twentieth century the doctrine had evolved from vicarious liability for the acts of employees to include direct liability for corporate actions.[103]

Most of the civil law systems of continental Europe have returned to corporate criminal liability, led by the Netherlands in the 1920s and 1930s.[104] The Council of Europe gave additional impetus to this movement in 1988, recommending that member states adapt their laws to permit corporate criminal prosecutions.[105] In response, France amended its laws in 1991, returning to the curiously modern principles of corporate crime that it had followed before the

---

100. *See generally* CRIMINAL LIABILITY OF CORPORATIONS (Hans de Doelder & Klaus Tiedemann eds., 1996) (XIVth International Congress of Comparative Law); CELIA WELLS, CORPORATIONS AND CRIMINAL RESPONSIBILITY (1993); L.H. Leigh, *The Criminal Liability of Corporations and Other Groups: A Comparative View*, 80 MICH. L. REV. 1508 (1982).

101. Guy Stessens, *Corporate Criminal Liability: A Comparative Perspective*, 43 INT'L & COMP. L.Q. 493, 494 (1994).

102. *Id.* at 494-95.

103. *See id.* at 495-98.

104. *Id.* at 500.

105. Council of Europe Recommendation No. R(88)18.

revolution.[106] The Inter-American system as well has recommended that states adapt their laws to permit criminal prosecution of corporations.[107] The environmental movement has further spurred the recognition of corporate crime, with widespread adoption of statutes imposing criminal sanctions for corporate violations of environmental safeguards.[108]

Exceptions to corporate criminal liability persist. Argentina, for example, maintains the doctrine of *societas delinquere non potest,* that is, an association cannot be the author of a crime.[109] Nevertheless, the concept continues to expand in Asia[110] and Latin America,[111] and the international trend is toward acceptance of the criminal liability of corporations.[112] Andrew Clapham offers an interesting indication of the increasing acceptance of the concept of corporate criminal liability—culled, ironically, from the defeat of a proposal to include corporate defendants within the statute of the proposed International Criminal Court.[113] Clapham details the procedural and definitional problems that led to the withdrawal of the proposal,[114] but notes that the negotiators demonstrated general support for the theoretical principle that corporations can be bound by criminal law, to the extent that "no delegation challenged the conceptual assumption that legal persons are bound by international criminal law."[115]

> The question *whether* legal persons are bound by international criminal law was never posed. The disagreements arose over the complexities involved in interna-

---

106. WELLS, *supra* note 100, at 122.

107. *See* Inter-American Juridical Committee, *Inter-American Model Legislation on Illicit Enrichment and Transnational Bribery*, OEA/Ser.Q CJI/doc.70/98 rev. 2, adopted Aug. 22, 1998, ("Although some legal systems do not allow for criminal sanctions the intention is that the legislating State will adapt its law to do so, so as to comply with the Convention.").

108. *See, e.g.,* Donald A. Carr & William L. Thomas, *Devising a Compliance Strategy under the ISO 14000 International Environmental Management Standards*, 15 PACE ENVTL. L. REV. 85, 93-94, 94 n.17 (1997) (describing increasing reliance on criminal sanctions for environmental violations); Sevine Ercmann, *Enforcement of Environmental Law in United States and European Law: Realities and Expectations*, 26 ENVTL. L. 1213, 1218-19 (1996) (detailing use of administrative, civil and criminal sanctions to enforce environmental law in the United States and Europe).

109. Romina Picolotti and Juan M. Picolotti, *Human Rights and Corporations: Legal Responsibility of Corporations for Human Rights Abuses in Argentina* (Maria-Candela Conforti trans., 2000) (on file with author).

110. *See* Kevin A. Gaynor & Thomas R. Bartman, *Criminal Enforcement of Environmental Laws*, 10 COLO. J. INT'L ENVTL. L. & POL'Y 39, 92-93 (1999) (describing corporate criminal sanctions for environmental injuries in Asia, including Thailand and Singapore).

111. *See id.,* at 92 n.330 (citing corporate criminal penalties in Brazil and other Latin American countries). *See also* Chijioke Okoli, *Criminal Liability of Corporations in Nigeria: A Current Perspective*, 38 J. AFR. L. 35 (1994) (1990 Nigerian statute explicitly provides for corporate criminal and civil liability).

112. *See, e.g.,* Theodor Meron, *Is International Law Moving Towards Criminalization?*, 9 EUR. J. INT'L L. 18, 20 (1998) (noting the international "movement towards this form of criminalization," so that "in the modern business world a corporation itself may be criminally liable for the actions or omissions of agents acting on the corporations behalf . . . ."); Klaus Tiedemann, *Rapport General, in* CRIMINAL LIABILITY OF CORPORATIONS, *supra* note 100, at 11, 12-13 (recognizing gradual adoption of corporate criminal liability, although the concept is not yet universally accepted).

113. Andrew Clapham, *The Question of Jurisdiction Under International Criminal Law Over Legal Persons: Lessons from the Rome Conference on an International Criminal Court, in* LIABILITY OF MULTINATIONAL CORPORATIONS, *supra* note 12, at 139-95.

114. *Id.* at 157-58.

115. *Id.* at 191.

tional trial of a non-natural person: *how* to serve the indictment, *who* would represent the interests of the legal person, *how much* intention need be proved, *how* to ensure that natural persons could not hide behind group responsibility.[116]

In fact, delegates were more concerned about the impact of corporate criminal responsibility on quasi-public corporate entities and non-governmental associations such as the Palestinian Liberation Organization than about the consequences for private corporations.[117]

Within the growing acceptance of corporate criminal liability, there are different approaches to determining when and how a corporation can be held to have committed a crime. According to U.S. federal law, corporations can be held liable when a corporate employee has committed a crime while acting within the scope of his or her authority, with an intent to benefit the corporation.[118] Each of these requirements has been interpreted broadly. Thus, if a crime includes a required knowledge or intent, a corporation may be held liable based on the collective knowledge of various employees. Virtually all job-related acts are considered within the scope of employment, and a broad range of neutral or even harmful acts are considered to have benefited the corporation.[119] By contrast, in some legal systems, only the acts of corporate officers or policymakers can be attributed to the corporation.[120] Yet another approach holds a corporation liable if "its procedures and practices unreasonably fail to prevent criminal violations."[121] Once again, however, these differences do not undermine the key building block of corporate accountability: corporations can be held liable for criminal violations committed by their employees, even if legal systems disagree about exactly what behavior by which employees will render the corporation liable.

One indication of the general acceptance of the need to expose corporations to the risk of criminal-like sanctions is that systems that do not directly recognize corporate criminal liability compensate by imposing similar alternatives, thus achieving something virtually identical to penal liability. As Stessens has detailed, such systems employ substitute, or "ersatz" corporate sanctions, "without attaching a 'criminal label'" to the penalty.[122] One such alternative is a system of administrative fines. These differ from criminal fines only in that they are imposed by an administrative agency, not a criminal court—with the conse-

---

116. *Id.*

117. *Id.*

118. John C. Coffee, *Corporate Criminal Responsibility, in* 1 ENCYCLOPEDIA OF CRIME AND JUSTICE 253, 255 (Sanford H. Kadish ed., 1983).

119. *Id.* at 255-56.

120. *Id.* at 254-55; Stessens, *supra* note 101, at 506-10; WELLS, *supra* note 100, at 94.

121. WELLS, *supra* note 100, at 95. Liability for corporate policies is an important response to the fact that the corporation's internal structures may be faulty, whether or not individual employees are also personally responsible for the violation. "[G]enerally the criminal acts of a modern corporation result not from the isolated activity of a single agent, but from the complex interactions of many agents in a bureaucratic setting." Note, *Corporate Crime: Regulating Corporate Behavior through Criminal Sanction, Part II: Rationale*, 92 HARV. L. REV. 1231, 1243 (1979).

122. Stessens, *supra* note 101, at 498. *See also* Leigh, *supra* note 100, at 1509-10, 1519-20, 1522-23, 1526. Leigh concludes, "Whether the range of sanctions is seen as penal or administrative in nature, the important point is that the sanctions be available." *Id.* at 1526.

quence that the corporate "defendant" is deprived of the protections associated with criminal prosecutions.[123] Another common provision provides that the corporation is civilly liable for a criminal fine assessed against an individual for actions taken on behalf of the corporation.[124] Through this maneuver, the criminal sanction is actually imposed on the corporation, while still maintaining the position that the corporation cannot be subjected to criminal prosecution.

Differences between legal systems that recognize corporate criminal liability and those that reject it, therefore, are more disagreements about theory than about practice:

> [Despite] start[ing] from first principles that are diametrically opposed, they often arrive in practice at a structure of liability that produces broadly similar answers to the problems of corporate crime. The coverage achieved by a system of administrative offenses, or by a system that permits corporations to be fined as a secondary party or assessed damages as a civil consequence of a crime, or by one that contains provisions imposing corporate liability only for certain offenses, for example, may differ little from that achieved under a system of full corporate liability.[125]

Under each of these systems, corporations can be held liable for the consequences of their wrongful acts, through penalties that are often identical, whether they be labeled criminal, civil or administrative.

Corporate criminal responsibility in national legal systems is more commonly applied to economic crimes. In practice, criminal prosecutions of corporations for traditional crimes of violence are rare.[126] This rarity, however, does not result from a theoretical problem but rather appears to be the result of a reluctance to view the corporation as being truly responsible for such crimes rather than the individuals who directly order, direct or commit violent acts.[127] Where corporate acts of violence fit within the legal requirements for attributing such conduct to the corporation, however, the corporation can be held criminally responsible. Attributing liability for violent human rights abuses to a corporation thus should not be problematic where corporate responsibility is based upon clear corporate policy, such as directing a security force to use violent abuse to repress opponents.

2. Liability by Any Other Name

Through the criminal and "ersatz criminal" liability of corporations, in combination with civil and administrative regulation, states assert their power to hold corporations accountable for transgressions of the law. For the purposes of

---

123. Stessens, *supra* note 101, at 502-06. The practice is so common that the European Court of Human Rights has considered the human rights consequences, concluding that certain administrative proceedings are "criminal in nature" and trigger the protections associated with criminal prosecutions, no matter the label assigned to the action by the national legal system. *Id.* at 504-05.

124. *Id.* at 501-02. "The technique of holding a corporation civilly liable for criminal fines imposed on natural persons acting on its behalf is widespread in continental legal systems." *Id.* at 501.

125. Leigh, *supra* note 100, at 1509-10.

126. *Id.* at 1512.

127. *Id.* at 1512-13.

corporate accountability, the exact category to which such accountability is assigned is not material. Corporations can be held accountable through awards of compensatory or punitive damages, through fines payable to the government, or through regulatory orders, up to and including dissolution. While criminal prosecution may have the advantages of greater moral condemnation and punishment in some legal systems, this is not uniformly the case. Regulatory crimes may not carry any moral impact, and in some situations, a finding of civil tort liability will entail both a hefty punishment and moral condemnation. In the U.S., the civil system of punitive damages will often produce more effective sanctions than the cumbersome, rarely used criminal prosecution of corporations.

Assumptions about inherent differences between civil and criminal procedures generally fail when applied to varied legal systems:

> [N]ational legal systems draw the line between civil and criminal in different ways. In some systems, criminal prosecutions are always public actions; in others they can be initiated and prosecuted by private parties. Conversely, governments can initiate civil actions that can be as onerous and "punishing" to the civil defendants as criminal prosecutions. . . . In some systems, damages for civil claims are always compensatory, in others they serve as a form of punishment as well. Some crimes are punishable only by fines, or orders to compensate the victim; some civil offenses can by "punished" by imprisonment. . . . The varieties of civil and criminal claims in domestic legal systems seeking redress for human rights violations span these different categories, with their exact categorization dependent on the definitions used by each system.[128]

Human rights abuses can be addressed in diverse ways. When handled in national legal systems, they must be "translated" into the procedures appropriate to each system.[129] The key in terms of international law and accountability is that all domestic systems hold corporations accountable, whether through criminal, civil or administrative proceedings.

International law can apply well-developed human rights norms to hold the various corporate entities responsible for their involvement in human rights abuses, and can rely on accepted principles of international jurisdiction to locate the domestic legal systems empowered to impose liability. These remaining topics—international norms and enforcement mechanisms—will be addressed in the following two parts of this article.

V.

DEFINING THE INTERNATIONAL HUMAN RIGHTS NORMS
GOVERNING CORPORATIONS

Human rights regulation entails both the articulation of norms and the enforcement of those standards. International law has made great strides in articu-

---

128. Beth Stephens, *Translating Filártiga: A Comparative and International Law Analysis of Domestic Remedies For International Human Rights Violations*, YALE J. INT'L L. (forthcoming 2002) (manuscript at 51, on file with author).
129. *See generally id.* (explaining "translation" of human rights accountability principles into varied national legal procedures).

lating the human rights norms applicable to corporations, far greater than often acknowledged. Although enforcement is still largely ineffectual, the existence of norms as a benchmark by which to evaluate corporate conduct plays an important role in the movement for corporate accountability.

In this part, I discuss the varied sources of international norms applicable to corporations, looking first at the rapidly growing set of treaties specifically directed at corporations. I then analyze generally binding human rights norms to demonstrate that they apply to corporations as fully as to private individuals. I conclude this part by demonstrating that so-called "voluntary" norms adopted by international and national governments and by corporations actually include many binding rules of law, and suggest that the broader, truly voluntary aspirational standards are likely to develop into binding rules as well.

A. *Specific Norms Aimed at Corporations*

An effort in the 1970s and 1980s to draft a comprehensive set of rules governing multinational corporations was unsuccessful. At that time, the underdeveloped and socialist countries sought to impose international rules regulating corporations doing business in their territory, including respect for local priorities and laws and reinvestment of profits in the host countries.[130] With the triumph of the global economy, such host country efforts have collapsed. In several specific areas, however, treaties define international law obligations that specifically apply to corporations.

Earliest among these was the Apartheid Convention, which established the international crime of apartheid and declared it a crime when committed by "organizations, institutions and individuals."[131] The Apartheid Convention was accompanied by a proposal—never implemented—for an international court to prosecute criminal violations of the treaty.[132] Most recently, the U.N. Convention Against Transnational Organized Crime, opened for signature on December 12, 2000, defined the international crimes of participation in an organized criminal group, money laundering, corruption, and obstruction of justice, all of which applied to corporations as well as natural persons.[133] In the intervening years,

---

130. *See* Development and International Economic Cooperation: Transnational Corporations, U.N. Economic and Social Commission, 2d Sess., Agenda Item 7(d), at 1, U.N. Doc. E/1990/94 (1990).

131. International Convention on the Suppression and Punishment of the Crime of Apartheid, art. I(2), U.N. Doc. A/2645 (1953) (entered into force July 18, 1976).

132. Draft Convention on the Establishment of an International Penal Tribunal for the Suppression and Punishment of the Crime of Apartheid and Other International Crimes, *reproduced in* M.C. BASSIOUNI, THE STATUTE OF THE INTERNATIONAL CRIMINAL COURT: A DOCUMENTARY HISTORY (1998). According to the proposal, persons, legal entities, groups and organizations would all have been subject to the jurisdiction of the court. *Id.* at arts. 5, 6, 21(4).

133. United Nations Convention Against Transnational Organized Crime (advance copy of the authentic text of the treaty), arts. 5, 6, 8, 23, *available at* http://www.uncjin.org/Documents/Conventions/dcatoc/final_documents_2/convention_eng.pdf (last visited Apr. 18, 2001). As of December 15, 2000, the treaty had been signed by 124 states, including the United States. *See* U.N. Office for Drug Control and Crime Prevention, Annex: United Nations Convention Against Transnational Organized Crime and the Protocols Thereto, *at* http://www.undcp.org/crime_cicp_signatures.html (last visited Apr. 18, 2001).

several treaties have established international corporate crimes connected to bribery and corruption.[134] The European Convention on Corruption, for example, calls for national prosecutions of "legal persons" for the crimes of bribery, trading in influence and money laundering.[135]

Another set of international treaties addresses corporate environmental violations. The Convention on Transboundary Movements of Hazardous Wastes criminalizes unauthorized movement of hazardous wastes committed by any "person"—including corporations as well as individuals.[136] In addition, a number of international agreements create *civil liability* for environmental damage caused by corporations.[137] The Convention on Civil Liability for Oil Pollution Damage, for example, imposes civil liability on ship owners for damage caused by oil pollution.[138]

Each of these treaties calls upon state parties to enact legislation making the prohibited conduct a crime under national law or imposing civil liability upon corporate violators. That is, rather than establishing an international enforcement mechanism, they instead require states to enact domestic measures of enforcement. The lack of international enforcement and the need for national action, however, should not be mistaken for the absence of an international norm. The standard of conduct, the definition of the crime or the civil wrong, is established by the international agreement; as is the case with most international norms, enforcement is left to the national legal system. As Professor Clapham points out, these treaties make clear that the international legal system is capable of defining international legal standards applicable to corporations. "[T]he international legal order has already adapted to define corporate crimes in international law and to oblige States to criminalize this behaviour."[139]

These detailed treaties demonstrate that states have the authority to develop rules specifically applicable to corporations. In addition, many human rights

---

134. *See, e.g.*, Council of Europe Criminal Law Convention on Corruption, opened for signature Jan. 27, 1999, art. 18, Europ. T.S. No. 173, at 6, 38 I.L.M. 505, 509 (active bribery, trading in influence and money laundering); Inter-American Convention Against Corruption, Mar. 29, 1996, art. 8, 35 I.L.M. 724, 730 (prohibiting offering article of monetary value to a government official of another state); OECD Convention on Combating Bribery of Foreign Public Officials in International Business Transactions, Dec. 17, 1997, art. 1, *available at* http://www.oecd.org/daf/nocorr-uption/20nov1e.htm (bribery of foreign public officials).

135. Council of Europe Criminal Law Convention on Corruption, *supra* note 134, at art. 18(1).

136. Basel Convention on the Control of Transboundary Movements of Hazardous Wastes and Their Disposal, Mar. 22, 1989, arts. 2, 4, 28 I.L.M. 657, 662. *See* discussion in Clapham, *supra* note 113, at 173-74.

137. *See, e.g.*, International Convention on Civil Liability for Oil Pollution Damage, Nov. 29, 1969, art. 3, 973 U.N.T.S. 4, 5 (entered into force June 19, 1975) (92 states ratified; United States signed) ("[T]he owner of a ship . . . shall be liable for any pollution damage caused by oil . . . "), as amended by the Protocol of 1992, art. 4; Convention on Civil Liability for Damage Resulting from Activities Dangerous to the Environment, June 21, 1993, arts. 6, 7, 32 I.L.M. 1228, 1233-34 (operator of polluting facility or waste dump liable for damage); Bamako Convention on the Ban of Import into Africa and the Control of Transboundary Movement and Management of Hazardous Wastes within Africa, opened for signature Jan. 30, 1990, art. 4(3)(b), 30 I.L.M. 773 (signed by 22 nations) (imposing strict liability on generators of hazardous wastes within states).

138. International Convention on Civil Liability for Oil Pollution Damage, *supra* note 137, at art. 3.

139. Clapham, *supra* note 113, at 178.

norms of general application bind private individuals and corporations, as well as state officials and states themselves. In the next section, I analyze the history of international regulation of corporate human rights abuses to demonstrate that corporations are bound by the core human rights norms.

B. *Universal Human Rights Norms and Corporations*

The international community has determined over the past fifty years that certain actions are prohibited and constitute violations of international law whether or not a state is a party to treaties outlawing the acts. These violations are prohibited by customary international law, binding on all regardless of state consent. The most egregious example is genocide, the intentional destruction, in whole or in part, of a national, ethnic, racial or religious group.[140] Others include summary execution, torture, and slavery and the slave trade.[141] Most of the international agreements that codify these and other human rights obligations are addressed to states, calling on states to enforce the listed obligations. But the norms embedded in the agreements bind the behavior of private individuals and corporations alike. International law has never been limited to regulating state behavior. Over the past fifty years, the international community has moved decisively to expand not only the rights of non-state actors but their responsibilities as well.

1. *Individuals*

The application of international law to individuals has been much debated, with "traditionalists" arguing that only states can be bound by international law's strictures.[142] This view, however, is both historically inaccurate and rejected by modern international law.

Historically, international law has long barred piracy, a violation that by definition is committed by stateless private actors.[143] The prohibition of the slave trade also applies to all actors, private as well as public.[144] Almost fifty years ago, the Nuremberg Tribunal reaffirmed the principle of individual responsibility, now a bedrock of modern international human rights law, in stirring language, stating, "[T]hat international law imposes duties and liabilities upon

---

140. Convention on the Prevention and Punishment of the Crime of Genocide, Dec. 9, 1948, art. 2, 102 Stat. 3045, 78 U.N.T.S. 277 [hereinafter Genocide Convention].

141. The full list adopted by the RESTATEMENT (THIRD) OF THE FOREIGN RELATIONS LAW OF THE UNITED STATES [hereinafter RESTATEMENT OF THE FOREIGN RELATIONS LAW] § 702 (1987), includes genocide; slavery or the slave trade; murder or causing disappearance; torture or other cruel, inhuman, or degrading treatment; prolonged arbitrary detention; systematic racial discrimination; and "a consistent pattern of gross violations of internationally recognized human rights."

142. Clapham describes—and rebuts—this "traditional" view. ANDREW CLAPHAM, HUMAN RIGHTS IN THE PRIVATE SPHERE 89-91, 93-133 (1993).

143. Piracy consists of "[a]ny illegal acts of violence, detention or any act of depredation, committed for private ends by the crew or the passengers of a private ship or a private aircraft . . . ." Convention on the High Seas, Apr. 29, 1958, arts. 15, 16, 13 U.S.T. 2312, 2317, 450 U.N.T.S. 82, 90; *see also* Convention on the Law of the Sea, Dec. 10, 1982, arts. 101, 102, 1833 U.N.T.S. 3, 436.

144. *See* Slavery Convention, Sept. 25, 1926, 60 L.N.T.S. 253; Supplementary Convention on the Abolition of Slavery, the Slave Trade, and Institutions and Practices Similar to Slavery, Sept. 7, 1956, 18 U.S.T. 3201, 266 U.N.T.S. 3.

individuals as well as upon States has long been recognized. . . . Crimes against international law are committed by men, not by abstract entities, and only by punishing individuals who commit such crimes can the provisions of international law be enforced."[145] The Nuremberg judgment thus took general international rules of behavior and applied them to individuals.[146]

Today, however, the application of international law to individuals is widely recognized. For example, The Genocide Convention, a modern outgrowth of the principles stated at Nuremberg, applies by definition to private actors as well as public officials. The Genocide Convention states that "persons committing genocide shall be punished, whether they are constitutionally responsible rulers, public officials or private individuals."[147] The preamble to the Universal Declaration of Human Rights states that "every individual and every organ of society" should promote respect for basic human rights.[148] Both the International Covenant on Civil and Political Rights and the International Covenant on Economic, Social and Cultural Rights recognize private obligations in their preambles, in the following terms: "Realizing that the individual, having duties to other individuals and to the Community of which he belongs, is under a responsibility to strive for the promotion and observance of the rights recognized in the present Covenant."[149] Moreover, all of the international agreements regulating corporations that were discussed in the prior section specifically govern the activities of private actors.

Clapham makes an additional argument for recognizing private rights and duties in the international human rights documents, based upon understanding the evolving context in which the documents were drafted and are currently interpreted. He argues for a broad, contextual interpretation of international agreements, stating that "it is neither a literal nor a teleological interpretation but a contextual/evolutive/dynamic one that is most appropriate" to an understanding of international law.[150] As stated by the International Court of Justice, "[A]n international instrument has to be interpreted and applied within the framework of the entire legal system prevailing at the time of the interpretation."[151] The ICJ concluded that the application of a fifty-year-old international agreement "must take into consideration the changes which have occurred in the supervening half century, and its interpretation can not remain unaffected by the

---

145.   Judgment of Oct. 1, 1946, Transcript of Proceedings.

146.   The Nuremberg judgments applied these general norms to corporations as well as to individuals, as discussed later in this part.

147.   Genocide Convention, *supra* note 140, at art. 4.

148.   Universal Declaration of Human Rights, Preamble, Dec. 10, 1948, U.N. Doc. A/810 [hereinafter Universal Declaration].

149.   International Covenant on Civil and Political Rights, Dec. 19, 1966, Preamble, para. 5, 999 U.N.T.S. 171, 173 (entered into force Jan. 3, 1976); International Covenant on Economic, Social and Cultural Rights, Dec. 19, 1966, Preamble, para. 5, 993 U.N.T.S. 3, 5 (entered into force Jan. 3 1976).

150.   CLAPHAM, HUMAN RIGHTS, *supra* note 142, at 98-99.

151.   *Id.* at 99, *citing* Advisory opinion of the ICJ on the Legal Consequences for States of the Continued Presence of South Africa in Namibia (South West Africa) [1971] ICJ Rep. 31, ¶ 53.

subsequent development of law," including customary international law as well as treaty law.[152]

The context in which international human rights norms must be interpreted and applied today is one in which such norms are routinely applied to private actors. Human rights law in the past several decades has moved decisively to prohibit violations by private actors in fields as diverse as discrimination, children's rights, crimes against peace and security, and privacy.[153] Significant provisions of international humanitarian law apply to non-state actors.[154] International and regional human rights bodies frequently call upon states to prevent human rights abuses committed by private actors.[155] It is clear that individuals today have both rights and responsibilities under international law. Although expressed in neutral language, many human rights provisions must be understood today as applying to individuals as well as to states.

2. *Complicity*

Certain international human rights prohibitions are triggered only with some level of state involvement or complicity. The Convention Against Torture, for example, prohibits torture "inflicted by or at the instigation of or with the consent or acquiescence of a public official or other person acting in an official capacity."[156] However, this and other international law prohibitions apply to those who are complicit in violations or participate in other ways.[157] The Genocide Convention, for example, prohibits both complicity and conspiracy to commit genocide, as well as prohibiting genocide itself.[158] The Torture Convention requires states to criminalize any act "that constitutes complicity or participation in torture."[159] Similarly, the Supplementary Slavery Convention establishes liability for "being an accessory thereto" of the enslavement of an-

---

152. *Id.*

153. *Id.* at 99-102.

154. *Id.* at 112-18. For example, common Article 3 of the four Geneva Conventions sets minimal rules applicable to all parties engaged in armed conflict, including private parties as well as states. Geneva Convention Relative to the Protection of Civilian Persons in Time of War, Aug. 12, 1949, art. 3, 6 U.S.T. 3516, 3518-3521, 75 U.N.T.S. 287, 288-289; Geneva Convention Relative to the Treatment of Prisoners of War, Aug. 12, 1949, art. 3, 6 U.S.T. 3316, 3318-3321, 75 U.N.T.S. 135, 136; Geneva Convention for the Amelioration of the Condition of the Wounded, Sick and Shipwrecked Members of Armed Forces at Sea, Aug. 12, 1949, art. 3, 6 U.S.T. 3217, 3220-3223, 75 U.N.T.S. 85, 86; Geneva Convention for the Amelioration of the Condition of the Wounded and Sick in Armed Forces in the Field, Aug. 12, 1949, art. 3, 6 U.S.T. 3114, 75 U.N.T.S. 31, 32. The Second Protocol to the Conventions similarly applies to private parties engaged in internal armed conflicts. Protocol Additional to the Geneva Conventions of 12 August 1949, and Relating to the Protection of Victims of Non-International Armed Conflicts, June 8, 1977, art. 13, 1125 U.N.T.S. 609.

155. CLAPHAM, HUMAN RIGHTS, *supra* note 142, at 107-12, 118-24.

156. Convention Against Torture and Other Cruel, Inhuman or Degrading Treatment or Punishment, Dec. 10, 1984, art. 1(1), 1465 U.N.T.S. 113, 113 (entered into force June 26, 1987) [hereinafter Torture Convention].

157. *See* sources cited *infra*, notes 158-60.

158. Genocide Convention, *supra* note 140, art. 3.

159. Torture Convention, *supra* note 156, art. 4(1).

other person, or "being a party to a conspiracy to accomplish any such acts."[160] Thus, private actors violate these international norms when they participate with official actors in acts constituting prohibited violations.

From the time of the Nuremberg Tribunals through recent decisions of the International Criminal Tribunals for the Former Yugoslavia and for Rwanda, international law has recognized that those who conspire to commit an international crime or aid and abet its commission are criminally liable along with the principals. Several World War II cases found defendants guilty of war crimes and crimes against humanity as accomplices to the crimes. In *The Zyklon B Case*,[161] for example, several German industrialists were convicted of supplying poison gas to Nazi concentration camps based on proof that they knew the purpose for which the gas was to be used.[162]

The modern international criminal tribunals have applied the holdings of the World War II cases to develop an international law definition of aiding and abetting.[163] In a case arising in Rwanda, the tribunal held that the required *actus reus* was "practical assistance, encouragement, or moral support which has a substantial effect on the perpetration of the crime."[164] The required *mens rea* was that the accomplice "have knowledge that his actions [would] assist the perpetrator in the commission of the crime;" it required neither intent to commit the crime nor even knowledge of the exact crime to be committed.[165] Reviewing the common understandings as to accomplice liability in domestic legal systems, the Rwanda tribunal concluded both that all criminal systems provide that an accomplice can be tried in absence of the principal perpetrator and that the accomplice need not intend the principal offense: "As a result, anyone who knowing of another's criminal purpose, voluntarily aids him or her in it, can be convicted of complicity even though he regretted the outcome of the offense."[166] The statute of the International Criminal Court similarly holds liable

---

160. Supplementary Convention on the Abolition of Slavery, the Slave Trade, Institutions and Practices Similar to Slavery, Sept. 7, 1956, art. 6 266 U.N.T.S. 3, 43.

161. *The Zyklon B Case (Trial of Bruno Tesch and Two Others)*, 1 Law Reports of Trials of War Criminals 93 (Brit. Mil. Ct. 1946).

162. *Id.* at 100. Similarly, Friederich Flick was convicted for knowingly contributing financial support to the Nazis. *U.S. v. Flick*, 6 Trials of War Criminals Before the Nuremberg Military Tribunals Under Control Council Law No. 10, at 1, 1216-23 (1949). In U.S. v. Krauch, pharmaceutical industrialists were convicted because they knowingly supplied experimental vaccines to the Nazis, knowing they would be used in illegal medical experiments on concentration camp inmates. 8 Trials of War Criminals, 1081, 1169-72 (1952).

163. *See generally* Brief of *Amici Curiae* International Human Rights Organizations and International Law Scholars in Support of Plaintiffs-Appellants, Doe v. Unocal Corp., 248 F.3d 915 (9th Cir. 2001), at 7-19 (international law recognizes concept of complicity and does not require actual participation), *available at* www.aclu.org/library/iclr/2000/iclr2000_6.pdf.; Andrew Clapham & Scott Jerbi, *Categories of Corporate Complicity in Human Rights Abuses* (Mar. 2001) (on file with author).

164. Prosecutor v. Furundzija, IT-95-17/1-PT (Dec. 10, 1998), ¶ 249. Moral support is sufficient where such support has "a significant legitimizing or encouraging effect on the principals." *Id.* ¶ 232.

165. *Id.* ¶ 246.

166. Prosecutor v. Akayesu, Case No. ICTR-96-4-T (Int'l Crim. Trib. for Rwanda, Trial Chamber I, Sept. 2, 1998), ¶¶ 531, 539, *at* http://www.ictr.org/ENGLISH/cases/Akayesu/judgement/akay 001.htm. Quoting an English case, the Rwanda tribunal stated:

a person who, "[f]or the purpose of facilitating the commission" of a crime, "aids, abets or otherwise assists in its commission. . . ."[167]

In the non-criminal context of state responsibility for violations of international law, international tribunals have also recognized the concept of complicity. Thus, both the European Court of Human Rights and the United Nations Human Rights Committee have held that a state violates international law where it extradites a person to a country where the fugitive is likely to be subjected to human rights violations.[168]

International human rights organizations also insist upon accountability that reaches beyond direct actions. Applying this principle to corporations, Human Rights Watch holds companies responsible for "human rights abuses that are being committed on their behalf and in their interest."[169] This responsibility goes beyond the "most egregious examples," such as when a company requests, pays for or supervises security operations that involve human rights violations.[170] Where company operations are "deeply intertwined" with repressive actions, the corporation has an obligation to take affirmative actions to ensure that abuses are not committed on its behalf.[171]

Non-state actors thus violate international norms when they are complicit in such abuses, as well as when they directly commit abuses. Moreover, private actors violate the norms requiring state action when they participate in acts taken in complicity with state actors. These principles apply to corporations as well as individuals, as discussed in the next section.

3. Corporations as well as Private Individuals

General human rights norms apply to individuals as well as to states. Although international enforcement mechanisms may be weak, with enforcement often left to domestic legal systems, the international rules of law prohibiting, for example, genocide, slavery and torture bar such conduct by individuals as well as by governments. Where some public action is required under interna-

---

[A]n indifference to the result of the crime does not of itself negate abetting. If one man deliberately sells to another a gun to be used for murdering a third, he may be indifferent about whether the third lives or dies and interested only in the cash profit to be made out of the sale, but he can still be an aider and abettor.

Akayesu, ¶ 539 (quoting National Coal Board v. Gamble, 1 Q.B. 11 (1959)).

167. Statute of the International Criminal Court, July 17, 1998, U.N. Doc. A/CONF.183/9 (1998), art. 25, §3(c).

168. *See generally* Soering v. United Kingdom, 11 E.H.R.R. 439 (1989) (European Court of Human Rights held that the United Kingdom would be responsible for violations where there was substantial reason to believe Soering would be subjected to torture or other inhuman or degrading treatment if extradited); Ng v. Canada, U.N. Doc. CCPR/C/49/D/469/1991 (1994) (U.N. Human Rights Committee found violation of international law where Canada extradited petitioner knowing that human rights violations might occur).

169. Human Rights Watch, *The Price of Oil: Corporate Responsibility and Human Rights Violations in Nigeria's Oil Producing Communities,* Summary, *at* http://www.hrw.org/hrw/press/1999/feb/nigsumm.htm (last visited June 5, 2001).

170. *Id.*

171. *Id.*

tional law, the norm applies to private individuals who act in complicity with state actors.

The same concepts underlie the application of international human rights norms to corporations.[172] Indeed, given the widespread recognition of corporate accountability within domestic legal systems, such an application is not surprising. International tribunals have applied human rights and humanitarian norms to corporations from the time of the Nuremberg Tribunals. That legacy, combined with the international consensus on corporate accountability, underlies the application of human rights provisions to corporate as well as individual persons.

The Nuremberg Tribunal made clear that norms applicable to "persons" applied to legal persons as well as individuals.[173] Thus, organizations were declared to be criminal where their purpose was to commit or facilitate crimes detailed in the Charter:

> A criminal organization is analogous to a criminal conspiracy in that the essence of both is cooperation for criminal purposes. There must be a group bound together and organized for a common purpose. The group must be formed or used in connection with the commission of crimes denounced by the Charter.[174]

The Nuremberg Charter authorized the criminal prosecution of only individuals, thus the groups labeled "criminal organizations" were not actually subject to criminal charges.[175] But, in applying the Charter in the area under its control, the United States Military Tribunal found that the I.G. Farben Corporation had violated international law:

> [W]e find that the proof establishes beyond a reasonable doubt that offences against property as defined in Control Council Law No. 10 *were committed by Farben,* and that these offences were connected with, and an inextricable part of the German policy for occupied territories.[176]

Farben in these passages is held to have violated international law prohibitions against pillage and plunder:

---

172. *See* Kamminga & Zia-Zarifi, *supra* note 12, at 8-9 (noting the "growing consensus that MNCs are bound by those few rules applicable to all international actors," including, *inter alia,* the prohibitions of slavery and forced labor, genocide, torture, extrajudicial murder, piracy, crimes against humanity and apartheid).

173. *See* Clapham, *supra* note 113, at 160-71 (discussing Nuremberg application of international law to corporations). Various international and national documents use the terms "juridical person," "legal person," "juristic persons" and "corporations" to refer to the organizations recognized as having legal status. *Id.* at 152, 152 n.24.

174. Nuremberg Judgment, *The Accused Organizations,* Oct. 1, 1946, *reprinted in* 41 AM. J. INT'L L. 172 (1947).

175. The jurisdiction of the International Military Tribunal included only prosecution of natural persons. Charter of the International Military Tribunal, annexed to Agreement for the Prosecution and Punishment of the Major War Criminals of the European Axis, Aug. 8, 1945, art. 6 59 Stat. 1544, 82 U.N.T.S. 279 (granting the Tribunal authority to evaluate the "individual responsibility" of "persons" who acted as "individuals or as members of organizations"). Organizations, however, could be held to be "criminal," subjecting certain members to prosecution for the crime of membership in a criminal organization. *Id.,* arts. 9, 10.

176. Case No. 57, The I.G. Farben Trial, U.S. Military Tribunal, Nuremberg, 14 Aug. 1947-July 29, 1948, 10 LAW REPORTS OF TRIALS OF WAR CRIMINALS 1; 8 TRIALS OF WAR CRIMINALS BEFORE THE NUREMBERG MILITARY TRIBUNALS 1108, 1140, INT'L L. REP. 676 (1948) (emphasis added) [hereinafter 8 TRIALS OF WAR CRIMINALS].

The result was the enrichment of Farben and the building of its greater chemical empire through the medium of occupancy at the expense of the former owners. Such action on the part of Farben constituted a violation of the rights of private property, protected by the Laws and Customs of War . . . .[177]

Thus, these general humanitarian law provisions governing the laws and customs of war applied to legal persons as well as individuals.

Despite some reluctance to apply international criminal law to corporations in the mid-twentieth century, the concept of international corporate crimes is now common.[178] As discussed above, several international treaties have expressly included corporate crimes, including the Apartheid Convention, and treaties governing corruption and bribery, hazardous wastes, and other environmental violations.

The absence of criminal prosecution as an enforcement mechanism does not detract from the conclusion that the norms bind corporate actors. International law and domestic legal systems may choose to enforce international norms through civil or administrative proceedings, as well as criminal prosecutions.[179] Moreover, discussion about criminal prosecution should not mask the more fundamental recognition that such conduct is prohibited—a violation of international law—even in the absence of specific enforcement mechanisms.

The preamble to the Universal Declaration of Human Rights contains a pointed application that goes beyond both states and individuals:

The General Assembly proclaims this Universal Declaration of Human Rights as a common standard of achievement for all peoples and all nations, to the end that every individual and *every organ of society,* keeping this Declaration constantly in mind, shall strive by teaching and education to promote respect for these rights and freedoms and by progressive measures, national and international, to secure their universal and effective recognition and observance, both among the peoples of Member States themselves and among the peoples of territories under their jurisdiction.[180]

As Professor Louis Henkin has emphasized, *"Every individual* includes juridical persons. *Every individual* and *every organ of society* excludes no one, no company, no market, no cyberspace. The Universal Declaration applies to them all."[181] Corporations are independent legal entities, subject to international and domestic regulation and capable of being held legally accountable for their actions. When an international agreement applies broadly to all actors, it applies

---

177. 8 TRIALS OF WAR CRIMINALS, *supra* note 176, at 1132, 1140 (emphasis added).

178. In both 1951 and 1953, the International Law Commission chose to exclude legal persons because some legal systems did not recognize penal responsibility on the part of legal entities. In the words of the 1953 report, the Commission decided to omit "so novel a principle as corporate criminal responsibility." U.N. Doc. A/2645 (1953). See Clapham, *supra* note 113, at 171-72, for a discussion of this history.

179. Similarly, the fact that the Statute of the International Criminal Court does not authorize international criminal prosecution of corporations implies nothing about the applicability of the norms covered by the court to legal persons: "[L]ack of ICC jurisdiction over legal persons for war crimes should not mislead us into thinking that the laws of war and international human rights law do not apply to companies." Clapham, *supra* note 113, at 178.

180. Universal Declaration, *supra* note 148, preamble (emphasis added).

181. Louis Henkin, *The Universal Declaration at 50 and the Challenge of Global Markets,* 25 BROOK. J. INT'L L. 17, 25 (1999) (emphasis in original).

78   *BERKELEY JOURNAL OF INTERNATIONAL LAW*   [Vol. 20:45

to corporations as well. In the realm of core human rights norms, multinational corporations "are bound by those few rules applicable to all international actors."[182]

The international committees that interpret human rights agreements increasingly apply them in this manner to corporations. Thus, the United Nations Committee on Economic, Social and Cultural Rights has said that:

> [A]ll members of society—individuals, families, local communities, non-governmental organizations, civil society organizations, *as well as the private business sector*, have responsibilities in the realization of the right to adequate food. . . . *The private business sector—national and transnational*—should pursue its activities within the framework of a code of conduct conducive to respect of the right to adequate food.[183]

The Committee has used similar language in reference to the right to health.[184] In addition, the Human Rights Committee has stated that private entities are governed by the protection of the right to privacy.[185] Non-binding resolutions at numerous international conferences have applied human rights obligations in the area of discrimination, the environment, human rights and development to private corporations.[186]

Although international law norms are often viewed as addressed only to states, many in fact apply to corporate persons as well as to private individuals and state officials and to states themselves.

C. *"Voluntary" Codes/Binding Rules*

Before discussing enforcement mechanisms, this section will address a curious phenomenon of the past decade: "voluntary" codes of corporate conduct. Such codes have their roots in a series of codes of conduct drafted by the United Nations and other international organizations in the 1970s, at a time when developing countries were most vocal in their concerns about the impact of multinational corporations on their economies.[187] The first of these, the draft U.N.

---

182. Kamminga & Zia-Zarifi, *supra* note 12, at 8.

183. U.N. Committee on Economic Social and Cultural Rights, General Comment 12, The Right to Adequate Food (Art. 11), May 12, 1999, para. 20.

184. U.N. Committee on Economic Social and Cultural Rights, General Comment 14, The Right to the Highest Attainable Standard of Health (Art. 12), July 4, 2000, para. 42.

185. U.N. Human Rights Committee, General Comment 16, The Right to Respect of Privacy, Family, Home and Correspondence, and Protection of Honor and Reputation (Art. 17), April 8, 1988.

186. International Council on Human Rights Policy, Business Rights and Wrongs: Human Rights and the Developing International Legal Obligations of Companies 39 (2001) (draft report), *at* http://www.ichrp.org.

187. "Between 1970 and 1981, virtually all major international governmental organizations interested in international trade and investment developed detailed proposals for MNE codes of conduct." Baker, *supra* note 39, at 409 (citing Hans V. Baade, *Codes of Conduct for Multinational Enterprises, in* 1 Legal Problems of Codes of Conduct for Multinational Enterprises 407, 412 (Norbert Horn ed., 1980)).

The concept of voluntary codes of conduct rests upon a historical tradition of corporate self-regulation, tracing back to medieval Europe, through to the beginnings of the U.S. industrial economy. *See* Antony Black, Guilds and Civil Society in European Political Thought From the Twelfth Century to the Present 4, 6 (1984); Harvey L. Pitt & Karl A. Groskaufmanis,

Code of Conduct for Transnational Corporations, aimed primarily at regulating corporate meddling in the internal affairs of developing countries, was never adopted.[188] The draft code included general human rights language, stating that "[t]ransnational corporations shall respect human rights and fundamental freedoms in the countries in which they operate" and prohibiting discrimination.[189]

Perhaps the most well-known of the private codes was the Sullivan Principles, a code of conduct for businesses operating in apartheid South Africa that prohibited discrimination.[190] Corporations were asked to pledge compliance and to report on their efforts. The author of the principles, Leon Sullivan, later criticized the code as ineffective, largely because of the lack of enforcement mechanisms.[191] Similar efforts in the 1980s addressed corporate activities in Northern Ireland, the Soviet Union and China.[192]

A host of such codes of conduct have been drafted by governmental and private organizations as well as by corporations over the past decade. Multilateral international efforts include the Compact for the New Century sponsored by U.N. Secretary General Kofi Annan[193] as well as a draft circulated by the subcommission of the U.N. Human Rights Commission.[194] The European Parliament has proposed a similar code, as well as calling for adoption of a binding code of conduct.[195] On a national level, the U.S. government has worked with business representatives on codes to govern both the apparel industry and mining and petroleum industries.[196] Private efforts include codes developed by corporations themselves and those drafted by a wide range of independent nongovernmental organizations.

Minimizing Corporate Civil and Criminal Liability: A Second Look at Corporate Codes of Conduct, 78 GEO. L. J. 1559, 1561, 1576-78 (1990); Baker, *supra* note 39, at 407.

188. *See* Development and International Economic Cooperation: Transnational Corporations, U.N. Economic and Social Commission, 2d Sess., Agenda Item 7(d), at 1, U.N. Doc. E/1990/94 (1990).

189. *Id.*

190. *Sullivan Principles for U.S. Corporations Operating in South Africa,* 24 I.L.M. 1496 (1985) (citing "The (Sullivan) Statement of Principles" (Fourth Amplification), Nov. 8, 1984).

191. *See* Leon Sullivan, *The Sullivan Principles and Change in South Africa, in* BUSINESS IN THE CONTEMPORARY WORLD 175 (Herbert L. Sawyer ed., 1988); Karen Paul, *The Inadequacy of Sullivan Reporting,* 57 BUS. & SOC. R. 61 (1986).

192. See discussion of these codes in Lance Compa & Tashia Hinchliffe-Darricarrere, *Enforcing International Labor Rights Through Corporate Codes of Conduct,* 33 COLUM. J. TRANSNAT'L L. 663, 671-72 (1995).

193. U.N. Secretary-General Kofi A. Annan, *A Compact for the New Century, at* http://www.un globalcompact.org/un/gc/unweb.nsf/content/thenine.htm (last visited Apr. 14, 2001) [hereinafter U.N. Compact].

194. *See generally* David Weissbrodt, *The Beginning of a Sessional Working Group on Transnational Corporations Within the UN Sub-Commission on Prevention of Discrimination and Protection of Minorities, in* LIABILITY OF MULTINATIONAL CORPORATIONS, *supra* note 12, at 119-38.

195. Resolution on EU Standards for European Enterprises Operating in Developing Countries: Towards a European Code of Conduct, European Parliament, Resolution A4-0508/98.

196. Bureau of National Affairs, Inc., Voluntary "Model Business Principles" Issued by the Clinton Administration, May 26, 1995, Daily Rep. For Executives, May 31, 1995, http://www.itcilo. it/english/actrav/telearn/global/ilo/guide/usmodel.htm (last visited Nov. 3, 2001) [hereinafter U.S. Dep't of Commerce].

80   *BERKELEY JOURNAL OF INTERNATIONAL LAW*   [Vol. 20:45

Perhaps the most striking fact about these "voluntary" codes is the extent to which they incorporate human rights norms that are, in fact, obligatory duties, not voluntary undertakings. The U.N. Compact, for example, calls on world business to "respect the protection of international human rights within their sphere of influence" and "make sure their own corporations are not complicit in human right abuses."[197] The Compact proceeds to ask business leaders to respect the four most fundamental labor rights principles that were adopted by unanimous consensus by the 170 members of the International Labor Organization: freedom of association and the effective recognition of the right to collective bargaining; the elimination of all forms of forced and compulsory labor; the effective abolition of child labor; and the elimination of discrimination in respect of employment and occupation.[198]

Similarly, the self-proclaimed voluntary Guidelines for Multinational Enterprises drafted by the Organization for Economic Cooperation and Development call on corporations to "[r]espect the human rights of those affected by their activities" and to "contribute to the effective elimination of child labor" and "forced or compulsory labor in their operations."[199] The ILO itself has adopted a non-binding declaration of principles that urges "All parties"— governments, employers and trade unions—to "respect the Universal Declaration of Human Rights" as well as the two International Covenants.[200] The Model Business Principles issued by the Clinton Administration follow this same pattern, terming their provisions voluntary, although they include a pledge to avoid forced labor and to comply with U.S. and local law.[201]

Despite the voluntary language in these codes, it is difficult to imagine a corporation arguing that it is not obligated to respect human rights and to refrain from using forced labor. The prohibition against forced labor has been a core, obligatory feature of international law for almost fifty years, since the adoption of the Supplementary Slavery Convention.[202] Use of forced labor violates international law—and there is nothing voluntary about a corporation's agreement to refrain from doing so. Similarly, paying a security force to commit torture violates international law; corporations do not "voluntarily" choose to abide by this international norm. This is not to deny that there is some importance to a pledge to abide by the law. Obviously, obligations are not actually honored in practice, and anything that contributes to greater compliance is useful. But, the fact that such obligations are included in "voluntary" codes should not obscure the obligatory foundation of many of the norms included in the codes.

---

197. U.N. Compact, *supra* note 193, §§ 1(a), (b).

198. *Id.* at § (2).

199. OECD Guidelines for Multinational Enterprises, II(2), IV(1)(c), *available at* http://www1. oecd.org/daf/investment/guidelines/mnetext.htm (last visited Nov. 3, 2001). The OECD guidelines were first drafted in 1976; this reference to respect for human rights was inserted in the most recent revision, in June 2000.

200. Tripartite Declaration of Principles Concerning Multinational Enterprises and Social Policy, International Labor Organization, art. 8, 17 I.L.M. 422, 425-28 (1978).

201. U.S. Dep't of Commerce, *supra* note 196.

202. Supplementary Convention on the Abolition of Slavery, the Slave Trade, and Institutions and Practices Similar to Slavery, Sept. 7, 1956, 226 U.N.T.S. 3.

The sad reality is that the weak language of most of these codes reflects the economic and political power of multinational corporations. The United Nations, for example, has acknowledged that the Global Compact is voluntary because corporations would not accept a binding commitment.[203] Critics have charged that the U.N. is "making peace with power," while abandoning the drive to strengthen legally binding norms.[204]

It is interesting to note, however, that the United Nations at the time of its foundation made a similar "peace with power" with surprising results, drafting an aspirational human rights code that has since evolved into a powerful human rights platform. The Universal Declaration of Human Rights was drafted as a non-binding document because the states belonging to the United Nations refused to agree to binding norms. As described by Eleanor Roosevelt, a key leader in the drafting and passage of the Declaration:

> In giving our approval to the declaration today, it is of primary importance that we keep clearly in mind the basic character of the document. It is not a treaty; it is not an international agreement. It is not and does not purport to be a statement of law or of legal obligation. It is a declaration of basic principles of human rights and freedoms, to be stamped with the approval of the General Assembly by formal vote of its members, and to serve as a common standard of achievement for all peoples of all nations.[205]

The United Nations described the Universal Declaration as originally "a manifesto with primarily moral authority."[206] Nevertheless, half a century later, the document is now considered to be binding, in important part, if not in total.[207]

Today's "voluntary" codes of business conduct are already, in part, statements of binding international law. To the extent that they extend beyond currently existing law, they may follow the path of the Universal Declaration, acquiring binding status through their incorporation into customary international law or international treaties.[208]

---

203. Irwin Arieff, *UN: One Year Later Global Compact Has Little To Show*, REUTERS, July 27, 2001 (U.N. Assistant Secretary-General Michael Doyle "acknowledged the program's [voluntary] form was in part dictated by a recognition that the corporate world was unwilling to accept binding global standards on corporate governance").

204. George Monbiot, *The United Nations is Trying to Regain its Credibility by Fawning to Big Business*, THE GUARDIAN, Aug. 31, 2000 (The U.N. is "helping western companies to penetrate new markets while avoiding the regulations which would be the only effective means of holding them to account. By making peace with power, the U.N. is declaring war upon the powerless.").

205. *Quoted in* 5 MARJORIE M. WHITEMAN, DIGEST OF INTERNATIONAL LAW 243 (Washington, D.C.: Dept. of State Publication # 7873, 1965).

206. United Nations, The International Bill of Human Rights 1 (U.N. Dept. of Public Information, 1988).

207. *See* Hurst Hannum, *The Status of the Universal Declaration of Human Rights in National and International Law*, 25 GA. J. INT'L & COMP. L. 287, 317-39 (1995/1996). Hannum concludes that although there is insufficient international support to find that the *entire* Declaration constitutes binding customary international law, there would seem to be little argument that many provisions of the Declaration today do reflect customary international law. *Id.*

208. *See* RESTATEMENT OF FOREIGN RELATIONS LAW, *supra* note 141, at § 213 note 7 (describing voluntary codes of conduct and concluding: "Such codes . . . may contribute to the development of international norms supporting state regulation of [multinational] enterprises.")

VI.

ENFORCEMENT: DOMESTIC AND INTERNATIONAL

There is no dispute about governmental authority to regulate corporations and to require that corporations abide by the rule of law. In fact, given corporate unwillingness to accept social obligations as part of the business ethic, governmental regulation is essential. Domestic legal regimes include myriad rules applicable to corporations and enforceable through the national legal systems. In addition, the international community has developed a considerable body of rules applicable to corporations. These international norms have the advantage of uniformity and consistency. Where domestic norms vary, multinational corporations have the ability to structure their operations so as to take advantage of the most favorable legal regime.

Many international norms are already well-developed; effective enforcement of those rules, however, remains the crucial missing piece of the regulatory puzzle. A great deal of effort has been spent developing enforceable rules to govern the *economic* behavior of multinational corporations: trade, patents, investment, financing are all the subject of existing international regulation or ongoing efforts to draft rules. These economic regulatory systems include well-elaborated enforcement mechanisms. Ironically, the human rights consequences of multinational corporate operations have received much less international attention, despite the fact that transnationals have an ongoing, and at times devastating, impact on human rights around the world.[209]

Uniform international norms prevent multinational corporations from evading regulation by transferring their operations to countries with weaker standards. Similarly, consistent international enforcement mechanisms would prevent multinationals from evading the consequences of their actions by avoiding nations with the most effective enforcement mechanisms. Such international efforts, however, are at the moment a rather distant goal. In the meantime, domestic enforcement can be at least partially effective, by enforcing either domestic laws or international norms. To the extent that enforcement becomes more widespread, evasive techniques will be correspondingly less successful.

A. *An Overview of Domestic Enforcement*

Domestic enforcement can take place either in the *home* state, the state of citizenship of the corporation, or in the *host* state, the place in which the relevant operations take place. Host state enforcement has seemingly clear advantages, because it permits local control over local events. Such enforcement is not possible, however, if the host government is complicit in the human rights abuses, as in Burma or Nigeria under the former military dictatorship. Moreover, the

---

209. As stated by Orentlicher and Gelatt:

>   The powerful influence of transnational corporations on human rights conditions in the countries where they invest makes it both appropriate, and necessary, to assure that the behavior of these private actors comports with the human rights standards established by public international law and enforced by national law.

Orentlicher & Gelatt, *supra* note 98, at 69.

unequal division of economic power within the global economy makes such regulation difficult for developing nations. Unequal bargaining power makes it difficult if not impossible for host countries to enforce restrictions on corporate activity. In addition, transnational businesses can often insulate themselves from liability in any one country by moving assets and operations to more favorable locations.

Although home country enforcement has disadvantages, it may nevertheless be a more viable alternative in many situations. Home state enforcement efforts may provoke opposition from host states, arguing that western efforts to impose higher labor and environmental standards will cost them jobs. These considerations may be valid in some settings. Moreover, regulation by the United States is often suspect, given the well-grounded suspicion that the U.S. only intervenes when such regulation is in the self-interest of the U.S. economy. Nevertheless, given the lack of an effective international regulatory system and the difficulties host countries face when trying to impose standards on the corporations acting within their territory, home country regulation may be the best short-term alternative. As Professor Vagts has said, a U.S. refusal to control the activities of U.S. corporations abroad would amount to "abdication" of a power that no other entity can, at this time, exercise.[210] He called for U.S. regulation in order to avoid a vacuum in which multinational corporations set their own rules, "without regard to their broader impact."[211]

Most legal systems assert jurisdiction over the activities of corporations based in their state, although many may either refuse jurisdiction where the activities at issue occurred in another country or apply the laws of that country to the claim.[212] The United States is more assertive, both in retaining jurisdiction over claims arising in another state and in applying substantive U.S. law to the activities of U.S. corporations in foreign countries. U.S. law permits Congress to impose its authority outside our borders but presumes that statutes do not have extraterritorial effect unless that presumption is overcome by a showing of congressional intent.[213] Jonathan Turley demonstrates the inconsistent manner in which this supposed presumption is applied: statutes regulating anti-trust, securities and criminal law have been found to apply extraterritorially, while statutes with near identical language in the areas of environmental or labor regulation have been denied extraterritorial application.[214] Nevertheless, the

---

210. Vagts, *supra* note 57, at 786.

211. *Id.*

212. Stephens, *Translating* Filártiga, *supra* note 128 (manuscript at 24-27, 36-39).

213. EEOC v. Arabian Am. Oil Co., 499 U.S. 244, 248 (1991) (Congress "legislates against the backdrop of the presumption against extraterritoriality," which can be overcome by "the affirmative intention of Congress clearly expressed.").

214. *See* Jonathan Turley, *"When in Rome": Multinational Misconduct and the Presumption Against Territoriality*, 84 NW. U. L. REV. 598 (1990). Turley suggests that extraterritoriality is upheld in areas involving protection of the free market, and rejected in cases involving non-market concerns. *Id.* at 601. More recently, Gibney and Emerick propose an even more blatant predictor of these otherwise inconsistent decisions: statutes are held to be extraterritorial when to do so would advance U.S. interests, and denied extraterritorial application when against our interests. *See* Mark Gibney & R. David Emerick, *The Extraterritorial Application of United States Law and the Protec-*

84   *BERKELEY JOURNAL OF INTERNATIONAL LAW*   [Vol. 20:45

power of the U.S. government to develop norms governing human rights-related behavior, and to impose those norms on corporations based in the United States, is clear.

A bill introduced into the U.S. Congress last year would have imposed a detailed set of international environmental, labor and human rights standards on U.S.-based corporations, with violators facing denial of access to a series of key government trade programs.[215] The European Parliament has also proposed imposing binding norms on European-based corporations.[216]

Norms governing corporate operations can also be enforced through litigation. A U.S. corporation, for example, can be sued in the United States by individuals harmed by its activities abroad. Such suits have been filed in England, Canada and Australia, asserting negligence claims arising out of corporate activities in foreign countries, where the firm is incorporated in the forum or has taken key decisions in its headquarters.[217] Such claims are possible only if the litigation satisfies the requirements of the domestic legal system.[218] The first hurdle is identifying a tort subject to suit. Claims based on domestic tort law are possible only when they fall within recognized domestic causes of action. Given that choice-of-law principles in most legal systems will direct the court to apply the law of the place where the events took place, host state laws may make it difficult or impossible to litigate claims based on human rights violations, labor rights or environmental norms.[219]

The national courts must also be authorized to assert personal jurisdiction over the defendant corporation. Where the forum state is the place of incorporation, that is, the state of nationality of the corporation, personal jurisdiction is generally not a problem. More difficult jurisdictional issues arise where the defendant is the parent company of the corporation charged with the abuses or related in some other way through the corporate group, an issue discussed later in this part.

Dismissal based on forum *non conveniens* is also a possibility, where all relevant events have taken place outside of the forum territory. However, in England, the House of Lords recently rejected an effort to dismiss a series of

---

tion of Human Rights: Holding Multinational Corporations to Domestic and International Standards, 10 TEMP. INT'L & COMP. L.J. 123 (1996).

> In our view, the case law falls together very neatly, depending not so much on what will promote a general principle such as the free market, but simply on what will benefit the United States. . . . In short, the law has been applied extraterritorially when it seeks to prevent negative phenomena from occurring in the United States, but generally not when an agent of the United States (or the government itself) pursues activities that might bring about "negative effects" in other countries.

Id. at 141.

215. The Transparency and Responsibility for U.S. Trade Health Act of 2001, .H.R. 460, 107th Cong. (2001).

216. Resolution on EU Standards for European Enterprises Operating in Developing Countries: Towards a European Code of Conduct, EUR. PARL. DOC. (Com 104) 108 (1999).

217. *See* Richard Meeran, *Accountability of Transnationals for Human Rights Abuses*, 148 NEW L.J. 1686 (Nov. 13, 1998), 148 NEW L.J. 1706 (Nov. 20, 1998).

218. *See generally* Stephens, *Translating* Filártiga, *supra* note 128.

219. *Id.* (manuscript at 36-39).

cases in favor of a forum in South Africa.[220] The Court found that South Africa did not offer a viable alternative forum given that the plaintiffs would be unable to find counsel capable of handling their claims. The *Lubbe* litigation is a significant example of a growing recognition by host states that their interests and those of their citizens may be served by litigation in the home states. Indeed, one reaction to such litigation is to argue that citizens of the developing world have a right to bring their claims in the more highly developed legal systems where the corporate defendants are based and where those defendants' assets are available for satisfaction of an eventual judgment. In *Lubbe,* the South African government supported the plaintiffs' efforts to maintain the lawsuit in England, arguing that South Africa's overtaxed, post-apartheid judiciary was not yet capable of handling such claims.[221] Similarly, although the government of Ecuador took varying positions as to litigation against Texaco for environmental damage, it eventually argued that the claims should be litigated in the United States.[222]

B. U.S. Human Rights Litigation

Domestic litigation can also, in some circumstances, apply international law to corporate violations. Many legal systems will not recognize civil international claims in the absence of authorizing legislation. Both civil and criminal claims for violations of fundamental rights, however, may be permitted under the authorization of universal jurisdiction.[223]

Civil claims for human rights violations are possible in the United States because of a unique statute that permits domestic litigation to enforce *international law.* The Alien Tort Claims Act[224] grants the federal courts jurisdiction over a "civil action by an alien for a tort only, committed in violation of the law of nations or by a treaty of the United States." In the first modern case to apply the statute, *Filártiga v. Peña-Irala,*[225] the Second Circuit held that the statute addresses violations of the law of nations as that body of law evolves over time and concluded that torture by a state of its own citizens violated modern norms of international law.[226] Since *Filártiga,* the statute has been consistently inter-

---

220. Lubbe v. Cape plc, 4 All E.R. 268 (2000).

221. *See* Statement of Case on Behalf of the Republic of South Africa (May 26, 2000) *in* Lubbe v. Cape plc, *supra* note 220 (arguing that consideration of "public interest" weighed in favor of deciding the case in England, not in South Africa) (copy on file with author).

222. See Jota v. Texaco, Inc., 57 F.3d 153, 156-58 (2d Cir. 1998), for discussion of the various Ecuadoran government submissions. One Ecuadoran legislator concluded that the United States represented the only possibility of "finding just treatment" for those injured by the oil company's operations. *Id.* at 157.

223. *See* Stephens, *Translating* Filártiga, *supra* note 128 (manuscript at 46-65).

224. 28 U.S.C. § 1350 (1994) [hereinafter ATCA].

225. Filártiga v. Peña-Irala, 630 F.2d 876 (2d Cir. 1980). Although cited in an early opinion by the U.S. attorney general, 1 Op. Att'y Gen. 57 (1795) (in response to complaint that U.S. citizens had attacked a British colony in Sierra Leone, attorney general suggested that those injured file civil suit for damages under ATCA), the statute was largely ignored until the Second Circuit decided the *Filártiga* case in 1980.

226. *Id.* at 881, 884-85. In *Filártiga,* the family of a young Paraguayan man who was tortured to death in Paraguay filed a lawsuit against a Paraguayan police officer. The district court dismissed the case, holding that the torture by a state official of that state's own citizen did not violate interna-

preted as applying to acts that violate "universal, obligatory and definable" norms,[227] including human rights and humanitarian law violations such as genocide, summary execution, war crimes and crimes against humanity, disappearance, slavery and forced labor.[228]

Two related principles permit ATCA litigation against corporations. First, private corporations are liable for violations of human rights norms such as genocide, slavery and war crimes that by definition apply to private actors as well

---

tional law, *see id.* at 880 (summarizing district court decision), the holding was then reversed by the Second Circuit.

227.   First articulated in Forti v. Suarez-Mason, 672 F. Supp. 1531, 1539-40 (N.D. Cal. 1987), this standard has since been widely accepted. *See, e.g.*, Martinez v. City of Los Angeles, 141 F.3d 1373, 1383 (9th Cir. 1998); *In re* Estate of Marcos Human Rights Litigation, 25 F.3d 1467, 1475 (9th Cir. 1994); BETH STEPHENS & MICHAEL RATNER, INTERNATIONAL HUMAN RIGHTS LITIGATION IN U.S. COURTS 51-52 (1995).

Filártiga has been followed by every Circuit and District Court to reach a decision on the issue. *See, e.g.*, Wiwa v. Royal Dutch Petroleum Co., 226 F.3d 88 (2d Cir. 2000), *cert. denied*, 121 S.Ct. 1402 (2001); Beanal v. Freeport-McMoran, Inc., 197 F.3d 161 (5th Cir. 1999); Martinez v. City of Los Angeles, 141 F.3d 1373 (9th Cir. 1998); Hilao v. Estate of Marcos, 103 F.3d 789 (9th Cir. 1996); Kadic v. Karadzic, 70 F.3d 232 (2d Cir. 1995), *cert. denied*, 518 U.S. 1005 (1996); Abebe-Jira v. Negewo, 72 F.3d 844 (11th Cir. 1996), *cert. denied*, 519 U.S. 830 (1996). In one decision by the D.C. Circuit, a three-judge panel rejected an ATCA claim without reaching agreement on the significance of the statute. Tel-Oren v. Libyan Arab Republic, 726 F.2d 774 (D.C. Cir. 1984), *cert. denied*, 470 U.S. 1003 (1985). One judge disagreed with the *Filártiga* holding, *id.* at 798-823 (Bork, J., concurring), while one agreed with it, *id.* at 775-98 (Edwards, J., concurring), and one would have dismissed the case on the basis of the political question doctrine, *id.* at 823-27 (Robb, J., concurring).

228.   *See, e.g.*, *Estate of Marcos*, 25 F.3d at 1475-76 (summary execution, torture, disappearance); *Kadic*, 70 F.3d at 246 (genocide, war crimes, and crimes against humanity); *Abebe-Jira*, 72 F.3d 844 (torture); Doe I v. Unocal Corp., 963 F. Supp. 880, 891-92 (C.D. Cal. 1997) (slavery and forced labor).

Claims have been rejected where the courts find no universal consensus as to the prohibition, including claims against private corporations for environmental harm, and claims based on expropriation of property, state contract law, fraud and free speech violations. *See, e.g.*, Beanal v. Freeport-McMoran, Inc., 197 F.3d 161, 166-67 (5th Cir. 1999) (rejecting environmental claim against corporation); Bigio v. Coco Cola Co., 239 F.3d 440, 447-50 (2d Cir. 2000) (rejecting ATCA jurisdiction over claim that defendant acquired property that had previously been expropriated by Egyptian government on basis of the owners' religion); Nat'l Coalition Gov't of the Union of Burma v. Unocal, 176 F.R.D. 329, 345 (C.D. Cal. 1997) (dismissing ATCA claim for loss of property); Wong-Opasi v. Tennessee State University, 229 F.3d 1155 (6th Cir. 2000), *available at* 2000 WL 1182827 at *2 (unpublished disposition) (rejecting ATCA jurisdiction over state law contract and tort claims); Hamid v. Price Waterhouse, 51 F.3d 1411, 1417-18 (9th Cir. 1994) (holding that claims of fraud, breach of fiduciary duty, and misappropriation of funds are not breaches of the "law of nations" for purposes of jurisdiction under the Alien Tort Statute); Guinto v. Marcos, 654 F. Supp. 276, 280 (S.D. Cal. 1986) ("violation of the First Amendment right of free speech does not rise to the level of such universally recognized rights and so does not constitute a 'law of nations'").

Post-*Filártiga* cases have recognized additionally the categories of defendants who can be held liable under the ATCA. *Filártiga* held liable the actual torturer. Defendants in several subsequent cases have included military commanders held responsible for violations committed by troops under their command. Philippine dictator Ferdinand Marcos, for example, was held responsible for thousands of executions, disappearances and torture committed by his military forces. *Estate of Marcos*, 25 F.3d 1467. *See also, e.g.*, *Kadic*, 70 F.3d 232 (leader of the Bosnian Serbs held responsible for violations committed by troops); Xuncax v. Gramajo, 886 F. Supp. 162 (D. Mass. 1995) (military commander held responsible for violations committed by troops); Paul v. Avril, 812 F. Supp. 207 (S.D. Fla. 1993) (same); *Forti*, 672 F. Supp. 1531 (same).

as official government agents.[229] Second, private corporations can be held liable for human rights violations when they act together with public officials.[230]

The concept of private corporate liability under the ATCA has been upheld in a handful of preliminary decisions, although none has resulted in a final judgment. In *Doe I v. Unocal Corp.*,[231] for example, the district court found that a corporation can be held liable for private acts of slavery and forced labor, because the international law prohibitions apply to all actors. Similarly, *Beanal v. Freeport*[232] found that a private corporation can be held liable for genocide, which by definition is barred whether committed by "public officials or private individuals."[233] These decisions have also recognized that corporations can be held responsible under the ATCA for international law violations that require state action, such as torture and summary executions. As stated by the court in *Beanal*, "[A] corporation found to be a state actor can be held responsible for human rights abuses which violate international customary law."[234] State action will be found when the private corporation acts in complicity with state actors; the courts apply the well developed standards of domestic civil rights cases to determine complicity.[235]

Where litigation is based on international norms, rather than domestic tort law, U.S. courts have found a heightened U.S. interest in offering a forum for the claims. Considering both the ATCA and a more recent U.S. statute, the Torture Victim Protection Act,[236] the court in *Wiwa v. Royal Dutch Petroleum Company* found that "Congress has expressed a policy of U.S. law favoring the adjudication of such suits in U.S. courts."[237] A coordinated international effort to provide access to national courts to litigate human rights claims would greatly further efforts to enforce the human rights obligations of transnational corporations.

---

229. The Second Circuit decision in *Kadic v. Karadzic*, 70 F.3d 232, addressed the responsibility of nonstate actors, rather than those committed by officials of recognized states. *Kadic* involved claims of genocide, torture and war crimes against Radovan Karadzic, the head of the unrecognized Bosnian Serb regime. The court held that the international prohibitions against genocide and certain war crimes apply to all actors, including private citizens. *Id.* at 241-43.

230. The *Kadic* court also found that international law norms that govern official action apply to private actors who act "in concert with" a state. *Id.* at 245. Plaintiffs alleged that Karadzic acted in concert with the recognized government of the former Yugoslavia.

231. 963 F. Supp. 880, 891-92 (C.D. Cal. 1997), dismissed on a motion for summary judgment, 110 F. Supp. 2d 1294 (C.D. Cal. 2000) (appeal pending).

232. Beanal v. Freeport-McMoran, Inc., 969 F. Supp. 362, 372-73 (E.D. La. 1997). In *Beanal*, however, the district court dismissed plaintiff's third amended complaint, holding that even as amended it still did not adequately allege genocide. Beanal v. Freeport-McMoran, Inc., 1998 WL 92246 (E.D. La. Mar. 3, 1998) (unpublished opinion), *aff'd* 197 F.3d 161 (5th Cir. 1999).

233. Genocide Convention, *supra* note 140, art. 4.

234. *Beanal*, 969 F. Supp. at 376.

235. *See, e.g.*, *Kadic*, 70 F.3d at 245; *Beanal*, 969 F. Supp. at 374-80; Doe I v. Unocal, 963 F. Supp. at 890-91.

236. Torture Victim Protection Act of 1991, 28 § U.S.C. 1350 note (1994).

237. Wiwa v. Royal Dutch Petroleum Co., 226 F.3d 88, 106 (2d Cir. 2000), *cert. denied*, 121 S.Ct. 1402 (2001).

88   *BERKELEY JOURNAL OF INTERNATIONAL LAW*   [Vol. 20:45

C. *Extraterritorial Jurisdiction and Enterprise Theory*

The *Wiwa* claims against Royal Dutch Petroleum illustrate a final obstacle to the use of domestic court systems to hold transnational corporations accountable. As stressed earlier, national law is ill-structured to regulate multinationals, whose operations, by definition, straddle many countries. Domestic judicial systems may be unable to obtain jurisdiction over the piece of the multinational that actually sets human rights policies and that has the resources to satisfy a judgment. In *Wiwa*, a magistrate originally concluded that the U.S. federal court in New York did not have jurisdiction over Royal Dutch Petroleum.[238] The district court judge disagreed, finding jurisdiction, a holding that was upheld by the Second Circuit on appeal.[239] However, jurisdiction was based not upon the presence of Shell gas stations throughout the United States; the court did not consider plaintiffs' argument that Shell U.S.A. was the alter ego of Royal Dutch Petroleum.[240] Jurisdiction instead was premised on a handful of direct contacts between Royal Dutch and New York State. The Shell components clearly have put tremendous effort into structuring their operations in such a way as to isolate themselves from the responsibilities of the other members of their corporate family—an effort that might have worked but for the direct contacts between the parent company and New York.

This same problem arises when applying international rules of jurisdiction. International law sets guidelines for exercise by national legal systems of both jurisdiction to prescribe, to determine the rules applicable to persons or activities, and jurisdiction to adjudicate, to subject persons or things to judicial process.[241] Both jurisdiction to prescribe and to adjudicate generally turn upon the contacts with the state seeking to assert jurisdiction.[242] Home state jurisdiction over multinational corporations is based upon the nationality of the corporation, that is, the fact that it is incorporated in the home state. However, where a multinational corporation is composed of multiple units, each incorporated in different states, each of these units may have a different "home state." As a result, multinational corporations argue that parents and subsidiaries are not subject to the jurisdiction of the other's home state. Once again, the reality of economic interdependence is masked by the legal fiction of separate corporate identities.

This highlights the importance of Professor Blumberg's call for application of enterprise law, looking at the reality of control, decision-making and economic benefit rather than the formalities of corporate legal structures. Blumberg highlights an emerging view of the corporate nature, one that recognizes that

---

238. *Id.* at 94.

239. *Id.* at 94-99.

240. *Id.* at 95 n.4.

241. RESTATEMENT OF FOREIGN RELATIONS LAW, *supra* note 141, § 401 (defining categories of jurisdiction under international law).

242. Both look at the location of the persons, things or activities central to the dispute; the nationality of the natural or legal persons involved; and the impact of the activities at issue on the state. *See id.* §§ 402 (listing bases of jurisdiction to prescribe), 421 (listing bases of jurisdiction to adjudicate).

corporations are no longer single-nation entities with a readily identifiable nationality:

> These very large corporations typically operate as multi-tiered multinational groups of parent and subsidiary corporations collectively conducting worldwide economically integrated enterprises that for legal or political purposes have been fragmented among the constituent companies of the group. In selected areas, the law is beginning to recognize corporate groups rather than a particular subsidiary company, as the juridical unit, and to impose group obligations and, less frequently, to recognize group rights as well.[243]

Such an approach was tried—and rejected—in response to the Union Carbide disaster in Bhopal, India, after a chemical leak in 1984 killed thousands of people and injured tens of thousands more.[244] The government of India, representing those injured by the chemical leak, argued in U.S. federal court that the multinational corporation must be viewed as "one entity" rather than as independent parts:

> In reality there is but one entity, the monolithic multinational, which is responsible for the design, development and dissemination of information and technology worldwide, acting through a neatly designed network of interlocking directors, common operating systems, global distribution and marketing systems, financial and other controls. . . . Persons harmed by the acts of [a] multinational corporation are [not] in a position to isolate which unit of the enterprise caused the harm, yet it is evident that the multinational enterprise that caused the harm is liable for such harm. The defendant multinational corporation has to bear this responsibility for it alone had at all material times the means to know and guard against hazards likely to be caused by the operation of the said plant, designed and installed or caused to be installed by it and to provide warnings of potential hazards.[245]

The district court flatly rejected this approach, dismissing the case on the basis of *forum non conveniens*, after concluding that there was insufficient connection between the U.S. parent company and the Indian operation to justify suit in U.S. courts.

Shortly after the Bhopal disaster, Westbrook noted the difficulty in applying notions of enterprise liability to an economic system built upon limiting liability:

> [A] central theme of the last two centuries of modern economic development has been the effort to harness enterprise capitalism without crushing it. . . . To choose to adopt or reject a theory of enterprise liability for personal injuries, or at least for mass disasters, is to confront once again the dilemma of capitalism.[246]

The concept of limited liability, however, arose long before corporations were permitted to expand to create the interlocking multinational enterprises that now dominate the international economy. As the Bhopal litigation illustrates, in the

---

243. Blumberg, *supra* note 83, at 298 (footnotes omitted).

244. See Jamie Cassels, *Outlaws: Multinational Corporations and Catastrophic Law,* 31 CUMB. L. REV. 311 (2000), for a summary of the facts and efforts to obtain legal redress.

245. *Id.* at 324 (quoting Complaint, Union of India v. Union Carbide Corporation (5 Sept., 1986), ¶ 19). The full complaint is reprinted in VALIANT VICTIMS AND LETHAL LITIGATION: THE BHOPAL CASE 3 (Upendra Baxi and Amita Dhanda eds., 1990).

246. Jay Lawrence Westbrook, *Theories of Parent Company Liability and the Prospects for an International Settlement,* 20 TEX. INT'L L. J. 321, 326 (1985).

absence of a pragmatic international approach, one that recognizes the reality of economic interdependence rather than relying on legal independence, multinationals will continue to evade regulation in domestic legal systems. International regulation and enforcement are necessary to regulate an international enterprise. To be fully effective, the corporate regulatory system must recognize enterprise principles so that it can deal with the global phenomenon of multinational corporations.

VII.
CONCLUSION

Multinational corporations are the driving force behind the global economy. Reining in their unchecked power, imposing regulations that force accountability for human rights abuses, is indeed a challenge to modern capitalism. International law has already developed applicable standards. The task ahead is to find effective mechanisms to enforce those norms, to ensure that the amorality of profit does not permit corporate human rights abuses to fester for another fifty years.

[3]

Human Rights Codes for Transnational Corporations: What Can the Sullivan and MacBride Principles Tell Us?

CHRISTOPHER McCRUDDEN*

Abstract—The development of codes of conduct for transnational corporations is considered, particularly those involving human and labour rights. The issue of compliance with such codes is examined through a detailed consideration of the development and operation of the Sullivan and MacBride Principles. The origin, evolution, and effects of these Principles is considered. Particular attention is paid to institutional and other features surrounding their enforcement, including the use of selective purchasing, shareholder activism, and linkage to government financial incentives. The paper considers what conclusions may be drawn from the operation of these Principles to inform current debates about the effectiveness of corporate codes of conduct.

1. Introduction

Codes of practice for transnational corporations are essentially guidelines setting out, usually in relatively general terms, what a corporation should do in a particular country, or when engaged in a particular type of operation, or where particular types of risk are apparent. This paper will be particularly concerned with codes of practice in the human rights field, including labour rights, but there are important codes of practice in the environmental area which raise many of the same issues.[1]

---

* Lincoln College, Oxford. The author was involved in some of the events described in this paper. He was commissioned by the Fair Employment Agency to report on its effectiveness in 1981. He served as a member of the Standing Advisory Commission on Human Rights between 1984 and 1988. He provided expert testimony on behalf of NYCERS in its dispute with American Brands. He acted as an informal advisor to Kevin McNamara, MP during the passage of the Fair Employment Bill in 1989 when Mr McNamara was Shadow Secretary of State for Northern Ireland. He has been an occasional advisor to the Fair Employment Commission. He testified to the US Congress, House of Representatives, International Relations Committee in March 1995 on economic justice in Northern Ireland. The article was originally prepared as a contribution to the American Society of International Law's Project on compliance with soft law, and another version will be published in the volume resulting from this project. I am grateful to Jill Murray, Pat Doherty, Heidi Welsh, and Sir Robert Cooper for detailed comments on an earlier draft.

[1] See Valerie Ann Zondorak, 'A New Face in Corporate Environmental Responsibility: The Valdez Principles', 18 *Boston College Environmental Affairs L Rev* 457 (1991).

168   *Oxford Journal of Legal Studies*   VOL. 19

Such codes have arisen from five different sources: from international organizations, from national governments, from private initiatives, from the corporations themselves, and (most recently) from negotiations between some or all of these interests.[2]

International organizations such as the International Labour Organization (ILO) and the Organization for Economic Cooperation and Development (OECD) produced codes of practice for multinational organizations during the 1970s.[3] However, as an embryonic system of international control of multinational corporations, the ILO and OECD codes are widely perceived to have failed, in part because their requirements are neither legally binding, nor effectively enforced.[4] Several governments produced codes of employment practice for firms operating in their countries with subsidiaries in South Africa during the 1970s and 1980s. In 1977 and 1985, the European Community[5] and Canada,[6] respectively, adopted such codes.

Private initiatives, notably the Sullivan Principles relating to South Africa and the MacBride Principles relating to Northern Ireland (the primary focus of this paper), came to prominence in the 1980s, and continue to be produced in other areas.[7] Other similar private-initiative codes include the Slepak Principles, the Miller Principles, the Maquiladora Standards of Conduct, the Valdez Principles, the Caux Principles, and the Kyosei Principles. In 1998, the Council on Economic Priorities launched a 'global standard' to be awarded to those businesses complying with a specified ethical stance in the production and sourcing of goods from the developing world.[8] Trade unions have also been active in producing similar codes. In 1997 the International Confederation of Free Trade Unions

---

[2] For a more detailed account of the history of codes of practice, see J. Murray, 'Corporate Codes of Conduct and Labour Standards', in Robert Kyloh (ed.), *Mastering the Challenge of Globalization* (ILO, Bureau for Workers' Activities, Working Paper, Geneva, 1998) 47, at 49–55.

[3] 'ILO Tripartite Declaration of Principles concerning MNEs and Social Policy, 1977', 17 *ILM* 422 (1978); 'OECD Guidelines for Multinational Enterprises, 1976', 15 *ILM* 967–79 (1976). For earlier considerations of Codes of Conduct see Raymond J. Waldmann, *Regulating International Business Through Codes of Conduct* (1980), and Norbert Horn (ed.), *Legal Problems of Codes of Conduct for Multinational Enterprises* (1980).

[4] For an analysis, see J. Murray, above n 2. See also, Peter Muchlinski, *Multinational Enterprises and the Law* (1996).

[5] 'Community Code of Conduct for Enterprises Having Affiliates, Subsidiaries or Agencies in South Africa' (20 September 1977), *EC Bulletin* 51 (1977, no 9). For a discussion, see R. Blanpain, *Labour Law and Industrial Relations of the European Community* (1991) at 207–10. For the effect of the Code in leading to action by the individual Member States, see K. C. Wellens and G. M. Borchardt, 'Soft Law in European Community Law' (1989) 14 *Eur L Rev* 267.

[6] 'Statements by the [Canadian] Secretary of State for External Affairs Regarding Sanctions Against South Africa', 24 *ILM* 1464 (1985).

[7] See *The Minnesota Principles: Toward an Ethical Basis for Global Business* (Minnesota Center for Corporate Responsibility, Minn, 1992). On the Valdez Principles which relate to the environment, see Daniel Pink, 'The Valdez Principles: Is What's Good for America Good for General Motors?', 8 *Yale L Policy Rev* 180 (1990). The Slepak Principles related to the former Soviet Union; the Miller Code related to China and Tibet, and the Maquiladora Standards of Conduct code relate the USA–Mexican border operations. On these codes, see Lance Compa and Tashia Hinchliffe-Darricarrère, 'Enforcing International Labor Rights through Corporate Codes of Conduct', 33 *Columbia J Transnat'l L* 663 at 672–3 (1995), and especially Jorge Perez-Lopez, 'Promoting International Respect for Worker Rights through Business Codes of Conduct', 17 *Fordham Int'l LJ* 1 at 12–23 (1993). In addition, the OECD has identified the Caux Principles and the Kyosei Principles, see OECD, *Trade, Employment and Labour Standards: A Study of Core Workers' Rights and International Trade* (OECD, 1996) at 198.

[8] 'Global Standard for Business Ethics Launched', *The Financial Times* (11 June 1998) at 10.

proposed its 'Basic Code of Conduct covering Labour Practices'.[9] A recent European example is the Code of Conduct agreed in 1997 between the European Trade Union Federation for Textiles, Clothing and Leather, and Euratex.

There has also been a flurry of activity by corporations themselves during the 1990s, with the production of codes aimed at self-regulation.[10] Three types of self-regulatory code can be identified. Some relate to minimum standards regarding conditions of work by the company and its associates. Some support increased involvement by the company in human rights in the larger community in which it operates. Some establish ethical criteria by which a company's investment should be guided.[11] There has been criticism of some of these codes as protective of the company rather than effective in furthering human rights.[12]

Recently, in a new development, codes have resulted from negotiations between corporations and other interests, whether trade unions, non-governmental organizations (NGOs), or governments. A Code of Practice was negotiated between a trade union coalition and FIFA (the international soccer regulatory body) regarding the production of goods licensed by FIFA.[13] In the 1990s, partly as a response to these developments, governments have also become increasingly involved in joint initiatives with companies and NGOs. In 1997, a US presidential task force that included human rights groups, labour unions, and apparel industry representatives reached an agreement to create a code of conduct on wages and working conditions in factories that American companies use throughout the world.[14] In the UK, the government, in an 'Ethical Trading Initiative' is 'supporting collaboration between business and the voluntary sector in promoting ethical businesses, including the development of codes of conduct and ways of monitoring and verifying these codes'.[15] Codes, therefore, in different guises,

---

[9] For text, see Steve Gibbons, *International Labour Rights—New Methods of Enforcement* (Institute of Employment Rights, 1998) Appendix 3.

[10] See, e.g. policies of Levi Strauss, Reebok Corp., and Starbucks Coffee Co. On these, see Lance Compa and Tashia Hinchliffe-Darricarrère, 'Enforcing International Labor Rights through Corporate Codes of Conduct', 33 *Columbia J Transnat'l L* 663 at 674–85 (1995), reprinted in a revised form in Lance A. Compa and Stephen F. Diamond, *uman Rights, Labor Rights, and International Trade* (University of Pennsylvania Press, 1996). For a more recent analysis, see Jean-Paul Sajhau, *Business Ethics in the Textile, Clothing and Footwear (TCF) Industries: Codes of Conduct* (ILO, Industrial Activities Branch, Sectoral Activities Programme, Working Paper, 1997).

[11] Barbara A. Frey, 'The Legal and Ethical Responsibilities of Transnational Corporations in the Protection of International Human Rights', 6 *Minn J Global Trade* 153 at 177 (1997). For an argument in favour of such codes, see Mark B. Baker, 'Private Codes of Corporate Conduct: Should the Fox Guard the Henhouse?', 24 *U Miami Inter-American L Rev* 399 (1993). For an up-to-date account, see Pamela Varle (ed.), *The Sweatshop Quandary: Corporate Responsibility on the Global Frontier* (IRRC, 1998).

[12] Consider the controversy surrounding Nike's and Shell's Codes, see, e.g. 'Nike's Asian Factories Pass Young's Muster', *New York Times* (25 June 1997) at D2; S. Glass, 'The Young and the Feckless', *The New Republic* (8 and 15 September 1997) at 20; Citizen Shell, *New York Times* (editorial) (31 March 1997) at A14 ('About 100 American companies now have such codes. They often go unenforced.') In May 1998, Nike published a new Code of Conduct. For text, see above n 9, Appendix 4.

[13] See text reproduced in *International Union Rights*, vol 3, issue 1 (1997).

[14] See Varle (ed.), above n 11 at 470–5 for text, and 464–7 for commentary. See also 'Apparel Industry Group Moves to End Sweatshops', *New York Times*, (9 April 1997) at A14.

[15] White Paper, *Eliminating World Poverty: A Challenge for the 21st Century* Cmnd 3789 (1997) at 64. See further, 'Cook Plans Ethics Guide for Companies', *The Financial Times* (2/3 January 1999) at 5.

and with varying degrees of approbation and criticism, have become the subject of increasing attention worldwide.[16]

As Gibbons has pointed out, however, the 'relative newness of what may be called the "modern" code of conduct means that there is little literature on the exact effect of such codes . . .'.[17] In studies evaluating the effectiveness of such codes, reference is frequently made to the Sullivan and MacBride Principles as well-researched examples of codes which indicate some ways in which voluntary codes may be made more effective.[18] This article focuses on the development and operation of the MacBride and Sullivan Principles, and 'compliance' with them. It argues that the two sets of Principles cast light on some current debates about the appropriateness and potential effectiveness of such codes.

The Sullivan Principles were originally a brief set of Principles, drafted by the Rev. Leon Sullivan, an African-American Baptist minister, whilst he was a member of the Board of Directors of General Motors Corporation in 1977. The Principles were intended to put pressure on American companies with operations in *apartheid*-era South Africa to comply with a set of labour and antidiscrimination standards in their South African operations. The focus of concern in South Africa was the position of the non-white workforce.

Some years later, in November 1984, and following the model of the Sullivan Principles, a separate private group promulgated the MacBride Principles. These are a set of Principles which are intended to put pressure on American companies operating in Northern Ireland to adopt a set of antidiscrimination and weak affirmative action goals in their Northern Ireland operations. The focus of concern in Northern Ireland is the need to ensure equality of opportunity in employment between the two main (religious) communities.

2. *The 'Principles' Approach in Context*

A. *Labour rights, human rights, and international trade*

The Sullivan and MacBride Principles focused primarily on labour standards, particularly equality of employment opportunities, in, respectively, South Africa and Northern Ireland. They are examples of attempts at transnational regulation of the workplace activities of employers. To that extent they can be viewed as examples of a lengthy tradition of international attempts at such regulation, seen most notably in the promotion of international labour standards by the ILO, in the form of its conventions and recommendations.[19] From this perspective,

---

[16] See, e.g. OECD, *Trade, Employment and Labour Standards: A Study of Core Workers' Rights and International Trade* (OECD, 1996) at 190–204.

[17] Above n 9 at 18.

[18] See, e.g. S. Charnovitz, 'The WTO and Social Issues', (1994) 28 *J World Trade L* 17; Jorge Perez-Lopez, 'Promoting International Respect for Worker Rights through Business Codes of Conduct', 17 *Fordham Int'l LJ* 1 (1993); Jonas Malmberg and David Johnsson, *Social Clauses and Other Means to Promote Fair Labour Standards in International Fora – A Survey* (Arbetslivsrapport, 1998:25, Arbetslivsinstitutet, Stockholm, 1998) at 28–30.

[19] See ILO, 'The ILO, Standard Setting and Globalization: Report of the Director-General' (International Labour Conference, 85th Session, 1997).

Human Rights Codes for Transnational Corporations

focusing on the activities of private sector employers is a primary *raison d'être* of such regulation.

Attempts at international labour relations regulation have also come to be seen by some as part of a more recent, broader movement—that advocating international human rights. The Sullivan and MacBride Principles were both heavily imbued with this perspective, although as we shall see, the content of the Principles owes more to American than international norms. To the extent that they are perceived to be part of international human rights developments, they fit uneasily into some more traditional conceptions of the appropriate role of that movement: that in which human rights have been regarded as primarily involving the control of states and governments, not private actors. However, as concern about human rights in the economic and social areas becomes a focus of concern, non-state actors become a major focus. As governments shed their responsibilities, the role of the private sector in human rights violations is exposed. As economic globalization of the world economy gathers apace, and with it an increase in the need for countries to encourage inward investment, the power of multinational corporations to pressure governments into behaving responsibly becomes even clearer. The role of private actors as they impinge on human rights is thus increasingly recognized.[20]

Labour and human rights standards can also be promoted through 'social clauses' in international trade and investment agreements.[21] Such social clauses involve the parties promising to comply with particular labour or human rights standards, or risk having trade sanctions being imposed. Such social clauses have been considered in connection, most recently, with the World Trade Organization (WTO) agreements, the North American Free Trade Agreement (NAFTA), and the (stalled) OECD Multilateral Agreement on Investment. Additionally, both the USA[22] and the European Community[23] unilaterally attach labour and other human rights provisions to their Generalized System of Preferences.

B. *Non-governmental activity*

A somewhat different approach in attempting to provide labour and human rights standards is through the activities of non-governmental activists, such as by consumers, shareholders, trade unions, and by single issue human rights and environmental pressure groups in several western countries.[24] Traditionally,

---

[20] See, e.g. Douglass Cassel, 'Corporate Initiatives: A Second Human Rights Revolution?', 19 *Fordham Int'l LJ* 1963 at 1984 (1996).

[21] See David Chin, *A Social Clause for Labour's Cause: Global Trade and Labour Standards – A Challenge for the New Millennium* (Institute of Employment Rights, 1998).

[22] In the Trade and Tarrif Act 1984, s 502(b).

[23] Council Regulation No 3281/94 of 19 December 1994, Council Regulation No 1256/96 of 20 June 1996, and Council Regulation No 1154/98, OJ No 160, 4 June 1998.

[24] See, in general, Barbara A. Frey, 'The Legal and Ethical Responsibilities of Transnational Corporations in the Protection of International Human Rights', 6 *Minn J Global Trade* 153 (1997).

activity by these groups was in the form of support for governmental or international regulation of private sector actors. Increasingly, however, such groups now seek additional means of putting pressure on corporations because of the perceived ineffectiveness of much traditional regulation. With this scepticism of governments' ability or willingness to regulate effectively has come the development of tactics by citizen groups to put pressure on companies directly through their own actions, rather than indirectly through advocating traditional governmental regulation. With the popularity of ethical business issues by sections of the general public has come a growing recognition by companies that issues of human rights and ethics are also, potentially, matters of business, and that to retain the loyalty of consumers, the cooperation of workers, or simply to avoid hassles at shareholder meetings, they need to (at least appear to) be taking such concerns seriously. One way in which this approach has been put into effect is by way of consumer boycotts, socially responsible investing, 'social labelling', and codes of practice.[25]

3. *The Sullivan Principles*

In early 1977, the Rev. Sullivan announced the endorsement of an initial 12 American firms to a set of six Principles to promote racial equality in employment practices for US firms operating in South Africa.[26] The Sullivan Principles were seen by the Rev. Sullivan as an alternative to corporate divestment from South Africa, which he had originally proposed to General Motors but had failed to achieve.[27] American corporations with operations in South Africa were invited to indicate their adherence to the Principles by signing a Declaration. The Statement of Principles was 'amplified' in June 1978 and again in May 1979. Amplifications required a more stringent implementation of the Principles including increased dimensions of activities, more sensitivity to employee concerns, a broadened scope of union recognition, further direction for training and promoting non-whites to all levels of company operation, and certified reporting. The fourth amplification, issued in November 1984, broadened the requirements on companies, calling for US companies to deal more directly with laws and customs which underpinned apartheid.

---

[25] OECD, *Trade, Employment and Labour Standards: A Study of Core Workers' Rights and International Trade* (OECD, 1996) at 199–204. On social labelling, see the recent study by Janet Hilowitz, *Labeling Child Labour Products* (ILO, 1997).

[26] On the operation of the Sullivan Principles, see D. Hauck, M. Voorhes, and G. Goldberg, *Two Decades of Debate: The Controversy Over US Companies in South Africa* (IRRC 1983); J. Leape, B. Baskin, and S. Underhill, *Business in the Shadow of Apartheid: US Firms in South Africa* (Lexington Books 1985). For studies which consider the Sullivan Principles in the wider context of sanctions against South Africa, see e.g. Robert M. Price, *The Apartheid State in Crisis: Political Transformation in South Africa, 1975–1990* (OUP, 1991); Richard W. Hull, *American Enterprise in South Africa: istorical Dimensions of Engagement and Disengagement* (New York University Press, 1990); Mark Orkin, *Sanctions Against Apartheid* (St Martins Press, 1990). For a more recent re-evaluation, see Kenneth A. Rodman, 'Think Globally, Punish Locally: Nonstate Actors, Multinational Corporations, and Human Rights Sanctions', 12 *Ethics and International Affairs* 19–41 (1998).

[27] OECD, *Trade, Employment and Labour Standards: A Study of Core Workers' Rights and International Trade* (OECD, 1996) at 197.

A. *An outline of the Sullivan Principles*

As thus amplified,[28] the Principles required (in Principle I), the 'non-segregation of the races in all eating, comfort, and work facilities'. Each signatory undertook immediately to eliminate all vestiges of racial discrimination, remove all race designation signs, and desegregate all eating, comfort, and work facilities. Principle II required equal and fair employment practices for all employees. Each signatory undertook immediately to implement equal and fair terms and conditions of employment; provide non-discriminatory eligibility for benefit plans; establish an appropriate and comprehensive procedure for handling and resolving individual employee complaints; support the elimination of all industrial racial discriminatory laws which impede the implementation of equal and fair terms and conditions of employment, such as abolition of job reservations, job fragmentation, and apprenticeship restrictions for blacks and other non-whites; support the elimination of discrimination against the rights of blacks to form or belong to government registered and unregistered unions, and acknowledge generally the rights of blacks to form their own unions or be represented by trade unions which already exist; secure rights of black workers to the freedom of association and assure protection against victimization while pursuing and after attaining these rights; and involve black workers or their representatives in the development of programmes that address their educational and other needs and those of their dependents and the local community.

Principle III required equal pay for all employees doing equal or comparable work for the same period of time. Each signatory undertook immediately to design and implement a wage and salary administration plan which is applied equally to all employees, regardless of race, who are performing equal or comparable work; ensure an equitable system of job classifications, including a review of the distinction between hourly and salaried classifications; determine the extent upgrading of personnel and/or jobs in the upper echelons is needed, and implement programmes to accomplish this objective in representative numbers, ensuring the employment of blacks and other non-whites at all levels of company operations; assign equitable wage and salary ranges, the minimum of these to be well above the appropriate local minimum economic living level.

Principle IV required the initiation of and development of training programmes that will prepare, in substantial numbers, blacks and other non-whites for supervisory, administrative clerical, and technical jobs. Each signatory undertook immediately to determine employee training needs and capabilities, and identify employees with potential for further advancement; take advantage of existing outside training resources and activities, such as exchange programmes, technical colleges, and, similar institutions or programmes; support the development of outside training facilities, individually or collectively—including technical centres,

---

[28] The 1984 text is reproduced in *ILM*, vol 24(5) (1985) at 1486.

professional training exposure, correspondence and extension courses, as appropriate, for extensive training outreach; and initiate and expand inside training programmes and facilities.

Principle V required increasing the number of blacks and other non-whites in management and supervisory positions. Each signatory undertook immediately to identify, actively recruit, train, and develop a sufficient and significant number of blacks and other non-whites to assure that as quickly as possible there will be appropriate representation of blacks and other non-whites in the management group of each company at all levels of operations; establish management development programmes for blacks and other non-whites, as needed, and improve existing programmes and facilities for developing management skills of blacks and other non-whites; and identify and channel high management potential blacks and other non-white employees into management development programmes.

Principle VI required employers to improve the quality of employees' lives outside the work environment in such areas as housing, transportation, schooling, recreation, and health facilities. Each signatory undertook immediately to evaluate existing and/or develop programmes, as appropriate, to address the specific needs of black and other non-white employees in the areas of housing, health care, transportation, and recreation; evaluate methods for utilizing existing, expanded or newly established in-house medical facilities or other medical programmes to improve medical care for all non-whites and their dependants; and participate in the development of programmes that address the educational needs of employees, their dependants, and the local community. Both individual and collective programmes should be considered, in addition to technical education, including such activities as literacy education, business training, direct assistance to local schools, contributions, and scholarships. Employers further undertook to support changes in influx control laws to provide for the right of black migrant workers to normal family life, and increase utilization of and assist in the development of black and other non-white owned and operated business enterprises including distributors, suppliers of goods and services, and manufacturers.

The 1984 amplification went further still, adding additional dimensions to employer activity outside the workplace. Employers undertook to use their influence and support the unrestricted rights of black businesses to locate in urban areas of South Africa; influence other companies in South Africa to follow the standards of equal rights Principles; support the freedom of mobility of black workers to seek employment opportunities wherever they exist, and make possible provisions for adequate housing for families of employees within the proximity of workers' employment; and support the ending of all apartheid laws.

Finally, signatory companies undertook to report progress on an annual basis to Rev. Sullivan through the independent administrative unit he has established; have all areas specified by Rev. Sullivan audited by a certified public accounting firm; and inform all employees of the company's annual periodic report rating and invite their input on ways to improve the rating. The utility of the Principles was increased by the decision in 1978 to appoint a firm of accountants (Arthur D. Little, Inc.) to monitor the effects of the Principles. Pressure was increased through media reporting and a perceived need to improve corporate image among consumers.

The content of the Principles clearly overlaps with several international law norms deriving from the human rights treaties,[29] and to that extent the Principles may be seen as attempting to secure compliance with these norms. However, it is equally clear that the breadth and depth of the obligations taken on by signatories goes beyond, in some cases (particularly the requirements of political engagement and funding of social projects) well beyond, obligations under the human rights treaties. Rather than reflecting international law norms, the Principles owe much of their inspiration and content to the view of the appropriate social responsibility of US corporations held at that time by American civil rights activists. The Sullivan Principles thus overlapped with international law norms but reflect much more a sustained attempt to export American conceptions of corporate social responsibility.

B. *Activities of institutional investors and state and local government*

Added weight was given to the Principles by the activities of church groups, human rights groups, institutional investors, college and university students, and several state and local governments in the USA, which used the Sullivan Principles as bench-marks against which to assess corporations with which they contracted, or in which they invested. Despite unanswered questions regarding their legality under US law,[30] the growth of investment and selective purchasing policies was particularly widespread.

A survey in 1993 found that 24 states had restrictions on South African investments by their public pension funds either by statute on by pension fund board policy.[31] At one extreme, the restrictions were absolute, requiring divestment from any firm doing business in or with South Africa. Another approach was to limit investment only to firms subscribing to the Sullivan Principles. Within this category, some laws required an active assessment of the degree of compliance, whilst others accepted promised adherence.[32] Where states and localities continued to hold stock in companies with South African

---

[29] Universal Declaration of Human Rights 1948, Art 23; International Convention on the Elimination of All Forms of Racial Discrimination 1966; International Covenant on Economic, Social, and Cultural Rights 1966, Arts 7 and 8; International Covenant on Civil and Political Rights 1966, Art 26; International Convention on the Suppression and Punishment of the Crime of Apartheid 1973. In addition, see the ILO Equal Remuneration and Discrimination (Employment and Occupation) Conventions of 1951 and 1958, respectively.

[30] The literature on this question was considerable. See, e.g. Richard B. Bilder, 'The Role of States and Cities in Foreign Relations', 83 *Am J Int'l L* 821 at 822, fn 6 (1989) which lists many of the main contributions.

[31] Roberta Romano, 'Public Pension Fund Activism in Corporate Government Reconsidered', 93 *Columbia L Rev* 795 (1993) at 809. For a severe criticism of this development, see John H. Langbein and Richard Posner, 'Social Investing and the Law of Trusts', 79 *Michigan L Rev* 72 (1980). For a defence, see Maria O'Brien Hylton, 'Socially Responsible Investing: Doing Good Versus Doing Well in an Inefficient Market', 42 *Am U L Rev* 1 (1992).

[32] See Howard N. Fenton, 'The Fallacy of Federalism in Foreign Affairs: State and Local Foreign Policy Restrictions', 13 *Northwestern J Int'l L Business* 563 at 569 (1993).

connections, shareholder resolutions were a favourite method of increasing the pressure to make changes, often by pressing for compliance with the Sullivan Principles. In addition to the activity of state and local bodies, other institutional investors also took up this approach, particularly several religious groups which became well-known thorns in the side of several companies, such as the Interfaith Center on Corporate Responsibility, based in New York. The possibility for the use of this mechanism for 'enforcement' arose from the rules of the Securities and Exchange Commission (SEC). These required public companies to include in the company-funded proxy statement all proper proposals by shareholders, and shareholders must be given the opportunity to vote on these proposals. (As we shall see subsequently, corporate distaste for social policy shareholder resolutions gave rise to efforts to pressure the SEC to change its policy.)

The history of state and local activity on South Africa also involved considerable recourse to the use of 'selective purchasing' as a tool to bring pressure for change. Indeed the first recorded economic initiative at a state or local level involved the adoption of a binding resolution by the city council of Madison, Wisconsin, to seek purchasing contracts with companies that did not have 'economic interests in South Africa'.[33] Many more localities and states were to follow suit, particularly during the mid-1980s. According to research carried out by the Investor Research Responsibility Center, at the height of such activity, six states had adopted selective purchasing laws or policies.[34] In addition, 53 cities and 14 other localities had adopted similar legislation or policies. In many cases, there was a simple ban imposed on contracting with companies which had business relations with South Africa, subject on occasion to exceptions, such as in the case of the non-availability of other suppliers. In some other cases, constructive engagement by companies was deemed permissible and the legislation referred specifically to the Sullivan Principles. The purpose of the reference to the Principles in the Maryland legislation, for example, was to provide a basic set of minimum requirements, compliance with which the purchasing authority was to regard as a necessary condition for state purchasing from that company. The Maryland law, for example, required any bidder for state contracts of more than $100,000 to certify either that it did no business in South Africa, *or* that it complied with specified parts of the Sullivan Principles.[35] In most cases, selective purchasing laws were merely one part of a much larger range of economic pressures which the state or locality sought to bring to bear, such as divestment of holdings in South Africa-related companies, restriction on which financial institutions a state or locality was able to use, and the ban on the purchase of South African made goods.

---

[33] William F. Moses, *A Guide to American State and Local Laws on South Africa* (IRRC, 1993) at 29.

[34] Maryland, Massachusetts, Michigan, New Jersey, North Carolina, and Rhode Island, see Peter DeSimone and William F. Moses, *A Guide to American State and Local Laws on South Africa* (IRRC, November 1995) at 17–22.

[35] Above n 33 at 27.

C. *Effects of the Principles*

There is some indication that the Principles had several positive effects: first, that corporations found them useful by providing a focus for their social and political activities in South Africa; second, that the Principles brought about some changes in conditions for black workers which may not otherwise have occurred; third, that the Principles led to increased funding by companies of social causes in the South African community, and fourth, that they may have increased pressure on government for the recognition of black trade unions, an important factor in the development of organized black politics.[36] It is difficult, however, for the effect of the Principles to be distinguished from the effect of other similar activity, outside the context of the Principles, such as that undertaken by other countries, or from larger political and economic forces operating at that time in South Africa.

Whatever effectiveness we may be able to attribute to the Principles, however, such corporate responsibility programmes could not hope to do other than affect South Africa at the margins. Less than half of the relevant US companies were signatories, and membership went into decline.[37] By 1982, there were 145 signatories to the Principles, and at the height of their popularity there were 178 signatory firms. By the mid-1980s, the Sullivan Principles came under increasing criticism, both within the USA, in South Africa itself,[38] and internationally. In 1985, for example, the UN Commission on Transnational Corporations criticized codes such as the Sullivan Principles for not helping the black majority.[39] Added to this was a sense of rising expectations about what was necessary in South Africa, expectations which the Principles could not hope to meet.

By the mid-1980s, the Principles were mostly side-lined, so far as American corporations were concerned. The decision of the US Congress to impose economic sanctions against South Africa by law hastened this. As pressure grew for Congress to take strong action, President Reagan sought to head off such action by issuing an Executive Order which included a requirement on larger American firms operating in South Africa to conform to a Code of fair employment practices modelled on the Sullivan Principles.[40] This tactic failed, however, and the Comprehensive Anti-Apartheid Act passed in 1986[41] prevented any new US investment in or loans to South Africa, banned the import of certain South African goods, and restricted the landing rights of South African aircraft. It also

[36] For assessments, see Note, 'US Labor Practices in South Africa: Will a Mandatory Fair Employment Code Succeed Where the Sullivan Principles Have Failed?', 7 *Fordham Int'l LJ* 358 at 363–5 (1983–4); D. C. Campbell, 'US Firms and Black Labor in South Africa: Creating a Structure of Change', VII(1) *Journal of Labor Research* 1 (1986); John M. Kline, *International Codes and Multinational Business* (Westport Con., 1985) at 95; R. T. de George, *Competing with Integrity in International Business* (OUP, 1993) at 57.

[37] Ibid at 366–7.

[38] The Code was 'widely derided by South African trade unionists as being completely ineffective against apartheid', *African Business* (January 1986) at 16, quoted by Murray above n 2 at 890.

[39] Examination of the Activities of Transnational Corporations in South Africa and Namibia, UN ESCOR (Agenda Item 3) at 10, 12–14, 20–1, UN Doc E/C.10/AC. 4/1985/5 (1985) cited in David Weissbrodt and Georgina Mahoney, 'International Legal Action Against Apartheid', IV *Law and Inequality* (1986) 485 at 501–2.

[40] Executive Order 12532 of 9 September 1985 (50 FR 36861).

[41] Comprehensive Anti-Apartheid Act of 1986 (Pub L 99–440).

Human Rights and Corporations

adopted a Code of Practice for American companies which continued to operate
in South Africa, and, to that extent, the Sullivan Principles became incorporated
into legislation. This became particularly clear when the implementing regulations
exempted from some reporting requirements under the Act those firms which
were signatories of the Sullivan Principles.[42] The main difference between the
Code of Conduct and the Principles lay in the sanctions attaching to the
requirements under the legislation. Failure to comply with the regulations could
lead to criminal penalties and administrative sanctions, action which those
administering the Sullivan Principles could not impose.

Whilst the thrust of the Sullivan Principles was one of engagement, however,
the thrust of the congressional action was one of disengagement. A Code of
Practice for companies operating in South Africa was an alternative to divestment,
but not really the preferred alternative. To the extent, therefore, that corporate
supporters sought to stave off pressure for divestment by adopting the Sullivan
Principles, the strategy had failed by the mid-1980s. Following congressional
action, many more companies left South Africa and the pressure on others to
do so increased. The credibility of the Principles was further undermined by the
decision of the Rev. Sullivan himself to disassociate himself from the programme
in 1987, urging divestment rather than engagement by companies and a total
US economic embargo against South Africa. Despite this, the programme
continued for some years under the administration of an Industry Support
Group, a group of executives representing those companies which had signed
up to the Principles.[43] By 1991/92, there were only 50 signatory firms. Since the
call in September 1993 by Nelson Mandela for the lifting of sanctions, most such
sanctions have been removed, including those involving selective purchasing.[44]

4. *The MacBride Principles*

Although in form similar to the Sullivan Principles, and strongly influenced
by their mechanisms for achieving compliance, the MacBride Principles were
developed in a context which was very different. To appreciate this, we need to
turn first to situate the development of the Principles in the context of the
Northern Ireland problem as a whole.

A. *Background to the Northern Ireland problem*

Northern Ireland was created in 1920 as a partially self-governing entity in the
UK, whilst the remainder of the island of Ireland became independent.[45] The
majority of the population (largely Protestant) supported continued membership

---

[42] 'US Department of State Regulations Implementing the Comprehensive Anti-Apartheid Act of 1986', 26
ILM 111 (1987).
[43] William F. Moses, *A Guide to American State and Local Laws on South Africa* (IRRC, 1993) at 195.
[44] See DeSimone and Moses, above n 34 at 17–22.
[45] There is a huge literature, see C. McCrudden, 'Northern Ireland and the British Constitution', in J. Jowell
and D. Oliver (eds), *The Changing Constitution* (3rd edn, OUP, 1994).

in the UK, while a minority (largely Catholic) continued to seek integration with the south. The experiment of devolved government lasted until the early 1970s. To the extent that the constitutional arrangements were intended to facilitate the coming together of Protestants and Catholics, the experiment was unsuccessful, in part because Catholics were regarded by Protestants as a threat to the continued existence of Northern Ireland as part of the UK, in part because Protestants were regarded by Catholics as suppressing not only their national identity but also their economic status through systematic discrimination, in employment, housing, education, and welfare.

By the early 1960s, a group of largely Catholic activists had formed a reform movement which concentrated on eradicating such discrimination, modelled on the US civil rights movement.[46] This led to some minor reforms by the late 1960s, but at the cost of increasing political instability. The reforms which were introduced by the local Northern Ireland Government were perceived by an influential group within the ruling party as going too far in the face of unjustified pressure, whilst a significant number of Catholics saw the measures as too little, and too late. Increasingly, views polarized, leading (in quick succession) to street demonstrations, civil unrest, the introduction of the British Army in a peace-keeping role, the resurgence of terrorism from both Protestant and Catholic paramilitary groups, the collapse of the Northern Ireland Government, the suspension of the experiment in devolution, and the imposition of 'direct rule' by the government of the UK in 1972. Since then there have been repeated attempts to secure a negotiated settlement.

Increasingly, the Government of Ireland has sought a role in influencing events, leading in turn to the Anglo-Irish Agreement in 1985, which formalized its continuing, but largely consultative role. In the absence of any settlement, terrorism continued until agreement was reached to have a cessation of para-military activity on both sides, leading eventually to multiparty talks involving all those Northern Ireland political parties which chose to attend, and the British and Irish Governments. The talks were chaired by former US Senator George Mitchell, indicating the close interest which the USA, particularly under the administration of President Clinton, has taken in attempting to reach a settlement. On 10 April 1998 (Good Friday), the talks eventually reached a successful conclusion.

This all too brief account is intended as an introduction to an equally brief description of the principal reforms introduced by the Northern Ireland Government and (more particularly) by successive British Governments after direct rule was introduced in 1972.[47] First, several pieces of voting rights reform removed the gerrymandering of local electoral districts which had been a feature of Northern Ireland politics during the period of devolution, and up-dated the qualifications for voting to remove property and other qualifications which had a discriminatory effect on Catholic voters. Second, responsibility for the allocation

[46] *Disturbances in Northern Ireland: Report of the Cameron Commission* Cmd 532 (1969).
[47] On reforms, see McCrudden, above n 45 *passim*.

of public housing was transferred from local authority control to a central housing authority (the Housing Executive) which largely eliminated the crude religious discrimination of the local authority allocations. Third, new constitutional guarantees against religious discrimination in the operation of government were introduced in the Northern Ireland Constitution Act 1972, replacing the previous, largely ineffective provisions in the Government of Ireland Act 1920. Fourth, reforms were introduced into recruitment procedures for the Northern Ireland Civil Service which aimed not only to reduce discrimination, but to result in a more representative bureaucracy. Most recently, the Good Friday Agreement included a strong element of human rights protection, particularly equality, as a significant part of an agreed peace process.[48] As a result, much has changed in terms of relationships, both political and economic, between Catholics and Protestants.

B. *Employment discrimination and inequality of opportunity*

One feature of relationships which remains a continuing problem, however, is the economic disparity between Catholics and Protestants, particularly in the labour market.[49] On almost all socio-economic indicators, Catholics are significantly worse off than Protestants. One of the most dramatic differences, and the one which has attracted significant local and international attention, is the unemployment differential between Catholics and Protestants. On average, a Catholic is around twice as likely as a Protestant to be unemployed, and this differential has remained fairly stable from when such statistics have become publicly available.

Legislation prohibiting employment discrimination (the Fair Employment (Northern Ireland) Act) was passed by Parliament in 1976 to address the extensive religious discrimination in the Northern Ireland labour market.[50] This mirrored closely the approach to employment discrimination which had been followed in the USA, including the establishment of an administrative agency to enforce the legislation, the Fair Employment Agency (FEA). Included in the legislative history of the Act was an indication that affirmative action was regarded as necessary if the inequality of employment opportunity between Catholics and Protestants was to be tackled. The legislation itself was unclear and ambiguous on the extent to which affirmative action was permitted, however. By the early 1980s, there emerged a significant body of opinion which viewed the legislation as insufficiently strongly enforced,[51] and increasing pressure was brought on the FEA to take a tougher enforcement stance. What pressure there was, however, came primarily from relatively fringe pressure groups and some (few) trade

---

[48] See C. McCrudden, 'Mainstreaming Equality in the Governance of Northern Ireland', *Fordham International Law Journal* (forthcoming).

[49] See, Standing Advisory Commission on Human Rights, *Employment Equality: Building for the Future* Cm 3684 (1997).

[50] On the 1976 Act, see Standing Advisory Commission on Human Rights, *Religious and Political Discrimination and Equality of Opportunity in Northern Ireland: Report on Fair Employment* Cm 237 (1987).

[51] See D. Smith and G. Chambers, *Inequality in Northern Ireland* (OUP, 1991).

unionists within Northern Ireland, rather than the established political parties in Northern Ireland, which largely avoided the issue, with the exception of the more extreme Unionist parties which strongly opposed both the legislation and its enforcement, alleging anti-Protestant bias at every turn.

Indeed, one of the major problems the Fair Employment Agency had was its isolation because of the lack of political pressure on the issue of fair employment from the mainstream political parties in Northern Ireland. Broadly speaking, the position of the main constitutional nationalist party, the Social Democratic and Labour Party (SDLP), was that the highest political priority was access to political power so that those they represented (mostly Catholics) would have their fingers on the levers of power and they were sceptical that access to justiciable rights, such as employment equality rights, would be seen as an alternative to this if it became a major focus of activity by them. In short, they considered that the problems of economic equality could only be dealt with when the minority participated in government. Sinn Féin, the political wing of the illegal Irish Republic Army (IRA), took the view at that time that Northern Ireland was inherently unable to be reformed. Any legislative attempt to bring about reform was intended to be merely cosmetic and was doomed to failure.

C. *The origins of the MacBride Principles*

The continuing disparities in the labour market led to several significant developments in the 1980s. The one which is the primary focus of this paper was the initiation of a campaign by Irish-American activists, and some human rights groups in the USA, to put pressure on the British Government to act more decisively in the area of equality of employment opportunity between Catholics and Protestants. A forerunner of the MacBride campaign lay in the activities of church-related groups and the Irish National Caucus (INC), 'a lobbying group in Washington, DC with a strongly nationalist perspective on the Northern Ireland question'.[52] The latter had been raising the issue of employment discrimination since 1981. This activism led to the introduction in 1983 of unsuccessful legislation in the US Congress, which would have required American companies with operations in Northern Ireland to follow a set of fair employment Principles, modelled after similar legislation then before Congress relating to South Africa.

The INC was also involved in unsuccessful protests over the award of US Government contracts to a Belfast aircraft firm, Short Bros. in 1983. Although unsuccessful in stopping the award of the contract, the campaign had a galvanizing effect on Shorts itself. The FEA had produced a critical report on the company's hiring practices, but it had had great difficulty in getting any response from (or even a meeting with) the company. On the day when the INC issued their first statement about the defence contracts, however, the company apparently called the FEA's chairman to arrange a meeting with the Managing Director that

---

[52] Helen E. Booth, *US Companies and Fair Employment Practices in Northern Ireland* (IRRC, 1988) at 39.

morning.[53] The lesson was not lost on fair employment activists: economic pressure seemed to work.

The immediate genesis of the MacBride Principles, however, has been said to have been the decision of the New York City Comptroller at that time, Harrison Goldin, to ask his staff to 'generate a Sullivan-type proposal'.[54] The New York City Comptroller's Office already had a high profile in socially responsible investment, including South Africa, but not previously on Northern Ireland. The staff member involved (Patrick Doherty, who has worked on the issue continuously since then under successive Comptrollers) drafted the final form of the Principles and approached the INC for their support. The MacBride Principles, as they became known, were launched in 1984. They requested American companies with subsidiaries in Northern Ireland to commit themselves to a series of non-discrimination and relatively weak affirmative action Principles in their operations in Northern Ireland. The model chosen was that previously adopted in the Sullivan Principles relating to South Africa. The Principles were named after, and sponsored by, Séan MacBride, a controversial Irish statesman who had led a chequered career, being variously a former leader of the IRA during the 1930s, a former Minister of Foreign Affairs in the Irish Republic, founder of Amnesty International, and recipient of the Lenin Peace Prize, the Nobel Peace Prize, and the American Medal of Honor.[55] His nationalist and human right credentials gave him unrivalled credibility among the constituency which the leaders of the campaign sought to mobilize—Irish-American groups and US human rights groups. Several Northern Ireland co-signatories joined in espousing the Principles: Inez McCormack (a prominent trade unionist—who is from a Protesant background married to a Catholic—continuously involved in employment equality issues), Fr Brian Brady (a Catholic priest who has since died), and John Robb (a respected surgeon from a Protestant background).

D. *The content of the Principles, and the controversy*

The clear and obvious model was that of the Sullivan Principles. Although in retrospect it may seem ironic that by then the Sullivan Principles were beginning to run out of steam and credibility, that was, perhaps, part of their attraction as a model—the model was relatively unthreatening, even conservative in appearance to human rights activists, whilst at the same time the linkage made between South Africa and Northern Ireland was of immense symbolic importance. The general appearance of reasonableness was furthered by the content of the Principles themselves, which drew heavily from the American employment discrimination law tradition, if a rather weak interpretation of it. This weakness was necessitated by the state of Northern Ireland and US law at that time. For

---

[53] Letter from R.G. Cooper, chairman of the Fair Employment Commission, to the author, 8 May 1998.
[54] Booth, above n 52 at 40. The competition between the INC and the Comptroller's Office over responsibility for the genesis of the Principles makes it difficult to reach a conclusion.
[55] Séan MacBride died in 1988.

institutional investor activism, using shareholder resolutions, to be effective the Principles has to require only 'lawful action'. Apart from this, the MacBride Principles also avoided the substantial commitments made by signatories of the Sullivan Principles to engage politically, and to fund social projects.

The purpose of the Principles was partly to ensure that an interpretation of equality of opportunity which incorporated the idea of affirmative action should be adopted by American companies with subsidiaries in Northern Ireland. The text is primarily addressed directly to private parties, that is, companies operating in Northern Ireland, who are invited to indicate their acceptance of them by 'signing' them. They call on employers both to abstain from specific conduct (religious discrimination) and to adopt affirmative action. The text is relatively unspecific in articulating what action is expected, prescribing goals and ends, rather than, except in a few cases, precise action to be taken in achieving these goals. It was clear that those drafting the Principles did not want to become embroiled in the raging American controversies surrounding affirmative action, and the approach taken in the drafting of the Principles was to adopt elements of affirmative action which were relatively uncontroversial in American eyes. The MacBride Principles were, like the Sullivan Principles, drafted as admonitions rather than as requirements. The Principles were opportunities for corporations to demonstrate their social responsibility. The non-binding form was adopted because they were drafted by a private group and therefore could have no direct legal force, either in Northern Ireland or in the USA.

The target was the American companies with subsidiaries in Northern Ireland. This is not to say that the employment practices in American subsidiaries were worse than that of local companies with no American parent; indeed, they are likely, if anything, to have been rather better. The reason for targeting American companies was because they were there in substantial numbers. (Currently, there are 61 publicly traded US companies with subsidiaries operating in Northern Ireland with more than 10 employees, but there are about another 40 firms that are either privately owned or publicly traded but with fewer than 10 employees, about 100 firms in all. These companies account for 6 per cent of the Northern Ireland workforce monitored by the Fair Employment Commission (FEC).[56]) They were, therefore, a useful peg on which to hang a campaign on the issue of employment equality, for two reasons. First, the need for inward investment means that Northern Ireland needs to project an image of attractiveness to American investors. Any threat to the continuation of existing American investment in Northern Ireland was deeply troubling to a government struggling with a high unemployment rate and the collapse of many of the core local industries such as textile manufacture and ship-building. Second, there was a justifiable view that if antidiscrimination policies became the norm in American companies in Northern Ireland, this was likely to spread to other firms.

---

[56] IRRC, *Fair Employment in Northern Ireland, Social Issues Service*, 1998 Background Report A (IRRC 1998) at 1.

Relatively quickly, however, the Principles ran into severe controversy in Northern Ireland for a whole host of reasons:[57] because of the explicit linking of South Africa and Northern Ireland, because of concern that effective American pressure might indeed develop on the employment discrimination issue, because of genuine concerns as to whether what was required of companies operating in Northern Ireland would be illegal under the law of Northern Ireland due to the affirmative action requirements (weak though they appeared), because of the composition of the group involved in drafting and promulgating the Principles (some were associated with Irish Republicanism, and the use of the MacBride name was deeply troubling to some given his previous IRA connections and to others because he was perceived as representative of the worst aspects of southern Irish Catholic social conservatism), and because of concerns that such activity might deter inward investment by new companies, or lead to divestment by companies already operating in Northern Ireland (here, again, the South African parallels were particularly troubling).

The political allegiance of some of its most vociferous supporters in the USA, coupled with the concern that inward investment could be deterred, gave rise also to some suspicion that the purpose of the campaign around the Principles in the USA was another attempt by Irish Republicans to carry out an 'economic war' against Northern Ireland. Not long before the campaign started, the IRA had begun a violent campaign against economic targets in Northern Ireland, and appeared specifically to target corporations with associations outside Northern Ireland. For example, during the 1970s executives from several such corporations were murdered or kidnapped. In these circumstances, some (including major SDLP figures who were campaigning for outside investment and who feared the effect on investment of the MacBride campaign) were concerned that some of those supporting the campaign saw it as another phase of these attacks.

Controversy over their legality under Northern Irish law led to an 'amplification' of the Principles being issued in 1986, again an obvious borrowing of the idea of the 'amplifications' which had been issued supplementing the Sullivan Principles. The MacBride 'amplifications' were intended to address specifically the affirmative action requirements, and to indicate more clearly their relatively weak content, but the controversy refused to go away.

The Principles provide as follows (the 1986 'amplifications' are in italics):
1. Increasing the representation of individuals from underrepresented religious groups in the work force, including managerial, supervisory, administrative, clerical, and technical jobs.

A work force that is severely unbalanced may indicate prima facie *that full equality of opportunity is not being afforded all segments of the community in Northern Ireland. Each signatory to the MacBride Principles must make every reasonable lawful effort*

---

[57] For a representative selection, see Northern Ireland Information Service, *What's Wrong With the MacBride Campaign?* (1990).

to increase the representation of underrepresented religious groups at all levels of its operations in Northern Ireland.

2. Adequate security for the protection of minority employees both at the workplace and while travelling to and from work.

While total security can be guaranteed nowhere today in Northern Ireland, each signatory to the MacBride Principles must make reasonable good faith efforts to protect workers against intimidation and physical abuse at the workplace. Signatories must also make reasonable good faith efforts to ensure that applicants are not deterred from seeking employment because of fear for their personal safety at the workplace or while travelling to and from work.

3. The banning of provocative religious or political emblems from the workplace.

Each signatory to the MacBride Principles must make reasonable good faith efforts to prevent the display of provocative sectarian emblems at their plants in Northern Ireland.

4. All job openings should be publicly advertised and special recruitment efforts should be made to attract applicants from underrepresented religious groups.

Signatories to the MacBride Principles must exert special efforts to attract employment applications from the sectarian community that is substantially underrepresented in the workforce. This should not be construed to imply a diminution of opportunity for other applicants.

5. Layoff, recall and termination procedures should not, in practice, favour particular religious groups.

Each signatory to the MacBride Principles must make reasonable good faith efforts to ensure that layoff, recall, and termination procedures do not penalize a particular religious group disproportionately. Layoff and termination practices that involve seniority solely can result in discrimination against a particular religious group if the bulk of employees with greatest seniority are disproportionately from another religious group.

6. The abolition of job reservations, apprenticeship restrictions, and differential employment criteria, which discriminate on the basis of religion or ethnic origin.

Signatories to the MacBride Principles must make reasonable good faith efforts to abolish all differential employment criteria whose effect is discrimination on the basis of religion. For example, job reservations and apprenticeship regulations that favour relatives of current or former employees can, in practice, promote religious discrimination if the company's workforce has historically been disproportionately drawn from another religious group.

7. The development of training programmes that will prepare substantial numbers of current minority employees for skilled jobs, including the expansion

of existing programmes and the creation of new programmes to train, upgrade and improve the skills of minority employees.

This does not imply that such programmes should not be open to all members of the workforce equally.

8. The establishment of procedures to assess, identify, and actively recruit minority employees with potential for further advancement.

This section does not imply that such procedures should not apply to all employees equally.

9. The appointment of a senior management staff member to oversee the company's affirmative action efforts and the setting up of timetables to carry out affirmative action Principles.

In addition to the above, each signatory to the MacBride Principles is required to report annually to an independent monitoring agency on its progress in the implementation of these Principles.

E. *Supervisory mechanisms*

The main force of the Principles lay not in their content, but in the political weight which was given to them by the institutional framework which was developed around them in the USA. No equivalent supervisory mechanism grew up in any other country; it was (and is) an almost entirely American phenomenon. Initially, the strategy developed by the New York City Comptroller's Office encouraged shareholder resolution approach, together with legislation short of divestment, following the Sullivan-type approach. Companies would be persuaded to sign up through shareholder resolutions as the Comptroller has been involved in doing previously in relation to South Africa. A strategy of pressing for federal, state, and local legislation in favour of the Principles was the preference of the INC; that is, what they had previously been most involved in. By 1986, a strategy based on both elements was in place. The news media, in particular newspapers and television in Ireland, were also actively drawn into the campaign, by directing attention to the issues, and plotting the growing acceptance of the Principles in the USA during the 1980s. There were several different elements to the activities involved which are worth distinguishing, since they indicate clearly the extent to which the Principles played a mobilizing role, and give some indication too of the effect of the Principles, an issue to which we return in more detail subsequently.

(i) *Action by institutional investors*
Several large pension funds controlled by state and local government embraced the Principles. Pressure was put on the American parent company through shareholder resolutions. Shareholder resolutions were submitted to companies'

annual meetings from 1985, with growing numbers and support emerging each year during the 1980s. The first shareholder resolution on Northern Ireland was organized by the Interfaith Center on Corporate Responsibility to General Motors in 1985. The New York City Comptroller's Office was also at the forefront of this approach. In particular, it supported successful litigation to challenge the refusal of American Brands to include the shareholder resolution (an issue we shall return to subsequently). Although none of the MacBride proposals were successfully adopted, they gave rise to a significant amount of publicity for the Principles, and some bargaining power for institutional investors to negotiate 'compliance' with the Principles outside the context of the share-holders' meetings. This occurred in the case of Ford Motor which agreed in 1987 to review and report on its operations in Northern Ireland, leading to the withdrawal of a shareholder resolution.[58] Ford's subsequently published report led to the adoption of several new fair employment policies in its Belfast operation, and agreement with the Comptroller in 1998. In 1989, the Comptroller's office persuaded Digital Equipment Corp. 'to become the first company to agree to take "lawful steps in good faith" to implement the Principles, and to allow independent monitoring of its Northern Ireland operations—in exchange for the withdrawal of the city's resolution'.[59] Several agreements along the lines of that reached with Digital Equipment were also concluded with other companies with subsidiaries in Northern Ireland.

Shareholder action activity continued every year. In 1997, for example, the 13th year in which resolutions asking firms to implement the MacBride Principles were submitted, the New York pension funds submitted seven resolutions asking companies to make lawful efforts to implement the Principles. As with Ford and Digital, the aim was to attempt to reach an agreement with the targetted company on implementing the Principles. As the Investor Responsibility Research Center (IRRC) observed, however, 'The agreements stop short of formal adoption of the Principles; generally, companies say they are implementing the Principles to the extent they lawfully can do so. Companies with agreements usually have indicated they would cooperate with independent monitoring of their Northern Ireland operations.'[60]

The collection of information about companies in Northern Ireland is an important part of the process. Initially, the information collected was sporadic, and was largely collected and disseminated by the New York City Comptroller's Office or the INC. There was an attempt to have the Arthur D. Little company involved, again mirroring the Sullivan Principles, but the company declined. By 1988, the IRRC, based in Washington, DC was closely monitoring the evolving campaign, and producing detailed analyses of the relevant companies. The IRRC had a long-standing relationship with the investor community due to its

[58] Above n 52 at 48.
[59] Heidi Welsh, *A Guide to US Laws and Legislation in Support of the MacBride Principles 1992* (IRRC, 1992) at 51.
[60] IRRC, *Fair Employment in Northern Ireland, Social Issues Service*, 1997 Background Report A (IRRC, 1997) at 3.

involvement in South African institutional investment issues. At the beginning of the 1990s, an agreement was reached between some of the institutional investors involved in the campaign and the IRRC to monitor compliance by employers with the Principles. This has involved the designation of a staff member to conduct inquiries in Northern Ireland on a periodic basis, and the publication of information on the basis of these inquiries for the benefit of the institutional investors and investment managers who handle the institutions' investment portfolios.

Two legal issues arose during the 'shareholder resolution' part of the MacBride campaign which should be noted. The first was of relatively limited general concern, though it was crucial to the continued vitality of shareholder action at the time. It involved the question of the legality of what the Principles required under the law of Northern Ireland. In other words, could a company adhere to the MacBride Principles, and still remain within Northern Ireland law? The issue arose in a case in 1986, because the Principles were alleged to require affirmative action which would result in reverse discrimination against the majority group and this, it was alleged, would be contrary to the law of Northern Ireland. The 1986 case involved the New York City Employees' Retirement System (NYCERS), which had put forward a shareholder resolution on the MacBride Principles, and American Brands, to which the resolution was directed. The company had successfully argued before the SEC that it could omit the resolution from consideration on this ground. The SEC decision was challenged in federal court, and resolved in favour of NYCERS. An injunction was issued requiring American Brands to include the resolution in its proxy ballot, on the basis that the Principles did not require unlawful action under the law of Northern Ireland.[61]

A second issue which arose was of more general importance. This involved the extent to which the SEC will not require shareholder resolutions to be tabled which relate to the company's 'ordinary business operations'. The standards, originally articulated in 1976,[62] provided an exception for certain proposals that raised significant social policy issues. However, in 1992 the SEC, in an no-action letter to Cracker Barrel Old Country Store Inc.,[63] included in its definition of 'ordinary business' those employment-related shareholder proposals which raised social-policy issues (including matters relating to discrimination and equality of opportunity within a company's workforce). This resulted in protracted litigation which the SEC eventually won in 1995, but the appeals court decision left open the possibility of further litigation on the issue. In 1996, one of the four SEC commissioners publicly advocated that the policy be revised. On MacBride-related resolutions, however, companies seldom refused either to include such resolutions in proxy statements on these grounds, or to reach a settlement with the sponsors. The IRRC has observed that 'Company's have been reluctant to

---

[61] *New York City Employees' Retirement System v American Brands*, 634 F Supp 1382 (SDNY, 1986).
[62] See Exchange Act Release No 12999 (22 November 1976), 41 FR 52994.
[63] SEC, 13 October 1992.

face possible litigation and/or bad publicity on the issue'.[64] Unless the SEC's position was changed, however, it was feared by shareholder activists that the shareholder resolution approach to the 'enforcement' of the Principles would be of limited utility in the longer term.[65] After protracted discussion and consultations, the SEC reversed its Cracker Barrel no-action letter position in 1998. This means that certain employment-related proposals raising significant social policy issues may now be included in companies' proxy materials. The SEC will return to its case-by-case approach which permits such resolutions provided they do not seek to micro-manage the company.[66]

(ii) *State legislation on investments*

The use of hearings at the US state legislative level was a popular means of generating support for the Principles. In part, this was the result of assiduous lobbying by several organizations, including the Irish National Caucus. In addition, the New York City Comptroller's Office, Irish-American-related trade union groups, and several religious groups have been active in promoting the Principles at the state and local levels. Successful efforts were made to underpin the ethical investment approach described above by persuading state legislatures and localities to adopt policies or legislation requiring American companies in which the state invests to ensure fair employment practices in their Northern Ireland subsidiaries. New York City pension funds were the first to do so in 1985. Massachusetts took the lead among states in 1985, followed by New York state in 1986. Connecticut, New Jersey, and Rhode Island followed in 1987. In 1988 Illinois, Michigan, Maine, Minnesota, and Florida adopted legislation. Then New Hampshire and Vermont adopted similar legislation in 1989.[67] During the 1980s, the campaign appeared to be 'moving faster than did the embracing of the anti-apartheid Sullivan Principles in the 1970s'.[68] By 1993, 18 states and the District of Columbia had adopted legislation of some kind, as had 31 cities.[69]

There was, however, something of a divergence of approach taken by states. In contrast with the approach which had quickly developed on South Africa, only one state (Connecticut) required disinvestment from firms not adopting the MacBride Principles. Massachusetts, prohibited investment in firms making weapons for use or deployment in Northern Ireland, as well as requiring compliance with the MacBride Principles. Most states, however, instead urged state fund managers to consider the firm's compliance before investing, required studies to be undertaken of compliance, and required shareholder efforts. The

---

[64] Above n 60.

[65] See Daniel E. Lazaroff, 'Promoting Corporate Democracy and Social Responsibility: The Need to Reform the Federal Proxy Rules on Shareholder Proposals', 50 *Rutgers L Rev* 33 (1997).

[66] SEC, Amendments to Rules on Shareholder Proposals, 21 May 1998 (Release No 34–40018), 63 FR 29106, 17 CFR Part 240.

[67] See above n 59. The competition between the Irish National Caucus and the Comptroller's Office over responsibility for the genesis of the Principles makes it difficult to reach a concluded view. See Sean McManus, *The MacBride Principles: Genesis and istory and the Story to Date* (Irish National Caucus, Washington, DC, n.d.).

[68] 'More Cities Sign on to MacBride Principles', *Bulletin of Municipal Foreign Policy*, (summer 1989) at 33.

[69] Above n 59 (1992) *passim*.

190   *Oxford Journal of Legal Studies*   VOL. 19

public reporting requirements of some of these laws has been important. This gave some teeth to the subsequent monitoring effort and has, in some measure, helped to keep the issue alive. It has institutionalized the campaign by making annual audits of corporate compliance a bureaucratic responsibility, and bureaucracies have budgets. The practice, in general, therefore, was constructive engagement with the issue, rather than disinvestment. This reflected closely the view of those in Northern Ireland who advised on strategy. It also reflected the views of the New York City Comptroller who wanted to avoid a repetition of the controversy surrounding divestment from South Africa if a non-disinvestment approach was as effective. There was no substantial move towards disinvestment, unlike South Africa.

(iii) *Selective purchasing by state and local governments*

From around 1989, selective purchasing, 'emerged as the major new plank of the MacBride campaign'.[70] By 1993, Cleveland, Chicago, and New York City, among others, had passed legislation linking contract eligibility to companies' actions on the MacBride Principles. In 1992 New York became the first state to do so. The New York City legislation was fairly typical. Under that law, prospective City contractors with operations in Northern Ireland could lose contract bids if their Northern Ireland subsidiaries are not implementing the MacBride Principles, an approach which appears to have concentrated the minds of some companies hitherto unwilling to engage with the MacBride advocates.[71] 'Since the law's enactment', reported the New York City Comptroller's Office, 'ten more corporations have reached agreements with New York City to implement MacBride and to cooperate with independent monitoring of their compliance'.[72] By 1993, a total of 14 localities had similar laws or resolutions.[73]

The selective purchasing approach by state and local governments has given rise to a host of domestic legal issues. It was argued by some that the imposition of equivalent requirements regarding the Sullivan Principles was unconstitutional under the US Constitution on the ground that it involved an impermissible entry by a state into an area of federal responsibility.[74] Although similar laws were in operation from the late 1970s and throughout the 1980s, beginning with protests against apartheid in South Africa, no major challenges were mounted on constitutional grounds against the linkage of purchasing with support for the MacBride Principles. However, more recently, the National Foreign Trade Counsel (NFTC), which represents about 580 US companies challenged the

---

[70] Ibid at 1.

[71] Administrative Code of the City of New York, s 6–115.

[72] City of New York, Office of the Comptroller, Office of Policy Management, *The MacBride Principles and Fair Employment Practices in Northern Ireland: A Status Report* (June 1993) at 2–3. By 1998, this number had risen to 45, according to Patrick Doherty in a telephone interview, June 1998.

[73] Above n 59 (1992) at 3.

[74] For example, P.J. Spiro, 'Note: State and Local Anti-South African Action as an Intrusion Upon the Federal Power in Foreign Affairs', 72 *Va LR* 813 (1986). However, in 1986 an opinion from the Office of Legal Counsel of the US Department of Justice concluded that the selective purchasing laws relating to South Africa were probably constitutional. 10 US Op Office of Legal Counsel 49 (9 April 1986).

constitutionality under the US Constitution of Massachusetts' selective purchasing legislation relating to Myanmar (formerly Burma). In November 1998, the US District Court for the District of Massachusetts held the legislation to be unconstitutional because it impermissibly infringed the federal government's power to regulate foreign affairs.[75] The state has, at the time of writing, appealed the decision.

Another issue is whether such requirements are contrary to the WTO Government Procurement Agreement, concluded as a side-agreement under the Uruguay Round. The latter issue has, again, been identified as an issue in the context of the Massachusetts Myanmar law. In January 1997, the European Commission and Japan formally complained to the USA regarding this legislation, and threatened to invoke the WTO dispute settlement procedure, if the issue was not resolved satisfactorily. The Commission's concern was heightened by the likelihood of similar legislation being enacted by Massachusetts and other states regarding other countries with a dubious human rights record. The issue was not settled diplomatically, despite consultations organized under the auspices of the WTO between the USA, the European Community, and Japan. In October 1998, a disputes panel was established to consider the complaint.[76] In February 1999 the panel suspended consideration of the complaint at the request of the EC and Japan because the law was technically not in effect pending the outcome of the constitutional case.[77]

(iv) *Linkage to federal aid programmes*
The MacBride Principles have come to be regarded as a relatively non-controversial matter for presidential candidates to support and many have done so, including President Clinton. Such support was initially forthcoming from Democratic presidential candidates, but support for the Principles was included in the Republican Party platform for the 1996 presidential campaign, and the Republican candidate Bob Dole specifically endorsed them. In addition, every year since the early 1980s, legislation has been introduced into the federal Congress to give the MacBride Principles some federal authority.

Different approaches have been taken. One approach was to prohibit the importation into the USA of an article from Northern Ireland unless documentation was presented at the time of entry indicating that the enterprise which manufactured or assembled such article complied at the time of manufacture with the MacBride Principles. Any US person with operations in Northern Ireland would be required to ensure the implementation of the Principles. Equivalent Bills were before the House and Senate for action in 1997–98.[78]

---

[75] *NFTC v Baker et al.*, 26 F. Supp. 2d 287 (D. Mass, 1998).

[76] For a consideration of the issues involved, see Christopher McCrudden, 'International Economic Law and the Pursuit of Human Rights: A Framework for Discussion of "Selective Purchasing" Laws Under the WTO Government Procurement Agreement', 2 *J Int'l Econ L* 3 (1999).

[77] Michael S. Lelyveld, 'Clinton refrains from intervening in Myanmar case', *Journal of Commerce*, 11 March 1999 at 3A.

[78] Northern Ireland Fair Employment Practices and Principles of Economic Justice Act 1997, s 184, HR 178; MacBride Principles of Economic Justice Act 1997, HR 2833, HR 150.

Another recent approach was to link adherence to the MacBride Principles (or their equivalent) to the receipt of federal aid to Northern Ireland, channelled through the International Fund for Ireland, which receives a federal grant each year. A rider to this effect was passed in 1995 by the US Senate and the House of Representatives, but the Bill in which it was contained was vetoed by President Clinton (for unrelated reasons) and thus failed to become law. The principle of adherence to the Principles, however, was accepted by the Administration so that when, in 1998, the US Congress again attached a set of Principles equivalent in most respects to the MacBride Principles to its approval of funding for the International Fund for Ireland, this was signed into law by President Clinton.[79]

This legislation specifies that US contributions to the Fund should be used in a manner that effectively increases employment opportunities in communities with rates of unemployment higher than the local or urban average of unemployment in Northern Ireland, and should be provided to individuals or entities in Northern Ireland which employ practices consistent with 'Principles of economic justice.' These Principles are defined in the legislation by incorporating the language of the MacBride Principles, with two notable exceptions. First, there is no provision similar to that in the second MacBride Principle requiring adequate security for the protection of employees 'while travelling to and from work'. Second, there is no specific reference to the concept of 'affirmative action' used in the ninth MacBride Principle, and there is a specific provision stating that '[n]othing . . . shall require quotas or reverse discrimination or mandate their use'. With these exceptions, the language is, in all major respects, identical. It is clear that the omissions were intended to respond to some of the criticisms made of the MacBride Principles in Northern Ireland, as was the omission of any specific reference to 'MacBride' in the legislation.

F. 'Compliance' with the MacBride Principles

The purpose of the MacBride campaign initially was to provide a private method of supervision of companies' compliance with fair employment standards, given the extent to which official methods of enforcement in Northern Ireland had proven unsatisfactory. Although the primary group addressed by the Principles were American employers with subsidiaries in Northern Ireland, the more important indirect addressees were the British Government, and its enforcement institutions. 'Compliance' with the Principles therefore involves considering the actions both of the companies directly addressed, and of the governmental bodies indirectly addressed. It is necessary, then, to distinguish between 'compliance' with the MacBride Principles in two different senses: first, the use of the Principles to put pressure on the British Government; second, the use of the Principles to put pressure on American employers with subsidiaries in Northern Ireland. We can also usefully distinguish between the use of the Principles in the USA, from

[79] Omnibus Consolidated and Emergency Supplemental Appropriations for Fiscal Year 1999 Act, 105 PL 277, s 2811, amending the Anglo-Irish Agreement Support Act 1986.

the use of the Principles in Northern Ireland itself. Finally, we can distinguish between the role that the Principles played prior to 1989–90, when the Northern Ireland Fair Employment Act 1976 was substantially strengthened by the Fair Employment Act 1989, from the role that the Principles have played subsequently. They have been influential in both periods, but particularly the former.

It is important, however, not to exaggerate the importance of the Principles, or indeed of the American political activity surrounding them. The MacBride campaign did not begin the campaign for the eradication of employment inequality in Northern Ireland. That was begun in the early 1960s. Local political activity on the issue by some (though not, as we have seen by the political parties) continued unbroken through the 1970s and 1980s. So too, local pressure on the issue is likely to continue irrespective of the continuing success of the MacBride campaign. Rather, the MacBride campaign was important, in UK terms, because of the extent to which it was taken up by those engaged in local political activity on the issue of employment discrimination. It was the synergy between American and Irish political activity which was of crucial importance.[80] In the absence of external political support, activists in Northern Ireland were relatively weak.

(i) *MacBride Principles and the pressure for new legislation*
This was particularly true in the context of the campaign in Northern Ireland for more effective government regulation. The success of the MacBride campaign in the USA was drawn on to put pressure on the British Government to introduce tougher new legislation, particularly in the period between 1984 and 1989, by several different organizations in the UK, including the British Labour Party when it was in Opposition, Northern Ireland trade union leaders, the government-appointed Standing Advisory Commission on Human Rights, the Fair Employment Commission, and the Irish Government. In this context, the Principles were used in part as an illustration of what could happen if the British Government did not handle the issue effectively. As a former British Government Minister responsible for fair employment issues has written: 'There was no doubt that the British Government had to introduce legislation to show the world (or rather Irish-America and Dublin) that employment practices were unbiased.'[81]

The MacBride Principles were strongly opposed by the British Government. Partly as a result of the MacBride campaign, however, the British Government initiated a process of reconsideration of the adequacy of the government's policies dealing with discrimination and equality between the two communities, particularly due to the UK's sensitivity to bad publicity in the USA about its role in Northern Ireland. In particular, it led to increased funding of the Fair Employment Agency, and to the funding of the Government-appointed Standing Advisory Commission on Human Rights to undertake a substantial investigation

---

[80] Vincent McCormack and Joe O'Hara, *Enduring Inequality* (Liberty, 1990) at 35.
[81] Richard Needham, *Battling for Peace* (Blackstaff Press, 1998) at 302.

of the effectiveness of the Northern Ireland Fair Employment Act 1976. The Commission produced an influential report which concluded that substantial reforms were necessary because the 1976 Act had proven less effective than was necessary.[82] This in turn led to new legislation being passed in 1989, the second Fair Employment Act.[83] This gave broader powers to the enforcement agency (renamed the Fair Employment Commission), required limited affirmative action, and compulsory monitoring, among other things.[84] In effect, the content of the MacBride Principles has been incorporated in Northern Irish law, but without any explicit mention of them.[85] Indeed, there has been no mention of the Principles in any legislation, or government regulations, in any country other than the USA.

(ii) *MacBride Principles and the effect on individual companies in Northern Ireland*

A principal aim of the MacBride campaign was to bring pressure to bear on American corporations to 'sign-up' to the Principles, and much of the early activities such as selective investment campaigns, ethical investment campaigns, etc. were designed to put pressure on particular companies. By April 1998, the IRRC reported that a total of 49 companies had reached agreement in some fashion to implement the MacBride Principles; 12 of them have ended their ties to Northern Ireland, leaving 37 companies now in Northern Ireland with agreements, out of the almost 100 eligible companies.[86] Campaigns were initiated against particular employers in Northern Ireland who were alleged to be con-travening the Principles, with criticisms being directed particularly to American audiences. This was the case with regard to the Ford Motor Corporation and Gallaher Ltd (then a subsidiary of American Brands). The attention given by the MacBride campaign to these companies in turn led to greater attention being given to them by the local official enforcement body, the FEA/FEC. Considerable pressure was exerted by the FEA/FEC on these companies, and agreements reached which were at least in part designed to take the pressure off the companies in the USA.

It might appear that the MacBride campaign is an example of a turf-battle between the American supporters of MacBride on the one hand, and the FEA/FEC on the other. However, this way of characterizing the relationship would be too simplistic. There developed, in practice, a curiously symbiotic relationship between the FEA/FEC and the MacBride campaign. On the one hand, the MacBride campaign in part depended on the FEA/FEC for information on

---

[82] Standing Advisory Commission on Human Rights, *Religious and Political Discrimination and Equality of Opportunity in Northern Ireland: Report on Fair Employment* Cm 237 (1987).

[83] On the passage of the legislation, see C. McCrudden, 'The Evolution of the Fair Employment (Northern Ireland) Act 1989 in Parliament', in R. J. Cormack and R. D. Osborne (eds), *Discrimination and Public Policy in Northern Ireland* (OUP, 1991) at 244.

[84] For the details, see C. McCrudden, *Fair Employment   andbook* (3rd edn, Eclipse, 1995).

[85] See Ken Bloomfield, *Stormont in Crisis: A Memoir* (Blackstaff Press, 1994) at 263–4.

[86] Above n 60.

companies, and instances of discrimination, in order to feed its American publicity machine. In addition, the IRRC 'piggy-backed' on the FEC's monitoring process. 'It's less threatening to companies (and less work for them) to say that we just want the same information that they give to the FEC.'[87] On the other hand, the FEA/FEC in part depended on the MacBride campaign for continued external pressure on the companies, thus giving it greater importance and weight than its somewhat weak political position in Northern Ireland itself would accord it. As we have seen, before the MacBride campaign, the FEA was politically isolated. With the development of the campaign, however, the FEA/FEC came to be seen as an organization attempting to carry out a necessary function: employers would be better off dealing with it, rather than face something worse.

iii The role of the MacBride Principles after 1989

Given its dual role, in pressuring the British Government, and in targetting particular companies, the campaign was able to adapt relatively easily to its relative success in contributing to the enactment of stronger legislation in Northern Ireland, and demonstrate that it had a continuing role to play. It was able to point to the strong reservations expressed by, among others, the British Labour Party in Parliament, as to whether the new legislation would be strong enough to accomplish its purposes. It was able to point, too, to continuing controversies surrounding particular companies once the new legislation was in operation. And it was able to argue that it had a continuing role in putting pressure on the British Government in ensuring that it did not renege on its legislative commitments. In the USA, its utility was undiminished both for politicians and pressure groups eager to demonstrate their commitment to a non-violent role for the USA in Northern Ireland. Although there has been continuing activity at the local and state levels,[88] however, and continuing shareholder activity, greater attention was given to the federal level during the 1990s. Presidential candidates, as we have seen, have continued to feel the need to endorse the Principles, and to avoid falling foul of those continuing to advocate the Principles. Also, as we have seen already, with the change in control of the House of Representatives passing from the Democrats to the Republicans, the House International Relations Committee, now chaired by a noted supporter of the Principles, Representative Ben Gillman, has held hearings on the issue,[89] and supported the passage in 1995 and 1998 of legislation requiring adherence

---

[87] Heidi Welsh in a letter to the author, 21 May 1998.

[88] An article in March 1997 mentions that the Principles had been adopted in 16 states and 30 cities. 'Sleepless in Seattle Over Ireland', *The Observer* (9 March 1997) at 26.

[89] Hearings Before the Committee on International Relations, House of Representatives, 104th Congress, 15 March 1995, US Economic Role in the Peace Process in Northern Ireland (US GPO, Washington, 1995); Hearings Before the Committee on International Relations, House of Representatives, 106th Congress, 13 March 1997. No similar hearings took place under the Democratic Congressional leadership since key members, including House Speaker Tom Foley and Senator Edward Kennedy were opposed to the MacBride campaign largely due to the influence of John Hume, leader of the Social Democratic and Labour Party in Northern Ireland.

to the Principles in the allocation of funds from the International Fund for Ireland.[90]

G. *Incentives and disincentives to compliance*

It will be useful to reflect the two purposes of the Principles (targetting individual firms, and targetting the British Government) by discussing the incentives and disincentives to compliance separately for each. In both cases, however, the crucial question is which actor's reactions and beliefs were thought to be important to their self-interest. The incentive structure for individual firms was often somewhat complicated. For American parent companies, the incentive to be seen to comply was based on two main considerations: first, the fear of losing state-government contracts or investment, where that was a possibility, and, second, in the context of investment, the desire to reduce the hassle of dealing with activists, particularly in the USA, when the bad publicity which would result could harm the company's image. There was no large campaign in the USA against compliance, which often boiled down initially to the relatively simple act of 'signing' the Principles. Particularly when monitoring of the workforce became compulsory under Northern Irish law in the 1989 Act, there was relatively little that a company had to do to comply with the MacBride Principles that it would not have done if it had sought to comply with the legislation, and so any difficulty of extra costs being generated to comply with the Principles was much reduced. There has, for example, been a relatively high rate of low-profile cooperation by companies with aspects of the MacBride campaign. There is a relatively high rate of cooperation, for example, with the IRRC's independent monitoring. Approximately 75 per cent of companies regularly respond (at least in some fashion) to the IRRC's annual surveys. This more comfortable relationship has evolved in part because there has been relatively little activity regarding particular companies as a result of disclosing the information, and in part because government authorities in Northern Ireland have demonstrated little opposition to such monitoring activities.[91]

Counterbalanced against these incentives to comply, however, was the reaction of the local population in Northern Ireland, where the Principles were seen as highly politicized and controversial. The MacBride campaign was opposed not only by the British Government, but also by the FEA, which alleged (before 1989) that they required unlawful action to be taken, by the main Catholic party (the SDLP) whose leader argued that they created extra barriers to inward investment from the USA, by the local business community, by sections of the Northern Ireland trade union movement, and (initially) by the Irish Government. It is likely, therefore, that advice from local managers would have been to attempt to avoid adverse reaction to the company in Northern Ireland from both the

---

[90] Foreign Relations Authorization Act, Fiscal Years 1998 and 1999, and European Security Act 1997, HR 1757, s 1737.

[91] Above n 87.

government and its own workforce (where that was primarily Protestant), by refusing explicitly to sign-up to the Principles.

Regarding the British Government, the incentive structure was somewhat different. The Government defined the issue relatively early on in the campaign as one involving its ability to defeat what it saw as an Irish Republican-based campaign against itself in the USA. It devoted considerable resources to attempting to defeat it, and therefore there was a strong incentive to deny that anything it was doing on the legislative front was occasioned in any way by the MacBride campaign. However, the relative success of the campaign in the USA contributed to the issue of employment equality in Northern Ireland remaining (during the 1980s) an issue of some importance in both Anglo-Irish and Anglo-American relations.[92] The incentive to be seen to be doing something in response to the campaign was the reduction of political pressure in this area, and somewhat soured relations with American public opinion, when good relations were important if the 'larger prize' of an overall constitutional settlement to the larger Northern Ireland problem was to be attained with American support. The result was the 1989 legislation which, whilst denying that it had anything to do with MacBride, nevertheless implemented its approach.

H. *Effectiveness assessed*

Was the MacBride campaign effective? In part, the answer depends on what it is that it is being compared with. We have concentrated earlier on the campaign's relationship with domestic law. What of other possible alternatives? If MacBride is compared to treaties and regional instruments, then MacBride was considerably more successful. The only treaty in the area which had been drawn on as a way of addressing employment discrimination in Northern Ireland (the European Convention on Human Rights) had proven itself unable to deal with the issue effectively because the discrimination concerned private sector employment, in the main, which was not covered by the Convention. If we compare the campaign surrounding MacBride to political activism without the Principles, then we can say that political activism with MacBride was more successful, because it gave a focus to the campaign which was easily identified, clear, and (from an American point of view) involved relatively uncontroversial standards. We have seen that, to the extent that the purpose of the MacBride Principles was to put pressure on the British Government, it was largely successful in the late 1980s, when new legislation was introduced. And it remains a potentially potent force for change in Northern Ireland should the British Government's own efforts, or those of its agencies, fail in the future.

Its added value in bringing about change in particular companies is more difficult to estimate, however, given the problem of determining causality, particularly in a context in which the nexus of pressure is mutually reinforcing. But, to the extent that it provided a focus for activity which might otherwise

---

[92] Compare Ken Bloomfield, above n 85 at 263.

have been more diverse and less targetted, it appears that some companies in Northern Ireland were pressed successfully to move further, and faster, than they would otherwise have done in the absence of the Principles and the campaign in the USA surrounding them.[93]

5. *Conclusion*

What, if any relevance, has all this for the proliferation of the codes of practice discussed at the beginning of this paper? An important point which emerges is the distinction between the use of such codes to create political pressure to change national laws and the use of such codes to change conditions in companies directly. If the latter is the aim, then such codes need to become institutionalized if they are to be effective. In particular, the institutionalization of effective monitoring, preferably by an independent body, is crucial.[94] This requires funding for such research, but this is often not available for transient issues which may attract publicity initially but die away relatively soon thereafter. The MacBride Principles have had a degree of staying power in the USA because of Irish-American political power, and because there has been no substantial countervailing force to which US politicians are beholden, early British lobbying efforts notwithstanding. Institutionalization of other codes seems less likely in the absence of these relatively favourable political conditions.

We can note, too, some features of the MacBride and Sullivan Principles, beginning with several areas of similarity. They have both been immensely plastic in their form, diverse in the purposes that they served, and adaptable over time. It is clear, too, that the form in which the Sullivan and MacBride Principles are expressed owes a lot to the traditional form of law, in that they are both rule-based in appearance. So too, the mechanisms for enforcement and pressure have been very similar: the importance of shareholder action, public procurement, and legislative backing in making them more effective should not be lost on those considering similar activism in other fields, or in other countries. These similarities, of course, are no accident: the MacBride Principles were explicitly based on the model of the Sullivan Principles. The similarities go deeper than this, however. In particular, each code's relationship to 'law' is similar, in some respects. Both codes operated in the twilight zone of legality. Both codes acted as a stimulus to the development of law in their areas of concern, operating like water that seeps into rock and, by continually freezing and unfreezing, creates fissures and cracks that contribute to collapse and its subsequent replacement by something different.

But despite their formal resemblance to law, and their relationship with law, they are not law. The differences between the two sets of Principles and law

---

[93] The hardest evidence for this can be found in changes introduced by companies involving policy on the display of offensive flags and emblems by the workforce.

[94] A point recognized in the recent agreement by Nike to permit independent observers into its plants in Asia, see 'Nike Pledges to End Child Labor and Apply US Rules Abroad', *New York Times* (13 May 1998) at D1.

does not arise from the lack of specificity of the way they are expressed, for law on occasion may be of a similarly indeterminate nature. The reason why the Principles are not law lies elsewhere. Under any definition of 'law' that requires governmental or intergovernmental approval or involvement in the creation of norms or their acceptance if created by others, the Principles cannot in themselves be regarded as law in South Africa or Northern Ireland, however broadly we define what 'government' is, because they were the product of private group activity, and were not subsequently 'adopted' as law by national or international entities capable of doing so. They have not, for example (to my knowledge), been seen by judges in any jurisdiction as a codification of existing law, nor as having created law, for example, by having been incorporated into individual contracts of employment. Indeed, this does not even appear to have been argued to be the case.

What, if any, relationship to law-creation do we think the activities of those drawing on the Principles has? Had these activities become so influential that the Principles became accepted almost automatically by the companies involved, then we might, at a pinch, view the Principles as having 'crystallized' into some form of 'common law' of US firms operating in Northern Ireland, or South Africa. But they have almost certainly not become this. There has been considerable resistance to signing them, and a significant number of eligible companies have not done so, despite the activities of investors and others. The controversy surrounding the Principles, particularly the MacBride Principles, has denied them any such comfortable status. The Principles have, however, been drawn on as guidelines by state and local governments in the USA for investment, procurement or other purposes, and in that very limited sense they may be considered to have been incorporated into law by reference in certain jurisdictions. They have never, however, been drawn on for these purposes in any other non-US jurisdiction, national or international. The Principles, then, are not in themselves soft law, though they may be said to have *become* soft law in some US jurisdictions through incorporation in governmental decision-making.

But to seek to emphasize this view of them is to miss the point, surely. They are essentially *political* Principles intended to mobilize, and be an expression of, *political* activity. For them to have the space to operate effectively as political tools, however, the *legal* system needs to give them space to operate in, and a certain tolerance. For those who see such political mobilization as desirable, the immediate danger lies in the possibility that the space for manoeuvre in which the MacBride and Sullivan Principles operated may be removed because the tolerance which the legal system needs to demonstrate for this type of activity to be effective has been withdrawn.

Now, the contrasts. Whereas the Sullivan Principles were explicitly established to encourage corporations to do things that were discouraged by South African law, the MacBride Principles were (ostensibly at least) meant to march in the same direction as existing Northern Ireland law. The MacBride Principles started largely as a follow-up to Northern Ireland law, although with a heavier dose of affirmative action than was then required under the local law; the Sullivan Principles were clearly contrary to the spirit of South African law at that time. Paradoxically, however, the South African Government tolerated the Sullivan Principles as alternatives to disinvestment, whilst the British Government opposed the MacBride Principles because they considered them likely to lead to disinvestment.[95]

More significant, however, is the difference in the public perception of the two sets of Principles. Whereas the Sullivan Principles came to be associated with a somewhat conservative political reaction to South Africa (engagement rather than withdrawal), the MacBride Principles have come to be seen as a somewhat radical tool for change, in part because of the British Government's miscalculation in drawing so much attention to them by so actively opposing them. This difference in perception has both followed, and contributed, to rather different interests lining up in support of the two sets of Principles. Whereas significant numbers of the business class in the USA saw the Sullivan Principles as a way of staying in South Africa whilst satisfying some external criticism of the role of business in South Africa, few business leaders have embraced the MacBride Principles. In part, this would appear to be due to differences in the legitimacy with which the two regimes are viewed. Whereas the British Government's role in Northern Ireland is perceived among a significant group of opinion formers as attempting in good faith to deal with a difficult problem, the South African Government was perceived to be part of the problem. Therefore, it had considerably less credibility in its opposition to Sullivan than the British Government has in its opposition to MacBride.

On the other hand, however, the lack of legitimacy of the MacBride Principles in these quarters has contributed to them being seen as of continuing utility by Irish-American and other human rights groups, and this has contributed to them being seen as of continuing relevance to the Northern Ireland situation. Ultimately, therefore, whereas a significant section of public opinion thought of the Sullivan Principles as acting as a barrier to pressure from outside, creating a defensive wall which protected rather than challenged corporations, this is not the case with regard to the MacBride Principles. The challenging role of the MacBride Principles remained even after significant changes in the area. They continue, unlike the Sullivan Principles, to act like putty that fills in the cracks of existing hard law, in this case the cracks in enforcement, making the hard law more effective and longer lasting. In this sense, the MacBride Principles now operate by shadowing hard law, ready to jump in when (or if) the enforcement of the hard law stumbles or falls.

The final contrast is, perhaps, the most important. The Sullivan Principles became largely irrelevant when they ceased to reflect the aims of any of the major political forces for change in South Africa. Once constructive engagement by US corporations had been rejected by those representing the black majority,

---

[95] Above n 80 at 37.

and economic sanctions became their mechanism of choice, the Sullivan Principles were rendered largely irrelevant to the larger picture, though the Principles continued in existence for some time after that. The relative success of the MacBride campaign lies in the extent to which it reflected and continues to reflect the preferences of an influential sector of human rights opinion formers in Northern Ireland. Constructive engagement by the USA is still the aim in general, and the MacBride campaign fits into that strategy.

This contrast, however, requires us to focus on a potentially troubling aspect of codes of conduct such as those of MacBride and Sullivan (and, indeed, corporate codes of conduct more generally): who should make judgments such as these? The two sets of Principles were devised and operated by interest groups in the USA. On the one hand, we may see this as a positive development, contributing to the democratization of norm generation and enforcement, replacing ineffective and compromised traditional mechanisms of law creation and enforcement. We can see, too, this development as a positive expression of growing grass roots involvement in effective rights enforcement. We may view hostility to such developments cynically, perceiving it to be motivated by the threat which it poses to the monopoly power of national and international legal bodies.

On the other hand, we may see the Principles and their enforcement as a rightly controversial development, relying on the aggregation and exercise of power by essentially unaccountable bodies, and permitting the application of national norms originating in one country on another in situations where the affected interests (particularly the workers affected) are neither consulted beforehand, nor agreed among themselves on the overall benefits to them of such norms, nor subsequently in control of the process of enforcement.[96] That there is at least a danger of such negative effects may leave us somewhat uncomfortable at the use of such strategies for ensuring compliance with these norms. The political reality is, however, that in the absence of more traditional mechanisms of effective national or international legal action, such developments are, perhaps, inevitable. As Arthurs has argued: 'the enfeeblement of the nation state and the failure to produce an effective substitute for the state at the transnational level may refocus attention on local struggles, on indigenous, implicit, and informal law-making, on movements which have not become juridified but which actually draw their strength and sustenance from grass-roots involvement'.[97]

---

[96] For a recent discussion of some of these issues, see Report of the Director-General, *The ILO, Standard Setting and Globalization*, International Labour Conference, 85th Session, 1997 (ILO, Geneva, 1997) at 29–32.

[97] H. Arthurs, 'Labour Law Without the State', 46 *U Toronto LJ* 1 at 45 (1996), quoted in B. Hepple, 'New Approaches to International Labour Regulation', 26 *Industrial LJ* 353 at 358 (1997).

[4]

BUSINESS AND HUMAN RIGHTS

*David Weissbrodt**

I. INTRODUCTION

Whether it is Nazi industrialists using slave labor from concentration camps or central African rebels exploiting local farmers and natural resources to supply international businesses, human rights atrocities are all too often committed in the name of corporate profitability. The international community's tendency to look the other way has been similarly, and regrettably, frequent. Although some treaties could be interpreted as applying to non-state entities, most of the development of international law has focused on state actors. As human rights abuses have persisted worldwide, so too have various attempts to establish international standards for corporate actions. Those efforts have been less than productive, however, because they have largely been without strong implementation methods or support from the United Nations.

But now, the United Nations has begun to develop a significant international standard: Norms on the Responsibilities of Transnational Corporations and Other Business Enterprises with Regard to Human Rights (the Norms). While maintaining a state's duty to enforce human rights, the Norms go a long way toward ensuring that international companies respect workers' equality of opportunity and treatment; avoid corruption; follow national and local laws; and protect the environments and residents where they operate. The U.N. Sub-Commission on the Promotion and Protection of Human Rights has approved the Norms and has submitted them to the U.N. Commission on Human Rights. While issues with the proposed Norms remain to be resolved, the Norms represent a crucial step toward ensuring international corporate social responsibility.

This Article begins with a discussion of why one should be concerned with, or at least interested in, the human rights conduct of corporations.

* Regents Professor and Fredrikson & Byron Professor of Law, University of Minnesota. The author served as a member of the U.N. Sub-Commission on the Promotion and Protection of Human Rights 1996–2003. He was elected the Chairperson of the Sub-Commission for 2001–2002. He also served as a member of the Sub-Commission's Working Group on the Working Methods and Activities of Transnational Corporations. This Article, however, reflects his views and not necessarily the positions of those institutions. The author wishes to thank Muria Kruger, Bridget Marks, and Mary Rumsey for their assistance in preparing this Article.

Hence, Part II presents some historical and current situations that require attention and standard setting. Part III focuses on past efforts of international law, particularly international human rights law, to treat non-state actors as corporations. Part IV discusses five major attributes of the U.N. Human Rights Norms that build upon the previous efforts to deal with the human rights conduct of corporations. Part V traces the process by which the Norms were prepared and are now being considered by the U.N. Commission on Human Rights. Part VI identifies three principal issues raised by the opponents to the Norms. And the Article concludes in Part VII with an account of how the Norms are already being used by businesses, mutual funds, and others.

II. HISTORICAL AND CURRENT HUMAN RIGHTS CONCERNS AS TO THE ACTIVITIES OF BUSINESS

This year marks the 60th anniversary of the initiation of the Nuremberg trials of the Major War Criminals after World War II.[1] During the trials, German industrialist Alfried Krupp and nine other officials of the huge Krupp industrial firm were convicted of charges relating to, *inter alia*, the use of slave labor. During that era, the Krupp firm became an inextricable part of the German policy for occupied countries such as France, Norway, and Poland. The Krupp corporate officers received terms of imprisonment with Krupp himself being sentenced to twelve years imprisonment. In addition, all his properties—public and private—were forfeited.[2] In a subsequent case, twenty-four directors and officers of the German conglomerate I.G. Farben Industry were convicted for using slave labor, for designing and producing poison gas used in the concentration camps of the Third Reich, and for other crimes.[3] Thirteen I.G. Farben corporate defendants

---

1. Agreement for the Prosecution and Punishment of the Major War Criminals of the European Axis, 82 U.N.T.S. 279, *entered into force* Aug. 8, 1945, *available at* http://www1.umn.edu/humanrts/instree/imt1945.htm.

2. United States v. Krupp, 9 Trials of War Criminals Before the Nuremberg Military Tribunals Under Control Council Law No. 10 (1950). As the trial court said in *Doe v. Unocal Corporation*, 110 F. Supp. 2d 1294, 1310 (C.D. Cal. 2000), *aff'd*, 395 F.3d 932 (9th Cir. 2002) (citations omitted): "The Tribunal found the defendants guilty of employing slave labor because their will was not overpowered by the Third Reich 'but instead coincide[d] with the will of those from whom the alleged compulsion emanate[d].' Moreover, the 'Krupp firm had manifested not only its willingness but its ardent desire to employ forced labor.'"

3. United States v. Krauch, 8 Trials of War Criminals Before the Nuremberg Military Tribunals Under Control Council Law No. 10 (1952) ("While the Farben organisation, as a corporation, is not charged under the indictment with committing a crime and is not the subject of prosecution in this case, it is the theory of the prosecution that the defendants individually and collectively used the Farben organisation as an instrument by and through which they committed the crime enumerated in the

were found guilty and were sentenced to terms of imprisonment.

A more recent example of corporate greed and crimes against humanity involves the brutal war in which more than three million lives have been lost over the past seven years in the Democratic Republic of Congo (DRC). In this war, companies engaged in forced labor practices reminiscent of World War II.[4] The U.N. Panel of Experts on the Illegal Exploitation of National Resources and Other Forms of Wealth of the Democratic Republic of the Congo identified more than eighty companies from developed nations[5] that exploited Congolese natural resources during the war. Some of those companies have used forced labor; others have facilitated the transfer of weapons to the warring parties that have been implicated in committing war crimes. The companies were evidently motivated by the mineral wealth of the DRC. For example, mineral columbo tantaline (coltan) is found in the eastern DRC and tantalum can be extracted from that ore for use in the production of electronic components commonly used in cell phones. Because of increases in the price of coltan in world markets, some rebel groups and unscrupulous businesses forced farmers and their families to leave their agricultural lands and compelled them to work in coltan mines.[6]

Companies may violate human rights not only in periods of armed conflict[7] but also by employing child laborers; discriminating against

---

indictment. All the members of the Vorstand or governing body of Farben who were such at the time of the collapse of Germany were indicted and brought to trial.").

4. Final Report of the Panel of Experts on the Illegal Exploitation of National Resources and Other Forms of Wealth of the Democratic Republic of the Congo, U.N. Doc. S/2002/1146 (2002), *available at* http://www.natural-resources.org/minerals/law/docs/pdf/N0262179.pdf. *See also* All Party Parliamentary Group on the Great Lakes Region, The OECD Guidelines for Multinational Enterprises and the DRC (February 2005).

5. Those identified were thirty developed nations of North America, Western Europe, and Asia that are members of the Organization for Economic Cooperation and Development (OECD).

6. The U.N. Panel brought to the attention of banks several companies and individuals that had engaged in illegal activities, causing the banks to close the relevant accounts. The U.N. Panel also worked closely with the National Contact Points of the Organization for Economic Cooperation and Development to seek information and to resolve identified problems.

7. "In the field of human rights, there are growing expectations that corporations should do everything in their power to promote universal human rights standards, even in conflict situations where governance structures have broken down." Andrew Clapham & Scott Jerbi, *Categories of Corporate Complicity in Human Rights Abuses*, 24 HASTINGS INT'L & COMP. L. REV. 339, 339 (2001); *see also* Ilias Bantekas, *Corporate Social Responsibility in International Law*, 22 B.U. INT'L L.J. 309 (2004); Surya Deva, *Human Rights Violations by Multinational Corporations and International Law: Where from Here?*, 19 CONN. J. INT'L L. 1 (2003); Surya Deva, *UN's Human Rights Norms for Transnational Corporations and Other Business Enterprises: An Imperfect Step in the Right Direction?*, 10 ILSA J. INT'L & COMP. L. 493 (2004); David Kinley & Junko Tadaki, *From Talk to Walk: The Emergence of Human Rights Responsibilities for Corporations at International Law*, 44 VA. J. INT'L L. 931 (2004); Harold Hongju Koh, *Separating Myth from Reality about Corporate Responsibility Litigation*, 7 J. INT'L

58   *UNIVERSITY OF CINCINNATI LAW REVIEW*   [Vol. 74

certain groups of employees (such as union members and women); attempting to repress independent trade unions and discourage the right to bargain collectively; failing to provide safe and healthy working conditions; and limiting the broad dissemination of appropriate technology and intellectual property. Companies also dump toxic wastes, and their production processes may have consequences for the lives and livelihoods of those in neighboring communities. One of the most visible examples of corporate human rights abuses occurred in Bhopal, India, in 1984, when forty-one tons of methyl isocyanate were released from a plant owned by Union Carbide Corporation.[8] At least 15,000 people were killed, and more than 170,000 people were disabled. Local water and soil still remain severely contaminated, and birth defects continue to be reported. Five years after the disaster, Union Carbide was held legally accountable by the Indian Supreme Court, which ordered the company to pay civil claims of $470 million. Twenty years after the disaster, however, many victims still have not received any compensation. Union Carbide has refused to release information about the chemicals that caused the harm, including the results of tests completed on the health effects of the spillage. In 2001, Union Carbide became a subsidiary of the Dow Chemical Company, which claims that it has no responsibility for the prior actions of its new subsidiary.

While corporations have the capacity to cause catastrophic damage, they also bring new jobs, capital, and technology capable of improving working conditions and raising local living conditions. They certainly have the capacity to assert a positive influence in fostering development and achieving prosperity. The issue becomes maximizing the good that companies do while eliminating the abuses they commit.

Whether one thinks of businesses as critical for the prosperity and economic success of the community or focuses upon the problems they may cause, companies are certainly powerful forces in local communities, around the nation, and throughout the world. The three hundred largest corporations account for more than one-quarter of the

---

ECON. L. 263 (2004); Jordan J. Paust, *Human Rights Responsibilities of Private Corporations*, 35 VAND. J. TRANSNAT'L L. 801 (2002); Ernst-Ulrich Petersmann, *Time for a United Nations 'Global Compact' for Integrating Human Rights into the Law of Worldwide Organizations: Lessons from European Integration*, 13 EUR. J. INT'L L. 621 (2002); Kerrie M. Taylor, *Thicker than Blood: Holding Exxon Mobil Liable for Human Rights Violations Committed Abroad*, 31 SYRACUSE J. INT'L. L. & COM. 273 (2004).

    8. Amnesty International, Union Carbide Corporation (UCC), DOW Chemicals and the Bhopal Communities in India: Amnesty International AI Index: ASA 20/005/2005 (2005), *available at* http://web.amnesty.org/library/eng-ind/reports (follow "India: Union Carbide Corporation (UCC), DOW Chemicals and the Bhopal Communities in India - The Case" hyperlink) (last visited Sept. 14, 2005).

world's productive assets.[9] For example, General Motors Corporation's sales in a single year are greater than the gross national product of 179 countries, including Malaysia, Norway, Saudi Arabia, and South Africa.[10]   Transnational corporations (TNCs) hold 90% of all technology and product patents worldwide,[11] and are involved in 70% of world trade.[12]   TNCs directly employ ninety million people (some twenty million of whom live in developing countries) and produce 25% of the world's gross product. The top thousand of these TNCs account for 80% of the world's industrial output.[13] TNCs are active in some of the most dynamic sectors of national economies, such as extractive industries, telecommunications, information technology, electronic consumer goods, footwear and apparel, transport, banking and finance, insurance, and securities trading.[14]

III. APPLICATION OF INTERNATIONAL HUMAN RIGHTS LAW TO NON-STATE ACTORS SUCH AS CORPORATIONS

Given their importance in the world, it is really remarkable that corporations have not received more attention in the evolution of international law, particularly international human rights law. International law and human rights law have principally focused on protecting individuals from violations by governments. There has been increasing attention, however, to individual responsibility for war crimes, genocide, and other crimes against humanity based on: the Nuremberg tribunals in the 1940s;[15] the criminal tribunals established in the 1990s for the former Yugoslavia[16] and Rwanda;[17] and the

---

9. MEDARD GABEL & HENRY BRUNER, GLOBAL INC.: AN ATLAS OF THE MULTINATIONAL CORPORATION 5 (2003) (citing *A Survey of Multinationals*, ECONOMIST, Mar. 27, 1993, at 9.).

10. *Id.* at 2.

11. "TNCs reportedly control 90% of the world's technology patents." Howard A. Kwon, *Patent Protection and Technology Transfer in the Developing World: The Thailand Experience*, 28 GEO. WASH. J. INT'L L. & ECON. 567, 570 n.13 (1995) (citing Suwanna Asavaroengchai, *Seeking a Fair Deal in Global Trade*, BANGKOK POST, Oct. 19, 1994, at 31).

12. TOM ATHANASIOU, DIVIDED PLANET: THE ECOLOGY OF RICH AND POOR 194 (1996); DAVID C. KORTEN, WHEN CORPORATIONS RULE THE WORLD 124 (1995).

13. *Id.* at 7 (citing UNITED NATIONS CONFERENCE ON TRADE AND DEVELOPMENT (UNCTAD), WORLD INVESTMENT REPORT 2001 at 9 (2001)).

14. GABEL & BRUNER, *supra* note 9, at 34. For an analysis of TNCs' activities in various economic sectors see *id.* at 36-119 (describing TNCs in motor vehicle, petroleum, chemical and pharmaceutical, construction, forest and paper products, computers, and other sectors).

15. *See* Agreement for the Prosecution and Punishment, *supra* note 1.

16. Statute of the International Tribunal for the Prosecution of Persons Responsible for Serious Violations of International Humanitarian Law Committed in the Territory of the Former Yugoslavia since 1991, S.C. Res. 847, U.N. SCOR, 48th Sess., 3217th mtg., U.N. Doc. S/RES/827 (1993), *reprinted in* 32 I.L.M. 1163 (1993).

International Criminal Court,[18] which has now been accepted by one hundred nations (although not by the United States).[19]

In addition to state responsibility and individual criminal responsibility, international humanitarian law has placed direct obligations on armed opposition groups—particularly in the context of civil wars and other non-international armed conflicts.[20] International criminal law has also been applied to terrorists[21] and traffickers in human beings.[22] Yet, there is one category of very powerful non-state actors that has not received sufficient attention. That category includes transnational corporations and, indeed, all businesses.

Some human rights treaties and other law-making instruments may be interpreted to apply to businesses. Most prominently, one can find a relevant passage in the Universal Declaration of Human Rights,[23] the primary non-treaty instrument that in 1948 first established an

---

17. Statute of the International Criminal Tribunal for the Prosecution of Persons Responsible for Genocide and Other Serious Violations of International Humanitarian Law Committed in the Territory of Rwanda, S.C. Res. 955, U.N. SCOR, 49th Sess., 3453d mtg. at 3, U.N. Doc. S/RES/955 (1994), *reprinted in* 33 I.L.M. 1598, 1600 (1994).

18. Rome Statute of the International Criminal Court, 2187 U.N.T.S. 3, *entered into force* July 1, 2002. The International Criminal Court has jurisdiction only over natural persons (including corporate officers), but not over legal persons, such as corporations. *Id.* art. 25. *See* Andrew Clapham, *The Question of Jurisdiction Under International Criminal Law Over Legal Persons: Lessons from the Rome Conference on an International Criminal Court*, LIABILITY OF MULTINATIONAL CORPORATIONS UNDER INTERNATIONAL LAW 143-45 (Menno T. Kamminga & Saman Zia-Zarifi eds. 2000).

19. Currently the Rome Statute of the ICC has 139 Signatories and 100 Ratifications, Coalition for the ICC, *available at* http://www.iccnow.org/countryinfo/worldsigsandratifications.html (last visited Apr. 3, 2005).

20. *See, e.g.*, Geneva Convention relative to the Protection of Civilian Persons in Time of War, Common Art. 3, Oct. 21, 1950, 75 U.N.T.S. 287, *entered into force* Oct 21, 1950.

21. *See, e.g.*, Convention against the Taking of Hostages, 1316 U.N.T.S. 205, *entered into force* Jun. 3, 1983; Convention for the Suppression of Terrorist Bombings, U.N. Doc. A/RES/52/164 (1997), *entered into force* May 23, 2001, 37 I.L.M. 249; Convention for the Suppression of the Financing of Terrorism, U.N. Doc. A/RES/54/109 (1999), *entered into force* Apr. 10, 2002, 39 I.L.M. 270; Convention for the Suppression of Unlawful Acts against the Safety of Civil Aviation, 974 U.N.T.S. 177, 24 U.S.T. 564, *entered into force* Jan. 26, 1973, 10 I.L.M. 1151; Convention for the Suppression of Unlawful Acts against the Safety of Maritime Navigation, 1678 U.N.T.S. 221, *entered into force* Mar. 10, 1988, 27 I.L.M. 668; Convention for the Suppression of Unlawful Seizure of Aircraft, 860 U.N.T.S. 105, *entered into force* Oct. 14, 1971.

22. Convention Against Transnational Organized Crime, G.A. Res. 55/25, 55 U.N. GAOR, Supp. No. 49, U.N. Doc. A/45/49 (2001), *entered into force* Sep. 29, 2003; Convention for the Suppression of the Traffic in Persons and of the Exploitation of the Prostitution of Others, 96 U.N.T.S. 271, *entered into force* Jul. 25, 1951; Protocol Against the Smuggling of Migrants by Land, Sea and Air, Supplementing the United Nations Convention Against Transnational Crime, G.A. Res. 55/25, 55 U.N. GAOR, Supp. No. 49 at 65, U.N. Doc. A/45/49 (Vol. I) (2001), *entered into force* Jan. 28, 2004; Protocol to Prevent, Suppress and Punish Trafficking in Persons, Especially Women and Children, Supplementing the United Nations Convention Against Transnational Organized Crime, G.A. Res. 55/25, 55 U.N. GAOR, 55th Sess., Supp. No. 49, U.N. Doc. A/45/49 (2001), *entered into force* Sep. 9, 2003.

23. Universal Declaration of Human Rights, G.A. res. 217A (III), U.N. Doc A/810 (1948).

authoritative, worldwide definition of human rights. While the Universal Declaration principally focuses on the obligations of states, it also mentions the responsibilities of individuals and "every organ of society,"[24] including businesses. The Universal Declaration thus provides that

> a common standard of achievement for all peoples and all nations, to the end that every individual and every organ of society, keeping this Declaration constantly in mind, shall strive by teaching and education to promote respect for these rights and freedoms and by progressive measures, national and international, to secure their universal and effective recognition and observance . . . .[25]

Under the International Covenant on Civil and Political Rights,[26] a treaty that has been ratified by 154 nations, including the United States, each state party "undertakes to respect and to ensure to all individuals within its territory and subject to its jurisdiction the rights recognized in the present Covenant . . . ."[27] Accordingly, if a corporation endangers the rights of an individual, the state has a duty to ensure respect of human rights and, thus, to take preventative action. In addition, the Covenant indirectly covers the responsibilities of companies in declaring "[n]othing in the present Covenant may be interpreted as implying for any State, group or person any right to engage in any activity or perform any act aimed at the destruction of any of the rights and freedoms recognized herein . . . ."[28]

Other treaties express the idea that the state can ensure that non-state entities respect human rights. For example, Article 2(d) of the International Convention on the Elimination of All Forms of Racial Discrimination[29] (ratified by 170 nations, including the United States) requires states to "prohibit and bring to an end, by all appropriate means, including legislation . . . racial discrimination by any persons, group or organization . . . ."[30] Hence, states have the indirect responsibility to prevent racial discrimination by corporations. Similarly, Article 2(e) of the Convention on the Elimination of All Forms of Discrimination

---

24. *Id.* preamble.

25. *Id.*

26. International Covenant on Civil and Political Rights, G.A. Res. 2200A (XXI), 21 U.N. GAOR, Supp. No. 16, U.N. Doc. A/6316 (1966), 999 U.N.T.S. 171, *entered into force* Mar. 23, 1976.

27. *Id.* art. 2.

28. *Id.* art. 5(1).

29. International Convention on the Elimination of All Forms of Racial Discrimination, G.A. Res. 2106 (XX), 20 U.N. GAOR, Supp. No. 14, U.N. Doc. A/6014 (1966), 660 U.N.T.S. 195, *entered into force* Jan. 4, 1969.

30. *Id.* art. 2(1)(d).

against Women[31] (ratified by 180 nations, but not the United States) requires states to "take all appropriate measures to eliminate discrimination against women by any person, organization or enterprise . . . ."[32] The Committee on the Elimination of Discrimination Against Women has interpreted that provision as including the responsibility of states "for private acts if they fail to act with due diligence to prevent violations of rights or to investigate and punish acts of violence, and for providing compensation."[33]

Accordingly, human rights treaties and interpretive pronouncements of treaty bodies at least provide for indirect human rights responsibilities of businesses.[34] The persistent occurrences of human rights abuses by businesses, however, have prompted several international efforts to define the direct responsibilities of companies. For example, the U.N. Commission on Transnational Corporations unsuccessfully attempted to draft an international code of conduct for TNCs in the 1970s and 1980s.[35] The Organisation for Economic Co-operation and Development (OECD) undertook a similar effort in 1976 (updated in 2000) when it established its Guidelines for Multinational Enterprises to promote responsible business conduct consistent with applicable laws, but the OECD Guidelines mentioned human rights only once in a single paragraph.[36] In 1977 (updated in 2000) the International Labor Organization (ILO) developed its Tripartite Declaration of Principles Concerning Multinational Enterprises, which calls upon businesses to

---

31. Convention on the Elimination of All Forms of Discrimination against Women, G.A. Res. 34/180, 34 U.N. GAOR, Supp. No. 46 at 193, U.N. Doc. A/34/46, *entered into force* Sept. 3, 1981.

32. *Id.* art. 2(e).

33. Committee on the Elimination of Discrimination against Women, General Recommendation 19, Violence against women (Eleventh session, 1992), U.N. Doc. A/47/38 (1993), *reprinted in* Compilation of General Comments and General Recommendations Adopted by Human Rights Treaty Bodies, U.N. Doc. HRI/GEN/1/Rev.6 at 243, para. 9 (2003).

34. For example, in interpreting the International Covenant on Civil and Political Rights, the Human Rights Committee observed, "Article 17 provides for the right of every person to be protected against arbitrary or unlawful interference with his privacy, family, home or correspondence as well as against unlawful attacks on his honour and reputation. In the view of the Committee this right is required to be guaranteed against all such interferences and attacks whether they emanate from State authorities or from natural or legal persons." Human Rights Committee, General Comment 16 (Twenty-third session, 1988), Compilation of General Comments and General Recommendations Adopted by Human Rights Treaty Bodies, U.N. Doc. HRI\GEN\1\Rev.1 at 21, para. 1 (1994).

35. *See* Development and International Economic Cooperation: Transnational Corporations, U.N. Doc. E/1990/94 (1990). *See also* United Nations Draft International Code of Conduct on Transnational Corporations, 23 I.L.M 626 (1984).

36. Organisation for Economic Co-operation and Development, Guidelines for Multinational Enterprises, 15 I.L.M. 967 (1976). The OECD updated these Guidelines in 2000. OECD Guidelines for Multinational Enterprises, Revision 2000, *available at* http://www.oecd.org/dataoecd/56/36/1922428.pdf.

follow the relevant labor conventions and recommendations.[37]

Further, in January 1999, U.N. Secretary-General Ko proposed a "Global Compact" of shared values and princip World Economic Forum in Davos, Switzerland.[38] The origin Compact asked businesses to voluntarily support and adopt nine succinctly expressed core principles, which are divided into categories dealing with the following: general human rights obligations, standards of labor, and standards of environmental protection. In 2004 the Global Compact added a tenth core principle on corruption.[39] The ILO, OECD, and Global Compact initiatives all indicate that they are voluntary, although the ILO[40] and the OECD[41] have established rarely used mechanisms for interpreting their guidelines.[42]

In addition, scrutiny of the activities of global businesses by civil society and an emerging concern of companies themselves for social responsibility have, since the 1980s, led hundreds of companies and several industry associations to adopt voluntary codes of conduct.[43] Some socially conscious businesspeople, such as the Minnesota

---

37. International Labour Organisation, Tripartite Declaration of Principles concerning Multinational Enterprises and Social Policy, 17 I.L.M. 422, ¶ 6 (1978), *available at* http://www.ilo.org/public/english/employment/multi/index.htm.

38. Secretary-General Kofi Annan, Address at the World Economic Forum in Davos, Switzerland (Jan. 31, 1999), in U.N. Doc. SG/SM/6448 (1999).

39. The principles are that businesses should:

> [(1) S]upport and respect the protection of internationally proclaimed human rights [within their sphere of influence]; [(2)] make sure they are not complicit in human right abuses[;] . . . [(3)] uphold the freedom of association and the effective recognition of the right to collective bargaining; . . . [(4)] eliminat[e] all forms of forced and compulsory labour; . . . [(5)] aboli[sh] child labour; . . . [(6)] eliminat[e] discrimination in respect of employment and occupation[;] . . . [(7)] support a precautionary approach to environmental challenges; . . . [(8)] undertake initiatives to promote greater environmental responsibility; . . . [(9)] encourage the development and diffusion of environmentally friendly technologies[;] . . . [and (10)] work against all forms of corruption, including extortion and bribery.

The Global Compact's Ten Principles, *available at* http://www.unglobalcompact.org/Portal/Default.asp? (follow "The Ten Principles" hyperlink) (last visited Sept. 14, 2005).

40. Tripartite Declaration, Interpretation Procedure, International Labor Organization, *available at* http://www.ilo.org/public/english/employment/multi/dispute.htm (last updated July 5, 2004).

41. Guidelines for Multinational Enterprises, Organisation of Economic Co-operation and Development, *available* *at* http://www.oecd.org/document/60/0,2340,en_2649_34889_1933116_1_1_1_1,00.html; http://www.oecd.org/document/43/0,2340,en_2649_34889_2074731_1_1_1_1,00.html (sites last visited Apr. 3, 2005).

42. *See* Kinley & Tadaki, *supra* note 7, at 956.

43. *See* PETER FRANKENTAL & FRANCES HOUSE, AMNESTY INTERNATIONAL & THE PRINCE OF WALES BUSINESS LEADERS FORUM, HUMAN RIGHTS: IS IT ANY OF YOUR BUSINESS? 23 (2000); *see also* Human Rights Codes of Conduct, *available at* http://www1.umn.edu/humanrts/business/codes.html (last visited Apr. 3, 2005).

Business Partnership and later the Caux Roundtable, developed voluntary principles applicable to a broad range of companies. Although there is a very important educational value in company codes and other voluntary initiatives, they often are very vague in regard to human rights commitments and lack mechanisms for assuring continuity or implementation. For example, only ninety-two corporations have even mentioned human rights in their respective company codes.[44]

Accordingly, one can summarize the situation when the U.N. Sub-Commission on the Promotion and Protection of Human Rights entered this field as follows: There existed significant concerns about the conduct of transnational corporations and other businesses. The OECD, an institution of thirty governments from only developed countries, had produced voluntary guidelines with a rudimentary implementation mechanism, but those guidelines only mentioned human rights once and lacked the support of a worldwide institution such as the United Nations. The ILO had issued another overlapping set of guidelines focusing almost exclusively on labor issues. Companies, industry groups, and nongovernmental organizations had prepared their own voluntary guidelines, but they rarely mentioned human rights, generally lacked implementation procedures, and could be posted on the Internet one day and taken down the next.

IV. THE U.N. HUMAN RIGHTS NORMS FOR BUSINESS AS THE NEXT LOGICAL STEP

Building upon the previous initiatives regarding corporate social responsibility, in August 2003 the U.N. Sub-Commission on the Promotion and Protection of Human Rights approved[45] the Norms on the Responsibilities of Transnational Corporations and Other Business Enterprises with Regard to Human Rights.[46] There are at least five significant attributes of the Norms that should be identified. First, the Norms evince a strong commitment that nothing in the Norms shall

---

44. Policies, Business & Human Rights Resource Center, *available at* http://www.business-humanrights.org (follow "Company policy/steps" hyperlink; then follow "Policies" hyperlink; then follow "Companies with human rights policies" hyperlink) (last visited Nov. 25, 2005).

45. Sub-Commission Resolution 2003/16, Responsibilities of transnational corporations and other business enterprises with regard to human rights, U.N. Doc. E/CN.4/Sub.2/2003/L.11 at 52 (2003), *available at* http://www1.umn.edu/humanrts/links/res2003-16.html.

46. Norms on the Responsibilities of Transnational Corporations and Other Business Enterprises with Regard to Human Rights, U.N. Doc. E/CN.4/Sub.2/2003/12/Rev.2 (2003); *see also* Commentary on the Norms on the Responsibilities of Transnational Corporations and Other Business Enterprises with Regard to Human Rights, U.N. Doc. E/CN.4/Sub.2/2003/38/Rev.2 (2003), *available at* http://www1.umn.edu/humanrts/links/commentary-Aug2003.html.

diminish the human rights obligations of governments. Accordingly, in its first and most important operative paragraph, the Norms establish that:

> States have the primary responsibility to promote, secure the fulfillment of, respect, ensure respect of and protect human rights recognized in international as well as national law, including ensuring that transnational corporations and other business enterprises respect human rights. Within their respective spheres of activity and influence, transnational corporations and other business enterprises have the obligation to promote, secure the fulfillment of, respect, ensure respect of and protect human rights recognized in international as well as national law, including the rights and interests of indigenous peoples and other vulnerable groups.[47]

Second, this core provision of the Norms further addresses an issue that not only was considered in preparing the Norms, but also arose in preparing the ILO,[48] OECD,[49] and Global Compact[50] guidelines: whether these standards apply only to TNCs or to all businesses. On the one hand, most media attention has focused on the activities and misdeeds of major corporations, such as Enron, Union Carbide, and Worldcom. Further, TNCs have the mobility and power to evade national laws and enforcement because they can relocate or use their political and economic clout to pressure governments to ignore corporate abuses.[51] On the other hand, if one applies human rights standards only to TNCs, that differential treatment could be considered discriminatory. Further, it is not easy to define a transnational corporation and there is a risk that sophisticated corporate lawyers will be able to structure any business so as to avoid the application of international standards. The Norms use one of the most comprehensive definitions of a transnational corporation, "an economic entity operating

---

47. *Id.* ¶ 1.

48. Paragraph 11 of the ILO Tripartite Declaration provides that "[m]ultinational and national enterprises, wherever the principles of this Declaration are relevant to both, should be subject to the same expectations in respect of their conduct in general and their social practices in particular." ILO, Tripartite Declaration, *supra* note 40, ¶ 11.

49. "Multinational and domestic enterprises are subject to the same expectations in respect of their conduct wherever the Guidelines are relevant to both." OECD Guidelines for Multinational Enterprises, Revision 2000, *supra* note 36, ¶ I-4 (emphasis omitted).

50. The Global Compact is aimed at "businesses," rather than multinational or domestic enterprises in particular. U.N. Global Compact, *supra* note 39.

51. Claudio Grossman & Daniel D. Bradlow, *Are We Being Propelled Towards a People-Centered Transnational Legal Order?*, 9 AM. U. J. INT'L & POL'Y 1, 8 (1993) ("The fact that they have multiple production facilities means that [transnational corporations] can evade state power and the constraints of national regulatory schemes by moving their operations between their different facilities around the world.").

in more than one country or a cluster of economic entities operating in two or more countries—whatever their legal form, whether in their home country or country of activity, and whether taken individually or collectively."[52] In the globalized economy of today, however, that definition is not adequate. For example, a company might employ only two hundred workers in Zurich and own only a single, but very popular, trademark. The company might contract with shirt manufacturers in China and India to purchase shirts and put the trademark on the front pocket. The Zurich company could then agree with a wholesaler to handle the transportation and distribution of the shirts for sale through retailers in Europe and the United States. The Zurich company could retain an advertising agency in London and New York to promote the sales worth many millions of dollars, pounds, euros, and eventually Swiss francs. In a real sense, the Zurich company should be considered a transnational corporation even though it has assets and employees in only one city.

Accordingly, the Norms apply not only to TNCs but also to national companies and local businesses in that each will be responsible according to "their respective spheres of activity and influence." This approach balances the need to address the power and responsibilities of TNCs and to level the playing field of competition for all businesses, while not being too burdensome on very small companies.

A third significant attribute of the Norms and the related Commentary[53] is that they take a very broad and comprehensive approach to human rights as compared with the ILO Guidelines that focus on labor standards, the OECD Guidelines that mention human rights only once, and the Global Compact that contains ten short sentences. The Norms comprise twenty-three paragraphs and are augmented by a more detailed Commentary to reflect the source of the principal provisions and to describe how the provisions apply to companies. As the most comprehensive set of standards developed thus far, the Norms and Commentary require TNCs and other business enterprises to respect the right to equality of opportunity and treatment; the right to security of persons; the rights of workers, including a safe and healthy work environment and the right to collective bargaining; respect for international, national, and local laws and the rule of law; a balanced approach to intellectual property rights and responsibilities; transparency and avoidance of corruption; respect for the right to health as well as other economic, social, and cultural rights; other civil and

---

52. Norms, *supra* note 46, ¶ 20.
53. Commentary, *supra* note 46.

political rights; consumer protection; and environmental prote
Regarding each of those subjects, the Norms principally reflect, re
and refer to existing international norms.

Fourth, while the Norms apply to all companies, they are not le_ _,
binding but are similar to many other U.N. declarations, principles,
guidelines, standards, and resolutions that interpret existing law and
summarize international practice without reaching the status of a treaty.
Eventually, of course, the Norms could be considered what international
law scholars call "soft law" and could also provide the basis for drafting
a human rights treaty on corporate social responsibility.

The fifth and final notable attribute of the Norms is that they endeavor
to include five basic implementation procedures and anticipate that other
techniques and processes may later supplement them. First, the Norms
anticipate that companies will adopt their own internal rules of operation
to assure the protections set forth in this instrument. Second, the Norms
indicate that businesses are expected to assess their major activities in
light of its provisions. Third, compliance with the Norms is subject to
monitoring that is independent, transparent, and includes input from
relevant stakeholders. Fourth, if companies violate the Norms and cause
damage, the Norms call for compensation, return of property, or other
reparations. And fifth, recognizing the significant responsibility of
governments, the Norms call upon those governments to establish a
framework for application of the Norms.

V. PROCESS BY WHICH THE NORMS WERE PREPARED AND ARE NOW BEING CONSIDERED BY THE COMMISSION ON HUMAN RIGHTS

The five-member U.N. Working Group on the Working Methods and
Activities of Transnational Corporations began preparing the Norms in
August 1999.[54] The Working Group held four public hearings on the
Norms during the summers of 2000, 2001, 2002, and 2003 as well as
meetings during March 2001 and 2003 in Geneva, at which
representatives of business, unions, nongovernmental organizations
(NGOs), the scholarly community, and other interested persons were
involved in reshaping the document.

The Working Group also posted the various drafts on the Internet[55]

---

54. David Weissbrodt & Muria Kruger, *Norms on the Responsibilities of Transnational
Corporations and Other Business Enterprises with Regard to Human Rights*, 97 A.J.I.L. 901, 904-07
(2003).

55. Previous Drafts of the Norms on the Responsibilities of Transnational Corporations and
Other Business Enterprises with Regard to Human Rights, *available at* http://www1.umn.edu/humanrts/
links/normsdrafts.html.

and issued them in U.N. publications, so that they were accessible and open to comment. All of the comments received have been taken into account in the drafting process.

After receiving the recommended text from its Working Group, the U.N. Sub-Commission unanimously approved the Norms on August 13, 2003. The Sub-Commission sent the Norms to its parent body, the U.N. Commission on Human Rights. Unlike the Sub-Commission, which is comprised of twenty-six more-or-less independent experts from twenty-six different nations representing all the regions of the world, the Commission is comprised of fifty-three government representatives. The Commission ordinarily meets each year from mid-March until the end of April, so that the Norms had their first hearing at the Commission in March-April 2004. The Commission accepted the Sub-Commission's primary procedural recommendation that the Norms should be disseminated broadly to all potentially interested governments, intergovernmental organizations, businesses, unions, nongovernmental organizations, and others, so that the Commission could receive comments in time for further consideration at its March-April 2005 session.[56] The deadline for comments was September 30, 2004. The Commission received more than ninety comments.[57] Also, on October 22, 2004, the Office of the High Commissioner for Human Rights, in cooperation with the U.N. Global Compact Office, held a one-day meeting in Geneva on the topic of the responsibilities of business with regard to human rights. In addition to soliciting comments and views so that the High Commissioner's Office could prepare a report for the 2005 session of the Commission on "the responsibilities of transnational corporations and related business enterprises with regard to human rights,"[58] the 2004 session of the Commission welcomed the Norms, while noting that the Commission had not actually asked for the document and that, as a draft before the Commission, the document does not on its own have any legal status. Simultaneously, however, the Commission recognized for the first time in its history that corporate social responsibility and human rights belong on the agenda of the Human Rights Commission. That was quite a success in itself.

It is extraordinarily unlikely that the Commission would act substantively upon the Norms without further drafting and several years of consideration—before the Norms or a successor instrument could

---

56. U.N. Comm. Human Rts. dec. 2004/16, U.N. Doc. E/CN.4/2004/L.11/Add.7 (2004), *available at* http://www.unhchr.ch/huridocda/huridoca.nsf/e06a5300f90fa0238025668700518ca4/169143c3c1009015c1256e830058c441/$FILE/G0413976.pdf.

57. *Available at* http://www.ohchr.org/english/issues/globalization/business/contributions.htm.

58. U.N. Doc. E/CN.4/2005/91 (2005).

eventually be submitted to the Economic and Social Council of the United Nations, and ultimately to the General Assembly for adoption. At the same time, however, any of these bodies could adopt the Norms or a similar standard as its view—carrying some degree of United Nations and thus world support. Obviously, the higher the U.N. institution and the more consensus achieved, the more authoritative would be the imprimatur the Norms should obtain.

At its 2005 session the Commission adopted a resolution[59] that welcomed the High Commissioner's report[60] and identified in an extraordinarily balanced fashion precisely the same number of criticisms of the Norms as it found positive attributes. The Commission also called for the appointment by the Secretary-General of a Special Representative on the issue of human rights and transnational corporations and other business enterprises. The Special Representative will serve for "an initial period of two years" implying that the Commission intends to continue the mandate beyond two years. The Special Representative received the following terms of reference:

(*a*) To identify and clarify standards of corporate responsibility and accountability for transnational corporations and other business enterprises with regard to human rights;

(*b*) To elaborate on the role of States in effectively regulating and adjudicating the role of transnational corporations and other business enterprises with regard to human rights, including through international cooperation;

(*c*) To research and clarify the implications for transnational corporations and other business enterprises of concepts such as "complicity" and "sphere of influence;"

(*d*) To develop materials and methodologies for undertaking human rights impact assessments of the activities of transnational corporations and other business enterprises;

(*e*) To compile a compendium of best practices of States and transnational corporations and other business enterprises; . . .[61]

The Commission also underlined that "the Special Representative of the Secretary-General should take into account in his or her work the report of the United Nations High Commissioner for Human Rights and the contributions to that report provided by all stakeholders, as well as

---

59. C.H.R. res. 2005/69, U.N. Doc. E/CN.4/2005/L.11/Add.7 at 68 (2005), was adopted April 20, 2005, by a vote of forty-nine in favor, three (Australia, South Africa, and the United States) against, and one (Burkina Faso) abstaining. The United States called for a vote and explained its vote against the resolution. http://www.humanrights-usa.net/2005/0420Item17TNC.htm.

60. U.N. Doc. E/CN.4/2005/91 (2005).

61. C.H.R. res. 2005/69, U.N. Doc. E/CN.4/2005/L.11/Add.7 at 68 (2005).

70   *UNIVERSITY OF CINCINNATI LAW REVIEW*   [Vol. 74

existing initiatives, standards and good practices."[62]

While the resolution does not mention the Norms, it focuses on the High Commissioner's report with regard to the Norms and the resolution underscores "existing initiatives, standards and good practices."

VI. Issues Regarding the Norms

A number of issues have been raised with regard to the Norms by the International Chamber of Commerce (ICC) and the International Organization of Employers (IOE)—bodies that represent some of the largest transnational corporations. While these two organizations were invited to participate in the drafting of the Norms and, to some extent, did participate, they have been most forceful in trying to stop the Norms ever since the Sub-Commission approved them in August 2003. The ICC and IOE lobbied hard to kill the Norms at the 2004 Commission sessions, but they did not succeed. They mounted a further lobbying effort for 2005 in which they have raised questions as to whether companies, as non-state actors, can be subjected to human rights standards. That argument ignores the trend of international human rights and humanitarian law towards applying standards not only to states, but also to armed opposition groups, individuals, and other entities. Even the ILO, OECD, and Global Compact guidelines, while voluntary, speak directly to business. The Norms take a clear and important step towards applying international standards to all business, and that step seems fully justified. Businesses should not be exempted from human rights responsibilities.

Another principal argument of the ICC and IOE has been that they will accept only voluntary guidelines. The voluntary Global Compact has been very successful in educating and encouraging nearly 2,300 companies to join, but there are an estimated 61,000 TNCs in the world.[63] What about the other 59,000 companies that are not covered by the Global Compact? The U.N. Human Rights Norms provide an answer to that question.

There is a third argument that the ICC and IOE are reluctant to make at the Commission on Human Rights because they know how unpopular the argument would be in an international forum. That argument has, however, been broached in American academic and political discourse. The argument is most closely associated with Professor Milton

---

62. *Id.*

63. United Nations Conference on Trade and Development (UNCTAD), World Investment Report 2004, Annex Table A.12 at 273-75 (2004) (61,582 TNCs in 2004), *available at* http://www.unctad.org/en/docs/wir2004_en.pdf.

Friedman who contended that "there is one and only one social responsibility of business—to use its resources and engage in activities designed to increase its profits so long as it stays within the rules of the game, which is to say, engages in open and free competition, without deception or fraud."[64] Notably, even Friedman's view that businesses should not pursue socially desirable objectives excluded two social policies—fraud and competition. Those exceptions may be explained by the need to maintain the quality of the free market that Friedman strenuously advocated. It is doubtful, however, that even Friedman would have argued that corporations should pursue profit by committing genocide or using slave labor. Indeed, Friedman would likely have agreed that corporations can only pursue profits in ways that are consistent with legal limitations. That position is consistent with the views of many businesses and business managers who wish to be informed of the law and would be willing to comply with the law.[65]

Focusing only on the self-interest of corporations, however, there is increasing reason to believe that greater respect for human rights by companies leads to greater sustainability in emerging markets[66] and better business performance.[67] For example, observance of human rights aids businesses by protecting and maintaining their corporate

---

64. MILTON FRIEDMAN, CAPITALISM & FREEDOM 133 (1962); *see also* Milton Friedman, *The Social Responsibility of a Business is to Increase Profits*, N.Y. TIMES MAG., Sept. 13, 1970 at 32, 125.

65. Professor Ronald Coase developed an alternative paradigm to Friedman's understanding of how businesses should act, arguing that businesses are best understood by observing carefully their actual conduct rather than creating artificial models of how they ought to act. *See* RONALD HARRY COASE, THE FIRM, THE MARKET AND THE LAW (1988). The past fifteen years have demonstrated that major businesses are, in fact, becoming aware of the interplay between their businesses and their impact on individuals, communities, and the environment; they realize that respect for human rights leads to better business performance and find it beneficial to issue their own codes of conduct that go far beyond a narrow profit motive or legal mandates. Hence, the creation of human rights standards that help attract the best and brightest employees, solicit investments from investors who place at least some socially responsible screen on their stock holdings, and attract consumers who prefer to purchase goods made without child labor or unnecessarily soiling the environment are not contrary to the primary purpose of transnational corporations and other business enterprises. The creation of a uniform set of international human rights standards would aid in this process by helping to make clear what human rights standards a company should follow and which business enterprises are meeting those standards.

66. A large-scale study of evidence from developing countries found that emerging-market companies gain financially from stability. *See* Press Release, International Finance Corporation, Groundbreaking Report Challenges Conventional Wisdom on Role of Business in Emerging Markets, (July 16, 2002), *available at* http://www.ifc.org/pressroom.

67. *See* ROGER COWE, ABI RESEARCH REPORTS, INVESTING IN SOCIAL RESPONSIBILITY: RISKS AND OPPORTUNITIES (2001) (supporting the proposition that corporate social responsibility has a positive impact on businesses by increasing their potential for competitive advantage and increasing shareholder value through promotion of risk management). *See also* Daniel Farber, *Rights as Signals*, 31 J. LEGAL STUD. 83, 98 (2002) (human rights protection properly encourages investment).

reputation,[68] as well as creating a stable and peaceful society in which they can prosper and attract the best and brightest employees.[69] Moreover, consumers have demonstrated that they are willing to purchase products based on a company's compliance with labor, environmental, and other human rights standards.[70] Similarly, there is evidence that a growing proportion of investors seeks to purchase shares only in socially responsible companies.[71]

VII. CONCLUSION: HOW THE NORMS ARE ALREADY BEING USED

While the Norms have yet to acquire legal standing or adoption by the Commission on Human Rights, even in their present format the Norms are beginning to form the basis for corporate action. For example, some investment institutions have begun applying the Norms to persuade

---

68. *Research: Corporate Reputation*, BRAND STRATEGY, Nov. 2004, at 40 (93% of senior executives believe that their customers and consumers consider corporate reputation to be extremely important or important. "There has also been a surge in the number of brands taking corporate social responsibility (CSR) seriously.")

69. *MBAs Want to Work for Caring and Ethical Employers*, BUS. & ENV. ISO 14000 UPDATES, Sept. 2004, at 15, 16 (citing a Stanford study in which "more than 97% of MBAs in the sample said that they would be willing to forgo financial benefits to work for an organization with a better reputation for corporate social responsibility and ethics"). *See also* CHRISTOPHER AVERY, AMNESTY INTERNATIONAL, BUSINESS AND HUMAN RIGHTS IN A TIME OF CHANGE (Feb. 2000), *available at* http://www.business-humanrights.org/Avery-Report.htm; United Nations High Commissioner for Human Rights, Business and Human Rights, *available at* http://www.unhchr.ch/global.htm.

70. Andrew Pendleton, *The Real Face of Corporate Social Responsibility*, CONSUMER POL'Y REV., May/June 2004, at 77, 79 (describing increase in consumer attention to corporate social responsibility). For example, consumer discontent that footballs were made through child labor led to a consumer boycott forcing the manufacturers to stop using child labor. *See* Robert J. Liubicic, *Corporate Codes of Conduct and Product Labeling Schemes: The Limits and Possibilities of Promoting International Labor Rights Standards Through Private Initiatives*, 30 LAW & POL'Y INT'L BUS. 111 (1998). Another example occurred in regard to the promotion of infant formula in developing countries. Certain companies were encouraging mothers in developing countries to use infant formula instead of breast-milk feeding. The use of infant formula led to increased infant mortality because of lack of clean water and because mothers were not properly instructed on how to use the formula. Once consumers learned about the increased infant mortality, they began boycotting Nestlé products. *See* Nancy E. Zelman, *The Nestlé Infant Formula Controversy: Restricting the Marketing Practice of Multinational Corporations in the Third World*, 3 TRANSNAT'L LAW. 697 (1990).

71. Paul M. Clikeman, *Return of the Socially Conscious Corporation*, STRATEGIC FIN., Apr. 2004, at 23, 24 (noting investors' demand for information on corporate social responsibility). The ethical market share in the United Kingdom grew 15% from 1999 to 2000. *See* Deborah Doane, New Economics Foundation, *Taking Flight: The Rapid Growth of Ethical Consumerism* (Oct. 2001), *available at* http://www.neweconomics.org (follow "publications" link; then follow link to page 12). A study in the United States found that one out of every eight professionally managed investment dollars is used in socially responsible investing. *See* SOCIAL INVESTMENT FORUM, 2001 REPORT OF SOCIALLY RESPONSIBLE INVESTING TRENDS IN THE UNITED STATES (Nov. 28, 2001), *available at* http://www.socialinvest.org/areas/research/trends/2001-Trends.htm.

companies to improve their social responsibility.[72] Some NGOs—such as Amnesty International,[73] Christian Aid,[74] Human Rights First,[75] Human Rights Watch,[76] and OXFAM[77]—have been using the Norms as the basis for their advocacy of corporate social responsibility. Some companies, such as Barclay's Bank and Novo Nordisk, as well as the International Business Leaders Forum, have expressed support for the Norms as a way of understanding their commitment to the Universal Declaration of Human Rights. Several leading companies have begun to road-test the Norms in their own businesses, such as Hewlett-Packard, Novartis, and the other companies that compose the Business Leaders Initiative on Human Rights.[78] Similarly, a major mobile phone company has inserted a clause in all its purchasing contracts requiring businesses with which it contracts or subcontracts (about a thousand of them) to comply with the terms of the U.N. Human Rights Norms for Business.[79] The U.N. Human Rights Norms for Business have initiated a process for further identifying, clarifying, and elaborating standards for the responsibility and accountability of transnational corporations and other business enterprises with regard to human rights.

---

72. Isis Asset Management (based in London) was involved in the drafting of the Norms, has supported the Norms since their inception, and has used the Norms in its efforts to persuade the companies in which it invested to improve its socially responsible conduct. In August 2004, Isis merged with Foreign & Commonwealth investment company and the new company, F&C, has followed the Isis approach to the Norms since the merger.

73. Amnesty International, *supra* note 8.

74. Christian Aid, Submission to the Office of the United Nations High Commissioner for Human Rights: Responsibilities of Transnational Corporations and Related Business Enterprises with Regard to Human Rights (Oct. 2004), http://www.christian-aid.org.uk/indepth/410unchcr/UNCHCR%20submission_formatted.pdf.

75. Human Rights First, Nongovernmental Organizations Welcome the New U.N. Norms on Transnational Business – Press Statement (Aug. 13, 2003), *available at* http://www.humanrightsfirst.org/workers_rights/wr_other/wr_press_st_081303.htm.

76. Human Rights Watch, The U.N. Norms: Towards Greater Corporate Accountability: Statement on the United Nations Norms on the Responsibilities of Transnational Corporations and Other Business Enterprises with Regard to Human Rights to the Office of the United Nations High Commissioner for Human Rights (Sept. 30, 2004), *available at* http://hrw.org/english/docs/2004/09/30/global9446.htm.

77. AI/Oxfam Open Call on Governments in Support of the U.N. Human Rights Norms for Business (Apr. 7, 2004), AI Index: IOR 42/010/2004, *available at* http://web.amnesty.org/library/Index/ENGIOR420102004?open&of=ENG-398.

78. Business Leaders Initiative on Human Rights, Submission to the Office of the U.N. High Commissioner for Human Rights Relating to the "Responsibilities of Transnational Corporations and Related Business Enterprises with Regard to Human Rights" (Sept. 28, 2004), *available at* http://www.blihr.org/Pdfs/The%20BLIHR%20submission%20to%20OHCHR.pdf.

79. Report of the Sessional Working Group on the Working Methods and Activities of Transnational Corporations on its sixth session, U.N. Doc. E/CN.4/2004/21 at 9 (2004).

[5]

Multinational Corporations and the Ethics of Global Responsibility: Problems and Possibilities

Mahmood Monshipouri*
Claude E. Welch, Jr.**
Evan T. Kennedy***

ABSTRACT

Multinational corporations (MNCs) have provoked considerable debate about the issues of "efficiency" and "social justice." The simultaneous surge in economic growth and inequality has led to serious implications for economic rights in developing countries. Using a rights-based perspective, we argue that in the human rights area the responsible party is generally the state. In the context of neoliberal globalization, however, the wrongdoers are often corporations. Reliance on state duties alone may not be sufficient

* *Mahmood Monshipouri* received his Ph.D. from the University of Georgia. He is Professor and Chair of the Political Science Department at Quinnipiac University. He specializes in human rights, democratization, comparative politics, Middle Eastern politics, and Western European politics. He is co-editor of *Constructing Human Rights in the Age of Globalization* (NY: M.E. Sharpe, 2003). His most recent articles have appeared in *International Peacekeeping, Yale Human Rights and Development Law Journal, Journal of Church and State,* and *Middle East Policy.*

** *Claude E. Welch, Jr.* received his B.A. from Harvard and his D.Phil. from Oxford. He is SUNY Distinguished Service Professor in the Department of Political Science at the University at Buffalo, where he also directs the Program in International and Comparative Law. Among his books are: *NGOs and Human Rights: Promise and Performance* (University of Pennsylvania Press, 2001), *Protecting Human Rights in Africa* (University of Pennsylvania Press, 1995) and *Human Rights and Development* (State University of New York Press, 1984). Professor Welch has published HRQ articles on the impact of the World Council of Churches' Program to Combat Racism, the effect of CEDAW and other treaties on the rights of African women, and the effectiveness of the African Commission on Human Rights.

*** *Evan T. Kennedy* received his B.A. in English and Political Science from Quinnipiac University in Hamden, Connecticut, where he served as Research Assistant for the Political Science Department during 1999–2000 academic year. He currently lives in Berkeley, California.

966 **HUMAN RIGHTS QUARTERLY** Vol. 25

to broadly protect human rights. Certain corporate behaviors are detrimental to internationally recognized norms of human rights. Although private actions, media exposure, and lawsuits based on civil law appear to be the only practical way to put the pressure on MNCs, it is important to examine the possibility of an outside governing body to hold in check unfettered global capitalism and to bring accountability to MNCs' policies that are socially detrimental.

I. INTRODUCTION

The global economy and the forces of globalization have become prominent characteristics of the current paradigm of world politics. In this context, the political spotlight has eventually rested on the balancing claims and criticisms of the multinational, or transnational, corporations (MNCs or TNCs). What makes MNCs a pertinent subject is their dynamic growth and influence on the world stage, and the ways in which they affect the life chances of millions of people around the world.

Human rights groups and organizations insist that free trade and its rules, or lack thereof, are insufficient to promote a fair game and that the push for greater social responsibility of the MNCs is necessary given their increasing influence and the trend toward further privatization.[1] Because MNCs have gained powers traditionally vested only in states, they should arguably be held to the same standards that international law presently imposes upon states. As Garth Meintjes put it, "the idea of a corporation as a legal fiction without responsibilities is no more sacred or accurate than the idea of unfettered state sovereignty."[2]

The MNCs' power to control international investment, especially portfolio investments, has had enormous bearing on the economies of developing countries. Faced with pressures to attract such investments, governments in the South have had little or no alternative but to be receptive to the terms of MNCs. The lack of leverage with the MNCs has meant, for example, that minimum wage has been set unrealistically low in developing countries so as to attract foreign investment. A related criticism of MNCs is that their overall strategy to relocate from the North has kept wages and living conditions down and resulted in the expansion of sweatshops in the South. This has led to the view that globalization is a euphemism for "sweatshop global economy."[3]

1. Garth Meintjes, *An International Human Rights Perspective on Corporate Codes*, in GLOBAL CODES OF CONDUCT: AN IDEA WHOSE TIME HAS COME 83–99, at 86 (Oliver F. Williams ed., 2000).
2. *Id.* at 87.
3. Steven Greenhouse, *Critics Calling U.S. Supplier In Nicaragua A Sweatshop*, N.Y. TIMES, Dec. 3 2000, at 9.

Critics argue that the current neoliberal global economy allows MNCs to utilize Southern workers as cheap labor and to exploit lower standards on working conditions, basic worker rights, and environmental regulations. MNCs have provoked considerable debate around the conflicting issues of "efficiency" and "fairness," and the resultant balance of economic growth and social injustice. The simultaneous surge in economic growth and inequity has led to serious implications for human rights in the developing world.

The MNCs' advocates, in contrast, regard them as benign engines of prosperity—enhancing local living conditions by generating employment, income, and wealth, as well as by introducing and dispensing advanced technology to the developing world.[4] There are three emerging perspectives that inform corporate social responsibilities. First is the so-called "reputation capital" view that sees corporate social responsibility as a strategy to reduce investment risks and maximize profits. The second view, referred to as the "eco-social" view, considers social and environmental sustainability crucial to the sustainability of the market. The third perspective is the "rights-based" view, which underscores the importance of accountability, transparency, and social/environmental investment as key aspects of corporate social responsibility.[5]

Using a rights-based perspective, we argue that in the human rights domain the responsible party is generally the state, and that, especially in the context of neoliberal globalization, the wrongdoers are often corporations. Some experts have argued that states are not and should not be the sole target of international legal obligations and that reliance on state duties alone may not be sufficient to broadly protect human rights.[6] A consensus has emerged that certain corporate behavior is detrimental to internationally recognized norms of human rights. This paper examines the possibility of an outside governing body to hold in check unfettered global capitalism and to bring accountability to MNC policies that are socially detrimental. Through an examination of the mixed results of globalization and an increased awareness of social responsibility, this paper concludes that MNCs will not address specific human rights violations if assigned only to a voluntary set of principles set up in the UN Global Compact of 1999. Although the Compact provides a helpful framework within which to examine ethical concerns,

---

4. CHARLES W. KEGLEY, JR. & EUGENE R. WITTKOPF, WORLD POLITICS: TREND AND TRANSFORMATIONS 230 (8th ed. 2001); *see also* John Stopford, *Multinational Corporations,* FOR. POL'Y, 12–24 (1998/1999).

5. John Samuel & Anil Saari, Whither Corporate Social Responsibility?, *available at* http://www.infochange.org/Corporaterslbp.jsp#csrh5.

6. We have borrowed the assumption developed in the seminal work of Steven R. Ratner, *Corporations and Human Rights: A Theory of Legal Responsibility,* 111 YALE L. J. 461 (2001).

968   **HUMAN RIGHTS QUARTERLY**   **Vol. 25**

without any teeth it serves only as public relations while delaying or blocking any real action to fundamentally address human rights deficiencies. While we leave open the argument as to where this governing body should be located institutionally, we argue that restructuring international organizations, such as the World Trade Organization (WTO), might be a good place to start. It is also worth mentioning that the United Nations may provide an appropriate base for mobilizing support for a code of conduct. For now, however, private actions, media exposure, and lawsuits based on civil law seem to be the only practical way to put the pressure on MNCs to consider observing global standards.

II. THE GLOBALIZATION–HUMAN RIGHTS INTERSECTION

Although there is no broadly accepted definition of the term "globalization," it is about the way in which the world is changing. A simple description is offered by Allan Cochrane and Kathy Pain: "Cultures, economies and politics appear to merge across the globe through the rapid exchange of information, ideas and knowledge, and the investment strategies of global corporations."[7] The main conceptual properties of globalization include: stretched social relations, intensification of flows, increasing interpenetration of economic and social practices, and institutional infrastructure of interaction made possible by information and communications technologies.[8]

Some popular interpretations of globalization include the view that it is "an evolutionary process of change driven by technological and scientific progress in the modern era."[9] A force behind this definition is the recent communication and information technology revolution, from which corporations operate in a world market outside of national boundaries. The new technologies have led to international corporate infrastructure, developed "in order to attain relative advantages among their global counterparts."[10]

Another popular definition of globalization maintains that it magnifies and intensifies the level of interaction and interdependence among nation-states and societies. As markets become available on a worldwide level, once-separate societies deepen their relationships, politically and economi-

---

7. Allan Cochrane & Kathy Pain, *A Globalizing Society, in* A GLOBALIZING WORLD? CULTURE, ECONOMICS, POLITICS 5–21; see esp. 6 (David Held ed., 2000).
8. *Id.* at 15–17.
9. Mahmood Monshipouri & Reza Motameni, *Globalization, Sacred Beliefs, and Defiance: Is Human Rights Discourse Relevant in the Muslim World?* 42 J. CHURCH & STATE 709–36, at 712 (2000).
10. *Id.* at 713.

cally. From a realist perspective, globalization is seen as a new hegemonic system upheld by the world's major capitalist economies of the post–Cold War world to promote their own political and economic interests. Seen in this light, globalization is a tool of the wealthy nations used to maintain their economic dominance. In its present mainly neoliberal course, globalization is connected with the rationalist structure of knowledge, the capitalist mode of production, technological innovation, and technical and procedural standardization. This last dynamic entails the establishment of regulatory measures that guarantee property rights for global capital and legalize global organizations and activities.[11]

Finally, some scholars see globalization as a paradigm shift, in which values, lifestyles, tolerance for diversity, and individual choice are simultaneously undergoing transformations on a global scale. Globalization as such relates not only to an increased interconnectedness between markets, but also to a shared culture of globalization, often effecting a social shift away from some traditional ideas and values.[12]

As the world moves into the twenty-first century, global interdependence has increased. At both the local and global levels, the protection and promotion of human rights have been caught up in this globalization process. But as more institutions function at the global level, organizations such as MNCs, the IMF, and the European Commission of the European Union have rarely, if ever, been held to the standard of democratic accountability.

The language of human rights has increasingly arisen to encounter such a neoliberal globalization. As the third millennium begins, an emerging normative consensus has begun to take shape on the realization of some fundamental human rights. We are nevertheless far from the creation of a single moral universe, shared by all cultures, nations, and civilizations. Rather, what has happened through conditions of chronic globalization, as one observer notes, is that the fate of communities throughout the world has become linked through complex and dynamic systems that create moral connections between the agents and the subjects of social action regardless of territorial and political boundaries. Although there still are varying conceptions of what constitute rights and what priorities should be assigned to varying types of rights, the philosophical and political debate underlying these disagreements is itself conducted in a global context.[13]

The concept of human rights entails a wide range of entitlements. For our analysis here, we divide human rights into three categories: first-

---

11.   Jan Aart Scholte, Globalization: A Critical Introduction 106 (2000).
12.   Monshipouri & Motameni, *supra* note 9, at 715–16.
13.   *Id.*

970   **HUMAN RIGHTS QUARTERLY**   **Vol. 25**

generation rights, with emphasis on civil-political rights (right to life, freedom from slavery and torture, right to participate); second-generation rights, the substance of which is based on economic, social, and cultural rights (right to health, education, and decent standards of living); and third-generation rights, the content of which stresses human "solidarity" (right to a clean environment, right to peace, right to self-determination, right to humanitarian intervention, and the right to the benefits of an international common heritage).

There are two sides to the human rights discourse. Western powers' domination of world politics for the past two centuries has affected the human rights discourse. Thus conceived, as one expert points out, "powerful western states have been in a central position to advance or retard ideas about the human being in world affairs."[14] From another angle, it seems reasonable to argue that "rights are increasingly seen as empowering weaker sections of communities and as the basis for social and political mobilization."[15] In such a view, both the privileged and disadvantaged in society share a common respect for the legitimacy of human rights. That is to say, the regime of rights is the best tool to advance these beliefs.[16]

The protection and promotion of the second-generation rights have focused attention on nonstate individuals and institutions such as the MNCs.[17] Although development should not be narrowly conceived as economic growth and output, the promotion and success of economic development should be judged by improvement in a wide range of effective capability and human choices.[18]

Because MNCs are not equipped to deal with the questions of international ethics themselves, they need the help of human rights NGOs and other actors to deal with various human rights concerns. The key to this process is making corporations realize the benefits that social responsibility will bring to them. Understandably, businesses have other concerns, such as profits and obligations to shareholders, that must be taken into account when discussing human rights issues.[19] But the true means to developing a sustainable global economy is to integrate the concerns of business and

---

14.   David P. Forsythe, Human Rights in International Relations 33 (2000).
15.   Yash Ghai, *Rights, Social Justice, and Globalization in East Asia, in* The East Asian Challenge for Human Rights 249 (Joanne R. Bauer & Daniel A. Bell eds., Cambridge Univ. Press 1999).
16.   *Id.* at 249–50.
17.   Lee A. Tavis, *The Globalization Phenomenon and Multinational Corporate Developmental Responsibility, in* Global Codes of Conduct: An Idea Whose Time Has Come 1336; see 21 (Oliver F. Willimans ed., Univ. of Notre Dame Press 2000).
18.   Amartya Sen, Development as Freedom (1999).
19.   Kevin T. Jackson, *The Polycentric Character of Business Ethics Decision Making in International Contexts*, J. Bus. Ethics (Jan. 2000).

human rights. Business and human rights interests are not necessarily in opposition. By emphasizing their mutual concerns, both communities may find themselves better positioned to concurrently advance their objectives.[20]

In this context, several questions must be raised. How will MNCs react to the rising tide of global human rights? What implications will lie ahead if MNCs choose to bypass such normative standards in the name of economic rationality and efficiency? Can MNCs be subject to some form of international regulation or litigation? Will mandatory/legal compliance work better than a voluntary approach to achieving corporate social responsibility? These questions are highly relevant to the discussions regarding the role that MNCs play in today's era of rising interconnectedness and globalization.

III. THE POWER OF CAPITAL

With the increased interaction and globalization of world markets, it is impossible to ignore the impact of MNCs on the human rights conditions worldwide. Like state action, global corporate action has an immense impact that stretches much further than the boardroom where the decisions are made. Consequently, there has been a recent upsurge in the opinion that MNCs are accountable for their actions and should transform their practices in lieu of the human rights debate.

Because MNCs have a direct impact on the economic, political, and social landscape of the countries in which they operate, their activities have considerable effect on individuals and human rights, both positively and negatively. Steven R. Ratner, who sees noticeable limits to holding states solely accountable for human rights violations in modern international affairs, asserts that "corporations may have as much or more power over individuals as governments."[21] Corporations control a great amount of capital, generating about one-fifth of the world's wealth. Only six nations (the United States, Germany, Japan, United Kingdom, Italy, and France) have tax revenues larger than the nine largest MNCs' sales. Wal-Mart, which is not regarded as one of the top ten revenue-earning MNCs, still profits more per year than the Canadian government's annual tax revenues, while relying on developing countries' labor to produce many of its products.[22] Wal-Mart is one of many MNCs with operations in Asia and Latin America, where MNC activity has come under increased scrutiny for its effect on the local economy and society.

---

20. Elliot Schrage & Anthony Ewing, *Engaging the Private Sector.*, Forum for Applied Res. & Pub. Pol'y (Spring 1999), *available at* http://proquest.umi.com.
21. Ratner, *supra* note 6, at 461.
22. All data taken from chart in Forsythe, *supra* note 14, at 192.

972   **HUMAN RIGHTS QUARTERLY**   **Vol. 25**

MNCs' activities in the developing world result in myriad rewards as well as costs. As a potent force for economic integration, MNCs can generate large amounts of income and wealth for host countries, while at the same time providing jobs in markets with high levels of unemployment. Some studies on MNC activity, including one by William Meyer, argue that the presence of MNCs in Third World economies is beneficial, leading to increased life expectancy and reductions in illiteracy and infant mortality rates, along with increases in first- and second-generation rights as a whole.[23]

Despite evidence that corporate activities in the developing world improve human rights standards, it is still fair to say that MNCs often react to human rights concerns slowly and callously. David P. Forsythe character- izes two groups in the international political economy—the "in" group, "us," the main beneficiary of money and goods; and the "out" group, "them," the laborers and governments that help to produce said goods. As long as the benefits of these operations continue to flow to "us," our concern for "them" is reduced: "On the one hand, the TNC must have cozy relations with the (all-too-often reactionary) government that controls access to the resource. The TNC and local government share an interest in a docile and compliant labor force. On the other hand, the TNC has little interest in other aspects of the local population."[24] Finished products, Forsythe asserts, are sold abroad, with a considerable portion of the profits going to the governmental elite. If that elite does not reinvest the profit into infrastruc- tures that improve the lot of the local population, such as education, health care, and ecological protection, this short-term profit will remain just that.[25]

MNCs have consistently held and continue to argue that the responsi- bility to improve the socioeconomic standards of living in Third World countries is that of the local government, not of a corporation. The chasm between maximizing economic self-interest and promoting human rights, which has separated the operations of TNCs from those of human rights activists, characterizes the existing tensions between the two. In the second half of the twentieth century, "the globalization of the economy and the globalization of human rights concerns developed separately from each other . . . ."[26]

MNC activity in the Third World has enhanced the inequitable tendencies of the market and further widened the gap between the rich and the poor. MNCs have also become the principal sites of economic and political power in the developing world. One Asian expert has argued that

---

23.   WILLIAM H. MEYER, HUMAN RIGHTS AND INTERNATIONAL POLITICAL ECONOMY IN THIRD WORLD NATIONS: MULTINATIONAL CORPORATIONS, FOREIGN AID, AND REPRESSION (1998).
24.   FORSYTHE, *supra* note 14, at 196.
25.   *Id.* at 196–97.
26.   *Id.* at 197.

the removal of barriers to trade as well as to the movement of capital has given MNCs "enormous flexibility in the organization of production and has made them 'footloose,' able to exploit economic opportunities around the world."[27]

Many other factors contribute to the increase in the power of corporations. These include international protection of their property and their prominent role in international institutions that regulate trade, such as the World Trade Organization (WTO). It is important to bear in mind the mounting power of corporations in the context of international trade. Throughout the world, trade, investment, and information technology are constraining governments' ability to provide social safety nets and public services to cushion the negative consequences of globalization.[28]

The power of capital is changing the relationship between states and the market. States are forced to lower their tax rates to entice capital to their economies, and are sacrificing public expenditures to do so. In order to get a company to invest in an area, the state has to provide conditions that the corporation prefers over those offered by other countries. States are inclined to do so because they see the opportunities for employment and revenues as investments in the future—not merely opportunities to skim off bribes. To the extent that the state has become increasingly subordinated to international capital, policy making has often been dictated by the exigencies of capital movement.[29] This imbalance of power gives capital and capitalists the advantage over the state and labor, but there are good reasons states are willing to take risks. The ability of MNCs to coerce states into lowering labor standards highlights the inequities of the global market. Globalization as such invites controversy.[30]

IV. CORPORATE HUMAN RIGHTS ABUSES

Corporations frequently infringe on human rights, but sometimes they are directly complicit in abuses. Steven R. Ratner argues that MNCs have the responsibility—"complicity-based duties"—to avoid any situation that would lead to abuse.[31] The duties of corporations are directly linked to their capacity to harm human dignity. In some cases, private actors prevent their employees from leaving the country, as evidenced by the problem of forced

---

27. Id. at 251.
28. Jeffrey E. Garten, Globalism Doesn't Have to be Cruel, Business Week, Feb. 9, 1998, available at http://proquest.umi.com.
29. Ghai, supra note 15, at 252.
30. Id. at 251.
31. Ratner, supra note 6, at 512.

prostitution.[32] Likewise, corporations are liable if they fail to exercise due diligence over their agents, including by not attempting corrective measures after the fact.[33]

Given the close connection between economic development and socioeconomic rights, it is argued, MNCs' operations in the developing world are likely to enhance human rights. To the extent that MNCs create jobs, bring new capital and new technology, and provide such employee benefits as health care, they necessarily advance economic and social rights.[34] The difficulty with such logic is that it overlooks the issue of uneven development. MNCs operations usually accentuate existing inequalities, both in terms of income and wealth, by simultaneously creating pockets of poverty and wealth, development as well as underdevelopment.[35]

Perhaps the most troubling aspect of MNCs' operations in the new global economy has to do with the inordinate amount of importance attached to the portfolio investment as compared to foreign direct investment (FDI). Critics claim that MNCs' preference for portfolio investment has had devastating impacts on the economies of developing countries, especially during the 1997 Asian crisis. Importance attached to portfolio investment, which is liquid capital, flies by night and is largely driven by profit, often resulting in crony capitalism. This type of capitalism was shown to be associated with the involvement of the Salinas and Suharto families in the banking systems of Mexico and Indonesia respectively. Portfolio investment spurs purely speculative economic activities such as arbitrage, causing further economic corruption and disruption.

Furthermore, the geographic flexibility that MNCs enjoy—mostly in the form of plant relocation—leaves local communities that are dependent on them for employment increasingly vulnerable. Wealthy MNCs in the new globalized economy routinely displace well-paid workers in the North in order to exploit Southern workers in what amounts to sweatshops characterized by low pay, hazardous working conditions, child labor, and the absence of basic worker rights.[36]

William Meyer's study on the effects of MNCs' involvement in the Third World gets to the essence of the ambivalent effect they have on Third World countries. While holding to his claim that MNCs have a "net beneficial impact" on rights, Meyer acknowledges that some corporations have a

---

32. *Id.*
33. *Id.* at 523–24.
34. Kathleen Pritchard is cited as the main advocate of such thesis. *See* MEYER, *supra* note 23 at 90.
35. *Id.* at 91.
36. GEORGE F. DEMARTINO, GLOBAL ECONOMY, GLOBAL JUSTICE: THEORETICAL OBJECTIONS AND POLICY ALTERNATIVES TO NEOLIBERALISM 181 (2000).

history of human right abuses.[37] It is easy enough to prove that a Wal-Mart factory in Honduras, for example, lowers unemployment in the region, providing jobs for persons that would not have them without such a factory. This improvement does not mean, however, that this hypothetical Wal-Mart operation is in compliance with universally accepted standards of human rights. As of yet, there is no universal protocol or method to weigh the benefits and drawbacks of MNCs' activity in the Third World.

Meyer cites specific examples of MNC operations that violate second- and third-generation rights in the Third World. The Bhopal environmental disaster in India; *maquiladoras* (export-oriented factories) in Mexico, Honduras, and El Salvador; and Nike sweatshops in Indonesia and Pakistan are prime examples of human rights "violations."[38] Meyer asserts that "some MNCs try to destroy labor unions. Many MNCs do harm to the environment."[39]

Currently, there are no guidelines that the international community can use to regulate corporate activity. Some have expressed a fear that MNCs, if left to themselves and without regulation, will "opt for short-term profits at the expense of human dignity for many persons affected directly and indirectly by their practices."[40] The evidence to support this claim comes about through increasing media coverage of human rights abuses in the developing world, especially concerning so-called "sweatshop" factories used by such companies as Nike, Wal-Mart, Gap, and Reebok. One situation often studied and cited as an example is Nike's operation in Indonesia. Jim Keady, a former soccer coach at St. John's University in New York City, a school that uses Nike apparel allegedly imported from Indonesian sweatshops, quit his post as coach and went to Indonesia in August 2000 to live on the average salary a factory laborer would earn, about US $1.26 a day. Keady and his assistants set up a website[41] and kept a diary detailing their stay.

Indonesia produces more Nike products than any other nation, manufacturing 36 percent of the sneaker and apparel giant's commodities.[42] Keady, in his online journal, breaks down his projected income for a month's work at a Nike factory in Indonesia and what his paycheck amounts to: "Tomorrow, we will begin to live on the monthly wage that Nike pays the workers in the factories here (325,000 Rp [Indonesian currency], or $37 a

---

37. Meyer, *supra* note 23, at 198.
38. *Id.* at 198, 202–03.
39. *Id.* at 199.
40. Forsythe, *supra* note 14, at 199.
41. *See available at* http://www.nikewages.org. Portions of Keady's journal excerpted from the *New Haven Advocate*, Sept. 21–27, 2000.
42. Meyer, *supra* note 23, at 202.

month)."[43] The 325,000 Rp is remuneration for eight-hour days, six days a week, excluding overtime.

After substituting for major expenses (rent, water, transportation, etc.), Keady reported having 214,000 Rp to spend for the month on food, or a little more than 7,000 Rp a day. An average meal of rice and vegetables will cost an estimated 2,500 Rp—leaving him only enough money per day for two meals, with the rest going to other necessities, such as toothpaste and soap. This leaves little if any money for other major expenses; health care, child care, or even clothing. "The reality is," Keady wrote in his diary, "even with 18–30 overtime hours per week, the workers still cannot make ends meet."

Along with the squalid living conditions Keady described, he filled his diary and website with first-hand stories from factory workers. Some laborers said they were told to lie to factory inspectors when asked if they used harmful chemical agents daily (they did, and reported not doing so to auditing firms such as PriceWaterhouse Coopers), and spoke of unsanitary conditions within the factories, with only five toilets for over 2,000 workers. If Keady's report is accurate, Nike laborers in Indonesia make barely enough money to survive on, and are subject to abuses of their second- and third-generation rights to health and a clean environment.

Companies other than Nike also find themselves under intense scrutiny from human rights organizations and other forces. Wal-Mart factories in China and Honduras have been found in violation of certain human rights in their operations, especially during the Kathie Lee Gifford clothing and handbag scandal that gave the anti-sweatshop movement considerable space in mainstream US media. In Honduras, workers in *maquiladoras* reported working up to twenty hours a day making only thirty-one cents an hour; and in China, a factory used by Wal-Mart set up a phony workshop that was up to Chinese labor code to mask conditions of illegally low pay and forced overtime.[44]

Human rights abuses are not limited to Asian and Latin American factories set up by Western mercantilists, evidenced by the charges against the Unocal Oil Corporation and its operations in Myanmar (formerly Burma). A group of Burmese citizens, in conjunction with some human rights organizations, say that in building a gas pipeline through Myanmar to Thailand, Unocal participates in a project that includes "slave labor, the

---

43. Taken from *Advocate* article paraphrasing Keady's online journal. Remainder of information for this paragraph and the next two taken either from Keady's website or the *Advocate* article.

44. Meyer, *supra* note 23, at 205. *See also* Dexter Roberts & Aaron Bernstein, *A Life of Fines and Beating*, Business Week, Oct. 2, 2000; Roberts & Bernstein article *available at* http://proquest.umi.com.

forced relocation of entire villages, and, in some cases, torture, rape, and murder by Burmese soldiers."[45] The pipeline is estimated to generate about $200 million a year in revenue, money that Unocal is not likely to turn away because of a few isolated human rights concerns. In a similar case, European Union member states have consistently acted through the European Parliament to embarrass British Petroleum (BP) over its policies in Colombia that allegedly led to the repression of labor rights through brutal actions by the Colombian army in constructing a BP pipeline.[46]

The case of Royal Dutch/Shell in Nigeria is another vivid example of how MNCs have been socially irresponsible in their operations. In 1958, Royal Dutch/Shell began its oil operation in one of the most densely populated regions of Nigeria, an area in the Niger River Delta named Ogoni after the region's dominant ethnic group. Though oil production dramatically increased Nigeria's GNP, this growth, experts note, came at a horrendous cost to the 6 million people living in the Niger River Delta. The region suffered severe environmental damage, and the inhabitants of the Ogonilands who protested were subjected to systematic violent repression at the hands of the ruling military dictatorship.[47]

According to some sources, twenty-seven incidents between 1982 and 1992 resulted in a total of 1,626,000 gallons of oil being spilled from Shell's Nigerian operations. Public health has suffered as a result of a massive pollution of farmlands, fishing areas, and water supplies. In addition to poor environmental and public health safeguards, regional negligence has aggravated the country's income disparities. Since 1958, Royal Dutch/Shell has extracted some $30 billion worth of oil from the region.[48] Despite this, the Ogoni are among the poorest in the country. Of Shell's 5,000 employees in Nigeria in 1995, only 85 were Ogoni.[49] Human rights activists, including the late Ken Saro-Wiwa and other Ogoni activists, who spoke out and organized protests against such continued environmental damages, were persecuted. Shell denied any involvement in such persecutions but admitted that it had imported arms for the Nigeria military. Shell refused to intercede with the Nigerian government to object to acts of violence against the Ogoni people.[50]

---

45. Morton Winston, *John Doe vs. Unocal: The Boardroom/Courtroom Battles for Ethical Turf,* Whole Earth (Summer 1999), *available at* http://proquest.umi.com
46. Forsythe, *supra* note 14, at 208.
47. *Id.* at 197; *see also* Joyce V. Millen & Timothy H. Holtz, *Dying for Growth, Part I: Transnational Corporations and the Health of the Poor, in* Dying for Growth: Global Inequality and the Health of the Poor 177–223; *see* 194–95 (Jim Yong Kim, Joyce V. Millen, Alec Irwin, & John Gershman eds., Common Courage Press 2000).
48. Charles W.L. Hill, *Royal Dutch/Shell: Human Rights in Nigeria, in* International Business 113–16; *see* 114 (London: Irwin McGraw Hill 2000).
49. *Id.*
50. Millen & Holtz, *supra* note 47, at 194.

V. DEVELOPING A REGIME OF CORPORATE RESPONSIBILITY

Perhaps due to a growing list of human rights abuses attributable to corporate activity in the developing world, a movement for a code of conduct for MNCs is gaining momentum internationally. The idea for a code of conduct for MNCs dates back to the mid-1970s, with the first meetings of the UN Commission on Transnational Corporations.[51] This commission considered, among other things, whether the code should be mandatory or voluntary, and whether or not MNC/TNCs were significant enough actors in international economic and political relations to warrant such a code.

With the increased international attention on corporate human rights abuses in the 1990s, the international community, headed by the United Nations, addressed the issue again in the form of the Global Compact. Outlined by UN Secretary-General Kofi A. Annan at the World Economic Forum on 31 January 1999, the Compact "provides a basis for structured dialogue between the UN, business, labor, and civil society on improving corporate practices in the social arena."[52] With roots in the Universal Declaration of Human Rights (1948), the fundamental principles and rights of the International Labour Organization, and the environmental backing of the Earth Summit's Agenda, the Global Compact has a prestigious basis of literature supporting it.

The Compact sets out its guidelines for corporate practices in its nine principles. The first two principles deal with human rights in a general sense, asking corporations to support the protection of universal human rights and ensure that they are not complicit in human rights abuses. Corporations that commit themselves to the human rights cause would ensure and adhere to human rights practices not only in the workplace, but would also condemn human rights violations in the wider community. The Compact advocates workplaces that have safe and healthy working conditions, rights to basic health, education, and housing, and an end to forced or child labor.[53] The Compact asserts that in the wider community corporations should prevent forced migration, protect the local economy, and most importantly, contribute to the public debate—MNCs have both the right and the responsibility to express their views on matters that affect their operations in the community.[54]

---

51. Seymour J. Rubin, *The Transnational Corporations*, 32 ACADEMY POL. SCIENCE 120–21 (1977).
52. *See available at* http://www.un.org.
53. This, and all information regarding the Nine Principles, *available at* http://www.unglobalcompact.org.
54. *See generally* Business and Human Rights Center, *available at* http://www.business-humanrights.org/categories/issues/other/housing.

Principles three through six deal exclusively with labor issues. In these labor principles, Secretary-General Annan asked MNCs to support workers' freedom of association and right to unionize, to eliminate forced labor (such as mandatory overtime), to abolish child labor, and to eliminate discrimination in the workplace. This labor-friendly proclamation argues that unions allow for increased dialogue between workers and managers, and lead to more efficient and effective problem solving. The Compact defines forced labor as "all work or service which is exacted from any person under the menace of any penalty and for which the said person has not offered himself voluntarily." Forced labor and child labor lower the level of productivity and can damage a company's reputation internationally, the Compact asserts. It also condemns discriminatory practices, as they restrict the pool of workers available to a corporation and generally promote social fractionalization.

Principles seven through nine of the Compact address environmental issues. These three principles emphasize that MNCs should promote environmental responsibility, encourage the development of environmentally friendly technologies, and support a "precautionary approach" to environmental challenges. A precautionary approach to environmental protection suggests that companies take early actions to ensure that irreparable environmental damage does not occur because of their practices, instead of waiting until the damage is done before addressing the problem. Doing this, the Compact suggests, is more cost-effective and also protects the corporation's public image.

VI. THE CASE FOR THE SYSTEMATIC REGULATION

Will codes of conduct offer a role for MNCs to play in promoting the human rights of their workers? It is generally believed that MNCs are profit-maximizing and profit-seeking corporations that use codes as public relations tools, not for the benefit of workers.[55] Urging corporate self-regulation is a false proposition: "it is untenable to expect companies to enforce their codes voluntarily."[56] Governments and international bodies should ultimately control the workers' rights by regulating companies through both national and international legislation. Medea Benjamin, executive director of Global Exchange, notes that "It is important to talk more about international codes rather than codes that each company designs. Most codes of conduct are based on internationally recognized

---

55. CARNEGIE COUNCIL ON ETHICS AND INTERNATIONAL AFFAIRS, HUMAN RIGHTS DIALOGUE 2 (2000).
56. *See An Interview with Medea Benjamin*, 2 HUMAN RIGHTS DIALOGUE 7–9 (2000).

980   **HUMAN RIGHTS QUARTERLY**   **Vol. 25**

rights, on the ILO's own standards. These codes have been forced on companies. The companies did not want to have the codes, so the code itself is not the companies' agenda."[57]

Cynicism about international codes and instruments is widespread. At present, the standards by which the conduct of MNCs should be judged are neither uniform nor effective. Strategies that human rights NGOs have employed against governments may, therefore, be the best hope for confronting irresponsible MNCs.[58] Although the Global Compact does represent a step toward curtailing human rights abuses by MNCs, the fact remains that it is voluntary—not a mandatory set of resolutions—and does not hold corporations accountable by way of penalties or sanctions for violating its principles. In its own words, the Compact "is not a code of conduct . . . it highlights the global citizenship qualities of corporations, and opens up opportunities for focused, mediated, directed, and constructive dialogue."[59] Its failure to demand enforceable standards has rendered the Compact only a voluntary endeavor.

Human Rights Watch maintains that three obstacles stand in the way of the Compact's effectiveness: "The lack of legally enforceable standards, the lack of a monitoring and enforcement mechanism, and a lack of clarity about the meaning of the standards themselves."[60] It follows that the UN may be tarnishing its image as a protector of universal human rights by issuing a document with broad definitions of complicity that fall far short of enforcing stricter guidelines or establishing a monitoring body to ensure corporate compliance with the human rights agenda.

To guard against the Compact becoming a forum for hypocrisy, the UN should also develop a mechanism for monitoring and evaluating corporate compliance. In the absence of such a mechanism, there is a troubling possibility that the guidelines could be misinterpreted, misapplied, or ignored. That would result in corporations being given what they might claim is a "UN Seal of Approval" without having taken meaningful steps to implement the Compact's standards.

A similar view echoes this concern: the UN should never align itself with MNCs that violate the human rights that the organization holds dear. "By embracing multinationals," it is argued, "the UN has tarnished its reputation and abdicated its role as a protector of human rights. . . . The United Nations should be establishing itself as a tough, independent monitor. Instead, it's jumped into bed with some of the most notorious

---

57.   *Id.* at 9.
58.   Meintjes, *supra* note 1, at 96.
59.   *See* http://www.un.org.
60.   *See* http://www.hrw.org.

companies in the world."[61] By embracing MNCs through the Global Compact, the UN is sending a message that companies will voluntarily abide by the principles of the Compact, even though history has proven otherwise. In taking this view, the Compact will do little more than burnish the reputations of companies that are complicit in human rights violations.

Corporations, however, are increasingly realizing that they cannot continue to ignore human rights concerns. There is an increasing realization among executives of large MNCs that in order for their companies to thrive, the communities in which they do business must prosper as well. British Petroleum, for instance, has made some adjustments. The oil conglomerate has invested in computer technology in Vietnam for flood-related damage control, provided refrigerators in Zambia for the storage of anti-malaria vaccines, and has helped to replant a forest destroyed by fire in Turkey, to name a few examples.[62]

This blossoming movement is likely to help transform the human rights practices of MNCs. The challenge remains, however, to find the most effective way (voluntary or coercive) to promote corporate social responsibility. Some experts have pointed to voluntary adoption of socially responsible policies as a vital component of running a business. They have sought ways in which to modify corporations' internal cultures. The key here, they argue, is to create an environment conducive to moving beyond the legal to the ethical realm of corporate social responsibility.[63] Such a voluntary approach to code formation and enforcement, they note, "would minimize the need for further governmental regulation, which is invariably more expensive and less efficient."[64]

Some have looked to the United Nations and its Global Compact, contending that the most encouraging part of the Compact is its emphasis on the social responsibility of corporations, an aspect critical to the protection of human rights. MNCs, according to the Compact, have a responsibility not only to obey the laws of the host communities, but also to contribute to the vitality of those communities. Judgments regarding MNCs operations are directly linked to their transparency and good governance.[65] The first principle of the Compact asks that MNCs support and respect internationally proclaimed human rights "within their sphere of

---

61. Anonymous, *The UN Sells Out*, Progressive (Sept. 2000), *available at* http://proquest.umi.com.
62. Garten, *supra* note 28.
63. Alan Jones, *Social Responsibility and the Utilities*, 34 J. Bus. Ethics 219–29 (2001).
64. S. Prakash Sethi, *Corporate Codes of Conduct and the Success of Globalization*, 16 Ethics & Int'l Aff. 89–106, esp. 106 (2002).
65. Anthony F. Lang, Jr., *Enhancing the Role of Ethics in Business*, Perspectives on Ethics & Int'l Aff. 4–5 (2000).

influence."[66] While the language is vague, the Compact makes it clear that corporations' responsibilities to protect human rights do not stop at the doorsteps of their factories. MNCs have a wider responsibility—through their efforts and actions—to promote human rights interests in the surrounding community.

Within this guideline, there are some suggestions for how companies can help to promote a human rights agenda. The Compact's recommendations include MNCs taking the lead in protecting the rights of unions, especially in countries with tight labor restrictions such as China, providing medical care for laborers who have fallen ill as a result of their work, raising awareness in the community about child labor, and providing education and training for working children.

The mere adoption of a code of conduct is only the first step in a long process.[67] International law has to protect these rights by holding corporations liable if they do not comply with universally accepted human rights standards, such as those outlined in the Global Compact. By focusing solely on the economic effects of the MNCs, international law has yet to hold these companies accountable for the social effects they have on developing countries.[68]

The issue of international regulation and transnational litigation, also known as "foreign direct liability," is gaining momentum and poses a real challenge for the MNCs' operations. MNCs should adopt minimum international standards throughout their operations. Global standards can and should be enforced. The 1789 Alien Tort Claims Act is an example. Legal recourse is based on allegations of corporate complicity in violations of fundamental human rights or principles of international environmental law in controversial regimes. Several cases against US multinationals for alleged violations occurring in other countries have been heard in US courts. The victims of India's Bhopal disaster sued Union Carbide in US courts. Texaco was sued by some indigenous Amazonians for environmental damage in Ecuador. What is more, litigation is based on a call for parent companies of the MNCs to ensure that their corporate activities abroad match standards held at home.[69]

There are signs that MNCs are realizing the importance, and value, of social responsibility. US-based corporations used to hold more of a "hands-

---

66. *See* http://www.unglobalcompact.org; all information in this paragraph taken from this website.

67. Doug Cahn & Tara Holeman, *Business and Human Rights,* Forum for Applied Res. & Pub. Pol'y (1999), *available at* http://proquest.umi.com.

68. Forsythe, *supra* note 14, at 201.

69. Halina Ward, *International Litigation: Joining Up Corporate Responsibility?* (7 Dec. 2000), *available at* http://www.dundee.ac.uk/cepmlp/journal/htm/article7–19.html; *see also* Tavis, *supra* note 17, at 22.

off" policy toward human rights abuses abroad, claiming they could not realistically be held responsible for abuses undertaken in foreign factories. With increased human rights activism, sharper media scrutiny, and the intensive communications made possible by information technology, US corporations find it immensely difficult and costly to sustain the old hands-off policies. Mounting pressure has compelled them to accept responsibility for the labor practices and human rights abuses of their foreign subcontractors.[70]

VII. FILLING THE ENFORCEMENT GAP

The rights of workers and the obligations of business to the community are arguably too important to be left to the voluntary good will of the corporations. Implementing socially responsible standards for MNCs is a significant task, which needs to be "backed up by effective sanctions to motivate corporations to take such standards seriously by detecting and preventing misconduct throughout their global operations."[71] It is imperative for an outside governing body to help monitor corporate practices, and to hold MNCs accountable for documented abuses of universally accepted human rights standards. Where will this come from? And will there ever be an international regime to govern corporate social responsibility?

The preceding discussions have revolved around four key points: (1) that companies cannot be trusted to monitor their own compliance to new human rights standards; (2) that there are no existing international legal obligations that require corporate social responsibility, let alone an effective legal regime to enforce such obligations[72]; (3) that the Global Compact has made great contributions, both in terms of setting standards and monitoring standards; (4) that the lack of enforcement mechanisms or its reliance on self-monitoring should not detract from the value of the Global Compact as a first step to developing and monitoring codes of conduct.[73]

There is a need for a monitoring system outside of the corporations themselves. In the past, some MNCs have themselves contracted factory-monitoring firms to check out their overseas operations; firms such as

---

70. Debora L. Spar, *The Spotlight and the Bottom Line: How Multinationals Export Human Rights*, 77 For. Aff. 7–12 (Mar./Apr. 1998).
71. Kevin T. Jackson, *A Cosmopolitan Court for Transnational Corporate Wrongdoing: Why its Time has Come*, J. Bus. Ethics 758 (May 1998), *available at* http://proquest.umi.com.
72. William H. Meyer & Boyka Stefanova, *Human Rights, the UN Global Compact, and Global Governance*, 34 Cornell Int'l L. J. 501–21, esp. 514–15 (2001).
73. Ambassador Betty King, *The UN Global Compact: Responsibility for Human Rights, Labor Relations, and the Environment in Developing Nations*, 34 Cornell Int'l L. J. 481–85, esp. 485 (2001).

Pricewaterhouse Coopers (PWC), which performs more than 6,000 factory inspections per year for corporations such as Nike.[74] Having a corporation pay a firm of its choosing to oversee its operations, however, is like holding an election in which only members of one party can vote—the results are basically pre-determined. When the corporation itself hires the firm to examine its Third World factories, the odds are high that inspecting the firm will return a favorable review. PWC has come under fire recently by various study groups and human rights NGOs for their conflicted role in these types of deals.

A recent independent study of factories in China and Korea indicates that PWC "had a pro-management bias, did not uncover the use of carcinogenic chemicals and failed to recognize that some employees were forced to work 80-hour weeks."[75] This same study indicated that PWC and other auditing firms have a decidedly pro-corporate tilt, and do not undertake very thorough inspections, overlooking problems such as tampered time cards and a lack of safety equipment to keep workers from injuring themselves.

Certainly a cosmopolitan body to adjudicate corporate wrongdoing will not spring up overnight, nor will it ever develop without finding a balance between corporate concerns and human rights concerns. Once the international community reaches a consensus on the need for such a system, the focus should turn to finding a balance between corporate and human rights concerns, and how to give the court the power it needs to hold corporations accountable. As noted above, the issue is where will the power for this international court come from—should it have its basis in the United Nations or should it be independent of all corporate, political, and nongovernmental organizations (NGOs)? With the introduction of the Global Compact (January 1999), some human rights NGOs such as Human Rights Watch saw the UN as the logical place to house an international, unbiased corporate monitoring system for human rights abuses. "The UN forum," Seymour Rubin wrote, "is *the* appropriate arena for the analysis of TNC issues in the context of global economic relations."[76] A marked imbalance, however, exists in the United Nations between the political side, exemplified by the General Assembly and Security Council, and the economic side, represented by ECOSOC and associated functional groups, notably the ILO, IMF, World Bank and WTO. An additional theme of the draft article could be reviewing and/or revising standard views of UN effectiveness and functional organization.

---

74. Steven Greenhouse, *Report Says Global Accounting Firm Overlooks Factory Abuses*, N.Y. Times, Sept. 28, 2000, at A12.
75. *Id.*
76. Rubin, *supra* note 51, at 126.

Other advocates of an international court visualize it as a system outside of the United Nations. Economist Stephen Hymer has, since 1979, advocated an alternative strategy for Third World development that cautions against reliance on MNCs: "move away from MNCs toward a system of regional economic integration."[77] Such a policy preference has been supported by the South Commission, chaired by Tanzania's Julius Nyerere, in its final report. The South Commission has embraced the notion of regional integration and new controls over MNCs through regulation of foreign investment.[78] Whether such regional integration would prove feasible in the wake of rising global corporate power remains to be seen. One nagging question persists: how would the controls over MNCs be established and implemented as part of the monitoring system at the regional level?

Another idea has been to link the ILO with the WTO, hoping that the ILO's rights-oriented culture might join with the WTO's enforcement power and sanctioning process.[79] The ILO has observer status at the WTO, making it possible for the two to coordinate their activities. The difficulty with the WTO is that while the organization has begun to address environmental issues, member states have shied away from considering human rights and labor issues as part of its mandate.[80]

An alternative suggestion has been to create an intermediate institution that is largely free from the WTO's exclusive trade orientation and the ILO's crippling tripartite system.[81] This idea, however, is called into question by those who argue that the functions necessary for the global governance can hardly be assigned to a single entity, regardless of its enforcement capacities.[82] Increasingly, some critics call for restructuring international organizations, such as the WTO, IMF, and the World Bank, so that they can perform more effective functions of monitoring labor and environmental standards across the globe. What is needed, they argue, is a major effort to democratize the WTO. A horizontal equity-of-voting system—reflecting disjunctures between one-country, one-vote and the distribution of wealth— may be an initial step toward achieving that goal. Only then can the WTO be entrusted with the task of crafting and implementing policies for better environmental and labor standards.[83]

---

77. *Quoted in* Meyer, *supra* note 23, at 93.
78. *Id.*
79. Human Rights Watch, World Report 2001: Events of 2000, at xviii (2000).
80. Ratner, *supra* note 6, at 538.
81. World Report 2001, *supra* note 79, at xviii.
82. Meyer & Stefanova, *supra* note 72, at 519.
83. Baushik Basu, *Compacts, Conventions, and Codes: Initiative for Higher International Labor Standards*, 34 Cornell Int'l L. J. 487–500, esp. 499 (2000).

The WTO is widely regarded "as a preserve of powerful and rich nations."[84] Many developing countries simply lack the resources, including money or expertise, to fight drawn out legal battles in Geneva. Almost one quarter of the members of the WTO cannot even afford representation in Geneva.[85] A case can be made that the hyper-legalization of the WTO process does more harm than good for poor countries. The trade-law expertise of developed countries gives them a disproportionate advantage over developing countries before WTO tribunals.[86] Such structural inequalities explain why developing countries are opposed to the idea of empowering the WTO.[87]

VIII. WHAT ROLE FOR THE NGOS?

Debate continues as to what impact NGOs may have on strengthening the democratic accountability of such international organizations as the WTO. Some experts insist that NGOs' direct influence on policy should be channeled through national governments, because governments usually are more accountable to their citizens.[88] It is nation-states that negotiate the rules within the WTO, an arena in which struggles take place over what form globalization should assume, and at whose benefits or costs.[89] Although NGOs are self-selected, and not democratically elected, they can play a positive role in increasing transparency in international organizations. They deserve an observer status and a voice, but not a vote.[90] Others observe that given the pluralistic and multidimensional nature of social responsibility, neither NGOs nor governments have the wisdom or the right to lay down what corporations must do.[91]

Many critics of international organizations have challenged the notion that the WTO as presently constituted can be reformed, arguing that as long

---

84. *Id.*
85. *See* Mike Moore, Director-General of the WTO, *Open Societies Do Better*, a speech given on 9 Feb. 2000, *available at* http://www.wto.org/english/news_e/spmm_e/spmm22_e.htm.
86. Claude E. Barfield, Free Trade, Sovereignty, Democracy: The Future of the World Trade Organization 35–36 (2001).
87. Basu, *supra* note 83, at 492.
88. Barfield, *supra* note 86.
89. Ron Labonte, *Globalization and Reform of the World Trade Organization*, 92 Canadian J. Pub. Health 248–49 (2001).
90. Joseph S. Nye, Jr., *Globalization's Democratic Deficit: How to Make International Institutions More Accountable*, For. Aff. (July/Aug. 2001), *available at* http://www.foreignaffairs.org/articles/Nye0701.html.
91. Jagdish Bhagwati, *Coping with Antiglobalization: A Trilogy of Discontents*, 81 For. Aff. 2–7 (Jan./Feb. 2002).

as power resides in the hands of large transnational corporations and the big powers that support them, the WTO is unreformable.[92] It is thus essential that NGOs pressure the WTO into observing global labor, environmental, and human rights standards. Human rights NGOs are exerting increasing pressure on the MNCs to rectify their human rights abuses. FoodFirst Information and Action Network (FIAN) has contributed to the strengthening of socioeconomic and cultural rights by drafting a code of conduct on the right to food. FIAN has demanded that MNCs be made accountable to this code.[93]

The pressure for progressive change will most likely come from private actions, civil society, media exposure, and lawsuits based on civil law. Such actions would endanger the corporations' brand name and profit margin, while exposing MNCs' Achilles' heel in any attempt to ignore criticism about their labor practices.[94] Evidence suggests that corporate behavior has been increasingly influenced by means of public stigmatization. As a result, more companies may seek to avoid such negative exposures by adopting and enforcing internationally recognized human rights codes of conduct before they have been targeted.[95] Ultimately, however, without national enforcement not much can be achieved by relying solely on consumers. It is the responsibility of national governments to enact and implement global labor, environmental and human rights standards for the MNCs.[96]

IX. CONCLUSION

Given the many questions and controversies surrounding the operations of MNCs, a case can be made for holding MNCs accountable to human rights standards and for pressuring MNCs to reorient their policies and practices. Two broad conclusions can be drawn. First, MNCs have thus far shown meager interest in the sociocultural welfare or human rights of the vast majority of the people living in host countries.[97] MNCs are under no legal— much less ethical—obligations to the governments of the countries within

---

92. Yash Tandon represents an NGO called International South Group Network, *Transparency—A Casualty of Democratic and Ethical Deficit WTO*, available at http://www.seatini.org/reports/transparency.

93. Brigitte Hamm, *FoodFirst Information and Action Network, in* NGOs AND HUMAN RIGHTS: PROMISE AND PERFORMANCE 167–81 (Claude E. Welch, Jr. ed., 2001).

94. FORSYTHE, *supra* note 14, at 209–10.

95. Morton Winston, *NGO Strategies for Promoting Corporate Social Responsibility*, 16 ETHICS & INT'L AFF. 71–87, esp. 86 (2002).

96. *Id.* at 87.

97. Robert McCorquodale & Richard Fairbrother, *Globalization and Human Rights*, 21 HUM. RTS. Q. 756–66 (1999).

988   **HUMAN RIGHTS QUARTERLY**   **Vol. 25**

which they operate, even as their policies and actions affect hundreds of millions of people. Conversely, it is states that are accountable to the transnational business forces and economic private regimes set by the MNCs.[98] In the absence of international regulatory agencies, MNCs have been entirely free to devise their own rules, creating an environment less hospitable or indifferent to human rights.[99]

Secondly, corporate policies and practices are arguably subject to constant evolution, as are corporate responsibilities and obligations. MNCs have an inherent responsibility to provide for their workers and the good of the community as a whole. Workers in developing countries' factories have the same inherent human rights as the company's shareholders, and need to be treated with the same amount of dignity and respect. The urgency of "growth" and "efficiency" need not detract from the importance of preserving the human rights and dignity of labor in the developing world. In the future, growth will be problematic if it further exacerbates existing disparities. Notwithstanding the recent surge in the rhetoric of social responsibility, many corporations cannot, and will not, apply the necessary human rights agendas to their developing countries' operations without an outside monitoring agent or structure enforcing a set of standards. The lack of consensus between states and the absence of leadership among MNCs have prevented the emergence of coherent and effective standards to assess the operation of the MNCs. The UN Global Compact is unlikely to completely end MNCs' misconduct, but it is a step in the right direction. The standards addressed therein necessitate a substantial supportive system to gain merit in the international community. Corporate codes of conduct are useful to the extent that they are an integral part of the employment contracts and the right to organize.[100] Such codes, however, lack mechanisms for implementation and external monitoring and audit.[101]

Views differ with respect to the effectiveness of NGOs' strategies. Some analysts, most notably Margaret Keck and Kathryn Sikkink, find success in a series of case studies. They focus on transnational advocacy networks, which seek to bring issues to the public agenda by framing them in innovative ways and by seeking hospitable venues. Keck and Sikkink isolate four approaches. *Information politics,* they argue, involves promoting change by reporting facts—whose impact is heightened if the information is timely and dramatic. *Symbolic politics* refers to major events, such as the

---

98. Peter Schwab & Adamantia Pollis, *Globalization's Impact on Human Rights, in* Human Rights: New Perspectives, New Realities 209–21, esp. 212 (Admantia Pollis & Peter Schwab eds., 2000).

99. *Id.* at 214.

100. United Nations Development Program, Human Development Report 2000, at 75 (2000).

101. *Id.* at 80.

1973 coup in Chile, that help create awareness of major international issues. *Leverage politics* allows weak NGOs to influence state practices directly, both materially and morally. Finally, *accountability politics* relies upon governments' public positions on democracy, human rights or (for purposes of this paper) corporate responsibility, to expose the distance between discourse and practice.[102]

Morton Winston utilized Keck and Sikkink's typology in his analysis of Amnesty International (AI), arguably the world's preeminent human rights advocacy organization.[103] However, he modified their concept of network, noting that formal movements like AI grew out of a pre-existing social movement within global civil society. This human rights network gave rise to AI and other such organizations or transnational advocacy networks. Winston also notes some inherent weaknesses in AI: its reliance on the mass media for attention and the limited political analysis of its reports; the limited thrill of its prisoner of conscience campaigns in recent years; the lack of action from its efforts to use MNCs for leverage on governments; and the need to focus on implementation of existing human rights norms, not on creation of new norms. AI urged MNCs to engage in dialogue and adopt codes of conduct. Human Rights Watch has also focused on corporations and human rights, although its main attention has been given to its five regional divisions and three thematic divisions.[104]

Whether the answer lies in restructuring international organizations, linking their strengths, enhancing private actions and media exposure, or creating a single intermediary institution, or regional or global governance, the case for the MNCs' self-policing is utterly unpersuasive. In the current global economy, MNCs and their shareholders are able to reap enormous benefits, and use their power to take advantages of workers and governments alike. If they can benefit from this increasingly interdependent global economy, it is only fair that they accept the responsibilities that go along with these economic gains.

---

102. Margaret E. Keck & Kathryn Sikkink, Activists Beyond Borders: Advocacy Networks in International Politics 16–25 (1998).
103. Morton E. Winston, *Assessing the Effectiveness of International Human Rights NGOs: Amnesty International, in* NGOs and Human Rights, *supra* note 93, at 26–54, esp. 31.
104. Widney Brown, *Human Rights Watch, in* NGOs and Human Rights, *supra* note 93, at 72–84.

[6]

Human Rights: The Emerging Norm of Corporate Social Responsibility

Claire Moore Dickerson[*]

The conduct of many multinational corporations suggests that corporate social responsibility means more than profit maximization. These companies are refraining from corrupt practices, are adopting minimum standards for treatment of workers, and are providing certain drugs at below-market prices. The changes in behavior reflect both the corporations' growing acceptance of responsibility toward more than shareholders, and their respect for the power of the collective, even when composed of individually vulnerable persons. Further, whatever the motive for these changes, the actual behavior has social influence.

Meantime, human-rights norms are now evolving toward an increased recognition of the collective as well. Included among the civil and political rights, and the economic, social, and cultural rights, are rights that are most effective when used by a group. The solidarity rights, including the right to development, are a natural culmination of that trend. These norms emerge from the larger society that extends beyond the developed world, and certainly far beyond the corporations' commercial environment. A democratic process of admittedly varying formality and effectiveness creates and legitimates these norms.

The feedback between (1) corporations' conduct in support of the collective and (2) the human-rights norms' move toward the collective, reinforce each other. Thus, the multinationals' behavior becomes more predictably compatible with human-rights norms, while these norms further support the corporations' move toward conduct consistent with human rights. The behavior and the norms, together, reflect a developing notion of corporate social responsibility that concerns the well-being of all those affected by the multinationals, and not only the shareholders.

* Professor of Law and Arthur L. Dickson Scholar, Rutgers University Law School. A.B. 1971, Wellesley College; J.D. 1974, Columbia University Law School; LL.M. in Taxation 1981, New York University Law School. Particular thanks go to Professors Berta Esperanza Hernández-Truyol and Gregory A. Mark for their generous and insightful comments. Thanks also to the Alfred P. Sloan Foundation and the George Washington University Law School, as well as the participants at their joint colloquium held June 24-27, 2002.

I. INTRODUCTION

The story is simple. In the past, the leaders of the commercial and corporate arena have defined the normative aspects of corporate social responsibility and have sought to control it as a positive matter.[1] This cannot be appropriate. These leaders have arrogated the power to themselves although the corporation owes its existence to a much larger community: to society as a whole.

Ironically, moreover, the practical reality today is that some multinational corporations' actual behavior is becoming more respectful of nonshareholder rights than the classic corporate social responsibility norm requires. As a matter of conduct, multinationals recognize the rights of persons other than shareholders,[2] and a growing appreciation of the power of groups influences this evolving behavior.[3] Both Nike and Wal-Mart, for example, have adopted codes of conduct

---

1.   *See infra* Part II.A.
2.   *See infra* Part II.B.
3.   *See infra* Part IV.A.

that articulate concern for the rights of developing-country workers.[4] What is the source of this different understanding of corporate social responsibility? It is a general change in perception, which increasingly conforms to norms of the East and South,[5] and which is reflected in the evolving human-rights norms.

Interestingly, as the human-rights norms are becoming worldwide as opposed to purely West/North-dominated, they are becoming more collective in nature. Collective both in the sense that some individual rights have a collective impact and in the sense that some of the most recently articulated rights belong to a group, not merely to an individual.[6] The emphasis on groups is a recognition that the more vulnerable are significant at least as a collective; the behavior of U.S.-based multinationals reflects this same understanding.

As multinationals' behavior becomes consistent with the emerging human-rights norms, the behavior reinforces the norms and vice versa. Further, because the human-rights norms emerge through a kind of unstructured, loose process akin to democracy, these norms—and the behavior consistent with them—acquire the type of legitimacy afforded to democratically approved conclusions. As corporate behavior begins to recognize the rights of a collective whose individuals are relatively powerless, the increasingly collective human-rights norms accord a reflected legitimacy to that behavior.[7]

This convergence of actual behavior and human-rights norms describes the new corporate social responsibility—a concept that is descriptive and normative, and is based on the will of a community far broader than the narrow commercial-corporate arena in which corporations have traditionally been thought to operate.[8] Further, as individuals as well as states gain rights under human-rights jurisprudence, this expression of corporate social responsibility increasingly becomes enforceable.[9]

---

4. *See* Nike, *Code of Conduct*, *at* http://www.nikebiz.com/labor/code.shtml (last visited Feb. 24, 2002). For the form current in 1996, see Bureau of Int'l Labor Affairs, U.S. Dep't of Labor, The Apparel Industry and Codes of Conduct: A Solution to the International Child Labor Problem? 165 (1996), *available at* http://www.dol.gov/dol/ilab/public/library/reports/iclp/apparel/apparel.pdf (last visited Feb. 22, 2002) [hereinafter Codes of Conduct]; *id.* at 200 (Wal-Mart Stores, Inc., Standards for Vendor Partners); *id.* at 165 (Nike Code of Conduct). For a discussion of the ambiguity of the multinationals' motives, see *infra* Part II.B.

5. *See infra* note 66 and accompanying text.

6. *See infra* Part III.A.

7. *See infra* Parts II.B, III.B.

8. *See infra* Part III.B.

9. *See infra* Part IV.B.

II.   EVOLUTION OF UNITED STATES MULTINATIONALS' BEHAVIOR IN
      THE GLOBAL ENVIRONMENT: THE NORMATIVE ARTICULATION
      (CORPORATE SOCIAL RESPONSIBILITY) AND THE DESCRIPTIVE
      OUTCOME

Statements about appropriate behavior, and behavior itself, are
two manifestations of a norm. Statements and behavior also influence
each other.[10] Thus, to understand corporate social responsibility, we
must review both the verbal expressions about appropriate behavior
and corporations' actual behavior.

A.   *A Recent History of the Normative Articulation: Corporate
      Social Responsibility*

Almost three decades ago, Milton Friedman asserted in simple,
blunt terms that the role of the corporation is to maximize shareholder
profits. The value underlying the implication is equally straightforward: managers who opt for goals other than shareholder profit
maximization may hurt the economy, and are arrogating to themselves
taxing powers granted only to the government.[11]

Later theorists, including, in particular, neoclassical law and
economics scholars, relied on the concept of efficiency to justify their
support of shareholder profit maximization. The socially responsible
corporation acts in an "efficient" manner.[12] This articulation masks the

---

10.   JOHN C. TURNER, SOCIAL INFLUENCE 16 (1991) (asserting that "social interaction"
creates social norms); *see also id.* at 4-5 (noting that compliance with norms can be willing,
i.e., driven by a desire to conform, or unwilling, i.e., coerced).

11.   *See* Milton Friedman, *A Friedman Doctrine–The Social Responsibility of
Business Is to Increase Its Profits*, N.Y. TIMES, Sept. 13, 1970, (Magazine), at 32 (stating that
efficiency considerations prohibit corporate management from spending corporate funds for
general social purposes); *id.* at 122 (stating that the manager who spends corporate money
other than to maximize shareholder profit is taxing the corporation; and in any event, the
manager is not in a position to know what action to take, for example, to reduce inflation); *id.*
at 126 ("[T]here is one and only one social responsibility of business–to use its resources and
engage in activities designed to increase its profits so long as it stays within the rules of the
game.").

12.   RICHARD A. POSNER, ECONOMIC ANALYSIS OF LAW § 4.11, at 460 (5th ed. 1998)
(asserting that profit maximization is the only viable purpose); *see also id.* § 1.2, at 13-15
(discussing efficiency and noting that the Kaldor-Hicks definition of efficiency is more
realistic than the Paredo measure); Chris William Sanchirico, *Deconstructing the New
Efficiency Rationale*, 86 CORNELL L. REV. 1003, 1005 (2001) (asserting that law and
economics's dominant principle is efficiency). The law and economics scholars are important
because they have been the dominant voice. *See, e.g.*, Donald C. Langevoort, *Theories,
Assumptions, and Securities Regulation: Market Efficiency Revisited*, 140 U. PA. L. REV.
851, 916 (1992) (stating that the law and economics school is dominant); David Millon, *New
Game Plan or Business as Usual? A Critique of the Team Production Model of Corporate
Law*, 86 VA. L. REV. 1001, 1003 (2000) (same).

existence of an underlying value, such as wealth maximization. Early responses to this neoclassical school challenged the implication that efficiency is value neutral. For example, if the value underlying efficiency is egalitarian, then the "efficient" act may be redistributional rather than profit-maximizing.[13]

Taking a different tack, within the last ten years the progressives have argued that social responsibility requires the corporation to consider all relevant stakeholders. In addition to shareholders, the stakeholders have typically included others who had made an investment in the corporation. Employees who have invested human capital are the classic example of a nonshareholder stakeholder. The progressives' perspective was bolstered by states' adoption of so-called "constituency statutes," which expressly permit the board of directors to consider constituents other than shareholders.[14]

If the statutes had mandated, rather than merely permitted, consideration of nonshareholder stakeholders, the progressives would in all likelihood have succeeded in broadening the articulation of corporate social responsibility.[15] As it was however, challenges to the shareholder profit maximization model have continued. The team production model is a recent attempt to raise the issue of shareholder primacy from a different perspective: what role do shareholders have anyway?[16] Another approach allows the corporation to maximize its shareholders' profit, but asks that it do so using a long-term

---

13. *See* Sanchirico, *supra* note 12, at 1006 n.3, 1069-70 (arguing for the importance of equity, of "equality of economic well-being," to the definition of efficiency); *see also* Richard S. Markovits, *Duncan's Do Nots: Cost-Benefit Analysis and the Determination of Legal Entitlements*, 36 STAN. L. REV. 1169, 1176-77, 1194 (1984) (suggesting either utilitarianism or egalitarianism as the values in connection with the efficiency analysis).

14. *See, e.g.*, Lawrence E. Mitchell, *Groundwork of the Metaphysics of Corporate Law*, 50 WASH. & LEE L. REV. 1477, 1477-88 (1993) (discussing stakeholders' rights); Marleen A. O'Connor, *The Human Capital Era: Reconceptualizing Corporate Law to Facilitate Labor-Management Cooperation*, 78 CORNELL L. REV. 899, 951 (1993) (discussing human capital, stakeholders, and stakeholder statutes). This progressive perspective antedates the last decade of the twentieth century. *See, e.g.*, William W. Bratton, *Berle and Means Reconsidered at the Century's Turn*, 26 J. CORP. L. 737, 761-62 (2001) (discussing the interchange between Dodd and Berle concerning the proper object of corporate benefits: the shareholders or a broader definition of constituencies, and noting that this interchange presaged disputes of the latter part of the twentieth century).

15. *See* O'Connor, *supra* note 14, at 951 (noting that all but one of the stakeholder statutes is permissive); *see also* Millon, *supra* note 12, at 1008-09 (acknowledging that the progressives have not been able to shake the law and economics school's dominance). This appears to be a declaration against interest; Professor Millon's credentials as a progressive are impeccable. *See* David Millon, *Communitarianism in Corporate Law: Foundations and Law Reform Strategies*, *in* PROGRESSIVE CORPORATE LAW 1 (Lawrence E. Mitchell ed., 1995).

16. *See* Margaret M. Blair & Lynn A. Stout, *A Team Production Theory of Corporate Law*, 85 VA. L. REV. 247 (1999). *But see* Millon, *supra* note 12.

perspective. This change in time horizon encourages the corporation to maximize labor's productivity by treating workers relatively well.[17]

Each of these perspectives, from the focus on the value underlying efficiency to the discussion of stakeholders and shareholders, focuses insistently on the corporation. In fact, however, the multinationals' actual behavior both reflects and demands a broader, society-wide point of departure.

B. *Multinationals' Actual Behavior Today Diverges from Shareholder Profit Maximization*

As a descriptive matter, the actual behavior of even highly visible corporations has already moved beyond the Friedman/neoclassical model. To appreciate the present, to understand that current standards are part of a progression, and generally to accept that standards are not immutable, it is useful to recognize that the corporation in the United States has already seen the public perception of its purpose evolve from purely public to increasingly private over the past two hundred years.[18] The question, then, is to identify what form this private purpose takes: does a review of corporate conduct reveal shareholder profit maximization, or some other standard?

Recently, prominent multinationals formed under the laws of U.S. states have behaved in ways that are consistent with responsibility to more than their shareholders. While this is not the only possible interpretation of multinational conduct, the corporations have demonstrated attention to the plight of workers through adoption of codes of conduct, the concern for payee-country residents through the anticorruption movement, and the recognition of obligations to actual and potential customers of, in particular, certain pharmaceuticals.[19] The motivation of the multinationals–of their management–is irrelevant when considering the impact of the multinationals' action. Initially, the significant question is how those who witness the

---

17.   *See* LAWRENCE E. MITCHELL, CORPORATE IRRESPONSIBILITY: AMERICA'S NEWEST EXPORT 116 (2001) (asserting that managers' very short time horizons contribute to their willingness to "skimp" on employees' well-being).

18.   The vast majority of corporations formed before 1800, including during the colonial period, were "essentially utilities . . . . almost 80 percent were for highways and local public services." Gregory A. Mark, *The Court and the Corporation: Jurisprudence, Localism, and Federalism,* 1997 SUP. CT. REV. 403, 413. However, as state laws allowed freer incorporation rather than requiring a special state grant, the corporation's purpose became less public in nature. Gregory A. Mark, Comment, *The Personification of the Business Corporation in American Law,* 54 U. CHI. L. REV. 1441, 1448 (1987). The discussion of private versus public purposes has continued over the past one hundred years.

19.   *See infra* notes 20-30 and accompanying text.

multinationals' performance interpret that behavior. In other words, it is appearance that matters.[20]

First, reviewing the treatment of developing-country workers: since the beginning of the 1990s, U.S.-based multinationals have adopted codes of conduct that purport to regulate their suppliers' labor practices with respect to those workers.[21] Although these codes are often honored in the breach,[22] and although the multinationals' managers may in fact have other motivations,[23] to the extent that the multinationals do insist on improved conditions, their behavior does display a concern for the workers' condition.[24] Indeed, there is some

---

20.   *See* TURNER, *supra* note 10, at 3, 40-42, 44 (defining "norms" and discussing internalized norms).

21.   For codes of conduct of three major multinational enterprises based in the United States, in the form current in 1996, shortly after the publicity began to have an impact, see, for example, CODES OF CONDUCT, *supra* note 4, at 200 (Wal-Mart Stores, Inc., Standards for Vendor Partners); *id.* at 165 (Nike Code of Conduct); *id.* at 155 (Levi Strauss & Co. Global Sourcing & Operating Guidelines). In 1991, Levi Strauss was the first multinational enterprise to write a code of conduct. Levi Strauss & Co., *Social Responsibility/Sourcing Guidelines, at* http://www.levistrauss.com/responsibility/conduct/ (last visited Feb. 24, 2002); *see also* Editorial, *Citizen Shell*, N.Y. TIMES, Mar. 31, 1997, at A14. Nike first adopted its code of conduct in 1992. *Nike Employing Andrew Young*, N.Y. TIMES, Feb. 26, 1997, at D2. *See generally* Claire Moore Dickerson, *Transnational Codes of Conduct Through Dialogue: Leveling the Playing Field for Developing-Country Workers*, 53 FLA. L. REV. 611, 613 n.8 (2001).

22.   *See, e.g., Group Links Pentagon, Firms to Child Labor*, WASH. POST, Dec. 22, 2000, at A9 [hereinafter *Group Links Pentagon*] (reporting accusations that Nike, Sharper Image, and Kohl's sell goods produced overseas under abusive working conditions and the companies' assertions that the conditions are appropriate to the region). Nike has a formal code of conduct. *See* Code of Conduct, *supra* note 4, at 165. Neither Kohl's nor Sharper Image publishes a code of conduct on their Web site. However, Kohl's appears to have one. *See Group Links Pentagon, supra*, at A9 (reporting that a spokeswoman for Kohl's says that PricewaterhouseCoopers reported violations of the "code" at an overseas factory). It is unclear whether Sharper Image has a formal code, but it assertedly investigates conditions. *Id.* (reporting that according to a Sharper Image spokeswoman, it conducts investigations of factories in China); *see also* Stephanie Strom, *A Sweetheart Becomes Suspect: Looking Behind Those Kathie Lee Labels*, N.Y. TIMES, June 27, 1996, at D1 (reporting that in 1996 Wal-Mart was again responsible for marketing clothes manufactured by children, this time by thirteen- and fourteen-year-old Hondurans). Thus, absent a concerted effort marshaled by an international agency such as the International Labour Organization (ILO), it is unlikely that the multinationals' behavior will predictably and consistently work to improve labor conditions. *See generally* Dickerson, *supra* note 21, at 614.

23.   The multinationals' managers may be motivated to comply with the perceived desire of developed-country consumers. *See generally* Dickerson, *supra* note 21.

24.   An international consensus can remain one even if honored in the breach. *See* Filártiga v. Peña-Irala, 630 F.2d 876, 884 n.15 (2d Cir. 1980) (holding that international customary law remains law even if breached). In any event, the multinationals' behavior has improved. *See, e.g., Group Links Pentagon, supra* note 22, at A9 (quoting a Nike spokesperson claiming that wages paid "far surpass regional or national minimum wages"); *see also* Jaime Sneider, Editorial, *Good Propaganda, Bad Economics*, N.Y. TIMES, May 16, 2000, at A23 (reporting that Nike wages in Vietnam are "more than twice the country's

evidence of improvement in the working conditions of workers after the multinationals have received media attention.[25]

Second, consider anticorruption. The developed countries engineered adoption of the Organization for Economic Cooperation and Development's (OECD) recent antibribery convention (OECD Convention);[26] at least to some degree, U.S.-based multinationals supported that effort.[27] This looks like an other-regarding move by the multinationals: although corruption subjects the bribe-receiving country's population to economic distortions, the ability to pay bribes can be advantageous to developed-country multinationals.[28] The

average annual income"). The watchdogs are unconvinced of the adequacy of improvements. *See, e.g., Group Links Pentagon, supra* note 22, at A9. If, however, the managers are unskilled or unlucky enough that a motivation for improving these conditions is visibly other than to help workers, then the behavior does not create social influence in favor of improving conditions. *See generally* Dickerson, *supra* note 21 (discussing other pressures, including in particular developed-country consumers, and thus other motivations for improving conditions).

25.   Nike claims that, having been battered by the media, it has improved its own performance, including the effectiveness of its monitoring. *See* Maureen Minehan, *Nike Offers Lessons on Corporate Responsibility*, 5 No. 24 HR POLICIES & PRACTICES UPDATE 1 (Nov. 24, 2001); *see also* William H. Meyer & Boyka Stefanova, *Human Rights, the UN Global Compact, and Global Governance*, 34 CORNELL INT'L L.J. 501, 502-03 (2001) (discussing the "spotlight effect" and its favorable impact on multinationals). *But see* Meyer & Stefanova, *supra*, at 513 n.35 (noting that Nike's insistence on self-monitoring allows critics to doubt Nike's claims of improvement in working conditions).

26.   *See, e.g.*, Convention on Combating Bribery of Foreign Public Officials in International Business Transactions, Dec. 18, 1997, 37 I.L.M. 1 (1998); International Anti-Bribery and Fair Competition Act of 1998, Pub. L. 105-366, 112 Stat. 3302 (amending the Foreign Corrupt Practices Act (FCPA), 15 U.S.C. §§ 78dd-1 to -2 (2000), to conform to the OECD Convention); *see also* Douglass Cassel, *Corporate Initiatives: A Second Human Rights Revolution?*, 19 FORDHAM INT'L L.J. 1963, 1970 (1996) (referring to twenty-six members; now there are twenty-eight); *see also* Paul B. Stephan, *Creative Destruction—Idiosyncratic Claims of International Law and the Helms-Burton Legislation*, 27 STETSON L. REV. 1341, 1343 (1998) (stating the United States' economic and strategic power are unparalleled).

27.   Mickey Kantor, who then was the United States Trade Representative, asserted that the FCPA cost U.S. business $45 billion in 1994 alone. His estimates came from the Central Intelligence Agency. Paul Lewis, *Corruption Is Now Under Global Attack*, COMMERCIAL APPEAL, Nov. 29, 1996, at 5B.

28.   *See id.* (reporting that the FCPA cost U.S. business $45 billion in 1994). Corruption may be, but is not necessarily, inefficient. *See* J.S. Nye, *Corruption and Political Development: A Cost-Benefit Analysis*, 61 AM. POL. SCI. REV. 417, 419-21 (1967); *see also* Susan Rose-Ackerman, *Reducing Bribery in the Public Sector, in* CORRUPTION & DEMOCRACY: POLITICAL INSTITUTIONS, PROCESSES AND CORRUPTION IN TRANSITION STATES IN EAST-CENTRAL EUROPE AND IN THE FORMER SOVIET UNION 21, 24-25 (Duc V. Trang ed., 1994). Corruption may give rise in some circumstances to the "efficient" result. *See, e.g.*, Rose-Ackerman, *supra*, at 24-25 (asserting that anticorruption is not dogmatic as corruption may be efficient, depending on the circumstances). However, it is only a second-best solution. *See* Susan Rose-Ackerman, *Corruption and Democracy*, 90 AM. SOC'Y INT'L L. PROC. 83, 84 (1996).

multinationals appear to be protecting the populations that would suffer from the distortions. To be sure, there also is evidence that the multinationals voiced support for the OECD Convention principally in order to reduce their own expenses by eliminating upward competition among suppliers of bribes.[29] Nevertheless, to the extent that multinationals have moderated their bribe payments since adoption of the OECD Convention,[30] the multinationals' conduct is optically consistent with a desire to benefit host-country residents, even at the multinationals' own expense. The anticorruption efforts ostensibly do continue, although it is too early to have proof of the OECD Convention's success in reducing bribe payment.[31]

Finally, we turn to the pharmaceutical manufacturers' expression of concern for actual and potential customers in the developing world. In 2001, the developed-country pharmaceutical companies, supported by home country governments, fought off demands that they drastically reduce the price of anti-HIV/AIDS drugs sold to South Africa.[32] The specific point of pressure was a South African law that encouraged use of generic drugs in that country.[33] The concern of the multinationals was not limited to loss of revenue from South Africa: they were also worried that drugs produced in South Africa would be imported as gray-market goods in the developed world, thereby cutting into the multinationals' highly profitable markets there.[34]

The pharmaceutical manufacturers' recalcitrance continued in the face of a worldwide pandemic that had already cost over sixteen

---

29.   *See* Jong Bum Kim, *Korean Implementation of the OECD Bribery Convention: Implications for Global Efforts to Fight Corruption*, 17 UCLA PAC. BASIN L.J. 245, 274 (2000) ("The OECD Bribery Convention . . . deals only with active bribery or the supply side of corruption. . . ."). *See generally* Dickerson, *supra* note 21, at 654.

30.   By mid-2001, all but three of the OECD Convention's signatories had enacted implementing legislation. *See* Enery Quinones, *Implementing the Anti-Bribery Convention: An Update from the OECD*, *in* TRANSPARENCY INTERNATIONAL, GLOBAL CORRUPTION REPORT 197, 198 (2001), *available at* http://www.globalcorruptionreport.org/download/gi_oecd_convention.pdf (last visited July 2, 2002).

31.   It is still too early to determine to what extent multinationals have in fact moderated bribe-payment: the first systematic review of performance under the OECD Convention will be the 2002 Transparency International Bribe Payers' Index. *See id.* at 202.

32.   *See, e.g.*, Rachel L. Swarns, *Fight Ends in S. Africa Over Cheaper AIDS Drugs*, SAN DIEGO UNION-TRIB., Apr. 20, 2001, at A1, *available at* 2001 WL 6455238.

33.   *See id.* (reporting that two months before they eventually capitulated, the pharmaceutical companies did finally lose support from the United States).

34.   *See, e.g.*, World Trade Organization (WTO), *Experts: Affordable Medicines for Poor Countries Are Feasible*, *at* http://www.wto.org/english/news_e/pres01_e/pr220_e.htm (Apr. 11, 2001) (acknowledging that in order to allow pharmaceutical companies' to recover costs while causing medicines to be available at lower prices in developing countries, the system must avoid imports of cheap drugs into "rich country markets").

million lives, and that had infected another thirty-three million people.[35]   Eventually, however, embarrassed by negative publicity worldwide, the pharmaceutical companies agreed to lower the price for sale of the antiviral and related drugs to South Africa, and to withdraw their suit triggered by the South African law permitting manufacture of generics.[36]   The pharmaceutical companies succumbed to pressure from many sources outside the narrow commercial world, running the gamut from consumer groups to the United Nations (U.N.), and the companies' ultimate behavior is consistent with a concern for the currently and potentially infected.[37]

These examples illustrate that certain highly visible multinationals may well not be ignoring all other players in favor of their shareholders.   Instead, the multinationals are behaving more generously–not less so–to nonshareholders than would be expected under a strict shareholder-profit model of corporate social responsibility.   The riposte is that in each of their situations, the multinationals' management is still seeking to maximize shareholder profits, and is merely incorporating changed circumstances into its strategy.   By treating developing-country workers better, the multinationals are responding to consumers in developed-country markets, and hence are protecting revenues; by ceasing to pay bribes, they are reducing their costs and thus increasing their profits; by reducing the price of anti-HIV/AIDS drugs sold to the developing

---

35.   *See, e.g.,* World Health Organization (WHO), *AIDS Not Losing Momentum— HIV Has Infected 50 Million, Killed 16 Million, Since Epidemic Began, at* http://www.who.int/inf-pr-1999/en/pr99-66.html (Nov. 23, 1999).   In South Africa, the average level of HIV infection is just over ten percent, but there are areas of the country with an infection rate as high as thirty-six percent.   Rachel L. Swarns, *South Africa's AIDS Vortex Engulfs a Rural Community,* N.Y. TIMES, Nov. 25, 2001, at A1 (reporting on the level of HIV infection in a community within Zululand).

36.   *See* Swarns, *supra* note 32 (reporting that the multinationals dropped their lawsuit).   *See generally* Claire Moore Dickerson, *Culture and Transborder Effects: Northern Individualism Meets Third-Generation Human Rights,* 54 RUTGERS. L. REV. § 2(b) (forthcoming 2002).

37.   For evidence of the U.N. involvement in the health crisis, see WHO, *supra* note 35.   For other pressure points, see generally Ben Barber, *Global Groups seek AIDS Drugs for Poor Patients; Drug Firms Back Off From Patents,* WASH. TIMES (D.C.), Mar. 19, 2001, at A13, *available at* 2001 WL 4149188 (reporting that consumer groups were planning to participate, together with AIDS advocacy groups and major drug companies, in the April 2001 joint meeting of the WHO and WTO in Norway); *see also Joint Communiqué from Secretary-General and Seven Leading Research-Based Pharmaceutical Companies on Access to HIV/AIDS Care and Treatment,* SG/SM/7982, AIDS/34, *at* http://www.un.org/News/Press/docs/2001/ sgsm7982.doc.htm (Oct. 4, 2001) (reflecting discussion leading to reduction of prices and increase in general health-care assistance).

world, the multinationals are protecting their reputations, and therefore their profits, in the developed world.

Consider this, however. Initially, the multinationals ignored developing-country workers, they paid bribes, and they charged the same high price for HIV/AIDS drugs worldwide. Then, at least as regards working conditions and anti-HIV/AIDS drugs, the multinationals changed their behavior when confronted by collective outrage emanating from a community far broader than the corporate world. This community pressure is new, and it did force the multinationals' management to take into account constituencies beyond the shareholders.

III. EVOLUTION OF THE HUMAN-RIGHTS NORMS: FROM THE INDIVIDUAL TO THE INCREASINGLY COLLECTIVE

Optically, the conduct of these multinationals has gotten ahead of traditional concepts of corporate social responsibility. A review of human-rights norms sourced in a community that extends beyond the commercial-corporate and beyond the West/North sets up a comparison of corporate behavior to current influences, rather than merely to traditional assumptions.

A. *A Brief History of the Three Generations' Move Toward Collective Rights*

Human rights are frequently categorized by "generations" representing the evolution of these norms.[38] These are only rough categories, and many rights do fit into more than one generation. The concept of generations nevertheless highlights the evolution of the group's, of the collective's status in the context of human rights.

Starting with the first so-called "generation" of human rights, and without going back before the eighteenth century,[39] it is fair to suggest that these civil and political rights focus on protecting individuals against abuse by governments.[40] They are memorialized in the

---

38. Berta Esperanza Hernández-Truyol, *Human Rights Through a Gendered Lens: Emergence, Evolution, Revolution, in* 1 WOMEN AND INTERNATIONAL HUMAN RIGHTS LAW 3, 25-29 (Kelly D. Askin & Dorean M. Koenig eds., 1999) (presenting a general overview of the three generations).

39. For a summary of earlier influences, see, for example, PAUL GORDON LAUREN, THE EVOLUTION OF INTERNATIONAL HUMAN RIGHTS: VISIONS SEEN 4-20 (1998) (discussing the early philosophical and religious origins of human rights).

40. *See, e.g.,* Louis B. Sohn, *The New International Law: Protection of the Rights of Individuals Rather Than States,* 32 AM. U. L. REV. 1, 22 (1982) (discussing civil and political rights as against the state).

International Convention on Civil and Political Rights (ICCPR)[41] and are principally negative: the state is, generally, asked to abstain from an exercise of power that compromises an individual's autonomy.[42] Included in the first generation are the right to free expression and the right to associate, which clearly are negative, but also the right to vote[43]—a right that, by its nature, requires affirmative governmental intervention.[44] Thus, although first-generation rights are primarily negative, they are not wholly so: as the United States illustrated during the presidential election of 2000, the state that fails to act affirmatively does not ensure its citizens' right to vote.[45] However useful the negative-positive dichotomy may be in describing an overall evolution, the distinction may be without a difference in other arenas.[46]

Among the three illustrations of corporate behavior, the first, relating to the treatment of overseas workers who are employees of a U.S.-based multinational's suppliers, is most clearly within the first generation: the rights of workers directly implicate freedom of expression and association.[47] To the extent that political corruption

41.   International Covenant on Civil and Political Rights (ICCPR), Dec. 16, 1966, 999 U.N.T.S. 171 (entered into force Mar. 23, 1976); Sohn, *supra* note 40, at 23 (discussing first-generation rights in the ICCPR).

42.   *See* ISAIAH BERLIN, FOUR ESSAYS ON LIBERTY 122-23 (1969) (discussing negative freedom as freedom from interference).

43.   *See* Sohn, *supra* note 40, at 24 (discussing rights included in the first generation).

44.   Berlin's positive freedom is different in that it describes the individual as master of self, without creating any state-based obligations. *See* BERLIN, *supra* note 42, at 131-32.

45.   *See* U.S. Comm'n on Civil Rights, *Executive Summary: Voting Irregularities in Florida During the 2000 Presidential Election, at* http://www.usccr.gov/pubs/vote2000/report/exesum.htm (last visited Feb. 22, 2002) (stating that 14.4% of "Florida's black voters cast ballots that were rejected," as compared with 1.6% of "nonblack Florida voters," and that the responsibility falls on an "overall lack of leadership" on the part of the state's political leaders). The Commission describes itself as "independent, bipartisan, fact-finding agency of the executive branch."   U.S. Comm'n on Civil Rights, *About the Commission, at* http://usccr.gov (last visited Aug. 4, 2002). However, others view it as partisan. *See, e.g.,* Katharine Q. Seelye, *U.S. Rights Commission Blocks Seating of Bush Nominee,* N.Y. TIMES, Dec. 8, 2001, at A10 (reporting that Democrats on the Commission "outmaneuvered" the White House); *see also Sleight of Hand at the Polls,* BUSINESS WK. ONLINE, Nov. 27, 2000, *at* http://www.businessweek.com/2000/00_48/b3709015.htm (last visited July 2, 2002) (arguing that government did not do enough to prevent manipulation of the absentee ballots). On the other hand, there also were allegations of affirmative governmental interference, including improper targeting of minorities by Florida's state police. *Id.*

46.   *See, e.g.,* Susan Bandes, *The Negative Constitution: A Critique,* 88 MICH. L. REV. 2271, 2279-85 (1990) (arguing, in the context of the United States Constitution, that the distinction between action and inaction is meaningless).

47.   *See, e.g.,* ICCPR, *supra* note 41, arts. 18, 22 (concerning freedom of expression and association, respectively). As of December 7, 2001, 145 states have ratified the ICCPR, fifty-six with some qualification; the United States ratified the ICCPR on June 8, 1992, noting in its Declarations, that "articles 1 through 27 are not self-executing," U.N., *International Covenant on Civil and Political Rights, at* http://untreaty.un.org/English/sample/

effectively disenfranchises citizens by creating an occult method of participating in government as a way of bypassing normal voting procedures, anticorruption efforts, also, fit under first-generation rights.[48] The anti-HIV/AIDS drug example implicates first-generation rights, too, including the rights to life, bodily integrity, and human dignity.[49]

In each of these categories of rights, the individual is definitely the focus of protection,[50] but, because the first generation of human rights really is about balancing the power of the state against the collective of the vulnerable,[51] some first-generation rights have distinctly collective aspects. The right to association emphasizes that directly, but freedom of expression's protection of the press and the right to vote similarly create a space in which the vulnerable can, by exercising their individual rights, mass against the state. These first-generation rights do belong to the individual, but they gain their impact through group cohesion. This traditional type of collectivity empowers the right holder as the holder joins with others. In this way, the collective nature of first-generation rights becomes effective when the

---

EnglishInternetBible/PartI/chapterIV/treaty5.asp (last visited Feb. 24, 2002). The International Labour Organization (ILO) Constitution, Preamble, and its 1944 reaffirmation, the Declaration of Philadelphia, Art. I(b) also discusses the freedom of expression and association. ILO, *Constitution, at* http://www.ilo.org/public/english/about/iloconst.htm (last visited Feb. 21, 2002).

48. *See, e.g.,* SUSAN ROSE-ACKERMAN, CORRUPTION AND GOVERNMENT: CAUSES, CONSEQUENCES, AND REFORM 22 (1999) (stating that bribery of a government official impedes the development of "effective mechanisms that translate popular demands into law"); *see also* ICCPR, *supra* note 41, art. 25 (granting the right to vote). It is not directly enforceable in the United States because the ICCPR is not self-executing in the United States. *See, e.g.,* Igartua De La Rosa v. United States, 32 F.3d 8, 10 n.1 (1st Cir. 1994) (holding that right to vote is not protected by ICCPR because convention is not self-executing); Christian A. Levesque, Comment, *The International Covenant on Civil and Political Rights: A Primer Raising a Defense Against the Juvenile Death Penalty in Federal Courts,* 50 AM. U. L. REV. 755, 778 n.137 (2001) (same); *supra* note 47 and accompanying text.

49. *See, e.g.,* Sohn, *supra* note 40, at 23-24 (discussing first-generation rights); *see also* ICCPR, *supra* note 41, arts. 6-10.

50. Nevertheless, traditionally only the nation-state has had the power to enforce human rights. *See, e.g.,* Kathryn L. Boyd, *Collective Rights Adjudication in U.S. Courts: Enforcing Human Rights at the Corporate Level,* 1999 B.Y.U. L. REV. 1139, 1147-53 (describing efforts in the last two decades of the twentieth century of private plaintiffs bringing suit in U.S. courts); *see also* Beth Stephens, *Taking Pride in International Human Rights Litigation,* 2 CHI. J. INT'L L. 485 (2001) (discussing private causes of action).

51. Jennifer A. Downs, Note, *A Healthy and Ecologically Balanced Environment: An Argument for a Third Generation Right,* 3 DUKE J. COMP. & INT'L L. 351, 364-65 (1993) (asserting that solidarity applies to all generations, in different ways).

right holders act as though they were unionized, whether or not they do so consciously.[52]

Second-generation rights—economic, social, and cultural rights— were championed principally by socialist regimes starting at the beginning of the twentieth century.[53] In general, these rights are considered to be affirmative: the state must act, rather than merely refrain from acting, in order to provide individuals with, for example, education, health care, or decent working conditions.[54] The United Nations Charter speaks of social and economic rights,[55] and the West has to a significant degree overcome its initial skepticism of these rights. At least from the perspective of the liberal democracies, second-generation rights represent a twentieth-century evolution of the human-rights universe. By the end of the twentieth century, three-quarters of the nations had ratified the International Convention on Economic, Social and Cultural Rights (ICESCR),[56] the treaty that most

---

52. It is hard to know exactly what "collectivity" means in the context of rights. Professor Sohn has described "collective rights" as those "exercised jointly by individuals grouped into larger communities, including peoples and nations," perhaps as distinguished from rights belonging to individuals who belong to a family, trade union, or a state. Sohn, *supra* note 40, at 48.

53. *See* LAUREN, *supra* note 39, at 292 (remarking that the socialist and Marxist revolutions of the nineteenth and early-twentieth centuries prompted discussion of the second generation of rights); Hernández-Truyol, *supra* note 38, at 26 (discussing the second generation and early-twentieth-century Socialist revolutions); Sohn, *supra* note 40, at 33 (stating that the second generation launched with Russian Revolution); *see also* Philip Alston, *U.S. Ratification of the Covenant on Economic, Social and Cultural Rights: The Need for an Entirely New Strategy*, 84 AM. J. INT'L L. 365, 369 (1990) (arguing that the United States in particular has had the most difficulty with articles 11 through 14, relating to the "rights to food, clothing and housing, the right of access to physical and mental health care, and the right to education").

54. *See* Alston, *supra* note 53, at 378-81 (describing the affirmative steps that the United States would obligate itself to take upon ratification of the International Covenant on Economic, Social and Cultural Rights (ICESCR), Dec. 16, 1966, 93 U.N.T.S. 3, *reprinted in* 6 I.L.M. 360 (1967) (entered into force Jan. 3, 1976)); ICESCR, *supra*, arts. 12-13 (covering health and education, respectively). The United States still has not ratified this treaty, although the Senate has had it to consider since 1978. *See, e.g.*, John C. Yoo, *Laws as Treaties?: The Constitutionality of Congressional-Executive Agreements*, 99 MICH. L. REV. 757, 808 n.196 (2001) (discussing the submission of ICESCR to the United States Senate). However, by the end of the twentieth century, three quarters of all nations had ratified the ICESCR. *See* Sharon K. Hom & Eric K. Yamamoto, *Collective Memory, History, and Social Justice*, 47 U.C.L.A. L. REV. 1747, 1789 n.194 (2000) (reporting that by 1997, 140 states had ratified the ICECSR, although forty with qualifications); *see also* Sohn, *supra* note 40, at 42 (explaining that second-generation rights are affirmative).

55. U.N. CHARTER art. 55; *see also* The Universal Declaration of Human Rights, G.A. Res. 217A, U.N. GAOR, 3d Sess., Supp. No. 127, at 71, U.N. Doc. A/810 (1948); *see also* Sohn, *supra* note 40, at 36 (discussing early U.N. documentation that includes second-generation rights).

56. *See supra* note 54 and accompanying text (describing the ICESCR).

broadly concerns second-generation rights.[57] With the notable exception of the United States, most Western countries have ratified the ICESCR, including almost all the European nations.[58]

The first illustration, relating to workers, implicates second-generation rights: the ICESCR expressly covers the issue of workers' rights, in particular conditions of work.[59] This focus reflects the same kind of collectivism implicated in the rights to free association and free expression: although the right is individual, the right holder derives power when other exploited workers exercise their individual rights simultaneously. The third illustration, too, the one describing the major pharmaceutical companies' slow embrace of an obligation to provide anti-HIV/AIDS drugs at low cost to the developing world, concerns the application of a second-generation right–the right to health care.[60] This right emphasizes the similar plight of all actually and potentially infected persons; the effectiveness of the actual and potential victims' individual right depends on collective action, as the illustration graphically underscores.[61] Although these victims suffer from the denial of HIV/AIDS drugs because they are ill or at risk, they are not being targeted just because they belong to a group of actual or potential victims. The right to health care thus represents the traditional type of collectivism.

The logical extension of this balancing of state or other concentrated power against the vulnerable population is the group of human rights called "solidarity" or "collective" rights; these are the third-generation rights. While the existence of these third-generation rights remains controversial, they are said to include a right to development, a right to a clean environment, rights of indigenous peoples, and even the right to peace and perhaps an emerging right to

---

57. *See* Hom & Yamamoto, *supra* note 54, at 1789 n.194.

58. *See* Alston, *supra* note 53, at 372 (reporting that as of March 1989, of the twenty-two nations in the Western European and Others grouping, only Ireland, Malta, and Turkey had not ratified the ICESCR). In December 1989, Ireland adopted the ICESCR. United Nations, *supra* note 47. Other than the United States, all the G-7 members including Russia, have adopted the ICESCR. *Id.* By August 21, 2002, Ireland and Malta have adopted the ICESR. Turkey and the United States have signed but not ratified the treaty (the United States signed in 1977, Turkey in 2000). Office of the High Comm'r for Human Rights, *Status of Ratifications of the Principal International Human Rights Treaties, at* http://www.unhchr. ch/pdf/report.pdf (Aug. 21, 2002).

59. *See* ICESCR, *supra* note 41, art. 7 (conditions of work).

60. *See id.* art. 12 (health care).

61. *See* Dickerson, *supra* note 36 (discussing the risk of contagion, including across borders).

democracy.[62]   A right that is collective may also belong to the individual. This kind of collectivity is different from the type we saw in the context of first- and second-generation rights because third-generation rights belong to the group or collectivity, not just to the individual.[63]   The second and third illustrations, concerning anticorruption activity and the availability of HIV/AIDS drugs, implicate the right to development. Corruption's economic distortions are incompatible with development,[64] and the HIV scourge has erased decades of development in the entire sub-Saharan region.[65] This right to development is both negative and affirmative: the state must avoid impeding development, and it must also take affirmative steps to support development.

---

62.   *See* Karel Vasak, *Pour une Troisième Génération des Droits de l'Homme*, *in* STUDIES AND ESSAYS ON INTERNATIONAL HUMANITARIAN LAW AND RED CROSS PRINCIPLES 837, 840 (Christophe Swinarski ed., 1984) (referring to rights to development, the environment, and peace); Sohn, *supra* note 40, at 48 (discussing rights related to self-determination, development, peace, and the environment); *see, e.g.*, S. James Anaya & Robert A. Williams, Jr., *The Protection of Indigenous Peoples' Rights Over Lands and Natural Resources Under the Inter-American Human Rights System*, 14 HARV. HUM. RTS. J. 33, 33-37 (2001) (cataloguing the evolution of the collective right of indigenous peoples); Robert A. Williams, Jr., *Encounters on the Frontiers of International Human Rights Law: Redefining the Terms of Indigenous Peoples' Survival in the World*, 1990 DUKE L.J. 660, 662-63, 680 (emphasizing the importance of hearing the indigenous peoples' own stories); *see also* Thomas M. Franck, *The Emerging Right to Democratic Governance*, 86 AM. J. INT'L L. 46, 79-80, 89-91 (1992) [hereinafter Franck, *Emerging Right*] (stating that while the right to democracy is perhaps not yet a separate human right, it does exist and can be based on the rights to self-determination, free expression, and peace); Thomas M. Franck, *The Democratic Entitlement*, 29 U. RICH. L. REV. 1 (1994) [hereinafter Franck, *Democratic Entitlement*] (same).

63.   *See, e.g.*, Anne Orford, *Globalization and the Right to Development*, *in* PEOPLES' RIGHTS 127, 136 (Philip Alston ed., 2001) (referring to the right to development and relying on the Declaration on the Right to Development, GA Res. 41/128 (Annex), UN GAOR, 41st Sess., Supp. No. 53, at 186, UN Doc. A/41/53 (1986), *available at* http://www1.umn.edu/humanrts/instree/s3drd.htm (last visited July 2, 2002), adopted by the United Nations General Assembly). For a brief description of the Declaration, see Berta Esperanza Hernandez-Truyol & Shelbi D. Day, *Property, Wealth, Inequality and Human Rights: A Formula for Reform*, 34 IND. L. REV. 1213, 1213-31 (2001).

64.   That, certainly, is the World Bank's stated view, as reported by a senior legal adviser of the Bank. *See* Sabine Schlemmer-Schulte, *The Impact of Civil Society on the World Bank, the International Monetary Fund and the World Trade Organization: The Case of the World Bank*, 7 ILSA J. INT'L & COMP. L. 399, 420-21 (2001) (stating that the World Bank's president has linked the negative effects of corruption on development for over five years).

65.   *See, e.g.*, Rene Loewenson & Alan Whiteside, U.N. Dev. Programme Policy Paper, *HIV/AIDS-Implications for Poverty Reduction* 7 (2001), *available at* http://www.undp.org/dpa/frontpagearchive/2001/june/22june01/hiv-aids.pdf (last visited June 4, 2002) (reporting that AIDS-related mortality is reducing life expectancy to 1950s levels in highly affected, sub-Saharan countries).

The move to third-generation rights, and thus, to increasingly collective rights, reflects the West/North's evolving acceptance of norms from the developing world.[66] It also reflects a natural progression in the West/North, from the first-generation rights through the more socialist second-generation rights, and finally to the collective rights. The inclusion of third-generation rights confirms that the human-rights regime no longer considers individualism to be the sole perspective, but, instead, recognizes the power and significance of the group. In the next Part, I will analyze the influence of the evolving human-rights regime on corporate social responsibility. At the threshold, however, lies the following question: are these changes in the human-rights regime legitimate, such that any influence they do exert on corporate behavior is defensible?

B. The Legitimacy of the Human-Rights Norms' Evolution: Emergence as Democracy

The evolution of human rights represents a change in norms. Whether the result is legitimate is a separate question. There are, of course, philosophic arguments in support of human rights, but I am instead proposing certain democratic principles as the legitimating force for human-rights norms. As a first step, democratic principles suggest that, because human rights belong to all persons, individually or as members of groups, all persons are affected and should weigh in the decision. Shareholders and prominent capitalists should not be the sole voices heard.

1. Democracy Legitimates, Subject to the Tyrannies of Majority and Minority

Nobel laureate Amartya Sen has famously stated that no famine ever occurred in a functioning democracy.[67] He points out that famines are inconsistent with democracies because the leaders must consider

---

66. *See, e.g.*, Makau Mutua, *Savages, Victims, and Saviors: The Metaphor of Human Rights*, 42 HARV. INT'L L.J. 201, 204 (2001) (asserting that historically, "[t]he human rights corpus, though well-meaning, is fundamentally Eurocentric"); Makau Wa Mutua, *The Ideology of Human Rights*, 36 VA. J. INT'L L. 589, 642-44 (1996) (stating that both in Africa and in Asia there is a strong emphasis on the community, as opposed to a focus on the individual).

67. AMARTYA SEN, DEVELOPMENT AS FREEDOM 16 (1999); *see also id.* at 43 (reporting that while China has had numerous famines, India has had none since its independence in 1947).

the future if they expect to stay in office.[68] This should be reason enough to espouse democracy when seeking society's definition of corporate social responsibility: inherent in the process is the leaders' incentive to consider the consequences to, and thus the reactions of, those whom they lead. First, however, we must face fundamental delegitimizing aspects of the democratic form, and in particular, the risk of tyranny by either the majority or the minority.

Corporate lawyers are familiar with these problems in the context of corporate governance. Whenever the minority acquires power, for example, if it has a veto, it can exercise that power just as abusively as any majority wields its own controlling position. The purpose of fiduciary duty is, at least in part, to control abusive majorities and minorities.[69] In the more classical, political context, democracy creates the risk of tyranny by both the majority and the interest group, each of which I will briefly consider in turn.[70]

James Madison saw the majority as dangerous and complained that democracy creates a risk for the "weaker party, or an obnoxious individual."[71] Proposals to temper the majority's power have included Lani Guinier's effort to provide minority voters at least some voice by appropriating the corporate cumulative voting mechanism.[72] Other suggestions have focused on education and, in particular, on educating the citizenry to "share in ruling." Madison proposed a representative government to defang the majority.[73]

---

68.   *Id.* at 49-50 (arguing that governments can easily prevent famines, and democratically selected leaders have the incentive to do so).

69.   *Compare* Donahue v. Rodd Electrotype Co., 328 N.E.2d 505, 515 (Mass. 1975) (discussing majority abuse), *with* Smith v. Atl. Props., Inc., 422 N.E.2d 798, 801 (Mass. App. Ct. 1981) (concerning minority with veto power).

70.   For a general over view of "illiberal democracies," i.e., democracies that neither protect the minority from the tyranny of the majority, nor the majority from the tyranny of an elected minority, see Fareed Zakaria, *The Rise of Illiberal Democracy*, FOR. AFF., Nov./Dec. 1997, at 22, *available at* 1997 WL 9287610.

71.   THE FEDERALIST NO. 10, at 61 (James Madison) (Jacob E. Cooke ed., 1961).

72.   *See* Lani Guinier, *Groups, Representation, and Race-Conscious Districting: A Case of the Emperor's Clothes*, 71 TEX. L. REV. 1589, 1617 (1993) (recommending cumulative voting as not being focused on any particular minority group).

73.   THE FEDERALIST NO. 10, at 62 (referring to citizens who have "wisdom . . . patriotism and love of justice"). *But see id.* at 63-64 (calling for a republic large enough so that factions do not control, but small enough so that the representatives retain a sense of the local, and preferring a federal form in order to insulate further the greater number from localized factions). Of course, for Madison the representatives have a heavy responsibility: rather than merely repeating the constituents' views, the representatives identify public interest and then communicate that information back to the constituents. *See, e.g.*, Herbert Hovenkamp, *Arrow's Theorem: Ordinalism and Republican Government*, 75 IOWA L. REV. 949, 955 (1990).

At the opposite end of the spectrum, the tyranny of the minority lurks. Interest groups can benefit from the larger group's—the majority's—collective action problems.[74] Indeed, smaller groups can have disproportionate power, especially if the group's members are finely focused.[75] There is an argument, of course, that vote weighted by interest is as legitimate as, for example, the vote granted per capita. For instance, a racial minority that is at risk from a diffuse majority's efforts to pass discriminatory legislation may be able to block passage if the members of the minority vote as a cohesive interest group.[76] To the extent that we applaud this result, we are not necessarily approving the distortion of the democratic process; rather, we are arriving at the independent, normative conclusion that to block discriminatory legislation is the preferable outcome.[77] Thus, we seek a democratic system that will allow the minority voice to be heard, but without encouraging full capitulation to an interest group.

What is needed is not just democracy, but a form of liberal, representative democracy, complete with checks and balances against tyranny by either the majority or the minority.[78]

2. Informal Democracy

We have seen that the human rights' three generations have evolved. Each generation has gained acceptance over time. For civil and political rights, the ICCPR is the culminating treaty, and for economic and social rights, it is the ICESCR.[79] For solidarity rights,

---

74. *See, e.g.,* MANCUR OLSON, THE RISE AND DECLINE OF NATIONS 31-34 (1982) (noting that a larger group has greater free-rider problems); *see also id.* at 46-48 (stating that a larger group has more difficulty organizing). *See generally* Einer R. Elhauge, *Does Interest Group Theory Justify More Intrusive Judicial Review*, 101 YALE L.J. 31, 38-39 (1991).

75. OLSON, *supra* note 74, at 127 (emphasizing the power of small, intense groups); *see also* Elhauge, *supra* note 74, at 50 (discussing small-interest groups).

76. *See* Elhauge, *supra* note 74, at 50 (discussing a smaller group blocking discriminatory legislation); *see also* Bruce A. Ackerman, *Beyond* Carolene Products, 98 HARV. L. REV. 713, 723-31 (1985) (discussing smaller groups' ability to overcome the free-rider problem); *see also* Daniel J.H. Greenwood, *Beyond the Counter-Majoritarian Difficulty: Judicial Decision-Making in a Polynomic World,* 53 RUTGERS L. REV. 781, 811 (2001) (discussing methods of limiting majoritarian excess).

77. *See* Elhauge, *supra* note 74, at 50 (discussing the role of the underlying normative view).

78. *See generally* Zakaria, *supra* note 70. There is a delightful circularity here, too. Democracy legitimates the human-rights norm as democracy becomes a human-rights norm. *See generally* Franck, *Emerging Right, supra* note 62 (analyzing democracy as an entitlement).

79. The Universal Declaration of Human Rights, a nontreaty precursor to the ICCPR and ICESCR, contains both first- and second-generation rights. *See, e.g.,* Hernández-Truyol, *supra* note 38, at 18, 20 (noting that the Declaration includes both civil and political rights,

we do not yet know the codification's full contours, but treaties of specific application, such as the International Labor Organization Convention No. 169[80] on indigenous and tribal peoples and the Banjul Charter,[81] have begun the process. The pre-codification part of the effort resembles emergence, an informal, spontaneous decision-making structure, roughly analogous to democracy.[82] The second part, the codification, more directly—but imperfectly—conforms to the classic understanding of representative government. Emergence is complex behavior that has a discernable pattern, but is created wholly from local rules of behavior.[83] If behavior is adaptive, the self-organizing system becomes smarter, that is, better able to accomplish the goal.[84] In this kind of bubbling up of structure, the action on the local level determines by feedback whether it is enhancing the community. In pure emergence, the feedback is not conscious: large cities grew in Europe during the Middle Ages because crop rotation increased productivity, and more food permitted greater population density, which in turn created more fertilizer, and subsequently, more food— and so forth.[85] By the time the behavior has emerged, it by definition has massive influence and, in this way, is majoritarian.[86] Once the majority has spoken, the minority may be overwhelmed.[87]

---

and economic, social, and cultural rights, and that the economic, social, and cultural rights were codified in the ICESCR).

80. *See, e.g.*, Indigenous and Tribal Peoples Convention, ILO Convention No. 169, June 27, 1989, 28 I.L.M. 1382 (entered into force Sept. 5, 1991), *available at* http://ilolex. ilo.ch:1567/english/convdisp1.htm (last visited Feb. 24, 2002). As of December 9, 2001, the convention has been ratified by fourteen countries. *Id.*

81. African Charter on Human and Peoples' Rights, June 27, 1981, 21 I.L.M. 58 (1982) (entered into force Oct. 21, 1986) [hereinafter Banjul Charter]. Its article 20 expresses a right of self-determination, article 22 grants a right to development, article 23 grants a right to peace, and article 24 combines the rights to a clean environment and to development by providing that "[a]ll peoples shall have the right to a general satisfactory environment favorable to their development."

82. For purposes of this discussion, I consider conventions to "codify" whether they are restating existing customary law or making new law. Thus, pretreaty norm-formation may not have risen to the level of customary law.

83. *See* STEVEN JOHNSON, EMERGENCE: THE CONNECTED LIVES OF ANTS, BRAINS, CITIES, AND SOFTWARE 19 (2001). Acting locally—considering only the immediate neighbors— creates a global behavior. *Id.* at 74 (discussing ant colonies).

84. *See id.* at 20.

85. *Id.* at 112-13. The feedback loop needs connectedness because the evaluation has to return. *See id.* at 134. However, decentralized systems, such as the Internet, connect without organizing; structure is necessary, too. *Id.* at 117-20. Cities provide both the density for connectedness and the clusters of tradespeople, who act as structures, for two-way connection. *See id.* at 107-08.

86. This eruption of herd behavior was thoroughly described in the mid-nineteenth century. *See* CHARLES MACKAY, EXTRAORDINARY POPULAR DELUSIONS AND THE MADNESS OF CROWDS 46-97 (1932) (1841) (recounting, among other excesses, the South-Sea Bubble of

Depending on the circumstances, emergence can also raise a concern about a minority's usurpation of majority prerogatives: not all emergence is pure, because sometimes a minority force guides the process.[88] The development of civil and political rights in the United States, for example, included conscious efforts by norm entrepreneurs to shape the developing social culture. The Federalist Papers are a prime exhibit of efforts to exert influence over an emerging public understanding about civil and political rights.[89] This type of feedback is more similar to "applied emergence" in which a person who controls the feedback structure and who values tolerance, can ensure that extreme views will not survive the otherwise self-organizing system.[90]

Development of the second-generation rights appears to be on this pattern, with a West/North minority initially resisting acceptance.[91]

1720 and the tulip mania of 1635). Once social influence has pushed the behavior over the tipping point, it grows exponentially. *See, e.g.*, Malcolm Gladwell, *The Tipping Point,* NEW YORKER, June 3, 1996, at 32-38 (discussing the theory of a tipping point); Philip G. Zimbardo, *The Human Choice: Individuation, Reason, and Order Versus Deindividuation, Impulse, and Chaos, in* NEBRASKA SYMPOSIUM ON MOTIVATION 237, 287-93 (William J. Arnold & David Levine eds., 1969) (referring to a "release signal" and rapid stripping of car). *See generally* Jonathan Crane, *The Epidemic Theory of Ghettos and Neighborhood Effects on Dropping Out and Teenage Childbearing,* 96 AM. J. SOC. 1226 (1991); Claire Moore Dickerson, *Political Corruption: Free-Flowing Opportunism,* 14 CONN. J. INT'L L. 393 (1999) (discussing the abandoned car at the tipping point); H. Range Hutson et al., *The Epidemic of Gang-Related Homicides in Los Angeles County from 1979 through 1994,* 274 J. AM. MED. ASS'N 1031, 1031-36 (1995).

87. It may be that, at least in some circumstances, the actions of the group in power are self-limiting: neither the majority nor the minority exercises its full power. Given that a norm expands exponentially, *see supra* note 86 and accompanying text, the viral analogy suggests that the group with power will strive not to kill the "host." *See, e.g.,* RICHARD PRESTON, THE HOT ZONE 84, 97, 99 (1994) (noting that the outbreak can die out on its own if the virus kills its host before it can infect another host).

88. When an entrepreneur applies the principles of emergence, an organization like Amazon.com collects information about what I, as a purchaser, might like based on my prior purchases, and those purchases of thousands of others. *See* JOHNSON, *supra* note 83, at 206-07 (discussing applied emergence); *see also infra* note 90 and accompanying text (same).

89. *See, e.g.,* Jacob E. Cooke, *Introduction in* THE FEDERALIST, at xi (Jacob E. Cooke ed., 1961) (conjecturing that Hamilton started writing the essays and contacting collaborators because he "concluded that if [the Constitution] were to be adopted, convincing proof of its merits would have to be placed before the citizens of New York"). There were at least more-or-less spontaneous uprisings opposing civil and political rights. *See, e.g.,* LAUREN, *supra* note 39, at 21 (describing an English mob hanging Thomas Paine in effigy in 1792).

90. JOHNSON, *supra* note 83, at 161 (discussing setting up a chat room by rewarding moderators who promote diverse views, instead of merely popular ones). Of course, this is easier to accomplish when a single person is setting up the rules for the chat room. In other words, although emergence occurs on its own, it can be shaped by successful norm entrepreneurs. This is what Johnson calls "applied emergence." *Id.* at 207; *see also supra* note 83 and accompanying text (discussing emergence).

91. They first emerged in revolutionary Russia. *See supra* note 53 and accompanying text (discussing Socialism, Marxism, and the Russian revolution as a launching point in the

Third-generation human rights similarly are subject to a risk of interest-group pressure, that is, to tyranny by the minority. The particular configuration of a right to development may be supported by an unrepresentative collection of activists.[92] Or, just as likely, that right is supported at least at an inchoate level by a large proportion of the Third World's population, but the articulation of the right meets determined opposition from multinationals who prefer the status quo.[93] Worldwide public opinion was marshaled in the South African HIV/AIDS drug debate as the engine for change, while the multinational pharmaceutical companies, supported by their home-nations, sought to attenuate efforts to impose a reduction in prices for the HIV/AIDS drugs.[94] The balance between majority and minority is imperfect and hard to predict.

3.   Formal Democracy

The codification process may provide a corrective to the risks of tyranny by the majority or the minority. A body such as the United Nations General Assembly, and other codification systems, can institutionalize a representative form of approval and thus begin to address both majority excess and interest-group pressures.

We know that the first generation of human rights simmered for at least two centuries before they were codified in the ICCPR. The progress from the second generation's first emergence[95] to its, at least

---

development of second-generation rights, and initial Western reluctance); *see also* James Gray Pope, *The First Amendment, The Thirteenth Amendment, and the Right to Organize in the Twenty-First Century*, 51 RUTGERS L. REV. 941, 944 (1999) (noting that significant labor militancy preceded every major reform in U.S. labor law and referring specifically to reforms in 1898 and 1935); LAUREN, *supra* note 39, at 112-13 (describing the relationship between worldwide misery during the Depression and the emergence of calls for economic and social rights). The Universal Declaration of Human Rights was split into the ICCPR and ICESCR at the time of drawing up the conventions because the West/North rejected second-generation rights as more than precatory. Hernández-Truyol, *supra* note 38, at 20.

    92.   Among scholars, Karel Vasak is an early proponent. *See* Vasak, *supra* note 62, at 837-53. He is considered the "author of the phrase 'third generation of human rights.'" Sohn, *supra* note 40, at 61.

    93.   *See* Sohn, *supra* note 40, at 56-58 (quoting Vasak as asserting that third-generation rights can be realized only by a conjunction of efforts of all relevant actors: the individual, the state, the public and private entities, and the international community).

    94.   *See generally* Swarns, *supra* note 32, at A1.

    95.   *See, e.g.*, Jack Donnelly, *In Search of the Unicorn: The Jurisprudence and Politics of the Right to Development*, 15 CAL. W. INT'L L.J. 473, 474 (1985) (explaining that the right to development was unknown in 1970, never discussed in the U.N. before 1975, first mentioned by the Commission on Human Rights in 1977, and by 1980 had been discussed even by the United Nations General Assembly). Seven years later the General Assembly had adopted Declaration on the Right to Development. *See supra* note 63 and accompanying text.

partial, codification in the ICESCR was more rapid, being effected in less than a century.[96] Third-generation rights are currently being codified selectively. As these rights move toward codification, the process offers some protection against minority excess, as the three illustrations help us understand.

The treaties most directly relevant to reducing the abuse of workers, cleaning up political corruption, and providing anti-HIV/AIDS drugs are, respectively, the ICCPR, the OECD Convention, and the ICESCR.[97] The first and third were initially adopted by the United Nations General Assembly and thus, indirectly, include decisions of the various state-members. To the extent that these states are liberal democracies, the people are indirectly represented through their own states, and then through the General Assembly. Unfortunately, forty-five percent of the world's population still lives under nondemocratic governments, which places the majority at risk of tyranny by the minority. And half of the democracies do not offer constitutional protections, which places the minority at risk of abuse by the majority.[98] For its part, the OECD Convention, engineered by disproportionately wealthy countries,[99] is arguably even less democratic in origin than the U.N. treaties. The OECD Convention is the decision of a representative democracy in the sense that most of the nation-members of the OECD are democracies; however, it codifies a norm imposed on the world by an unrepresentative group of nations, being primarily the developed countries in which the great multinationals are based. These efforts to codify human rights are at best very imperfect democracies, with inadequate protection against the twin tyrannies of majority and minority.

There are some further correctives against these twin tyrannies. International organizations, for example, are offering fora for discussion. The International Labor Organization provides a forum for workers through its tripartite structure that includes not only

---

More classic examples of partial codification include the ILO Convention No. 169, *supra* note 80 (rights of indigenous peoples).

96. *See supra* Part III.A (providing a brief history of the generations).

97. *See supra* Part II.B (providing three illustrations).

98. *See* Zakaria, *supra* note 70 (noting that in 1997, 118 of the 193 extant countries, representing 54.8% of the world's population, had democratically elected governments, and half of those governments were illiberal).

99. *See, e.g.,* Cassel, *supra* note 26, at 1970 (referring to the twenty-six—now twenty-eight—OECD members as "affluent"); Stephan, *supra* note 26, at 1343 (asserting that the United States' economic and strategic power are unparalleled).

government representatives and employers, but also workers.[100] The international financial institutions are spearheading demands for clean government, and their processes are making increasing use of nongovernmental organizations as proxies for persons who are affected by these institutions' decisions, but who otherwise would be under- or unrepresented.[101] The U.N. and its agencies are now involved in discussions concerning the pricing of anti-HIV/AIDS drugs; they, too, are reaching out to constituent groups.[102] These organizations are not providing the worldwide town meeting, nor even a true representative democracy, but they do offer one more context for consultations between the majorities and minorities, however defined on any specific issue.

This clearly is not a perfect system. However, both the informal and the formal process have democratic undertones and, together, have the potential to address at least some of the risks of abuse. Thus, as

---

100. The ILO has a tripartite organization, including representatives of employees. ILO Constitution, *supra* note 47, art. 3, § 5 ("The Members [the States] undertake to nominate non-Government delegates and advisers chosen in agreement with the industrial organizations, if such organizations exist, which are most representative of employers or workpeople, as the case may be, in their respective countries."). Who will represent the employees is important, because representation by a union leader is often not available in developing countries. *See, e.g.*, Frances Lee Ansley, *Rethinking Law in Globalization Labor Markets*, 1 U. PA. J. LAB. & EMP. L. 369, 371 (1998) (asserting that in the developing world, workers tend not to be "seasoned and organized").

101. *See, e.g.*, The World Bank Group, *Helping Countries Reduce Corruption*, at http://www1.worldbank.org/publicsector/anticorrupt/helping.htm (last visited Feb. 24, 2002) (noting that the World Bank has pursued a "comprehensive anti-corruption policy" since 1997); *see also* Daniel Citrin, Ass't Dir., Asia & Pacific Dept., IMF, *Statement at Consultative Group Meeting for Indonesia*, para. 22 (Nov. 7-8, 2001), *at* http://www.imf.org/external/np/dm/2001/110701.htm (last visited Feb. 20, 2002) (noting the importance of institution building and governance in general and anticorruption efforts, in particular). Further, the World Bank has issued an advisory Good Practices statement expressly acknowledging the importance of interaction with nongovernmental organizations as interested and knowledgeable parties. *See* World Bank, *Good Practices: Involving Nongovernmental Organizations in Bank-Supported Activities*, *in* THE WORLD BANK OPERATIONAL MANUAL GP 14.70 (Feb. 2000), *at* http://wbln0018.worldbank.org/Institutional/Manuals/OpManual.nsf/GPraw (last visited June 4, 2002).

102. U.N. Special Session on HIV/AIDS, *"Global Crisis–Global Action": Declaration of Commitment on HIV/AIDS*, *at* http://www.unaids.org/whatsnew/others/un_special/Declaration020801_en.htm (Aug. 2, 2001) (providing declaration following the United Nations General Assembly's June 2001 session on HIV/AIDS). This is the first United Nations General Assembly session ever devoted entirely to the HIV/AIDS pandemic. Michael Specter, *Annals of Medicine: India's Plague*, NEW YORKER, Dec. 17, 2001, at 74, 77. The WHO is an agency of the U.N. *See* U.N., *Organization Chart of the United Nations*, *at* http://www.un.org/aboutun/chart.html (last visited June 4, 2002). The WHO displays prominently a list of the nongovernmental organizations who are its "partners." *See* WHO, *Directory of NGOs in Official Relations with WHO*, *at* http://www.who.int/ina-ngo (last visited June 4, 2002).

human-rights norms are evolving toward a more collective conception they carry with them not only whatever legitimacy traditional philosophical perspectives can offer, but also the legitimacy that an admittedly flawed form of democracy provides. This is a democracy that is broader than the West/North, and far broader than the corporate-commercial arena.

IV.   FEEDBACK BETWEEN MULTINATIONALS' BEHAVIOR AND
      EVOLVING HUMAN-RIGHTS NORMS

The actual behavior of prominent multinationals is moving toward the human-rights norms. We see this both in the specific behavior described in the three illustrations, and in the general trend toward recognition of collectives. The similarity of behavior and norms reflects an existing norm of corporate social responsibility, one that has evolved in the greater community, not just among the commercial-corporate arena's opinion makers.

A.   *Both Corporate Behavior and Human-Rights Norms Are
     Increasingly Recognizing the Significance of the Vulnerable as a
     Collective*

This multinational conduct is consistent with an acknowledgment that workers in developing countries have a right to working conditions that exceed certain, stated minimum standards. Multinationals support their governments' efforts to criminalize occult payoffs to developing countries' political officials. Multinationals have agreed to provide developing countries with HIV/AIDS drugs at a fraction of the price in the developed world.[103] This behavior is a "norm" in the technical, sociological sense even if the multinationals behave in this way only because of different motives.[104] Thus, the behavior is a "norm" even if the multinationals seek only to increase profits by eliminating the cost of bribery, or to placate developed-country consumers outraged by cold calculation in the face of sweatshops and the modern plague.[105]

The multinationals' behavior, whatever the motive, casts its own social influence on society at large. When the behavior conforms to the three generations of human-rights norms, it reinforces those norms

---

103. *See supra* Part II.B (providing the three illustrations).

104. *See* TURNER, *supra* note 10, at 4-5 (discussing different reasons for compliance).

105. Or even if the multinationals are ostensibly supporting the right to development only as a means of weakening the civil and political rights by arguing that the former trumps the latter. *See* Orford, *supra* note 63, at 136. *See generally* TURNER, *supra* note 10, at 40-42, 144 (discussing internalized norms).

among all members of the community, including, for example, developed-country consumers.   Consider how this plays out concerning political corruption: even if bribery were culturally acceptable both in the payor's and payee's country,[106] the very fact that the behavior becomes nonpayment of bribes creates a sociological "norm" with social influence. If the influence takes hold, both the residents of the payee's country and the consumers in the payor's markets will insist that multinationals cease contributing to political corruption. In the case of labor conditions and HIV/AIDS drugs, consumers and workers already are on the multinationals' radar screens influencing behavior.[107] Thus, a feedback loop evolves that, in its turn, reinforces human-rights norms, which then encourages the multinationals to respect the human rights of workers and of HIV/AIDS victims.[108] The loop continues.

This complicated feedback between multinationals' behavior and human-rights norms applies not just to specific rights, such as the right to reasonable work conditions, to education, or to vote. It also applies to the larger trends, including the movement toward an appreciation of the collective. The beginnings of that recognition exist already for labor and health care, but with respect to political corruption, the multinationals are still in the process of acquiring a conscious recognition that residents of the payee's country have, collectively, a right to development remains a work in progress.[109] Nevertheless, that multinational behavior becomes consistent with a recognition of the collective right to development, that conduct does support third-generation rights, too. These new norms confirm the West/North's

---

106. *See, e.g.*, Steven R. Salbu, *Extraterritorial Restriction of Bribery: A Premature Evocation of the Normative Global Village*, 24 YALE J. INT'L L. 223, 232-40 (1999) (discussing cultural subtleties in defining corruption); *see also* Barbara Crutchfield George et al., *The 1998 OECD Convention: An Impetus for Worldwide Changes in Attitudes Toward Corruption in Business Transactions*, 37 AM. BUS. L.J. 485, 496 (2000) (noting that a trigger for the OECD Convention was the fact that France and Germany had allowed tax deductions for bribes paid to foreign officials).

107. *See generally* Dickerson, *supra* note 21 (influence of developed-world consumers on multinationals); Del Jones, *Unions Call for Fair Trade, Practices WTO Should Protect Rights of Workers*, USA TODAY, Dec. 1, 1999, at 3B, *available at* 1999 WL 6860091 (reporting that workers see the multinationals as using the WTO to "drive a wedge" between workers from the developed and developing world); *see supra* note 36 and accompanying text (discussing pressures of, inter alia, consumers on the major pharmaceutical manufacturers).

108. *See* TURNER, *supra* note 10 (concerning the modalities of social influence). *See generally* Dan M. Kahan, *Social Influence, Social Meaning, and Deterrence*, 83 VA. L. REV. 349 (1997) (discussing social influence); *supra* note 86 and accompanying text (discussing the tipping point).

109. *See supra* Part III.B (describing the three illustrations in the context of the evolving human-rights generations reflecting a move toward a more collective perspective).

increasing acknowledgment of the collective–not just of the individual. The behavior, whatever the motive, reflects an implicitly democratic acceptance that the collective "other" has a relevant voice.

This combination of the evolving behavior and the evolving human-rights norms describes corporate social responsibility: how corporations behave tags up to the larger community's normative expression. Because the rights are positive as well as negative, the norm calls for affirmative, corrective action, not merely the avoidance of a directly exploitative act. Increasingly, this norm of corporate social responsibility is undergirded by legal enforceability.[110]

B. *Human-Rights Norms Are Real: Enforceability*

The human-rights duties are both negative and affirmative; thus, the multinationals subject to the concomitant duties must both avoid certain actions and affirmatively take others. To the extent that corporate social responsibility is reflected in the actual behavior of multinationals, enforceability is not necessary, but it does serve as a framework to support the norm.[111] When multinationals do not conform to the norm, however, enforceability obviously has direct application. There are two separate issues to consider in this connection: are human-rights norms enforceable at all in the United States? Even if the answer is affirmative, are they enforceable against a private, nonstate party, such as a multinational corporation?[112]

The most straightforward source of enforceable human-rights law is through treaties. There, the United States scene is bleak: first-generation rights are not enforceable under the ICCPR because the treaty is not self-executing in the United States;[113] second-generation

---

110. *See, e.g.*, Edward B. Rock & Michael L. Wachter, *Islands of Conscious Power: Law, Norms, and the Self-Governing Corporation*, 149 U. PA. L. REV. 1619 (2001) (discussing the role of law as the framework for norms); Claire Moore Dickerson, *Bracketed Flexibility: Standards of Performance Level the Playing Field*, 26 J. CORP. L. 1001 (2001) (discussing the law as a support for standards of performance).

111. *See, e.g.*, Ariela Gross, *Beyond Black and White: Cultural Approaches to Race and Slavery*, 101 COLUM. L. REV. 640, 686-87 (2001) (emphasizing the difference between (1) treating law and norms as though they are on parallel tracks but affect each other and (2) recognizing that they are on an infinite feedback loop); *see also* Cass R. Sunstein, *On the Expressive Function of Law*, 144 U. PA. L. REV. 2021, 2025 (1996) (asserting the influence of law on norms); *supra* note 110 and accompanying text (discussing law and norms).

112. *See generally* Steven R. Ratner, *Corporations and Human Rights: A Theory of Legal Responsibility*, 111 YALE L.J. 443 (2001) (concerning the enforceability of human-rights laws against corporations).

113. Although the United States has ratified the ICCPR, the United States claims that it is not self-executing. *See supra* note 47 and accompanying text. Of course certain

rights are not enforceable under the ICESCR because the United States has never ratified it;[114] third-generation rights are not enforceable even in jurisdictions traditionally more hospitable than the United States to human-rights adjudication.[115] The alternate ground for enforceability is that at least first-generation rights are part of customary law.[116] By the same analysis, second-generation rights, too, may be customary because very few nations other than the United States have failed to sign the ICESCR. Third-generation rights remain problematic. Nevertheless, recent regional conventions, and even the illustrations of the pro-development aspects of the fight against corruption and of the fight to reduce the price of HIV/AIDS drugs, indicate an increasing recognition of third-generation rights.[117]

Assuming, then, that at least certain human rights are enforceable, are they enforceable against a multinational? Although historically only states could be actors in international public law, recent cases in the United States have allowed causes of action against individuals for violation of human-rights law.[118] To avoid dismissal, however, these cases must concern egregious, human-rights violations as to which there is worldwide consensus. To date, torture or genocide suffice; claims for fraud or breach of fiduciary duty do not.[119]

---

violations of human rights are independently prohibited in the United States. Bribery of foreign officials, for example, is illegal under the FCPA.

114. *See supra* note 54 and accompanying text (noting that the United States has not ratified the ICESCR).

115. *See* Laurence R. Helfer & Anne-Marie Slaughter, *Toward a Theory of Effective Supranational Adjudication*, 107 YALE L.J. 273, 276-79 & n.13 (1997) (arguing that Europe is more hospitable than the United States to private actions asserting violations of first-generation rights, but is not hospitable to the second- or third-generation rights). Specific conventions do, however, provide for third-generation rights. *See, e.g., supra* Part III.B.2 (discussing the ILO Convention No. 169 and the Banjul Charter).

116. Customary international law is federal law. *The Paquete Habana,* 175 U.S. 677, 700 (1900); *The Nereide,* 13 U.S. (9 Cranch) 388, 423 (1815).

117. *See supra* Part II.B for the illustrations; *supra* Part III.B.2 for discussion of the Banjul Charter, a regional convention.

118. These causes of action are based on the Alien Tort Claims Act, 28 U.S.C. § 1350 (1994), granting jurisdiction to federal courts over "[a] tort only, committed in violation of the law of nations." *See* Filártiga v. Pena-Irala, 630 F.2d 876 (2d Cir. 1980) (involving case where Paraguayan citizens brought a civil suit in the United States against a citizen of Paraguay living in the United States); *see also* Kadic v. Karadzic, 70 F.3d 232, 239-41 (2d Cir. 1995) (allowing a cause of action against a nonstate actor). *But see* Curtis A. Bradley, *Customary International Law and Private Rights of Action,* 1 CHI. J. INT'L L. 421 (2000) (asserting the impropriety of bringing a private cause of action even if customary international law exists, absent a specific authorizing statute). *See generally* Stephens, *supra* note 50 (discussing private causes of action and criticizing Bradley).

119. *Filártiga,* 630 F.2d at 878 (allowing a cause of action for torture); *Karadzic,* 70 F.3d at 236 (allowing a cause of action for genocide); Hamid v. Price Waterhouse, 51 F.3d

Directors of U.S. corporations may, today, have less risk of legal liability in the U.S. courts for violating the human rights of a developing-country worker than they have for violating the duty of care or loyalty to a shareholder, but the trend is toward increased liability.

Worldwide consensus emerges as the evolution of behavior and norms continues to emphasize the collective aspects of first- and second-generation rights, and the collective nature of third-generation rights. The larger community is both the source of the evolving norm and its beneficiary. This form of corporate social responsibility, already in evidence as a behavior and as human-rights norms, recognizes obligations to the collective, based on the will of the larger community. Consequently, the multinationals are faced with duties that are increasingly likely to be the subject of legal enforcement.

V. CONCLUSION

In the past, the leaders of the commercial-corporate domain determined what is corporate social responsibility, and the definition included, famously, profit maximization for shareholders. Globalization of trade and the sheer size of modern multinationals have expanded the reach of such corporations from their base in the developed world, into the recesses of the developing world's labor markets and homes. In consequence, it is no longer these leaders who, alone, determine the multinationals' conduct, because home-market consumers and complex pressures from the developing world combine to influence the multinationals' behavior.

Multinationals' conduct is moving beyond the traditional concept of corporate social responsibility, which narrowly focuses on shareholder primacy. Prodded from beyond the traditional commercial-corporate realm, many multinationals have adopted codes of conduct that, at least to some degree, regulate the treatment of developing-country workers, and support pro-development actions relating to corruption and healthcare. By their actual behavior, the multinationals evidence their appreciation of the power of vulnerable individuals when acting collectively.

At the same time, evolving human-rights norms, including for development, reflect an awareness, born both of the developed world's traditions and of those of the developing world, that people who are

---

1411, 1418 (9th Cir. 1995) (disallowing, because it is not against the "law of nations," a cause of action for fraud and breach of fiduciary duty); *see also* Stephens, *supra* note 50, at 487-88.

individually vulnerable have collective significance. The emergence of these norms is a kind of unstructured, democratic process and, therefore, benefits from the legitimacy imparted by a system akin to democratic voting. That system is further bolstered by the more formal, international codification process.

Meantime, the feedback loop kicks in. As the actual behavior of multinationals becomes increasingly consistent with the evolving human-rights norms, the behavior both reinforces the norms, and is reinforced by them. The human-rights norms, supported by and supporting actual corporate behavior, redefine corporate social responsibility–and they do so in accordance with the most broadly held perception of the appropriate corporate role.

Benefiting from this broader input into the definition, neither the multinationals' behavior nor human-rights norms have adopted shareholder profit maximization as the core value for corporate social responsibility. Instead, the emerging understanding of corporate social responsibility recognizes the interests of persons beyond the corporation's shareholders, beyond traditional stakeholders, and certainly beyond the West and North. And the trend is toward enforceability of this new definition of corporate social responsibility based on human-rights norms.

Part II
Conceptual Perspectives

[7]

PROTECTING HUMAN RIGHTS IN A GLOBALIZED WORLD

Dinah Shelton*

Abstract: The shift in sovereignty accompanying globalization has meant that non-state actors are more involved than ever in issues relating to human rights. This development poses challenges to international human rights law, because for the most part that law has been designed to restrain abuses by powerful states and state agents. While globalization has enhanced the ability of civil society to function across borders and promote human rights, other actors have gained the power to violate human rights in unforeseen ways. This Article looks at the legal frameworks for globalization and for human rights, then asks to what extent globalization is good for human rights and to what extent human rights are good for globalization. It then considers several legal responses to globalization as they relate to the promotion and protection of human rights. This Article concludes that responses to globalization are significantly changing international law and institutions in order to protect persons from violations of human rights committed by non-state actors.

INTRODUCTION

International human rights law aims primarily to protect individuals and groups from abusive action by states and state agents.[1] Recent developments throughout the world, including failed states, economic deregulation, privatization, and trade liberalization across borders—components of what has come to be known as globalization—have led to the emergence of powerful non-state actors who have resources sometimes greater than those of many states.[2] Two opposing views of globalization and its relationship to human rights have emerged: some see the two topics as mutually reinforcing and positive in improving human well-being, while others view globalization as posing new threats not adequately governed by existing international human rights law.

---

* Professor of Law, Notre Dame Law School. The author would like to thank Aaron Shelton for his assistance in the preparation of this Article.

[1] *See infra* note 42, et seq.

[2] *See infra* notes 31–25.

274   *Boston College International & Comparative Law Review*   [Vol. 25:273

The legal relationship between globalization and human rights can be analyzed from the perspective of economic regulation as well as that of human rights law, examining first whether international economic law sufficiently supports or takes into account human rights concerns, then considering the extent to which human rights law takes into account globalization and economic interests. In respect to both inquiries, the fundamental question is whether a human rights system premised on state responsibility to respect and ensure human rights can be effective in a globalized world.

This Article will discuss the framework of international human rights law and that related to globalization, i.e., international trade, technology, and investment law. It studies the relationship between globalization and human rights, assuming that international society accepts human rights as a fundamental goal and globalization as a generally positive phenomenon. After considering whether or not globalization is favorable to the promotion and protection of human rights, and whether or not the promotion and protection of human rights is favorable to globalization, the Article examines several approaches for the promotion and protection of human rights in the era of globalization: (1) emphasizing state responsibility for the actions of non-state actors; (2) imposing international legal obligations directly on non-state actors, including international institutions, multilateral enterprises, and individuals; (3) encouraging private regulation through corporate codes of conduct, product labeling, and other consumer or corporate actions; and (4) involving non-state actors directly in the activities of international organizations to promote and protect human rights.

The Article concludes that responses to globalization are significantly changing international law and institutions in order to protect persons from violations of human rights committed by non-state actors. To the extent that these changes have brought greater transparency to and participation in international organizations, globalization has produced unintended benefits and further challenges to the democratic deficit in global governance.[3] At the same time, an emphasis on subsidiarity and a strengthening of weak states and their institutions may be necessary to ensure that globalization does not mean a decline in state promotion and protection of human rights. To ensure that such strengthening does not lead to further

---

[3] *See* Eric Stein, *International Integration and Democracy: No Love at First Sight,* 95 Am. J. Int'l L. 489, 489 (2001).

human rights violations, the international community should make concerted multilateral efforts to enhance its ability to respond to human rights violations, rather than unleashing each state to control what it views as the sins of the private sector.

I. THE MEANINGS OF GLOBALIZATION

Globalization is a multidimensional phenomenon, comprising "numerous complex and interrelated processes that have a dynamism of their own."[4] It involves a deepening and broadening of rapid transboundary exchanges due to developments in technology, communications, and media.[5] Such exchanges and interactions occur at all levels of governance[6] and among non-state actors,[7] creating a more interdependent world.

Globalization is not new,[8] although its forms and the technology that spurs it have changed. Globalization today is most often associ-

---

[4] *Globalization and its Impact on the Full Enjoyment of All Human Rights: Preliminary Report of the Secretary-General,* U.N. GAOR, 55th Sess., ¶ 5, U.N. Doc. A/55/342 (2000). On the various meanings of globalization, see Wolfgang H. Reinicke & Jan Martin Witte, *Interdependence, Globalization and Sovereignty: The Role of Non-binding International Legal Accords, in* COMMITMENT AND COMPLIANCE: THE ROLE OF NON-BINDING NORMS IN THE INTERNATIONAL LEGAL SYSTEM 75 (Dinah Shelton ed., 2000). *See generally* A.G. MCGREW ET AL., GLOBAL POLITICS: GLOBALIZATION AND THE NATION STATES (1992); STATES AGAINST MARKETS: THE LIMITS OF GLOBALIZATION (R. Boyer & D. Drache eds., 1996); J.N. Rosenau, *The Dynamics of Globalization: Toward an Operational Formulation,* 27 SEC. DIALOGUE 247 (1996).

[5] The U.N. General Assembly has called globalization "not merely an economic process but [one that] has social, political, environmental, cultural and legal dimensions which have an impact on the full enjoyment of all human rights." *Globalization and its Impact on the Full Enjoyment of All Human Rights,* G.A. Res. 55/102, U.N. GAOR 3d Comm., 55th Sess., 81st plen. mtg., at 2, U.N. Doc. A/RES/55/02 (2001); *see also Globalization and its Impact on the Full Enjoyment of All Human Rights,* G.A. Res. 54/165, U.N. GAOR 3d Comm., 54th Sess., 83d plen. mtg., at 2, U.N. Doc. A/RES/54/165 (2000). Both resolutions recognize "that globalization affects all countries differently and makes them more exposed to external developments, positive as well as negative, including in the field of human rights." *Id.*

[6] *See generally* D.M. JOHNSTON, CONSENT AND COMMITMENT IN THE WORLD COMMUNITY (1997). Examples include the memoranda of understanding of port state authorities, judicial cooperation, and border city agreements. *Id.*

[7] HENRY STEINER & PHILIP ALSTON, INTERNATIONAL HUMAN RIGHTS IN CONTEXT 940 (2d. ed. 2000). Non-state actors include individuals, scientific and academic associations, international criminal syndicates, corporations, religious bodies, human rights organizations, and international organizations. *Id.* The U.N. estimates that there were some 36,000 non-governmental organizations in 1995. *Id.*

[8] Some see globalization as beginning around the end of the fifteenth century, with Europe's expansion through mercantile capitalism into America and Asia. *See* Statement of Rubens Ricupero, Secretary-General, UNCTAD, *Financial Globalization and Human Rights: Written Statement Submitted by the International Organization for the Development of Freedom of Education to the Commission on Human Rights,* U.N. Doc. E/CN.4/1998/NGO/76 (1998).

ated with economic interdependence, deregulation, and a dominance of the marketplace that includes a shifting of responsibilities from state to non-state actors.[9] Economic globalization has been accompanied by a marked increase in the influence of international financial markets and transnational institutions, including corporations, in determining national policies and priorities.[10] In addition, information and communications technology has emerged as a dominant force in the global system of production, while trade in goods, services, and financial instruments are more prevalent than any time in history.[11]

Some see this emergence of cross-border networks of production, finance, and communications as posing profound challenges to traditional concepts of state sovereignty. Richard Falk has spoken of the "disabling of the state as guardian of the global public good"[12] in the face of a shift of power and autonomy from the state to markets. Kenichi Ohmae refers to a "borderless world" in which "[m]ore than anything else, the burgeoning flow of information directly to consumers is eroding the ability of governments to pretend that their national economic interests are synonymous with those of their people."[13] He adds that, "[i]n today's world there is no such thing as a purely national economic interest."[14] Perhaps the same may be said for national political interests. Other authors refer to the decline of the western nation state.[15] The presence of weakened and failed states is an unde-

---

Others consider it to be a phenomenon with even longer roots, beginning with the invention of money and the emergence of trade links around the Mediterranean. *See* Grzegorz W. Kolodko, *Technical Paper No. 176: Globalisation and Transformation: Illusions and Reality*, at 7, *available at* http://www.oecd.org/dev/publication/tp1a.htm (last visited Dec. 12, 2001).

   [9] *See* W.H. REINICKE, GLOBAL PUBLIC POLICY: GOVERNING WITHOUT GOVERNMENT 11–18 (1998).

   [10] *See* Philip Alston, *The Universal Declaration in an Era of Globalization, in* REFLECTIONS ON THE UNIVERSAL DECLARATION OF HUMAN RIGHTS: A FIFTIETH ANNIVERSARY ANTHOLOGY 29 (Barend van der Heijden & Bahia Tahzi-Lie eds., 1998).

   [11] *See, e.g.*, John O. McGinnis, *The Decline of the Western Nation State and the Rise of the Regime of International Federalism*, 18 CARDOZO L. REV. 903, 918 (1996). The rate of information exchange has drastically reduced transaction costs, enabling expansion of transboundary communications. In 1860, sending two words across the Atlantic cost the equivalent of $40 in current money. Today this amount would be enough to transmit the contents of the entire Library of Congress. Kolodko, *supra* note 8, at 11–12.

   [12] RICHARD FALK, LAW IN AN EMERGING GLOBAL VILLAGE: A POST-WESTPHALIAN PERSPECTIVE, at xxiv (1998); *see also* Enrico Colombatto & Jonathan R. Macey, *A Public Choice Model of International Economic Cooperation and the Decline of the Nation State*, 18 CARDOZO L. REV. 925, 925 (1996).

   [13] KENICHI OHMAE, THE BORDERLESS WORLD 185 (1991).

   [14] *Id.* at 197.

   [15] McGinnis, *supra* note 11, at 918; KENICHI OHMAE, THE END OF THE NATION STATE: THE RISE OF REGIONAL ECONOMIES 1 (1995).

niable modern phenomenon,[16] yet there is no clear causal link between globalization and failed states.[17] Moreover, state sovereignty remains the international frame of reference,[18] even if the exact contours of sovereignty change over time, as they have throughout history.[19]

Paul Streeten has pointed out that globalization can come "from above," in the form of multinational firms, international capital flows, and world markets, or it can come "from below," reflecting the concerns of individuals and groups throughout the world.[20] It seems evident that globalization has enhanced the ability of civil society to function across borders and promote human rights. The past two decades have seen a shift to multi-party democratic regimes, as more than 100 countries ended rule by military dictatorships or single parties. Pressed by an international network of non-governmental organizations and activists, the international protection of human rights itself can be seen as an aspect of globalization, reflecting universal

---

[16] "An estimated five million people died in intrastate conflicts in the 1990s. In 1998, there were more than ten million refugees and five million internally displaced persons." U.N. DEVELOPMENT PROGRAMME, HUMAN DEVELOPMENT REPORT 2000, at 6 (2000), *available at* http://www.undp.org/hrd2000/english/hdr2000.htm [hereinafter UNDP]. On internal conflicts, race, and ethnicity, see NEW TRIBALISMS: THE RESURGENCE OF RACE AND ETHNICITY 1 (Michael W. Hughey ed., 1998).

[17] Dinah Shelton, *Droit et justice pour chaque citoyen de la planète?*, in MARINA RICCIAR-DELLI ET AL, MONDIALISATION ET SOCIÉTÉS MULTICULTURELLES: L'INCERTAIN DU FUTURE 305, 313 (2000). The weakening of the state is at the origin of numerous ethnic conflicts, sustained by unregulated commerce in conventional arms and by the growth in numbers of armed mercenaries. *Id.* Of the sixty-one conflicts that appeared during the years 1989–1998, all but three were internal armed conflicts. In states where the government has collapsed, armed tribes, and ethnic and political groups control territories without the rule of law and in the absence of public authorities. *Id.* In those states, human rights, like other legal constraints, have given way to anarchy and the exercise of unlimited power. *Id.*

[18] *See* Jason Burke et al., *Asylum in Crisis: All Australia Can Offer is Guano Island*, THE OBSERVER (LONDON), Sept. 2, 2001, at 3. Some 460 refugees on board the Norwegian freighter the MV Tampa discovered the on-going importance of borders and state sovereignty in September, 2001, when they were denied entry and held off the coast of Australia for six days before being routed to Nauru and New Zealand. *Id.*

[19] On the various meanings of sovereignty, see T.J. BIERSTECKER & C. WEBER, STATE SOVEREIGNTY AS A SOCIAL CONSTRUCT 1-4, 11, 123, 283 (1996); R. JACKSON & A. JAMES, STATES IN A CHANGING WORLD 8, 19 (1993); HENDRIK SPRUYT, THE SOVEREIGN STATE AND ITS COMPETITORS 36, 37 (1994). *See generally* JENS BARTELSON, A GENEALOGY OF SOVEREIGNTY (1995); STEPHEN KRASNER, SOVEREIGNTY: ORGANIZED HYPOCRISY (1999).

[20] Paul Streeten, *Globalization and its Impact on Development Co-operation*, 42 DEV. 11, 11 (1999).

278   *Boston College International & Comparative Law Review*   [Vol. 25:273

values about human dignity that limit the power of the state and reduce the sphere of sovereignty.[21]

Global technology and the information revolution have limited
the ability of governments to control the right to seek, receive, and
transmit information within and across boundaries. Ideas and information can circulate more freely, as can individuals. The number of
televisions per 1000 persons doubled between 1980 and 1995, while
the number of Internet subscribers exceeds 700 million persons. Free
circulation enhances the ability to inform all persons about rights and
avenues of redress. It also makes it more difficult for governments to
conceal violations and allows activists more easily to mobilize shame in
order to induce changes in government behavior.[22] Information
technology and the media also can be used, however, to violate human rights when the government is weak. In Rwanda, the radio and
television channel "Radio-Télévision Libre des Mille Collines" was an
important avenue for inciting genocide.[23] Internet too has been used
for hate speech.[24]

The multiple and sometimes contradictory impacts of globalization are reflected in the complete disagreement of views over the pattern and direction of globalization. Proponents point to a rise in average incomes for the world as a whole. Opponents note that there is
persistent inequality and poverty. The World Bank Development Report estimates that, at purchasing power parity, the per capita GDP in
the richest twenty countries in 1960 was eighteen times that of the

---

[21] Prior to the founding of the United Nations (U.N.), human rights were seen largely
as internal matters within the sovereignty of the state. Early debates in the U.N. over human rights usually centered on the question of whether or not Article 2(7), prohibiting
the U.N. from intervening in matters essentially within the domestic jurisdiction of a state,
excluded human rights issues from the agenda of the organization. For the debate over
South Africa's apartheid policies as a matter of international concern, see U.N. GAOR
Comm. on the Racial Situation in the Union of South Africa, 8th Sess., Supp. No. 16, at 16–
22, U.N. Doc. A/2505 (1953). Today, the claim of domestic jurisdiction is largely rejected.
See, e.g., Document of the Moscow Meeting of the Conference on the Human Dimension
of the Conference on Security and Cooperation in Europe, Oct. 3, 1991, *reprinted in* 30
I.L.M. 1670, 1672 (1991) ("[C]ommitments undertaken in the field of the human dimension of the CSCE are matters of direct and legitimate concern to all participating States
and do not belong exclusively to the internal affairs of the State concerned.").

[22] *See, e.g.,* Upendra Baxi, *Voices of Suffering and the Future of Human Rights,* 8 TRANS-
NAT'L L. & CONTEMP. PROBS. 125, 159–61 (1998).

[23] *See* Jamie Frederic Metzl, *Rwandan Genocide and the International Law of Radio Jam-
ming,* 91 AM. J. INT'L L. 628, 629 (1997).

[24] *See* Christiane Chombeau, *Des Juifs D'extrême Droite Déversent Leur Haine Antiarabe Sur
Internet,* LE MONDE, Oct. 12, 2001, at 11.

poorest twenty countries.[25] By 1995, the gap had widened to thirty-seven times.[26] According to the International Labor Organization (ILO), only 24%of the world's foreign direct investment (FDI) went to developing countries in 1999, down from 38% over the period 1993–97, and 80% of recent investment went to only ten developing countries.[27] Wealth concentration is not only seen among countries, but among individuals as well. According to the *UNDP Human Development Report 1999*, the assets of the three wealthiest individuals in the world is more than the combined gross national product of all least developed countries, while the annual sales of one transnational corporation exceeds the combined gross domestic product of Chile, Costa Rica, and Ecuador.[28]

Globalization, thus, has created powerful non-state actors that may violate human rights in ways that were not contemplated during the development of the modern human rights movement.[29] This development poses challenges to international human rights law, because, for the most part, that law has been designed to restrain abuses by powerful states and state agents, not to regulate the conduct of non-state actors themselves or to allow intervention in weak states when human rights violations occur.[30] An increasingly globalized civil society is likely to respond to economic globalization by opposing liberalized trade and investment regimes that are not accompanied by accountability, transparency, public participation, and respect for fundamental rights.

---

[25] INTERNATIONAL LABOR OFFICE, REDUCING THE DECENT WORK DEFICIT: A GLOBAL CHALLENGE–REPORT OF THE DIRECTOR GENERAL 49 (2001), *available at* http://www.ilo.org (citing WORLD BANK, WORLD BANK DEVELOPMENT REPORT 2000/2001: ATTACKING POVERTY (2001)) (last visited Jan. 29, 2002) [hereinafter ILO Report of the Director General].

[26] *Id.* The 1998 U.N. Development Program report has even more extreme figures, focusing on individual wealth: the 20% of the world's people who live in the richest countries had thirty times the income of the poorest 20% in 1960, and by 1995, had eighty-two times as much income. U.N. DEVELOPMENT PROGRAMME, HUMAN DEVELOPMENT REPORT 1998, at 29 (1998).

[27] *See* ILO Report of the Director General, *supra* note 25, § 3.1.

[28] U.N. RESEARCH INSTITUTE FOR SOCIAL DEVELOPMENT, STATES OF DISARRAY: THE SOCIAL EFFECTS OF GLOBALIZATION, REPORT ON THE WORLD SUMMIT FOR SOCIAL DEVELOPMENT 13 (1995), *available at* http://www.unrisd.org (last visited Mar. 11, 2002).

[29] Although there were issues such as the slave trade and war crimes that were raised during the nineteenth century and concern for some economic and social rights emerged in the early twentieth century, most human rights law developed in the period following World War II.

[30] *See generally* LOUIS HENKIN, THE AGE OF RIGHTS (1990).

280   *Boston College International & Comparative Law Review*   [Vol. 25:273]

The result may be viewed as a "clash of globalizations."[31] The clash plays out in the international institutional and normative system that has separated human rights matters from economic policy and regulation, creating distinct institutions, laws, and values for each field. Integrating them is no easy task; indeed, some commentators view a conflict as inevitable.[32]

A. *The Framework of International Human Rights Law*

The development of human rights law in response to globalization is not new, and there is nothing inherent in the international system that would prevent further protective measures. The movement against the slave trade, which was largely a private enterprise, and to combat the more indiscriminate or destructive forms of weaponry, such as gas warfare and dum-dum bullets, are early examples of international movements to counter the negative side of international trade and technology. Broader efforts to establish international protection for human rights can be traced to the surge of globalization and the emergence of international markets that occurred at the end of the nineteenth century.[33] During this period, the telephone, the telegraph, and radio transmissions first opened the world to rapid transboundary communications; the development of railroads and steamships allowed trade to move more quickly from one market to another, while the abuses associated with industrialization provoked efforts to improve working conditions and the standard of living in many countries.

Efforts to avoid competitive distortions and enhance the protection of fundamental rights of workers necessitated international labor standards. The resulting movement led to the creation of the ILO in 1919.[34] Unlike all subsequent international organizations, the ILO

---

[31] Stephen Kobrin, *The MAI and the Clash of Globalizations*, 112 FOREIGN POL'Y 97, 97 (1998).

[32] *See* Philip M. Nichols, *Trade Without Values*, 90 NW. U. L. REV. 658, 672–73 (1996) (noting that the basic values of globalization may conflict with other values of society); *see also* Frank Garcia, *The Global Market and Human Rights: Trading Away the Human Rights Principle*, 25 BROOK. J. INT'L L. 51, 51 (1999); Alex Seita, *Globalization and the Convergence of Values*, 30 CORNELL INT'L L.J. 429, 470 (1997).

[33] JACK DONNELLY, UNIVERSAL HUMAN RIGHTS IN THEORY AND PRACTICE 64 (1989) ("Modern markets also created a whole new range of threats to human dignity and thus were one of the principal sources of the need and demand for human rights.").

[34] The ILO's Constitution may be accessed at INTERNATIONAL LABOR ORGANIZATION CONST., *available at* http://www.ilo.org/public/english/about/iloconst.htm (last visited Mar. 11, 2002). The original constitution of the ILO comprises Part XIII of the Treaty of

engaged all the relevant actors in its operations from the beginning. Using a tripartite structure of representation, the ILO ensured the participation of business, labor, and governments in developing worker rights and minimum labor standards for member states.[35] While the standards adopted are addressed to member states for implementation, compliance requires the cooperation of the non-state actors as well, because the organization primarily aims to respond through regulation to poor treatment of labor by private industry. Such regulation is made easier by the participation of labor and business in the law-making and supervisory procedures of the ILO.

The international protection of civil and political rights emerged later, becoming an aim of the international community at the end of World War II in response to the atrocities committed during that conflict. While human rights theory supports the claims of rights holders against all others,[36] international human rights law treats the

---

Versailles of June 28, 1919, of the Treaty of Saint Germain of Sept. 10, 1919, of the Treaty of Trianon of June 4, 1920, and Part XII of the Treaty of Neuilly of Nov. 27, 1919. In 1944, the Declaration Concluding the Aims and Purposes of the ILO redefined the aims and purposes of the ILO to emphasize that: (1) labor is not a commodity: (2) freedom of expression and association is essential to sustained progress; and (3) all human beings have a right to pursue their material and spiritual well-being in conditions of freedom, dignity, and equal opportunity. The Declaration now forms an annex to the ILO Constitution. For further information on the ILO, see International Labor Organization, *at* http://www.ilo.org (last visited Mar. 11, 2002).

[35] Between 1919 and 2001, the ILO adopted 182 conventions and 180 recommendations covering basic human rights such as abolition of forced labor, freedom of association, and elimination of child labor, as well as conventions on occupational safety and health, industrial relations, and other conditions of employment.

[36] Among the fundamental theoretical issues respecting human rights is the question of who rights may be claimed against, i.e., identifying the duty-holder corresponding to the rights-holder. The French Declaration of the Rights of Man and the Citizen proclaims that, "the end in view of every political association is the preservation of the natural and imprescriptable rights of man." Declaration of the Rights of Man and the Citizen, French National Assembly, Aug. 27, 1789, art. II. This may imply rights held against all private and public interests. H.L.A. Hart describes "general rights" as those which "have as correlatives obligations not to interfere to which everyone else is subject and not merely the parties to some special relationship or transaction, though of course they will often be asserted when some particular persons threaten to interfere as a moral objection to the interference." H.L.A. Hart, *Are There Any Natural Rights? in* Jeremy Waldron, Theories of Rights 77, 87–88 (1984). In his view the assertion of general rights directly invokes the principle that all men equally have the right to be free; the assertion of a special right invokes the same concept indirectly. Gerwith also posits that rights are claim-rights, in the Hohfeldian sense, that they "are justified claims or entitlements to the carrying out of some correlative duties, positive or negative. A duty is a requirement that some action be performed or not be performed; in the latter, negative case, the requirement constitutes a prohibition." A. Gewirth, *Are There Any Absolute Rights?, in* Waldron, *supra,* at 93. Government's function is to ensure that rights and duties are fulfilled. Winston agrees that, "when individuals enter

282   *Boston College International & Comparative Law Review*   [Vol. 25:273]

state as the principal threat to individual freedom and well being.[37] In the post-World War II paradigm, the state and its agents are obliged to respect and ensure rights. Indeed, some acts are explicitly defined as human rights violations only if committed by state agents or those acting in complicity with them.[38] If rights are violated, the state is obligated to ensure domestic remedies to correct the harm are available.[39] A failure to do so may allow the individual to bring a complaint against the state before an international tribunal. No *international* procedures exist at present whereby an injured individual may directly hold responsible the individual perpetrator of the harm.[40]

Despite the emphasis on state responsibility, international human rights instruments continue to recognize human rights that are violated predominately by non-state actors, for example, freedom from slavery and forced labor. The duty imposed in such instances, however, remains primarily on the state to ensure the right against the slave holders and employers of forced labor. Human rights instruments also speak to the obligations of non-state actors. The first gen-

---

into the social compacts by which governments are created, they in effect deputize their governments to discharge their duties to protect human rights on their behalves. This would explain why it is customary to treat governments as the addressees of human rights, but also why, when governments fail to fulfill their roles in protecting these rights, the responsibility to see that they are protected devolves on individuals." MORTON E. WINSTON, THE PHILOSOPHY OF HUMAN RIGHTS 9 (1988).

[37] *See* Anne Orford, *Contesting Globalization: A Feminist Perspective on the Future of Human Rights, in* THE FUTURE OF INTERNATIONAL HUMAN RIGHTS 157, 157 (Burns H. Weston & Stephen P. Marks eds., 1999) (noting human rights law was not designed to consider as human rights violations those abuses that take place in the private sector).

[38] *See, e.g.,* Convention Against Torture and Other Cruel, Inhuman or Degrading Treatment or Punishment, Dec. 10, 1984, art. 1, G.A. Res. 39/46, U.N. GAOR, Supp. No. 51, at 197, U.N. Doc. E/CN.4/1984/72 (1984), *reprinted in* 23 I.L.M. 1027 (entered into force June 26, 1987) ("[Torture] means any act by which severe pain or suffering . . . is intentionally inflicted on a person . . . by or at the instigation of or with the consent or acquiescence of a public official or other person acting in an official capacity."); Inter-American Convention to Prevent and Punish Torture, Dec. 9, 1985, art. 3, O.A.S.T.S. No. 67, O.A.S. Doc. OEA/ser. P., AG/doc. 2023/85, *reprinted in* 25 I.L.M. 519 (1986) (entered into force Feb. 28, 1987) (describing those who shall be guilty of torture as including a public servant or employee or a person acting at the instigation of a public servant or employee).

[39] *See generally* DINAH SHELTON, REMEDIES IN INTERNATIONAL HUMAN RIGHTS LAW (2000).

[40] According to Michael Riesman, one of the "crueler ironies" of human rights law is that the system allows the actual wrongdoers to escape responsibility while the victims pay taxes the state uses to compensate such victims for the harms they have suffered. Michael Reisman & Janet Koven Levit, *Reflections on the Problem of Individual Responsibility for Violations of Human Rights, in* THE MODERN WORLD OF HUMAN RIGHTS: ESSAYS IN HONOR OF THOMAS BUERGENTHAL 419, 421 (Pedro Nikken & Antonio Cancado Trindade eds., 1996).

eral international human rights instrument, the American Declaration of the Rights and Duties of Man (American Declaration), begins its preamble with an exhortation to all individuals to conduct themselves with respect for the rights and freedoms of others. It clearly views individuals as having duties towards each other.[41] The Universal Declaration of Human Rights (Universal Declaration), adopted some six months later, refers to itself as "a common standard of achievement for all peoples and all nations, to the end that every individual, and every organ of society" shall strive to promote respect for, and observance of, the rights.[42] Article 1 of the Universal Declaration specifically refers to the behavior of individuals towards each other.[43] This is complemented at the close of the Universal Declaration with a firm statement that, "[n]othing in this Declaration may be interpreted as implying for any [s]tate, group or person any right to engage in any activity or to perform any act aimed at the destruction of any of the rights and freedoms set forth herein."[44] Human rights law also imposes individual responsibility for some human rights violations[45] and other acts[46] designated as crimes under international law. These offenses require the state where the offender is found to try or extradite the individual, and in a few instances may allow prosecution before an

---

[41] *See* American Declaration of the Rights and Duties of Man, Ninth International Conference of American States, O.A.S. Res. XXX, art. XXIX, O.A.S. Off. Rec. OEA/ser. L./V/I.4 Rev. (1965). ("It is the duty of the individual to so conduct himself in relation to others that each and every one may fully form and develop his personality.").

[42] Universal Declaration of Human Rights, G.A. Res. 217A (III), U.N. GAOR, 3d Sess., at 71, U.N. Doc. A/810 (1948) [hereinafter Universal Declaration].

[43] *Id.* art. 1.

[44] *Id.* art. 30.

[45] Human rights treaties that call for criminalization of specific acts include the Convention on the Prevention and Punishment of the Crime of Genocide, the U.N. Convention Against Torture, the Inter-American Convention against Torture, the Inter-American Convention on Forced Disappearance of Persons, and the International Convention on the Suppression and Punishment of the Crime of Apartheid.

[46] *See, e.g.,* Convention for the Suppression of Unlawful Seizure of Aircraft, Dec. 16, 1970, 22 U.S.T. 1641, 860 U.N.T.S. 105, 10 I.L.M. 133 (1971) (entry into force Oct. 14, 1971); Convention for the Suppression of Unlawful Acts Against the Safety of Civil Aviation, Sept. 23, 1971, 24 U.S.T. 564, 10 I.L.M. 1151 (1971) (entry into force Jan. 26, 1973); Convention on the Prevention and Punishment of Crimes against Internationally Protected Persons, Including Diplomatic Agents, Dec. 14, 1973, 28 U.S.T. 1975, 1035 U.N.T.S. 168, 13 I.L.M. 41 (1974) (entry into force Feb. 20, 1977); European Convention on the Suppression of Terrorism, Nov. 10, 1976, Europ. T.S. No. 90, 15 I.L.M. 1272 (1976) (entry into force, Aug. 4, 1978); International Convention against the Taking of Hostages, June 3, 1983, G.A. Res. 34/146, at xxxiv, U.N. GAOR, Supp. No. 46, at 245, U.N. Doc. A/34/786 (1979), *reprinted in* 18 I.L.M. 1456 (1979).

international tribunal.[47] More generally, Article 28 of the Universal Declaration recognizes that, "[e]veryone is entitled to a social and international order in which the rights and freedoms set for in th[e] Declaration can be fully realized."[48] From this may emerge the principle that respect for human rights applies to all societal relations locally, regionally, and globally. Thus, although positive human rights law generally addresses state action or inaction, the theoretical and positive foundation is there to apply human rights guarantees to non-state actors.

In recent years, the many facets and importance of the complex interplay of human rights and globalization are reflected in the multiple studies conducted on aspects of globalization by the human rights organs of the United Nations (U.N.). The Sub-Commission on the Promotion and Protection of Human Rights (Sub-Commission) has undertaken studies on transnational corporations,[49] on the impact of globalization on the enjoyment of human rights generally,[50] the impact of globalization on racism and xenophobia,[51] the relationship between the enjoyment of human rights and income distribution,[52] and on human rights as the primary objective of international trade,

---

[47] For crimes committed in the former Yugoslavia and in Rwanda, the U.N. created special international tribunals, but a permanent international court does not exist.

[48] Universal Declaration, *supra* note 42, at 71.

[49] *See The Relationship Between the Enjoyment of Economic, Social and Cultural Rights and the Right to Development, and the Working Methods and Activities of Transnational Corporations*, Sub-Commission on Prevention of Discrimination and Protection of Minorities Res. 1998/8, U.N. ESCOR, 50th Sess., 26th mtg., U.N. Doc. E/CN.4/Sub.2/Res/1998/8 (1998) [hereinafter Sub-Commission Resolution 1999/8].

[50] *See* J. Oloka-Onyango & Deepika Udagama, *The Realization of Economic, Social and Cultural Rights: Globalization and Its Impact on the Full Enjoyment of Human Rights*, U.N. ESCOR, 52d Sess., U.N. Doc. E/CN.4/Sub.2/2000/13 (2000) (submitted in accordance with Sub-Commission Resolution 1999/8) [hereinafter Oloka-Onyango & Udagama, *Globalization* I]; J. Oloka-Onyango & Deepika Udagama, *Economic, Social and Cultural Rights: Globalization and Its Impact on the Full Enjoyment of Human Rights*, U.N. ESCOR, 53d Sess., U.N. Doc. E/CN.4/Sub.2/2001/10 (2001) (submitted in accordance with Sub-Commission Resolution 1999/8 and Commission on Human Rights Decision 2000/102). In decision 2000/102, the Commission on Human Rights decided to approve the nomination of Mr. J. Oloka-Onyango and Ms. Deepika Udagama as Special Rapporteurs to undertake a study on the issue of globalization and its impact on the full enjoyment of all human rights.

[51] *See* J. Oloka-Onyango, *Comprehensive Examination of Thematic Issues Relating to the Elimination of Racial Discrimination: Globalization in the Context of Increased Incidents of Racism, Racial Discrimination and Xenophobia*, U.N. ESCOR, 51st Sess., U.N. Doc. E/CN.4/Sub.2/ 1999/8 (1999) [hereinafter Oloka-Onyango, *Racism*].

[52] *See* Jose Bengoa, *The Realization of Economic, Social and Cultural Rights: The Relationship Between the Enjoyment of Human Rights, in Particular Economic, Social and Cultural Rights, and Income Distribution*, U.N. ESCOR, 49th Sess., U.N. Doc. E/CN.4/Sub.2/1997/9 (1997).

investment, and finance policy and practice.[53] Beginning in 1998, the Commission on Human Rights (Commission) established a working group on the impact of structural adjustment programs on economic, social, and cultural rights.[54] The working group is largely composed of developing countries, with France, Germany, and Italy representing industrialized countries among the sixteen states participating. The Commission also has appointed an independent expert on the topic.[55]

Both the Commission and the Sub-Commission have adopted resolutions on globalization and human rights.[56] The Sub-Commission also unanimously adopted a resolution on trade liberalization and its impact on human rights,[57] in which it asked all governments and forums of economic policy to take fully into consideration the obligations and principles of human rights in the formulation of international economic policy. At the same time, the resolution expressed opposition to unilateral sanctions and to negative conditionality on trade as a means to integrate human rights into the policies and practices governing international economic matters. The resolution requested the High Commissioner for Human Rights to cooperate with the World Trade Organization (WTO) and its member states to underline the human dimension of free trade and investments and to take measures to see that human rights principles and obligations are fully taken into account in future negotiations in the framework of the WTO.

Finally, it is noteworthy that human rights law not only potentially imposes duties on non-state economic actors, it guarantees rights es-

---

[53] *See* J. Oloka-Onyango & Deepika Udagama, *The Realization of Economic, Social and Cultural Rights: Human Rights as the Primary Objective of International Trade, Investment and Finance Policy and Practice,* U.N. ESCOR, 51st Sess., U.N. Doc. E.CN.4/Sub.2/1999/11 (1999).

[54] *See Economic, Social and Cultural Rights: Report of the Open-ended Working Group on Structural Adjustment Programmes and Economic, Social and Cultural Rights on Its Second Session.,* U.N. ESCOR, 55th Sess., U.N. Doc. E/CN.4/1999/51 (1999).

[55] *See* Fantu Cheru, *Economic, Social and Cultural Rights: Effects of Structural Adjustment Policies on the Full Enjoyment of Human Rights,* U.N. ESCOR, 51st Sess., U.N. Doc. E/CN.4/1999/50 (1999).

[56] For more information on this matter, see the Commission on Human Rights, Resolution 1999/59 of April 27, 1999, and the Sub-Commission on the Promotion and Protection of Human Rights, on globalization and its impact on the full enjoyment of all human rights. U.N. ESCOR, 51st Sess., 58th mtg., U.N. Doc. E/CN.4/Res/1999/59 (1999); U.N. ESCOR, 52d Sess., 32d mtg., U.N. Doc E/CN.4/Sub.2/Res/2000/7 (2000).

[57] See *Trade Liberalization and Human Rights,* Sub-Commission on the Promotion and Protection of Human Rights Res. 1999/30, U.N. ESCOR, 51st Sess., U.N. Doc. E/CN.4/Sub.2/ Res/1999/30 (1999) [hereinafter Res. 1999/30].

sential for the furtherance of globalization. It protects the right to property, including intellectual property, freedom of expression and communications across boundaries, due process for contractual or other business disputes, and a remedy before an independent tribunal when rights are violated. Furthermore, the rule of law is an essential prerequisite to the long-term conduct of trade and investment.

B. *The Framework of International Trade Law*

Intrinsic to globalization is the contemporary legal and institutional framework within which the regimes of international trade, finance, and investment are being conducted. In general, economic globalization has a focus on economic efficiency, the goal being to improve economic well being through efficient market exchanges.[58] The system is based upon enhancing the economic well being of nations through trade, on the theory that gains are maximized through the unrestricted flow of goods across national boundaries.[59] The system rests upon a view of humans as economic beings that seek to maximize wealth and self-interested satisfaction of personal preferences.[60] In a pure economic model, values outside efficiency are irrelevant, even pernicious because they complicate or hamper the trading system.[61]

---

[58] *See* JOHN H. JACKSON, THE WORLD TRADING SYSTEM: LAW AND POLICY OF INTERNATIONAL ECONOMIC RELATIONS 8–9 (2d ed. 1989).

[59] *See* DOUGLAS A. IRWIN, AGAINST THE TIDE: AN INTELLECTUAL HISTORY OF FREE TRADE 3 (1996).

[60] On economic values, see Daniel M. Hausman & Michael S. McPherson, *Taking Ethics Seriously: Economic and Contemporary Moral Philosophy,* 31 J. ECON. LITERATURE 671, 671 (1993).

[61] The consequences of the economic approach can be tested by considering the issue of child labor. The ILO estimates that there are approximately 250 million children working worldwide. ILO Report of the Director General, *supra* note 25, § 1.3. From the human rights perspective, a ban on child labor is necessary for the well-being, dignity, and proper development of the child. It is also legally required to implement the ILO Convention and the Convention on the Rights of the Child which reflect these goals. Convention on the Rights of the Child, Nov. 20, 1989, 28 I.L.M. 1456 (1989). Every state except the United States has ratified the latter Convention and some states have enacted child labor bans, in total or in part. For example, the United States prohibits the importation of products "mined, produced and manufactured by forced or indentured child labor." Treasury and General Government Appropriations Act of 1998, Pub. L. No. 105–61, § 634, 111 Stat. 1272, 1316 (1998). From the perspective of international economic theory, it can be argued that such bans should be discouraged because they are inefficient. Child labor produces goods more cheaply and gives an economic advantage to the producing state. On the other hand, economic analysis also shows that productivity increases with the educational level of workers and in the long run is likely to be more economically beneficial than child labor. Within the international trading regime, such trade bans could be found

The legal dimensions of the framework are expressed in international economic law and the institutional structure of the Bretton Woods multilateral lending institutions and the WTO. International trade and finance institutions were created largely to operate on the economic model and generally exclude from consideration other values of international society, like human rights and environmental protection.

The international trade regime is clearly marked by a commitment to open markets.[62] The Uruguay Round agreements that concluded with the establishment of the WTO[63] expanded the substantive reach of international trade regulation to include trade-related aspect of intellectual property,[64] trade in services,[65] and trade-related investment measures.[66] Yet, within the legal instruments and policies related to trade and investment there can be found some considerations of human rights. The General Agreement on Tariffs and Trade (GATT) allows states to ban the importation of products stemming from prison labor.[67] In addition, GATT Article XX(a) permits trade measures "necessary to human morals."[68] GATT Article XX(b) allows

---

to be in violation of the most-favored-nation and national treatment requirements unless they are justified by one of the exceptions found in GATT article XX. The jurisprudence of the WTO suggests that only products themselves are the subject of the restrictions, not the processes by which they are made. *See* GATT Dispute Panel Report on Thailand–Restrictions on Imp. of and Internal Taxes on Cigarettes, Nov. 7, 1990, GATT B.I.S.D. (37th Supp.) at 200, DS 10/R-375/200 (1991); GATT Dispute Panel Report on U.S. Restrictions on Imp. of Tuna, 33 I.L.M. 1594 (1991).

[62] Frank Garcia argues that, "the regulatory framework which international economic law provides for globalization operates according to a view of human nature, human values and moral decision-making fundamentally at odds with the view of human nature, human values and moral decision-making which underlies international human rights law." Garcia, *supra* note 28, at 53 (1999).

[63] *See* Agreement Establishing the World Trade Organization, Apr. 15, 1994, 108 Stat. 4809, 4815, 33 I.L.M. 1125, 1144 (1994) [hereinafter WTO Agreement].

[64] *See* Agreement on Trade-Related Aspects of Intellectual Property Rights, Apr. 15, 1994, Marrakesh Agreement Establishing the World Trade Organization, Annex 1C, LEGAL INSTRUMENTS—RESULTS OF THE URUGUAY ROUND vol. 31, 33 I.L.M. 81 (1994), *available at* http://www.wto.org [hereinafter TRIPs Agreement].

[65] *See* General Agreement on Trade in Services, Apr. 15, 1994, 108, Stat. 4809, 4815, 33 I.L.M. 1167 (1994), *available at* http://www.wto.org [hereinafter GATS Agreement].

[66] *See* Agreement on Trade-Related Investment Measures, Apr. 15, 1994, 108 Stat. 4809, 4815 (1994), *available at* http://www.wto.org.

[67] General Agreement on Tariffs and Trade, Oct. 30, 1947, art. XX(e), 61 Stat. 5, A3, T.I.A.S. 1700, 55 U.N.T.S. 187, *available at* http://www.wto.org [hereinafter GATT Agreement]; General Agreement on Tariffs and Trade-Multilateral Trade Negotiations, Final Act Embodying the Results of the Uruguay Round of Multilateral Trade Negotiations, Apr. 15, 1994, art. XX(e), 33 I.L.M. 1125 (1994).

[68] GATT Agreement, *supra* note 67, art. XX(a).

measures "necessary to protect human, animal or plant life or health."[69] All of these exceptions are limited by the Article XX *chapeau* that requires the measures taken not be a means of arbitrary or unjustifiable discrimination or a disguised restriction on trade.[70]

The agreement establishing the WTO refers to "reciprocal arrangements" for tariff reductions and the "elimination of discriminatory treatment in international trade relations."[71] Yet, the annexes to the WTO Agreement comprise seventeen interwoven trade agreements that accord rights indirectly to individuals and other non-state actors.[72] Among the rights protected are those of intellectual property.[73] The General Agreement on Trade in Services (GATS) applies most-favored nation and national treatment principles to service suppliers, requiring that governments accord non-national service suppliers treatment no less favorable than that granted to suppliers from any other country.[74] The earlier GATT Article X requires remedies before independent tribunals for those affected by the application of national laws and public information about those laws and regulations.[75] The WTO extends these procedural rights to the agreements on antidumping, subsidies, intellectual property, and services.[76]

In jurisprudence and statements of international officials, the rights of non-state actors are beginning to be considered. In a 1999 panel decision, the panel stated that, "the multilateral trading system is, per force, composed not only of States but also, indeed mostly, of individual economic operators" whose needs should be a factor in deciding disputes brought to the WTO.[77] The U.N. Secretary-General

---

[69] *Id.* art. XX(b).

[70] *Id.* art. XX. For an interpretation of the *chapeau* and Article XX exceptions, see GATT Appellate Body Report on U.S.–Imp. Prohibition of Certain Shrimp and Shrimp Prod., § VI(c), WT/DS58/AB/R (Oct. 12, 1998), *available at* 1998 WL 720123, at *41.

[71] WTO Agreement, *supra* note 63, pmbl.

[72] *See* Steve Charnowitz, *The WTO and the Rights of the Individual,* 36 INTERECONOMICS 98 (2001).

[73] *See* TRIPs Agreement, *supra* note 64, arts. 1.3, 2.1, 9.1, 10.2, 11, 14.2, 16.1, 25.1, 27.1, 35.

[74] GATS Agreement, *supra* note 65, arts. I:2(d), II:1.

[75] GATT Agreement, *supra* note 67, art. X.

[76] For the application of such procedural rights to anti-dumping, see the WTO Agreement on Implementation of Article VI of the General Agreement on Tariffs and Trade 1994, arts. 6.1, 12.1, 12.2, 6.2, 6.9, 8.3, 13, 11.2, *available at* http:// docsonline.wto.org (last visited Mar. 1, 2002), and for the application of subsidies. *See* TRIPs Agreement, *supra* note 64, arts. 22.2, 23.1, 26.1, 28.1, 31, 39.2, 41, 42, 46; GATs Agreement, *supra* note 65, arts. VI, VII.5.

[77] GATT Dispute Panel Report on U.S.–Sections 301–310 of the Trade Act of 1974, ¶¶ 7.76, 7.90, 7.94, 7.167, WT/DS152/R (Dec. 22, 1999).

has found that the goals and principles of the WTO agreements and those of human rights law have much in common in part because the WTO agreements "seek to create a liberal and rules-based multilateral trading system" according to which states can trade under conditions of fair competition.[78]

Yet, efforts to strengthen human rights protections in trade law have run into difficulties. The WTO Singapore Ministerial Declaration made reference to international labor standards, yet primarily affirmed the jurisdiction of the ILO over the matter.[79] Before and during the meeting of member states of the WTO in Seattle, developing countries opposed any discussion or negotiation on worker rights. Industrialized countries recommended enhanced cooperation between the secretariats of the WTO and the ILO, while the United States called for the elaboration of a working program dedicated to employment standards. It seems clear that at present the WTO would oppose the use of unilateral or multilateral trade sanctions for human rights violations. Regional economic bodies have more easily raised human rights matters.[80]

With globalization, the International Monetary Fund (IMF) and the World Bank have received considerable attention because of the substantial impact they can have on human rights, although both initially resisted taking human rights into account in their operations.[81] The General Counsel of the World Bank at first rejected the idea that the Bank should take into account human rights concerns, arguing a need to honor the Bank's Charter[82] "and to respect the specialisation of different international organisations."[83] Recently, the World Bank

---

[78] The goals of the WTO include the objectives of increasing living standards, full employment, the expansion of demand, production and trade in goods and services, linked to optimal use of the world's resources according to the objective of sustainable development. WTO Agreement, *supra* note 63, pmbl.

[79] World Trade Organization, *Singapore Ministerial Declaration* ¶ 4, WTO Doc. WT/MIN(96)DEC/W (Dec. 13, 1996), *reprinted in* 36 I.L.M. 218, 221 (1997).

[80] NAFTA has created a Labor Commission to monitor national enforcement of labor laws. North-American Agreement on Labor Cooperation, Sept. 8, 1993, Can.-Mex.-U.S., art. 8.1, 32 I.L.M. 1499, 1504 (1993). The European Union makes respect for human rights a condition of membership via the Treaty of Amsterdam.

[81] *See* James Gathii, *Human Rights, The World Bank and the Washington Consensus: 1949-1999*, 94 AM. SOC'Y INT'L L. PROC. 144, 144 (2000); Anne Orford, *The Subject of Globalization: Economics, Identity and Human Rights*, 94 AM. SOC'Y INT'L L. PROC. 146, 147 (2000).

[82] The Articles of Agreement of the International Bank for Reconstruction and Development, July 22, 1944, 60 Stat. 1440, 2 U.N.T.S. 134, *as amended*, 16 U.S.T. 1942, 606 U.N.T.S. 294 (1965) (providing in Article IV, section 10 that, "[o]nly economic considerations shall be relevant" in the Bank's lending decisions and operations).

[83] Ibrahim Shihata, *Democracy and Development*, 46 INT'L & COMP. L.Q. 635, 638 (1997).

has begun to consider the human dimension of its work and it has declared that the alleviation of poverty is its main objective. The Bank has also been active in designing mechanisms to address the issue of the debt burden, culminating in the highly indebted poor countries (HIPC) initiative.

These efforts mark a shift from the "Washington Consensus" methods of structural adjustment and economic liberalization that were applied in the 1980s and early 1990s to the macroeconomic policies of developing countries.[84] The Washington Consensus privileged market forces, and the Bank followed by promoting privatization programs that took the state out of health, education, and housing. Reduced social spending transferred resources to the private sector and, in some cases, to the military. Human rights activists responded by demanding greater attention to human rights and a social safety net to meet the basic needs of individuals.

Largely as a result of scrutiny from non-governmental organizations and activists concerned about increasing wealth disparity, increased unemployment and other failures to improve the human condition in the countries subject to Bank operations, the Bank has begun to pay attention to social safety nets, human rights, and the notion of good governance. By 1990, the General Counsel determined that, "[v]iolation of political rights may . . . reach such proportions as to become a Bank concern due to significant direct economic effects or if it results [in violation of] international obligations."[85] In 1998, the Bank published a report on development and human rights emphasizing equality and development and the protection of vulnerable groups.[86] It also instituted its Inspection Panel to hear a narrow spectrum of complaints about violations of Bank policy.

The IMF has been less accommodating and remains under pressure to incorporate human rights concerns in its activities. After a difficult public encounter in May, 2001 between the IMF and the U.N. Committee on Economic, Social and Cultural Rights (CESCR), the latter invited three members of the CESCR to meet with the IMF in

---

[84] *See* Cord Jakobeit, *The World Bank and Human Development: Washington's New Strategic Approach*, 6 DEV. & COOPERATION 1, 4 (1999).

[85] IBRAHIM SHIHATA, ISSUES OF "GOVERNANCE" IN BORROWING MEMBERS: THE EXTENT OF THEIR RELEVANCE UNDER THE BANK'S ARTICLES OF AGREEMENT (1990), *quoted in* JOHN STREMLAU & FRANCISCO SAGASTI, PREVENTING DEADLY CONFLICT: DOES THE WORLD BANK HAVE A ROLE? 45 (1998).

[86] WORLD BANK GROUP, DEVELOPMENT AND HUMAN RIGHTS: THE ROLE OF THE WORLD BANK (1998), *available at* http://www.worldbank.org/html/extdr/rights/hrintro.htm (last visited Mar. 11, 2002).

Washington on October 31, 2001, to have informal, private discussions to try to find some common ground and build confidence.

The IMF argues that its founding Charter mandates that it pay attention only to issues of economic nature. The IMF has issued a document on "Good Governance,"[87] said to respond to the fact that, "a much broader range of institutional reforms is needed if countries are to establish and maintain private sector confidence and thereby lay the basis for sustained growth."[88] The IMF's concerns still appear confined to:

> Issues such as institutional reforms of the treasury, budget preparation and approval procedures, tax administration, accounting, and audit mechanisms, central bank operations, and the official statistics function. Similarly, reforms of market mechanisms would focus primarily on the exchange, trade, and price systems, and aspects of the financial system. In the regulatory and legal areas, IMF advice would focus on taxation, banking sector laws and regulations, and the establishment of free and fair market entry.[89]

The "Good Governance" document emphasizes combating corruption and the need to establish transparent operational systems within states; there is no mention of human rights. The Guidelines also say nothing about the IMF itself and its operations.

While both the World Bank and the IMF have modified their policy stances to reduce the emphasis on structural adjustment policies to give greater emphasis to poverty reduction, the ILO still faults them for failing to give enough importance to employment. In its view, a number of country experiences clearly show that integration in global markets is compatible with successful social policy, provided there are adequate national social security systems, functioning systems of social dialogue and relatively low income inequality.[90]

II. Is Globalization Good for Human Rights?

There is considerable debate over the question of whether or not globalization is good for human rights. One view is that globalization

---

[87] *See generally* INTERNATIONAL MONETARY FUND, GOOD GOVERNANCE: THE IMF's ROLE (1997).

[88] *Id.* at v.

[89] *Id.* at 4.

[90] *See generally* ILO Report of the Director General, *supra* note 25, at 9.

enhances human rights, leading to economic benefits and consequent political freedoms.[91] The positive contributions of globalization have even led to the proposal that it be accepted as a new human right.[92] In general, trade theory predicts a significant increase in global welfare stemming from globalization, indirectly enhancing the attainment of economic conditions necessary for economic and social rights. Many thus believe that market mechanisms and liberalized trade will lead to an improvement in the living standards of all people. Some also posit that free trade and economic freedom are necessary conditions of political freedom, or at least contribute to the rule of law that is an essential component of human rights.[93] Certainly, globalization facilitates international exchanges that overcome the confines of a single nation or a civilization, allowing participation in a global community. There is also the possibility that economic power can be utilized to sanction human rights violators more effectively.[94] Ease of movement of people, goods, and services are enhanced. Increased availability and more efficient allocation of resources, more open and competitive production and improved governance could lead to faster growth and more rights. In sum, Judith Bello argues that:

> Trade liberalization promotes the growth of stability-promoting middle class all over the globe; trade enhances efficiency and wealth and thereby creates potential revenue for environmental protection. Trade creates jobs in developing as well as developed countries, thereby reducing the pressure on both illegal immigration and illicit drug trafficking. Trade liberalization is not a panacea for the world's problems, but it can be part of a solution for many of them.[95]

The pro-globalization assumption that globalization is in the common good and market forces will achieve general well being is

---

[91] *See* Anthony Giddens, Runaway World: How Globalization Is Reshaping Our Lives 30–35 (1999).

[92] M.D. Pendleton, *A New Human Right—The Right to Globalization*, 22 Fordham Int'l L.J. 2052, 2052 (1999).

[93] *See* Garcia, *supra* note 32, at 60.

[94] *See* Patricia Stirling, *The Use of Trade Sanctions as an Enforcement Mechanism for Basic Human Rights: A Proposal for Addition to the World Trade Organization*, 11 Am. U. J. Int'l L. & Pol'y 1, 42–45 (1996).

[95] Judith Bello, *National Sovereignty and Transnational Problem Solving*, 18 Cardozo L. Rev. 1027, 1029 (1996).

not a consensus view. Anne Orford, for example, argues that, "[t]he trade and investment liberalization furthered by the Uruguay Round agreements entrenches a relationship between states and transnational corporations that privileges the property interests of those corporations over the human rights of local peoples and communities."[96] As such, the economic and technological changes associated with globalization may lead to a world in which the state is no longer the principal threat to human rights, but one where the threats are more posed by multinational corporations, multilateral intergovernmental organizations, and transnational criminal syndicates or organized terrorists. The U.N. Development Program devoted its 2000 *Human Development Report* to "Human Development and Human Rights" in which it pointed out that, "global corporations can have enormous impact on human rights—in their employment practices, in their environmental impact, in their support for corrupt regimes or in their advocacy for policy changes."[97]

It has been argued that values associated with human rights emerge with multinational free market growth, as the rule of law follows investors who seek predictability and safeguarding of investments, leading to strengthened independent institutions for civil and political rights, but human rights advocates assert that liberalization in trade, investment, and finance does not necessarily lead to general economic development or better human rights performance. According to the Oxfam Poverty Report:

> Trade has the power to create opportunities and support livelihoods; and it has the power to destroy them. Production for export can generate income, employment, and the foreign exchange which poor countries need for their development. But it can also cause environmental destruction and a loss of livelihoods, or lead to unacceptable levels of exploitation. The human impact of trade depends on how goods are produced, who controls the production and marketing, how the wealth generated is distributed, and the terms upon which countries trade. The way in which the international trading system is managed has a critical bearing on all of these areas.[98]

---

[96] Orford, *supra* note 37, 169.
[97] UNDP, *supra* note 16, at 1.
[98] KEVIN WATKINS, THE OXFAM POVERTY REPORT 109–110 (1995).

294   *Boston College International & Comparative Law Review*   [Vol. 25:273

Opponents of globalization see it as a threat to human rights in several ways. First, local decision-making and democratic participation are undermined when multinational companies, the World Bank, and the IMF set national economic and social policies. Second, unrestricted market forces threaten economic, social, and cultural rights such as the right to health, especially when structural adjustment policies reduce public expenditures for health and education. Third, accumulations of power and wealth in the hands of foreign multinational companies increase unemployment, poverty, and the marginalization of vulnerable groups.

Some criticism has been particularly strong. In resolution 1997/11, the U.N. Sub-Commission on the Promotion and Protection of Human Rights asked El Hadji Guissé to prepare a working document on the impact of the activities of transnational corporations on the realization of economic, social, and cultural rights. The report, delivered in June, 1998, is a wholesale condemnation of economic globalization.[99] It begins, "[t]oday's economic and financial systems are organized in such a way as to act as pumps that suck up the output of the labour of the toiling masses and transfer it, in the form of wealth and power, to a privileged minority."[100] Given this opening, it is not surprising that Guissé finds little in globalization that assists in the realization of human rights. Yet, he agrees that the pursuit of profit is not necessarily incompatible with the promotion and protection of human rights.

Globalization is leading to greater problems of state capacity to comply with human rights obligations, particularly economic, social, and cultural rights,[101] such as trade union freedoms,[102] the right to work, and the right to social security. It also may have a dispropor-

---

[99] El Hadji Guisse, *The Realization of Economic, Social and Cultural Rights: The Question of Transnational Corporations*, U.N. ESCOR, 50th Sess., U.N. Doc. E/CN.4/Sub.2/1998/6 (1998).

[100] *Id.* ¶ 1.

[101] *See* Statement by the United Nations Committee on Economic, Social and Cultural Rights, *Globalization and Economic, Social and Cultural Rights* (May, 1998), *at* http://www.unhchr.ch/tbs/doc.nsf/385c2ad ... a?OpenDocument&Highlight=0, globalization (last visited Oct. 22, 2001); *see also* UNCTAD, WORLD INVESTMENT REPORT 1994: TRANSNATIONAL CORPORATIONS, EMPLOYMENT AND THE WORKPLACE 260 (1994).

[102] ILO Report of the Director General, *supra* note 25, at 9. According to the 2001 report of the ILO Director General, close to two of every five countries have serious or severe problems of freedom of association. *Id.*

tionate effect on minorities.[103] Cooperation internationally and from non-state actors is needed in the face of an undoubted concentration of wealth in the hands of multinational enterprises, greater than the wealth of many countries. Globalization is a particular issue for women, because they often bear a disproportionate burden of poverty, which may be exacerbated by economic restructuring, deregulation,[104] and privatization.[105] Investors have demonstrated a preference for women in the "soft" industries such as apparel, shoe- and toy-making, data-processing, and semi-conductor assembling—industries that require unskilled to semi-skilled labor, leading women to bear the disproportionate weight of the constraints introduced by globalization.[106] The process of economic liberalization has also led to growth in the informal sector and increased female participation therein. Employment in the informal sector generally means that employment benefits and mechanisms of protection are unavailable.[107] Underemployment seems to be as big a problem as open unemployment.

It also has been asserted that states feel compelled to ease labor standards, modify tax regulations, and relax other standards to attract foreign investment,[108] seen especially in the export production zones (EPZs) where employment may be plentiful, but working conditions poor. Labor unions claim that EPZs are sometimes designed to undermine union rights,[109] deny or restrict rights to free association, expression, and assembly.[110] There are some twenty-seven million work-

---

[103] *See* Marc W. Brown, *The Effect of Free Trade, Privatization and Democracy on the Human Rights Conditions for Minorities in Eastern Europe: A Case Study of the Gypsies in the Czech Republic and Hungary*, 4 BUFF. HUM. RTS. L. REV. 275, 275 (1998).

[104] *See* LIN LEAN LIM, MORE AND BETTER JOBS FOR WOMEN: AN ACTION GUIDE 18–20 (Int'l Labour Office 1999). Deregulation and the privatization of state enterprises have been key components of structural adjustment programs (SAPs) introduced by multilateral lending agencies as conditionals attached to aid packages to developing countries. *Id.*

[105] *See generally* Bharati Sadasivam, *The Impact of Structural Adjustment on Women: A Governance and Human Rights Agenda*, 19 HUM. RTS. Q. 630 (1997).

[106] For more information on these effects, see Riham el-Lakany, *WTO Trades off Women's Rights for Bigger Profits*, 12 WOMEN'S ENV'T & DEV. ORG. 1, 32 (1999), *available at* www.wedo.org/news/Nov99/wtotradeoff.htm.

[107] LIM, *supra* note 104, at 19–20.

[108] *See* Deborah Spar & David Yoffie, *Multinational Enterprises and the Prospects for Justice*, 52 J. INT'L AFF. 557, 557 (1999).

[109] International Confederation of Free Trade Unions, *Background Paper: Implementation of International Covenant on Economic, Social and Cultural Rights*, ¶ 4, U.N. Doc. E/C.12/1998/4 (1998) [hereinafter ICFTU].

[110] *See, e.g.,* John Eremu, *Uganda Warned on EPZ Strategy*, NEW VISION, Dec. 7, 1998, at 54 (noting that exclusive protection zones in many African countries are characterized by human rights abuses).

ers employed in such zones worldwide.[111] It is estimated that the number of developing countries with EPZs increased from twenty-four in 1976 to ninety-three in 2000, with women providing up to 80% of the labor force.[112]

Another impact observed in many countries is a shift from companies hiring permanent employees with job security and benefits, to the use of contingent or temporary workers lacking health care, retirement, collective bargaining arrangements, and other security available to the permanent work force.[113] As with other negative impacts of globalization, this one also has more severe impacts on women,[114] minorities, and migrant workers.[115] Women comprise the largest segment of migrant labor flows, both internally and internationally. States often do not include migrant workers in their labor standards, leaving women particularly vulnerable.[116] Overall, only some 20% of the world's workers have adequate social protection.[117] In addition, some 3000 people a day die from work-related accidents or disease.[118]

Globalization also has produced an important new type of transboundary criminal enterprise. International crimes that involve or impact human rights violations are increasing: illegal drug trade, arms trafficking, money laundering, and traffic in persons are all facilitated by the same technological advances and open markets that assist in human rights. Traffic in women for sexual purposes is estimated to involve more than $7 billion a year, but the sex trade is not

---

[111] ILO Report of the Director General, *supra* note 25, at 10.

[112] LIM, *supra* note 104, at 30.

[113] *See* Aaron B. Sukert, Note, *Marionettes of Globalization: A Comparative Analysis of Protections for Contingent Workers in the International Community,* 27 SYRACUSE J. INT'L L. & COM. 431, 431 (2000).

[114] *See 1999 World Survey on the Role of Women in Development: Globalization, Gender and Work: Report of the Secretary General,* at 9, 54th. Sess., U.N. Doc. A/54/227, U.N. Sales No. E.99.IV.8 (1999). Women have entered the workforce in large numbers in states that have embraced liberal economic policies. *Id.* "It is by now considered a stylized fact that industrialization in the context of globalization is as much female-led as it is export led." The overall economic activity rate of women for the age group 20–54 approached 70% in 1996. *Id.* at 8. One estimate is that 90% of the twenty-seven million people employed in EPZs worldwide are women. *See* JOHN HILARY, GLOBALIZATION AND EMPLOYMENT: NEW OPPORTUNITIES, REAL THREATS 1 (1999).

[115] Hilary, *supra* note 114, at 440–41.

[116] *See generally* Laurie Nicole Robinson, *The Globalization of Female Child Prostitution: A Call for Reintegration and Recovery Measures Via Article 39 of the United Nations Convention on the Rights of the Child,* 5 IND. J. GLOBAL LEGAL STUD. 239 (1997).

[117] ILO Report of the Director General, *supra* note 25, at 9.

[118] *Id.*

the only market for humans. Coercion against agricultural workers, domestic workers, and factory workers also is evident.

Crime syndicates are rivaling multinational corporations for economic power, threatening the security and well being of large numbers of persons. The free movement of capital, which is a prior condition to the growth in foreign investment, permits money laundering in the absence of exchange controls or other appropriate regulation. The free circulation of goods can bring stolen automobiles, smuggled sex workers, and torture implements, as well as fresh fruit and vegetables. At the same time, new technologies also permit the easier pirating of intellectual property. Indigenous groups and local communities challenge the very foundations of intellectual property protection, particularly when applied to pharmaceuticals necessary to ensure the right to life and to health.

Certain human rights are particularly threatened by globalization. Respect for private life needs protection against personal data collection. Cultural and linguistic rights can also suffer under global assault, but the evidence seems contradictory. There is no doubt that globalization facilitates the transfer of cultural manifestations and cultural property. A study by the U.N. Economic and Social Council (UNESCO) indicates that commerce in cultural property tripled between 1980 and 1991 under the impulse of satellite communications, Internet, and videocassettes.[119] Yet, in this field, as in others, mergers and acquisitions have concentrated ownership to the detriment of local industry. The Hollywood film industry represented 70% of the European market in 1996, more than double what it was a decade earlier, and constituted 86% of the Latin American market. In the opposite direction, traditional cultures across the world are being transmitted and revived in multiethnic states through the movement of peoples, their languages, and their beliefs.

Economic globalization has been criticized for protecting investors to the detriment of local people, arguably increasing unemployment and underemployment. To make conditions better for investors, the World Bank and IMF impose economic "reform" that may lead to human rights violations, including an increase in infant and child mortality rates.[120] In addition, structural reform usually mandates

---

[119] *See generally* U.N. Economic and Social Council, Study on International Flows of Cultural Goods Between 1980–1998 (2000).

[120] *See* Danilo Turk, *The Realization of Economic, Social and Cultural Rights*, U.N. GAOR, Hum. Rts. Comm., 44th Sess., Agenda Item 8, ¶ 1-37, U.N. Doc. E/CN.4/Sub2/1992/16 (1992); *see also* Statement by the Committee on Economic, Social and Cultural Rights,

298   *Boston College International & Comparative Law Review*   [Vol. 25:273]

trade liberalization, something industrialized countries have not been similarly pressured to do. States may or may not be weakened, but the weakest within states are further marginalized. Lack of accountability results from the inability to exercise rights of political participation or information about key decisions. Structural adjustment may require cutting public expenditure for health and education, social security, and housing. Labor deregulation, privatization, and export-oriented production increase income disparity and marginalization in many countries.[121] This leaves the main function of the state to be policing and security, which may lead either to increased political repression or to violent protests and political destabilization.

According to the independent expert appointed by the U.N. to study the impact of structural adjustment programs on human rights, there are two main consequences of such programs. First, they have led to a significant erosion of the living standards of the poor and investment in the productive sectors of many countries; second, such countries have ceded their right to independently determine their country's development priorities . According to the expert, structural adjustment shifted from being a mechanism to handle national debt into a vehicle for deregulation, trade liberalization, and privatization—all reducing the role of the state in national development. Properly structured debt relief is essential to alleviate poverty and build democratic institutions.[122]

The formation and enhancement of transboundary religious, tribal, corporate, or associational allegiances are aspects of globalization that have both positive and negative aspects. They may challenge the nationality link and loyalty of individuals towards the territorial state. Networks of human rights activists forming an international civil society are an important component in the protection of human rights. Their formation and work is enhanced by information technology and ease of movement. Networks linked by air, telecommunications, media, and the Internet allow shared ideas and the formation of shared values. The human rights activists of the world share values with each other and a commitment to universal compliance with human rights norms that transcend nationality and particular cultural

---

Globalization and Economic, Social and Cultural Rights (May, 1998), *at* http://www.unhchr.ch/html/menu2/6/cescrnote.htm#note18h [hereinafter Statement, *Globalization*].

[121] *See* Sadasivam, *supra* note 105, at 630.

[122] The debt burden of the thirty-three poorest countries of the world collectively amounts to $127 billion owed to industrialized countries and institutions. In Mozambique, one of the poorest countries in the world, 30% of all revenue goes to debt servicing.

values. These activists have in turn pressured corporations to accept social responsibility in their global dealings. On the negative side, international criminal syndicates and terrorist groups form the same transboundary allegiances and threaten the security of all. The problems then become those of states that are too weak, not states that are too strong.

III. ARE HUMAN RIGHTS GOOD FOR GLOBALIZATION?

The dominant view among economists and policy makers in multilateral financial institutions appears to be that any hindrances to global trade and investment are bad for development in general. Recent studies, however, suggest that business and economic indicators are better in developing countries that have more favorable civil and political rights than in repressive regimes.[123] Mancur Olson explains that the majority in whose interests a democratic government is ruling demand smaller growth-retarding exaction from the minority and pay greater attention to the supply of growth-promoting public goods than does a dictatorship, even when the majority is acting out of pure self-interest.[124] According to his analysis, the dispersal of political power and the emergence of representative government have often been the trigger for faster economic growth. So, prosperity is not only good for democracy, but democracy seems good for prosperity. A feature in the poorest countries is the absence or poor enforcement of contract and property rights, which are necessary for advanced markets and rapid growth.

It also seems clear that establishment of the rule of law with protection for contracts and property rights is essential to maintaining security for international investment and trade. Tourism is the world's fastest-growing industry, generating more than 10% of total international GNP, and is particularly harmed by images of repression, acts of terrorism, and the political instability that usually result from widespread human rights abuses. Judicial reform and the establishment of the rule of law with respect for human rights should be a priority, even if only for the instrumental reason to secure investment, prop-

---

[123] *See* A. Bernstein, *Labor Standards: Try a Little Democracy*, BUS. WK., Dec. 13, 1999, at 42.

[124] *See generally* MANCUR OLSON, POWER AND PROSPERITY: OUTGROWING COMMUNIST AND CAPITALIST DICTATORSHIPS (2000). On development and human rights, see generally AMARTYA SEN, DEVELOPMENT AS FREEDOM (1999).

erty, contracts, debts, and profits.[125] As the U.N. Development Program's *Human Development Report 2000* proclaims, "[r]ights make human beings better economic actors."[126]

Like human rights, economic liberalization is concerned with restraining the power of the state. At the special session of the U.N. General Assembly to review progress since the 1995 Copenhagen World Summit for Social Development, the final document, adopted on July 1, 2000, makes special reference to the role and responsibilities of the private sector to work with governments to eradicate poverty, promote full employment and universal access to social services, and ensure that everyone has equal opportunities to participate in society. In turn, democratic rule and the rule of law inspires further global business activity, generating an upward spiral in rights protection. The text encourages corporate social responsibility and promotes dialogue among government, labor, and employer groups. It also expresses a belief in the relationship between economic growth and social development.[127] The Copenhagen Declaration and Program of Action affirmed that social development and social justice cannot be attained in the absence of respect for all human rights and fundamental freedoms. The Sub-Commission on Promotion and Protection of Human Rights finds in major human rights instruments "obligations and goals which are fundamental to the development process and to economic policy."[128]

None of the international human rights instruments imposes an economic model, free trade, or deregulation. Yet, as Anne Orford points out, there is a link between human rights and a liberal economic regime that may facilitate globalization.[129] Liberal concepts of human rights identify the individual with property ownership and are linked with the emergence of capitalism.[130] In contrast, the failure by some governments to respect core labor standards is likely to provoke

---

[125] In Bosnia, foreign investment and donor support have been stifled because of rampant corruption and judges too fearful of retribution to enforce the law. *See* Chris Hedges, *Leaders in Bosnia Are Said to Steal up to $1 billion,* N.Y. TIMES, Aug. 17, 1999, at A1; *see also* Benn Steil & Susan L. Woodward, *A European 'New Deal' for the Balkans,* FOREIGN AFF., Nov.-Dec. 1999, at 95–96 (noting that reports of financial corruption and delays in creating economic institutions have driven away corporate investors).

[126] UNDP, *supra* note 16, at iii.

[127] For clarification on this relationship, see United Nations, *Copenhagen+5 Review, at* http://www.un.org/esa/socdev/geneva2000/index.html (last visited Mar. 10, 2002).

[128] Res. 1999/30, *supra* note 57.

[129] Orford, *supra* note 81.

[130] *See* JOHN LOCKE, SECOND TREATISE OF GOVERNMENT ch. V, § 27 (C.B. McPherson ed., Hackett Publishing Co. 1980) (1690).

trade tensions and lead to protectionist efforts. The stability of the world's trading system may thus depend upon ensuring that an open trading system does not come at the price of human rights.

IV. INTERNATIONAL RESPONSES TO THE PROBLEMS OF GLOBALIZATION AND HUMAN RIGHTS

Globalization has led to an increased concern about the responsibility of all international actors to ensure the promotion and protection of human rights. International institutions and scholars have responded with various proposals for strengthening the international regime. First, human rights activists and institutions have begun to posit the primacy of human rights law. The Committee on Economic, Social and Cultural Rights (CESCR) has emphasized that, "the realms of trade, finance and investment are in no way exempt from these general principles [on respect for human rights] and that international organizations with specific responsibilities in those areas should play a positive and constructive role in relation to human rights."[131] The CESCR also asserts that competitiveness, efficiency, and economic rationalism must not be permitted to become the primary or exclusive criteria against which governmental and inter-governmental policies are evaluated.[132]

Second, state responsibility for failing to control the actions of private parties has received considerable attention in the case law of international tribunals[133] and the work of the U.N.[134] Third, international law is increasingly regulating non-state behavior directly. Fourth, private market mechanisms such as codes of conduct or consumer purchasing schemes have sought to influence corporate behavior. Finally, restructured international governance mechanisms are

---

[131] Statement, *Globalization, supra* note 120, ¶ 5.

[132] *Id.* ¶ 4.

[133] *See, e.g.*, Inter-Am. C.H.R., Velasquez Rodriguez Case, Judgment of July 29, 1988, Ser. C, No. 4, ¶ 159–77, *available at* http://www.corteidh.or.cr/sericing/C_4_Eng.html (last visited Mar. 11, 2002). *See generally*, Dinah Shelton, *Private Violence, Public Wrongs, and the Responsibility of States*, 13 FORDHAM INT'L L.J. 1, 1 (1990).

[134] The General Assembly has affirmed that while globalization, by its impact on the role of the state, may affect human rights, the promotion and protection of all human rights is first and foremost the responsibility of the state. The Assembly has called for an environment at both the national and global levels that is conducive to development and to the elimination of poverty through, *inter alia*, good governance within each country and at the international level, transparency in the financial, monetary and trading systems and commitment to an open, equitable, rule-based, predictable, and non-discriminatory multilateral trading and financial system. G.A. Res. 102/54, U.N. GAOR, 54th Sess., U.N. Doc. A/RES/54/102 (2000).

302   *Boston College International & Comparative Law Review*   [Vol. 25:273

bringing a variety of international actors together to achieve common goals.

The first general trend, seen particularly among human rights advocates, has been to affirm the priority of human rights over other international legal regimes. According to this view, international economic policies cannot be exempt from conformity to international human rights law. States and international organizations are directly obliged to comply with those principles and obliged to ensure that private economic actors within their jurisdictions do not act in violation of those rights.[135] In a 1998 statement on globalization and economic, social, and cultural rights, the CESCR expressed its concerns over the negative impact of globalization on the enjoyment of economic, social, and cultural rights, and called on states and multilateral institutions to pay enhanced attention to taking a rights-based approach to economic policy-making.[136] The CESCR declared that the realms of trade, finance, and investment are in no way exempt from human rights obligations. Those concerns were raised again in the statement the CESCR addressed to the WTO Third Ministerial Conference in Seattle in November, 1999. The CESCR urged WTO members to adopt a human rights approach at the conference, recognizing the fact that, "promotion and protection of human rights is the first responsibility of Governments."[137] The CESCR's language echoes that of the Vienna Declaration and Program of Action,[138] which affirmed that, "the promotion and protection of human rights and fundamental freedoms is the first responsibility of government" and that, "the human person is the central subject of development." Similarly, the Copenhagen Declaration and Program of Action[139] recommended to

---

[135] According to Diller and Levy, referring specifically to the issue of coercive forms of child labour, where fundamental human rights norms are implicated, "international law requires that treaty obligations, such as trade undertakings, be maintained only to the extent of consistency with these norms." Janelle Diller & David Levy, *Child Labor, Trade and Investment: Toward the Harmonization of International Law*, 91 AM. J. INT'L L. 678, 678 (1997).

[136] Statement, *Globalization, supra* note 120.

[137] *Statement of the United Nations Committee on Economic, Social and Cultural Rights to the Third Ministerial Conference of the World Trade Organization*, Committee on Economic, Social and Cultural Rights, 21st Sess., Agenda item 3, ¶ 6, U.N. Doc. E/C.12/1999/9 (1999).

[138] World Conference on Human Rights, *Vienna Declaration and Programme of Action*, U.N. Doc. A/CONF.157/23; *see also* Commission on Human Rights, *Globalization and its Impact on the Full Enjoyment of All Human Rights*, U.N. Doc. E/CN.4/RES/1999/59 (1999) ("While globalization by its impact on, *inter alia*, the role of the State, may affect human rights, the promotion and protection of all human rights is first and foremost the responsibility of the State.").

[139] *Final Act, World Summit for Social Development: Report of the World Summit for Social Development*, U.N. Doc. A/CONF.166/9 (1995) [hereinafter *Final Act*].

states the need to intervene in markets to prevent or counteract market failure, promote stability and long-term investment, ensure fair competition and ethical conduct, and harmonize economic and social development. The Sub-Commission on Promotion and Protection of Human Rights has expressly asserted the "centrality and primacy" of human rights obligations in all areas of governance and development, including international and regional trade, investment and financial policies, agreements, and practices.[140] The Commission on Human Rights, for its part, has affirmed that, "the exercise of the basic rights of the people of debtor countries to food, housing, clothing, employment, education, health services and a healthy environment cannot be subordinated to the implementation of structural adjustment policies and economic reforms arising from the debt."[141] The special rapporteurs on globalization and its impact on the full enjoyment of human rights flatly assert that, "the primacy of human rights law over all other regimes of international law is a basic and fundamental principle that should not be departed from."[142]

Can the primacy of human rights be justified in international law? An argument can be posited on the basis of treaty law. The U.N. Charter refers to human rights in its second preamble paragraph and lists human rights as the third of its purposes in Article 1, after maintenance of peace and security, and the development of friendly relations among nations based on equal rights and self-determination of peoples.[143] The Charter not only makes human rights an aim of the organization, it obligates all member states to take joint and separate action with the U.N. to achieve universal respect for and observance of human rights and fundamental freedoms, as in Articles 55 and 56.[144] Article 103 of the Charter provides that, "in the event of a conflict between the obligations of the members of the United Nations under the present Charter and their obligations under any other international agreement, their obligations under the present Charter

---

[140] Sub-Commission on Promotion and Protection of Human Rights, *Human Rights as the Primary Objective of Trade, Investment and Financial Policy*, U.N. Doc. E/CN.4/Sub.2/RES/1998/12 (1998); *Report of the Sub-Commission on its 50th Sess.*, U.N. ESCOR, 50th Sess., at 39, U.N. Doc. E/CN.4/Sub.2/1998/45 (1998).

[141] Commission on Human Rights, *Effects of Structural Adjustment Policies and Foreign Debt on the Full Enjoyment of All Human Rights, Particularly Economic, Social and Cultural Rights*, U.N. Doc. E/CN.4/RES/2000/82 (2000).

[142] Oloka-Onyango & Udagama, *Globalization* I, *supra* note 50.

[143] U.N. CHARTER pmbl., art. 1.

[144] *Id.* arts. 55–56.

shall prevail."[145] This "supremacy clause" has been invoked to suggest that the aims and purposes of the U.N., maintenance of peace and security, and the promotion and protection of human rights, constitute an international public order to which other treaty regimes must conform.[146] It may be argued, however, that there is no conflict between human rights and the international trade and financial regime because they regulate separate areas of human activity. In addition, some may point to the "later in time" rule of the Vienna Convention on the Law of Treaties.[147] However, the Vienna Convention is not retroactive and, in any case, the provisions of Article 30 expressly provide that the later in time rule is "without prejudiced to [A]rticle 103 of the United Nations Charter."[148] As with domestic bills of rights, international human rights law may limit the implementation of other social goals to means and methods compatible with its contents. In practice, states and international organizations are taking action to increase the responsibility of state and non-state actors when their economic activities impact on human rights.

The second response to globalization is found in efforts to insist on state responsibility for the behavior of non-state actors. As far as human rights are concerned, this means the state is responsible for its acts and its omissions. The Restatement of U.S. Foreign Relations Law makes it clear that a state violates international law if it commits, encourages, or condones genocide, slavery, torture, or inhuman or degrading treatment.[149] Complicity in human rights violations between state and non-state actors is a growing subject of interest and litigation.

The next question posed is whether or not a state is responsible for the acts of international organizations in which it participates. The International Covenant on Economic, Social and Cultural Rights (ICESCR),[150] Article 2(1), provides that each state party will "take steps, individually and through international assistance and coopera-

---

[145] *Id.* art. 103.

[146] *See id.*

[147] Vienna Convention on the Law of Treaties, May 27, 1969, art. 59, 1155 U.N.T.S. 331, 8 I.L.M. 679 (1969).

[148] U.N. Charter art. 30.

[149] Restatement (Third) of the Foreign Relations Law of the United States § 601–02 (1987).

[150] *International Covenant on Economic, Social, and Cultural Rights*, G.A. Res. 2200A (XXI), U.N. GAOR, Supp. No. 16, at 49, U.N. Doc. A/6316 (1966), *reprinted in* 6 I.L.M. 360.

tion" to achieve the rights in the Covenant.[151] This means that voting in the World Bank or IMF for programs or policies that will lead to human rights regression in one or more states could be deemed to violate the voter's obligations under the Covenant.[152]

Traditional interpretations of the ICESCR, Article 2, permit states to determine how and when they allocate resources for the realization of economic, social, and cultural rights.[153] However, in its General Comment No. 3 on the nature of the states parties' obligations under the ICESCR, the CESCR declared that concrete legal obligations are imposed by the Covenant under Article 2.[154] State parties are obliged to realize minimum standards relating to each of the rights utilizing available resources in an effective manner. Violations can occur either through commission or omission.

The jurisprudence of the CESCR also recognizes "minimum core obligations" on the part of state parties that have to be fulfilled irrespective of resource or other constraints. In determining whether a state party has utilized the "maximum of its available resources," attention shall be paid to the equitable and effective use of and access to available resources. States also may be responsible if they fail to exercise due diligence in controlling the behavior of non-state actors, such as transnational corporations, over which they exercise jurisdiction, when such behavior deprives individuals of their economic, social, and cultural rights.

The CESCR has consulted with multilateral institutions, specialized agencies, and non-governmental organizations (NGOs) in developing its approach to the issue of globalization. Other treaty-based human rights mechanisms have also shown concern over rising economic disparities that impact on their individual mandates. For example, the Committee examining periodic country reports under the Convention on the Elimination of All Forms of Discrimination against Women (CEDAW), has shown great concern over the evidence of the feminization of poverty and the impact of economic policies on the rights of women.[155] The Human Rights Committee, in General Com-

---

[151] *Id.* art. 2(1). Other references to international cooperation are found in Articles 11, 15, 22, and 23.

[152] *Id.*

[153] *Id.* art. 2.

[154] *See* Committee on Economic, Social and Cultural Rights, *Report on the Fifth Session, Economic and Social Council*, U.N. ESCOR, Supp. No. 3, Annex III, General Cmt. No. 3, U.N. Doc. E/1991/23-E/C.12/1990/8 (1991).

[155] *See Report of the Committee on the Elimination of Discrimination against Women*, U.N. GAOR, 52d Sess., Supp. No. 38, ¶¶ 295, 345, U.N. Doc. A/52/38/Rev.1 (1997); *see also*

ment No. 28 dealing with equality of rights between men and women, gives some consideration to issues such as the feminization of poverty, declining social indicators, and gender inequity in employment within the framework of globalization.

A number of U.N. specialized agencies have also addressed the question of globalization. The ILO has long tackled the phenomenon. From the Copenhagen Social Summit in 1995 to the 1998 Declaration on Fundamental Principles and Rights at Work, the ILO has pressed for an international consensus on the content of the core labor standards that provide a social floor to the global economy.[156] In 1998, the ILO adopted the Convention concerning the Prohibition and Immediate Action for the Elimination of the Worst Forms of Child Labour (Convention No. 182).[157] It also adopted its Declaration on Fundamental Principles and Rights at Work together with a follow-up procedure based upon technical cooperation and reporting. The principles have been incorporated into codes of conduct by the private sector and also used as a basis for action by various regional communities, such as the Southern African Development Community, MERCOSUR, and the Caribbean Community. U.N. bodies and specialized agencies, such as the U.N. Children's Fund (UNICEF), the U.N. Educational, Scientific and Cultural Organization (UNESCO), the Office of the U.N. High Commissioner for Refugees (UNHCR), and the U.N. Environment Programme (UNEP), have all carried out work that has implications for the overall response by the U.N. to the phenomenon of globalization. On the regional level, the European Union, in the context of negotiations for the fourth Lomé Agreement with countries of Africa, the Caribbean, and the Pacific (ACP states), sought to include good governance in public affairs, democracy, respect for human rights, and respect for the rule of law, essential in the elements of the accord, with the termination of assistance for non-respect of any of the elements.

Committee on the Rights of the Child, *Report on the Twentieth Session*, U.N. ESCOR, ¶¶ 211–13, U.N. Doc. CRC/C/84 (1999) (recording a statement made by a representative of the IMF at the session acknowledging the link between child rights and a stable macroeconomic environment).

[156] The rights guaranteed are: freedom of association and the effective recognition of the right to collective bargaining; elimination of all forms of compulsory or forced labor; effective abolition of child labor; elimination of discrimination in occupation and employment. For more information, see the ILO website, *at* http://www.ilo.org.

[157] *See generally* Michèle Jackson, *A New Convention to Eliminate the Economic Exploitation of Children*, 6 TRIBUNE DES DROITS HUMAINS 36 (1999).

Finally, it may be asserted that both the home and the host states have obligations to regulate the conduct of multinational companies. The *Trail Smelter Arbitration*,[158] the *Corfu Channel Case*,[159] and the U.N. Survey of International Law all state the same principle: every state's obligation not to allow knowingly its territory to be used contrary to the rights of other states.[160] The *Trail Smelter Arbitration* involved a privately owned Canadian company that caused harm through its activities to farmers in the United States.[161] Corporate decisions in one state to undertake activities in another state that involve human rights violations could similarly lead to recognition that both states have a duty to control the conduct of the multinational company.

In a third approach, the international community has been moving towards greater ascription of individual responsibility for human rights violations, both by state and by non-state actors. While states remain primarily responsible for ensuring the promotion and protection of human rights, increasing attention is being given to the responsibility under international law of inter-governmental organizations, business enterprises, and individuals. In this regard, the international legal system can no longer be described as one governing states alone. The Universal Declaration of Human Rights opened the door to this development by providing, in Article 30, that, "[n]othing in this Declaration may be interpreted as implying for any [s]tate, group or person any right to engage in any activity or to perform any act aimed at the destruction of any of the rights and freedoms set forth herein."[162] Conceptually linked to this, the preceding article stipulates that, "everyone has duties to the community in which alone the free and full development of his personality is possible."[163]

The special rapporteur on the relationship between the enjoyment of human rights, in particular economic, social, and cultural rights, and income distribution, views economic, social, and cultural rights as "the set of basic rights which determines the limits of globalization."[164] In Bengoa's view, "lack of education, early school leaving and structural poverty are not only general ethical issues but also vio-

---

[158] 3 U.N. R.I.A.A. 1905 (1931–41) [hereinafter *Trail Smelter Arbitration*].

[159] 1949 I.C.J. 22.

[160] *Id. See generally supra* notes 158–159.

[161] *Trail Smelter Arbitration, supra* note 158.

[162] Universal Declaration, *supra* note 42, art. 30.

[163] *Id.* art. 29.

[164] Jose Bengoa, *Poverty, Income Distribution and Globalization: A Challenge for Human Rights, Addendum to the Final Report*, at ¶ 28, U.N. ESCOR, 50th Sess., U.N. Doc. E/CN.4/Sub.2/1998/8 (1998).

lations of the human rights proclaimed by international law."[165] He concludes that the great legal, political, and ethical challenge for the coming century will be the codification and enforceability of human rights in an internationalized market.[166] Such an action requires taking into consideration the fact that the state is neither the sole agent nor the sole economic actor, despite its central responsibility, for the realization of economic, social, and cultural rights. Other important actors are transnational corporations, international organizations, trading and financial enterprises, and even such groups as private agencies providing assistance to the poor and needy.[167] He suggests further development of codes of conduct for these non-state actors and in particular the formation of a "Social Forum" with the participation of all such actors. It is somewhat surprising that the suggestion is this modest, given his characterization of the globalized world as one where:

> There is not only the enormous wealth of a few thousand, but also the corruption of many [s]tate authorities, the failure of [s]tate mechanisms and services to discharge their functions, the unregulated and uncontrolled presence of transnational corporations and companies, the authoritarian and unconsidered operation of international financial institutions, and the frequently futile action of organizations and institutions which are well-intentioned but which do not coordinate their activities in a stable and sustained manner.[168]

Another special rapporteur has remarked upon the lack of effective mechanisms to enforce the accountability of non-state actors.[169] He asserts that enforcing respect for codes of conduct, trade union laws, and rights of association and expression may prove difficult, citing the example of the code on marketing breast milk substitutes.[170]

In respect to intergovernmental organizations, the theoretical basis for insisting that they adhere to human rights standards in their

---

[165] *Id.*

[166] *Id.* ¶ 29.

[167] *Id.* ¶ 31. Bengoa also notes that it is very important that development NGOs, international cooperation agencies, and charitable foundations participate, "as they are acquiring ever greater relevance in relations between north and south, as part of the growing 'privatization' of cooperation." *Id.*

[168] *Id.* ¶ 30.

[169] Oloka-Onyango, *Racism, supra* note 51, ¶ 35.

[170] *Id.*

programs derives from their international legal personality.[171] International organizations are entities created by states delegating power to achieve certain goals and perform specified functions. While not states, and not having the full rights and duties of states, international organizations take on rights and duties under international law. It would be surprising if states could perform actions collectively through international organizations that the states could not lawfully do individually.[172] In other words, if states cannot confer more power on international organizations than they themselves possess, international organizations are bound to respect human rights because all the states that create them are legally required to respect human rights pursuant to the U.N. Charter and customary international law.

The Commission on Human Rights has begun to suggest, albeit very cautiously, that multilateral institutions must conform their policies and practices to human rights norms. In its Resolution 2001/32, the Commission recognized:

> That multilateral mechanisms have a unique role to play in meeting the challenges and opportunities presented by globalization and that the process of globalization must not be used to weaken or reinterpret the principles enshrined in the Charter of the U.N., which continues to be the foundation for friendly relations among states, as well as for the creation of a more just and equitable international economic system.[173]

The resolution affirms not only the individual responsibility of states for human rights but "also recognizes that, in addition to [s]tates' separate responsibilities to their individual societies, they have a collective responsibility to uphold the principles of human dignity, equality and equity at the global level."[174] Subsequent to this, and in the most recent statement of the human rights bodies on the issue, the Sub-Commission adopted a resolution in which it considers that, "at-

---

[171] *See* Reparation for Injuries Suffered in the Service of the United Nations, Advisory Opinion, 1949 I.C.J. 174, 178-79. *See generally,* Louis Henkin, *Responsibility of International Organizations, in* HENKIN ET AL., INTERNATIONAL LAW, CASES AND MATERIALS 359–60 (3d ed. 1993).

[172] The U.N. Charter, Chapter VII, does allow international peace-keeping actions, however, for threats to the peace, breaches of the peace, and acts of aggression—actions that would generally not be legal if performed unilaterally except in self-defense.

[173] Commission on Human Rights, *Globalization and its Impact on the Full Enjoyment of All Human Rights,* U.N. Doc. E/CN.4/RES/2001/32 (2001).

[174] *Id.*

tention to the human rights obligations of governments participating in international economic policy formulation will help to ensure socially just outcomes in the formulation, interpretation and implementation of those policies."[175] The Sub-Commission expresses its gratitude for discussions with the WTO, the IMF, and the World Bank, and attempts to walk a difficult line in reaffirming "the importance and relevance of human rights obligations in all areas of governance and development, including international and regional trade, investment and financial policies and practices, while confirming that this in no way implies the imposition of conditionalities upon aid to development."[176] It urges all governments and "international economic policy forums" to take international human rights obligations fully into account in international economic policy formulation.[177]

In its 1998 comment on globalization, the CESCR called for a renewed commitment to respect economic, social, and cultural rights, emphasizing that international organizations, as well as governments that have created and managed them, have a strong and continuous responsibility to take whatever measures they can to assist governments to act in ways that are compatible with their human rights obligations, and to seek to devise policies and programs that promote respect for those rights.[178] The CESCR addressed itself in particular to the IMF and the World Bank, calling upon them to pay enhanced attention to human rights, including "through encouraging explicit recognition of these rights, assisting in the identification of country-specific benchmarks to facilitate their promotion, and facilitating the development of appropriate remedies for responding to violations."[179] The WTO also should "devise appropriate methods to facilitate more systematic consideration of the impact upon human rights of particular trade and investment policies."[180] The CESCR's recent General Comment on the right to food concerns food security within the context of globalization.[181] It draws attention to the responsibilities of private actors, aside from the obligation of states parties to regulate appropriately their conduct, in the realization of the right to adequate

---

[175] *Id.*

[176] *See id.*

[177] *See id.*

[178] Statement, *Globalization, supra* note 120, ¶ 5.

[179] *Id.* ¶ 7.

[180] *Id.*

[181] *The Right to Adequate Food: Report of the Committee on Economic, Social and Cultural Rights,* General Comment No. 12, at 102, 106, U.N. ESCOR., Supp. No. 2, U.N. Doc. E/2000/22 (2000).

food.[182] The comment goes on to stipulate that, "[t]he private business sector—national and transnational—should pursue its activities within the framework of a code of conduct conducive to respect of the right to adequate food, agreed upon jointly with the Government and civil society".[183] Furthermore, it calls upon the IMF and the World Bank to pay attention to the protection of the right to food in drawing up lending policies, credit, and structural adjustment programs.[184] This approach by a treaty-based mechanism, focusing on the responsibilities of multilateral organizations as well as private actors in protecting human rights, is a significant step in international law.

International conferences also have called on international financial institutions to pay greater attention to human rights, through promotion and through assisting in the development of benchmarks to monitor compliance and remedies to respond to violations.[185] In particular, "social safety nets should be defined by reference to these rights and enhanced attention should be accorded to such methods to protect the poor and vulnerable in the context of structural adjustment programs."[186] Social monitoring and impact assessments, similar to that done for the environment, are recommended to international financial institutions and to the WTO. Labor unions have called for including core labor standards in the future WTO work program.[187]

For individuals, international responsibility is also increasing. The U.N. Development Program *Human Development Report 2000* calls for greater accountability of non-state actors, pointing out that, "global corporations can have enormous impact on human rights—in their employment practices, in their environmental impact, in their support for corrupt regimes or in their advocacy for policy changes."[188] The most egregious acts are proscribed as international crimes. The Nuremberg Military Tribunal[189] and subsequent princi-

---

[182] *Id.*

[183] *Id.* ¶ 20.

[184] *Id.* ¶ 41.

[185] *See Final Act, supra* note 139 (calling for a reorientation of the work of the international community including the IMF and the World Bank to establish full employment, the eradication of poverty and popular participation as the primary goals of global development policy); ICFTU, *supra* note 109.

[186] ICFTU, *supra* note 109, ¶ 7.

[187] *Id.* ¶ 17.

[188] UNDP, *supra* note 16, at 10.

[189] *See* Charter of the International Military Tribunal, Aug. 8, 1945, 82 U.N.T.S. 280, 58 Stat. 1544 [hereinafter *London Charter*].

ples prepared by the U.N. International Law Commission[190] made clear that neither government position nor government orders will free an individual from responsibility for the commission of an international crime.[191] As was said in the Nuremberg judgment: "crimes against international law are committed by men and not by abstract entities and it is only by punishing individuals who commit such crimes" that international law can be upheld.[192] The U.N. Security Council also has made clear the international liability of non-state as well as state actors who commit war crimes and other international crimes

The list of international crimes at Nuremberg were war crimes, crimes against peace, and crimes against humanity.[193] The Convention on the Prevention and Punishment of the Crime of Genocide affirms that genocide, whether committed in peacetime or wartime, is a crime under international law and that, "[p]ersons committing genocide . . . shall be punished, whether they are constitutionally responsible [rulers], public officials, or private individuals."[194] In 1973, the U.N. similarly declared apartheid a crime against humanity and broadly imposed responsibility on "individuals, members of organizations, institutions and State representatives."[195] The International Law Commission's Draft Code of Crimes against the Peace and Security of Mankind holds that systematic or widespread violations of human rights constitute international crimes for which non-state as well as state actors may be responsible.[196] Article 21 of the Draft Code of Crimes imposes individual responsibility for the commission of "murder; torture; establishing or maintaining over persons a status of slav-

---

[190] *Principles of International Law Recognized in the Charter of the Nuremberg Tribunal and in the Judgment of the Tribunal,* [1950] Y.B. Int'l L. Comm'n 374–78, ¶¶ 95–127, U.N. Doc. A/1316; *Draft Code of Crimes Against the Peace and Security of Mankind: Report of the International Law Commission on the Work of its Forty-third Session,* [1991] 2 Y.B. Int'l L. Comm'n 79, U.N. Doc. A/CN.4/L 464.Add.4 (1991) [hereinafter *Draft Code of Crimes*].

[191] *London Charter, supra* note 189, arts. 7–8; *Draft Code of Crimes, supra* note 190, arts. 11, 13.

[192] INTERNATIONAL MILITARY TRIBUNAL, 22 TRIALS OF THE MAJOR WAR CRIMINALS BEFORE THE INTERNATIONAL MILITARY TRIBUNAL 466 (1948).

[193] *London Charter, supra* note 189, art. 6.

[194] Convention on the Prevention and Punishment of the Crime of Genocide, Dec. 9, 1948, 78 U.N.T.S. 277 (entry into force Jan. 12, 1951).

[195] International Convention on the Suppression and Punishment of the Crime of Apartheid, Nov. 30, 1973, art. III, G.A. Res. 3068 (XXVIII), 28 U.N. GAOR, Supp. No. 30, U.N. Doc. A/9030 (1974), *reprinted in* 13 I.L.M. 50.

[196] *Draft Code of Offenses Against the Pease and Security of Mankind: Report of the Int'l Law Comm'n on the Work of its 48th Session,* U.N. GAOR, 51st Sess., art. 21, U.N. Doc. A/51/10 (1996).

ery, servitude, or forced labor; persecution on social, political, racial, religious, or cultural grounds in a systematic manner or on a mass scale; and deportation or forcible transfer of the population."[197]

Recently, member states of international organizations have sought to reach misconduct that is transnational in character, but not specifically designated as an international crime. The Inter-American Convention on Violence against Women calls on state parties thereto to take action against state and non-state actors that commit violence against women in the public and private spheres, including family violence.[198] On November 15, 2000, the U.N. General Assembly adopted a Convention against Transnational Organized Crime and a Protocol to Prevent, Suppress and Punish Trafficking in Persons, Especially Women and Children.[199] This Convention calls on states to criminalize listed offenses, including money laundering and corruption, and to cooperate to combat transnational crime and to protect victims of crime.[200] The Protocol on Trafficking expressly refers to the human rights of victims[201] and to various human rights abuses such as forced labor, slavery, or practices similar to slavery.[202] Natural and legal persons may be liable, and the proceeds of crimes confiscated and seized are to be used for the benefit of victims.

International organizations have taken up several problems where trade and human rights are linked, in the process enhancing global governance by bringing together state and non-state actors. The U.N. Security Council has expressed its concern about the role of the illicit diamond trade supporting the conflict in Sierra Leone and called upon the international diamond industry to cooperate on a ban on all rough diamonds from Sierra Leone.[203] The Council requested the U.N. Secretary-General to appoint a panel of experts to monitor implementation of the ban.[204] In addition, the resolution calls upon states, international organizations, the diamond industry,

---

[197] Id.

[198] Inter-American Convention for the Prevention, Punishment and Eradication of Violence against Women, June 9, 1994, 33 I.L.M. 1334 (1994) (entry into force Mar. 3, 1995).

[199] United Nations Convention Against Transnational Organized Crime; Protocol to Prevent, Suppress and Punish Trafficking in Persons, Especially Women and Children; Protocol Against the Smuggling of Migrants by Land, Sea and Air, Nov. 15, 2000, U.N. Doc. A/55/383 (2000), reprinted in 40 I.L.M. 335 (2001).

[200] Id. arts. 14(2), 25.

[201] Id., pmbl., art. 2(b)6.

[202] See id. art. 3(a).

[203] S.C. Res. 1306, U.N. SCOR, 55th Sess., 4168th mtg., U.N. Doc. S/RES/1306 (2000).

[204] Id.

314   *Boston College International & Comparative Law Review*   [Vol. 25:273

and other relevant entities to assist the government of Sierra Leone to develop a well-structured and well-regulated diamond industry.[205] The World Diamond Congress, meeting in 2000 in Antwerp, proposed the creation of an international diamond council made up of producers, manufacturers, traders, governments, and international organizations to oversee a new system to verify the provenance of rough diamonds.

If the behavior of non-state actors violates international norms directly applicable to their conduct, they may be held responsible to their victims. Efforts to hold corporations accountable for conduct occurring in overseas operations have recently become prevalent in U.S. courts. Using the Alien Tort Claims Act, plaintiffs have sought to hold multinational companies liable for customary human rights violations and environmental harm in Burma, Nigeria, Ecuador, and India. In England as well, the House of Lords has upheld an action brought against an English-based multinational company by South African mineworkers suffering from asbestos related diseases. The use of international human rights law in presenting claims directly against industry is a relatively recent phenomenon and reflects the growing attention being paid to non-state actors in international law and the expectations that their behavior will be tested by norms previously directed at states and state agents. The draft Hague Convention on Jurisdiction and Foreign Judgments in Civil and Commercial Matters refers to human rights in Article 18, in reference to war crimes and grave violations of fundamental rights.

Further action is being taken by human rights bodies. In 1998, the U.N. Sub-commission for the Prevention of Discrimination and Protection of Minorities voted to establish a Working Group to examine over three years the effects of the working methods and activities of transnational corporations on human rights.[206] The mandate of the Working Group is extensive and includes identification and examination of the effects of the activities of transnational corporations on the enjoyment of civil, cultural, economic, political, and social rights, the right to development, the right to a healthy environment, and the right to peace.[207] It is to gather and examine information and reports, and prepare an annual list of transnational corporations to provide examples of the positive and negative impacts on human rights of their activities in the countries in which they operate.[208] In addition,

---

[205] *Id.*
[206] Sub-Commission Resolution 1999/8, *supra* note 49.
[207] *Id.*
[208] *Id.*

the Working Group is to assess how existing human rights standards apply to transnational corporations, including private initiatives and codes of conduct, and collect for study international, regional, and bilateral investment agreements.[209]

The Working Group has prepared a draft code of principles relating to the human rights conduct of companies, based upon relevant language from the codes of conduct by the U.N., the Organization for Economic Co-Operation and Development (OECD), the ILO, corporations, unions, and non-governmental organizations.[210] The principles address a wide range of human rights issues, including nondiscrimination, and freedom from harassment and abuse, slavery, forced labor and child labor, healthy and safe working environments, fair and equal remuneration, hours of work, freedom of association, and the right to collective bargaining, as well as war crimes and other international crimes.[211] The fundamental rationale for the draft principles was to impose responsibility on companies commensurate with their increased power.[212] During the meetings of the Working Group leading up to the principles, many non-governmental organizations argued in favor of drafting a legally binding instrument, on the basis that another voluntary code of conduct would be insufficient.[213]

The ILO remains the key institution concerned with the rights of workers throughout the world. To the extent that other organizations have become involved, the ILO seeks to determine whether or not their standards conform to those of the ILO and adopt a similar human rights approach. The ILO Tripartite Declaration of Principles Concerning Multinational Enterprises and Social Policy addresses the obligations of four groups: the enterprises themselves; workers' groups; employers' organizations; and governments. Its aims are to encourage the positive contributions of multinational companies to economic and social progress and to minimize the negative consequences that might accompany their activities. The Declaration provides that all four groups should respect the Universal Declaration of Human Rights and the two U.N. Covenants on Human Rights. The

---

[209] *Id.*

[210] *See* Commission on Human Rights, *Report of the Working Group on the Effects of the Working Methods and Activities of Transnational Corporations on Human Rights*, at 4, U.N. Doc. E/CN.4/Sub.2/2000/WG.2/WP.1 (2000).

[211] *Id.*

[212] *Id.*

[213] Commission on Human Rights, *The Realization of Economic, Social and Cultural Rights: The Question of Transnational Corporations: Second Report of the Working Group*, ¶ 52, U.N. Doc. E/CN.4/Sub.2/2000/12 (2000).

316   *Boston College International & Comparative Law Review*   [Vol. 25:273

ILO also surveys the positive and negative effects of multinational activities based on information from workers, employers, and governments.

The OECD became a focus of controversy during its unsuccessful
efforts to draft a Multilateral Agreement on Investment (MAI), a process that ended in December, 1998.[214] Strikingly, both the investors
pressing the MAI and those opposed to it were part of the globalized
community and, according to one view, "compromise the concept of
national sovereignty and local control."[215] Many of the issues raised
concerned human rights, including some related to the negotiating
process itself and its lack of transparency.[216] In addition, NGOs were
concerned about several substantive areas that seemed to seriously
limit the sovereignty of states in favor of foreign investors.

Before and after the MAI negotiations, the OECD addressed issues of human rights. First, in 1995, it published guidelines on participatory development and good governance[217] in which the members reiterated their adherence to international human rights
norms.[218] In 1996, OECD studied trade and labor standards, looking
at core worker rights.[219] Later, it adopted revised Guidelines for Multinational Enterprises on June 27, 2000,[220] supported by follow-up
procedures in the twenty-nine member states and four non-member
states participating in the process.[221] The Guidelines concern multinational enterprises operating in or from the thirty-three countries and

---

[214] For differing accounts about why the effort was unsuccessful, see Kobrin, *supra* note
31, at 97.

[215] *Id.* at 99.

[216] *See* Milloon Kothari & Tara Krause, *Human Rights or Corporate Rights? The MAI Challenge*, 5 TRIBUNE DES DROITS HUMAINS 16 (1998).

[217] *See generally* Development Assistance Committee of the Organization for Economic
Co-Operation and Development, *Final Report of the Ad Hoc Working Group on Participatory
Development and Good Governance*, at 1, OECD Doc. OCDE/GP/93/191 (1997), *available at*
http://www.oecd.org/dac [hereinafter OECD, *Working Group*].

[218] *Id.* ¶ 66.

[219] *See generally* Organization for Economic Co-operation and Development, TRADE,
EMPLOYMENT AND LABOUR STANDARDS: A STUDY OF CORE WORKERS' RIGHTS AND INTER-
NATIONAL TRADE (1996).

[220] OECD, *Working Group*, *supra* note 217, ¶¶ 12–13.

[221] The revision process demonstrated the impact of the Internet on prospects for participation in international organizations. A draft text of the guidelines were posted on the
web with an invitation for the public to comment. After comments were received from
businesses, labor unions, environmental groups, academic institutions, individuals, and
non-member states, the draft was revised and the second version also posted on the Internet. A second round of public comment followed before the Guidelines were finalized. *See*
James Salzman, *Labor Rights, Globalization and Institutions: The Role and Influence of the Organization for Economic Cooperation and Development*, 21 MICH. J. INT'L L. 769, 847 (2000).

apply to all operations worldwide. The revision added a human rights obligation, stating that, "enterprises should . . . [r]espect the human rights of those affected by their activities consistent with the host government's obligations and commitments." It is significant that the Guidelines do not refer to policies or practices, but rather to the legal obligations of the host state. Every state has such obligations under the U.N. Charter, customary international law, and such human rights treaties as the state has ratified. The Guidelines impose a duty upon businesses to inform themselves of the relevant obligations and conform their conduct to them. The follow-up foresees a series of procedures involving consultations, good offices, conciliation, and mediation.

The U.N. Declaration Against Corruption and Bribery in International Commercial Transactions encourages social responsibility and ethical behavior, calling on partners to international transactions to observe the laws of the host countries, and take into account the impact of their activities on economic and social development and protection of the environment and human rights.

Yet another response to the intersecting issues of globalization and human rights has been to utilize market mechanisms and other forms of private regulation to impact corporate behavior. Pressure from international and national groups, as well as perceived long-term interests, have led many companies to take up the issue of human rights. A survey by the Ashridge Centre for Business and Society found that human rights issues caused more than one in three of the 500 largest companies to abandon a proposed investment project and nearly one in five to divest its operations in a country. Nearly half have codes of conduct that refer to human rights. The record is not clear, however, on implementation. The U.N. Development Program *Human Development Report 2000* calls for better implementation of corporate codes of conduct, stating that, "many fail to meet human rights standards, or lack implementation measures and independent audits."[222] It suggests that the use of human rights indicators be extended to include the role of corporations.

Codes of conduct for human rights often result from pressure on companies to divest from countries with widespread and systematic human rights violations.[223] Consumer boycotts and labeling initiatives

---

[222] UNDP, *supra* note 16, at 80.

[223] Examples are the Sullivan Principles concerning South Africa during apartheid and the McBride Principles for Northern Ireland. *See* Lance Compa & Tashia Hinchliffe-Darricarrère, *Enforcing International Labor Rights Through Corporate Codes of Conduct*, 33 Co-

such as "Rugmark"[224] provide a means for persons concerned with labor conditions and human rights to use their purchasing power to influence corporate policy. Effective mobilization of international consumer pressure can substitute for regulation.[225] A writer in the *Economist* has observed that, "a multinational's failure to look like a good global citizen is increasingly expensive in a world where consumers and pressure groups can be quickly mobilised behind a cause."[226] Such marketplace regulation has been criticized as lacking in the accountability and transparency that normally accompany the formation of laws.[227]

The final approach concerned with enhancing human rights in a globalized world is one that has broad implications for global governance generally. It seeks to enhance non-state participation in international organizations and other fora concerned with international regulation. While international organizations other than the ILO have limited participation for non-governmental entities, efforts are being made to develop more collaborative efforts between state and non-state actors within the framework of international organizations.

The U.N. Millennium Declaration[228] resolves to give greater opportunities to the private sector, NGOs, and civil society in general "to contribute to the realization of the Organization's goals and programs."[229] The U.N. Global Compact Initiative aims to develop policy networks of international institutions, civil society, private sector organizations, and national governments to further human rights.[230] The Initiative has taken up such issues as trade in diamonds in zones of conflict, corporate social responsibility generally, the inclusion of corporate behavior in the studies conducted by U.N. special rappor-

---

LUM. J. TRANSNAT'L L. 663, 671 (1995); *see also* J. Perez-Lopez, *Promoting International Respect for Worker Rights Through Business Codes of Conduct,* 17 FORDHAM INT'L L.J. 1, 47 (1993).

[224] "Rugmark" is a program to label carpets that have been made free from child labor. *See* J. Hilowitz, *Social Labelling to Combat Child Labor: Some Considerations,* 136 INT'L LAB. REV. 215, 224 (1997).

[225] Peter J. Spiro, *New Global Potentates: Nongovernmental Organizations and the "Unregulated" Marketplace,* 18 CARDOZO L. REV. 957, 959 (1996).

[226] *See Multinationals and Their Morals,* ECONOMIST, Dec. 2, 1995, at 18.

[227] Spiro, *supra* note 225, at 962–63 (criticizing NGOs for lack of accountability and transparency).

[228] *United Nations Millennium Declaration,* G.A. Res. 55/2, U.N. GAOR, 55th Sess., U.N. Doc. A/Res/55/2 (2000) (issuing on behalf of the heads of state and government attending the U.N. Millennium General Assembly).

[229] *Id.* ¶ 30.

[230] *See* Office of the High Commissioner for Human Rights, *Business and Human Rights: An Update* (June 26, 2000), *at* http://www.unhchr.ch/businesupdate.htm.

teurs on various human rights issues, and the impact of national litigation on corporate liability for human rights abuses in countries
where the companies have operations.[231] It is also concerned with the
work of international financial institutions like the World Bank and
regional organizations, such as the OECD.[232]

U.N. special rapporteurs have held discussions with private actors
in exercising their mandates. The special rapporteurs on Sudan and
on Afghanistan held dialogues with oil companies conducting activities in these countries; the special rapporteur on toxic waste met with
a pharmaceutical company.[233] The special rapporteur on the sale of
children has worked with the International Chamber of Commerce
requesting information about company initiatives benefitting children
that could be proposed for action in various parts of the world.

Multinational companies also have been important in conflict
resolution, especially in mobilizing information and communications
technology. This was the case with the U.N. High Commissioner for
Refugees in, for example, Kosovo.[234] Successful partnership will require companies to shun corrupt leaders and work to build viable
states that respect human rights.[235] The joint U.N.-World Bank effort
in East Timor demonstrates a broad engagement in rebuilding, including the development of judicial institutions and processes.[236]
Given the insecurity in many conflict and post-conflict areas, the cooperation of the U.N. and the World Bank with private enterprise will
be necessary to ensure that the risks are properly shared, perhaps
through more favorable terms for political-risk insurance.[237] Humanitarian and human rights NGOs also must be part of the coalition, with
the aim of overcoming the mutual distrust with which the business
sector and NGOs view each other. To fully work, such a coalition may

---

[231] *Id.*

[232] *Id.*

[233] The mandate of the special rapporteur on toxic waste includes complaints brought
by and against states and non-state actors for the transboundary movement of toxic wastes
and she is to identify specific companies and states involved in such traffic.

[234] *See* JANE NELSON, THE BUSINESS OF PEACE: THE PRIVATE SECTOR AS A PARTNER IN
CONFLICT PREVENTION AND RESOLUTION 20 (2000), *available at* http://www.international-
alert.org/corporate/Pubs.htm (last visited Dec. 22, 2001).

[235] *See* Jonathan Berman, *Boardrooms and Bombs: Strategies of Multinational Corporations in
Conflict Areas,* 22 HARV. INT'L REV. 28, 28 (2000), *available at* http://www.hir.harvard.edu
(last visited Mar. 11, 2002).

[236] *See generally* Hansjörg Strohmeyer, *Collapse and Reconstruction of a Judicial System: The
United Nations Missions in Kosovo and East Timor,* 95 AM. J. INT'L L. 46 (2001).

[237] *Id.*

320　　　*Boston College International & Comparative Law Review*　　　[Vol. 25:273]

require restructuring international institutions to allow more effective participation by non-state actors.

Several multinational agreements have been concluded between international industry associations and workers' organizations.[238] These include the collective agreement between the International Transport Workers Federation and the International Maritime Employers' Committee, an agreement that covers wages, minimum standards, and other terms and conditions of work, including maternity protection. In January, 2001 the two partners agreed upon the future development of labor standards in the international shipping industry to permit such standards to become the third pillar of the shipping industry, alongside maritime environmental and safety standards.[239] The Spanish-based telecommunications company Telefonica and the Union Network International (UNI) similarly signed an agreement that covers some 120,000 workers represented by eighteen labor unions affiliated to UNI. Both sides agreed to respect ILO core labor standards covering freedom of association and the right to collective bargaining, non-discrimination, and freedom from forced labor and child labor. In all, the agreement referred to some fifteen ILO conventions and recommendations.

The question of whether or not non-economic, e.g., human rights values, are or should be incorporated in the trade regime remains debated. Richard Shell has proposed a "stakeholder model" of international government in which "private commercial parties, indigent citizens in developing countries with weak governments, environmentalists, labor interests, . . . consumer groups," and others affected by trade would have a role in economic policy-making and dispute settlement in order to integrate non-economic values with economic ones.[240] Human rights interest groups and other NGOs having consultative status[241] have been prominent in various U.N. human

---

[238] In addition to the two agreements mentioned here, other international agreements signed include the code of labor practice signed between the International Federation of Association Football (FIFA) and the International Confederation of Free Trade Unions (ICFTU), the International Federation of Commercial, Clerical, Professional and Technical Employees (FIET) and the International Textile, Garment and Leather Workers' Federation (ITGLWF). ILO, Report of the Director General, *supra* note 25, at 43–44.

[239] *Id.* at 42.

[240] *See* G. Richard Shell, *Trade Legalism and International Relations Theory: An Analysis of the World Trade Organization*, 44 DUKE L.J. 829, 908–09 (1995).

[241] Article 71 of the U.N. Charter authorizes ECOSOC to consult with NGOs concerned with matters within ECOSOC competence. Article 71 has been implemented through procedures adopted in ECOSOC resolutions. *See General Review of Arrangements for Consultations with Non-Governmental Organizations: Report of the Secretary-General, Open-ended*

rights meetings and in other international fora, but have had far less success in participating in the WTO.[242] In general, more transparency and participation are needed.

CONCLUSION

The key international legal developments that appear to be emerging as a result of globalization, as discussed above, seem to be the following. First, human rights institutions and activists are asserting a primacy of human rights law over other fields of international law. Whether or to what extent this assertion will be accepted remains to be seen. Second, the international legal personality of inter-governmental organizations is seen to carry with it the obligation to conform to general international law norms, above and beyond the requirements of the constituting charters or constitutions of the organizations. Third, the imposition of responsibility for human rights violations on non-state actors appears to be increasing. This all leads to asking: does the state need strengthening?

Globalization has created centers of power that are alongside, even in competition with the power of states. Accountability for human rights violations and prevention of future ones must today and in the future take into account these non-state actors: the media, corporations, and international organizations such as the WTO and the World Bank. States and their agents are no longer the only or sometimes even the key actors responsible for ensuring that human rights and freedoms are guaranteed. As recent international developments have shown, there are multiple avenues to respond to this problem. The first is to strengthen the state and to insist on its responsibility for ensuring that non-state actors do not commit human rights violations.

There is no doubt a need to strengthen weak states that lack the institutions necessary to protect and ensure human rights. Institutions such as independent judiciaries must be formed and executive power, including the police and military, must be brought under the rule of law. At the same time it must be recognized that there are two problems with solely relying on strengthened individual state action. First, it raises the specter of powerful state agents again capable of and perhaps willing to use and abuse state power to prolong their time in

---

Working Group on the Review of Arrangements for Consultation with Nongovernmental Organizations, U.N. GAOR, 1st Sess., U.N. Doc. E/AC.70/1994/5 (1994).

[242] *See* Kenneth W. Abbott, *"Economic" Issues and Political Participation: The Evolving Boundaries of International Federalism,* 18 CARDOZO L. REV. 971, 1005-06 (1996).

322   *Boston College International & Comparative Law Review*   [Vol. 25:273

office. The wisdom of political philosophers who called for a balance of and restraints on power must not be forgotten because "the good old rule, [s]ufficeth them, the simple plan, [t]hat they should take, who have the power, [a]nd they should keep who can."[243] The second problem is that even strong states are unable to deal unilaterally with all the challenges posed by globalization, especially when dealing with international crime, including terrorism. The amount of individual state strengthening that would be necessary to combat these problems would probably require an unacceptable retreat from basic human rights.

The alternative is to strengthen the weak states to enable them to protect human rights, while at the same time imposing increased international obligations on non-state actors through multilateral mechanisms. Thus, even though states will retain the primary responsibility for ensuring the promotion and protection of human rights, non-state actors will be held accountable when they undermine state efforts to do so or are complicit in violations undertaken by the state. Non-state actors have always had a pivotal role in developing the law of human rights; they now may take a further role as a result of globalization.

---

[243] Wordsworth, *Rob Roy's Grave,* stanza 9, *available at* http://www.bartleby.com/145/ww242.html (last visited Mar. 10, 2002).

[8]

Corporations and Human Rights:
A Theory of Legal Responsibility

Steven R. Ratner[†]

CONTENTS

† Albert Sidney Burleson Professor in Law, University of Texas School of Law. I appreciate comments from Jose Alvarez, Hans Baade, Eyal Benvenisti, Sarah Cleveland, Francesco Francioni, Mark Gergen, John Knox, Douglas Laycock, Gerald Neuman, Peter Spiro, Russell Weintraub, Jay Westbrook, and David Wippman. The Article also benefited from questions from participants at colloquia and conferences at Columbia Law School, New York Law School, the University of Chicago Law School, the University of Texas School of Law, and the University of Melbourne Faculty of Law, where I presented earlier versions in November 2000, February 2001, and May 2001.

446   The Yale Law Journal   [Vol. 111: 443

The last decade has witnessed a striking new phenomenon in strategies to protect human rights: a shift by global actors concerned about human rights from nearly exclusive attention on the abuses committed by governments to close scrutiny of the activities of business enterprises, in particular multinational corporations. Claims that various kinds of corporate activity have a detrimental impact on human welfare are at least as old as Marxism, and have always been a mantra of the political left worldwide. But today's assertions are different both in their origin and in their content. They emanate not from ideologues with a purportedly redistributive agenda, but from international organizations composed of states both rich and poor; and from respected nongovernmental organizations, such as Amnesty International and Human Rights Watch, whose very credibility turns on avoidance of political affiliation. Equally importantly, these groups do not seek to delegitimize capitalism or corporate economic power itself, but have criticized certain corporate behavior for impinging on clearly accepted norms of human rights law based on widely ratified treaties and customary international law.

Consider the following small set of claims challenging private business activity and the arenas in which they occur:

- The United Nations Security Council condemns illegal trade in diamonds for fueling the civil war in Sierra Leone and asks private diamond trading associations to cooperate in establishing a regime to label diamonds of legitimate origin.[1]

- The European Parliament, concerned about accusations against European companies of involvement in human rights abuses in the developing world, calls upon the European Commission to develop a "European multilateral framework governing companies' operations worldwide" and to include in it a binding code of conduct.[2]

- In response to public concern that American companies and their agents are violating the rights of workers in the developing world, the U.S. government endorses and oversees the creation of a voluntary code of conduct for the apparel industry.[3]

---

1. S.C. Res. 1306, U.N. SCOR, 55th Sess., 4168th mtg., U.N. Doc. S/RES/1306 (2000).

2. Resolution on EU Standards for European Enterprises Operating in Developing Countries: Towards a European Code of Conduct, 1999 O.J. (C 104).

3. Fair Labor Ass'n, Workplace Code of Conduct, *at* http://www.fairlabor.org/html/CodeOfConduct/index.html (last visited Oct. 15, 2001).

- The South African Truth and Reconciliation Commission, in a searching study of apartheid, devotes three days of hearings and a chapter of its final report to the involvement of the business sector in the practices of apartheid.[4]

- Human Rights Watch establishes a special unit on corporations and human rights; in 1999, it issues two lengthy reports, one accusing the Texas-based Enron Corporation of "corporate complicity in human rights violations" by the Indian government,[5] and another accusing Shell, Mobil, and other international oil companies operating in Nigeria of cooperating with the government in suppressing political opposition.[6]

- Citizens of Burma and Indonesia sue Unocal and Freeport-McMoRan in United States courts under the Alien Tort Claims Act and accuse the companies of violating the human rights of people near their operations. The corporations win both suits without a trial.[7]

- Holocaust survivors sue European banks, insurance companies, and industries for complicity in wartime human rights violations, and, with the aid of the U.S. government, achieve several multimillion-dollar settlements.[8]

The creation of a new target for human rights advocates is a product of various forces encompassed in the term globalization: the dramatic increase in investment by multinational companies in the developing world; the sense that the economic might of some corporations has eroded the power of the state; the global telecommunications revolution, which has brought worldwide attention to the conditions of those living in less developed countries and has increased the capacity of NGOs to mobilize public opinion; the work of the World Trade Organization (WTO) and International Monetary Fund (IMF) in requiring states to be more

---

4. 4 TRUTH & RECONCILIATION COMM'N, FINAL REPORT ch. 2 (1998), http://www.polity.org.za/govdocs/commissions/1998/trc/4chap2.htm.

5. HUMAN RIGHTS WATCH, THE ENRON CORPORATION: CORPORATE COMPLICITY IN HUMAN RIGHTS VIOLATIONS (1999), at http://www.hrw.org/reports/1999/enron.

6. HUMAN RIGHTS WATCH, THE PRICE OF OIL: CORPORATE RESPONSIBILITY AND HUMAN RIGHTS VIOLATIONS IN NIGERIA'S OIL PRODUCING COMMUNITIES (1999), at http://www.hrw.org/reports/1999/nigeria.

7. *See* Doe v. Unocal Corp., 110 F. Supp. 2d 1294 (C.D. Cal. 2000), *aff'd*, 248 F.3d 915 (9th Cir. 2001); Beanal v. Freeport-McMoRan, Inc., 969 F. Supp. 362 (E.D. La. 1997), *aff'd*, 197 F.3d 161 (5th Cir. 1999). For an updated list of suits, see Christopher Avery, Lawsuits Against Companies, *at* http://www.business-humanrights.org/Lawsuits.htm (last visited Oct. 1, 2001).

8. *See* Sean D. Murphy, *Nazi-Era Claims Against German Companies*, 94 AM. J. INT'L L. 682 (2000).

448   The Yale Law Journal   [Vol. 111: 443

hospitable to foreign investors; and the well-documented accounts of the activities of a handful of corporations. These advocacy efforts build on earlier attempts by concerned actors to focus attention on private business activity, ranging from the trials of leading German industrialists for war crimes after World War II to campaigns in the United States in the 1970s and 1980s to encourage divestment from corporations doing business in South Africa. All are based on the view that business enterprises should be held accountable for human rights abuses taking place within their sphere of operations. Corporations, for their part, have responded in numerous ways, from denying any duties in the area of human rights to accepting voluntary codes that could constrain their behavior.

But is there an objective standard by which to appraise both the claims that various business activities are illegitimate from the perspective of international human rights and the corresponding responses of business actors? For example, are corporations responsible for human rights abuses if they simply invest in a repressive society? What if they know that the government will violate human rights in order to make an investment project succeed? What if they share with the government information on suspected troublemakers? What if, illegally, but with the tacit consent of the government, they pay a very low wage or provide bad working conditions?

Any answer not depending exclusively on diverse and possibly parochial national visions of human rights and enterprise responsibility must come from international law. International law offers a process for appraising, and in the end resolving, the demands that governments, international organizations, and nongovernmental organizations are now making of private enterprises. Without some international legal standards, we will likely continue to witness both excessive claims made against such actors for their responsibility and counterclaims by corporate actors against such accountability. Decisionmakers considering these claims—whether legislatures or international organizations contemplating regulation, courts facing suits, or officials deciding whether to intervene in a dispute involving business and human rights—will respond in an ad hoc manner, driven by domestic priorities or by legal frameworks that are likely to differ significantly across the planet. The resultant atmosphere of uncertainty will be detrimental to both the protection of human rights and the economic wealth that private business activity has created worldwide.[9]

---

9. This uncertainty is reflected in a corporate policy statement of the Royal Dutch/Shell group of companies. *See* ROYAL DUTCH/SHELL GROUP OF COS., HUMAN RIGHTS—THE ROLE OF BUSINESS, *at* http://www.shell.com/royal-en/content/0,5028,25470-51032,00.html (last visited Sept. 2, 2001) ("It has often been difficult for [NGOs, the media, and others] to agree on . . . a theoretical framework for a new understanding of business's role in . . . human rights. . . . As a result it has been difficult for business to respond to expectations that appear to be changing significantly . . . .").

This Article posits a theory of corporate responsibility for human rights protection. Building upon the traditional paradigm whereby international law generally places duties on states and, more recently, individuals, I consider whether and how the international legal process might provide for human rights obligations directly on corporations. My thesis is that international law should and can provide for such obligations, and that the scope of these obligations must be determined in light of the characteristics of corporate activity. In particular, business enterprises will have duties both insofar as they cooperate with those actors whom international law already sees as the prime sources of abuses—states—and insofar as their activities infringe upon the human dignity of those with whom they have special ties. My approach thus marries principles of international law concerning foreign investment, as well as principles of corporate law more generally, with the theory and practice of human rights law.

This proposal will not be without its detractors. Corporate and governmental leaders might find the idea simply unnecessary, viewing the state as a sufficient guarantor of the human rights of its population. They and others, including those sympathetic to the human rights agenda, might find a philosophical objection to the idea that human rights law should regulate private actors. Some traditional international legal scholars might see corporate duties as unprecedented or even doctrinally prohibited, asserting that only states, and perhaps individuals, are holders of obligations. And still others may find such an approach inherently unworkable given the differences between state and corporate structures. In addressing these concerns, my argument fits within broader academic and policy debates about the power of transnational corporations and nongovernmental organizations, the role of the state in protecting human rights, and the extent to which international law can and should regulate nonstate actors.

I lay out my argument in six Parts. Part I examines the approach international law has taken to corporations as independent actors. It describes a swinging pendulum in the attention that the law has given to the relations between corporations and the states where they undertake their activities. This process will prove critical to understanding international law's views on corporate duties. In light of this historical review, Part II seeks to justify the need for corporate responsibility, rather than state or individual responsibility, as a means for protecting human rights. Given that most human rights abuses continue to be committed by governments, organized insurgencies, and the individuals in them, the answer is by no means obvious. Inherent in this issue is also the tension between the imposition of duties on business enterprises and the conventional view that only violations of human dignity sponsored by governments or quasi-governmental actors engage international responsibility. With the concept

450   The Yale Law Journal   [Vol. 111: 443

of corporate responsibility defended, Part III considers a variety of ways in which key international actors have already accepted duties on corporations, particularly in areas other than human rights. Their actual recognition of corporate responsibility undercuts any conceivable doctrinal bar to such duties.

Part IV launches the theory by examining whether existing international law doctrines, which make states and individuals responsible for violations of human rights, can provide a basis for deriving corporate duties. Part V, the core of my theory, proposes deriving such duties based on four factors: the corporation's ties with the government, its nexus to affected populations, the particular human right at issue, and the structure of the corporate entity. In Part VI, I review the theory and provisionally apply it to some of the factual claims currently leveled at corporations. In Part VII, I offer an overview of the means by which the theory of responsibility might be implemented within various arenas in which key actors prescribe, invoke, and apply international law. This includes a discussion of enforcement options, which represent one of the great challenges to international human rights law and international law generally. I conclude by engaging anticipated criticisms of the theory and discussing the theory's implications for international law and human rights.

Before beginning, it is worth putting up four guideposts for the reader. First, the theory offered here is grounded in international law rather than the domestic law of one state. Others have begun to consider the reasoning of U.S. courts handling corporate cases under the Alien Tort Claims Act (ATCA), which gives federal courts jurisdiction to hear claims of aliens for violations of international law.[10] These cases are important evidence of the trend toward corporate accountability—indeed, with concrete results.[11] Yet exclusive or excessive focus on them would be mistaken, because American principles of state action, which were developed in U.S. civil rights law and have proved critical in corporate ATCA cases, cannot simply be transferred to the international arena. This United States-centered view is likely to undermine the entire enterprise. The businesses at issue in this problem are predominantly multinational or foreign, and primarily

---

10. 28 U.S.C. § 1350 (1994); *see, e.g.,* Kathryn L. Boyd, *Collective Rights Adjudication in U.S. Courts: Enforcing Human Rights at the Corporate Level,* 1999 BYU L. REV. 1139; *Developments in the Law—International Criminal Law,* 114 HARV. L. REV. 1943, 2025-49 (2001); Richard L. Herz, *Litigating Environmental Abuses Under the Alien Tort Claims Act,* 40 VA. J. INT'L L. 545 (2000).

11. *See, e.g.,* Roberta C. Yafie, *Freeport in Deal with Irian Java* [sic] *Citizens,* AM. METAL MARKET, Aug. 22, 2000, at 6, LEXIS, Nexis Library, American Metal Market File (discussing a memorandum of understanding between Freeport and local citizens' groups, which was prompted by the suit in *Beanal v. Freeport-McMoRan, Inc.,* 969 F. Supp. 362, *aff'd,* 197 F.3d 161, and which addressed human rights and environmental concerns).

headquartered outside the United States.[12] The abuses of concern also take place principally outside the United States. Not surprisingly, international law rejects such a one-dimensional basis for the creation of international norms. Indeed, domestic legal principles matter only to the extent they are shared by many different legal systems and, even then, are subsidiary to treaties and customary law.[13]

Second, this Article seeks to develop an approach to corporate responsibility that can be applied in numerous international fora, not merely courts. International law, including human rights law, is invoked, interpreted, and applied in diverse arenas.[14] Some norms based on the principles of international responsibility will be incorporated by businesses themselves under economic pressure from interested shareholders and consumers, who serve as private enforcers of the law. Some claims will be addressed in domestic fora as legislators and government officials draft statutes, regulations, or governmental policy. Some prescription and application of law will take place in international arenas as diplomats, perhaps prodded by NGOs, prepare treaties or nonbinding legal instruments. And both domestic and international courts and other dispute resolution bodies may play a role. But excessive focus on the activities of courts diverts attention from the principal venues in which international legal argumentation is made and matters.[15]

Third, this Article's advocacy of a theory of responsibility for business enterprises under international law should in no way suggest any sort of unilateral imposition of rules on corporations. International norms are not—indeed cannot be—prescribed through such a process. Wherever lawmaking occurs, the detailed elaboration of norms must directly involve all interested actors, whether governments, businesses, or human rights groups. A theory of responsibility under international law in no way precludes, but rather invites and assumes, a role for states and their citizens (individual and corporate) in developing appropriate norms and enforcement mechanisms.

---

12. U.N. CONFERENCE ON TRADE & DEV., WORLD INVESTMENT REPORT 1999, at 78-80, U.N. Sales No. E.99.II.D.3 (2000) (ranking top multinational firms by "transnationality index," of which the leading five were headquartered in Canada (Seagram and Thomson), Switzerland (ABB and Nestle), and the Netherlands (Unilever)).

13. 3 SHABTAI ROSENNE, THE LAW AND PRACTICE OF THE INTERNATIONAL COURT, 1920-1996, at 1605 (3d ed. 1997) (construing general principles of law as "particularizations of a common underlying sense of what is just in the circumstances"); *see also* BIN CHENG, GENERAL PRINCIPLES OF LAW AS APPLIED BY INTERNATIONAL COURTS AND TRIBUNALS 24 (Grotius Publ'ns 1987) (1953) (defining general principles of law as "general propositions underlying the various rules of law which express the essential qualities of juridical truth itself").

14. Myres S. McDougal & W. Michael Reisman, *The Prescribing Function in the World Constitutive Process: How International Law Is Made, in* INTERNATIONAL LAW ESSAYS 353, 374-77 (Myres S. McDougal & W. Michael Reisman eds., 1981).

15. *See, e.g.,* Steven R. Ratner, *International Law: The Trials of Global Norms,* FOREIGN POL'Y, Spring 1998, at 65, 70-71.

452   The Yale Law Journal   [Vol. 111: 443

Finally, the use of the term "corporations" or "transnational enterprises" (TNEs) in this Article does not reflect an assumption of a particular structure of business enterprises. Rather, the terms are chosen to respond to the current debates among governments, human rights NGOs, and businesses, which essentially highlight the duties of multinational corporations in countries where they invest or otherwise do business. The theory I develop is, however, applicable broadly to business enterprises—whatever their form (e.g., partnership or family-owned business) and whatever the degree of transnationality (from completely local to highly transnational).[16] I thus use a variety of terms interchangeably and maintain a focus on multinational enterprises, but do not suggest that there is a principled distinction among such entities and other economic actors.

I. THE SWINGING PENDULUM: A HISTORICAL REVIEW OF INTERNATIONAL LAW'S APPROACH TO THE BUSINESS-HUMAN RIGHTS DYNAMIC

The approach international law has taken and can take to business enterprises and the protection of human rights flows from relationships among four sets of key actors involved in the process of international economic activity and, in particular, of foreign investment: the home state of a transnational enterprise (a concept that has, of course, itself changed as corporations have become more multinational); the host state(s) for the activities of the enterprise; the enterprise or individual investor; and the affected population of the host state(s).[17] The law's characterization of these relationships has changed significantly in the last century, reflecting global political and economic transformations.

A. *Action: The Colonial Era*

During the period of European colonialism, the home state retained the greatest power among the relevant actors. Its relationship with the host state was defined as one of direct control through the various mechanisms and legalisms of the colonial relationship. Far from undermining this dynamic, international law affirmatively recognized and supported it.[18] The host state

---

16. For a similar starting point within the UN context, see David Weissbrodt, *Principles Relating to the Human Rights Conduct of Companies: Working Paper*, Commission on Human Rights, Sub-Commission on the Promotion and Protection of Human Rights, 52d Sess., para. 16, U.N. Doc. E/CN.4/Sub.2/2000-WG.2/WP.1 (2000).

17. One might wish to picture these four actors as sitting at the corners of a quadrangle, with home states and corporations the endpoints on the top left and right, and host states and their populations the endpoints at the bottom left and right, with the legal relationships among them viewed as lines between them.

18. *See* 1 LASSA OPPENHEIM, INTERNATIONAL LAW 99 (1st ed. 1905) (equating civilized states with fully independent ones); *id.* at 219 ("Colonies rank as territory of the

might exist as a de jure matter, with treaties officially defining its relationship with the metropole,[19] but in fact the home state could generally dictate to its own colonies whatever terms it chose. Of course, colonial powers did not enjoy these powers vis-à-vis the colonies of other states. Nonetheless, for the sake of a snapshot description of the international economic and political order of the period, the overall relationship between home states and host states could be regarded as colonial. The black African membership of the League of Nations, limited to two independent states—Liberia and Ethiopia, suffices to make this clear.

As for TNEs, they were creatures of domestic law. They varied in status, ranging from some that were purely private (including individual investors) to others that were effectively controlled by the government. The latter included the British East India Company, Hudson's Bay Company, Dutch East India Company, and other trading companies that helped—or in some cases de facto did—administer India, Canada, Indonesia, southern Africa, and other parts of the world. In matters concerning the overseas possessions, the business or individual could generally count on the support of the home state. European companies became the principal agents for the economic exploitation of the colonial territory.[20] That support gave enterprises and individuals access to the wealth of the colonies on extraordinarily favorable terms. Local communities received few economic benefits for their work and had no basis to complain. The colonial legacy included swaths of African farmland owned by whites, African mineral wealth controlled by Europeans, and significant petroleum sources in the Middle East granted to Western oil companies. The very legal term used to describe these foreign investments—concessions—crystallized the relationship between the home state and its companies, on the one hand, and the host territory, on the other.[21] The same general practice held sway even with respect to independent states in the developing world, notably in Latin America, where the United States and European nations at times

motherland . . . ."); *see also* Antony Anghie, *Finding the Peripheries: Sovereignty and Colonialism in Nineteenth-Century International Law*, 40 HARV. INT'L L.J. 1 (1999) (demonstrating the incorporation of colonialism within legal doctrine).

19. *Cf.* Western Sahara, 1975 I.C.J. 12, 39 (Oct. 16) (noting the legal status of nineteenth-century territories). *But see* Malcolm Shaw, *The* Western Sahara *Case*, 49 BRIT. Y.B. INT'L L. 119, 133-34 (1978) (noting theories of the time, which denied international legal personality to non-European entities).

20. *See, e.g.,* MICHAEL W. DOYLE, EMPIRES 176-77, 189-91 (1986) (describing the rise of "company colonialism"); THOMAS PACKENHAM, THE SCRAMBLE FOR AFRICA 386-87, 491-94 (1992) (discussing the British South Africa Company's role in Rhodesia). On King Leopold of Belgium's privatization of colonial control over the Congo through the creation of the so-called Congo Free State, see generally ADAM HOCHSCHILD, KING LEOPOLD'S GHOST (1998).

21. *See* M. SORNARAJAH, THE INTERNATIONAL LAW ON FOREIGN INVESTMENT 9-10 (1994).

resorted to gunboat diplomacy or covert intervention to protect economic interests.[22]

The remaining actors—individuals in the host state—were, as a legal matter, marginal to the entire process. They enjoyed few rights with respect to the host state government (to the extent it might exist independently), the colonial power, or the TNE. The colonial authorities or their host state agents supplied workers to the TNEs. In sum then, home states and TNEs working with them had substantial rights vis-à-vis host states and (to the extent anyone in the North noticed) their populace, while the latter two enjoyed few rights with respect to the former two.

B. *Reaction: Decolonization and Its Aftermath*

The global transformation that resulted in the independence of nearly all colonial territories within thirty years after World War II drastically altered these political relationships and the corresponding legal relationships. First, states accepted that the legal links between the developed world and the developing world would be based on the notion of the sovereign or juridical equality of independent states.[23] Although certain territories remained non-self-governing, states agreed that any such relationship had to stem from a clear choice by the people of the territory.[24] Moreover, as more developing world states became members of international organizations, they succeeded in passing resolutions demanding greater economic equality between the North and the South and in creating mechanisms to study the realization of this goal. The apogee of this process took place in the 1970s, when the United Nations General Assembly passed a series of resolutions aimed at the establishment of a "New International Economic Order." These included a Charter of Economic Rights and Duties of States that emphasized the obligations of the North to the South.[25] The United Nations Conference on Trade and Development held numerous meetings in which the grievances of the South

---

22. EDWARD M. GRAHAM, FIGHTING THE WRONG ENEMY 168 (2000); SORNARAJAH, *supra* note 21, at 9-11.

23. U.N. CHARTER art. 2, para. 1.

24. G.A. Res. 2625, *Declaration on Principles of International Law Concerning Friendly Relations and Co-operation Among States in Accordance with the Charter of the United Nations*, U.N. GAOR, 25th Sess., Supp. No. 28, at 121, 124, U.N. Doc. A/8028 (1970).

25. G.A. Res. 3281, *Charter of Economic Rights and Duties of States*, U.N. GAOR, 29th Sess., Supp. No. 31, at 50, U.N. Doc. A/9631 (1974); G.A. Res. 3201, *Declaration on the Establishment of a New International Economic Order*, U.N. GAOR, 6th Spec. Sess., Supp. No. 1, at 3, U.N. Doc. A/9959 (1974); G.A. Res. 3171, U.N. GAOR, 28th Sess., Supp. No. 30, at 52, U.N. Doc. A/9030 (1973).

received great attention, even though North-South disagreements prevented any significant restructuring of global economic relations.[26]

Second, alongside the decolonization process occurred another sea change in international law—the elaboration of a body of international human rights law that placed direct duties on states toward their own people. Although the UN Charter itself enshrined the notion of noninterference in the internal affairs of states,[27] this provision did not prevent the UN and its members from promoting the protection of human rights through international law. In the two decades after the Charter, states promulgated the Universal Declaration on Human Rights and codified many of its principles in the International Covenant on Civil and Political Rights (ICCPR), the International Covenant on Economic, Social, and Cultural Rights (ICESCR), and additional treaties on racial discrimination, women's rights, children's rights, and torture.[28] States and other actors thus came to see the relationship between a state and its inhabitants as governed by a set of human rights norms. At the same time, implementation of these norms remained sporadic, as most of the newly decolonized states ended up being ruled by regimes that resisted international inquiry into their domestic politics.[29] The Cold War contributed to this neglect, as each superpower sought to shore up client states without much concern for their human rights records.

The period of decolonization and its immediate aftermath also changed the relationship between multinational enterprises and host state governments. The host states in the developing world that were lobbying for a new North-South dynamic also sought to redefine the ties between themselves and the TNEs based in the North. Seeing the TNEs or individual foreign investors as agents of the North in the economic and political domination of the South, they wanted to even the scales.[30] The attempt at equalization had several dimensions. First, developing world states began to engage in significant expropriations of foreign investment. The best known of these took place in the petroleum industry, when Middle Eastern states

---

26. *See* ROBERT L. ROTHSTEIN, GLOBAL BARGAINING: UNCTAD AND THE QUEST FOR A NEW INTERNATIONAL ECONOMIC ORDER 106-216 (criticizing UNCTAD as a forum for commodity negotiations); Edwin P. Reubens, *An Overview of the NIEO, in* THE CHALLENGE OF THE NEW INTERNATIONAL ECONOMIC ORDER 1, 2-6 (Edwin P. Reubens ed., 1981) (discussing the increasing demands of the South).

27. U.N. CHARTER art. 2, para. 7.

28. *See generally* U.N. DEP'T OF PUB. INFO., THE UNITED NATIONS AND HUMAN RIGHTS, 1945-1995, at 3-91, U.N. Sales No. E.95.I.21 (1995) (reviewing the UN's role in creating treaties and implementation mechanisms for human rights); *see also* JACK DONNELLY, INTERNATIONAL HUMAN RIGHTS 5-17 (1993) (reviewing the role of NGOs in the creation of international human rights law).

29. *See, e.g.,* GEORGE B.N. AYITTEY, AFRICA BETRAYED 142-52 (1992) (highlighting significant human rights abuses in African countries); ARNOLD RIVKIN, NATION-BUILDING IN AFRICA 112-30 (1969) (discussing challenges to the rule of law in newly independent states).

30. GRAHAM, *supra* note 22, at 167-72.

nationalized concessions held by Western companies.[31] (Latin American states had already attempted to adjust the TNE-host state relationship before World War II, for instance, when Mexico expropriated U.S. agricultural holdings.)[32] Intimately tied with this action was the insistence by the developing world that international law did not grant foreigners any right to receive the economic value of their investment as compensation and that the amount of compensation was determined solely through domestic law. This position manifested itself most clearly in the aforementioned General Assembly resolutions, which contained expropriation provisions that were harshly resisted by the West.[33]

Second, host states and TNEs adjusted their economic and legal relationship through economic development agreements. These agreements provided in great detail the rights enjoyed by the host state and the duties of the foreign investor, in particular, with respect to payments by the former to the latter.[34] They also spelled out rights of investors, such as the right to institute international arbitration in the event of a contractual dispute. International lawyers devoted many pages to considering whether these agreements were governed by international law, domestic law, or something else.[35] Whatever their answer, the agreements clearly defined a set of legal rights and duties between the TNE and the host state. As the political and economic power of the South increased, these states demanded and achieved renegotiation of the agreements to increase their share of the wealth generated by the investment.[36]

---

31. *E.g.*, Gov't of Kuwait v. Am. Indep. Oil Co. (Aminoil), 66 I.L.R. 519 (Int'l Arb. Trib. 1982); Texaco Overseas Petroleum Co. v. Libyan Arab Republic, 17 I.L.M. 1 (Int'l Arb. Trib. 1978).

32. For the diplomatic correspondence on this episode, in which the United States formally asserted its views on the standard of compensation for expropriation, see Property Rights, 3 Hackworth DIGEST § 288, at 655-65 (1942).

33. *See, e.g.*, G.A. Res. 3281, *supra* note 25, at 52 (resolving that the right to nationalize is subject only to compensation by the state "taking into account *its* relevant laws and regulations and all circumstances that *the state* considers pertinent" with no reference to international law) (emphasis added). The commentary on these developments is voluminous. *See generally* Rudolf Dolzer, *New Foundations of the Law of Expropriation of Alien Property*, 75 AM. J. INT'L L. 553 (1991) (proposing the balancing of interests of host states and investors); Burns H. Weston, *The Charter of Economic Rights and Duties of States and the Deprivation of Foreign-Owned Wealth*, 75 AM. J. INT'L L. 437 (1981) (endorsing the thrust of General Assembly resolutions from the 1970s).

34. For an example, see Oil Concession Agreement Between the Government of Abu Dhabi and Amoco Abu Dhabi Exploration Company (Oct. 13, 1980), *in* 2 THE PETROLEUM CONCESSION AGREEMENTS OF THE UNITED ARAB EMIRATES 122 (Mana Saeed Al Otaiba ed., 1982).

35. *E.g.*, Richard B. Lillich, *The Law Governing Disputes Under Economic Development Agreements: Reexamining the Concept of "Internationalization,"* *in* INTERNATIONAL ARBITRATION IN THE 21ST CENTURY 61 (Richard B. Lillich & Charles N. Brower eds., 1993) (evaluating various positions).

36. *See* Gov't of Kuwait v. Am. Indep. Oil Co., 66 I.L.R. at 519-28; *see also* Samuel K.B. Asante, *Restructuring Transnational Mineral Agreements*, 73 AM. J. INT'L L. 335, 341-49 (1979) (reviewing the host states' practice of gaining control through joint ventures); Thomas W. Waelde

Third, host states sought to rein in the power of TNEs by drafting a multinational code of conduct for transnational corporations. This goal had for a long time been a part of the agenda of socialist political leaders in both the North and the South. It received its primary impetus from the revelations about United Fruit Company's and International Telephone and Telegraph's roles in destabilizing, respectively, the governments of Guatemala in the 1950s and Chile in the early 1970s.[37] In 1974, the United Nations established a Centre for Transnational Corporations to prepare the Code; it completed a draft in 1983 and another in 1990.[38] While recognizing some rights for investors, these Codes emphasized the need for foreign investors to obey host country law, follow host country economic policies, and avoid interference in the host country's domestic political affairs.[39] In a response to this development, the Organization for Economic Cooperation and Development (OECD), the principal international institution composed of wealthy states, drafted its own set of guidelines for multinational enterprises. These contained far fewer and weaker obligations on TNEs and were not intended to be binding.[40]

The overall effect of the decolonization period with respect to corporate-host state relations was thus to emphasize the rights of states and the duties of TNEs. Developing states asserted a right to expropriate with little or no compensation and to gain favorable economic development agreements that they could renegotiate on better terms. They also proposed duties on investors to comply with host country law and policies. The next phase in the relationship among foreign investors, home states, and host states would see a seismic shift in these patterns.

& George Ndi, *Stabilizing International Investment Commitments: International Law Versus Contract Interpretation*, 31 TEX. INT'L L.J. 215 (1996) (reviewing the modern practice of contract renegotiation).

37. *See, e.g., Multinational Corporations and United States Foreign Policy: Hearing on the International Telephone and Telegraph Company and Chile, 1970-71, Before the Subcomm. on Multinational Corps. of the S. Comm. on Foreign Relations*, 93d Cong. 1 (1973).

38. *Development and International Economic Co-operation: Transnational Corporations*, U.N. ESCOR, 2d Sess., U.N. Doc. E/1990/94 (1990) [hereinafter *1990 Code*]; *Draft United Nations Code of Conduct on Transnational Corporations*, U.N. ESCOR, Spec. Sess., Supp. No. 7, Annex II, U.N. Doc. E/1983/17/Rev.1 (1983); *see also* Peter T. Muchlinski, *Attempts To Extend the Accountability of Transnational Corporations: The Role of UNCTAD, in* LIABILITY OF MULTINATIONAL CORPORATIONS UNDER INTERNATIONAL LAW 97, 98-102 (Menno T. Kamminga & Saman Zia-Zarifi eds., 2000).

39. *See, e.g., 1990 Code, supra* note 38, at 6-8.

40. Declaration on International Investment and Multinational Enterprises annex 1 (1976), *reprinted in* THE OECD GUIDELINES FOR MULTINATIONAL ENTERPRISES 57 (1994) [hereinafter 1976 OECD Guidelines]; *see also* Hans W. Baade, *The Legal Effects of Codes of Conduct for Multinational Enterprises, in* 1 LEGAL PROBLEMS OF CODES OF CONDUCT FOR MULTINATIONAL ENTERPRISES 3 (Norbert Horn ed., 1980) (demonstrating how codes might produce binding norms under domestic and international law).

C. *Counterreaction: Globalization and the Emphasis on Corporate Rights*

As hard as the developing world fought to rectify the imbalance of economic power between North and South, its leaders also realized that developing countries desperately needed foreign direct investment from the developed world. When the Cold War wound down in the late 1980s, many developing-world states could no longer count either on economic aid from one side of the iron curtain or the other, or on political support in the North-South battles at the UN. International banks, stung by the failure of many developing-world nations to service their debts, stopped much of their lending.

As a result, the lure of foreign investment became even greater,[41] which led to a shift in the relationships among home states, host states, and investors. The rhetoric of the New International Economic Order faded in favor of one promoting free trade and investment, albeit with a hope of the developing world for development aid and forgiveness of foreign debt. Many developing-world states concluded bilateral investment treaties (BITs) with home states and thus undertook significant obligations to protect foreign investment. These included guarantees of fair and equitable treatment as determined by international law, national treatment, and most favored nation treatment; the right of investors to hire their own senior personnel; a guarantee of free repatriation of profits and liquidated proceeds; and, most significantly, the duty to pay full economic value in the event of an expropriation.[42] The United States even succeeded in including in its later BITs and in the North American Free Trade Agreement (NAFTA) a ban on certain so-called performance requirements, prohibiting treaty partners from asking investors for certain concessions, including technology transfers and promises to sell a certain amount of output locally or abroad.[43] The Draft UN Code of Conduct, which, its advocates hoped, would become a treaty, was effectively discarded in the early 1990s as the South retreated from assertive policies regarding economic development.[44] Indeed, in the General Assembly's 1990 Declaration of International

---

41. GRAHAM, *supra* note 22, at 172; *see also* Sagat Tugelbayev, *Come and Exploit Us*, FAR E. ECON. REV., Jan. 28, 1993, at 25 (consisting of a plea from the governor of a province in Kazakhstan for foreign investment).

42. *See, e.g.*, Treaty Concerning the Reciprocal Encouragement and Protection of Investment, Nov. 14, 1991, U.S.-Arg., arts. II-V, S. TREATY DOC. NO. 103-2, at 3-6 (1993), 31 I.L.M. 124, 129-32 [hereinafter United States-Argentina BIT]; *see also* Kenneth J. Vandevelde, *The Political Economy of a Bilateral Investment Treaty*, 92 AM. J. INT'L L. 621 (1998) (evaluating BITs as vehicles for promoting economic liberalism).

43. *See, e.g.*, United States-Argentina BIT, *supra* note 42, art. II(5), S. TREATY DOC. NO. 103-2, at 4, 31 I.L.M. at 130; North American Free Trade Agreement, *done* Dec. 17, 1992, art. 1106, 32 I.L.M. 605, 640 [hereinafter NAFTA].

44. Muchlinski, *supra* note 38, at 102-05.

Economic Cooperation, governments urged developing nations to achieve "favourable conditions for domestic and foreign investment."[45]

This transformation, of course, directly affected the host state-foreign investor relationship as well. Bilateral investment treaties are heavily skewed in favor of foreign investors. Beyond the substantive rights noted above, the BITs and NAFTA also provided investors a critical procedural right—to institute international arbitration without the consent of the host state to the individual arbitration and thereby bypass domestic courts entirely.[46] The OECD's proposal for a Multilateral Agreement on Investment would have provided these rights on a multilateral basis to companies from its various signatory states. The prospect of such rights for companies galvanized a coalition of nongovernmental organizations to press governments to abandon the pact, which was laid to rest (at least for now) in 1998.[47]

On the ground in host states, the results from the change in attitude about foreign investment have been staggering. Annual increases in foreign investment have significantly outpaced growth in international trade.[48] Furthermore, foreign investment has changed, moving from the traditional concession to new relationships between corporation and host state. These include joint ventures, innovative licensing and franchising regimes, turn-key operations, and other forms.[49] These arrangements predate the 1990s and indeed flowed from the shift of foreign investment—as a result of the expropriations in the 1960s and 1970s—away from concessions. But they have clearly accelerated since that time.[50] The result is a different, far denser relationship between the corporation and the host state. Instead of relying upon relatively unskilled labor to carry out mining or farming operations, the TNE is now an active player in the economy, hires many types of workers, and relies upon local offices to do much of its work. It is more embedded in the economy of the host state than ever before.

---

45. G.A. Res. S-18/3, U.N. GAOR, 18th Spec. Sess., Supp. No. 2, at 6, U.N. Doc. A/S-18/15 (1990).

46. *See, e.g.,* United States-Argentina BIT, *supra* note 42, art. VII, S. TREATY DOC. NO. 103-2, at 6, 31 I.L.M. at 132-34; NAFTA, *supra* note 43, arts. 1115-1121, 32 I.L.M. at 642-44.

47. For the last text before negotiations ceased, see ORG. FOR ECON. COOPERATION & DEV., THE MULTILATERAL AGREEMENT ON INVESTMENT: NEGOTIATING TEXT (1998), *at* http://www.oecd.org/daf/investment/fdi/mai/negtext.htm. On the debacle, see, for example, GRAHAM, *supra* note 22, at 1-49.

48. *Compare* U.N. CONFERENCE ON TRADE & DEV., WORLD INVESTMENT REPORT 2000, at 4 (2000) (showing a twenty-seven percent increase in foreign direct investment inflows in 1999), *with* WORLD TRADE ORG., INTERNATIONAL TRADE STATISTICS 2000, at tbl.I.1 (Bernan CD-ROM, 2000) (showing a five percent increase in trade in 1999).

49. CHARLES OMAN, NEW FORMS OF INTERNATIONAL INVESTMENT IN DEVELOPING COUNTRIES 14-21 (1984).

50. SUSAN STRANGE, THE RETREAT OF THE STATE 47 (1996).

D. *The Missing Link: Business Relations with Individuals*

In terms of the four actors involved in the foreign investment-human rights interactions, the contemporary situation is thus defined as follows in terms of international law: host states and home states enjoying juridical equality, with economic forces and international economic law now promoting free trade and investment as a recipe for progress; host states (as well as home states) having obligations to their populations under human rights law; and host states having significant obligations to TNEs and individual investors pursuant to various international legal instruments. But something is clearly missing from this description: Has this evolution created any role for international law in the relationship between business enterprises and the citizens in the states in which they operate? Is such a relationship solely a function of the employment contract between the worker and the TNE, or do the corporations have any duties under international law?

This link was until recently not the subject of much interest for either the host states or the corporations. During the decolonization period, host states were primarily concerned with control over foreign investors by requiring obedience to the host states' laws and policies. The government sought to achieve these goals through expropriation of assets, special laws aimed at regulating TNEs, the Draft UN Code of Conduct, and other measures.[51] More recently, the host states' goals have shifted to attracting foreign investment. Host states have adjusted domestic laws to make them more attractive to corporations, handed over tracts of land to de facto control by corporations, or simply turned a blind eye to violations of domestic law.[52] In responding to corporate demands for a hospitable investment environment, they have essentially turned the South's agenda for the Draft UN Code of Conduct on its head. Compliance with host country law has been enough—indeed, often more than enough—to ask of the foreign investor. For the corporations, the relationship with the citizenry became a matter of getting the best terms out of the employment contract. The citizenry's human rights were the government's responsibility, not theirs. In short, the race to the bottom was on.[53]

---

51. On the use of nonpublic codes to effect these policies, see Michael W. Gordon, *Of Aspirations and Operations: The Governance of Multilateral Enterprises by Third World Nations*, 16 U. MIAMI INTER-AM. L. REV. 301, 325-40 (1984).

52. *See, e.g.*, U.N. CTR. ON TRANSNATIONAL CORPS., THE DETERMINANTS OF FOREIGN DIRECT INVESTMENT, U.N. Doc. ST/CTC/121, U.N. Sales No. E.92.II.A.2 (1992); *As a River Runs Over, the Rain Forest Is Besieged*, TIMES-PICAYUNE, Jan. 28, 1996, at A18.

53. *See* Eyal Benvenisti, *Exit and Voice in the Age of Globalization*, 98 MICH. L. REV. 167 (1999) (analyzing the problem as one of a global "prisoner's dilemma"); *see also* Jeffrey L. Dunoff & Joel P. Trachtman, *Economic Analysis of International Law*, 24 YALE J. INT'L L. 1, 54-55 (1999) (endorsing an economic analysis of the race to the bottom).

II. WHY CORPORATE RESPONSIBILITY?

Protecting human rights solely through obligations on governments seems rather uncontroversial if host states represented the only threat to human dignity, or if states could be counted on to restrain conduct within their borders effectively. However, a system in which the state is the sole target of international legal obligations may not be sufficient to protect human rights. In this Part, I justify the need for corporate responsibility first by examining the shortcomings of placing human rights duties solely on states, the primary holders of international legal obligations. Corporations are powerful global actors that some states lack the resources or will to control. Other states may go as far as soliciting corporations to cooperate in impinging human rights. These realities make reliance on state duties inadequate. Beyond the practicalities of corporate power, human rights theory rejects efforts to limit dutyholders to states or to those carrying out state policy. This Part then examines the shortcomings of individual responsibility as an alternative to state responsibility. In this context, corporate law provides guidance to international law on the need to view corporations, and not simply those working for them, as dutyholders. Thus, both the corporate entity's potential impact on human rights, and theoretical understandings of the nature of human rights and of business enterprises, render corporate responsibility practically necessary and conceptually possible.

A. *The Limits to Holding States Accountable for Human Rights Violations*

International human rights law principally contemplates two sets of actors who may be held liable for abuses—states, through the concept of state (primarily civil) responsibility, and individuals, through the concept of individual (primarily criminal) responsibility. States are dutyholders for the full range of human rights, whether defined in treaties or customary law. Individual responsibility applies to a far smaller range of abuses, principally characterized by the gravity of their physical or spiritual assault on the individual.[54]

1. *Corporations as Global Actors*

The inadequacy of state responsibility stems fundamentally from trends in modern international affairs confirming that corporations may have as  much or more power over individuals as governments. In analyzing the

---

54. STEVEN R. RATNER & JASON S. ABRAMS, ACCOUNTABILITY FOR HUMAN RIGHTS ATROCITIES IN INTERNATIONAL LAW 13 (2d ed. 2001).

power of TNEs today, Susan Strange emphasizes the need to conceptualize power beyond political power to include economic power and accordingly concludes that markets matter more than states.[55] Whether or not the "retreat of the state" is as great as she states,[56] corporations clearly exercise significant power over individuals in the most direct sense of controlling their well-being. Of course, corporations have always wielded significant power over their employees; and governments have to enforce their own laws as well as to protect the human rights of their citizens. So why does such power require moving beyond state responsibility?

First, the desire of many less developed states to welcome foreign investment means that some governments have neither the interest nor the resources to monitor corporate behavior, either with respect to the TNEs' employees or with respect to the broader community.[57] Their views on investment might lead them to assist companies in violations, for instance, through deployments of security forces. In extreme cases, governments actually grant corporations de facto control over certain territories. For instance, whatever one may believe of the merits of claims against Freeport-McMoRan of human rights abuses in Irian Jaya or against Texaco in the Colombian rainforest, there seems little doubt that those entities exercise significant power in certain regions, often with little interference by the government.[58]

Second, regardless of its position on foreign investment, the government might also use various corporate resources in its own abuses of human rights. The South African experience represents the epitome in recent times of such nefarious cooperation between public and private sectors.[59] Because repressive governments (or opposition movements) may need to rely on businesses to supply them with material for various

---

55. STRANGE, *supra* note 50, at 16-43.

56. For a dissenting view, see Gregory H. Fox, *Strengthening the State*, 7 IND. J. GLOBAL LEGAL STUD. 35 (1999).

57. *See* AMNESTY INT'L & PAX CHRISTI INT'L, MULTINATIONAL ENTERPRISES AND HUMAN RIGHTS 17-18 (2000). Indeed, labor unions would point out that the problem is not limited to less developed countries.

58. *Criticism Undermines Freeport-McMoRan Image*, TIMES-PICAYUNE, Jan. 28, 1996, at A16; Laurie Goering, *Pollution Test Case Pits Ecuadoreans Against U.S. Firm*, CHI. TRIB., June 25, 1996, at 1; *see also* Freeport McMoRan & Gold, Inc., Military Security: Does Freeport Provide the Military with Food, Shelter, and Transportation?, *at* http://www.fcx.com/mr/issues&answers/ia-m&s.html (last visited Oct. 1, 2001) ("Irian Jaya (Papua) is one of the most undeveloped regions in the world. In its area, Freeport is the only infrastructure."). For an overall assessment of the effect of mining on local communities in the Philippines and Indonesia, see Michael C. Howard, *Mining, Development, and Indigenous Peoples in Southeast Asia*, 22 J. BUS. ADMIN. 93 (1994).

59. *See* 4 TRUTH & RECONCILIATION COMM'N, *supra* note 4, ch. 2, paras. 23-36 (relating the degrees of involvement of industry with the government).

unacceptable activities, corporations may work in tandem with governments in abusing human rights.[60]

Third, as firms have become more international, they have also become ever more independent of government control.[61] Many of the largest TNEs have headquarters in one state, shareholders in others, and operations worldwide. If the host state fails to regulate the acts of the company, other states, including the state of the corporation's nationality, may well choose to abstain from regulation based on the extraterritorial nature of the acts at issue.[62] Corporations can also shift activities to states with fewer regulatory burdens, including human rights regulations. Recognition of duties on corporations under international law could encourage home states to regulate this conduct or permit others to do so; at the very least, it would suggest a baseline standard of conduct for corporations themselves that could be monitored by interested constituencies.

If private entities might be contributing to a deleterious human rights situation, then those concerned with the behavior of such enterprises are left with three options—to continue to focus exclusively on the state, encouraging it eventually to control such enterprises; to enforce obligations against individuals (the limits of which I discuss below); or to identify and prescribe new obligations upon those private entities in international law and develop a regime of responsibility for violations they might commit.

Indeed, multinational enterprises are themselves recognizing the limits of duties on states. Unocal, for instance, has stated publicly that "human rights are not just a matter for governments."[63] In 2000, the United Kingdom's Prince of Wales Business Leaders Forum and Amnesty International teamed up to issue *Human Rights: Is It Any of Your Business?*, a glossy 144-page human rights guide for senior corporate policymakers. The publication notes: "While a company is not legally obliged under international law to comply with [human rights] standards, those companies

---

60. *See* S.C. Res. 1306, *supra* note 1 (condemning the role of diamond companies in Sierra Leone's civil war).

61. STRANGE, *supra* note 50, at 49-50; *see also* Nick Butler, *Companies in International Relations*, SURVIVAL, Spring 2000, at 149, 155 (describing the lack of national identity of TNEs); Jonathan I. Charney, *Transnational Corporations and Developing Public International Law*, 1983 DUKE L.J. 748, 770-72 (examining the role of corporations as global actors).

62. Peter J. Spiro, *New Players on the International Stage*, 2 HOFSTRA L. & POL'Y SYMP. 19, 28-30 (1997).

63. Human Rights and Unocal: Our Position, *at* http://www.unocal.com/responsibility/humanrights/hr1.htm (last visited Oct. 1, 2001); *see also* PRINCE OF WALES BUS. LEADERS FORUM & AMNESTY INT'L, HUMAN RIGHTS: IS IT ANY OF YOUR BUSINESS? 83-85 (2000) [hereinafter PWBLF & AI] (summarizing major corporate statements); Enron, Statement of Principles of Human Rights, *at* http://www.enron.com/corp/pressroom/responsibility/human_rights_statement.html (last visited Oct. 1, 2001) ("We do not and will not tolerate mistreatment or human rights abuses of any kind by our employees or contractors."). *But see* Goering, *supra* note 58, at 1 (quoting a Texaco spokesman stating that the company "complied with existing laws and regulations" of Ecuador).

who have violated them have found, to their cost, that society at large will condemn them."[64] And, as discussed in Section VII.A below, corporate-initiated codes of conduct represent clear evidence that normative expectations of all relevant actors—not just NGOs or governments—are now shifting.

In this sense, the need for corporate responsibility parallels the evolution of the existing corpus of law beyond state liability to cover individual responsibility, under which individuals are criminally responsible for exceptionally serious human rights abuses.[65] Individual responsibility emerged primarily from the sense of governments and nonstate actors that holding states accountable proved inadequate to address those acts.[66] Unlike state responsibility, accountability for individual violators might provide victims of atrocities with a sense of justice and a possibility to put the past behind them (the amorphous notion of closure). It might also help deter future abuses more effectively,[67] send a powerful message of moral condemnation of heinous offenses, and help a society traumatized by massive human rights violations to identify perpetrators and thereby promote national reconciliation.[68] In its ability to advance these goals, individual responsibility has become a promising alternative along a continuum of enforcement mechanisms for international human rights or international humanitarian law.[69]

Some of the reasons for the inadequacy of state responsibility for individual human rights abuses—for example, the impact on victims of identifying and punishing their individual perpetrators (as opposed to merely blaming the state)—differ from the reasons for its inadequacy for corporate actions. But the deterrence rationale remains common to both contexts and points to the need to place obligations on entities that have the resources to violate human rights and whose conduct cannot properly be policed by the state where they operate. If international law provided for a regime whereby the corporations had duties themselves and incurred some

---

64. PWBLF & AI, *supra* note 63, at 23.

65. *See infra* text accompanying notes 74-81.

66. *See* 22 TRIALS OF THE MAJOR WAR CRIMINALS BEFORE THE INTERNATIONAL MILITARY TRIBUNAL 466 (1948) [hereinafter IMT TRIALS] ("Crimes against international law are committed by men, not by abstract entities, and only by punishing individuals who commit such crimes can the provisions of international law be enforced.").

67. On the efficacy of individual accountability as a deterrent, see David Wippman, *Atrocities, Deterrence, and the Limits of International Justice*, 23 FORDHAM INT'L L.J. 473 (1999); and Aryeh Neier, *What Should Be Done About the Guilty?*, N.Y. REV. BOOKS, Feb. 1, 1990, at 32, 35.

68. For an overview of theories of punishment in the context of human rights abuses, see Jaime Malamud-Goti, *Transitional Governments in the Breach: Why Punish State Criminals?*, 12 HUM. RTS. Q. 1, 6-11 (1990).

69. *See* M. Cherif Bassiouni, *An Appraisal of the Growth and Developing Trends of International Criminal Law*, 45 REVUE INTERNATIONALE DE DROIT PÉNAL 405, 405-06 (1974).

penalty for violations of them, it would place the incentives on the party with the greatest ability and interest in addressing corporate conduct.

In one historically significant instance, the justifications for individual accountability and business accountability, and the corresponding limits of state responsibility, all came together—international efforts to outlaw the slave trade. The slave trade represented, in a sense, the worst form of private enterprise abuse of human rights. To end it, abolitionists eschewed sole reliance upon state responsibility, both because traders operated on the high seas and because many states tolerated the practice. Instead, they convinced governments to conclude a series of treaties that allowed states to seize vessels and required them to punish slave traders.[70] Thus the first true example of international human rights law was a response to commercially oriented violations of rights.

Beyond these three reasons lies a fourth and, for some readers, I suspect, more compelling reason. Even if one believes that the state should be the sole object of obligations regarding the behavior of businesses operating on its soil based on its unique competence to control private behavior within its borders, one would still need to determine *which* acts of corporations render the state liable. As discussed in the following Subsection, international human rights courts and other bodies have begun to hold states responsible for failing to prevent private activity that violates human rights. In order to hold states accountable for corporate conduct in a coherent fashion, however, one would still need a theory of understanding when a corporation's violation of human rights rises to such a level that the state is responsible for preventing or suppressing it.

2. *The Problem of State Action*

A more profound argument against corporate duties in international human rights law would question the possibility of even conceiving of human rights as creating duties in actors other than states. For although the post-World War II elaboration of human rights law destroyed any notion that only states had rights under international law (or, in other words, that states had duties only to other states), it did seem to rest on the premise that

---

70. *See* Protocol to the 1926 Slavery Convention, *opened for signature* Dec. 7, 1953, art. 6, 212 U.N.T.S. 17, 22 (requiring that parties "whose laws do not at present make adequate provision for the punishment of infractions [under the Convention] . . . undertake to adopt the necessary measures in order that severe penalties may be imposed"); *see also* MYRES S. McDOUGAL ET AL., HUMAN RIGHTS AND WORLD PUBLIC ORDER 482-508 (1980) (discussing the historical treatment of slavery internationally and mentioning agreements permitting the seizure of slave ships); A. Yasmine Rassam, *Contemporary Forms of Slavery and the Evolution of the Prohibition of Slavery and the Slave Trade Under Customary International Law*, 39 VA. J. INT'L L. 303, 329-42 (1999) (showing the evolution of international law on slave trade to cover a broad array of practices).

466   The Yale Law Journal   [Vol. 111: 443

the rights individuals have are principally against states. Of course, human rights may give rise to a variety of obligations of states, depending in part upon the particular right. These include the duty to avoid certain conduct that impinges on the right, the duty of equal treatment in guaranteeing the right, the duty to create institutional machinery (like courts) to secure the right, the duty to prevent abuses, the duty to provide a remedy for abuses, the duty to provide certain goods or services, and the duty to promote human rights.[71] But the unstated understanding during the growth of the human rights movement was that the duties were still those of states.[72]

This seemingly originalist position regarding human rights emphasizes that international law should distinguish between, on the one hand, ordinary crimes (e.g., murder) or torts (e.g., slander) between private actors—which are outside its province and belong to domestic law—and, on the other hand, governmental action, which is the true subject of international law. State (or quasi-state) action elevates violations of human rights to the international plane on the theory that domestic law is not sufficient to regulate the behavior of governments (or de facto authorities). In that sense, to talk about corporate duties is arguably to redefine international human rights—and international law—in an unacceptable way. To the extent that one contemplates recognizing in law a large number of duties on entities other than the state, one has potentially asked international law to do too much and ignored the expectation that states should enjoy the prerogative to regulate most areas of private conduct on their territory.[73]

The short answer to this argument is that international law has already recognized human rights duties on entities other than states. International humanitarian law (the law of war) places duties on rebel groups (qua groups, rather than individuals) to respect certain fundamental rights of persons under their control.[74] States have also accepted the idea of duties of

---

71. *See* HENRY J. STEINER & PHILIP ALSTON, INTERNATIONAL HUMAN RIGHTS IN CONTEXT 182-84 (2d ed. 2000) (listing five kinds of duties); *see also* HENRY SHUE, BASIC RIGHTS 51-64 (1980) (discussing the duties that accompany various rights); James W. Nickel, *How Human Rights Generate Duties To Protect and Provide*, 15 HUM. RTS. Q. 77 (1993) (discussing duties to avoid deprivation of the right, to protect against deprivation, and to aid those deprived).

72. *E.g.*, ROSALYN HIGGINS, PROBLEMS AND PROCESS: INTERNATIONAL LAW AND HOW WE USE IT 105 (1994) (stating that human rights are "demands of a particularly high intensity made by individuals *vis-à-vis* their governments"); *see also* William N. Nelson, *Human Rights and Human Obligations*, *in* HUMAN RIGHTS 281, 281-82 (J. Roland Pennock & John W. Chapman eds., 1981) (labeling this the "standard assumption"). *But see* McDOUGAL ET AL., *supra* note 70, at 4 (stating that "rudimentary demands for freedom from despotic executive tyranny have gradually been transformed into demands for protection against not only the executive but all institutions or functions of government and all private coercion").

73. I appreciate this argument from David Wippman.

74. Protocol Additional to the Geneva Conventions of 12 August 1949, and Relating to the Protection of Victims of Non-International Armed Conflicts (Protocol II), *adopted* June 8, 1977, 1125 U.N.T.S. 609. On the convergence of human rights and humanitarian law, see, for example, Louise Doswald-Beck & Sylvain Vité, *International Humanitarian Law and Human Rights Law*, 293 INT'L REV. RED CROSS 94 (1993).

nonstate actors through the corpus of international criminal law on human rights atrocities.[75] Thus, war crimes, genocide, crimes against humanity, torture, slavery, forced labor, apartheid, and forced disappearances are all crimes under international law. Some treaties make an individual criminally responsible only if he was an agent of the state or some other entity controlling territory,[76] but others—including the slavery treaties—provide that wholly private actors incur individual responsibility.[77] In any case, these treaties and customary norms clearly provide individual responsibility by setting forth a variety of strategies to hold the individual responsible. These include explicit recognition of certain acts as international crimes (genocide under the Genocide Convention or crimes against humanity under customary law); requirements that states prosecute or extradite individuals committing certain crimes (as in the Geneva Conventions on armed conflict and the Torture Convention); and authorizations to states to prosecute certain offenses notwithstanding normal jurisdictional limits.[78] By authorizing punishment for *individuals* who commit especially egregious abuses, the law imposes duties directly upon them to refrain from this behavior.

Yet this answer falls short, insofar as international criminal law and humanitarian law conventions have thus far recognized only a relatively small category of human rights abuses as crimes, most notably true atrocities, or, as Agnes Heller put it, "manifestations of evil."[79] Several of these—genocide, crimes against humanity, and war crimes—have particular elements that were intended to internationalize the offenses and thus distinguish them from ordinary crimes, namely, a special intent to destroy a protected group of people, a systematic attack on a civilian population, and the presence of an armed conflict.[80] Other conventions—on torture and forced disappearances—require a clear nexus to official

75. *See* RATNER & ABRAMS, *supra* note 54.

76. *See* Inter-American Convention on the Forced Disappearance of Persons, *done* June 9, 1994, art. II, 33 I.L.M. 1529, 1530 (1994); Convention Against Torture and Other Cruel, Inhuman or Degrading Treatment or Punishment, *adopted* Dec. 10, 1984, art. 1, S. TREATY DOC. NO. 100-20, at 1 (1988), 1465 U.N.T.S. 85, 113-14 [hereinafter Torture Convention].

77. *E.g.*, Supplementary Convention on the Abolition of Slavery, the Slave Trade, and Institutions and Practices Similar to Slavery, *done* Sept. 7, 1956, 18 U.S.T. 3201, 266 U.N.T.S. 3; Convention on the Prevention and Punishment of the Crime of Genocide, *adopted* Dec. 9, 1948, S. EXEC. DOC. O, 81-1 (1949), 78 U.N.T.S. 277 [hereinafter Genocide Convention]; *cf.* Kadic v. Karadzic, 70 F.3d 232 (2d Cir. 1995) (holding the president of an unrecognized state liable for human rights violations under the Alien Tort Claims Act).

78. RATNER & ABRAMS, *supra* note 54, at 11.

79. Agnes Heller, *The Limits to Natural Law and the Paradox of Evil*, *in* ON HUMAN RIGHTS: THE OXFORD AMNESTY LECTURES 149, 154-55 (Stephen Shute & Susan Hurley eds., 1993).

80. *E.g.*, Rome Statute of the International Criminal Court, July 17, 1998, arts. 6-8, U.N. Doc. A.CONF/189/9 [hereinafter ICC Statute].

468   The Yale Law Journal   [Vol. 111: 443

conduct.[81] International criminal law does not simply incorporate human rights law.

A fuller answer accepts that the notion of corporate duties represents a departure from the emphasis on the state as dutyholder and seeks to justify that new direction. That position starts from a jurisprudential premise—that the rights of individuals give rise to not only a variety of duties but also a variety of *dutyholders*. As Joseph Raz has stated, "there is no closed list of duties which correspond to the right .... A change of circumstances may lead to the creation of new duties based on the old right."[82] Moreover, he goes on, "one may know of the existence of a right ... without knowing who is bound by duties based on it or what precisely are these duties."[83] Raz and others thus emphasize that rights come first—that they ground duties.[84] The focus on rights preceding duties is, of course, not the only way of relating the two. Kant derived his moral theory from a duty-based starting point.[85] But even from that framework, dutyholders still encompass a broad range of entities.

Natural rights theory took the starting point of individual rights and attempted to derive a moral code from it. Yet it readily accepted that those fundamental rights enjoyed by all peoples were rights vis-à-vis each other.[86] Locke thus never saw natural rights as creating duties only on government; he believed that any duties on government were derivative insofar as (1) governments were set up to protect rights of individuals against each other; and (2) governments might, in the process of possessing power to protect those rights, have duties to the citizenry not to abuse that power.[87] Over time, however, the rhetoric of natural rights came to focus on duties of the state, because of the state's agglomeration of both power and authority over

---

81. *See* Torture Convention, *supra* note 76, art. 1, S. TREATY DOC. NO. 100-20, at 1, 1465 U.N.T.S. at 113-14. For a critique of these distinctions, see Steven R. Ratner, *The Schizophrenias of International Criminal Law*, 33 TEX. INT'L L.J. 237 (1998).

82. JOSEPH RAZ, THE MORALITY OF FREEDOM 171 (1986).

83. *Id.* at 184; *see also id.* at 170-72, 184-86 (discussing the relationship between rights and duties).

84. *See, e.g.*, JEREMY WALDRON, THE RIGHT TO PRIVATE PROPERTY 79-87 (1988); Neil MacCormick, *Children's Rights: A Test-Case for Theories of Right, in* LEGAL RIGHT AND SOCIAL DEMOCRACY 154, 161-83 (1982).

85. *See* IMMANUEL KANT, THE GROUNDWORK OF THE METAPHYSICS OF MORALS 10-18 (Mary Gregor ed. & trans., Cambridge Univ. Press 1996) (1785); *see also* RONALD DWORKIN, TAKING RIGHTS SERIOUSLY 171-73 (1978) (stating that Kant's moral theory was "duty-based").

86. JOHN LOCKE, TWO TREATISES OF GOVERNMENT 271 (Peter Laslett ed., Cambridge Univ. Press 1988) (1690) ("The *State of Nature* has a Law of Nature to govern it, which obliges every one[;] ... no one ought to harm another in his Life, Health, Liberty, or Possessions.").

87. *Id.* at 351, 353, 357-63; *cf.* THE DECLARATION OF INDEPENDENCE para. 2 (U.S. 1776) ("[A]ll men are created equal, that they are endowed by their Creator with certain unalienable rights; that among these are life, liberty and the pursuit of happiness. ... [T]o secure these rights, governments are instituted among men . . . ."); DECLARATION OF THE RIGHTS OF MAN AND OF THE CITIZEN art. 2 (Fr. 1789), *translated at* http://www.hrcr.org/docs/frenchdec.html (last visited Nov. 15, 2001) ("The aim of all political association is the preservation of the natural and imprescriptible rights of man.").

its citizens.[88] And when the idea of natural rights moved into the international arena, this focus continued.[89]

Accordingly, the League of Nations oversaw a regime of treaties that provided ethnic and religious minorities with a variety of rights against the governments of the new or reconstituted states of Central and Eastern Europe.[90] The immense power of the state to cause harm to human dignity was revealed as never before in World War II and thus justified the continued concentration on rights of individuals against the state. Although the Universal Declaration of Human Rights does not on its face limit dutyholders to states, the premise of that instrument and of the treaties that eventually flowed from it was that states held the obligations.[91]

Thus, while human rights law has focused on state duties, the two are by no means tied to each other jurisprudentially or even historically. The link is rather a product of a decision by those concerned with human rights, including those in government, that (1) states represent the greatest danger to the individual; (2) domestic law cannot alone effectively constrain state action; (3) domestic law can effectively regulate private action; and probably (4) states will never accept international regulation of private entities. I do not wish to challenge the first two propositions, nor do I need to.[92] Rather, I posit the view that other entities may also pose a threat to human dignity—either acting with the state or alone—so that any contemporary notion of human rights must contemplate duties on those entities as well. This step does not entail the recognition or development of new human rights, which is quite popular among some scholars and activists.[93] Instead, it requires the identification of new dutyholders.

As Andrew Clapham discusses in his remarkable book, *Human Rights in the Private Sphere*, the European Court of Human Rights (ECHR),

---

88. Burns H. Weston, *Human Rights, in* HUMAN RIGHTS IN THE WORLD COMMUNITY 14, 14-16 (Richard Pierre Claude & Burns H. Weston eds., 2d ed. 1992).

89. *See* David Sidorsky, *Contemporary Reinterpretations of the Concept of Human Rights, in* ESSAYS ON HUMAN RIGHTS 88, 90-95 (David Sidorsky ed., 1979).

90. FRANCESCO CAPOTORTI, U.N. ECON. & SOC. COUNCIL, COMM'N ON HUMAN RIGHTS, SUB-COMM'N ON THE PREVENTION OF DISCRIMINATION & PROTECTION OF MINORITIES, STUDY OF THE RIGHTS OF PERSONS BELONGING TO ETHNIC, RELIGIOUS AND LINGUISTIC MINORITIES 16-26, U.N. Doc. E/CN.4/Sub.2/384/Rev.1, U.N. Sales No. E.78.XIV.1 (1979); David Wippman, *The Evolution and Implementation of Minority Rights*, 66 FORDHAM L. REV. 597, 599-602 (1997); *see, e.g.,* Convention Concerning Upper Silesia, Mar. 15, 1922, Ger.-Pol., 16 Martens Nouveau Recueil (ser. 3) 645 (enumerating rights for the Polish minority).

91. *Universal Declaration of Human Rights*, G.A. Res. 217A, U.N. Doc. A/810, at 71 (1948); JOHANNES MORSINK, THE UNIVERSAL DECLARATION OF HUMAN RIGHTS 36-91 (1999); *see also* HERSCH LAUTERPACHT, INTERNATIONAL LAW AND HUMAN RIGHTS 155-57 (1950) (limiting dutyholders to states, but arguing that states have a duty to prevent racial discrimination by private actors).

92. On the feminist critique of the first and third assumptions, see *infra* notes 109-110 and accompanying text.

93. For one example, see Mohammed Bedjaoui, *The Right to Development, in* INTERNATIONAL LAW 1177, 1182 (Mohammed Bedjaoui ed., 1991).

European Court of Justice (ECJ), Inter-American Court of Human Rights (IACHR), and UN human rights bodies have repeatedly found that abuses of human dignity by private actors in private relations can give rise to international human rights violations.[94] In most instances, they have worked within the paradigm of state responsibility by asserting that the state's tolerance of a private human rights abuse actually violates the state's duty to protect the right through legislation, preventive measures, or provision of a remedy (or, in other cases, that the private actor involved is actually the organ of a state). For instance, the ECHR has held that the Netherlands' failure to prosecute sexual assault by a private person against a mentally handicapped ward violated the victim's right to privacy;[95] that Italy's failure to prevent a fertilizer company from releasing toxic gases also violated the right to privacy;[96] that the United Kingdom's plan to deport an AIDS patient to St. Kitts, where he would receive inadequate medical treatment, violated his right to life;[97] and that the United Kingdom's failure to protect two boys against child abuse violated their right to be free from torture and cruel treatment.[98] The Inter-American Court of Human Rights, in its famous *Velásquez Rodríguez* decision of 1988, found the Honduran government responsible for the failure to prevent and punish a forced disappearance committed by persons whom it could not associate with the state (even though in all likelihood they were state agents).[99] In requiring states to prevent or punish certain acts by private entities, those bodies have implicitly concluded that some private activities are a legitimate area for international concern.[100]

This trend of decisions suggests that state responsibility can still go very far in addressing actions in the private sphere. Holding governments accountable may create important incentives for them to prevent private infringements, and governments might have the means to do so. Thus corporate responsibility through state responsibility remains an important

---

94. ANDREW CLAPHAM, HUMAN RIGHTS IN THE PRIVATE SPHERE 89-133 (1993); Evert Albert Alkema, *The Third-Party Applicability or "Drittwirkung" of the European Convention on Human Rights, in* PROTECTING HUMAN RIGHTS: THE EUROPEAN DIMENSION 33, 33-36 (Franz Matscher & Herbert Petzold eds., 2d ed. 1990).

95. X and Y v. The Netherlands, 91 Eur. Ct. H.R. (ser. A) at 11 (1985) (stating that the Convention may require "the adoption of measures designed to secure respect for private life even in the sphere of the relations of individuals between themselves").

96. Guerra v. Italy, 1998-I Eur. Ct. H.R. 210.

97. D. v. United Kingdom, 1997-III Eur. Ct. H.R. 777.

98. A. v. United Kingdom, 1998-VI Eur. Ct. H.R. 2692.

99. Velásquez Rodríguez Case, Inter-Am. Ct. H.R. (ser. C) No. 4 (1988).

100. For an example of the reluctance of a domestic constitutional court to adopt a similar stance at the national level, see *DeShaney v. Winnebago County Department of Social Services*, 489 U.S. 189 (1989). The Court dismissed a suit against a state welfare agency for its failure to prevent severe child abuse and held that the Due Process Clause was only designed "to protect the people from the State, not to ensure that the State protected them from each other." *Id.* at 196.

part of the process of accountability.[101] Yet, as discussed earlier, relying upon state responsibility still begs a key question: What sorts of abuses by private actors does the state have a duty to prevent and remedy?[102]

Beyond holding states responsible for abuses by private actors, other courts in Europe have found violations of human rights even when the defendant is not a state. The European Court of Justice has held that provisions of the Treaty of Rome (the EU's founding document) that prohibit states from discriminating based on nationality and require equal pay for equal work apply directly to private entities. Adopting an overtly teleological interpretation of the Treaty, in key cases in the 1970s, it found that the elimination of employment discrimination, whether nationality-based or gender-based, is central to the purpose of the European Community and required private entities to terminate it.[103] Long before those cases, German courts had developed the notion of third-party (or horizontal) effect (*Drittwirkung*), holding that some German constitutional rights affect private legal relationships.[104] Dutch courts have relied upon similar doctrines to find international obligations relevant to private disputes;[105] Israeli courts have applied Israel's Basic Law in private litigation;[106] and after Britain's passage of domestic legislation incorporating the European Convention into British law, courts in that country will soon be facing the issue of third-party effects as well.[107]

---

101. *See* INT'L COUNCIL ON HUMAN RIGHTS POLICY, BUSINESS WRONGS AND RIGHTS paras. 44-80 (draft report 2001), *at* http://www.ichrp.org/excerpts/30.pdf (calling such duties "indirect obligations"). The ICHRP study is the most sophisticated to date to emerge from the NGO community.

102. *See* Francesco Francioni, *Exporting Environmental Hazard Through Multinational Enterprises: Can the State of Origin Be Held Responsible?, in* INTERNATIONAL RESPONSIBILITY FOR ENVIRONMENTAL HARM 275, 288 (Francesco Francioni & Tullio Scovazzi eds., 1991) (calling for the state of origin of a company that causes a toxic spill in another country to be held responsible, and proposing substantive contours to the duties of that state).

103. *See, e.g.,* Case 36/74, Walrave v. Association Union Cycliste Internationale, 1974 E.C.R. 1405; Case 43/75, Defrenne v. Société Anonyme Belge de Navigation Aérienne Sabena, 1976 E.C.R. 455.

104. Lüth Case, BverfGE 7, 198 (1958), *translated in* DONALD P. KOMMERS, THE CONSTITUTIONAL JURISPRUDENCE OF THE FEDERAL REPUBLIC OF GERMANY 361 (2d ed. 1997); *see also* B.S. MARKESINIS, *The Applicability of Human Rights as Between Individuals Under German Constitutional Law, in* 2 ALWAYS ON THE SAME PATH 175 (2001) (reviewing and endorsing trends in case law); Kenneth M. Lewan, *The Significance of Constitutional Rights for Private Law: Theory and Practice in West Germany,* 17 INT'L & COMP. L.Q. 571 (1968). For U.S. laws that make private individuals liable for constitutional violations, see *infra* note 222.

105. André Nollkaemper, *Public International Law in Transnational Litigation Against Multinational Corporations: Prospects and Problems in the Courts of the Netherlands, in* LIABILITY OF MULTINATIONAL CORPORATIONS UNDER INTERNATIONAL LAW, *supra* note 38, at 265, 270-76.

106. Gabriela Shalev, *Constitutionalization of Contract Law, in* TOWARDS A NEW EUROPEAN IUS COMMUNE 205 (A. Gambaro & A.M. Rabello eds., 1999).

107. Authorities have debated the legislation's likely impact. *Compare* Gavin Phillipson, *The Human Rights Act, "Horizontal Effect" and the Common Law: A Bang or a Whimper?,* 62 MOD. L. REV. 824 (1999) (opining that the legislation is unlikely to have a major effect in private

Clapham builds upon these important trends, in terms of both direct and indirect duties on private entities to respect human rights, to support a human rights regime that challenges the exclusive focus on the state. He writes:

> [T]he emergence of new fragmented centres of power, such as associations, pressure groups, political parties, trade unions, corporations, multinationals . . . and quasi-official bodies has meant that the individual now perceives authority, repression, and alienation in a variety of new bodies. . . . This societal development has meant that the definition of the public sphere has had to be adapted to include these new bodies and activities.[108]

In addition, and not surprisingly, the call for the blurring of the public/private distinction has received particular attention from some women's rights advocates and feminist legal scholars, who are concerned that a focus on state responsibility eliminates various sexual assaults from the purview of human rights protection.[109] Strategies for responding to this perceived bias vary, however, with some favoring a complete reconceptualization of international law to govern private behavior, and others finding the link to state action malleable enough to cover the most important private conduct.[110]

In light of the above-mentioned increase in corporate power and of the concomitant inadequacy of state responsibility, Clapham's arguments would appear to apply strongly to activities by corporations. If human rights are aimed at the protection of human dignity, the law needs to respond to abuses that do not implicate the state directly. As discussed further below, this does not mean that everything that a corporation does that might deleteriously affect the welfare of those in the corporation's sphere of operations is a human rights abuse—just as, for example, a tax increase that makes some people worse off financially is not a human rights abuse. Nor does it require ignoring the nexus to state action, as such a linkage may well serve to help clarify certain duties of corporations. But it does suggest that the recognition of some duties of corporations, far from being at odds with the purpose of international human rights law, is wholly consonant with it.

---

litigation), *with* Dawn Oliver, *The Human Rights Act and Public Law/Private Law Divides*, 4 EUR. HUM. RTS. L. REV. 343 (2000) (stating that significant impacts are possible).

108. CLAPHAM, *supra* note 94, at 137. For a critical and eloquent argument for this view from a generation ago, see Jean Rivero, *La protection des Droits de l'Homme dans les rapports entre personnes privées, in* 3 RENÉ CASSIN AMICORUM DISCIPULORUMQUE LIBER 311 (1971).

109. *See, e.g.*, Hilary Charlesworth et al., *Feminist Approaches to International Law*, 85 AM. J. INT'L L. 613, 625-30 (1991).

110. Karen Engle, *After the Collapse of the Public/Private Distinction: Strategizing Women's Rights, in* RECONCEIVING REALITY: WOMEN AND INTERNATIONAL LAW 143 (Dorinda G. Dallmeyer ed., 1993).

B. *The Limits to Holding Individuals Accountable for Human Rights Violations*

Decisionmakers in the international legal process have developed an adjunct to the idea of states as dutyholders through their acceptance of individual responsibility. If individuals, such as corporate officers, can in theory be held responsible for abuses (under existing or perhaps expanded norms of international criminal law), then why the need for corporate responsibility? A response to this question comes from those who have examined the need to hold corporations, rather than individuals within them, liable for certain conduct. While international law works from the starting point that states should be held responsible for human rights abuses, and only then acknowledges the need for duties on others, theorists of corporate liability have worked from the opposite position—that of domestic civil and criminal law holding individuals accountable—to make a case for corporate liability. Their insights thus have direct relevance to our task.

Scholars of corporate accountability have proffered a variety of policy rationales for holding corporations responsible for undesirable conduct. The economic rationale has received particular attention.[111] It holds that liability upon enterprises deters corporate managers better than liability upon individuals, because corporate agents are judgment-proof and cannot bear the costs of sanctions, and because corporate liability encourages shareholders to monitor corporate actions. Richard Gruner has summarized the rationales for criminal sanctions in particular, as follows: punishing unacceptable conduct by corporate agents, coercing corporations into complying with the law, creating economic incentives for proper conduct, signaling to third parties the limits of acceptable corporate behavior, punishing the corporation, reforming the corporation, and compensating victims.[112] Nations implementing criminal schemes have grappled with whether they actually accomplish these goals.[113]

Brent Fisse and John Braithwaite have offered a compelling normative account of the shortcomings of individual liability with respect to corporate misconduct, and their theory seems pertinent to the inquiry regarding

---

111. *See, e.g.*, RICHARD A. POSNER, ANTITRUST LAW: AN ECONOMIC PERSPECTIVE 225-36 (1976); John Collins Coffee, Jr., *Corporate Crime and Punishment: A Non-Chicago View of the Economics of Criminal Sanctions*, 17 AM. CRIM. L. REV. 419, 456-65 (1980); Lewis A. Kornhauser, *An Economic Analysis of the Choice Between Enterprise and Personal Liability for Accidents*, 70 CAL. L. REV. 1345 (1982); Reinier H. Kraakman, *Corporate Liability Strategies and the Costs of Legal Controls*, 93 YALE L.J. 857 (1984); Alan O. Sykes, *The Economics of Vicarious Liability*, 93 YALE L.J. 1231 (1984).

112. RICHARD S. GRUNER, CORPORATE CRIME AND SENTENCING 84-160 (1994).

113. *See, e.g.*, William S. Laufer, *Corporate Liability, Risk Shifting, and the Paradox of Compliance*, 52 VAND. L. REV. 1343 (1999) (regarding the shifting of liability from firms to agents in the United States).

human rights. They argue that corporations act as organizations and are not simply the sum of individuals working for them; because they have autonomy of action, including the capacity to change their policies, they can be held responsible for the outcomes resulting from these policies.[114] Fisse and Braithwaite reject any notion that blameworthiness requires a prior determination that the relevant actor have "philosophical personality" (which, in the view of some philosophers, only individuals possess).[115]

Thus, if a corporation's internal decisionmaking process results in morally irresponsible behavior, the corporation may be blameworthy, either civilly or criminally. The degree of fault required for such responsibility might be as high as intent to cause an outcome, but could just as easily be a negligence or strict liability standard. Justifying the liability of Union Carbide for the disaster at Bhopal, Fisse and Braithwaite note that even if the executives of the corporation individually did not engage in criminal conduct, "higher standards of care are expected of such a company given its collective might and resources."[116] As for claims that only individuals, and not corporations, will be deterred by liability or punishment, they note correctly that a collective cost on the corporation from having been found responsible for unacceptable conduct does affect corporate behavior.[117] Peter French, Celia Wells, and others have built on these normative premises to argue for a theory of criminal responsibility that takes into account defects in corporate decisionmaking structures rather than simply individual fault. In the process, they have developed different standards of corporate fault.[118]

In focusing on what societies might legitimately expect from corporations as a basis for holding them responsible, these scholars have built on the work of Robert Goodin. Goodin rejects a concept of responsibility that is centered on blame and that holds actors with evil intent

---

114. Brent Fisse & John Braithwaite, *The Allocation of Responsibility for Corporate Crime: Individualism, Collectivism and Accountability*, 11 SYDNEY L. REV. 468, 483-88 (1988).

115. *Id.* at 481-82 & n.63. A similarity exists between this criticism of personality and that pertinent to international law. *Compare id.* at 482 n.63 ("[T]he moral responsibility or blameworthiness of corporate entities . . . is most unlikely to be resolved by resort to the question-begging notion of philosophical 'personality.'"), *with* HIGGINS, *supra* note 72, at 50 (attacking the subject-object dichotomy as overly simplistic).

116. Fisse & Braithwaite, *supra* note 114, at 486.

117. *Id.* at 488-90.

118. *See* PETER A. FRENCH, COLLECTIVE AND CORPORATE RESPONSIBILITY 156-63 (1984) (endorsing the idea of "reactive fault" based on a corporation's failure to institute procedures to prevent the repetition of a harmful act); CELIA WELLS, CORPORATIONS AND CRIMINAL RESPONSIBILITY 143-46 (1993) (discussing liability based on aggregating the responsibility of certain officers and considering internal decisionmaking structures); *see also* J.E. PARKINSON, CORPORATE POWER AND RESPONSIBILITY 358-59 (1993) (focusing on criminal liability, but arguing that the mens rea of a corporation should be replaced by the concept of defective decisionmaking); V.S. Khanna, *Corporate Liability Standards: When Should Corporations Be Held Criminally Liable?*, 37 AM. CRIM. L. REV. 1239 (2000) (calling for a mixed liability regime).

per se more blameworthy than actors who are merely negligent in their actions. Instead, he emphasizes the actors' responsibility for different tasks and their ex ante duties to ensure that certain harms do not happen.[119] As a consequence, the distinction between civil responsibility and criminal responsibility is ultimately of second-order importance. This stress on ex ante duties also provides an important starting point for a theory of corporate duties under international law. These duties will turn not on any concept of ill will by the corporation. but rather on its potential for violating human rights. In the end, all these theorists of corporate responsibility point to the futility of targeting norms only at individual employees who commit wrongs. Instead, the business enterprise as such must assume its own responsibilities.

III. TRENDS OF INTERNATIONAL DECISION IN FAVOR OF CORPORATE DUTIES

If a legal regime regulating corporations, rather than only states or individuals, is necessary to address the nature of corporations as actors in the human rights field, a final step must be taken before seeking to offer a theory. This step entails examining international practice to see whether states, international organizations, and other key participants are, in a sense, ready for such an enterprise. In reviewing recent trends, one discovers that international law has already effectively recognized duties of corporations.[120]

As an initial matter, it bears brief mention that international law doctrine poses no significant impediment to recognition of duties beyond those of states. Some writers insist that private persons cannot, in general, be liable under international law because the state is a "screen" between them and international law;[121] or that only states are full subjects of international law (with so-called legal personality) because only they can enjoy the full range of legal rights and duties and make claims for violations of rights.[122] Yet the orthodoxy now accepts that nonstate entities may enjoy forms of international personality. For a half-century it has been clear that the United Nations may make claims against states for violations

---

119. Robert E. Goodin, *Apportioning Responsibilities*, 6 LAW & PHIL. 167, 181-83 (1987).

120. *Cf.* INT'L COUNCIL ON HUMAN RIGHTS POLICY, *supra* note 101, paras. 81-156 (offering an independent account of this practice).

121. *See, e.g.*, NGUYEN QUOC DINH, DROIT INTERNATIONAL PUBLIC 618 (Patrick Daillier & Alain Pellet eds., 5th ed. 1994).

122. *See, e.g.*, Nkambo Mugerwa, *Subjects of International Law*, in MANUAL OF PUBLIC INTERNATIONAL LAW 247, 249 (Max Sørenson ed., 1968); Giuseppe Sperduti, *L'individu et le droit international*, 90 RECUEIL DES COURS 733 (1956).

of their obligations to it.[123] International lawyers have argued about the extent of personality enjoyed by individuals and corporations in light of treaties allowing victims of human rights to sue states in regional courts or permitting foreign investors to sue states in the International Centre for the Settlement of Investment Disputes.[124] And the corpus of international criminal law makes clear that actors other than states have duties under international law.[125] The question is not whether nonstate actors have rights and duties, but what those rights and duties are.

The lack of an international court in which businesses can be sued does not alter this conclusion. Of course, mechanisms for compliance—or, as the New Haven School puts it, control mechanisms—are central, for law cannot exist without them.[126] But in most areas of the law, states have obligations without either the possibility or probability that they might be called before an international court. Instead, the diverse methods of enforcement include self-restraint based on states' reluctance to create adverse precedents,[127] reciprocal action, protest, diplomatic responses, nonforcible sanctions, and, in highly limited circumstances, recourse to force.[128] In the human rights area, the presence of a court holding states responsible has never been the linchpin of the obligation itself. The International Covenant on Civil and Political Rights (ICCPR) contains no provisions granting either individuals or interested states the right to take a violating state to the ICJ or any other court.[129] Instead, many states and regional organizations take human rights

---

123. Reparations for Injuries Suffered in the Service of the United Nations, 1949 I.C.J. 174 (Apr. 11).

124. *See* WOLFGANG FRIEDMANN, THE CHANGING STRUCTURE OF INTERNATIONAL LAW 223 (1964) (calling for "a limited *ad hoc* subjectivity" for TNEs); CARL AAGE NØRGAARD, THE POSITION OF THE INDIVIDUAL IN INTERNATIONAL LAW 180-82 (1962). Rosalyn Higgins has made a convincing attack on the entire notion of legal personality. *See supra* note 115.

125. *See supra* text accompanying notes 74-78.

126. *See* McDougal & Reisman, *supra* note 14, at 377-78; Carlos S. Nino, *The Duty To Punish Past Abuses of Human Rights Put into Context: The Case of Argentina*, 100 YALE L.J. 2619, 2621 (1991) ("[A] necessary criterion for the validity of any norm of . . . positive international law . . . is the willingness of . . . states and international bodies . . . to enforce it.").

127. Georges Scelle, *Le phénomène juridique de dédoublement fonctionnel*, *in* RECHTSFRAGEN DER INTERNATIONALEN ORGANISATION 324 (Walter Schatzel & Hans-Jürgen Schlochauer eds., 1956).

128. LUNG-CHU CHEN, AN INTRODUCTION TO CONTEMPORARY INTERNATIONAL LAW 10 (1989); OLIVER J. LISSITZYN, THE INTERNATIONAL COURT OF JUSTICE 5-6 (1951) (stating that international law is enforced primarily in a horizontal, rather than vertical, manner).

129. International Covenant on Civil and Political Rights, *adopted* Dec. 19, 1966, S. EXEC. DOC. E, 95-2, at 23 (1978), 999 U.N.T.S. 171 [hereinafter ICCPR]. The closest provision is Article 44, S. EXEC. DOC. E, 95-2, at 37, 999 U.N.T.S. at 184, which merely provides that the ICCPR's procedures for implementation do not prevent parties from utilizing "other procedures for settling a dispute in accordance with general or special international agreements in force." A state could appear before the ICJ for violations of the ICCPR if it and the applicant state had both accepted the court's compulsory jurisdiction. *See* ICCPR, *supra*, arts. 40-42, S. EXEC. DOC. E, 95-2, at 33-37, 999 U.N.T.S. at 181-84; *see also* Optional Protocol to the International Covenant on Civil and Political Rights, *adopted* Dec. 19, 1966, 999 U.N.T.S. 302 (enabling the Human Rights Committee to comment on reports submitted by states and to issue opinions in response to individual complaints, if a state accepts the individual petition procedure).

into account in their foreign policy, and the United Nations has other mechanisms (of varying degrees of effectiveness) for putting pressure on violators.[130]

As we move from doctrine to the more important realm of the actions of global decisionmakers, the following developments evince a clear trend in favor of corporate duties.

A. *The World War II Industrialist Cases*

Although the universe of international criminal law does not reveal any prosecutions of corporations per se, an important precedent nonetheless shows the willingness of key legal actors to contemplate corporate responsibility at the international level. This episode concerns the trials of German industrialists by American courts sitting in occupied Germany in the so-called second Nuremberg trials under the Allied forces' Control Council Law No. 10.[131] In three cases, *United States v. Flick*, *United States v. Krauch* (the *I.G. Farben Case*), and *United States v. Krupp*, the leaders of large German industries were prosecuted for crimes against peace (i.e., initiating World War II), war crimes, and crimes against humanity.[132] The charges stemmed from the active involvement of the defendants in Nazi practices such as slave labor and deportation. A British court also tried those manufacturing Zyklon B gas for complicity in war crimes.[133]

Although in all these cases the courts were trying individuals, they nonetheless routinely spoke in terms of corporate responsibilities and obligations. For example, in the *I.G. Farben Case,* the court wrote:

> With reference to the charges in the present indictment concerning Farben's activities in Poland, Norway, Alsace-Lorraine, and France, we find that the proof establishes beyond a reasonable doubt that offenses against property as defined in Control Council Law No. 10 were committed by Farben, and that these offenses were connected with, and an inextricable part of the German policy for occupied countries. . . . The action of Farben and its

---

130. *See generally* OAS Res. AG/RES.1080, OAS Gen. Ass., 21st Sess., Proceedings, vol. I, at 4, OAS Doc. OEA/Ser.p/XX1.0.2 (1991) (discussing responses to "sudden or irregular disruption of the democratic political institutional process"); HUMAN RIGHTS AND COMPARATIVE FOREIGN POLICY (David P. Forsythe ed., 2000) (appraising practices of various states); Bruno Simma et al., *Human Rights Considerations in the Development Co-operation Activities of the EC*, *in* THE EU AND HUMAN RIGHTS 571 (Philip Alston ed., 1999) (discussing linkages of human rights to EU development aid).

131. Control Council Law No. 10 (Dec. 20, 1945), *reprinted in* 1 TRIALS OF WAR CRIMINALS BEFORE THE NUERNBERG MILITARY TRIBUNALS, at xvi (photo. reprint 1998) (1949) [hereinafter CCL NO. 10 TRIALS].

132. *See generally* CCL NO. 10 TRIALS, *supra* note 131, vols. 6-9 (1950-1953).

133. The *Zyklon B Case*: Trial of Bruno Tesch and Two Others, 1 LAW REPORTS OF TRIALS OF WAR CRIMINALS 93 (1997) (Brit. Mil. Ct. 1946).

representatives, under these circumstances, cannot be differentiated from acts of plunder or pillage committed by officers, soldiers, or public officials of the German Reich. . . . Such action on the part of Farben constituted a violation of the Hague Regulations [on the conduct of warfare].[134]

The court used these various activities as a starting point for determining the guilt of the individuals based on their knowledge and participation.[135] The courts' focus on the role of the firms shows an acceptance that the corporations themselves had duties that they had breached.

B. *International Labor Law*

Second, states have promulgated a series of international labor conventions, recommendations, and other standards to promote the welfare of employees. In line with the traditional paradigm, governments and the International Labour Organization (ILO) view the standards as creating duties on states, and thus the focus of ILO and governmental attention is on the duties of states to implement them.[136] But both the purpose of the conventions and their wording make clear that they do recognize duties on enterprises regarding their employees. For instance, one of the ILO's so-called core conventions, the 1949 Convention Concerning the Application of the Principles of the Right To Organise and To Bargain Collectively, states simply, "Workers shall enjoy adequate protection against acts of anti-union discrimination in respect of their employment." [137] While clearly an injunction to governments to enact legislation against certain behavior by industry, the obligation also entails, indeed presupposes, a duty on the

---

134. United States v. Krauch, 8 CCL No. 10 TRIALS, *supra* note 131, at 1081, 1140 (1952) (U.S. Mil. Trib. VI 1948); *see also* United States v. Krupp, 9 CCL No. 10 TRIALS, *supra* note 131, at 1327, 1352-53 (1950) (U.S. Mil. Trib. III 1948) ("[T]he confiscation of the Austin plant [a French tractor plant owned by the Rothschilds] . . . and its subsequent detention by the Krupp firm constitute a violation of Article 43 of the Hague Regulations . . . [and] the Krupp firm, through defendants[,] . . . voluntarily and without duress participated in these violations . . . .").

135. United States v. Krauch, 8 CCL No. 10 TRIALS, *supra* note 131, at 1081, 1153 (1952) (U.S. Mil. Trib. VI 1948) ("[C]orporations act through individuals and, under the conception of personal individual guilt . . . the prosecution . . . must establish . . . that an individual defendant was either a participant in the illegal act or that, being aware thereof, he authorized or approved it."); Matthew Lippman, *War Crimes Trials of German Industrialists: The "Other Schindlers,"* 9 TEMP. INT'L & COMP. L.J. 173 (1995).

136. *See* Constitution of the International Labour Organisation, *adopted* Oct. 9, 1946, pmbl., 15 U.N.T.S. 35, 40-42 ("[T]he failure of any nation to adopt humane conditions of labour is an obstacle in the way of other nations which desire to improve the conditions in their own countries."); *see also* NICOLAS VALTICOS, INTERNATIONAL LABOUR LAW 225-36 (1979) (focusing on state obligations).

137. Convention Concerning the Application of the Principles of the Right To Organise and To Bargain Collectively, *adopted* July 1, 1949, art. 1, http://ilolex.ilo.ch:1567/english/convdisp2.htm.

corporation not to interfere with the ability of employees to form unions. In Raz's conception, the rights to form a union and to strike are rights against the employer, even if the treaties themselves place the duties on the state.[138] States preparing other conventions have, in fact, recognized this truism in textual terms. For example, the 1981 Occupational Safety and Health Convention contains six articles specifically obligating employers to attain certain standards.[139]

The labor rights treaties assume special significance with respect to the possibility of duties on corporations in the human rights area. They have a long historical pedigree, dating back to the 1920s, well before the development of most modern human rights law, and thereby they show that states have accepted the need to regulate corporate conduct through international law. Today, most states view labor rights as a subset of human rights and, in particular, of economic and social rights.[140] This global recognition that the rights of employees create duties for corporations represents a stepping stone to an acceptance by states that the rights of the citizenry can create other duties for corporations.

C. *International Environmental Law and Polluter Responsibility*

Beyond labor law, decisionmakers prescribing international environmental law have gone even further in holding private enterprises liable for harms. Governments and environmentalists understand that state responsibility—even under a strict liability regime—may not work to provide appropriate reparation for the harm done.[141] As a result, the "polluter pays" principle has exerted a strong impact on governmental policies toward prevention and responses to pollution, moving international

---

138. *See supra* text accompanying notes 82-84.

139. Convention Concerning Occupational Safety and Health and the Working Environment, *adopted* June 22, 1981, http://ilolex.ilo.ch:1567/english/convdisp2.htm; *see, e.g., id.* art. 16(1) ("Employers shall be required to ensure that, so far as is reasonably practicable, the workplaces, machinery, equipment and processes under their control are safe and without risk to health."); *see also* Convention Concerning Forced or Compulsory Labour, as Modified by the Final Articles Revision Convention of the International Labour Organisation, *done* Aug. 31, 1948, art. 25, 39 U.N.T.S. 55, 56-74 (obligating states to criminalize any forced labor, but not imposing such an obligation directly on corporations).

140. Virginia A. Leary, *The Paradox of Workers' Rights as Human Rights, in* HUMAN RIGHTS, LABOR RIGHTS, AND INTERNATIONAL TRADE 22 (Lance A. Compa & Stephen F. Diamond eds., 1996). On the U.S. government's acceptance of labor rights notwithstanding its rejection of much of the logic of economic and social rights, see *id.* at 24. *See generally* Philip Alston & Gerard Quinn, *The Nature and . Scope of States Parties' Obligations Under the International Covenant on Economic, Social and Cultural Rights*, 9 HUM. RTS. Q. 156 (1987) (providing an overview of perceptions on economic, social, and cultural rights and discussing states parties' obligations).

141. Alan E. Boyle, *Making the Polluter Pay? Alternatives to State Responsibility in the Allocation of Transboundary Environmental Costs, in* INTERNATIONAL RESPONSIBILITY FOR ENVIRONMENTAL HARM, *supra* note 102, at 363, 363-66.

environmental law well beyond exclusive reliance on state responsibility.[142] The principle in the abstract has been reiterated in various important, though nonbinding, instruments.[143] More important, states have made it operational through an array of treaties that place liability directly upon polluters. These include the 1960 Paris Convention on Third Party Liability in the Field of Nuclear Energy,[144] the 1962 Brussels Convention on the Liability of Operators of Nuclear Ships,[145] the 1963 Vienna Convention on Civil Liability for Nuclear Damage,[146] the 1969 International Convention on Civil Liability for Oil Pollution Damage and the 1984 Protocol thereto,[147] the 1971 Brussels Convention Relating to Civil Liability in the Field of Maritime Carriage of Nuclear Material,[148] and the 1976 Convention on Civil Liability for Oil Pollution Damage Resulting from Exploration for and Exploitation of Seabed Mineral Resources.[149] For instance, the 1969 Brussels Convention states:

> [T]he owner of a ship at the time of an accident, or where the incident consists of a series of occurrences at the time of the first such occurrence, shall be liable for any pollution damage caused by oil which has escaped or been discharged from the ship as a result of the incident.[150]

These treaties thus impose an international standard of liability on the corporation. Indeed, one key environmental treaty recognizes some pollution damage as a bona fide international crime. The 1989 Basel Convention on the Control of Transboundary Movements of Hazardous

---

142. PATRICIA W. BIRNIE & ALAN E. BOYLE, INTERNATIONAL LAW AND THE ENVIRONMENT 201 (1992).

143. *See, e.g.*, 1 U.N. CONFERENCE ON ENV'T & DEV., RIO DECLARATION ON ENVIRONMENT AND DEVELOPMENT 9, 10-11, U.N. Doc. A/CONF.151/26, U.N. Sales No. E.93.I.11 (1993) ("National authorities should endeavour to promote the internalization of environmental costs and the use of economic instruments, taking into account the approach that the polluter should, in principle, bear the cost of pollution, with due regard to the public interest and without distorting international trade and investment."); Implementation of the Polluter-Pays Principle, OECD Council Res. C(74)223 (Nov. 14, 1974), *reprinted in* ORGANIZATION FOR ECON. COOPERATION & DEV., OECD AND THE ENVIRONMENT 26 (1986). On the notion of soft law, see *infra* text accompanying note 179.

144. Paris Convention on Third Party Liability in the Field of Nuclear Energy, *done* July 29, 1960, 956 U.N.T.S. 251.

145. Brussels Convention on the Liability of Operators of Nuclear Ships, *done* May 25, 1962, *reprinted in* 57 AM. J. INT'L L. 268 (1963).

146. Vienna Convention on Civil Liability for Nuclear Damage, *done* May 21, 1963, 1063 U.N.T.S. 265.

147. International Convention on Civil Liability for Oil Pollution Damage, *done* Nov. 29, 1969, 26 U.S.T. 765, 973 U.N.T.S. 3 [hereinafter 1969 Convention].

148. Brussels Convention Relating to Civil Liability in the Field of Maritime Carriage of Nuclear Material, *done* Dec. 17, 1971, 974 U.N.T.S. 255.

149. Convention on Civil Liability for Oil Pollution Damage Resulting from Exploration for and Exploitation of Seabed Mineral Resources, *done* Dec. 17, 1976, 16 I.L.M. 1450.

150. 1969 Convention, *supra* note 147, at 5.

Wastes and Their Disposal declares that "illegal traffic in hazardous wastes or other wastes is criminal" and requires all parties to introduce legislation to prevent and punish it.[151]

Although environmental treaties demonstrate a willingness of states to impose responsibility directly on corporations, they are still very much influenced by the traditional paradigm of international law. Thus, governments and commentators routinely refer to them as "civil liability" treaties, rather than corporate responsibility schemes, reflecting the extent to which the term "responsibility" is tied up with the idea of state responsibility.[152] Indeed, scholars largely exclude these regimes from the ambit of public international law and instead regard them as private law regimes.[153] Commentators use these terms because all the treaties above provide for implementation by national courts, wherein victims of the pollution may sue; they are thus merely, as Alan Boyle puts it, "transboundary civil litigation" regimes.[154]

But this once again confuses the existence of responsibility with the mode of implementing it. It suggests that international law does not itself impose liability on the corporations—even though this is the very language of some of the treaties—because the mechanism for enforcement is through a private lawsuit in one or more states. The treaties do impose responsibility upon the polluters, however; the use of domestic courts to implement this liability does not change this reality, just as the use of such courts to implement international criminal responsibility—through, for example, obligations on states to extradite or prosecute offenders—does not detract from the law's imposition of individual responsibility.[155]

---

151. Basel Convention on the Control of Transboundary Movements of Hazardous Wastes and Their Disposal, *done* Mar. 22, 1989, arts. 4(3), 9(5), 1673 U.N.T.S. 57, 132, 137; *see also id.* art. 2(14), 1673 U.N.T.S. at 130 ("'Person' means any natural or legal person."); Andrew Clapham, *The Question of Jurisdiction Under International Criminal Law over Legal Persons, in* LIABILITY OF MULTINATIONAL CORPORATIONS UNDER INTERNATIONAL LAW, *supra* note 38, at 139, 173-75 (discussing EU and U.K. implementation).

152. *See, e.g.*, Environmental Liability: White Paper from the European Commission Directorate-General for the Environment, COM(00)66 final (proposing a civil liability regime for Europe); Boyle, *supra* note 141, at 363-70. In orthodox usage, the term liability is thus used to describe a form of accountability that does not entail a finding of an international law violation. *See* Pemmaraju Sreenivasa Rao, *First Report on Prevention of Transboundary Damage from Hazardous Activities*, U.N. GAOR, Int'l Law Comm'n, 50th Sess., U.N. Doc. A/CN.4/487 (1998); Karl Zemanek, *Causes and Forms of International Liability, in* CONTEMPORARY PROBLEMS OF INTERNATIONAL LAW 319 (Bin Cheng & E.D. Brown eds., 1988).

153. *See* Zemanek, *supra* note 152; *see also* Sean D. Murphy, *Prospective Liability Regimes for the Transboundary Movement of Hazardous Wastes*, 88 AM. J. INT'L L. 24, 48-56 (1994) (analyzing the "negotiated private law regime").

154. Boyle, *supra* note 141, at 367.

155. RATNER & ABRAMS, *supra* note 54, at 11-12. *But see* Bruno Simma & Andreas L. Paulus, *The Responsibility of Individuals for Human Rights Abuses in Internal Conflicts: A Positivist View*, 93 AM. J. INT'L L. 302, 308 (1999) (distinguishing between *delicta juris gentium* and direct international responsibility, where the former applies to crimes in which states are authorized or required to prosecute and the latter to a smaller category of crimes).

482 The Yale Law Journal [Vol. 111: 443

D. *Anti-Corruption Law*

Beyond environmental treaties, states have developed international law creating binding obligations on corporations with respect to discrete economic activities. In 1997, the states in the OECD concluded under its auspices the Convention on Combating Bribery of Foreign Public Officials in International Business Transactions.[156] The Convention requires state parties to criminalize bribery of foreign public officials, when committed in whole or in part in their territory.[157] Moreover, the Convention makes clear that each party must ensure that such criminal liability extends to corporations.[158] While adhering to the orthodox distinction between duties of governments under international law and duties of enterprises under domestic law, the treaty nonetheless makes clear that the responsibility of businesses is recognized and may be regulated by international law.[159] The Organization of American States and the Council of Europe have similar treaties with provisions on enterprise liability.[160] The United Nations, IMF, World Bank, and other organizations have also taken steps toward standards for corporations in this area.[161]

The Bribery Conventions are also an important precedent insofar as they do not aim simply to penalize corporate conduct that governments and their citizenry regard as illegitimate (namely, bribe-giving) or to avoid disadvantaging companies whose home states prohibit bribery (such as the United States). Rather, the states sought to create a process leading to the

---

156. Convention on Combating Bribery of Foreign Public Officials in International Business Transactions, Dec. 17, 1997, http://www.oecd.org/daf/nocorruption/20nov1e.htm [hereinafter OECD Bribery Convention]. The Convention has twenty-six parties, including five non-OECD states.

157. *Id.* arts. 1, 4.

158. *Id.* art. 2 (requiring parties to "establish the liability of legal persons").

159. This treaty states that:

The bribery of a foreign public official shall be punishable by effective, proportionate and dissuasive criminal penalties. The range of penalties shall be comparable to that applicable to the bribery of the Party's own public officials and shall, in the case of natural persons, include deprivation of liberty sufficient to enable effective mutual legal assistance and extradition.

Id. art. 3.

160. *See* Inter-American Convention Against Corruption, *done* Mar. 29, 1996, art. VIII, 35 I.L.M. 724, 730 (stating that states must prohibit bribes by "businesses domiciled there"); Criminal Law Convention on Corruption, *done* Jan. 27, 1999, art. 18, 38 I.L.M. 505, 509 [hereinafter Council of Europe Corruption Convention] (requiring parties to legislate "to ensure that legal persons can be held liable" for various offenses); *see also* Second Protocol to the Convention on the Protection of the European Communities' Financial Interests, 1997 O.J. (C 221) 12 (requiring members to hold legal persons liable for misuse of EU resources).

161. *See, e.g.*, Int'l Monetary Fund, Revised Code of Good Practices on Fiscal Transparency, *at* http://www.imf.org/external/np/fad/trans/code.htm#code (last visited Oct. 15, 2001); World Bank Group, Supporting International Efforts To Reduce Corruption, *at* http://www1.worldbank.org/publicsector/anticorrupt/supporting.htm (last visited Sept. 2, 2001).

diminution of corruption in the target states.[162] By recognizing that foreign individuals and companies are complicit—indeed an indispensable element—in the obnoxious behavior, the OECD hopes to cut off the resources for bribery and reduce the incidence of corrupt activities.[163] One can thus ask why, if corporations can be regulated to reduce the incidence of corruption, they have not been regulated to reduce the incidence of human rights abuses. Possible reasons include the lack of the type of causal nexus between corporate behavior and governmental abuses that is present in cases of corruption, and the clear interest of corporations from states that banned bribery in creating an international regime that would eliminate their competitive disadvantage—a factor missing from the human rights dynamic.[164]

E. *United Nations Sanctions*

Haltingly during the Cold War and with increasing frequency thereafter, the members of the United Nations have used the General Assembly and the Security Council to recommend or impose economic sanctions against a variety of states, or, on occasion, insurgent groups.[165] Such sanctions resolutions are, by their terms, formally directed at states. But their implementation requires the cooperation of private business as well, and both UN organs have at times recognized that, in the end, sanctions create a duty upon corporations. During its long efforts to isolate apartheid-era South Africa, the General Assembly repeatedly noted that private businesses have duties to respect the sanctions it had recommended.[166] The Security Council, in creating a comprehensive

---

162. *See, e.g.*, OECD Bribery Convention, *supra* note 156, pmbl., para. 1 (noting that bribery "undermines good governance and economic development"). I appreciate this insight from Jeffrey Gordon.

163. The OECD has thus established a broad outreach program with nonmember states to help with the implementation of the Convention. *See* OECD Online: Anti-Corruption Div., Non-Member Activities, *at* http://www.oecd.org/daf/nocorruption/outreach.htm (last visited Sept. 1, 2001).

164. *See* David A. Gantz, *Globalizing Sanctions Against Foreign Bribery: The Emergence of a New International Legal Consensus*, 18 J. INT'L L. & BUS. 457 (1998).

165. U.N. CHARTER arts. 11, 25 (empowering the General Assembly to make recommendations concerning peace and security and the Security Council to make binding decisions).

166. *See, e.g.*, G.A. Res. 2671F, U.N. GAOR, 25th Sess., Supp. No. 28, at 33, 34, U.N. Doc. A/8028 (1970) (deploring "the continued co-operation by certain States and foreign economic interests with South Africa . . . as such co-operation encourages the Government of South Africa in the pursuit of its inhuman policies"); *Programme of Action Against Apartheid*, U.N. SCOR, 38th Sess., Supp. for Oct.-Dec.. 1983, at 58, 63, U.N. Doc. S/16102 (1983) (calling on "corporations and employers" to "withdraw from any commercial operations in South Africa"); Appeal by Leaders of the African National Congress, the South African Indian Congress and the Liberal Party of South Africa for a Boycott of South African Produce by the British People (Dec. 1959), *in* U.N. DEP'T OF PUB. INFO., THE UNITED NATIONS AND APARTHEID 1948-1994, at 243, U.N. Doc. DPI/1568, U.N. Sales No. E.95.I.7 (1994).

sanctions regime for Iraq following the conclusion of the 1991 Gulf War, endorsed a plan by the Secretary-General that placed strict requirements on corporations regarding their purchases of oil from Iraq.[167] Indeed, in order to gain permission for trade with Iraq, the oil companies themselves must apply to the Council's sanctions committee and comply with its directives.[168] While it may appear that sanctions obligations are confined to UN member states, the reality has suggested otherwise.

F. *European Union Practice*

Alongside the foregoing attempts to create duties upon corporations through the paradigm of state duties, the states of the European Union have gone significantly further. Both the Treaty Establishing the European Community (i.e., the 1957 Treaty of Rome, as amended) and the binding decisions of the European Council and Commission have created a vast body of legal obligations which apply directly to corporate entities. For instance, Article 81 of the Treaty forbids anticompetitive behavior.[169] Further, the Council and Commission have issued numerous regulations and directives with which private companies must comply, and the European Court of Justice has heard many cases in which one private party has sought to enforce the Treaty against another.[170] As noted earlier, in a series of highly significant cases, the European Court of Justice directly imposed on companies not only legal duties, but also human rights duties regarding nondiscrimination. The *Walrave and Koch* and *Defrenne* cases rely upon the language of the Treaty of Rome, which does not distinguish between public and private entities in banning nationality- and gender-based discrimination. These decisions also emphasize the purpose of the European Community in promoting free movement (thus prohibiting

---

167. S.C. Res. 986, U.N. SCOR, 50th Sess., at 101, U.N. Doc. S/INF/51 (1995) (approving a report of the Secretary-General that required private purchasers of oil from Iraq to follow certain procedures, including depositing proceeds in an escrow account); *Report by the Secretary-General Pursuant to Paragraph 5 of Security Council Resolution 706*, U.N. SCOR, 46th Sess., para. 58, U.N. Doc. S/23006 (1991).

168. *See, e.g.*, Annual Report of Security Council Committee Established by Resolution 661, paras. 7-13 (1990), *annexed to* Letter from the Chairman of the Security Council Committee to the President of the Security Council (July 26, 2001), U.N. Doc. S/2001/738 (2001) (discussing the oil-for-food program).

169. TREATY ESTABLISHING THE EUROPEAN COMMUNITY, Nov. 10, 1997, art. 81, O.J. (C 340) 3 (1997) [hereinafter EC TREATY].

170. *See generally* David J. Gerber, *The Transformation of European Community Competition Law?*, 35 HARV. INT'L L.J. 97 (1994) (analyzing successes of and tensions among EU actors).

nationality-based discrimination) and social equality between the sexes (thereby barring gender-based discrimination).[171]

That European Community law—a category of international law— provides both direct rights and duties on corporations (i.e., without the intervention of individual states) follows both from the language of the Treaty of Rome itself[172] and from the acceptance of direct effect by both the European Court of Justice and the EU member states.[173] Indeed, direct effect is now a cornerstone of the EU legal system.[174] It might be argued that this "new legal order of international law" (to quote the ECJ in its key decision on direct effect[175]) makes the EU unique and demonstrates that other, seemingly more ordinary treaty regimes can at best provide for the indirect sort of liability seen in the environmental or bribery conventions. Yet the European Community's practice shows that states can conclude treaties providing for direct corporate responsibility and implement those treaties effectively. The leap of faith is one of political will; the legal doctrine follows inevitably.

G. *Treaty Interpretation Bodies*

Most of the standing expert bodies established under global human rights treaties have refrained from addressing corporate duties, although they have on occasion reinforced the view of the European and Inter-American courts that the state has a duty to prevent certain private abuses.[176] It is worth noting, however, that in 1999, the Committee on Economic, Social, and Cultural Rights, which oversees implementation of the International Covenant on Economic, Social, and Cultural Rights, interpreted an individual's right to food under Article 11 of that Covenant

---

171. Case 36/74, Walrave v. Association Union Cycliste Internationale, 1974 E.C.R. 1405, 1419; Case 43/75, Defrenne v. Société Anonyme Belge de Navigation Aérienne Sabena, 1976 E.C.R. 455, 457-63; CLAPHAM, *supra* note 94, at 248-52.

172. EC TREATY, *supra* note 169, art. 249 (establishing EU regulation as "binding in its entirety and directly applicable in all Member States").

173. *See* Case 26/62, Van Gend en Loos v. Nederlandse Administratie Der Belastingen, 1963 E.C.R. 3, 12 ("[T]his Treaty is more than an agreement which merely creates mutual obligations between the contracting states .... [T]he Community constitutes a new legal order of international law for the benefit of which the states have limited their sovereign rights, albeit within limited fields, and the subjects of which comprise not only Member States but also their nationals.... Community law therefore not only imposes obligations on individuals but is also intended to confer upon them rights which become part of their legal heritage."); Case 6/64, Costa v. Ente Nazionale per l'Energia Elettrica (Enel), 1964 E.C.R. 585; *see also* P.S.R.F. MATHIJSEN, A GUIDE TO EUROPEAN UNION LAW 26-32, 41-45 (7th ed. 1999) (explaining the legal status of regulations and directives).

174. *See* J.H.H. Weiler, *The Transformation of Europe*, 100 YALE L.J. 2403, 2413-15 (1991) (describing the direct effect as key to the "constitutionalization" of EU law).

175. *Van Gend en Loos*, 1963 E.C.R. at 12.

176. *See* CLAPHAM, *supra* note 94, at 108-12.

as giving rise to responsibilities by private actors.[177] Nonetheless, the Committee's interpretive comments, while often influential upon both governments and nonstate actors, are not binding, and it is hard to interpret that comment as more than aspirational. The UN Human Rights Commission's Subcommission on the Promotion and Protection of Human Rights (which does not address a particular treaty but human rights observance generally) has established a panel to study and make proposals on the activities of TNEs, but its work is in an early stage.[178]

H. *Soft Law Statements of Direct Duties*

Finally, governments have recognized duties of corporations through a number of significant soft law instruments. These documents result when governments wish to make authoritative statements about desired behavior; these statements typically correspond to the expectations of most states, even though states may not be prepared to state that such behavior is legally mandated.[179] In the area of corporate responsibilities, two soft law instruments stand out. First, in 1977 the ILO adopted the Tripartite Declaration of Principles Concerning Multinational Enterprises and Social Policy.[180] This instrument remains important insofar as it was adopted by the three component groups of the ILO's governing body—governments, industry, and labor—and has been cited by governments and industry since that time as reflecting a fair balance among the interests of all three.[181] The

---

177. International Covenant on Economic, Social, and Cultural Rights, *adopted* Dec. 16, 1966, art. 11, 993 U.N.T.S. 3, 7 [hereinafter ICESCR]; *see* General Comment No. 12, para. 20, *in Report of the Committee on Economic, Social, and Cultural Rights*, U.N. ESCOR, Supp. No. 2, at 102, 106, U.N. Doc. E/2000/22 (2000) ("While only States are parties to the Covenant and are thus ultimately accountable for compliance with it, all members of society—individuals, families, local communities, non-governmental organizations, civil society organizations, as well as the private business sector—have responsibilities in the realization of the right to adequate food."). For an argument that the Universal Declaration of Human Rights itself creates obligations on corporations, see INT'L COUNCIL ON HUMAN RIGHTS POLICY, *supra* note 101, paras. 94-106.

178. *See* Res. 1998/8, U.N. ESCOR, Subcomm'n on Prevention of Discrimination & Protection of Minorities, para. 4, U.N. Doc. E/CN.4/SUB.2/RES/1998/8 (1998); Weissbrodt, *supra* note 16 (presenting a report for the Subcommission on developing a human rights code of conduct for companies). (The Subcommission on the Promotion and Protection of Human Rights was formerly known as the Subcommission on Prevention of Discrimination and Protection of Minorities.)

179. *See, e.g.*, Christine Chinkin, *Normative Development in the International Legal System, in* COMMITMENT AND COMPLIANCE: THE ROLE OF NON-BINDING NORMS IN THE INTERNATIONAL LEGAL SYSTEM 21, 25-31 (Dinah Shelton ed., 2000); *see also* Michael Reisman, *The Concept and Functions of Soft Law in International Politics, in* 1 ESSAYS IN HONOUR OF JUDGE TASLIM OLAWALE ELIAS 135, 135-36 (Emmanuel G. Bello & Bola A. Ajibola eds., 1992) (positing three ways in which a legal instrument might be soft).

180. Declaration Adopted by the Governing Body of the International Labour Office at Its 204th Session (Nov. 1977), http://www.ilo.org/public/english/standards/norm/sources/mne.htm [hereinafter Tripartite Declaration].

181. U.S. DEP'T OF LABOR, THE APPAREL INDUSTRY AND CODES OF CONDUCT § II.B.1, http://www.dol.gov/dol/ilab/public/media/reports/iclp/apparel/2b.htm (noting the Tripartite

document contains a variety of principles for both governments and corporations. It urges corporations to cooperate with governmental development policies, to adopt a hiring policy favorable to local nationals, to look out for the employees' health and safety, and to recognize the rights of workers to organize and bargain collectively.[182] Most of these precepts restate various obligations on governments, but the reformulation of some as creating duties (albeit soft ones) on corporations is significant. Given the source of the instrument and its repeated recitation, it is not merely wishful thinking, but reflects a sense among those three constituencies that corporations have duties toward their employees.

Second, the OECD has developed various sets of guidelines for multinational enterprises. The first such guidelines, from 1976, contained rather anodyne statements regarding a corporation's duties to follow the policies of the host country.[183] In 2000, the OECD issued a long-awaited and far more detailed set of guidelines to respond to growing concerns by nongovernmental organizations about the power of TNEs.[184] Though principally addressing business-related issues such as disclosure, employment practices, pollution, and bribery, the principles do cover human rights specifically. Among the general policies for corporations to follow, the OECD Guidelines state that corporations should " [r]espect the human rights of those affected by their activities consistent with the host government's international obligations and commitments." [185] At the same time, the Guidelines go no further than this statement and give corporations no sense of what rights are included and how broadly the group of " those affected by their activities" extends. In addition to the ILO and the OECD, the European Community issued a set of nonbinding guidelines concerning business in apartheid-era South Africa and is, as noted, considering a broader code of conduct.[186]

* * *

The overall picture thus far presented shows a somewhat inconsistent posture among decisionmakers over the role of corporations in the international legal order. On the one hand, they accept that business

---

Declaration with favor); U.S. Council on Int'l Bus., USCIB Position Paper on Codes of Conduct, http://www.uscib.org/code1298.asp (same).

182. Tripartite Declaration, *supra* note 180, §§ 10, 16, 37, 41.

183. 1976 OECD Guidelines, *supra* note 40, paras. 1-2.

184. OECD Guidelines for Multinational Enterprises (2000), http://www.oecd.org/daf/investment/guidelines/mnetext.htm [hereinafter 2000 OECD Guidelines].

185. *Id.* § II.2.

186. *See* Menno T. Kamminga, *Holding Multinational Corporations Accountable for Human Rights Abuses: A Challenge for the EC, in* THE EU AND HUMAN RIGHTS, *supra* note 130, at 553, 564.

enterprises have *rights* under international law, whether the economic right under investment treaties to receive nondiscriminatory treatment and to bring a state to international arbitration, or clearly recognizable political rights such as freedom of speech.[187] Yet most governments appear to remain somewhat ambivalent about accepting corporate duties, and, in particular, duties that corporations might have toward individuals in states where they operate.[188] They have, however, indirectly recognized duties upon corporations by prescribing international labor law, environmental law, anti-corruption law, and economic sanctions. And the European Union, through treaties, legislation, and decisions of the European Court of Justice, has gone further, directly placing duties on businesses. States have provided for enforcement of those duties through the civil liability regime of the environmental agreements, the criminal liability regime of the OECD Bribery Convention, and recourse to the European Court of Justice. The cumulative impact of this lawmaking and application suggests a recognition by many decisionmakers that corporate behavior is a fitting subject for international regulation.

If states and international organizations can accept rights and duties of corporations in some areas, there is no theoretical bar to recognizing duties more broadly, including duties in the human rights area. The soft law instruments like the OECD Guidelines show that governments at least talk about duties upon corporations with respect to human rights, as does the UN's current focus on illicit diamond trading,[189] or the Human Rights Commission's discussions of the issue. And even corporations themselves, while generally disdaining the idea of increased international regulation, have come to accept the idea of duties to protect human rights.[190] Nonetheless, to move beyond the current stage and prescribe law in this area in a coherent fashion requires a theory of corporate responsibility for human rights under international law.

---

187. *See* Asakura v. City of Seattle, 265 U.S. 332 (1924) (holding that a friendship treaty with Japan overrode a Seattle ordinance against Japanese businesses); Sunday Times v. United Kingdom, 30 Eur. Ct. H.R. (ser. A) (1979) (upholding a newspaper's right to free speech). *See generally* Michael K. Addo, *The Corporation as a Victim of Human Rights Violations, in* HUMAN RIGHTS STANDARDS AND THE RESPONSIBILITY OF TRANSNATIONAL CORPORATIONS 187 (Michael K. Addo ed., 1999) (reviewing cases in human rights bodies brought by corporate entities).

188. *See* Charney, *supra* note 61, at 767 (noting how the "nonstatus" of corporations allows them to enjoy rights but not duties and thus to "have it both ways").

189. The operative paragraph of the Security Council's resolution directed toward private entities is not worded in the form of an obligation, presumably because of a belief that the Council cannot place obligations on them. *See* S.C. Res. 1306, *supra* note 1, at 3 (encouraging "the International Diamond Manufacturers Association . . . to work with the Government of Sierra Leone"). *But see supra* notes 166-167 (citing UN resolutions on South Africa and Iraq).

190. *See supra* note 63 (noting statements of Enron).

IV. PRIMARY RULES AND SECONDARY RULES: INTERNATIONAL LAW'S DOCTRINAL STARTING POINT

Any theory of corporate responsibilities in the human rights area that seeks to gain some acceptance among international decisionmakers—whether states, international organizations, corporations, diverse nongovernmental organizations, or even academic advisers to these groups—must have some grounding in contemporary understandings about international law. In that regard, it becomes necessary to examine the law's approach to liability—state and individual—and to inquire into its suitability for the new enterprise. This Part first outlines the basic doctrines of state and individual responsibility. It then appraises whether these principles can be transposed to a clearly different sort of entity—the transnational corporation.

A. *The Responsibility of States: A Primer*

The task of appraising the expectations of states and other decisionmakers regarding the contours of state responsibility benefits from the systematic study of the subject undertaken by the UN's International Law Commission (ILC), a standing body of thirty-four independent experts. In 1949, the ILC decided to begin work on a project to draft a treaty on the responsibilities of states for injuries to aliens and their property. States have long agreed that, if one state harmed the citizens of another who might be traveling or setting up a business there, the host state was committing a harm against the home state. Such acts had been the subject of countless interstate disputes and numerous arbitrations, and the ILC and the UN's members believed that elaboration of the duties of host states might prevent future incidents.[191] By the early 1960s, however, the Commission was plagued by disagreements among its members as to the substance of those duties. A key divergence concerned the duties of states regarding the protection of alien property, the very issue that proved so divisive during the developing world's efforts to construct a New International Economic Order.[192]

Stymied in its original mandate, the Commission made an explicit decision to refocus its project on developing a set of "principles which govern the responsibility of States for internationally wrongful acts, maintaining a strict distinction between this task and the task of defining the rules that place obligations on States."[193] International law doctrine has

---

191. *See* 1 IAN BROWNLIE, STATE RESPONSIBILITY 60-84, 90-131 (1983).

192. *See supra* text accompanying note 25.

193. *Report of the Special Rapporteur*, [1970] 2 Y.B. Int'l L. Comm'n 306, U.N. Doc. A/8010/Rev.1. As the ILC's Special Rapporteur wrote, "it is one thing to define a rule and the

490   The Yale Law Journal   [Vol. 111: 443

come to accept this distinction by referring to both primary and secondary rules of state responsibility. Primary rules are the substantive obligations of states in the myriad subject areas of international law, from the law of the sea to jurisdiction to the use of force. Secondary rules are those, as stated by the ILC, that elaborate what it means for a state to be legally accountable for violations of these duties.[194]

Thus, many secondary rules concern principles of attribution—namely, rules for determining the responsibility of the state or individuals for acts of agents or others. For example, the state is responsible for the acts of its organs, even if they act beyond their authority, for the acts of nongovernmental groups exercising governmental authority in the absence of the official government, for the conduct of others that it adopts after the fact, and for knowingly assisting another state in its illegal acts.[195] Other rules concern circumstances that preclude a finding of wrongful conduct by the state despite a prima facie violation by the state of its duties; these rules include consent, lawful self-defense, lawful countermeasures, force majeure, distress, and a state of necessity.[196] The ILC's decades-long codification project has, as a result, sought to refrain—not always with complete success—from elaborating primary rules in international law. Those norms continue to proliferate as new subjects of international relations emerge and require regulation.[197]

The ILC's bifurcated approach to state responsibility reflects the practice of decisionmakers authorized to determine whether a state has breached its duties, insofar as they have addressed primary and secondary rules separately, analyzing both the content of a given norm and the links between the unlawful conduct and the state. The International Court of Justice, for instance, extensively addressed secondary rules in determining whether the acts of Iranian students in taking over the U.S. Embassy in

---

content of the obligation it imposes, and another to determine whether that obligation has been violated and what should be the consequence of the violation." *Id.*

194. *See Report of the International Law Commission*, [1991] 2 Y.B. Int'l L. Comm'n, pt. 2, at 1, U.N. Doc. A/CN.4/Ser.A/1991/Add.1 (1991 Draft Articles); *Report of the International Law Commission*, [1980] 2 Y.B. Int'l L. Comm'n, pt. 2, at 30-34, U.N. Doc. A/CN.4/SER.A/1980/Add.1 [hereinafter *1980 ILC Report*] (1980 Draft Articles). As a shorthand, when international lawyers refer to the doctrine of state responsibility, they are referring to the set of secondary rules and processes. For a broader definition of secondary rules, see H.L.A. HART, THE CONCEPT OF LAW 89-96 (1961) (defining secondary rules as rules that set up the principles by which the primary rules are formed, amended, or terminated).

195. *Responsibility of States for Internationally Wrongful Acts*, U.N. GAOR, Int'l Law Comm'n, 53d Sess., pt. I, ch. 1, arts. 4-11, 16, U.N. Doc. A/CN.4/L.602/Rev.1 (2001) [hereinafter *ILC 2001 Draft Articles*].

196. *Id.* pt. I, ch. 1, arts. 20-27.

197. *See, e.g.*, HIGGINS, *supra* note 72, at 161, 162-65 (criticizing the ILC for mixing primary rules and secondary rules). The most recent Special Rapporteur has proposed some major changes to the project to preserve the focus on secondary rules. *See* James Crawford, *First Report on State Responsibility*, U.N. GAOR, Int'l Law Comm'n, 50th Sess., paras. 12-18, U.N. Doc. A/CN.4/490 (1998).

1979 were attributable to Iran, and whether the acts of the Contras against Nicaragua were acts of the United States.[198] (The primary rules in those two cases concerned, respectively, the law of diplomatic immunity and the law on the use of force.) The Inter-American Commission and Court of Human Rights, as well as the European Commission and Court of Human Rights, have repeatedly engaged in this process as well.[199] Beyond these bodies, arbitral tribunals, UN committees that oversee implementation of human rights treaties, and other decisionmakers routinely make reference to concepts of state responsibility, at times quoting the ILC's Draft Articles as if they were a restatement of customary international law.[200]

Thus an examination of corporate responsibility must begin with these two sets of norms and consider their applicability to companies. For our purposes here, the primary rules at issue are those in the law of human rights. A number of secondary rules will prove pertinent, particularly with regard to attribution of and complicity in wrongful conduct.

B. *The Responsibility of Individuals: A (Shorter) Primer*

International law approaches to individual responsibility have not benefited from the sort of systematic, academic examination provided by the International Law Commission with respect to state responsibility. Nonetheless, a clear set of primary and secondary norms has emerged since the days of the International Military Tribunal through international criminal law treaties, domestic statutes, state practice, and important domestic and international court decisions (most recently those of the International Criminal Tribunals for the Former Yugoslavia and for Rwanda).

For individual accountability, the primary rules are human rights protections that recognize various offenses, such as genocide, war crimes, crimes against humanity, and torture. They define a set of acts that give rise to individual criminal responsibility. As discussed above, the corpus of primary rules of individual responsibility is quite limited compared to the primary rules of state responsibility.[201]

---

198. Military and Paramilitary Activities (Nicar. v. U.S.), 1986 I.C.J. 14, 63-65 (June 27); U.S. Diplomatic and Consular Staff in Tehran (U.S. v. Iran), 1980 I.C.J. 3, 30 (May 24).

199. X v. Federal Republic of Germany, 1958 Y.B. Eur. Conv. on H.R. 256, 304 (Eur. Comm'n on H.R.) (holding that the Federal Republic of Germany was not responsible for acts of East German courts); Loizidou v. Turkey, 310 Eur. Ct. H.R. (ser. A) (1995); Velásquez Rodríguez Case, Inter-Am. Ct. H.R. (ser. C) No. 4 (1988).

200. *See, e.g.,* Yeager v. Iran, 17 Iran-U.S. Cl. Trib. Rep. 91, 103 (1987); General Comment No. 3, para. 1, *in Report of the Committee on Economic, Social, and Cultural Rights,* U.N. ESCOR, 1st Sess., Supp. No. 3, Annex III, at 83, U.N. Doc. E/1991/23 (1991).

201. *See supra* text accompanying notes 80-82.

492   The Yale Law Journal ·   [Vol. 111: 443

The secondary rules of individual (criminal) responsibility, often termed the general principles of criminal law, essentially concern attribution of conduct to the individual, defenses, and other principles such as *nullum crimen sine lege*.[202] Derived from principles of criminal law common to many states, decisionmakers have recognized secondary rules widely through treaties and international court judgments. Among the most significant attribution rules are complicity and conspiracy, which hold that an individual may be guilty for aiding and abetting an offense that he did not directly commit; and command responsibility, which attributes certain acts of subordinates to the superior. Among the critical defenses recognized in international criminal law are coercion (or duress) and mental incapacity.[203] The law has also sharply limited one commonly asserted defense, namely, following orders.[204]

C. *The Corporate Parallel*

Looking at this rich doctrine, one is naturally inclined to ask if it can address the problem of determining the scope of corporate duties. In a word, can decisionmakers transpose the primary rules of international human rights law and the secondary rules of state and individual responsibility onto corporations? If corporations are such significant actors in international relations and law, then can they not assume the obligations currently placed on states or individuals, based on those sets of rules of responsibility? I consider the challenges to applying primary and secondary rules in turn.

1. *The Barriers to Transposing Primary Rules*

Any decision to extend primary human rights rules to corporations faces several problems. With respect to those human rights norms binding on states (the larger category), if, for the moment, we confine their scope to the provisions of the International Covenant on Civil and Political Rights, then some of the obligations specified therein are obviously not within the province of corporate activity. As an obvious example, the ICCPR grants criminal defendants numerous rights, such as the presumption of innocence, a speedy and fair trial, free counsel, the ban on self-incrimination, and

---

202. For one useful grouping of these principles, see ICC Statute, *supra* note 80, pt. 3.

203. *Id.* arts. 25, 28, 31; RATNER & ABRAMS, *supra* note 54, at 129-42.

204. *See, e.g.*, ICC Statute, *supra* note 80, art. 33 (permitting the defense only if the defendant can show a legal obligation to obey the order and excluding its application to genocide and crimes against humanity on the theory that such orders are manifestly unlawful).

nonretroactivity of the law.[205] Some of these rights create duties only on the state insofar as guaranteeing these rights is within the unique province of states as part of their function of maintenance of public order. In that sense, it is, for instance, difficult and perhaps impossible to say that an individual's right to be informed of the reasons for her arrest or right to confront her accusers in a criminal trial can create any duty upon a corporation, as only the state can ensure these rights.[206]

Nonetheless, one can imagine hypothetical situations in which a private enterprise might somehow involve itself in the criminal process. For example, a company seeking to remove a union activist from the scene might conceivably provide false testimony or a fake document to the prosecutor (with or without the latter's knowledge) in order to support charges of illegal activity by the activist. Here the corporation has in some sense helped to deprive the defendant of a fair trial. Thus, the unique role for states in securing some rights (such as the right to free counsel) does not preclude duties for corporations with respect to other, related rights (such as other rights in the criminal field). The principal role for the state in securing some rights—for instance, its role as primary dutyholder in guaranteeing a fair trial—does not exclude extending duties to others for securing those rights.[207]

Second, simply extending the state's duties with respect to human rights to the business enterprise ignores the differences between the nature and functions of states and corporations. Just as the human rights regime governing states reflects a balance between individual liberty and the interests of the state (based on its nature and function), so any regime governing corporations must reflect a balance of individual liberties and business interests.[208] The rights of an individual to privacy and to free expression—rights that on their face create duties in both the state and

---

205. ICCPR, *supra* note 129, arts. 9(2), 14, S. EXEC. DOC. E, 95-2, at 26-28, 999 U.N.T.S. at 176-77.

206. *Cf.* Laurence Dubin, *The Direct Application of Human Rights Standards to, and by, Transnational Corporations*, 61 INT'L COMMISSION JURISTS REV. 35, 41 (1999) (asserting that other rights—to asylum, to take part in government, and to a nationality—cannot be "reformulated" as applying to corporations); INT'L COUNCIL ON HUMAN RIGHTS POLICY, *supra* note 101, para. 148 ("More work will be needed to show how [many civil and political rights] can be applied directly to non-state actors including businesses.").

207. *Cf.* RAZ, *supra* note 82, at 182-86 (discussing the possibility of multiple dutyholders for any given right).

208. *See* ICCPR, *supra* note 129, arts. 4, 14(1), 18(3), 19(3), 21, 22(2), S. EXEC. DOC. E, 95-2, at 24, 27, 29-30, 999 U.N.T.S. at 174, 176, 178 (permitting derogations and restrictions to some rights); *see also* FRANCIS G. JACOBS & ROBIN C.A. WHITE, THE EUROPEAN CONVENTION ON HUMAN RIGHTS 304-06 (2d ed. 1996) (describing legitimate bases for interfering with individual rights under the Convention); MCDOUGAL ET AL., *supra* note 70, at 158-59 (categorizing acceptable derogations). For a recent application of this idea to the corporate context, see Sarah Joseph, *An Overview of the Human Rights Accountability of Multinational Enterprises, in* LIABILITY OF MULTINATIONAL CORPORATIONS UNDER INTERNATIONAL LAW, *supra* note 38, at 75, 90-92.

494   The Yale Law Journal   [Vol. 111: 443

private actors—surely create a different, and in all likelihood smaller, set of duties on the corporation (a point developed further in Section V.C below). In the end, we can say that duties on states are not simply transferable to corporations, but the same human rights that create duties for states may create the same or different duties upon corporate actors.

Third, the limited scope of the primary rules of individual responsibility makes their application to corporations conceptually easier than the application of the primary rules of state responsibility to corporations. Just as individuals might act alone to commit international crimes, so they might choose to act through corporate entities and thus justify decisionmakers to hold the entities responsible. *I.G. Farben* and other post-World War II cases discussed above effectively reached this conclusion under international law; many domestic legal systems have also accepted corporate criminal liability.[209] The difficulty, however, with building a theory of corporate responsibility solely upon these rules is that they are highly limited as a result of their evolution through the process of international *criminal* law. As discussed earlier, most human rights abuses do not give rise to individual responsibility.[210] More generally, as state responsibility makes clear, the criminal route does not exhaust the possibilities for creating duties.

It might be argued that the primary rules on individual responsibility under international criminal law are, in fact, perfectly adaptable to the corporate context—that corporate responsibility ought to extend no further than (although as far as) individual responsibility.[211] The recognition of the corporate entity as a juridical person in both domestic law and international law might support the idea of treating it the same as a natural person, with the result that businesses would be responsible for the same international crimes as individuals.[212] This limited view of corporate responsibility would certainly represent a conservative approach to the issue, although the states drafting the ICC Statute refused to take even this step.[213] But again it assumes that the norms developed through the criminal process are sufficient to address acts when noncriminal forms of responsibility are possible. It also ignores the potential differences between natural persons and juridical persons in terms of their access to resources, ability to harm

---

209. *See supra* text accompanying notes 134-135. On corporate criminality in domestic law, see *infra* notes 326-327 and accompanying text. For one endorsement of this position, see Weissbrodt, *supra* note 16, para. 13.

210. *See supra* text accompanying notes 79-81.

211. I appreciate this argument from Gerald Neuman.

212. *See* Barcelona Traction, Light & Power Co. (Belg. v. Spain), 1970 I.C.J. 3, 34-36 (Feb. 5).

213. For an account, see Clapham, *supra* note 151, at 143-60.

human dignity, and ability to avoid the control of the state.[214] In effect, then, just as the primary human rights rules binding on states are so broad and diverse as to make impossible any notion of simply transferring them to corporations, so the primary rules binding on individuals are so narrow as to make transferring them to corporations insufficient. Corporations might in theory commit war crimes or crimes against humanity, but as a practical matter, history does not suggest this is a prevalent practice; and NGOs and others monitoring corporate practices do not appear to be limiting their concerns to such massive or systematic abuses of basic human rights.

2. *The Barriers to Transposing Secondary Rules*

With respect to secondary rules, the answer to the problem of transferability is less obvious. At one level, some of the secondary rules of state responsibility are not transferable for the same reason that the primary rules are not transferable—because they are defined in terms of actions that only the state can carry out. For example, the preclusion of wrongfulness based on self-defense under the UN Charter would be inapplicable to corporations, which lack such a right under the Charter.[215]

The attribution principles can, however, play an important part in a theory of corporate responsibility. Some of them might easily apply in the corporate context, but others might not. For instance, one of the core rules of attribution to states posited by the ILC provides that the "conduct of an organ of a State or of a person or an entity empowered to exercise elements of the governmental authority" is an act of the state even if it "exceeds its authority or contravenes instructions."[216] If we simply replace the word "state" with "corporation" (or "business enterprise") and the phrase "governmental authority" with "corporate authority," we have generated a new secondary rule, although one that raises new issues because of differences between states and corporations—notably the meaning of an "organ of a corporation" or an "entity empowered to exercise elements of corporate authority." Defining these terms will be more challenging than with respect to the state, where constitutional, statutory, or regulatory provisions typically describe these relationships (although there is some international law jurisprudence finding state action by nongovernmental actors even in the absence of formal ties to the state[217]). Corporate theory

---

214. On the conceptual problems that arise as the corporate entity approaches the individual, see the Conclusion.

215. U.N. CHARTER art. 51; *ILC 2001 Draft Articles, supra* note 195, pt. I, ch. 1, art. 21.

216. *ILC 2001 Draft Articles, supra* note 195, pt. I, ch. 1, art. 7; *see also* 1 BROWNLIE, *supra* note 191, at 145-50 (citing numerous cases); 1 OPPENHEIM'S INTERNATIONAL LAW 545-48 (Robert Jennings & Arthur Watts eds., 9th ed. 1992) (same).

217. *See* United States Diplomatic and Consular Staff in Tehran (U.S. v. Iran), 1980 I.C.J. 3, 35 (May 24) (holding that hostage-takers were agents of Iran).

496 The Yale Law Journal [Vol. 111: 443

assists in understanding the numerous ways in which the business entity may be defined, inviting questions as to whether organs and entities empowered to exercise elements of corporate authority include subsidiaries, contractors, suppliers, distributors, or dedicated customers.[218]

3. *A Methodology for Deriving Norms of Corporate Responsibility*

The route to building a theory of corporate responsibility that does not simply ignore decades of practice and doctrine about state and individual responsibility is to recognize explicitly where decisionmakers could apply such principles to corporations and where they could not. This determination will turn on the similarity or differences between corporate behavior in the area of human rights and individual or state behavior. In essence, the challenge is to construct a theory both *down* from state responsibility and *up* from individual responsibility that, in the end, develops new primary and secondary rules. Some principles of state and individual responsibility (both primary and secondary rules) are quite similar, permitting us to rely upon them in the corporate context. Such a methodology acknowledges that, in general terms, a corporation is, as it were, more than an individual and less than a state.

Lastly, it bears mentioning that this process will have benefits beyond the corporate human rights context. In particular, the secondary rules derived here, especially the principles of attribution, would likely work with other primary rules, for example, with those concerning the environment. Although the goal of this project is not to develop a comprehensive set of secondary rules for corporations, an incidental benefit of the theory would be the creation of such rules.

V. CIRCUMSCRIBING CORPORATE DUTIES: A THEORY IN FOUR PARTS

Building upon these doctrinal foundations, the theory adopted here for developing a model of enterprise liability is based on an inductive approach that reflects the actual operations of business enterprises. It appraises the ways in which corporations might affect the human dignity of individuals and posits a theory that is sensitive to the corporations' diverse structures and modes of operating within a particular country. This theory asserts that corporate duties are a function of four clusters of issues: the corporation's relationship with the government, its nexus to affected populations, the

---

218. *See, e.g.,* PHILLIP I. BLUMBERG & KURT A. STRASSER, THE LAW OF CORPORATE GROUPS 9-18 (1998) (categorizing various relationships within the corporate group); Hugh Collins, *Ascription of Legal Responsibility to Groups in Complex Patterns of Economic Integration*, 53 MOD. L. REV. 731 (1990) (urging a revision of common-law principles of liability with respect to integrated economic enterprises).

particular human right at issue, and the place of individuals violating human rights within the corporate structure.

A. *The Company's Relationship to the Government*

As discussed above, the doctrine of state responsibility has recognized that the government may act through a variety of actors in breaching its international obligations. International decisionmakers evaluate the connections between these actors and the government to determine whether the state has violated international law.[219] The reverse applies as well, i.e., the ties between the government and the TNE play a major role in determining the obligations of the corporation. Where an enterprise has close ties to the government, it has prima facie a greater set of obligations in the area of human rights.[220] This proposition follows from the government's possession of the greatest set of resources capable of violating human dignity—police and military forces, with accompanying weapons, as well as judicial processes capable of curtailing human rights. It also reflects the likelihood that such ties reduce the state's desire and ability to regulate the conduct effectively, necessitating the recognition of responsibility under international law. The critical issue then becomes determining the sort of ties to the state that are relevant for deriving corporate duties. I begin my analysis from the standpoint of state responsibility rules that describe the consequences of ties between states and private actors; I then consider the relationships that states and corporations are most likely to have and the legal ramifications of these relationships for the company.

1. *State Responsibility—The Mirror Image*

As an initial matter, the extant rules of state responsibility that make the state liable for the acts of some private actors can provide for the responsibility of those private actors as well. That is, because the state is responsible for certain acts of private actors, those actors can also be held responsible for that same conduct under international law. This principle already has some basis in domestic law. For instance, certain important U.S. statutes hold private defendants civilly and criminally liable for violations of civil rights on the theory that such entities may be acting

---

219. *See, e.g.*, Military and Paramilitary Activities (Nicar. v. U.S.), 1986 I.C.J. 14 (June 27); Loizidou v. Turkey, 310 Eur. Ct. H.R. (ser. A) (1995).

220. *Cf.* Costello-Roberts v. United Kingdom, 247 Eur. Ct. H.R. (ser. A) 50, 58 (1993) (holding that a state cannot "absolve itself from responsibility by delegating its obligations to private bodies").

"under color of law."[221] U.S. courts have applied a variety of tests to determine whether the acts of private individuals were so closely linked with the state as to make them liable.[222] These cases demonstrate the rather obvious proposition that when a private entity acts, in some sense, on behalf of the state, it is as liable as the state for violations of human rights. In recent years, courts have applied these tests to determine whether acts of private corporations violate international law for purposes of the Alien Tort Claims Act (based on the view among those courts that most violations of international law require state action). For the most part, these tests set a relatively high standard, as a result of which plaintiffs have lost key cases alleging, for instance, that Unocal acted under color of law in Burma and Freeport acted under color of law in Indonesia.[223]

As significant as these cases are, any international law theory must transcend American notions of state action. International decisionmakers have also recognized a variety of ways in which private entities can become agents of the state. Some of these decisions do not entail affirmative findings of liability by the private actor because the particular forum—an international court or arbitral body—permits only suits against states; but other venues, such as international criminal courts, do reach such conclusions directly. Yet the multitude of arenas for law interpretation at the international level renders the task more difficult than simply restating clearly accepted principles of domestic law. I consider here three sets of relationships.

---

221. *E.g.*, 18 U.S.C. § 242 (1994); 42 U.S.C. § 1983 (1994). U.S. civil rights laws also prohibit various forms of private discrimination, although the constitutional basis for those provisions does not involve the Fourteenth Amendment and its requirement of state action. *See, e.g.*, Jones v. Alfred H. Mayer Co., 392 U.S. 409, 420-44 (1968) (holding that 42 U.S.C. § 1982, which bans racial discrimination in real property transactions, was a proper exercise of congressional power under the Thirteenth Amendment).

222. *Compare, e.g.*, Gallagher v. "Neil Young Freedom Concert," 49 F.3d 1442, 1447 (10th Cir. 1995) ("In order to establish state action, a plaintiff must demonstrate that the alleged deprivation of constitutional rights was 'caused by exercise of some right or privilege created by the State or by a rule of conduct imposed by the State or by a person for whom the State is responsible.'" (quoting Lugar v. Edmonson Oil Co., 457 U.S. 922, 937 (1982))), *with* George v. Pac.-CSC Work Furlough, 91 F.3d 1227, 1230 (9th Cir. 1996) ("'If a private actor is functioning as the government, that private actor becomes the state for purposes of state action.'" (quoting Gorenc v. Salt River Project Agric. Improvement & Power Dist., 869 F.2d 503, 508 (9th Cir. 1989))).

223. *See* Doe v. Unocal Corp., 110 F. Supp. 2d 1294, 1307 (C.D. Cal. 2000), *aff'd*, 248 F.3d 915 (9th Cir. 2001) ("In order to establish proximate cause, a plaintiff must prove that the private individuals exercised *control* over the government official's decision to commit the section 1983 violation."); Beanal v. Freeport-McMoRan, Inc., 969 F. Supp. 362 (E.D. La. 1997), *aff'd*, 193 F.3d 161 (5th Cir. 1999); *see also* Craig Forcese, Note, *ATCA's Achilles Heel: Corporate Complicity, International Law and the Alien Tort Claims Act*, 26 Yale J. Int'l L. 487 (2001) (examining shortcomings of the U.S. approach).

2. *Corporations as Governmental Agents*

Governments, international courts, and others have devoted significant time to appraising the legal implications of a state serving as a principal to private agents. A key issue here is the degree of control that a government must have over private actors in order to be responsible for their actions. In the *Nicaragua* case, the International Court of Justice held that the United States could be held responsible for the acts of the Contras in their war against the Nicaraguan government in the 1980s only if it had "effective control of the military or paramilitary operations in the course of which the alleged violations were committed."[224] In 1999, in *Prosecutor v. Tadic*, the first appeal brought before the International Criminal Tribunal for the Former Yugoslavia (ICTY), the Appeals Chamber had to determine whether the Bosnian Serb army was part of the armed forces of Serbia; a positive finding would mean that the war in Bosnia was an interstate war and would thereby trigger the protections of civilians in the 1949 Geneva Conventions and make certain breaches of that treaty war crimes. The court criticized the *Nicaragua* test and adopted a looser formula—that the acts of an armed group are attributable to a state as long as the state "has a role in organising, coordinating or planning the military actions" of the group, not necessarily controlling its particular operations.[225] At the same time, the Chamber said that the acts of nonmilitary private groups were attributable to the state only if "specific instructions concerning the commission of that particular act had been issued" by the state, or the state "publicly endorsed or approved ex post facto" the conduct, a test very close to the ICJ's *Nicaragua* test.[226]

In another forum, the European Court of Human Rights adopted an even looser test for attribution. It found Turkey responsible for the acts of the authorities of the self-styled "Turkish Republic of Northern Cyprus" on the basis of the Turkish army's "effective" and "overall" control of that part of the island.[227] The members of the International Law Commission, for their part, seem to favor the strictness of the *Nicaragua* test, with the ILC's latest proposal on state responsibility positing responsibility of the state if a person or group is "in fact acting on the instructions of, or under the direction or control of, that State in carrying out the conduct."[228]

As a least common denominator, then, if we posit that the responsibility of the principal entails the responsibility of the agent, this jurisprudence

---

224. Military and Paramilitary Activities (Nicar. v. U.S.), 1986 I.C.J. at 64-65.
225. Prosecutor v. Tadic, Case No. IT-94-I-A, para. 137 (Int'l Crim. Trib. for Former Yugoslavia Appeals Chamber July 15, 1999), http://www.un.org/icty/tadic/appeal/judgement/index.htm.
226. *Id.*
227. Loizidou v. Turkey, 310 Eur. Ct. H.R. (ser. A) at 23-24 (1995).
228. *ILC 2001 Draft Articles, supra* note 195, pt. I, ch. 1, art. 8.

means that private enterprises would be liable for human rights violations where the government has instructed them to engage in those violations. This may well have been the case with some of the World War II business defendants.[229] But as a practical matter, such a relationship probably characterizes a fairly small category of corporate activity, either because governments do not typically make many such bald requests or because corporations do not comply with them. It would, however, cover an episode where the government has asked a company, through its private security force, to detain someone for interrogation where there is reason to believe that the detention will lead to a violation of human dignity (e.g., torture, disappearance, summary execution, or unfair trial).

Beyond responsibility emanating from governmental control over the particular violator, the secondary rules of state responsibility also provide that the state is responsible if private groups more broadly exercise governmental authority as empowered by the law of the state, or in the absence or default of official authorities.[230] (U.S. law on state action recognizes similar tests.)[231] The first category covers a very important class of parastatal actors; while the second covers those filling in for the government, a situation that the doctrine has considered quite exceptional on the theory that governments do not typically relinquish such power.[232] Yet with respect to corporations, both scenarios prove more than speculative. The practices of South American states and Indonesia with respect to foreign corporations would appear to amount, in essence, to granting these companies de jure or de facto control over the areas of the concessions. Under this view, private corporations have duties to protect the human rights of those under their control when they exercise quasi-state authority. The extent of the duties would depend on the extent of control.

3. Corporations as Complicit with Governments

Beyond situations where the private entity is an agent—de facto or de jure—of the state, other links might characterize the state-enterprise relationship. International law also accepts notions of complicity, whereby one entity engages in otherwise lawful conduct that serves to aid other

---

229. See supra text accompanying notes 131-135.

230. Yeager v. Iran, 17 Iran-U.S. Cl. Trib. Rep. 92, 104 (1987); ILC 2001 Draft Articles, supra note 195, pt. I, ch. 1, arts. 5, 9.

231. See, e.g., Jackson v. Metro. Edison Co., 419 U.S. 345, 352-53 (1974) (recognizing state action where a private entity exercises powers traditionally reserved to the state, but finding that the defendant did not do so); Marsh v. Alabama, 326 U.S. 501 (1946) (determining that the freedoms of speech and religion apply in a company town).

232. James Crawford, First Report on State Responsibility: Addendum, U.N. GAOR, Int'l Law Comm'n, 50th Sess., paras. 217-221, U.N. Doc. A/CN.4/490/Add.5 (1998); 1980 ILC Report, supra note 194, art. 11.

entities in violating norms. With respect to state responsibility, numerous decisionmakers have held, either in the course of deriving or interpreting primary or secondary rules of conduct, that a state can be responsible for the acts of another state, based on a variety of tests involving its cooperation. Statements of the liability of states for complicity in illegal acts have emanated from decisions of the ICJ,[233] authoritative resolutions of the General Assembly and Security Council,[234] and ample state practice.[235] The ILC has attempted to codify such a standard too and has recently suggested that responsibility hinges upon a requirement that the state "aids or assists" another state "with knowledge of the circumstances" of the illegal act.[236]

The law on individual responsibility has long recognized notions of complicity as well. Thus, for example, Article III of the 1948 Genocide Convention states that conspiracy to commit genocide and complicity in genocide also constitute crimes.[237] The statutes of the International Criminal Tribunals for the Former Yugoslavia and for Rwanda make culpable those who "planned, instigated, ordered, committed or otherwise aided and abetted in the planning, preparation or execution" of one of the enumerated crimes.[238] The 1998 Statute of the International Criminal Court offers a detailed schema, providing for responsibility for a broad range of associated crimes, but conditioning guilt for certain of these crimes on completion of various acts or possession of various mental states.[239] The ICTY has interpreted its statute to mean that an accomplice is guilty if "his participation directly and substantially affected the commission of that

233. Legal Consequences for States of the Continued Presence of South Africa in Namibia (South West Africa) Notwithstanding Security Council Resolution 276 (1970), 1971 I.C.J. 15, 55-56 (June 21).

234. G.A. Res. 3314, U.N. GAOR, 29th Sess., Supp. No. 31, at 142-43, U.N. Doc. A/9631 (1974) (holding that "the action of a State in allowing its territory, which it has placed at the disposal of another State, to be used by that other State for perpetrating an act of aggression against a third State" constitutes illegal aggression); S.C. Res. 301, U.N. SCOR, 26th Sess., at 7-8, U.N. Doc. S/INF/27 (1971) (calling on states not to cooperate with South Africa's occupation of Namibia).

235. See the lengthy discussion in John Quigley, *Complicity in International Law: A New Direction in the Law of State Responsibility*, 57 BRIT. Y.B. INT'L L. 77 (1986).

236. *ILC 2001 Draft Articles, supra* note 195, pt. I, ch. 1, art. 16.

237. Genocide Convention, *supra* note 77, art. III, S. EXEC. DOC. O, 81-1, at 7, 78 U.N.T.S. at 280.

238. Statute of the International Criminal Tribunal for the Former Yugoslavia, art. 7(1), *annexed to Report of the Secretary General Pursuant to Paragraph 2 of Security Council Resolution 808 (1993)*, U.N. SCOR, 48th Sess., U.N. Doc. S/25704 (1993) [hereinafter ICTY Statute]; Statute of the International Criminal Tribunal for Rwanda, art. 6(1), *in* S.C. Res. 955, U.N. SCOR, 49th Sess., at 15, U.N. Doc. S/INF/50 (1994); *see also Report of the International Law Commission to the General Assembly on the Work of Its Forty-Eighth Session*, [1996] 2 Y.B. Int'l L. Comm'n, pt. 2, at 18-22 (reprinting Article 2 of the 1996 Draft Code of Crimes Against the Peace and Security of Mankind and showing seven categories of participation); Torture Convention, *supra* note 76, art. 4(1), S. TREATY DOC. NO. 100-20, at 20, 1465 U.N.T.S. at 114.

239. *See* ICC Statute, *supra* note 80, art. 25.

offence through supporting the actual commission before, during, or after the incident," and that guilt extends to "all that naturally results" from the act; as for mens rea, the court required that the defendant act with knowledge of the underlying act.[240]

Deriving duties of corporations from the law's recognition that states are responsible for their complicity in illegal acts by others states, and that individuals are responsible for complicity in illegal acts by other individuals, must be done with care. Nevertheless, at a minimum, both the state (civil) and individual (criminal) standards clearly recognize such responsibility as long as the underlying activity is illegal and the state or individual involved in the illegal activity has, in some sense, knowledge of it. With respect to corporate activity, this view would suggest that if a business materially contributes to a violation of human rights by the government with knowledge of that activity, it should be held responsible as a matter of international law—to put it conversely, that a business has a duty not to form such complicit relationships with governments.[241]

Such a standard does not suggest that any ties, or even any significant ties, between the government and the corporation per se create corporate responsibility for the government's acts (although other standards might suggest so). The international legal standards for complicity would, for instance, require a corporation not to lend its equipment to government forces with knowledge that it will be used to suppress human rights. Recognition of such duties would address many, perhaps most, of the ongoing concerns about corporate involvement in human rights abuses, for example, accusations of corporate involvement in harassment of government critics and loans of corporate equipment to military units suspected of human rights abuses.[242] But it would not require a corporation to divest, or not invest in the first place, in a country whose government

240. Prosecutor v. Tadic, Case No. IT-94-I-T, para. 692 (Int'l Crim. Trib. for Former Yugoslavia Trial Chamber II May 7, 1997), http://www.un.org/icty/tadic/trialc2/judgement/index.htm; *see* Prosecutor v. Aleksovski, Case No. IT-95-14/1-T, para. 61 (Int'l Crim. Trib. for Former Yugoslavia Trial Chamber I June 25, 1999), http://www.un.org/icty/aleksovski/trialc/judgement/index.htm; Prosecutor v. Delalic, Case No. IT-96-21-T, paras. 326-329 (Int'l Crim. Trib. for Former Yugoslavia Trial Chamber II Nov. 16, 1998), http://www.un.org/icty/celebici/trialc2/judgement/index.htm, *aff'd*, Case No. IT-96-21-A (Int'l Crim. Trib. for Former Yugoslavia Appeals Chamber Feb. 20, 2001), http://www.un.org/icty/celebici/appeal/judgement/index.htm; Prosecutor v. Kayishema, Case No. ICTR-95-1-T, paras. 191-207 (Int'l Crim. Trib. for Rwanda Trial Chamber II May 21, 1999), http://www.ictr.org; Prosecutor v. Akayesu, Case No. ICTR-96-4-T, paras. 474-484 (Int'l Crim. Trib. for Rwanda Trial Chamber I Sept. 2, 1998), http://www.ictr.org.

241. To the extent that regional human rights courts have derived from the duty of states to protect human rights a duty to protect citizens against abuse by private actors, *see supra* text accompanying notes 94-100, complicity in such a failure would also engender responsibility.

242. *See, e.g.*, HUMAN RIGHTS WATCH, *supra* note 5, § VII (alleging use of a company helicopter); Neela Banerjee, *Lawsuit Says Exxon Aided Rights Abuses*, N.Y. TIMES, June 21, 2001, at C1; Paul Lewis, *After Nigeria Represses, Shell Defends Its Record*, N.Y. TIMES, Feb. 13, 1996, at A1.

abuses its citizens. Nor would it require, for instance, a paper company (or a soft drink company for that matter) to stop selling to a governmental bureaucracy that violates human rights insofar as this activity does not "directly and substantially" contribute to the violations. Nor would it even suggest that close personal or business ties between the government and the TNE give rise to the latter's responsibility. More would have to be shown than such loose ties.[243]

Indeed, these sorts of distinctions proved critical to the South African Truth and Reconciliation Commission's appraisal of the role of business in apartheid. The Commission drew lines establishing three levels of involvement: (1) companies that "played a central role in helping design and implement" apartheid, in particular, mining firms; (2) companies "that made their money by engaging directly in activities that promoted state repression," with knowledge thereof, such as the arms industry; and (3) companies that "benefited indirectly by virtue of operating" in apartheid society.[244] The TRC found the first two levels reprehensible per se and thereby rejected many claims by business leaders of innocence based on their nonstate status.[245] Yet its nuanced conclusions regarding other businesses reflected an appreciation of the extent to which apartheid clearly benefited them and of the complexity of business interactions with the government.[246] In the end, while concluding that government and business "co-operated in the building of an economy that benefited whites,"[247] it rejected both a condemnation of all business people as collaborators as well as an exculpation of them for taming and helping end the system.[248] Although the TRC was not in a position to impose—or eliminate—legal, let alone criminal, liability upon corporations,[249] its sophisticated analysis represents an important element of state practice in favor of a duty on corporations to avoid complicit relationships.

One could go much further than the existing norms of international law for deriving corporate duties—for instance, by working from a moral starting point that a corporation has a duty not to invest at all in a repressive society, or a duty to ensure that it does not in any way benefit from the

---

243. *Cf.* Beanal v. Freeport-McMoRan, Inc., 969 F. Supp. 362 (E.D. La. 1997) (dismissing claims because of the plaintiff's failure to allege sufficient ties between actual abuses by the government and Freeport), *aff'd*, 197 F.3d 161 (5th Cir. 1999).

244. 4 TRUTH & RECONCILIATION COMM'N, *supra* note 4, ch. 2, paras. 23, 26, 28, 32.

245. *See* Beth S. Lyons, *Getting to Accountability: Business, Apartheid and Human Rights*, 17 NETH. Q. HUM. RTS. 135, 144-54 (1999).

246. 4 TRUTH & RECONCILIATION COMM'N, *supra* note 4, ch. 2, paras. 81-147.

247. 4 *id.* ch. 2, para. 97.

248. 4 *id.* ch. 2, paras. 140-147.

249. Section 20 of Promotion of National Unity and National Reconciliation Act 34 of 1995 (S. Afr.) (limiting the amnesty provisions to individuals).

government's lax human rights policy.[250] During the years of apartheid, many states and nonstate actors asserted such a duty with respect to South Africa, resulting in the divestment of many corporations from that country.[251] And those opposing investment in Burma today might well be seeking to advance such a legal duty. A note of caution, however, is required. To the extent that international actors have accepted the notion of complicity, they have generally hinged it on the direct involvement of the individual or state in violations of law. To extend complicity to corporations seems a reasonable—although, certainly in the view of many, unorthodox—step in the development of international norms.[252] To ignore completely the extant notions of legal responsibility in favor of a concept of accomplice liability that has little support in state practice risks defeating the entire enterprise.[253] I do not wish to exclude such responsibility as a possibility for the future, nor would I advise corporations to develop ties with repressive regimes that fall short of legal complicity.[254] But this version of corporate responsibility would need to derive from an acceptance by governments and other actors of a broader notion of complicity than they have expressed to date.

4. Corporations as Commanders?

The need for care in transposing notions of individual responsibility into the corporate area is demonstrated by a special, significant form of culpability that international law recognizes for acts of omission—the doctrine of superior or command responsibility. It extends the liability of a military commander or civilian superior for acts of subordinates beyond those covered through the notion of accomplice liability to those where the superior plays a more passive role by failing to prevent certain actions of

---

250. *See, e.g.,* AMNESTY INT'L & PAX CHRISTI INT'L, *supra* note 57, at 51 ("To accept the benefits of measures by governments or local authorities to improve the business climate which themselves constitute violations of human rights, makes a company a party to those violations."); HUMAN RIGHTS WATCH, *supra* note 5, at 105 ("Complicity occurs . . . when corporations benefit from the failure of government to enforce human rights standards.").

251. *See supra* note 166 and accompanying text.

252. See *infra* Section V.C for a discussion of corporate responsibility for acts without governmental conduct.

253. *Cf.* The Global Compact: From Policy to Practice: Human Rights, *at* http://www.unglobalcompact.org/un/gc/unweb.nsf/content/trhr2.htm (last visited Oct. 20, 2001) (noting decisions by some states and governments not to invest in repressive states or use their influence "have not yet yielded a commonly-accepted guideline for determining whether and how companies can operate in countries where human rights violations are widespread").

254. *See* ANDREW CLAPHAM & SCOTT JERBI, TOWARDS A COMMON UNDERSTANDING OF BUSINESS COMPLICITY IN HUMAN RIGHTS ABUSES (2001), *at* http://www.globaldimensions.net/ articles/cr/complicity.html (noting that companies need to avoid accusations of direct complicity, indirect complicity, and silent complicity); Margaret Jungk, *A Practical Guide to Addressing Human Rights Concerns for Companies Operating Abroad, in* HUMAN RIGHTS STANDARDS AND THE RESPONSIBILITIES OF TRANSNATIONAL CORPORATIONS, *supra* note 187, at 171, 177-78.

subordinates. The rationale for such responsibility is that, by virtue of a hierarchical relationship between superior and subordinate, the former should be held criminally liable for failure to exercise his duties when the result is the commission of offenses by subordinates. In general, the doctrine holds that a superior is responsible for the acts of subordinates if (1) he knew or should have known that the subordinate had committed, or was about to commit, the acts, and (2) he did not take necessary and reasonable measures to prevent the acts or punish the subordinate.[255] This general starting point nonetheless leaves unanswered numerous questions regarding the precise scope of the superior's responsibility, including the definition of a superior[256] and the scope of his duty to be aware of activities by subordinates.[257]

NGOs have made claims against corporations based on the corporations' failure to inform themselves of certain conduct by the government.[258] Because all traditional forms of complicity assume knowledge of the illegal activity, the NGO claims stem essentially from a notion of superior responsibility. And inherent in such a claim is the belief that the company is effectively the superior and the state the agent. This starting point flips the traditional doctrine of state responsibility on its head insofar as the law generally works from the presumption that nonstate actors are the agents rather than the principal.[259] But it may accurately reflect some enterprise-state relations. If, for instance, the company utilized governmental forces to maintain security around the perimeter of a mine,

---

255. For excellent overviews, see Ilias Bantekas, *The Contemporary Law of Superior Responsibility*, 93 AM. J. INT'L L. 573 (1999); L.C. Green, *Command Responsibility in International Humanitarian Law*, 5 TRANSNAT'L L. & CONTEMP. PROBS. 319 (1995); and William H. Parks, *Command Responsibility for War Crimes*, 62 MIL. L. REV. 1 (1973).

256. *See, e.g.*, Prosecutor v. Delalic, Case No. IT-96-21-A, paras. 188-198 (Int'l Crim. Trib. for Former Yugoslavia Appeals Chamber Feb. 20, 2001), http://www.un.org/icty/celebici/appeal/judgement/index.htm; Prosecutor v. Blaskic, Case No. IT-95-14-T, paras. 300-301 (Int'l Crim. Trib. for Former Yugoslavia Trial Chamber I Mar. 3, 2000), http://www.un.org/icty/blaskic/trialc1/judgement/index.htm; Prosecutor v. Kayishema, Case No. ICTR-95-1-T, paras. 217-223 (Int'l Crim. Trib. for Rwanda Trial Chamber II May 21, 1999), http://www.ictr.org.

257. *Compare* Protocol Additional to the Geneva Conventions of 12 August 1949, and Relating to the Protection of Victims of International Armed Conflicts, *adopted* June 8, 1977, art. 86(2), 1125 U.N.T.S. 3, 43 (imposing liability on those who "knew, or had information which should have enabled them to conclude in the circumstances at the time" of the activities), *with* ICC Statute, *supra* note 80, art. 28(a)(i) (imposing liability on military commanders if they "either knew or, owing to the circumstances at the time, should have known" of the activities), *and id.* art. 28(b)(i) (imposing liability on other superiors who "either knew, or consciously disregarded information which clearly indicated" that a crime was being committed). *See also* Prosecutor v. Delalic, Case No. IT-96-21-A, paras. 235-241 (Int'l Crim. Trib. for Former Yugoslavia Appeals Chamber Feb. 20, 2001), http://www.un.org/icty/celebici/appeal/judgement/index.htm (finding a superior responsible only where the superior had information putting him on notice of subordinates' offenses).

258. *See, e.g.*, HUMAN RIGHTS WATCH, *supra* note 6, pt. IX, at 6 (stating that oil companies have the responsibility to "monitor security force activity in the oil producing region"); HUMAN RIGHTS WATCH, *supra* note 5, at 110-11.

259. *See supra* notes 224-228 and accompanying text.

506   The Yale Law Journal   [Vol. 111: 443

and those forces engaged in serious human rights abuses, one can speak of a form of superior responsibility of the company for the acts of the governmental forces.[260] Utilizing, as an example, the standard in the ICC Statute for the responsibility of civilian superiors for acts of subordinates, the corporation would be liable for acts of those under its "effective authority and control" where it "knew, or consciously disregarded information which clearly indicated, that the subordinates were committing or about to commit such crimes" and where "the crimes concerned activities that were within the effective responsibility and control of the superior."[261]

Determining "effective responsibility and control" and what sort of information "clearly indicates" the commission of human rights abuses is, of course, no simple matter. Hard cases would arise if, for instance, the business agreed to invest in exchange for a government promise to "secure" (so to speak) an area from opponents of the investment or the regime, and if the investor knew what that term in fact meant. Human rights NGOs involved in the drafting of the Rome Statute found even its standard of knowledge too high.[262] Indeed, if my theory is to derive a set of duties applying to corporations generally rather than simply those duties that give rise to criminal liability, a lower standard of knowledge seems justifiable, one more akin to the negligence standard imposed on military commanders.[263] But, regardless of how these details are resolved, command responsibility itself seems a justifiable basis for corporate duties in situations where corporations are indeed superiors to governmental actors.

B. *The Corporation's Nexus to Affected Populations*

The second element in a theory of corporate responsibility arises from a fundamental distinction between states and companies. States generally have human rights obligations toward all persons on their territory, although some duties do not run to nonnationals.[264] This stems from an assumption that governmental control and jurisdiction is determined on a territorial basis. For TNEs, however, a territorial scope for determining the

---

260. For a practical set of principles for corporations reflecting these ideas, see PWBLF & AI, *supra* note 63, at 13, 45-47.

261. ICC Statute, *supra* note 80, art. 28(b).

262. *See, e.g.*, Amnesty Int'l, The International Criminal Court: Making the Right Choices— Part V: Recommendations to the Diplomatic Conference 43 (Jan. 5, 1998), *at* http://www.amnesty.org/ailib/index.html; Human Rights Watch, Summary of the Key Provisions of the ICC Statute § 8 (Sept. 1998), *at* http://www.hrw.org/campaigns/icc/docs/icc-statute.htm.

263. ICC Statute, *supra* note 80, art. 28(a)(i) (finding guilt when a commander "knew or, owing to the circumstances at the time, should have known" of abuses).

264. *See, e.g.*, ICCPR, *supra* note 129, art. 25, S. Exec. Doc. E, 95-2, at 30-31, 999 U.N.T.S. at 179 (limiting the right to participate in public affairs to citizens); ICESCR, *supra* note 177, art. 2(3), 993 U.N.T.S. at 5 (allowing developing-world states to limit economic rights to nationals).

universe of relevant rightholders will not work insofar as businesses do not exercise such a geographically fixed form of jurisdiction. Therefore, the determination of enterprise duties must address the company's links with individuals possessing human rights. My analysis of this factor is grounded in premises from moral philosophy about interpersonal duties and is buttressed by extant international practice.

The extent to which obligations of one actor toward other actors turn on the former's ties with the latter has engaged moral philosophers for centuries.[265] Contemporary scholars have framed the debate in terms of partiality and impartiality. In its purist (and indeed most extreme or absurd) form, impartiality is seen by its supporters to flow inevitably from Kant's Categorical Imperative and to endorse equal treatment of all persons under all circumstances (regardless of family or group connections); partiality, on the other hand, would favor overt identification with close relatives and limited moral duties toward others.[266] Nonetheless, many philosophers have rejected pure impartiality as unrealistic and pure partiality as immoral, and have instead found common ground that explicitly acknowledges the morality of certain preferences toward family, community, association, or country. Arguing in different ways, scholars such as Alan Gewirth and Brian Barry have shown that partialist conceptions of duties are not inconsistent with—and indeed can flow from—an overall moral theory of impartiality and equal respect for all persons.[267] Communitarian political philosophers such as Michael Walzer and Yael Tamir have adopted similar ideas to demonstrate how liberalism and nationalism need not collide.[268] Without delving into the philosophical differences among these and other thinkers, the overall conclusion remains that the idea of equal respect for all humans, central in human rights theory and law, is consistent with the notion that, under certain circumstances, individuals and institutions owe

---

265. For the debate among classical schools, see JULIA ANNAS, THE MORALITY OF HAPPINESS 249-90 (1993), which discusses Aristotelian and Stoic views of self-concern and other-concern, and John Cottingham, *The Ethics of Self-Concern*, 101 ETHICS 798 (1991), which discusses Christian and Continental thinkers.

266. For helpful reviews of the modern debate, see Marilyn Friedman, *The Practice of Partiality*, 101 ETHICS 818 (1991); Barbara Herman, *Agency, Attachment, and Difference*, 101 ETHICS 775 (1991); and Hugh LaFollette, *Personal Relationships, in* A COMPANION TO ETHICS 327 (Peter Singer ed., 1993). The principal modern advocate of the partialist stance is Bernard Williams. *See* BERNARD WILLIAMS, MORAL LUCK (1981).

267. *See, e.g.,* BRIAN BARRY, JUSTICE AS IMPARTIALITY 217-33 (1995); Alan Gewirth, *Ethical Universalism and Particularism*, 85 J. PHIL. 283 (1988); *see also* ROBERT E. GOODIN, PROTECTING THE VULNERABLE 109-44 (1985) (grounding duties in the need to protect those vulnerable to our acts).

268. MICHAEL WALZER, SPHERES OF JUSTICE 31-46 (1983); *see also* YAEL TAMIR, LIBERAL NATIONALISM 95-116 (1993) (arguing for the "morality of community"); WALZER, *supra*, at 33 ("People who do share a common life have much stronger duties."); *cf.* IMMANUEL KANT, THE METAPHYSICS OF MORALS 89-90 (Mary Gregor ed. & trans., Cambridge Univ. Press 1996) (1797) (describing the need for a system of law because of the proximity of people to one another).

greater duties to those with whom they have special associative ties than to others beyond that sphere.

In the corporate context, this premise argues for viewing the ties as falling within concentric circles emanating from the enterprise, with spheres enlarging from employees to their families, to the citizens of a given locality otherwise affected by their operation (admittedly a broad and amorphous category), and eventually to an entire country. This, of course, represents an oversimplification in the case of TNEs, since by their very nature they operate in different localities and different countries. But in general, as the circles widen, the duties of the corporation will diminish. In Gewirth's terms, these circles represent social groupings, with the bonds (and corresponding intra-group structures and rules) strongest among the corporation and its employees and weaker with respect to other communities. (Certain members of the groupings, such as neighbors of a plant, may not have chosen to be part of the social group, just as family members do not choose to be a part of a social group, but this does not diminish—indeed it arguably increases—the enterprise's duties toward them.)[269]

The nexus factor thus suggests, all other things being equal, that as the proximity of the corporation to individuals—the extent to which the enterprise and the population form a meaningful association—lessens, the duties of the corporation toward those individuals lessen as well. For example, the ICCPR's requirement that the law prohibit any discrimination based on "race, colour, sex, language, religion, political or other opinion, national or social origin, property, birth or other status"[270] would suggest a duty upon corporations not to discriminate on these grounds in their employment practices—their relations with the group enjoying the closest nexus to the corporation.[271]

Moving further out in the spheres of influence, the corporation's duties to its customers might well suggest an obligation to ensure that the product is sold (perhaps through its franchisers or distributors) in a way that does not entail those invidious forms of discrimination. At a certain point, however, the nexus to the affected population fails to generate duties concerning this right—it would be difficult to conclude, for example, that the corporation has a duty to ensure that its product is sold in all parts of the

---

269. Gewirth, *supra* note 267, at 292-94.

270. ICCPR, *supra* note 129, art. 26, S. EXEC. DOC. E, 95-2, at 31, 999 U.N.T.S. at 179; *see also* General Comment No. 18, para. 12, *in Report of the Human Rights Committee*, U.N. GAOR, 45th Sess., Supp. No. 40, vol. I, Annex VI, at 173, 175, U.N. Doc. A/44/40 (1990) (noting that the article "prohibits discrimination in law or in fact in any field regulated and protected by public authorities").

271. I leave aside here the question of how the content of a given right affects the particular duties on corporations and how they may be different from the duties on states, an issue discussed *infra* Section V.C.

country in order to ensure access for all different religious, national, or social groups.

The nexus factor might also have a purely territorial element to it, such that a corporation's duties depend upon the extent to which the corporation physically controls a certain area. Thus, where the enterprise effectively manages a particular piece of territory, as in the case of mineral or timber concessions, it would have a certain, presumably larger, set of duties to those living within that territory, distinct from those to persons living outside it. The enterprise operates as a quasi-state whose special obligations to those under its control are accepted in both moral philosophy and international law doctrine.[272] On the other hand, insofar as the corporation has important ties with persons within a broader area, it would have some duties to them as well. For instance, if the activities of the corporation poisoned the only supply of drinking water of an adjacent area, then the human right to "the highest attainable standard of physical and mental health"[273] would appear to place some duties on the corporation to prevent or respond to such damage.[274] Similar examples might apply to the duties of the corporation to those persons in the immediate vicinity of a factory as compared to those living further away from it.

States have already accepted this concept through the development of international labor standards. Whatever one's view on whether those treaties place direct or merely indirect duties on companies, their promulgation by institutions such as the ILO suggests that governments, labor unions, and business leaders view the sphere of employer-employee relations as an appropriate target for detailed international regulation (one that, as noted, preceded the international human rights movement by a generation). International law has not, for the most part, extended these duties to cover larger spheres potentially influenced by private enterprises, although ILO Convention No. 169 Concerning Indigenous and Tribal Peoples in Independent Countries,[275] while principally drafted to impose

---

272. See TAMIR, supra note 268, at 111-16; Legal Consequences for States of the Continued Presence of South Africa in Namibia (South West Africa) Notwithstanding Security Council Resolution 276 (1970), 1971 I.C.J. 16, 54 (June 21) ("Physical control of a territory, and not sovereignty or legitimacy of title, is the basis of State liability for acts affecting other States.").

273. ICESCR, supra note 177, art. 12, 993 U.N.T.S. at 8.

274. As discussed infra Section V.C, the precise duties remain somewhat unclear, because the Covenant's recognition of the right does not equate with a requirement on states to guarantee the right. Rather, the obligations of the state are much more ones of best efforts. See ICESCR, supra note 177, art. 2(1), 993 U.N.T.S. at 5 (requiring the state to "take steps . . . to the maximum of its available resources, with a view to achieving progressively the full realization of the rights" in the Covenant); General Comment No. 3, supra note 200 (providing an interpretation of the idea of progressive realization). For key cases under tort law, see Dow Chemical Co. v. Castro Alfaro, 786 S.W.2d 674 (Tex. 1990), cert. denied, 498 U.S. 1024 (1991); and Charan Lal Sahu v. Union of India, 118 I.L.R. 452 (India 1989).

275. Convention Concerning Indigenous and Tribal Peoples in Independent Countries, adopted June 27, 1989, http://ilolex.ilo.ch:1567/english/convdisp2.htm.

obligations on governments, does at least hint of corporate duties toward those groups.[276]

More recently, the United Nations, the OECD, the EU, and human rights and corporate NGOs have endorsed such an approach. For instance, the UN Secretary-General, in establishing in 1999 the UN's Global Compact program (a joint project of the UN and world business leaders), noted two distinct sets of duties of corporations: to respect human rights "within their sphere of influence" and to avoid being "complicit in human rights abuses"[277]—the latter term referring to corporate involvement in governmental action. The OECD's 2000 Code of Conduct for TNEs urges companies to "[r]espect the human rights of those affected by their activities consistent with the host government's international obligations and commitments."[278] The European Commission's Directorate of Employment and Social Affairs has noted, in the context of the reach of corporate codes of conduct, that "[w]hat seems to matter is the degree of control a company has over the employment conditions of all workers employed by its subcontractors."[279] Both Amnesty International and the Prince of Wales Business Leaders Forum have distinguished corporate responsibility for a company's own operations from duties extending to the broader environment in the state.[280]

But is there a circularity here? Are these institutions and I simply asserting that as long as the corporation engages in activities that trigger duties, it will have duties? Is not the notion of ties so amorphous that the spheres themselves are not fixed but merely move with the given human right? For example, what happens if corporate agents were physically to attack persons who were seemingly unrelated to the company's operations but were in fact representing some sort of threat to the company? Would the theory argue that these persons are beyond some objective sphere of influence and thus the corporation owes no duty to them, or that the

---

276. *Id.* art. 15 ("The rights of the peoples concerned to the natural resources pertaining to their lands shall be specially safeguarded."); *id.* art. 16 ("[T]he peoples concerned shall not be removed from the lands which they occupy.").

277. The Global Compact: The Nine Principles, *at* http://www.unglobalcompact.org/un/gc/unweb.nsf/content/thenine.htm (last visited Oct. 20, 2001).

278. 2000 OECD Guidelines, *supra* note 184, § II.2.

279. Eur. Comm'n Directorate for Employment & Soc. Affairs, *Codes of Conduct and Social Labels*, EUR. SOC. DIALOGUE, May 1999, at 7, http://www.europa.eu.int/comm/employment_social/soc-dial/social/newsletter/special_en.pdf.

280. AMNESTY INT'L, HUMAN RIGHTS PRINCIPLES FOR COMPANIES (1998), *at* http://www.amnesty.org; PWBLF & AI, *supra* note 63, at 28-29; *see also* AMNESTY INT'L & PAX CHRISTI INT'L, *supra* note 57, at 47-54 (noting three "levels of influence": (1) where the TNE has "control," (2) where it "can exercise influence over a situation," and (3) where it "can contribute to the creation of an enabling environment"); INT'L COUNCIL ON HUMAN RIGHTS POLICY, *supra* note 101, paras. 161-163 (describing the spectrum of potential victims from employees and consumers to broader society); Douglass Cassel, *Corporate Initiatives: A Second Human Rights Revolution?*, 19 FORDHAM INT'L L.J. 1963, 1981-84 (1996) (proposing five "gradations of responsibility").

corporation would have effectively extended its sphere of influence, and thus the violation of their physical integrity would render the company liable? The theory addresses this question in the important "all other things being equal" qualification to the premise noted above. In general, the corporation's duties can be defined in spheres. However, there may well be circumstances (or certain rights) for which the spheres of influence factor is irrelevant. Gewirth and Raz, for instance, have both written of certain absolute rights, such that, in the former's words, "agents and institutions are absolutely prohibited from degrading persons, treating them as if they had no rights or dignity."[281] For such rights, the corporation may well have equal duties toward all.

C. *The Substantive Rights at Issue*

Once decisionmakers identify the corporation's connections to the government and to affected populations, they must turn to the nature of the right being impinged. For any particular human right may well place a different set of duties upon a corporation than the sort of duties that the primary rules of state responsibility place on states. I argue below that, for those rights that business enterprises can infringe, corporate duties turn on a balancing of individual rights with business interests and rights. This approach circumscribes corporate duties in a manner that considers the nature of business activity.

1. *Can the Corporation Infringe the Right?*

A preliminary issue in appraising how particular rights give rise to duties is whether the corporation can even have a duty with respect to all human rights. As discussed above in Part IV regarding primary and secondary rules, for some human rights, the government represents the principal dutyholder insofar as only the government can directly infringe upon those rights. Thus, I sought to differentiate between those sorts of rights that the corporation can directly infringe and those that only the government can directly infringe, for example, between the right against cruel, inhuman, or degrading treatment and the right to cross-examination in criminal trials.[282] The duties of the corporation with regard to the latter

---

281. Alan Gewirth, *Are There Any Absolute Rights?*, *in* THEORIES OF RIGHTS 91, 108 (Jeremy Waldron ed., 1984); *see also* RAZ, *supra* note 82, at 182 (observing that some rights, such as personal security, are against the world while others are against "certain persons in virtue of a special relation they have to the right-holder").

282. *See supra* text accompanying notes 205-206; *see also* ICCPR, *supra* note 129, arts. 7, 14, S. EXEC. DOC. E, 95-2, at 25, 27-28, 999 U.N.T.S. at 175-77; *cf.* Torture Convention, *supra* note 76, art. 1(1), S. TREATY DOC. NO. 100-20, at 19, 1465 U.N.T.S. at 113-14 (defining torture

are only the complicity-based duties discussed in Section V.A above. Thus, for those rights that only the government can directly infringe, the links between the corporation and government (the first factor in the theory) are a necessary factor for the derivation of company duties. Indeed, the links with the government would seem to be a sufficient factor for determining enterprise duties so that the issue of the corporation's nexus to the victims (the factor in Section V.B above) becomes irrelevant. In such cases, the state is violating the rights of its citizens, and the enterprise has a duty not to be complicit in this effort, whether the affected population consists of its own employees or individuals far from its normal sphere of influence.

Which other rights belong in this category? In addition to many rights concerning criminal defendants, others would include the right to enter one's country without arbitrary restrictions; the right of a child to nationality, registration, and a name; the right to marry; the right to vote and run for office; and the right to equality before the law.[283] Of course, the scope of this list can itself be the subject of some dispute. Purists opposed to a notion of corporate duties might argue that the vast majority of human rights, especially in the civil and political realm, are capable of being violated only by the state. They might argue that the right to leave one's country can be directly infringed only by the state (through its interior ministry or immigration bureaucracy) and that it therefore gives rise to corporate duties only through the notion of complicity.[284] Yet private actors are capable, through physical force, of preventing their employees from leaving the country, as the problem of forced prostitution makes clear.[285]

But what of the large number of rights that do not belong in this category, that is, those that are capable of direct infringement by private actors and corporate entities, as well as by the state?[286] As a preliminary matter, it bears clarifying that the complicity-based duties that arise when the government can directly abuse rights also arise when both the government and the corporation can abuse the rights. As long as the state can violate the right, the corporation has a duty not to be complicit in such conduct.

---

that states are required to punish as that with a nexus to state action, though the perpetrator need not be a governmental official).

283. ICCPR, *supra* note 129, arts. 12(4), 23(2), 24, 25(b), 26, S. EXEC. DOC. E, 95-2, at 27, 30-31, 999 U.N.T.S. at 176, 179.

284. *See id.* art. 12(2), S. EXEC. DOC. E, 95-2, at 27, 999 U.N.T.S. at 176.

285. *See generally* ASIA WATCH & THE WOMEN'S RIGHTS PROJECT, A MODERN FORM OF SLAVERY (1993) (discussing the trafficking of Burmese women and children to Thailand for prostitution); Janie Chuang, *Redirecting the Debate over Trafficking in Women: Definitions, Paradigms, and Contexts*, 11 HARV. HUM. RTS. J. 65 (1998) (discussing the trafficking of women beyond prostitution).

286. At least one right in the ICCPR, while it can be infringed by both state and corporation, seems to place duties primarily on private actors—the right against slavery and forced labor. ICCPR, *supra* note 129, art. 8, S. EXEC. DOC. E, 95-2, at 25-26, 999 U.N.T.S. at 175.

More important, because other human rights are capable of direct infringement by business actors, they give rise to obligations on those actors beyond the duty to avoid complicity in the government's violation of them. But in order to derive the duties from all those other rights—whether the right to life, liberty, and security of the person, to free association, free assembly, and free speech, or to participation in public affairs—we need to take into account the differences between corporations and states, as well as the various types of duties that can arise from the same right.

2. The Imperative of Balancing Interests

Human rights law is generally based on a balancing between the interests of the state and the rights of the individual. As Raz notes from a jurisprudential perspective, a right does not simply translate into some corresponding duty. Rather, "[i]t is the ground of a duty, ground which, if not counteracted by conflicting considerations, justifies holding that other person to have the duty." [287] The ICCPR (and its regional counterparts in Europe and Latin America) identifies these interests—national security (including preservation of the nation in the event of a national emergency), public order, public health or morals, and the rights or freedoms of others—although it also recognizes that some rights cannot be suspended under any circumstances. [288] Business enterprises, however, have different goals and interests that fundamentally rest on the need to maintain a profitable income stream. To talk about duties of business entities vis-à-vis individuals necessitates taking into account not only the rights of the individuals, but also these interests. Indeed, as noted earlier, businesses themselves have some human rights, including privacy and association rights that, when exercised, inevitably have an impact upon individuals with whom they interact. [289]

Consequently, the company's responsibility must, as an initial matter, turn on a balancing of the individual right at issue with the enterprise's interests and on the nexus between its actions and the preservation of its interests. Such a view simply parallels the basic notion of human rights law that the state may limit many rights to the extent "necessary in a democratic

---

287. RAZ, *supra* note 82, at 171; *cf.* Dennis v. United States, 341 U.S. 494, 524-25 (1951) (Frankfurter, J., concurring) ("The demands of free speech in a democratic society as well as the interest in national security are better served by candid and informed weighing of the competing interests . . . .").

288. *See, e.g.*, ICCPR, *supra* note 129, arts. 4, 12(3), S. EXEC. DOC. E, 95-2, at 24, 27, 999 U.N.T.S. at 174, 176.

289. *See supra* note 187 and accompanying text; *see also* Andrew Clapham, *The "Drittwirkung" of the Convention, in* THE EUROPEAN SYSTEM FOR THE PROTECTION OF HUMAN RIGHTS 163, 202-03 (R. St. J. Macdonald et al. eds., 1993) (discussing theoretical difficulties of duties on entities other than states).

society," with its concomitant notion of proportionality between means and ends.[290] To give a simple example, the right to free speech requires governments to refrain from penalizing individuals for speech critical of the government (as well as much other speech);[291] but it would not require a company to refrain from penalizing employees for public speech that insults the company to consumers, lures away employees, or gives away trade secrets, since these actions impinge on core interests of the company. In general, however, it would bar a company from taking disciplinary measures against an employee for his speech critical of the government.

Just as domestic constitutional courts, regional human rights courts, and UN human rights bodies grapple with determining the limits of lawful governmental interference with individual liberties, so the balancing of corporate interests and individual rights may prove difficult. For example, with respect to the right against arbitrary or unlawful interference with privacy, family, home, or correspondence, a corporation would not be able to use its resources to break into anyone's home, wiretap conversations there, or intercept mail, since the means are disproportionate to the ends.[292] The corporation would not, however, be violating the human rights of employees by videotaping them surreptitiously while on the job in order to prevent pilfering of products.

Decisionmakers would also apply the balancing test if the corporation's rights were at issue. One difficult example would concern whether a media company's rights to free speech violated the individual's right to privacy if it published embarrassing information about celebrities, politicians, or criminal suspects. One might argue that the individual is too far removed from the corporation—that their associative ties are too weak—to create any duties in the latter. Some decisionmakers might, however, regard their ties (given the nature and purpose of the media company's business) as close enough to justify corporate duties; in that case, they would have to balance the reputational harm to the individual against the right of a business to speak.[293] This individual rights/business rights balancing—what might be called horizontal balancing—seems by its nature more difficult than the individual rights/business interests—i.e., vertical—balancing more akin to the sort done by human rights bodies and domestic constitutional

290. *See, e.g.*, ICCPR, *supra* note 129, art. 21, S. EXEC. DOC. E, 95-2, at 29-30, 999 U.N.T.S. at 178; European Convention for the Protection of Human Rights and Fundamental Freedoms, Nov. 4, 1950, art. 9(2), 213 U.N.T.S. 221, 230; Silver v. United Kingdom, 61 Eur. Ct. H.R. (ser. A) at 37-38 (1983).

291. *See, e.g.*, Lingens Case, 103 Eur. Ct. H.R. (ser. A) at 36-38 (1986) (discussing a journalist's right to criticize a government official).

292. *Cf.* General Comment No. 16, para. 8, *in Report of the Human Rights Committee*, U.N. GAOR, 43rd Sess., Supp. No. 40, Annex VI, at 181, 182, U.N. Doc. A/43/40 (1988) (discussing a state's responsibilities during searches).

293. *Cf.* RAZ, *supra* note 82, at 170 ("In matters of libel, the right to free expression may be completely defeated by the interests of people in their reputation.").

courts. Yet the former sort of balancing takes place all the time when legislatures and courts grapple with issues of libel and other so-called private law.[294] Indeed, the use of the third-party effect doctrine by German and Dutch courts as well as by the European Court of Justice in cases concerning exclusively private parties suggests that balancing that considers the rights (or interests) of private parties faces no larger theoretical bar than do the more paradigmatic cases of balancing governmental interests with individual rights.[295]

In the end, the balancing test offers a uniform approach for those deriving specific corporate duties—whether through domestic statute, treaty, or soft law. Of course, one set of decisionmakers, such as a legislature, might prove unwilling to do the balancing itself, leaving the final determinations to administrative officials or courts. That balancing does not guarantee uniform outcomes is no more an argument against corporate duties than it is against governmental duties in the human rights area, which are derived by the same methodology and may assume different contours from region to region.

Beyond balancing, certain rights with which the state may never interfere—such as the right to life and physical integrity and the rights against torture, slavery, or debt imprisonment—would be just as nonderogable against the corporation. The nature of those rights determines their nonderogability, such that no state or corporate interests can override them.[296]

While some readers may see such balancing as too theoretically complex for its own good, decisionmakers may well find as a practical matter that deriving a set of corporate duties based on balancing is hardly an unmanageable exercise. Corporations have already begun this task. For instance, the Norwegian Confederation of Business and Industry has derived a list of twelve human rights, primarily based on the Universal Declaration, and suggested various obligations they might put on corporations. The list notably prohibits corporations from interfering with individual political freedoms and proscribes corporal punishment.[297]

---

294. I appreciate this insight from Eyal Benvenisti.

295. *See supra* text accompanying notes 103-107; *see also* MARKESINIS, *supra* note 104, at 194-213 (discussing German principles on the limits of the third-party effect doctrine).

296. *See, e.g.*, Selmouni v. France, 1999-V Eur. Ct. H.R. 149, 181 (justifying the absolute ban on torture).

297. *See* PWBLF & AI, *supra* note 63, at 124-26; *see also* ROYAL DUTCH/SHELL GROUP OF COMPANIES, *supra* note 9 ("A company should . . . ensure that its own personnel, and any security forces engaged by them, are thoroughly familiar with and committed to international guidelines and standards for the use of force in policing . . . ."); Weissbrodt, *supra* note 16.

516   The Yale Law Journal   [Vol. 111: 443

3. *Derivative Duties on Corporations*

Beyond not violating rights directly, how far do corporate duties extend? Under the International Covenant on Civil and Political Rights and its regional counterparts, states must not only directly refrain from abuses; they must also "respect and ensure" the rights in the Convention, which include in particular the obligation to provide an "effective remedy" in the event of a violation of the right.[298] The UN Human Rights Committee has, for instance, stated that many rights give rise not only to duties on the government not to impinge them directly, but positive duties as well (e.g., the right against torture implies a state duty to train police and prison guards in order to prevent torture).[299] The question thus arises whether, for example, the right against torture creates a duty on corporations to train their security personnel properly. Or does the human right to form a family create a duty upon a corporation to provide a certain amount of paid or unpaid maternal and paternal leave to the parents? Or a duty not to discriminate on the basis of pregnancy or maternal status in hiring and promotion? Beyond these derivative duties, as noted in Section II.A above, regional human rights courts have required states to prevent certain abuses by private actors on their territory.[300]

The scope of such related duties turns in part on the extent to which fulfillment of the derivative duty is necessary for compliance with the principal duty. In the case of torture, the close link between training security personnel and preventing torture argues strongly for such a duty. As for the right to form a family, this right does not, in the current state of international human rights law, create an obligation on states to provide parental leave, so it would not create such an obligation on businesses.[301] In addition, these duties turn on the enterprise's nexus to affected individuals, as discussed in Section V.B above. The closer the nexus, the greater the

---

298. ICCPR, *supra* note 129, arts. 2(1), 2(3)(a), S. Exec. Doc. E, 95-2, at 24, 999 U.N.T.S. at 173-74.

299. *See* General Comment No. 20, para. 10, *in Report of the Human Rights Committee*, U.N. GAOR, 47th Sess., Supp. No. 40, Annex VI, at 193, 194, U.N. Doc. A/47/40 (1992) ("Enforcement personnel, medical personnel, police officers and any other persons involved in the custody or treatment of any individual subjected to any form of arrest, detention or imprisonment must receive appropriate instruction and training."); General Comment No. 21, *in Report of the Human Rights Committee*, *supra*, at 195.

300. *E.g.*, A. v. United Kingdom, 1998-VI Eur. Ct. H.R. 2692; Velásquez Rodríguez Case, Inter-Am. Ct. H.R. (ser. C) No. 4, at 91 (1988).

301. General Comment No. 19, para. 5, *in Report of the Human Rights Committee*, U.N. GAOR, 45th Sess., Supp. No. 40, Annex VI, at 175, 176, U.N. Doc. A/45/40 (1990). On protection against termination of employment based on pregnancy as gender discrimination, see U.S. Nat'l Admin. Office, Public Report of Review of NAO Submission No. 9701 (1998), http://www.dol.gov/dol/ilab/public/media/reports/nao/pubrep9701.htm, a report by the U.S. Department of Labor under the North American Agreement on Labor Cooperation finding that Mexican employer practices in maquiladora industries violated Mexican and international labor law.

extent of corporate duties. If, for example, the corporation enjoys control over territory equivalent to that of a state, it has duties beyond the duty not to infringe directly the right itself, more akin to those of states. It would also have some duties to protect the welfare of those closest to it, such as employees, and to ensure that actors, whether private or governmental, do not violate their human rights. The Prince of Wales Business Leaders Forum and Amnesty International, for example, have asserted that if labor activists are arrested, state security forces abuse rights at a TNE site, or a worker disappears, "for a [company] not to raise these concerns . . . with government officials, while adopting the argument of political neutrality or cultural relativism, is to fail to fulfill its responsibility to uphold international human rights standards."[302] In the many situations short of these sorts of ties, the company's duties will be significantly less.

As a practical matter, the nexus analysis suggests that the company will usually have only negative duties or those positive measures clearly necessary to effect them.[303] That is, the company's duties will typically be to avoid directly infringing upon the right based on the balancing test above, including through some prophylactic measures. Other derivative duties might be appropriate where the nexus between the enterprise and the individual is particularly close. But to go further than this position would effectively ignore the functional differences between states and businesses; it would thereby ask too much of the corporation, especially at this stage of the international legal process, when the broad notion of business duties in the human rights area is just emerging.

This position a fortiori calls into question the applicability to business entities of state duties under human rights law to go beyond immediate preventive action (such as the training of security forces) and promote respect for human rights generally.[304] Promotion is a secondary duty compared to directly respecting or protecting rights, as it calls upon the dutyholder to create a general atmosphere or public consciousness of human rights, rather than to refrain from the conduct itself or to undertake necessary measures to ensure that it will not engage in the conduct.[305] In the end, improvement of the overall human rights situation of the population seems attenuated from the corporation's key purposes, whereas it is one of

---

302. PWBLF & AI, *supra* note 63, at 29.

303. For a critique of the negative/positive duties distinction in human rights law, see SHUE, *supra* note 71, at 35-64; and Alston & Quinn, *supra* note 140, at 172-73.

304. *See, e.g.,* Convention on the Elimination of All Forms of Discrimination Against Women, *adopted* Dec. 18, 1979, art. 5, 1249 U.N.T.S. 13, 17 (imposing a duty to "take all appropriate measures . . . to modify the social and cultural patterns of conduct of men and women"); Convention on the Elimination of All Forms of Racial Discrimination, *opened for signature* Mar. 7, 1966, art. 2, S. EXEC. DOC. C, 95-2, at 2 (1978), 660 U.N.T.S. 195, 216, 218 (imposing a duty to "pursue by all appropriate means and without delay a policy of . . . promoting understanding among all races").

305. STEINER & ALSTON, *supra* note 71, at 180-82.

518   The Yale Law Journal   [Vol. 111: 443

the central purposes of government (or at least of liberal government).[306] The business enterprise might have resources at its disposal that, if improperly used, could violate human rights, thus necessitating the derivation of duties to ensure that it does not do so; and it may well be both good corporate policy as well as good human rights policy to encourage corporations to promote human rights, especially when they operate in countries with poor human rights records.[307] But to extend their duty away from a dictum of "doing no harm"—either on their own or through complicity with the government—toward one of proactive steps to promote human rights outside their sphere of influence seems inconsistent with the reality of the corporate enterprise.

D. *Attribution Principles: The Relevance of Corporate Structures*

The final element of the theory of responsibility addresses the structure of the enterprise as an actor and the place of the human rights violator (or person(s) complicit with the government) within that structure. This Section derives a set of attribution principles that connect individual violators to the company. These critical secondary rules of corporate responsibility must confront the reality of the modern business organization.

As noted above, part of the difficulty of transplanting notions of state responsibility to the corporate area lies in the differences between states and corporations. The former are constituted and organized in overtly legal terms—through constitutions, statutes, regulations, policies, and practices, all defining the relationship of the various parts to the whole. This characteristic of states forms the basis for a core secondary rule of state responsibility—that states are responsible for the acts of all state organs and state officials acting as such, however low or high in the governmental hierarchy and however close or far from the state's governmental center.[308]

The business entity, however, is defined in more diverse ways. The status of many individuals as direct employees justifies attribution of their company-related acts to the corporation based on ideas of state responsibility (although questions of the standard of fault arise in this connection, an issue considered below[309]). Beyond employees, other

---

306. *See, e.g., Universal Declaration of Human Rights, supra* note 91, pmbl., para. 6; LOCKE, *supra* note 86.

307. *See* AMNESTY INT'L, *supra* note 280. For one example of an exceptionally forward-looking view, see Body Shop, Human Rights, *at* http://www.bodyshop.com/usa/aboutus/body-hrights.html (last visited Nov. 1, 2001).

308. *See, e.g.,* Elletronica Sicula S.p.A. (ELSI), 1989 I.C.J. 3, 52 (July 20) (assuming acts of the mayor of Palermo are attributable to Italy); *ILC 2001 Draft Articles, supra* note 195, pt. I, ch. 1, art. 4; Crawford, *supra* note 232, para. 158 (discussing the principles of the "unity of the State").

309. *See infra* Section V.E.

relationships are more complex. As Blumberg and Strasser note, the subsidiary's relationship with the corporation turns upon a number of distinct factors, namely, stock ownership, economic integration, administrative, financial, and employee interdependence, and a common public persona.[310] The corporate group may extend beyond this paradigm to include a variety of enterprises with which the main corporation maintains close relations, such as franchisees and licensees.[311]

The relations among parts of a business enterprise can make the determination of the very boundaries of that entity difficult. A corporate entity may operate through joint ventures with other businesses, contractors, and subcontractors; and it may rely upon obtaining inputs from certain suppliers and selling outputs to certain buyers, each creating a variety of economic ties.[312] In some cases, these links originate in contracts establishing long-term relationships; in others, the economic interactions result from the economic importance of the corporation to the supplier or purchaser. A theory of corporate duties must take these relationships into account through some guidelines regarding attribution.

The touchstone for determining the relevance of enterprise structures for duties must be the element of control. As Hugh Collins writes, corporate relations are not merely a function of ownership (subsidiaries) or contractual ties (contractors, distributors, or franchisees). Rather, they extend to a variety of what he calls "authority relations" that "arise wherever the economic dependence of one party upon the other effectively requires compliance with the dominant party's wishes."[313] In such situations, attributing to the controller actions of the controlled entity is entirely appropriate. This concept, of course, resonates with principles of state and individual responsibility noted above; in the corporate realm, it is gaining some acceptance as a basis for assessing corporate responsibility under domestic law.[314]

Several issues immediately arise concerning the role of control. First, control is not a monolithic concept. A corporation's control over its wholly-owned subsidiary might be total, requiring the former to assume

---

310. BLUMBERG & STRASSER, *supra* note 218, at 9-12.

311. *Id.* at 13-17.

312. *Id.* at 19 (describing a tripartite scheme of domination or control by one unit of another, economic integration between the units, or both).

313. Collins, *supra* note 218, at 734; *see also* INT'L COUNCIL ON HUMAN RIGHTS POLICY, *supra* note 101, para. 166 (endorsing this view).

314. *Compare* Phillip I. Blumberg, *The Increasing Recognition of Enterprise Principles in Determining Parent and Subsidiary Corporation Liabilities,* 28 CONN. L. REV. 295 (1996) (reviewing U.S. law incorporating intra-enterprise liability based on control), *with* Ian M. Ramsay, *Allocating Liability in Corporate Groups: An Australian Perspective,* 13 CONN. J. INT'L L. 329 (1999) (highlighting inconsistencies of the Australian approach to corporate groups).

responsibility for all the latter's acts.[315] But what of a corporation's control over a joint venture partner, subcontractor, supplier, or buyer?[316] As a first take, one might distinguish between the corporation's control over the contractor and subcontractor for human rights abuses related to the particular contract, and its control over the contractor for acts on a project not involving that corporation. With respect to the former, the corporation might be said to control the contractor; with respect to the latter, it would not.

Yet such a dichotomy is too simple insofar as it might not accurately take into account the question of economic interdependence central to Collins's theory. Thus, what if demand for particular contractors so exceeded supply that the corporation effectively had to work with the contractor on the latter's terms and had no real control of its operations? Do the contractual links between them alone serve to make the enterprise responsible for the acts of the contractor? Conversely, what if supply for particular contractors so exceeded demand, or the corporation provided such a large part of the contractor's business, that the contractor effectively had to work with the corporation on the latter's terms? In that case, the corporation would appear in a position to control the contractor, even on the contractor's projects not involving that corporation.[317]

One approach to this problem would lie in a set of rebuttable presumptions: The corporation would be prima facie responsible for acts of contractors and subcontractors concerning the contracted-for projects, and prima facie not responsible for other acts by those entities. The two presumptions could be overcome if it were shown, respectively, that the corporation did not exercise real control over the execution of the contracted-for project, or, conversely, that it had actual dominion over the contractor.

Dependence may also turn upon technical cooperation arrangements among entities. If, for example, one TNE lends numerous expert personnel to a local entity such that the latter becomes dependent upon it for its

---

315. For a British case addressing this issue currently, see *Lubbe v. Cape PLC*, 4 Law Reports 268 (H.L. 2000) (appeal taken from S. Afr.). In a suit by South African laborers against a U.K. company for asbestos-related damage caused by a wholly-owned subsidiary, the court held that the "[r]esolution of this issue will be likely to involve an inquiry into what part the defendant played in controlling the operations of the group." *Id.* at 276. For a practical perspective on this question in which a former TNE official notes that responsibility should be "very high," but not legal in nature, see Worth Loomis, *The Responsibility of Parent Corporations for the Human Rights Violations of Their Subsidiaries, in* HUMAN RIGHTS STANDARDS AND THE RESPONSIBILITIES OF TRANSNATIONAL CORPORATIONS, *supra* note 187, at 145, 145.

316. Collins also discusses the possibility that a creditor might have control over a corporation, a question I leave for another day. Collins, *supra* note 218, at 733-34.

317. For a more broadsided attack on the notion of responsibility for the work of contractors, which argues that "[t]he preponderance of the business community rejects the notion that companies can be held responsible for the overall behavior and policies of their subcontractors and suppliers throughout the supply chain," see U.S. Council on Int'l Bus., *supra* note 181.

effective functioning, then the TNE is, for all intents and purposes, exercising control over the latter. But even here, actions by individuals within the local entity who have no real connection to the expert personnel would not give rise to responsibility by the corporation.

Deriving such presumptions for suppliers and purchasers based on a linchpin of control proves more difficult. Does one attribute to the corporation the abuses of a buyer of its products simply by virtue of the corporation's having supplied a core input? Are the acts of a seller to the company attributable to the latter simply if the company is the seller's largest customer? These difficulties might be resolved by ascribing a certain knowledge standard to the company. Indeed, at a certain point, the rules of attribution—determining the scope of the corporation's component entities—begin to merge with the principles of agency and complicity discussed above.[318] (The difference between this scenario and that discussed in Section V.A is that we are now considering the liability of a company for acts of another company, rather than complicity by one company in the acts of the government.) The test for determining the responsibility of a company for acts of a buyer or seller (or even of a contractor or subcontractor) may thus turn on the mindset of the company rather than merely on economic ties. I do not seek to resolve these issues here, but merely point out the possible limitations of a test that hinges on control.

Of course, such a proposition could also be attacked from the other side, i.e., that the mere presence of economic contacts between the corporation and other entities suffices to attribute to the corporation the acts of all those with whom it works. But this seems far too slender a reed upon which to hang a theory of responsibility. It would require as a general matter that enterprises cut off all ties from entities that might abuse human dignity, even if the abuses stem from activities completely unrelated to the enterprises' connection with the violator entities. To extract a general notion of attribution (just like complicity) from economic ties alone has no basis in domestic or international law.[319]

Second, economic dependence must take account of the attenuated influence of the corporation as one moves further down the chain of production. If a multinational corporation making shoes in Vietnam hires a contractor to make the cotton laces, who hires a subcontractor to provide the cotton cloth, who hires a subcontractor to grow the cotton, who hires a subcontractor to actually pick the cotton, and this last actor uses forced labor in his practices, can the corporation be said to be responsible for his activities—even if each was somehow dependent upon the entity directly

---

318. *See supra* Section V.A; *see also infra* Section V.E (discussing duties of care).

319. *Cf. supra* text accompanying note 166 (taking a broad view of complicity with the South African government, though not suggesting that entities buying or selling from companies doing business in South Africa were themselves responsible).

522   The Yale Law Journal   [Vol. 111: 443

above it for its continuing livelihood? If one were to base a theory of responsibility upon multiplying the degree of dependency, an eighty-five percent dependency for four levels of dependency translates to just over fifty percent.[320] (If the cotton-picker were acting in his spare time, the conduct would clearly be totally private.)

Finally, the control test might not suffice for determining the responsibility of joint venture partners for the activities of their newly created entity. If four companies joined forces to create a local mining company, with each owning twenty-five percent of the company's shares and appointing a quarter of its directors or senior managers, none might control the entity in the sense of being able to force through decisions or block the decisions of others. Yet state responsibility principles increasingly recognize the concept of joint and several liability for such joint acts by states.[321] The extension of this principle to joint ventures seems justified on the same underlying ground, namely that because the companies have created the joint venture specifically for the purpose of gaining the benefits of cooperation from its conduct, they assume the risks should the venture violate human dignity.

E. A Brief Word on Fault

Lastly, any discussion of corporate duties must address the degree of fault (if any) that creates enterprise responsibility. Governments, international institutions, and legal scholars have long wrestled with the standards of fault required for determining whether the state has violated international law. Treaties, courts, arbitral bodies, individual governments, and other decisionmakers have adopted various standards in elaborating primary rules of state and individual responsibility.[322] As a general matter, fault is not required for violations by states. Thus, for instance, human

---

320. *See, e.g.*, Stephanie Strom, *A Sweetheart Becomes Suspect: Looking Behind Those Kathie Lee Labels*, N.Y. TIMES, June 27, 1996, at D1 (noting that Wal-Mart's blouses were made by a New York company that subcontracted to an Alabama company, which then subcontracted to a New Jersey company, which in turn subcontracted to another New York company with apparently poor conditions for employees).

321. *See, e.g.*, Convention on International Liability for Damage Caused by Space Objects, *opened for signature* Mar. 29, 1972, art. V, 24 U.S.T. 2389, 2394, 961 U.N.T.S. 187, 190 (declaring that states jointly participating in the launch of a space object are "jointly and severally liable for any damage caused"); *see also* John E. Noyes & Brian D. Smith, *State Responsibility and the Principle of Joint and Several Liability*, 13 YALE J. INT'L L. 225 (1988) (reviewing situations of multiple state responsibility for breaches of international law); *cf.* James Crawford, *Third Report on State Responsibility*, U.N. GAOR, Int'l Law Comm'n, 52d Sess., paras. 267-278, U.N. Doc. A/CN.4/507/Add.2 (2000) (recognizing each state's responsibility in the case of joint action, but not equating this principle with common-law joint and several liability).

322. 1 BROWNLIE, *supra* note 191, at 40-46; *ILC 2001 Draft Articles*, *supra* note 195, pt. I, ch. 1, arts. 4, 9 (dictating attribution for activities of state organs having acted in that capacity). On standards of fault as primary and not secondary rules, see Crawford, *supra* note 197, paras. 12-18.

rights courts do not require victims to demonstrate that the government was negligent in restraining its officials; rather, the acts of such officials are simply attributed to the state (a secondary rule) and the state is liable for the violation.[323] For other primary rules binding on states, such as duties to prevent certain injuries to individuals by wholly private actors, courts and other decisionmakers have found violations only after finding the state at fault in its failure to exercise due diligence.[324]

With respect to individual responsibility, international criminal law conventions and cases include the defendant's mens rea as part of the definition of a crime. Intent and knowledge are typically required, although the extent of the defendant's knowledge and intent regarding each element of the crime can vary from crime to crime; and under the concept of superior responsibility, the defendant need not have had either intent or knowledge regarding the underlying act.[325]

Can either of the above approaches to standards of care be shifted to the corporate sector? On the one hand, the individual accountability standards require such a significant level of fault as to be inappropriate for a general scheme of corporate responsibility that goes beyond criminal sanctions. Even with respect to criminal liability, different national systems have adopted sharply contrasting concepts of the degree of fault (if any) required of the corporation for criminal liability, suggesting the absence of general principles of law upon which one might rely.[326] On the other hand, we can ask whether the state responsibility standard, which generally does not require fault, should apply to corporations. Perhaps, as the discussion on attribution makes clear, the business enterprise is different enough from the state that the former should be liable only if it fails to exercise due diligence

---

323. *See* Ireland v. United Kingdom, 25 Eur. Ct. H.R. (ser. A) at 64 (1978) (holding that a state is "strictly liable" for the conduct of subordinates); 1 OPPENHEIM'S INTERNATIONAL LAW, *supra* note 216, at 511 n.15 (noting the difference between liability and attribution). For an example from the environmental field, see Convention on International Liability for Damage Caused by Space Objects, *supra* note 321, art. II, 24 U.S.T. at 2392, 961 U.N.T.S. at 189, which makes a state liable for damage caused by its space objects to aircraft and to objects on Earth.

324. *See, e.g.*, Velásquez Rodríguez Case, Inter-Am. Ct. H.R. (ser. C) No. 4 (1988); British Property in Spanish Morocco Case, 2 R.I.A.A. 616, 636 (1925); Janes Case, 4 R.I.A.A. 82, 86 (1925); BRIAN D. SMITH, STATE RESPONSIBILITY AND THE MARINE ENVIRONMENT 36-43 (1988); *see also* General Comment No. 3, *supra* note 200, para. 10 (discussing economic limitations as a factor in determining due diligence in meeting obligations under the ICESCR).

325. *See* ICC Statute, *supra* note 80, arts. 28, 30; *Finalized Draft Text of the Elements of Crimes*, Preparatory Commission for the International Criminal Court, U.N. Doc. PCNICC/2000/1/Add.2 (2000).

326. *See* WELLS, *supra* note 118, at 94-122; Guy Stessens, *Corporate Criminal Liability: A Comparative Perspective*, 43 INT'L & COMP. L.Q. 493 (1994). The Council of Europe's anti-corruption convention requires states to punish corporations only if someone who "has a leading position" within the enterprise commits the acts or is an accessory thereto, or if he fails to supervise someone under his authority. In either case, the act must be committed for the company's benefit. Council of Europe Corruption Convention, *supra* note 160, art. 18, 38 I.L.M. at 509. The line between principles of fault and principles of attribution becomes a bit thin here, as the corporation is effectively liable for the acts of certain employees but not for those of others.

524   The Yale Law Journal   [Vol. 111: 443

over its agents, including by not engaging in corrective measures after the fact.[327] Moreover, business enterprises will likely resist any standard of strict liability.

In the end, it would seem that the ultimate standard of care will turn upon the particular forum in which the norms are formulated, whether civil, penal, administrative, or otherwise. The state responsibility approach seems most appealing as a general matter insofar as it views the business enterprise, like the state, as a unit engaged in a particular function, with its own internal structures. In that sense, it seems appropriate that it should be per se responsible for all its components acting under color of corporate authority without any separate requirement of fault by the business.[328] For those duties for which the corporation might have to prevent actions by persons not connected with the business enterprise, a lesser standard, such as due diligence, would apply, as the human rights courts have recognized. If, however, severe sanctions were envisioned, it would seem justifiable to limit the enterprise's responsibility to situations where it failed to exercise due diligence over its agents.

VI. A RECAPITULATION AND SOME APPLICATIONS

The above analysis offers a framework for global and domestic actors to begin to derive a set of duties under international law for business enterprises regarding the protection of human rights. In essence, it posits that the duties of a company are a direct function of its capacity to harm human dignity. Consequently, corporate responsibility will depend upon the enterprise's proximity to the violation as determined by its relationship to the government, its nexus to the affected populations, the individual right at issue, and principles of attribution that connect those committing the violations to the company. These propositions can be summarized as follows:

> (1) All other things being equal, the corporation's duties to protect human rights increase as a function of its ties to the government. If the corporation receives requests from the government leading to violations, knowingly and substantially aids and abets governmental abuses, carries out governmental functions and causes abuses, or, in some circumstances, allows governmental actors to commit them, its responsibility flows from that of the state.

---

327. *See* FRENCH, *supra* note 118, at 156 (discussing the requirement that the responsible party adopt a course of action to prevent repetition).
328. *See* WELLS, *supra* note 118, at 130-35; Fisse & Braithwaite, *supra* note 114, at 483-88.

(2) All other things being equal, the corporation's duties to individuals increase as a function of its associative ties to them. These connections may, for example, emanate from legal ties (as with employees), physical proximity, or possession of de facto control over a particular piece of territory. As these connections dissipate, the duties do as well. For certain severe abuses, the corporation's duties will not turn on such ties.

(3) In situations not involving cooperation with the government in its own human rights violations, the enterprise's duties turn on a balancing of the right at issue with the corporation's interests (and in some cases, rights), except for certain nonderogable human rights. The nexus factor will need to be taken into account in determining any derivative duties. The company's derivative duties will not extend to duties to promote observance of the rights generally.

(4) The attribution of responsibility within the corporate structure depends upon the degree of control exercised by the corporation over the agents involved in the abuses, not simply financial or contractual links with them.

(5) The extent to which the corporation must have some fault to be responsible will depend upon the particular sanction envisioned. It is not a required element of responsibility with respect to corporate agents acting under corporate authority, but should be an element regarding the duty of the corporation to prevent violations by actors not connected with it.

Viewed differently, the theory attempts to answer three basic questions: (1) Who is violating the right—the government, the corporation, or both? And which actors within the corporate structure? (2) Whose rights are violated—those of people with special ties or not? and (3) Which rights are violated, in terms of the particular duties that they impose on corporate actors?

The theory ultimately results in two sets of duties upon the corporation. First are the complicity-based duties that the corporation not involve itself in illegal conduct by the government; these duties rise, in those circumstances in which the corporation's links to the government are akin to those in the doctrine of superior responsibility, to a duty to prevent abuses by governmental forces. For these duties, the factor of the nexus to affected populations drops out. Second is a set of duties on the corporation not to infringe directly on the human rights of those with whom it enjoys certain ties, with the possibility of greater duties depending upon the scope of those links.[329] The duties in the first group are conceptually simpler insofar as they are grounded in the sort of human rights abuses that fall within the existing paradigm, namely those committed by governments. The duties in the second set are more complex insofar as they do not assume governmental involvement and move human rights more into the private sphere.[330]

The utility of this theory ultimately turns on its effectiveness as a tool for decisionmakers in domestic and international arenas to appraise and resolve the competing claims regarding corporate conduct in the human rights area. With this challenge in mind, one can examine several claims asserted against corporations in recent years. For purposes of this appraisal only, I will take as given the facts asserted by the relevant NGOs, not because I know them to be true, but simply because the absence of impartial decisions or independent investigation (by the author or others) renders an independent evaluation impossible, and, more importantly, because the utility of the theory does not turn on the truth or falsity of the underlying claims. I will also not rehash all the claims made against those TNEs, but simply those most relevant to the theory.

A. *Enron Corporation in Maharashtra State (India)*

In its lengthy January 1999 report, Human Rights Watch (HRW) accused Enron of "complicity in human rights violations" regarding the operations of the Dahbol Power Corporation (DPC), a joint venture of Enron, General Electric, and Bechtel Corporation, that had a contract with the Indian state of Maharashtra to build an electrical power plant.[331] HRW discussed the extensive opposition to the plant from the local community and the actions of the Indian government in suppressing this dissent. It ultimately accused Enron of complicity based on (1) having benefited from human rights violations by the state government; (2) having paid and materially supported state forces that committed human rights abuses, insofar as Enron compensated the state for the salaries of state police protecting the site and allowed state police to use company helicopters to monitor and harass local labor and human rights activists; (3) not having responded to complaints that DPC contractors directly attacked or threatened local villagers opposed to the project.[332]

---

329. The case of corporations serving as de facto governmental authorities over territory probably falls under both categories of duties, as their authority emanates from the state, yet they can directly infringe the rights without the involvement of the state in the immediate violation.

330. *See supra* text accompanying notes 94-110.

331. HUMAN RIGHTS WATCH, *supra* note 5, § VII.

332. *Id.*

Under the theory, two of the claims, if true, would point to violations of Enron's duties under international law. The first is claim (2), which is, under the scheme above, a paradigmatic claim of a violation of a complicity-based duty. HRW has alleged that the links between DPC and the Maharashtra state police—financing of their operations and lending of equipment—point to a case of complicity in human rights violations committed by those forces. (As noted earlier, such accusations were also leveled at Freeport McMoRan's operations in Indonesia,[333] although in that case, the accusations that Freeport exercises de facto control over a large part of Irian Jaya require, under my theory, a discussion of a larger set of duties.) The principles of attribution also make Enron's duties clear insofar as the actors involved are all employees of DPC, which HRW asserts was largely an Enron entity.[334]

The second is claim (3), which concerns a direct infringement of the rights to physical integrity and freedom of opinion without any governmental involvement. The affected populations are close to Enron— the villagers in the area of the power plant. (In the case of the right to physical integrity, the nexus may not be relevant at all.) The actors alleged to have engaged in the conduct are contractors of DPC, although HRW noted that a number of the attacks were by pro-DPC villagers not clearly linked to the company.[335] With respect to the first of the two rights, because the right to physical integrity is nonderogable, the corporation would have a duty not to engage in such conduct. With respect to freedom of opinion, although a corporation might be permitted to fire employees who publicly criticize the company, intimidation of villagers affected by the operations of the plant (and thus still with a close nexus to the corporation) is not a proportionate response to further a legitimate goal. As to attribution, it would be necessary to determine the degree of control over the contractors to determine whether their activities are attributable to Enron. Those attacks by villagers who were not contractors cannot be attributed directly to Enron. And because Enron's operations seem more in the form of routine business construction than de facto territorial control, it seems difficult to conclude that it has a responsibility (even under the due diligence standard) to prevent violations by those unrelated actors.

Claim (1) would clearly not rise to the level of a corporate violation of human rights. The claim is based on a concept of complicity not accepted in international or domestic law—that if one party merely benefits from the misdeeds of another without more, it has breached some legal duty owed to

---

333. *See* Beanal v. Freeport-McMoRan, Inc., 969 F. Supp. 362, 374-75 (E.D. La. 1997), *aff'd*, 197 F.3d 161 (5th Cir. 1999).

334. HUMAN RIGHTS WATCH, *supra* note 5, § II ("In the eyes of the public, the DPC was Enron, and it is often colloquially referred to as 'the Enron project' . . . .").

335. *Id.* § V.

the victims of the misdeeds. Although it is desirable for the promotion of human rights for corporations in such situations to object to such conduct, and even in some circumstances divest, it seems premature to allege that this sort of conduct violates a legal duty.

B. *Diamonds and the Sierra Leone Civil War*

United Nations actions with respect to diamond companies stem from a concern by interested governments that these businesses are purchasing diamonds from the Revolutionary United Front (RUF), which has committed gross human rights violations during Sierra Leone's civil war. (These same charges have been leveled against companies for aiding the UNITA guerrillas in their long insurgency against the government of Angola.) Were companies that bought the diamonds violating human rights? The above approach suggests treating this problem as one of a potential violation of complicity-based duties, since governments and NGOs do not generally allege that the diamond companies themselves or their agents are directly violating human rights.[336] Nonetheless, one would not wish to rule out the possibility that those engaged in human rights violations are de facto agents of the diamond companies due to long-term sales relationships and the possibility of the violators' dependence upon the diamond companies. Participants and observers offer differing views on this question.[337]

Under the complicity-based set of duties, the diamond companies would be violating human rights if they substantially aided or abetted the commission of human rights violations by the RUF, with knowledge of the underlying abuses.[338] The notoriety of the RUF's atrocities—especially amputations of the limbs of innocent civilians—suggests, as a prima facie matter, that the diamond companies that knew they were trading with the RUF also knew of the abuses. More difficult factual determinations would be required with respect to activities of diamond companies that did not know the origin of the diamonds. In such cases, they may not have known that their activities were contributing to the RUF's activities, although a somewhat lower standard for complicity would suggest responsibility insofar as, in many circumstances, they would have very good reason to

---

336. *See, e.g.*, S.C. Res. 1306, *supra* note 1, pmbl., para. 1 (expressing concern at the role of the diamond trade in "fuelling the conflict in Sierra Leone").

337. *See, e.g.*, Norimitsu Onishi, *Africa Diamond Hub Defies Smuggling Rules*, N.Y. TIMES, Jan. 2, 2001, at A1 (reporting disagreement over the relations between traders and rebels).

338. For purposes of analysis, I apply the complicity principles applicable to complicity with the government, since the RUF claims to be one. On international law's imposition of human rights obligations on such insurgent groups, see *supra* text accompanying note 74. *See also* S.C. Res. 1315, U.N. SCOR, 55th Sess., 4186th mtg., at 2, U.N. Doc. S/1315 (2000) (endorsing a special court for prosecuting atrocities by all sides in Sierra Leone).

suspect the origin of the diamonds.[339] As to whether purchasing of diamonds constitutes material assistance to the group rising to the level of aiding and abetting, one can lean in favor of a positive answer as it seems that the RUF depended heavily upon the diamonds as a source of income.[340] In domestic criminal law in many states, the financiers of criminal enterprises are routinely held responsible for complicity in the underlying activity.[341] But as noted earlier, merely doing business with the diamond traders is not sufficient.

C. *Clothing Production in Latin America and Asia*

A third example concerns the numerous claims made by unions and NGOs against industry regarding conditions of work at apparel and other factories in the developing world, in particular Latin America and South and Southeast Asia. Such concerns prompted the U.S. government, businesses, and NGOs to establish the Apparel Industry Partnership, which prepared the Workplace Code of Conduct noted in the Introduction.[342] Although a full discussion is beyond the scope of this Article, a number of thoughtful commentators have examined the sweatshop phenomenon and challenged the common understanding that such factories create oppressive conditions for workers and doom them to a life of poverty.[343] The question here is more limited: whether any human rights abuses in these settings point to a violation of duties by the multinational corporations.

Here the accusations are primarily leveled at the corporations as actors directly abusing human rights, rather than as actors complicit in government violations (although such accusations are made as well).[344] In this case, the theory would appraise the allegations of inhuman working conditions as follows. First, the nexus to the affected population—typically the employees working in factories—is very close. With respect to

339. *Compare Illegal Diamond Trade Funds War in Sierra Leone*, UNITED METHODIST NEWS SERVICE, Apr. 19, 2000, *at* http://umns.umc.org/00/april/210.htm ("By accepting Liberian exports as legitimate, the international diamond industry actively colludes in crimes . . . ." (internal quotation marks omitted)), *with Illegal Trafficking in Sub-Saharan Diamonds: Hearing Before the Trade Subcomm. of the House Ways and Means Comm.*, 106th Cong. 39 (2000) (statement of Matthew Runci, President and Chief Operating Officer of Jewelers of America, Inc.) (noting that diamonds may pass through a dozen hands before reaching the retail counter and asserting the impossibility of tracking them accurately).

340. *See* S.C. Res. 1306, *supra* note 1.

341. *See, e.g.*, Racketeer Influenced and Corrupt Organizations Act, 18 U.S.C. §§ 1961-1962 (1994).

342. *See supra* text accompanying note 3.

343. *See, e.g.*, THE SWEATSHOP QUANDARY (Pamela Varley ed., 1998); Nicholas D. Kristof & Sheryl WuDunn, *Two Cheers for Sweatshops*, N.Y. TIMES, Sept. 24, 2000, § 6 (Magazine), at 70.

344. *Special Issues: Corporations and Human Rights: The Apparel Industry*, *in* HUMAN RIGHTS WATCH, HUMAN RIGHTS WATCH WORLD REPORT 1998, *at* http://www.hrw.org/hrw/worldreport/Back-06.htm (last visited Sept. 1, 2001).

530 The Yale Law Journal [Vol. 111: 443

attribution, the place of the potential violators within the corporate structure seems clear in many situations—typically the factories are owned by contractors of the TNE. In such situations, the presumption above is that the TNE is able to control the activities of the contractor on these projects, although this could be rebutted in individual cases.

As for the rights affected, the concerns tend to center around the extent to which sweatshops undermine worker safety and health. These claims necessitate an inquiry as to the exact rights of laborers in such circumstances. International labor law is generally quite weak in guaranteeing individuals any particular wage, with ILO treaties (which lack many ratifications) giving states great flexibility.[345] With respect to health and sanitary rights, international labor law has created somewhat more detailed standards,[346] though ratification numbers are still low on most of the relevant conventions. In the end, a detailed inquiry regarding the solidity of current international labor norms will be needed. If the NGOs are able to demonstrate that working conditions are significantly detrimental to health to the point of harming physical integrity, the corporation will have a duty to refrain from such conduct.

VII. IMPLEMENTING THE THEORY—SOME PRELIMINARY POSSIBILITIES

The theory posited above offers a starting point for global actors to develop a corpus of law that would recognize obligations on businesses to protect human rights. The modes by which this theory can be implemented are numerous and reflect the diverse processes by which international norms develop and are applied. This Part briefly sketches out five principal methods, from those originating within the corporation to those created by governments at the international level. As noted at the beginning of this Article, whatever the arena, all key claimants—corporations, governments, and victims' representatives (including NGOs)—will need to participate together in prescribing and applying the law.

---

345. For example, the Minimum Wage Fixing Convention states that the elements for determining minimum wage

> so far as possible and appropriate in relation to national practice and conditions, include (a) the needs of workers . . . taking into account the general level of wages in the country, the cost of living, social security benefits, and the relative living standards of other social groups; [and] (b) economic factors, including the requirements of economic development, levels of productivity and the desirability of . . . a high level of employment.

Convention Concerning Minimum Wage Fixing, with Special Reference to Developing Countries, *adopted* June 22, 1970, art. 3, http://ilolex.ilo.ch:1567/scripts/convde.pl?C131. The Convention has been ratified by forty-three states. *Id.*

346. *See* International Labour Standards on Safety and Health, *at* http://www.ilo.org/public/english/standards/norm/whatare/stndards/osh.htm (last visited Sept. 1, 2001); *see also* PWBLF & AI, *supra* note 63, at 52 ("Companies should have explicit policies and procedures in place to ensure that they do not violate any of [the seven key ILO conventions].").

A. *Corporate-Initiated Codes of Conduct*

The most basic starting point for implementing the above theory is through a form of self-regulation. Indeed, many businesses have adopted formal policies and practices in order to avoid any form of external regulation.[347] In many cases, they may be responding to market pressures from consumers or demands of key shareholders. Ideally, self-regulation based on acceptance of duties from the theory, coupled with transparency, would best address the overall issue. In the end, for optimal effect, corporations will need to internalize such norms in their decisionmaking.[348] This point resonates with the key insight from international relations theorists and others that internalization is critical to successful implementation of international norms, whether in human rights or other areas of the law.[349]

The corporate-initiated code of conduct represents industry's most public response to the claims leveled against corporations in the area of human rights. These codes are voluntary commitments made by companies, business associations, or other entities, which put forth standards and principles for business activities.[350] Although such codes date back at least to the beginning of the twentieth century, they have proliferated in the last twenty years due to shareholder and consumer interest in corporate behavior, and now number in the hundreds.[351] One recent study found that these codes focused on labor and environmental issues and that many included consumer protection, bribery, competition, and information disclosure.[352] The codes typically address a limited range of human rights issues—forced labor, child labor, conditions of employment, and the right to unionize. One offshoot of the corporate code of conduct is social

---

347. Lance Compa & Tashia Hinchliffe-Darricarrère, *Enforcing International Labor Rights Through Corporate Codes of Conduct*, 33 COLUM. J. TRANSNAT'L L. 663, 677-89 (1995).

348. Weissbrodt, *supra* note 16, para. 22.

349. *See generally* THE POWER OF HUMAN RIGHTS (Thomas Risse et al. eds., 1999) (presenting case studies analyzing the impact of international norms); Harold Hongju Koh, *Bringing International Law Home*, 35 HOUS. L. REV. 623 (1998) (suggesting that nations obey international law when they internalize norms); Weissbrodt, *supra* note 16, para. 22 (noting that any UN code "will be most effective if it can be internalized as a matter of company policy and practice").

350. KATHRYN GORDON & MAIKO MIYAKE, DECIPHERING CODES OF CORPORATE CONDUCT 31 (OECD Directorate for Fin., Fiscal & Enter. Affairs, Working Paper on International Investment No. 1999/2, 2000). This definition would also cover codes drafted by international organizations.

351. *Overview of Global Developments and Office Activities Concerning Codes of Conduct, Social Labeling and Other Private Sector Initiatives Addressing Labour Issues*, ILO Working Party on the Social Dimensions of the Liberalization of International Trade, ILO Doc. BG.273/WP/SDL/1 (Rev.1) (Nov. 1998), http://www.ilo.org/public/english/standards/relm/gb/docs/gb273/sdl-1.htm.

352. GORDON & MIYAKE, *supra* note 350, at 12. For a sample list, see Weissbrodt, *supra* note 16, para. 10 nn.23-25.

labeling, whereby industry groups agree, often in cooperation with NGOs, to certify products as resulting from processes that do not involve certain deleterious practices (e.g., "dolphin-safe" tuna and the Rugmark label on carpets from the Indian subcontinent that are not produced with child labor).[353]

Inclusion of a larger set of human rights commitments within corporate codes of conduct could have a positive impact on corporate behavior. Many corporations are now ensuring that their internal decisionmaking processes, including their relations with contractors, reflect the commitments undertaken in their codes.[354] At the same time, business groups are reluctant to accept uniform standards of behavior, claiming that each industry must develop its own set of guidelines.[355] And the voluntary nature of corporate codes of conduct creates the clear potential for some TNEs to treat them as purely a public relations exercise, leading human rights NGOs to downplay their effectiveness.[356] NGOs and labor unions have pressed corporations to address this shortcoming by including procedures for independent monitoring. Yet this effort has fallen short, as many TNEs resist such provisions; and while some monitoring provisions have clearly improved conditions of workers, even those codes with monitoring provisions have fallen prey to industry capture.[357] The overall impact of such codes on corporate behavior is thus unclear, with different companies and industries adopting stronger or weaker codes, each of which is observed with varying degrees of seriousness.

The route of corporate-initiated codes of conduct nonetheless seems useful in the process of addressing violations of human rights, as it will at least raise corporate awareness of these issues and permit the possibility of monitoring (either by independent monitors paid by the industry or by NGOs). Undoubtedly, corporations will adopt various, even inconsistent, codes as a substantive matter, and human rights NGOs will object to that

353. Compa & Hinchliffe-Darricarrère, *supra* note 347, at 673-74, 677-89.

354. Gary Gereffi et al., *The NGO-Industrial Complex*, FOREIGN POL'Y, July-Aug. 2001, at 56.

355. U.S. Council on Int'l Bus., *supra* note 181, at 3 ("The business community rejects the notion that standardization is necessary or desirable.").

356. *E.g., Who Can Protect Workers' Rights?: The Workplace Codes of Conduct Debate*, HUM. RTS. DIALOGUE, Fall 2000, at 1; California Global Corporate Accountability Project, Summary of Concerns (1999), *at* http://www.nautilus.org/cap/codes/summary.html.

357. *E.g.*, U.S. DEP'T OF LABOR, THE APPAREL INDUSTRY AND CODES OF CONDUCT: A SOLUTION TO THE INTERNATIONAL CHILD LABOR PROBLEM? § II.F.3 (1998), http://www.dol.gov/dol/ilab/public/media/reports/iclp/apparel/main.htm#Table (noting the absence of monitoring from most codes); Steven Greenhouse, *Report Says Global Accounting Firm Overlooks Factory Abuses*, N.Y. TIMES, Sept. 28, 2000, at A12 (describing a report finding that the world's largest factory-monitoring firm did a "shoddy" job). For a pro-labor critique, see David Moberg, *Bringing Down Niketown: Consumers Can Help, but Only Unions and Labor Laws Will End Sweatshops*, NATION, June 7, 1999, at 15. For a review noting successes and failures, see CHRISTOPHER L. AVERY, BUSINESS AND HUMAN RIGHTS IN A TIME OF CHANGE ch. 3.4 (1999), http://www.business-humanrights.org/Chapter3.htm.

inconsistency. But the process of international lawmaking often begins with such private codes, which create expectations of appropriate conduct among diverse actors and can lead over time to other forms of lawmaking.

B. *NGO Scrutiny*

NGOs have already demonstrated their interest in monitoring corporate activity and recognized it as a priority for future work.[358] They should consider the adoption of more detailed norms for business enterprises than have been developed to date, and seek to ground their scrutiny of corporate behavior in those principles. In addition, to the extent other institutions develop law regarding corporate duties, NGOs can help with the monitoring process—just as they do regarding state obligations in the area of human rights. They remain central actors in mobilizing shame upon violators, leading to the termination of offensive conduct.[359] At the same time, NGOs have clear responsibilities in light of their lack of accountability to anyone other than their members or donors.[360] Though organizations like Amnesty International and Human Rights Watch are accustomed to making arguments based on legal principles and insisting on high standards of accuracy in reporting, other NGOs seem to fall prey to a visceral anti-TNE bias that only arouses suspicions by TNEs of the bona fides of the human rights agenda.[361]

C. *National Legal Regimes*

If self-regulation and NGO scrutiny prove insufficient, decisionmakers will need to consider the expansion of domestic public and private legal regimes to create duties upon businesses along the model specified above. National regimes would take advantage of the state's power over its territory and respond to those critics who might view corporate responsibility as an abdication of the role of the state. By developing a regulatory scheme through statutes, regulations, and policy directives, governments could monitor corporate human rights activity in the same

---

358. *See* Robin Broad & John Cavanagh, *The Corporate Accountability Movement: Lessons and Opportunities*, 23 FLETCHER F. WORLD AFF. 151 (1999).

359. *See* ALFRED ZIMMERN, THE LEAGUE OF NATIONS AND THE RULE OF LAW 1918-1935, at 460 (1936).

360. *See generally* Peter J. Spiro, *New Global Potentates: Nongovernmental Organizations and the "Unregulated" Marketplace*, 18 CARDOZO L. REV. 957 (1996) (appraising consequences of increased NGO roles).

361. *See, e.g.*, U.S. Council on Int'l Bus., *supra* note 181, at 4 ("[B]usiness rejects as a matter of principle the imposition of a right to outside monitoring by groups with no responsibility with regard to a company's performance and with no accountability."); *see also* Ethan B. Kapstein, *The Corporate Ethics Crusade*, FOREIGN AFF., Sept.-Oct. 2001, at 105 (criticizing NGOs for having short-sighted demands).

534   The Yale Law Journal   [Vol. 111: 443

way they monitor corporate environmental, anticompetitive, securities, or bribery-related activity. Indeed, parts of this model could be incorporated into existing labor laws. Companies violating their duties could face sanctions ranging from mere publication of a list of companies whose practices appear to fall below acceptable standards, to loss of particular benefits, such as preferential loans for overseas investments or permits for the import or export of commodities, up to criminal fines. Although private litigation might prove a cumbersome way to enforce such duties, legislatures or courts could also develop law recognizing private rights of action for victims of human rights abuses.

The effectiveness of national regimes will turn in part on international expectations regarding the scope of a state's jurisdiction to legislate. Most governmental regulation is based upon either the principle of territoriality, whereby a state can make and apply law that covers acts committed within its borders (which are often broadly defined), or the principle of nationality, which gives a state jurisdiction over a business incorporated there, regardless of the situs of the conduct.[362] Yet states differ sharply on some jurisdictional issues. The United States—whether the President, Congress, or the courts—has argued with much of the rest of the world over the extent of the reach of the territoriality principle,[363] the applicability of the nationality principle to foreign-incorporated wholly owned subsidiaries,[364] and the requirement of an overall test of reasonableness that would limit a state's jurisdiction if other states had a greater interest in regulating the particular activity.[365] Some treaties attempt to overcome these differences; for instance, in the bribery context, the OECD's Convention requires states to criminalize based on the territoriality principle, but does not preclude use of the nationality principle, and calls for consultations in the event of

---

362. *E.g.*, IAN BROWNLIE, PRINCIPLES OF PUBLIC INTERNATIONAL LAW 303-06 (5th ed. 1998); Christopher L. Blakesley, *Extraterritorial Jurisdiction*, *in* 2 INTERNATIONAL CRIMINAL LAW 33 (M. Cherif Bassiouni ed., 2d ed. 1999) (giving other bases of jurisdiction).

363. *Compare* Joined Cases 89, 104, 114, 116, 117 & 125-129/85, Ahlström v. Commission, 1988 E.C.R. 5193 (approving the application of EU anticompetition law to overseas producers based on the implementation of the plan within the EU), *with* Hartford Fire Ins. Co. v. California, 509 U.S. 764, 796 (1993) (holding that the Sherman Act "applies to foreign conduct that was meant to produce and did in fact produce some substantial [domestic] effect"). *See also Opinion of the Inter-American Juridical Committee in Response to Resolution 3375/96 of the General Assembly of the Organization*, OAS Doc. No. CJI/SO/II/doc.67/96rev.5 (Aug. 23, 1996), *reprinted in* 35 I.L.M. 1329 (rejecting the legality of the 1996 U.S. legislation permitting suits against foreign companies doing business in Cuba on previously expropriated land).

364. *See* European Communities: Comments on the U.S. Regulations Concerning Trade with the U.S.S.R. (July 1982), 21 I.L.M. 891 (arguing that certain U.S. sanctions violated international law).

365. *Compare Hartford Fire*, 509 U.S. 764 (recognizing a limitation on U.S. jurisdiction only if compliance with U.S. law would violate foreign law), *with* RESTATEMENT (THIRD) OF FOREIGN RELATIONS LAW § 403 (1987) (endorsing a reasonableness test).

disputes,[366] while the Council of Europe's Convention requires the use of territoriality- and nationality-based jurisdiction in most situations.[367]

As a result, national regulation has both promises and pitfalls. States would agree that each state can regulate the human rights abuses that take place on its territory (even by foreign-based TNEs) as well as the activities of TNEs headquartered on the territory (even if the abuses take place overseas). If both the state of nationality and the territorial state (which is also likely to be the state of any victims of abuses) choose to regulate the activity, the result may well be an effective regime if the two states did not place different demands on corporations. But the developing world states might well place fewer requirements on businesses, in which case companies would seek to challenge the more restrictive laws. Litigation or diplomatic disputes over the limitations of jurisdiction—in particular the relevance of the reasonableness test—would inevitably arise.

What of the possibility to regulate conduct based on universal jurisdiction, which permits a state to legislate over offenses particularly harmful to mankind, regardless of any nexus the state may have with the offense, the offender, or the victim?[368] Beyond the potential for conflicts of jurisdiction noted above, two obstacles lie in the way of expecting states to endorse this option. First, it is not at all clear that universal jurisdiction extends beyond the grave human rights abuses noted in Section II.A and a small number of transnational crimes such as aircraft hijacking and sabotage. If a state tried to regulate corporate conduct over a broad range of human rights activities (e.g., violations of free speech), it might face protests from other states. Such protests would suggest an absence of acceptance of universal jurisdiction.[369] Second, as a practical matter, despite the increased tendency in recent years of states to prosecute foreign nationals for human rights abuses committed abroad, they remain, on the whole, rather hesitant to legislate or prosecute based on universal

---

366. OECD Bribery Convention, *supra* note 156, art. 4.

367. Council of Europe Corruption Convention, *supra* note 160, art. 17. For a treaty failing to overcome differences and thus providing only a weak division of jurisdiction, see Agreement on the Application of Positive Comity Principles in the Enforcement of Their Competition Laws, June 4, 1998, U.S.-E.C., State Dep't No. 98-106, 37 I.L.M. 1070.

368. *See* Brigitte Stern, *À propos de la compétence universelle, in* LIBER AMICORUM JUDGE MOHAMMED BEDJAOUI 735 (Emile Yakpo & Tahar Boumedra eds., 1999); *see also* Blakesley, *supra* note 362, at 70-73 (discussing offenses that any nation obtaining personal jurisdiction over the perpetrator may prosecute). Offenses subject to universal jurisdiction include: piracy, slave trade, war crimes, genocide, crimes against humanity, torture, crimes against diplomats, and aircraft hijacking and sabotage. *See, e.g.*, Prosecutor v. Furundzija, Case No. IT-95-17-T, para. 156 (Int'l Crim. Trib. for Former Yugoslavia Trial Chamber II Dec. 10, 1998), http://www.un.org/icty/furundzija/trialc2/judgement/index.htm; 1 OPPENHEIM'S INTERNATIONAL LAW, *supra* note 216, § 435; RESTATEMENT (THIRD) OF FOREIGN RELATIONS LAW § 404 (1987); Blakesley, *supra* note 362, at 70-73.

369. *See* RATNER & ABRAMS, *supra* note 54, at 165 n.19.

jurisdiction.[370] Some governments fear foreign policy repercussions of trials based on universal jurisdiction; others are concerned about the diversion of resources entailed by such prosecutions or civil suits, especially since the evidence and witnesses are typically located abroad. These factors would suggest an even greater hesitancy by states to regulate purely extraterritorial activity by foreign corporations. Even if a state had jurisdiction, a court might dismiss the case based on forum non conveniens or analogous grounds.[371]

D. *Soft International Law*

Shifting to interstate arenas of lawmaking, international organizations could elaborate corporate duties through soft law instruments. To identify the appropriate fora for the development of such law, and for harder forms as well, one must consider the views of states, international organizations, corporations, and human rights NGOs as to an institution's legitimacy or authority in this area. This, in turn, will depend on its ability to represent the views of key participants and garner their acceptance, as well as its expertise on the subject.[372]

At least four organizations are promising candidates for prescribing soft law. First, the International Labour Organization would constitute a useful arena because its tripartite structure overtly incorporates labor and business viewpoints, and because it has previously produced significant hard and soft law regarding corporate behavior. Nonetheless, with the exception of the unions, the ILO does not include the potential groups of rightholders in the debate over corporate accountability. Second, the OECD, because it includes the home states of most significant TNEs, has a credibility that would aid the process. However, the absence of developing world states—the home of a sizeable share of businesses and potential victims—and the general lack of transparency of its methods cast some doubt on its authority, as shown during the 1998 debacle over the proposed Multilateral Agreement on Investment.[373] Third, the United Nations, due to its universal membership and long history as the leading international organization for the promulgation of human rights standards, represents a possible venue for soft lawmaking. Nonetheless, the UN's authority in this area is significantly tarnished in the eyes of TNEs and some Western states, particularly the

---

370. *Id.* at 185-86.

371. *See* INT'L COUNCIL ON HUMAN RIGHTS POLICY, *supra* note 101, paras. 74-77; *see also* Wiwa v. Royal Dutch Petroleum Co., 226 F.3d 88, 99-108 (2d Cir. 2000), *cert. denied*, 121 S. Ct. 1402 (2001) (discussing the limits of forum non conveniens in suits under the Alien Tort Claims Act).

372. *Cf.* McDougal & Reisman, *supra* note 14, at 356-57 (discussing the importance of authority in prescriptive arenas).

373. *See supra* note 47 and accompanying text.

United States, as a result of the debates of the 1970s and 1980s over the New International Economic Order and the planned UN Code of Conduct.

Fourth, the World Bank enjoys respect not only from its near-universal membership but in particular from its promulgation of the most important modern soft law instrument regarding foreign investment—the 1992 Guidelines for the Treatment of Foreign Investment.[374] Those guidelines, the result of a process within the Bank that included consultation with states both North and South, elaborate norms for states regarding foreign investment in a way that balances many of the competing claims of host states and investors. The Guidelines appear to have gained significant acceptance from key decisionmakers.[375] The Bank's competence in the area of foreign investment and development would make it a potentially promising candidate for drafting guidelines regarding corporate conduct as well. Its key shortcoming lies in its lack of deep expertise and experience with human rights issues, which might cause its product to reflect state and corporate views to the detriment of human rights concerns. Nonetheless, in recent years, the Bank has begun to make some strides in considering quite explicitly the human rights implications of the projects that it finances.[376] Its views could also be incorporated into the decisionmaking of regional development banks in Asia, Africa, and Latin America.

Soft law can even result from bilateral understandings. In December 2000, the United States and British governments, companies, and NGOs agreed on Voluntary Principles on Security and Human Rights in the Extractive Sectors. This document reiterates that public forces should follow international human rights law and includes strong recommendations to companies to ensure that private security forces also respect human rights, relying on soft law United Nations documents concerning law enforcement personnel.[377]

---

374. WORLD BANK, REPORT TO THE DEVELOPMENT COMMITTEE AND GUIDELINES FOR THE TREATMENT OF FOREIGN INVESTMENT (1992), *reprinted in* 31 I.L.M. 1363, 1379. *See generally* IBRAHIM F.I. SHIHATA, LEGAL TREATMENT OF FOREIGN INVESTMENT: "THE WORLD BANK GUIDELINES" (1993) (discussing the process leading to the development of the Guidelines and placing the Guidelines in the broader context of continuing international efforts to improve investment climates).

375. *See, e.g.*, Fedax N.V. v. Republic of Venezuela, ICSID Case No. ARB/96/3, para. 35, 37 I.L.M. 1378, 1385 (July 11, 1997) (identifying the Guidelines as a "major multilateral instrument[]").

376. *See, e.g.*, Richard E. Bissell, *Recent Practice of the Inspection Panel of the World Bank*, 91 AM. J. INT'L L. 741 (1997).

377. *See* Voluntary Principles on Security and Human Rights in the Extractive Sectors (Dec. 2000), *at* http://www.state.gov/www/global/human_rights/001220_fsdrl_principles.html.

E. *The Treaty Process—A Binding Code of Conduct*

States could promote uniformity of regulation of TNEs for activities
with human rights implications through a multilateral instrument
recognizing certain obligations upon corporations. The OECD's Bribery
Convention and the various environmental conventions noted earlier
represent the clearest examples of multilateral efforts to regulate corporate
activity. And the World Health Organization's ongoing efforts to draft a
Framework Convention on Tobacco Control evidence further moves in this
direction.[378] Such a convention could obligate enterprises based on the
theory above; it could also work through the framework of state
responsibility by imposing duties on states to regulate corporate conduct, as
is the case with much international labor law.

For an international institution to serve as the arena for the prescription
and application of hard law, decisionmakers must agree not only upon its
legitimacy and expertise (as is the case with soft law); they must also view
the organization as capable of creating and overseeing a regime with
enforcement mechanisms that will prove effective.[379] The ILO, OECD, and
United Nations could also serve as fora for treaty-drafting as well as soft
lawmaking, although their shortcomings noted above remain of concern.
Moreover, despite success in achieving widespread ratification of its
fundamental conventions, the overall record of the ILO on ratification and
implementation of its conventions is rather poor, and another convention
forgotten over time would undermine the purpose of the exercise.[380]
Another possibility is the World Trade Organization, which enjoys near-
universal membership and is now the leading global institution concerning
international commerce. At the same time, the WTO and its members have
started to consider the impact of trade on other issues only in the last
decade; and while the organization has begun to address environmental
issues in both intergovernmental discussions and dispute-settlement
decisions, members have been reluctant to consider human rights and labor
issues as part of its mandate.[381]

A component of a hard law instrument, of course, would be its control
or enforcement mechanisms. Several options are possible. First, the
convention could set up a monitoring body akin to the committees

---

378. *See, e.g., Elements of a WHO Framework Convention on Tobacco Control*, WHO Doc.
A/FCTC/WG1/6 (Sept. 8, 1999); *Proposed Draft Elements for a WHO Framework Convention on
Tobacco Control: Provisional Texts with Comments of the Working Group*, WHO Doc.
A/FCTC/INB1/2 (July 26, 2000).

379. McDougal & Reisman, *supra* note 14, at 356-57.

380. *See* PWBLF & AI, *supra* note 63, at 52 (discussing the ratification of ILO conventions).

381. Sarah H. Cleveland, *Human Rights Sanctions and the World Trade Organization, in*
ENVIRONMENT, HUMAN RIGHTS AND INTERNATIONAL TRADE 199, 201-02 (Francesco Francioni
ed., 2001).

established under the various global human rights instruments and the ILO Constitution.[382] The treaty could authorize the body to receive reports from states, NGOs, or multinational corporations, or even hear complaints about conduct from local community representatives or NGOs. Its findings, while not judicial in nature, would create a public—and, one hopes, objective— record of the activities of certain companies, allowing other actors, state and nonstate, to mobilize shame against them.

Second, the convention could call for domestic enforcement as do the Bribery Convention, the environmental conventions, and the international criminal law conventions that incorporate obligations to prosecute. States would be encouraged or required to investigate suspected abusers and impose appropriate sanctions—through administrative or criminal procedures—on the corporation. They could also be required to permit civil suits by those alleging violations of the treaty. The treaty would have to include jurisdictional provisions to clarify which states incur these obligations. One obvious model to follow is that employed in the modern international criminal law conventions, which typically obligate states to pass criminal laws based on several types of jurisdiction (e.g., territoriality, nationality, and passive personality), without prejudice to the right of states to criminalize based on any other links with the offending activity.[383]

Third, it is at least conceivable that such an agreement could set up a free-standing body composed of representatives of the parties (and perhaps others) authorized to determine corporate violations of duties and impose sanctions. This body might, for instance, have the power to order or authorize states to fine the offending company or increase tariff barriers on the exports and imports of the firm; to order or request that international arbitral bodies, such as the International Centre for the Settlement of Investment Disputes, refuse to hear claims brought by those companies; to order or request intergovernmental bodies that include corporate participants to preclude participation of violating entities;[384] or to prohibit international organizations from signing contracts with the offending firm.[385] If enacted under the auspices of the WTO, such an agreement could

---

382. *See generally* THE FUTURE OF U.N. HUMAN RIGHTS TREATY MONITORING (Philip Alston & James Crawford eds., 2000) (discussing institutional arrangements designed to monitor compliance with UN human rights treaties). For other suggestions on the use of existing monitoring bodies, including OECD and World Bank panels, see INT'L COUNCIL ON HUMAN RIGHTS POLICY, *supra* note 101, paras. 237-255.

383. *See, e.g.,* Torture Convention, *supra* note 76, art. 5, S. TREATY DOC. NO. 100-20, at 20, 1465 U.N.T.S. at 114; OECD Bribery Convention, *supra* note 156, art. 4.

384. *E.g.,* Int'l Telecomm. Union, Sector Membership—Participation, *at* http://www.itu.int/ members/sectmem/participation.html (last visited Sept. 1, 2001) (explaining the role of the telecommunications companies in ITU rulemaking).

385. *E.g.,* United Nations System: General Business Guide for Potential Suppliers of Goods and Services, *at* http://www.un.org./partners/business/procure.htm (last visited Sept. 1, 2001) (noting that the UN issues 135,000 contracts and purchase orders annually).

employ that organization's existing—and robust—mechanism for compliance, which allows states that prevail in dispute settlement proceedings to suspend benefits of the General Agreement on Tariffs and Trade against the losing party.[386] That process might allow for findings of violations against the state of incorporation of a particular enterprise, or even against the enterprise itself.[387] Again, however, the new nature of this concept suggests that states would be unlikely to contemplate such a robust enforcement process immediately.

VIII. CONCLUSION

The path of international law over the last century has been one of increasing both the breadth and the depth of its coverage. Its breadth has grown through the addition of new areas for regulation, whether the environment, telecommunications, health, or human rights; and its depth has expanded through erosion of much of the notion of the *domaine reservé*, the area seen as falling exclusively within the domestic jurisdiction of states.[388] Proposing international norms of corporate responsibility for violations of human dignity continues the trajectory that the law has taken, but it also represents new challenges for the enterprise. It challenges the state's exclusive prerogative (what some might call sovereignty) to regulate business enterprises by making them a subject of international scrutiny; it makes them entities that have their own duties to respect human rights.

With the theory now justified, elaborated, and applied in at least some preliminary ways, I would anticipate that it has sown the seeds of a number of core objections to the project of enterprise accountability. I thus conclude by treating four objections that demand a considered response. First, it might be argued that even if, as a matter of moral philosophy, human rights give rise to duties by more than just states, the inevitable result of my theory is essentially to make all private wrongs into human rights abuses. The theory effectively merges human rights law with private tort law. As a result, human rights are no longer special, human rights claims are no longer distinctive, and human rights law is inhibited from its primary goal,

---

386. Understanding on Rules and Procedures Governing the Settlement of Disputes, Apr. 15, 1994, art. 22, Marrakesh Agreement Establishing the World Trade Organization, Annex 2, LEGAL INSTRUMENTS—RESULTS OF THE URUGUAY ROUND vol. 31, 33 I.L.M. 1125, 1239-41 (1994).

387. For endorsements of this venue, see INT'L COUNCIL ON HUMAN RIGHTS POLICY, *supra* note 101, paras. 200-214; and Daniel S. Ehrenberg, *From Intention to Action: An ILO-GATT/WTO Enforcement Regime for International Labor Rights*, in HUMAN RIGHTS, LABOR RIGHTS, AND INTERNATIONAL TRADE, *supra* note 140, at 163.

388. Steven R. Ratner & Anne-Marie Slaughter, *Appraising the Methods of International Law: A Prospectus for Readers*, 93 AM. J. INT'L L. 291, 291 (1999). *But see* David Kennedy, *International Law and the Nineteenth Century: History of an Illusion*, 65 NORDIC J. INT'L L. 385 (1996) (emphasizing the need to reject the idea of international law as making inevitable progress).

the protection of individuals against governments. One concrete concern might be that human rights bodies would be overwhelmed with complaints about corporate behavior and diverted from considering complaints against states.[389]

Several responses are in order. First, to the extent an individual can point to a specific internationally recognized human right that he or she claims has been violated, that person has made a bona fide human rights claim; it is still special in that sense. The victim of, for instance, privately initiated torture or private discrimination based on religion is not a mere plaintiff in a tort case; that person's human rights—stated in core human rights instruments—were violated. Second, the theory is one based on human rights, not human desires. International human rights law has developed limits as to what certain rights against the state actually mean. For example, the individual right of members of national minorities to have their own schools does not require the state to pay for a religious establishment, nor would it require corporations to do so.[390] Because corporate duties derive from existing rights, not new ones, the danger of outrageous claims is diminished.

Third, and most critically, the possibility that relevant international decisionmakers will derive human rights duties for corporations does not mean that those obligations will be coextensive with the obligations on states. The differences between corporations and states regarding both their internal structures and those to whom they owe duties, as well as the need to respect corporate interests and rights, will inevitably limit the list of duties. For example, with respect to the right to privacy, those applying the theory might well find a duty not to invade people's homes, but not a duty to avoid publishing embarrassing information about public figures. The focus by respected NGOs, corporations, and governments on business behavior directly affecting physical integrity suggests a recognition of the need to proceed cautiously in making claims of corporate duties. I suspect that, over time, decisionmakers are likely to find a set of duties on corporations larger than those on individuals under international criminal law but noticeably smaller than those on states under existing human rights law.

A second, related, criticism is that this enterprise cannot be logically separated from an attempt to address duties by all other nonstate actors. In other words, if corporations can violate human rights, then why not sports clubs, unions, NGOs, universities, churches, and, ultimately, individuals? Of course, that individuals have some legal duties in the human rights area

---

389. I appreciate this critique from John Knox.

390. *See, e.g.*, Framework Convention for the Protection of National Minorities, *done* Feb. 1, 1995, art. 13(1), 34 I.L.M. 351, 356; *see also supra* note 301 and accompanying text (noting limitations on the right to form a family).

has been obvious since Nuremberg.[391] The concern must then be that new categories of dutyholders will inevitably arise, or new duties will fall on individuals. Indeed, this criticism suggests that my project inadvertently advances the cause of some world leaders who seek to give the state new powers over individuals through, for instance, the idea of a code of human responsibilities to complement the various codes of human rights.[392]

Clearly, the theory does broach the private-public divide in a way that invites the possibility that the law will recognize new dutyholders in the future. But why the concern? If, for example, the Rwandan Catholic Church participated in the 1994 genocide in that country, as has been alleged by respected observers, why not regard it as having violated the human rights of the victims?[393] If other entities have the ability to deprive individuals of recognized human rights, this theory might provide a framework for doing so, or the basis for a broader framework addressing more actors. If, at some point, decisionmakers end up recognizing more duties for the individual than those now encompassed in international criminal law, they need not have brought about an increase in state power relative to the individual. For any duties of individuals derive only from *human* rights; because the government does not and cannot itself have human rights, the individual has no new duties toward the government. If the concern is that new individual duties would empower the government to limit the human rights of some in order to guarantee the rights of others (and thus fulfill the former's duties to the latter), the prerogative—indeed the responsibility—of the state to protect individuals from each other is well enshrined in human rights law.[394]

Other skeptics could make claims not about the danger of the doctrine, but of its futility. First, it could be argued that tort law remains equipped to deal with corporate abuses of rights, and that reformulating corporate duties

---

391. *See supra* text accompanying notes 74-78.

392. *See, e.g.*, Universal Declaration of Human Responsibilities (Sept. 1, 1997), http://www.asiawide.or.jp/iac/UDHR/EngDecl1.htm; Theo van Boven, *A Universal Declaration of Human Responsibilities?*, *in* REFLECTIONS ON THE UNIVERSAL DECLARATION OF HUMAN RIGHTS 73 (Barend van der Heijden & Bahia Tahzib-Lie eds., 1998). For a balanced evaluation, see INT'L COUNCIL ON HUMAN RIGHTS POLICY, TAKING DUTIES SERIOUSLY (1999).

393. INT'L PANEL OF EMINENT PERSONALITIES TO INVESTIGATE THE 1994 GENOCIDE IN RWANDA AND THE SURROUNDING EVENTS, SPECIAL REPORT ch. 14, para. 14.66 (2000), http://www.oau-oua.org/document/ipep/report/Rwanda-e/EN-14-CH.htm; *see also* PHILIP GOUREVITCH, WE WISH TO INFORM YOU THAT TOMORROW WE WILL BE KILLED WITH OUR FAMILIES: STORIES FROM RWANDA 135-42 (1998) (discussing the involvement of clergy in the 1994 Rwandan genocide).

394. *See, e.g.*, *Universal Declaration of Human Rights*, *supra* note 91, art. 29(2), at 77 ("In the exercise of his rights and freedoms, everyone shall be subject only to such limitations as are determined by law solely for the purpose of securing due recognition and respect for the rights and freedoms of others . . . ."); ICCPR, *supra* note 129, art. 5(1), S. EXEC. DOC. E, 95-2, at 25, 999 U.N.T.S. at 174 (stating that there is no right of a state, group, or person to "perform any act aimed at the destruction of any of the rights and freedoms" in the Covenant); *id.* arts. 12(3), 18(3), 19(3), 21, 22(2), S. EXEC. DOC. E, 95-2, at 27, 29-30, 999 U.N.T.S. at 176, 178 (permitting states to limit rights as necessary to protect rights and freedoms of others); *see also* RAZ, *supra* note 82, at 184 (exploring conflicts of rights and conflicts of duties).

as human rights duties accomplishes nothing. But such a position assumes too much about tort law and too little about human rights law. While high-profile tort cases in the United States against corporations for human rights and environmental harms may be proceeding, the practice is hardly uniform. Most states provide no realistic possibility of such recovery. Transforming the controversy into a human rights issue is hardly a cure-all, as victims will always face such barriers to recovery as recalcitrant legislatures, inept courts, and powerful economic pressures. But reformulating the problem of business abuses as a human rights matter might well cause governments and the population to view them as a legitimate issue of public concern and not as some sort of private dispute.[395] In addition, using human rights, rather than tort law, as the prism through which to examine certain business abuses offers some possibility of more uniform global treatment of the issue rather than reliance upon the divergences of domestic tort law.

Second, skeptics might well seize on the cautious tone of Part VI and ask why, assuming that governments are unable or unwilling to regulate business activity now, the proposed scheme will somehow improve matters. In the end, does not resistance by the state doom the prospects for enterprise accountability? What possible incentives could states have to get such a process started? Will not corporations simply move to states that refuse to impose new obligations on them? It is, of course, unexceptionable that if states are so uninterested in regulating the activities of corporate actors, they will neither create domestic regimes nor cooperate to prescribe more hard or soft international law. The corporation can no more easily replace the government as having the first duty to protect human rights than can an international organization.

But even if states remain reluctant for the short term to prescribe new domestic or international norms on this issue, the derivation of enterprise duties still serves a critical function, insofar as it sets standards for businesses that can be monitored by nongovernmental organizations, international organizations, or the corporations themselves. The changing of expectations regarding appropriate behavior by transnational actors must often begin with civil society before governments can be expected to respond. Recognizing duties on enterprises, rather than merely on governments, also has the advantage of putting pressures directly on them not to seek refuge in some state that may be lax about enforcement. Thus even if the host states do not enforce the new duties, the outside scrutiny

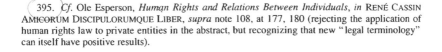

395. *Cf.* Ole Esperson, *Human Rights and Relations Between Individuals, in* RENÉ CASSIN AMICORUM DISCIPULORUMQUE LIBER, *supra* note 108, at 177, 180 (rejecting the application of human rights law to private entities in the abstract, but recognizing that new "legal terminology" can itself have positive results).

544   The Yale Law Journal   [Vol. 111: 443

will elicit compliance.[396] Moreover, it is possible that courts, domestic and international, that remain somewhat insulated from such economic pressures could jump-start this process through the sorts of rulings the European Court of Justice has issued regarding nondiscrimination in the private sector.[397]

Indeed, the same broad claim about government reluctance could be (and has been) leveled at the entire enterprise of human rights law, which is premised on the notion that domestic law may not offer sufficient protections for human dignity. And yet states have still come together over the last fifty years to draft an impressive corpus of human rights instruments and empower various institutions to monitor compliance and even adjudicate violations. This revolution has clearly affected the way that governments act toward their citizens and even promoted wide-scale changes in governmental structures to promote democracy.[398] As for the obvious reluctance of many governments to curb their abuses in practice even as they promulgate and promise to adhere to human rights norms, this cognitive dissonance represents one of the ways in which international law and institutions can improve state and nonstate behavior over time, as targets of norms find it increasingly difficult to walk away from their professed commitments.[399]

In the end, this exercise's strongest defense is its possibility of providing a framework and rationality to the dialogue of the deaf that seems to be transpiring among businesses, those affected by their operations, governments, and NGOs. One of law's great purposes is to provide a set of bookends that exclude certain claims by various sides from the table and thereby narrow the range of differences.[400] If these four participants in the accountability dynamic can focus their debate on what are truly human rights violations, the possibilities for constructive solutions loom larger. As the South African Truth and Reconciliation Commission said when it rejected both the view that all apartheid-era businesses should be condemned and that they were blameless, the duties of corporations turn on "[i]ssues of realistic choice, differential power and responsibility."[401]

---

396. I appreciate this argument from David Wippman.

397. *See supra* note 94 and accompanying text.

398. Steven R. Ratner, *Does International Law Matter in Preventing Ethnic Conflict?*, 32 N.Y.U. J. INT'L L. & POL. 591 (2000).

399. Peter M. Haas, *Choosing To Comply: Theorizing from International Relations and Comparative Politics, in* COMMITMENT AND COMPLIANCE, *supra* note 179, at 43, 45, 58-61; *see also* Thomas Risse & Kathryn Sikkink, *The Socialization of International Human Rights Norms into Domestic Practices: Introduction, in* THE POWER OF HUMAN RIGHTS, *supra* note 349, at 1, 14-17 (discussing the reaction of states to outside pressures).

400. *See* Ratner, *supra* note 398, at 627-29 (discussing the use of minority-rights norms to reject extreme claims by government and minorities).

401. 4 TRUTH & RECONCILIATION COMM'N, *supra* note 4, ch. 2, para. 146.

This is not to suggest that the law is the end of the story: Political and economic interests will surely drive the various actors as they make their claims and work to accommodate them, just as they do in other areas where international law is relevant. And both corporations and NGOs will have reasons for discussing enterprise activities that do not breach legal standards. Nonetheless, the law can, as it does in countless other areas of international affairs, offer a common language in this debate, as well as a set of standards that can be enforced. The duties resulting when these actors work through the above theory will clearly satisfy no group fully. But if prescribed and applied by legitimate and effective institutions, or enforced through corporate self-regulation, these norms represent the beginning of a more global and coherent response to new challenges to human dignity.

[9]

Meta-regulation: legal accountability for corporate social responsibility

CHRISTINE PARKER

I. Introduction: legal accountability and corporate social responsibility

The very idea that law might make business responsible for corporate social responsibility (CSR) is paradoxical. We might argue that ideally CSR includes compliance with business' legal responsibilities but goes 'beyond compliance'[1] to encompass the *economic* ('to produce goods and services that society wants and to sell them at a profit'), *ethical* ('additional behaviours and activities that are not necessarily codified into law but nevertheless are expected of business by society's members') and even *discretionary* ('those about which society has no clear-cut message for business', but society does expect business to assume some discretionary role, for example making philanthropic contributions) expectations of society.[2] If so, how is it possible for the *law* to make companies accountable for going *beyond the law*?

Research for this chapter was funded by the Australian Research Council Discovery Grant DP0344638 'Meta-regulation and the regulation of law'. I am grateful to my colleagues on that project – John Braithwaite, Colin Scott and Nicola Lacey – for discussions and ideas that have contributed to this paper. I am also grateful to Pamela 'Responsibilisation' Hanrahan, Doreen McBarnet, Greg Restall, Rob Rosen, Ronen Shamir and Aurora Voiculescu for helpful comments and discussions.

[1] See N. Gunningham, R. Kagan and D. Thornton, 'Social Licence and Environmental Protection: Why Businesses go Beyond Compliance?', *Law and Social Inquiry* 29 (2004), 307.

[2] A. B. Carroll, 'A Three-dimensional Conceptual Model of Corporate Performance', *Academy of Management Review* 4 (1979), 497, 500 (italics added). Carroll's definition recognises that all four overlap, some obligations may simultaneously fall into more than one category and obligations may move from being purely ethical to legal over time. They are all aspects of *society's* expectations of what corporations are obligated to do, and hence are *social* responsibilities.

On the other hand, we might argue that CSR is a set of vague, discretionary and non-enforceable corporate responses to social expectations.[3] If so, then might not companies use CSR to stave off more demanding legal regulation? Does not the idea of corporations' taking responsibility themselves for meeting society's expectations undermine the very idea of legal accountability for meeting substantive standards?

This chapter is concerned with the way in which law could (and sometimes does) seek to hold businesses *accountable* for taking their *responsibilities* seriously by using various mechanisms to encourage or enforce businesses to put in place internal governance structures, management practices and corporate cultures aimed at achieving responsible outcomes. Law attempts to constitute corporate 'consciences'[4] – getting companies 'to want to do what they should do'[5] – not just legally compliant outputs or actions. I have previously labelled regulatory initiatives that seek to do this 'meta-regulation' because they represent the (attempted) regulation of internal self-regulation.[6] Meta-regulation – the proliferation of different forms of regulation (whether tools of state law or non-law mechanisms) each regulating one another – is a key feature of contemporary governance.[7] The focus of this chapter, however, is on the meta-regulatory potential only of law.

---

[3] R. Shamir, 'Mind the Gap: The Commodification of Corporate Social Responsibility', *Symbolic Interaction* 28 (2005), 229; and R. Shamir, 'Between Self-regulation and the Alien Tort Claims Act: On the Contested Concept of Corporate Social Responsibility', *Law and Society Review* 38 (2004), 635. For a discussion of the ambiguity of 'corporate social responsibility', see D. Vogel, *The Market for Virtue: The Potential and Limits of Corporate Social Responsibility* (Washington, DC: Brookings Institution Press, 2005), pp. 4–6.

[4] Selznick uses the term 'corporate conscience': P. Selznick, *The Communitarian Persuasion* (Washington, DC: Woodrow Wilson Center Press, 2002), p. 101. See also n. 25 below.

[5] *ibid.*, p. 102

[6] C. Parker, *The Open Corporation* (Cambridge: Cambridge University Press, 2002). For similar uses of 'meta-regulation' or cognate terms, see J. Braithwaite, 'Meta-risk Management and Responsive Regulation for Tax System Integrity', *Law and Policy* 25 (2003), 1; C. Coglianese and D. Lazer, 'Management-based Regulation: Prescribing Private Management to Achieve Public Goals', *Law and Society Review* 37 (2003), 691 (government as 'meta-manager'); P. Grabosky, 'Using Non-governmental Resources to Foster Regulatory Compliance', *Governance* 8 (1995), 527, 543 ('meta-monitoring'). For commentary, see R. Baldwin, 'The New Punitive Regulation', *Modern Law Review* 67 (2004), 351, 374–82; J. Black, 'The Emergence of Risk-based Regulation and the New Public Risk Management in the United Kingdom', *Public Law* Autumn (2005), 512, 543–5; M. Power, *The Risk Management of Everything: Re-thinking the Politics of Uncertainty* (London: Demos, 2004), p. 21.

[7] C. Parker, J. Braithwaite, C. Scott and N. Lacey (eds.), *Regulating Law* (Oxford: Oxford University Press, 2004).

To the extent that law focuses on companies' *internal responsibility processes* rather than *external accountability outcomes*, law runs the risk of becoming a substanceless sham, to the delight of corporate power-mongers who can bend it to their interests. Law might be hollowed out into a focus on process that fails to recognise and protect substantive and procedural rights.[8] If the law itself fails to recognise and protect substantive and procedural rights, then business will doubly fail to do so.

Putting the critique so starkly anticipates the response. This chapter argues that it is possible, in principle at least, to imagine (and even to see partial examples of) legal meta-regulation that holds business organisations accountable for putting in place corporate conscience processes that are aimed at substantive social values. However, this requires that procedural and substantive rights of customers, employees, local communities and other relevant stakeholders, as against businesses,[9] are adequately recognised and protected. 'Meta-regulatory' accountability for corporate responsibility is possible – but it may have little to do with most current business and government 'corporate social responsibility' initiatives.

This chapter:

(1) Sets out what meta-regulating law must do and be in order to hold companies accountable for their responsibility, and briefly explains how this notion of meta-regulating law relates to the plurality of legal, non-legal and quasi-legal 'governance' mechanisms at work in a globalising, 'post-regulatory' world.

(2) Sets out the critique that law which attempts to meta-regulate corporate responsibility will focus on internal governance processes in a way that allows business to avoid the conflict between self-interest and social values, and therefore to avoid accountability.

(3) Argues that law or regulation that falls into this critique does not fall within the criteria I have defined for meta-regulation of corporate responsibility. My conception of legal meta-regulation is a useful tool for evaluating proposals to use law to encourage or enforce CSR precisely because it addresses the main critiques of attempts to regulate CSR.

[8] W. Heydebrand, 'Process Rationality as Legal Governance: a Comparative Perspective', *International Sociology* 18 (2003), 325.

[9] Including their senior managers and shareholders: see, for example, Gideon Haigh, *Bad Company: The Strange Cult of The CEO* (London: Aurum Books, 2004) (how remuneration of CEOs affects corporate behaviour); Christopher Kutz, *Complicity: Law and Ethics for a Collective Age* (Cambridge: Cambridge University Press, 2000) (an argument for shareholder liability for corporate irresponsibility).

II. Meta-regulation: legal regulation of corporate conscience

A. Meta-regulation

The concept of meta-regulation can be fitted into a broader literature in which governance is seen as increasingly about 'collaborations', 'partner-ships', 'webs' or 'networks' in which the state, state-promulgated law, and especially hierarchical command-and-control regulation, is not neces-sarily the dominant, and certainly not the only important, mechanism of regulation.[10] States, businesses, non-governmental organisations (NGOs) and people operating even outside these three sectors may all be active in constituting various governance networks that steer (or attempt to steer) different aspects of social and economic life.[11] States and law may be important to a greater or lesser extent in each of these networks, with overlapping forms of governance coming together in different ways to frustrate or accomplish various regulatory goals.[12]

The term 'meta-regulation' itself has been used as a descriptive or explanatory term within the literature on the 'new governance' to consider the way in which the state's role in governance and regulation is changing and splitting. The state is regulating its own regulation as a consequence of policies to apply transparency, efficiency and market competition prin-ciples to itself for example: government units that assess the social and economic impact of regulation proposed by other departments before allowing new legislation to be proposed;[13] regulating or auditing the quality assurance mechanisms of semi-independent government agencies (such as schools or universities), newly privatised or corporatised entities (such as prisons, rail operators or telecommunications companies), and

---

[10] See, e.g., J. Braithwaite, 'The New Regulatory State and the Transformation of Criminology', *British Journal of Criminology* 40 (2000), 222; J. Braithwaite and P. Drahos, *Global Business Regulation* (Cambridge: Cambridge University Press, 2000); M. Dorf and C. Sabel, 'A Constitution of Democratic Experimentalism', *Columbia Law Review* 98 (1998), 267; J. Freeman, 'The Private Role in Public Governance', *New York University Law Review* 75 (2000), 543, and 'Collaborative Governance in the Administrative State', *UCLA Law Review* 45 (1997), 1; R. Lipschutz, *Globalization, Governmentality and Global Politics: Regulation for the Rest of Us?* (Abingdon: Routledge, 2005); O. Lobel, 'The Renew Deal: the Fall of Regulation and the Rise of Governance in Contemporary Legal Thought', *Minnesota Law Review* 89 (2004), 342; H. Schepel, *The Constitution of Private Governance: Product Standards in the Regulation of Integrating Markets* (Oxford: Hart Publishing, 2005).

[11] C. Shearing and J. Wood, 'Nodal Governance, Democracy, and the New "Denizens"', *Journal of Law and Society* 30 (2003), 400, 405.

[12] See C. Scott, 'Analysing Regulatory Space: Fragmented Resources and Institutional Design', *Public Law* Summer (2001), 283.

[13] B. Morgan, 'The Economisation of Politics: Meta-regulation as a Form of Nonjudicial Legality', *Social and Legal Studies* 12 (2003), 489.

government departments.[14] 'Meta-regulation' can also entail any form of regulation (whether by tools of state law or other mechanisms) that regulates any other form of regulation. Thus it might include legal regulation of self-regulation (for example, putting an oversight board above a self-regulatory professional association), non-legal methods of 'regulating' internal corporate self-regulation or management (for example, voluntary accreditation to codes of good conduct and so on), the regulation of national law-making by transnational bodies (such as the European Union), and so on.

Some of this governance literature is mainly analytical or descriptive. Some writers are critical of the 'hollowing out of the state' by plural governance mechanisms. Some actively encourage it. Others are cautiously optimistic about the possibilities for increased participation in decision-making entailed by changes in governance. Some seek to suggest ways in which governance networks might be made more democratic, just, and/or fair, starting from the assumption that plural governance mechanisms are (and always have been) a reality for good or for ill. There is no consensus (among either scholars or practitioners) about what substantive values, if any, the techniques of meta-regulation and the new governance represent.[15] Nor is there any consensus about what role, if any, law at the national, and especially international, level can and should play in facilitating, enforcing, regulating or supplanting governance networks.[16]

Why, then, might we be interested in thinking about law 'meta-regulating' corporate responsibility?

First, and most practically, we would expect that law (or indeed other forms of regulation/governance) that can focus itself on the inside of

---

[14] M. Power, 'Evaluating the Audit Explosion', *Law and Policy* 25 (2003), 185; C. Scott, 'Speaking Softly without Big Sticks: Meta-regulation and Public Sector Audit', *Law and Policy* 25 (2003), 203. Also see C. Hood, O. James, C. Scott, G. Jones and T. Travers, *Regulation Inside Government* (Oxford: Oxford University Press, 1999); J. Jordana and D. Levi-Faur, 'The Politics of Regulation in the Age of Governance', in J. Jordana and D. Levi-Faur (eds.), *The Politics of Regulation: Institutions and Regulatory Reforms for the Age of Governance* (Cheltenham: Edward Elgar, 2004), p. 1.

[15] See Jordana and Levi-Faur, *The Politics of Regulation*, p. 11 ('the true colours of the regulatory state are still to be determined').

[16] Contrast, for example, Vogel, *The Market for Virtue* (cautious support for the possibility of achieving CSR at an international level through market mechanisms and civil society action); Lipschutz, *Globalization* (a substantial argument that current transnational governance mechanisms and CSR reform proposals are both based on market regulation that exclude political participation and regulation aimed at the common good); Schepel, *The Constitution of Private Governance* (detailed analysis of law and practice to show that 'private' governance already represents the 'centre' of product safety-setting in a way that is ineluctably intertwined with 'public' law on the periphery).

corporations to constitute corporate consciences that go beyond compliance might be able to achieve more sustainable compliance with traditional regulatory goals more effectively and efficiently because it latches onto companies' inherent capacity to manage themselves.[17] Recognition of the plurality of governance provides an opportunity. Meta-regulating law could connect with communities, networks and organisations that are rich with the possibility of regulating themselves and one another responsibly, and work with that possibility to invigorate and enliven their inner commitment to responsibility.

Second, even if meta-regulation cannot be shown to have practical effectiveness and efficiency benefits, we might still think it is good to develop a meta-regulatory aspect to law because it makes the law track more accurately the way we think about organisational responsibility for identifying, preventing and correcting legal and ethical wrongdoing – meta-regulatory law recognises the complex ways in which organisational processes and structures can sometimes lead to wrong actions or outputs, and gives us techniques for holding organisations and their management responsible for the wrongness of those processes, as well as for the wrongness of their outputs.[18]

Finally, in the context of the new governance, meta-regulation might be one of the ways in which the practice and theory of law must be transformed and reconceptualised in order for us to work out how law interacts with other strands of governance.[19] Meta-regulatory law might recognise, incorporate or empower initiatives developed by non-state actors or

---

[17] See references at n. 6 above, and at n. 30 below. See also B. Fisse and J. Braithwaite, *Corporations, Crime and Accountability* (Cambridge: Cambridge University Press, 1993). Note this argument assumes a certain level of management competence and coherence, assumptions that are not always justified in practice (see critique of meta-regulating corporate responsibility in section III below).

[18] I have set out previously the ways in which more traditional command-and-control regulation of business frequently fails to achieve these first two objectives, and how meta-regulation does: see Parker, *The Open Corporation*.

[19] See C. Sabel and W. Simon, 'Epilogue: Accountability Without Sovereignty', in G. de Búrca and J. Scott (eds.), *New Governance and Constitutionalism in Europe and the US* (Oxford: Hart Publishing, 2006) (on the 'transformation' or 'hybridisation' of law in the context of the 'new governance'). The concept of meta-regulation would be aimed towards similar ideals as those represented by Teubner's idea of 'reflexive' law: G. Teubner, 'Corporate Fiduciary Duties and their Beneficiaries: A Functional Approach to the Legal Institutionalization of Corporate Responsibility', in K. Hopt and G. Teubner, *Corporate Governance and Directors' Liabilities: Legal, Economic and Sociological Analyses of Corporate Social Responsibility* (Berlin: Walter de Gruyter, 1985); Nonet and Selznick's 'responsive' law: P. Nonet and P. Selznick, *Law and Society in Transition: Toward Responsive Law* (2nd edn New Brunswick, NJ: Transaction Publishers, 2001) and, earlier, Durkheim's notion of law as coordinating between different social roles and functions, especially as represented

partnerships of actors that can regulate corporate governance processes (for example by enforcing management system standards developed by international NGOs). Taking a meta-regulatory approach to law might also allow us to recognise that some governance mechanisms that we might not have traditionally thought of as law could in fact be thought of as 'law' in an extended sense, and evaluated according to criteria of legality.[20] And, vice versa, we might understand better the ways in which law's regulatory goals are achieved or frustrated via regulatory forces outside the law (for example pollution limits are only observed by companies to the extent that relevant technology is available and management implements that technology appropriately in corporate production processes), and we might better understand the limits of law's regulatory reach. Meta-regulatory law is a response to the recognition that law itself is regulated by non-legal regulation, and should therefore seek to adapt itself to plural forms of regulation.

B. What would law need to do in order to meta-regulate corporate social responsibility?

Legal regulation characteristically works by holding people *accountable* for meeting 'threshold criteria of good conduct or performance' after the fact.[21] Legal regulation of business has typically involved imposing liability for conduct that has an impact or manifestation external to the business that fails to meet the legal standard, for example pollution, the death or injury of a worker, price-fixing, harmful products and so on.[22] CSR requires *responsibility*. As Philip Selznick puts it, *responsibility* goes beyond accountability to ask 'whether and how much you care about your duties. An ethic of responsibility calls for reflection and understanding, not mechanical or bare conformity. It looks to ideals as well as obligations, values as well as rules ... Responsibility internalizes standards by building them into the self-conceptions, motivations, and habits of individuals and into the organization's premises and routines.'[23]

---

in associational governance regimes: see R. Cotterrell, *Emile Durkheim: Law in a Moral Domain* (Edinburgh: Edinburgh University Press, 1999), pp. 111, 176–80.

[20] See, for example, Schepel's study of product standards developed outside formal legal mechanisms yet incorporated into law and much more important than law in many ways: Schepel, *The Constitution of Private Governance*.

[21] Selznick, *The Communitarian Persuasion*, p. 29

[22] Of course, law does not always regulate by setting standards, monitoring compliance and prosecuting and punishing non-compliance: see Parker, *et al.* (eds.), *Regulating Law*.

[23] Selznick, *The Communitarian Persuasion*, pp. 29, 102.

Responsible institutions, like responsible individuals, must have an inner commitment to doing the right thing[24] – they must have a corporate 'conscience'. For a corporation we need to look at its governance, management and culture in order to see whether, or what kind of, corporate conscience, it has. Selznick puts this well:

> A corporate conscience is created when values that transcend narrow self-interest are built into the practice and structure of the enterprise. This can be done in several ways: by clarifying policies and making them public; by practicing sensitive recruitment of staff; by inculcating appropriate attitudes and habits; by establishing special units to implement policies affecting the well-being of employees, or environmental and consumer protection; and by cooperating with relevant outside groups, such as trade unions and public agencies. All this becomes an 'organisational culture,' a framework within which the main goals of the enterprise are pursued. Although self-interest is by no means rejected, the realities of interdependence are accepted, the benefits of belonging acknowledged. Self-interest is moderated and redirected, not forgotten or extinguished.[25]

Selznick's morally 'thick' conception of what meta-regulation should aim to do set out here can be contrasted with the morally 'thin' reasons for which the critics argue meta-regulation has been adopted. For example, Kim Krawiec argues that meta-regulatory techniques aimed at internal compliance systems have grown in popularity in the United States because policy-proposers and makers see corporate compliance breaches too narrowly as a principal–agent problem – that is, that 'misconduct within organizations results from the acts of single, independent agents who disregard the preferences of shareholder principals and their representatives – the board of directors and senior management'.[26] According to her, meta-regulation is therefore aimed narrowly at giving organisational principals incentives to police their agents more carefully, rather than addressing substantively the ways in which organisational management, systems and culture shape and/or implicitly encourage misconduct. She also argues that 'heightened organizational liability in exchange for a "safe harbor" in the form of mitigation based on internal compliance structures' is 'far

---

[24] P. Selznick, *The Moral Commonwealth* (Berkeley, CA: The University of California Press, 1992), p. 345. See also K. Goodpaster, 'The Concept of Corporate Responsibility', *Journal of Business Ethics* 2 (1983), 1 (corporations should be expected to take ethical responsibility through internal decision-making processes analogous to individual ethical reasoning).

[25] Selznick, *The Communitarian Persuasion*, p. 101.

[26] K. Krawiec, 'Organizational Misconduct: Beyond the Principal–agent Model', *Florida State Law Review* 32 (2005), 1, 28.

less onerous' to business than actually 'altering current business practices or paying damages for agent misconduct', and in that sense it is a public choice response to organisational liability (that is, business preferences have shaped the nature of organisational liability).[27] She may be right or wrong about the factual reasons why US law has incorporated so many apparently meta-regulatory initiatives. But, even if she is right, this does not mean that meta-regulation cannot be justified, and evaluated, on the ethically thicker grounds proposed by Selznick and adopted in this chapter.

In order to instigate, catalyse and hold accountable corporate social *responsibility*, law would have to be aimed at 'regulating' the internal self-regulation of businesses. Following Selznick's formulation of what 'corporate conscience' requires in the quotation above, I suggest that legal 'meta-regulation' of internal corporate self-regulation (or conscience) requires the following three things. Achieving these three things in combination is what would distinguish legal regulation that 'meta-regulates' CSR from other types of legal regulation.[28] If it means anything to hold companies legally accountable for CSR, this is what it must mean:

(1) *Law that meta-regulates CSR must be aimed at making sure that companies meet 'values that transcend narrow self-interest'*
Law that meta-regulates CSR must be aimed clearly at values or policy goals for which companies can take responsibility, not merely compliance with output rules.[29] Social and economic regulation is usually promulgated for specific, articulated policy purposes (albeit vague and/or contested to a greater or lesser extent) – a healthy environment, a fair and competitive market, a high degree of security of financial investment for individuals. Relevant values or policy goals might also come from other sources such as human rights or labour rights instruments at a global level, whether they are seen as law or 'soft law', or neither.

(2) *Law that meta-regulates CSR must be aimed at making sure these values are 'built into the practice and structure of the enterprise'*
An organisation, not being an individual, can only be responsible by building responsibility into its practice and structure. Selznick mentions a

---

[27] *Ibid.*, 41. See also the references at n. 3 above.

[28] Note this chapter is concerned only with considering the *legal* regulation of CSR, not (meta-)regulation by other means.

[29] See J. Braithwaite and V. Braithwaite, 'The Politics of Legalism: Rules versus Standards in Nursing Home Regulation', *Social and Legal Studies* 4 (1995), 307.

number of ways in which responsibility might be 'institutionalised' within a business enterprise. This echoes an extensive literature on what it takes for organisations to be internally committed to legal compliance,[30] and indeed to go 'beyond compliance'.[31] The aim is that each company would have an organisational culture that supports and sustains responsibility, and that management would be carried out in practice in a way that demonstrates responsibility. Generally, in order to achieve these objectives, meta-regulating law would require companies to put in place formal governance structures and management systems that help to produce a responsible culture and management in practice. These might include high-level statements and demonstrations of commitment to compliance with legal and/or ethical obligations; institutionalised in management and worker accountability and performance measurement systems and standard operating procedures; communication and training programmes for disseminating information about these policies and systems; internal reporting and monitoring systems for gathering information about compliance with those obligations and procedures; processes for gathering and resolving relevant complaints, grievances, suggestions and whistle-blowing reports from those both internal and external to the organisation; and internal and external reviews or audits of the functioning and performance of the whole system that feeds back to the highest level and into the design and operation of the systems.[32] I have previously argued that these are all ways of making corporate management 'open' or 'permeable' to external values.[33]

---

[30] J. Braithwaite, *Corporate Crime in the Pharmaceutical Industry* (London: Routledge and Kegan Paul, 1984); J. Braithwaite, *To Punish or Persuade: Enforcement of Coal Mine Safety* (Albany, NY: State University of New York Press, 1985); F. Haines, *Corporate Regulation: Beyond 'Punish or Persuade'* (Oxford: Oxford University Press, 1997); B. Hutter, *Regulation and Risk: Occupational Health and Safety on the Railways* (Oxford: Oxford University Press, 2001), pp. 301–12; D. McCaffrey and D. Hart, *Wall Street Polices Itself: How Securities Firms Manage the Legal Hazards of Competitive Pressures* (New York: Oxford University Press, 1998); Parker, *The Open Corporation*, pp. 43–61, 197–244; J. Rees, *Reforming the Workplace: A Study of Self-regulation in Occupational Safety* (Philadelphia, PA: University of Pennsylvania Press, 1988).

[31] N. Gunningham, R. Kagan and D. Thornton, *Shades of Green: Business, Regulation and Environment* (Stanford, CA: Stanford University Press, 2003); A. Prakash, *Greening the Firm: The Politics of Corporate Environmentalism* (Port Chester, NY: Cambridge University Press, 2000).

[32] Parker, *The Open Corporation*, pp. 197–244, includes a more sophisticated analysis of what such systems are likely to require in order to be effective. See also the other references in nn. 30 and 31 above.

[33] See Parker, *The Open Corporation*.

⟶ *(3) Law that meta-regulates CSR must recognise that 'the main goals of the organisation' are still to be pursued within the responsibility framework*

The stance of meta-regulating law is to recognise that the main goals of a company are not merely to make sure that it acts socially responsibly, but also to meet its main goals of producing particular goods and/or services, providing a return to its investors, and/or providing paid employment to its workers and managers. Meta-regulating law should allow space for the company itself to take responsibility for working out how to meet its main goals within the framework of values set down by regulation, provided its main goals can be carried on consistently with social responsibility values. Meta-regulating law should be careful to leave space, to the greatest extent possible, to allow the companies it regulates to decide for themselves how to institutionalise responsibility. This means meta-regulating law does not assume command-and-control is the only appropriate technique for regulating social responsibility. It is willing to experiment with more indirect or facilitative techniques for engendering responsibility, including through requiring or capacitating non-state agencies (such as auditors, NGOs or the public at large) to help regulate corporate behaviour (for example, through audit requirements, provision of information about corporate performance to the public and so on). It is also willing to treat firms that show different levels of inner commitment to responsibility in different ways.[34] Note the rider, as much room 'as possible' consistent with ensuring companies do operate within a responsibility framework – meta-regulating law is law, not merely self-regulation.

In summary

Meta-regulation should be about requiring organisations to implement processes (point 2 above) that are aimed at making sure they reach the right results in terms of actions that impact on the world (point 1 above). It recognises, however, that law-makers and regulators may not know exactly what the 'right' processes, and even the right results, will look like in each situation. The people who are involved in the situation are best placed to work out the details in their own circumstances, *if* they can be motivated to do so responsibly (point 3 above). Whenever we see these criteria being met, we see law seeking to make companies responsible – that

---

[34] See N. Gunningham and P. Grabosky, *Smart Regulation: Designing Environmental Policy* (Oxford: Clarendon Press, 1998) and N. Gunningham and R. Johnstone, *Regulating Workplace Safety: Systems and Sanctions* (Oxford: Oxford University Press, 1999) for comprehensive examinations of the various techniques available in two regulatory arenas.

is, meta-regulating companies' internal consciences.[35] Meta-regulating law can also recognise that motivation, standards, and even monitoring and enforcement systems, for responsibility come from places other than law – from consumer activism, voluntary industry codes, the desire to protect organisational reputation and so on – and that regulators and regulation can usefully facilitate, coordinate, extend and simply recognise these other forms of governance.[36] The details of corporate responsibility processes and their goals will often be 'negotiated' to one extent or another with industry – by explicitly negotiating standards and goals with individual companies or industry, leaving it for individual companies to decide exactly how to design a compliance management system for their own situation, by incorporating into legal requirements voluntary standards developed by industry, or simply because the relevant law or policy instrument provides only for management systems in the most general terms.

C. *Examples of techniques of legal meta-regulation*

At a *national level* we will generally find clear examples of legal meta-regulation of CSR within specific domains of social and economic regulation of business.

The most common method is through determinations of corporate liability, damages or penalties in civil or criminal law by reference to whether the corporation has implemented an appropriate compliance system. Meta-regulating law makes it a good legal risk management practice to implement processes to ensure internal corporate responsibility for meeting regulatory goals. One of the oldest examples is probably the duty to provide a safe system of work in relation to occupational health and safety liability in tort and statutory regulation. The most famous is the US Federal Sentencing Guidelines for organisations, which state that the existence of an effective compliance system (as defined in the Guidelines) will provide companies or individuals with a reduction of penalty if they are found to have breached the law.[37] A variety of other regulatory liability regimes in the United States are now predicated on similar considerations.[38] In other jurisdictions implementation of a compliance system is an important aspect in determining liability or penalties in relation to competition and consumer protection law, and vicarious liability

---

[35] For a similar conception, see Coglianese and Lazer, 'Management-based Regulation'.

[36] See Braithwaite and Drahos, *Global Business Regulation*; Vogel, *The Market for Virtue*.

[37] See D. Murphy, 'The Federal Sentencing Guidelines for Organizations: A Decade of Promoting Compliance and Ethics', *Iowa Law Review* 87 (2002), 697.

[38] For a comprehensive overview, see Krawiec, 'Organizational Misconduct', 14–21.

for sexual harassment and discrimination or unequal employment opportunity.[39] Recent UK and Australian proposals to introduce an offence of corporate manslaughter could also be seen as examples of meta-regulation through the use of liability. For example, the 2005 UK Home Office's Draft Corporate Manslaughter Bill provides that an organisation will be guilty of corporate manslaughter 'if the way in which any of the organisation's activities are managed or organised by its senior managers (a) causes a person's death, and (b) amounts to a gross breach of a relevant duty of care owed by the organisation to the deceased'.[40]

A second technique of legal meta-regulation of corporate responsibility is when regulators 'settle' potential regulatory enforcement actions with businesses only on condition that they implement internal changes to identify, correct and prevent future wrongdoing. Or, where courts make corporate 'probation' orders that require the company to do so as part of the organisation's sentence. The US Sentencing Guidelines state that organisations that do not have an effective compliance programme should be placed on probation to implement one.[41] Regulators in the United Kingdom and other Commonwealth jurisdictions have used discretionary powers to make informal settlements requiring compliance system implementation for years. Similarly, US prosecutors under a number of regulatory regimes consider whether a business has implemented an effective compliance programme or not in deciding whether to prosecute or not.[42] Australian regulatory law seems to be specialising in formalising these types of settlements as 'enforceable undertakings' in legislation.[43]

Another common method of meta-regulation is to make the implementation of internal corporate conscience mechanisms a condition of licences or permissions required before a company can engage in a certain business,

---

[39] See Parker, *The Open Corporation*, pp. 249–51.

[40] But for a thorough evaluation of the limits of the UK Bill, see Centre for Corporate Accountability, *Response to the Government's Draft Bill on Corporate Manslaughter* (June 2005), available at www.corporateaccountability.org/dl/manslaughter/reform/crownlegal2005.doc (accessed 30 April 2007); see generally A. Hall, R. Johnstone and A. Ridgway, 'Reflection on Reforms: Developing Criminal Accountability for Industrial Deaths' (April 2004), *National Research Centre for Occupational Health and Safety Working Paper* 33, available at www.ohs.anu.edu.au/publications/pdf/WorkingPaper26pdf.pdf (accessed 30 April 2007).

[41] In Australia, see Trade Practices Act 1974 (Cth), s. 86C for provision for corporate probation orders in relation to competition and consumer protection offences.

[42] See C. Parker, *The Open Corporation*, p. 260.

[43] The first was Trade Practices Act 1974 (Cth), s. 87B. See C. Parker, 'Restorative Justice in Business Regulation? The Australian Competition and Consumer Commission's use of enforceable undertakings', *Modern Law Review* 67 (2004), 209.

or build facilities in a certain location. The most common examples are the environmental management systems and local community consultations often required as part of the licence obligations for permissions required from environmental regulators for manufacturing facilities. The licence requirements for financial services firms usually include broad-ranging internal systems for ensuring integrity of funds (preventing fraud, ensuring proper investment decisions, avoiding conflicts of interest and so on) and investor disclosure (including consumer protection measures such as 'know your client' principles) regulation.[44] In New South Wales, the regulator of the corporatised/privatised gas and electricity providers regularly audits their internal compliance systems to make sure they comply with licence obligations, with the frequency of audits partially dependent on the results of the previous audit.[45]

Then there are a number of more voluntary meta-regulatory initiatives that seek to encourage or reward 'beyond compliance' internal management systems by granting extra regulatory flexibility to firms that voluntarily adopt superior internal systems that go 'beyond compliance' – for example, by fast-tracking the granting of permissions or licences to such firms, scheduling inspections less frequently for them, or providing public recognition for them through allowing them to use a seal or logo that is publicised as a mark of superior performance. US environmental and occupational health and safety regulators have been particularly active in experimenting with such schemes.[46]

The law might also seek more indirect or partial methods of meta-regulation. Often more indirect, less coercive, methods of meta-regulation are used (or proposed) for schemes aimed more at the ethical and discretionary aspects of CSR, or for schemes aimed at improving CSR as a whole (rather than focused on the goals of a specific regulatory regime). For example, laws, such as the US *Sarbanes-Oxley Act* (2002), that require certain corporate employees to report suspected corporate fraud to senior management and that require or encourage companies to put in place

---

[44] See, for example, Black, 'The Emergence of Risk-based Regulation'; P. Hanrahan, '(Ir)responsible Entities: Reforming Manager Accountability in Public Unit Trusts', *Company and Securities Law Journal* 16 (1998), 76; H. Lauritsen, 'Enforced Self-regulation under the Financial Services Reform Act: Ensuring the Competency of Financial Intermediaries', *Company and Securities Law Journal* 21 (2003), 468.

[45] See 'Licence Compliance' page in section on Electricity Licensing at www.ipart.nsw.gov.au (accessed 30 April 2007).

[46] See N. Gunningham and D. Sinclair, *Leaders and Laggards: Next-Generation Environmental Regulation* (Sheffield: Greenleaf Publishing, 2002), pp. 111–15; O. Lobel, 'Interlocking Regulatory and Industrial Relations: The Governance of Workplace Safety', *Administrative Law Review* 57 (2005), 1071.

whistleblower policies are a form of partial encouragement to internal corporate conscience, since a corporate policy encouraging and protecting whistleblowers (generally in relation to any breach of legal or ethical obligations, not just financial fraud) would be one element of the sort of processes that companies would need to have in place to ensure their own responsibility.[47] But much more would also be necessary. Laws that simply protect whistleblowers (for example, by providing that they should not be sacked or sued for their actions, and giving them the right to sue for compensation if they are sacked), rather than mandating implementation of policies, provide indirect encouragement to internal corporate conscience.[48] The availability of damages indirectly holds businesses accountable for allowing a culture or management system that ignores and punishes whistleblowers to go unchecked, and encourages whistleblowers to make their concerns known. Other examples might include government 'approved' or sponsored voluntary CSR management accreditation and auditing schemes,[49] voluntary undertakings to implement CSR management systems given to government and enforceable by contract, tax incentives, and government procurement decisions predicated on implementation of CSR systems.[50]

In the final section, we will evaluate some of these more ambiguous examples.

Much discussion about CSR is about corporate observation of human rights at the *transnational level*. It is hard to find good examples of transnational *legal* meta-regulation of CSR because, as is well-known, there are few avenues for holding corporations accountable under international law at all, and none in relation to human rights, the main focus of CSR at the transnational level.[51] (There are many attempts at *non-legal* regulation

---

[47] On the US Sarbanes-Oxley reforms, see R. Rosen, 'Resistances to Reforming Corporate Governance: The Diffusion of QLCC's', *Fordham Law Review* 74 (2005), 1251.

[48] Corporations Act (Cth), Part 9.4AAA (commenced 1 July 2004).

[49] For example EMAS, the Eco-Management and Audit Scheme, a voluntary initiative established by the European Commission (Council Regulation 761/01/EC, OJ No. L114/1. 24 April 2001): see ec.europa.eu/environment/emas/index_en.htm (accessed 30 April 2007).

[50] These had both been proposed by the European Community, but not even that level of legal 'enforceability' is being given to CSR by the European Community at this stage: see Commission of the European Communities, *Communication from the Commission concerning Corporate Social Responsibility: A Business Contribution to Sustainable Development*, Brussels, 2 July 2002 COM (2002) 347 final.

[51] See D. Kinley and J. Tadaki, 'From Talk to Walk: the Emergence of Human Rights Responsibilities for Corporations at International Law', *Virginia Journal of International Law* 44 (2004), 931 (concluding that there is no binding transnational law on human rights obligations for corporations; but there is 'an expanding body of extraterritorial domestic jurisprudence that focuses on the human rights implications of actions taken by

of transnational CSR, with varying degrees of success.)[52] In order to find examples of *legal* regulation of transnational CSR, we will generally need to look for situations where nations legally regulate the conduct of transnational corporations (TNCs) in accord with international obligations, or adopt or enforce voluntary global corporate responsibility standards,[53] or where national law has an extra-jurisdictional impact on TNCs.[54] In the future multilateral institutions might also seek to enforce obligations on TNCs directly, rather than relying on member states to do so.[55] We might also find international 'networks' of regulation in which state law, transnational voluntary codes, global civil society organisations and so on reinforce one another to regulate corporate conscience.[56]

corporations overseas' (at 935); and a number of multilateral institutions have created 'soft-law' human rights standards for the conduct of TNCs, although these have generally not been implemented, monitored or enforced in any way: at 949–52).

[52] See n. 36 above.

[53] Things like SA8000 (an accreditable and auditable social accountability standard), and possibly ISO14000, have a focus on internal corporate management systems, but barely count as law of any kind, even 'soft law'. In the future they might be adopted or encouraged by national laws by being used for reporting standards, liability or incorporated by contract (by government or by private companies): see Kinley and Tadaki, 'From Talk to Walk', 957; A. Wawryk, 'Regulating Transnational Corporations through Corporate Codes of Conduct', in J. Frynas and S. Pegg (eds.), *Transnational Corporations and Human Rights* (Basingstoke: Palgrave Macmillan, 2003), p. 53; K. Webb and A. Morrison, 'The Law and Voluntary Codes: Examining the "Tangled Web"', in K. Webb (ed.), *Voluntary Codes: Private Governance, the Public Interest and Innovation* (Ottawa: Carleton University Research Unit for Innovation, Science and the Environment, 2002), p. 93. For a comprehensive overview of the ways in which environmental management system certification programmes can be incorporated into, enforced or facilitated by the law, see E. Meidinger, 'Environmental Certification Programs and U.S. Environmental Law: Closer than you may Think', *Environmental Law Reporter* 31 (2001), 10162.

[54] See, e.g., Alien Torts Claims Act liability in the United States and equivalents in other jurisdictions and the proposed (but failed) attempts to legislate by the Australian, UK and US government for companies based in those respective countries to be required to observe certain human rights standards in overseas operations: Kinley and Tadaki, 'From Talk to Walk', 939–42. So far these initiatives do not have a meta-regulatory aspect.

[55] See R. Mayne, 'Regulating TNCs; the Role of Voluntary and Governmental Approaches', in S. Picciotto and R. Mayne (eds.), *Regulating International Business* (Basingstoke: Macmillan Press, 1999), p. 235; cf. T. McInerney, 'Putting Regulation before Responsibility: the Limits of Voluntary Corporate Social Responsibility' (2005), *The George Washington University Law School Public Law and Legal Theory Working Paper No.* 123, available at ssrn.com/abstract = 658081 (accessed 30 April 2007) (voluntary CSR is not enough and global business regulation should develop national capacity to regulate).

[56] See Braithwaite and Drahos, *Global Business Regulation*. The same types of networks regulate at a national level too, of course (see references at n. 10 above). See also R. O'Brien, 'NGOs, Global Civil Society and Global Economic Regulation', in S. Picciotto and R. Mayne (eds.), *Regulating International Business* (Basingstoke: Macmillan Press, 1999), p. 257.

Our concern in this chapter is the extent to which any of these forms of transnational legal regulation of business might be meta-regulatory – that is, aimed at the corporate conscience, not just corporate outputs.[57] One partial example of meta-regulation at the transnational level is the Basel Accord on Banking Regulation, a voluntary multilateral agreement by which G10 nations agree to harmonised standards for national banking regulation. Under this accord, the robustness of banks' internal systems for managing operational risk (a concept that includes breach of legal compliance requirements and reputational loss through breach of ethical obligations to stakeholders and other CSR failures) should be an element in deciding their capital adequacy ratios (the proportion of the investments they hold for customers that they must have available in cash in order to be able to operate).[58]

The World Health Organisation's *International Code of Marketing of Breast Milk Substitutes*[59] is probably the most successful example of international regulation that applies to business organisations. It includes a primitive meta-regulatory aspect: 'manufacturers and distributors of products within the scope of this Code should regard themselves as responsible for monitoring their marketing practices according to the principles and aims of this Code, and for taking steps to ensure that their conduct at every level conforms to them'.[60]

National governments have implemented it to differing degrees but usually only partially as labelling regulation. They have not legally enforced the internal corporate responsibility aspect. An NGO, however, the International Baby Food Action Network has been extremely active in monitoring compliance with the code (including the meta-regulatory provision quoted above) by Nestlé and other baby food companies (as well as governments), and enforcing it through social and political action.[61]

---

[57] For one proposal for a meta-regulatory initiative to be enforced by the World Bank or International Labour Organisation, see A. Fung, D. O'Rourke and C. Sabel, 'Realizing Labour Standards', *Boston Review* 26 (2001), 1, available at www.bostonreview.net/BR26.1/fung.html (accessed 30 April 2007).

[58] Basel Committee on Banking Supervision, *Basel II: International Convergence of Capital Measurement and Capital Standards: A Revised Framework* (June 2004), available at www.bis.org/publ/bcbs107.htm (accessed 30 April 2007). See also D. Ho, 'Compliance and International Soft Law: Why do Countries Implement the Basle Accord?', *Journal of International Economic Law* 5 (2002), 647.

[59] World Health Organisation, 1981.   [60] ibid., para. 11.3.

[61] See the critiques of implementation of the code in internal systems and documents by Nestlé (but also other manufacturers) at the International Baby Food Action Network (IBFAN) webpage: www.ibfan.org (accessed 30 April 2007). Despite its relative success, see the critique of this regime in J. Richter, *Holding Corporations Accountable: Corporate Conduct, International Codes and Citizen Action* (London: Zed Books, 2001).

III. Critique: process at the expense of substance?

The main critique of meta-regulatory-style developments in the law is that they will focus on corporate responsibility processes in a way that allows companies to avoid accountability for substance.[62] Meta-regulatory law runs the danger of hollowing itself out into a focus merely on corporate governance processes that avoid necessary conflict over the substantive values that should apply to corporations. In her work on risk regulation by financial services regulators that utilises firms' internal risk management systems, Julia Black (rather gently) criticises the idea of meta-regulation:

> the firm's internal controls will be directed at ensuring the firm achieves the objectives it sets for itself: namely profits and market share. Whilst proponents of meta-regulation are correct to argue that its strength lies in the ability to leverage off a firm's own systems of internal control, and indeed that regulators should fashion their own regulatory processes on those controls, this *difference in objectives* means that regulators can never rely on a firm's own systems without some modifications. The problem then arises, however, of *locating those differences*, and ensuring both regulator and regulated understand them.[63]

The ability of regulators and stakeholders to locate and hold businesses accountable for those 'differences' – that is, potential conflict between social values and corporate self-interest – is likely to be frustrated in several overlapping ways by companies:

(1) *Companies will avoid conflict over substantive change to their internal management, structure and practices by implementing 'corporate conscience' requirements in a half-hearted, partial and surface-level way.*

---

[62] The critique from the other side (those who are less sympathetic to CSR obligations, and also those who are wary of rule of law values being undermined) is that meta-regulation will appear to focus on allowing companies to set processes that meet their own needs, but so much unaccountable power and discretion will be given to regulators and other stakeholders (who might be given the right to participate in or influence corporate decision-making) that inappropriate and illegitimate substantive values will in fact be imposed on corporations in ways that would not be possible under more traditional legal regulation. See, for example, K. Yeung, *Securing Compliance – A Principled Approach* (Oxford: Hart Publishing, 2004), pp. 204–14. See Lobel, 'Interlocking Regulatory and Industrial Relations', for an examination of the way in which US meta-regulatory initiatives in occupational health and safety have been stymied by administrative laws that impose unsuitable regulatory accountability requirements on them. I have previously addressed Yeung's critique in Parker, 'Restorative Justice in Business Regulation?' (2004).

[63] Black, 'The Emergence of Risk-based Regulation'. For a more robust articulation of a similar critique, see F. Pearce and S. Tombs, *Toxic Capitalism: Corporate Crime and the Chemical Industry* (Aldershot: Ashgate, 1998). (Emphases added by author.)

Companies will implement management systems to the extent necessary to ensure legitimacy, but will make no substantive change to their ordinary modus operandi, if not necessary.[64] As Lauren Edelman and her co-authors argue, 'organizations create symbolic structures as visible efforts to comply with law, but their normative value does not depend on effectiveness so they do not guarantee substantive change'.[65] They will be able to satisfy regulators and prosecutors by 'ticking the boxes' that show they have gone through prescribed processes, but regulators and prosecutors will not assess whether management systems are producing outputs that meet the policy goals of the relevant regulatory regime – indeed, policy goals may not even be defined.[66] It has been suggested that the whole push for meta-regulation, rather than strict output liability, is an attempt by corporate interests to avoid substantive internal change by focusing liability instead on meaningless processes.[67]

(2) *The implementation of corporate conscience requirements may be subsumed into the risk management of legal liability in ways that have little to do with commitment to social values and which obscure possibilities for corporate accountability.*[68]

---

[64] Parker, *The Open Corporation*, p. 145; S. Simpson, *Corporate Crime, Law and Social Control* (Cambridge: Cambridge University Press, 2002), pp. 103–6.

[65] L. Edelman, S. Petterson, E. Chambliss and H. Erlanger, 'Legal Ambiguity and the Politics of Compliance: Affirmative Action Officers' Dilemma', *Law and Policy* 13 (1991), 73, 75. See also S. Beder, *Global Spin: The Corporate Assault on Environmentalism* (Melbourne: Scribe Books, 1997), pp. 128–30; L. Cunningham, 'The Appeal and Limits of Internal Controls to Fight Fraud, Terrorism, other Ills', *The Journal of Corporate Law* 29 (2004), 267; K. Krawiec, 'Cosmetic Compliance and the Failure of Negotiated Governance', *Washington University Law Quarterly* 81 (2003), 487, 514, 542; D. McBarnet, 'Legal Creativity: Law, Capital and Legal Avoidance', in M. Cain and C. Harrington (eds.), *Lawyers in a Postmodern World: Translation and Transgression* (New York: New York University Press, 1994), p. 73; S. Tombs, 'Understanding Regulation', *Social and Legal Studies* 11 (2002), 113; G. Weaver, L. Trevino and P. Cochran, 'Corporate Ethics Practices in the mid-1990's: An Empirical Study of the Fortune 1000', *Journal of Business Ethics* 18 (1999), 283 (finding that the vast majority of US Fortune 1000 firms have committed to the low-cost, possibly symbolic, side of ethics management).

[66] W. Laufer, 'Social Accountability and Corporate Greenwashing', *Journal of Business Ethics* 43 (2003), 253, 254. See, for example, the critiques of regulators' inadequate use of audit of required internal management systems in M. Power, *The Audit Society: Rituals of Verification* (Oxford: Oxford University Press, 1997); C. Parker, 'Regulator-required Corporate Compliance Program Audits', *Law and Policy* 25 (2003), 221.

[67] Krawiec, 'Organizational Misconduct'.

[68] R. Rosen, 'Risk Management and Corporate Governance: The Case of Enron', *Connecticut Law Review* 35 (2003), 1157, 1180.

As Baldwin says of the 'challenges' of meta-regulation, 'Managers may see regulatory liabilities as risks to be managed, not as ethically reinforced prescriptions'.[69] For example, the internal management systems required by meta-regulating law may be used to obscure senior management/entity responsibility for breaches, and/or to shift blame for breaches onto individual employees (workers, line managers or compliance staff). Thus Laufer suggests that corporations may 'game' regulators to fully insulate the company as an entity and top management from liability by 'reverse whistle-blowing' – offering up culpable subordinate employees, or at least putting all the responsibility for compliance onto employees and line managers.[70] Similarly, regulatory responsibilities might be identified by internal 'corporate conscience' processes but then managed by 'outsourcing' the risk of not acting responsibly – performing ethically or legally questionable activities through separate legal entities that bear the risk of any failure of responsibility. For example, Enron used its joint venture partners to bear responsibility for questionable financial transactions. Brand name retailers have done the same by leaving it to manufacturers in other countries to work out how to comply with labour standards *and* meet production demands at the same time. Insurance, electricity and gas, and telecommunications companies frequently outsource compliance obligations to independent sales agents who must also meet tight sales targets in order to be paid. In Australia, James Hardie famously completely separated off its asbestos compensation responsibilities into a separate legal company set adrift from the rest of the corporate group without adequate financial provision. Socio-legal scholars' critiques of risk management imply that the management of potential legal/regulatory liability is a motivating factor for companies in their adoption of a risk management approach to business.[71] But potential legal accountability may barely rate a passing thought – risk management can be a whole approach to business decision-making, in which it is assumed that legal and compliance risks, like all other risks, can be transformed, hedged or insured against,

---

[69] Baldwin, 'The New Punitive Regulation', 378. See also Power, *Risk Management*.

[70] W. Laufer, 'Corporate Liability, Risk Shifting and the Paradox of Compliance', *Vanderbilt Law Review* 52 (1999), 1341, and 'Corporate Prosecution, Cooperation and the Trading of Favours', *Iowa Law Review* 87 (2002), 643. See also J. Braithwaite, *Corporate Crime*, p. 308 (on the 'vice-president responsible for going to jail'); Hutter, *Regulation and Risk*, pp. 145–7 (British Rail employees believe the purpose of health and safety systems was to shift responsibility away from the Board and pass the buck to staff); Parker, *The Open Corporation*, pp. 149–56.

[71] We are all tempted to think that our own special area of interest is just as important to others as it is to ourselves!

rather than eliminated (by substantive compliance).[72] Meta-regulatory law therefore falls into the trap of giving company lawyers a set of process rules perfectly designed to be manipulated into meaninglessness in the context of a risk management culture.

(3) *Management systems that ostensibly put in place a corporate conscience may be used to contain, mollify and transform dissent about whether the company has followed appropriate values in particular instances without addressing the conflict and allowing it to be authoritatively and accountably resolved.*[73]

Internal corporate governance processes may simply not be capable of resolving such conflict appropriately because of management incompetence or failures of strategic imagination to overcome deadlocks and stultification over dissent.[74] The mollification of dissent and conflict within internal processes may also be more strategic. For example, internal sexual harassment and equal employment opportunity complaints systems have been shown to be a way of containing contestations of equality and reframing appeals to rights as human resources management issues that avoid court action.[75] Similarly stakeholder engagement programmes may simply be a way of 'cooling out' protesters.[76] We normally like to think that legal accountability (ideally anyway) can be a way in which conflicts about corporate behaviour can be brought into open court and determined. Law that mandates corporate responsibility processes gives management the perfect 'legal' cover for keeping conflict out of the public eye and the accountability processes of the courts. Meta-regulatory law requires and rewards them for 'managing' conflict internally.

According to this critique, the development of meta-regulating law in practice and in scholarly writing shows that businesses might be succeeding in shaping the notion of CSR to suit themselves. Meta-regulating law is seen as the spearhead of a corporate campaign to pull back the reach of regulatory accountability through existing command and control regulation of business. Thus, Shamir argues that multinational corporations are responding to the heat of protests against them by seeking to shape the

---

[72] See Rosen, 'Risk Management'.
[73] See Parker, *The Open Corporation*, pp. 156–64.   [74] Baldwin, 'Punitive Regulation', 379.
[75] Edelman, *et al.*, 'Legal Ambiguity'; L. Edelman, H. Erlanger, and J. Lande, 'Internal Dispute Resolution: The Transformation of Civil Rights in the Workplace', *Law and Society Review* 27 (1993), 497; J. Kihnley, 'Unraveling the Ivory Fabric: Institutional Obstacles to the Handling of Sexual Harassment Complaints', *Law and Social Inquiry* 25 (2000), 69.
[76] See J. Conley and C. Williams, 'Engage, Embed, Embellish: Theory versus Practice in the Corporate Social Responsibility Movement', *Journal of Corporate Law* 31 (2005) 1.

notion and practice of CSR in terms of 'a voluntary and altruistic spirit and with notions implying honesty toward investors, with charity-oriented "good citizenship" campaigns, and with more or less elaborate schemes of voluntary self-regulation'.[77] To the extent that scholars and policy-makers focus on achieving CSR through corporate governance processes (i.e., meta-regulation), it 'signifies a decisive move in the direction of abandoning traditional "command and control" state regulatory schemes in favor of "responsive regulation," which is supposed to facilitate – yet not enforce and dictate – self-regulation programs and "compliance-oriented" regulation, which is to be carried out through corporate consent and voluntary organizational processes of reflexive learning'.[78]

The application of substantive standards[79] to corporations is not facilitated, but conflict forestalled by this 'responsibilisation of subjects who are empowered to discipline themselves'.[80]

Kim Krawiec makes the same point from a different angle. She argues that internal compliance-based liability regimes (meta-regulation) are 'negotiated' – the gaps are filled by firms and their legal compliance professionals, and they are likely to do so in ways that are favourable to them.[81]

> In short, the incompleteness of law creates room for interpretation and manipulation by a variety of public and private actors. As such, it presents a political opportunity for those with a stake in regulation to push their agenda through renegotiation during the implementation and enforcement phases of governance by constructing a gap-filling interpretation that serves the group's self-interest.[82]

Corporations (their managers, lawyers and compliance professionals) will be able to take advantage of the fact the law is focusing on process to avoid conflict over substantive change.

These critiques of meta-regulating law would apply regardless of whether the meta-regulating law includes enforcement mechanisms or not (and what kind they are – direct or indirect, rewards or sanctions). The

---

[77] Shamir, 'The Alien Tort Claims Act', 644. See also Conley and Williams, 'Theory Versus Practice in the CSR Movement'.

[78] Shamir, 'The Alien Tort Claims Act', 660.

[79] Shamir's concern is with human rights standards.

[80] Shamir, 'The Alien Tort Claims Act', 660. He concludes that 'the idea that human rights standards will be imposed by the courts (whether national or international) and the idea that corporations may be coerced into compliance in this area through formally binding regulations (whether national or transnational) are still far on the horizon' (at 660–1).

[81] Krawiec, 'Cosmetic Compliance', 494.   [82] *ibid.*, 542.

point of the criticisms is that there is nothing worthwhile to be enforced anyway. The problem is that the process orientation of the meta-regulating law leaves too many gaps and too much room for interpretation, in a context where some interests are more equal than others, and relevant social values heavily contested.[83] These are a principled set of objections to meta-regulation.[84]

IV. Response: meta-regulation as a process aimed at a substance

The key feature of each of the three critiques of the idea of meta-regulating CSR above is that meta-regulation runs the risk of creating legal accountability for a vague process without substantive goals because it leaves it up to business itself to define the details of responsibility processes, and then leaves it to the process to define the appropriate outcomes or goals: 'the substance of CSR seems to be process'.[85] Neither the process nor the goals are adequately set from outside business, and therefore we cannot

---

[83] See Scheuerman, 'Reflexive Law and the Challenges of Globalization' *Journal of Political Philosophy* 9 (2001), 101. See also Shearing and Wood, 'Nodal Governance' (for a similar argument that inequality of access to purchasing power is the basis for a governance disparity that means some people are unable to participate in governance processes); Lipschutz, *Globalization* (the new governance is based too much on people participating through markets rather than politics aimed at the public good); cf. Braithwaite and Drahos, *Global Business Regulation* (arguing that seeming powerless interests can sometimes find the right strand to pull in regulatory webs to have a big influence).

[84] Note there is also another set of (related) arguments about whether it is possible to specify standards for internal management systems and how to identify the features of management systems, governance structures or corporate cultures that reliably 'work' to achieve more responsible outcomes in different contexts; how to monitor whether these internal processes have been implemented effectively; what enforcement mechanisms (rewards and sanctions, direct and indirect, persuasive and coercive, formal and informal, etc.), if any, to use; or whether it is better to rely on other diffusion mechanisms that do not rely on legal enforcement. These issues will not be dealt with in detail in this chapter. See R. Kagan, N. Gunningham and D. Thornton, 'Explaining Corporate Environmental Performance: how does Regulation Matter', *Law and Society Review* 37 (2003), 51; V. Nielsen and C. Parker, 'Chapter 4: Degree of Compliance', in *The ACCC Enforcement and Compliance Survey: Report of Preliminary Results* (Canberra: RegNet, ANU, 2005), available at cccp.anu.edu.au/projects/project1.html (accessed 30 April 2007); M. Potoski and A. Prakash, 'Covenants with Weak Swords: ISO14001 and Facilities' Environmental Performance', *Journal of Policy Analysis and Management* 24 (2005), 745. cf. Krawiec, 'Organizational Misconduct'; Krawiec, 'Cosmetic Compliance', 542; M. McKendall, B. De Marr and C. Jones-Rikkers, 'Ethical Compliance Programs and Corporate Illegality: Testing the Assumptions of the Corporate Sentencing Guidelines', *Journal of Business Ethics* 37 (2002), 367.

[85] Conley and Williams, 'Engage, Embed, Embellish'.

expect meta-regulation to make business accountable for anything – there is nothing to be accountable for, no one to be accountable to.

Meta-regulation could be seen as an aspect of a broader shift in the way law regulates in the context of the new governance – 'the creation of a new type of rationality or mode of governance based on a logic of informal, negotiated processes within social and socio-legal networks'.[86] However, as Heydebrand points out, this 'process rationality' can come 'at a heavy cost, namely the emergent deconstruction of procedural and substantive rights, the dissolution of the normative legality that is historically embedded in formal justice, and the deformation of constitutional protections and safeguards':[87] And again, 'Process rationality shares neither the rule-governed, proceduralist schemata of formal legal rationality nor the consensual goal-directedness of substantive rationality. Process drives substance, not the other way around . . . Whatever goals are associated with process rationality tend to emerge dialectically from within the process itself rather than directing it from outside'.[88]

Yet there is nothing inherent in the idea of meta-regulation as a technique that means this must be true, that business must drive the process and the process must drive the substance. We can discriminate between a substance-oriented process (consistent with the distinctives of meta-regulation as defined above) and process driving substance.[89]

Certainly, meta-regulation is about setting a process. *But* it must be a process that is 'going somewhere'.[90] That means it must be set in a context in which it is clearly aimed at social policy goals (or responsibility values) that are defined by the law or by some other mechanism that can garner widespread legitimacy. Conflicts over the meaning of those values must be

---

[86] Heydebrand, 'Process Rationality', 326. See also Scheuerman's assessment of Teubner's notion of reflexive law applied to global business regulation: W. Scheuerman, 'Reflexive Law', 81.

[87] Heydebrand, 'Process Rationality', 334 although Heydebrand does see substantive rationality continuing to operate in areas of administrative regulation where 'social policy and substantive rights protection remain relatively intact' (at 337). Contrast Selznick's idea of 'responsive law' as built upon the foundations of formal justice rather than dissolving it: Nonet and Selznick, *Law and Society in Transition*; Selznick, *The Moral Commonwealth*, pp. 463–5.

[88] Heydebrand, 'Process Rationality', 328.

[89] Compare also Heydebrand, 'Process Rationality', 341 (describing Habermasian communicative rationality as a 'kind of substantively oriented process rationality' and commenting '[i]t is not yet clear, however, to what extent these normative conceptions will remain utopian visions, or else, can be realized and implemented in a concrete, empirical context').

[90] Borrowing Thomas Shaffer's phrase for describing what the 'ethics of care' requires of deliberation between a lawyer and client: T. Shaffer and R. Cochran, *Lawyers, Clients and Moral Responsibility* (Eagan, MN: West Publishing Co., 1994).

capable of external authoritative resolution where corporate management fails to do so appropriately. People who are affected by corporate failure to observe the relevant values or reach the policy goals must be able to contest them within the organisation. If management cannot work out how to resolve cooperatively conflicts over value identified by contestation in this way within the organisation, then the conflict needs to be made obvious and dealt with authoritatively by law or some other mechanism external to the organisation.

In other words, the *substantive goals* at which internal processes are aimed must be adequately specified and enforced external to the company. Moreover, the standards for the companies' internal processes must be specified sufficiently to make sure that those values are represented within internal decision-making processes. This will often involve making sure that stakeholders who might otherwise be excluded from contesting corporate decisions are given specific rights to do so. Meta-regulating law must meet 'traditional formalistic ideals' at least 'by insisting that procedural and organizational norms are relatively clear and cogent'.[91] The aim of meta-regulation in this conception is precisely that substantive conflict between social values and corporate ways of doing things is forced to be dealt with and resolved inside the organisation, or the organisation forced to respond to external resolution.

By stating it that way, we should be able to evaluate some of the proposals for law to be involved in holding companies accountable for CSR and come to a conclusion on whether they are likely to be worthwhile or not.

A. *Using 'meta-regulation' to evaluate corporate social responsibility initiatives*

The ideal form of meta-regulating law I have set out here is a normative standard that we can use to evaluate various existing approaches and proposals. Whether particular legal mechanisms meet the requirements of meta-regulation that is more than mere process is likely to be highly context-dependent. We will need to examine the surrounding law and governance for each initiative in order to determine whether substantive and procedural rights are adequately specified, or able to be adequately debated and determined in democratically legitimate ways (whether by traditional formal law or by other mechanisms), before we can come to a conclusion on the meta-regulatory value of particular attempts to build CSR.

---

[91] Scheuerman, 'Reflexive law', 99 (rephrasing and referring to I. Maus, 'Sinn und Bedeutung der Volkssouveranitet in der modernen Gesellschaft', *Kritische Justiz* 24 (1991), 137).

Most examples of what governments are doing to promote CSR, beyond traditional business regulation, can barely be stretched to count as law or regulation at all. And where they can, they are not meta-regulatory – that is, they are not focused on constituting corporate consciences internally. One area where government proposals to reform the law might be perceived as meta-regulatory is corporate governance proposals to require companies/directors to report on CSR issues, or even to expand directors' duties to allow them to take into account stakeholder interests.[92] One example was the (now repealed) requirement introduced in the United Kingdom in 2005 that directors of quoted companies should prepare an operating and financial review (OFR) each year in addition to their normal reporting requirements.[93] The OFR included a 'balanced and comprehensive analysis' of:

- the business's development and performance during the financial year;
- the company's (or group's) position at the end of the year;
- the main trends and factors underlying the development, performance and position of the company (or group) and which are likely to affect it in the future.

> This will include a company's (or group's) objectives, strategies and the key drivers of the business, focusing on more qualitative and forward-looking information than has traditionally been included in annual reports in the past. It must include a description of the resources available to the company (or group), and of the capital structure, treasury policies and objectives and liquidity of the company (or group).
>
> In fulfilling these general requirements, directors will need to consider whether it is necessary to provide information on a range of factors that may be relevant to the understanding of the business, including, for example, environment, employee and social and community issues.[94]

---

[92] For an overview of Anglo-American developments in this area, see C. Williams and J. Conley, 'An Emerging Third Way? The Erosion of the Anglo-American Shareholder Value Construct', *Cornell Journal of International Law* 38 (2005), 493. See, for example, the Australian parliament's Joint Committee on Corporations and Financial Services inquiry into corporate responsibility: www.aph.gov.au/senate/committee/corporations_ctte/corporate_responsibility/tor.htm (accessed 30 April 2007).

[93] The Companies Act 1985 (Operating and Financial Review and Directors' Report, etc.) Regulations 2005 (SI 2005 No. 1011); See also *Guidance on the OFR and Changes to the Directors' Report* (Department of Trade and Industry, April 2005). The OFR requirement has now been repealed by the Companies Act 1985 (Operating And Financial Review) (Repeal) Regulations (SI 2005 No. 3442) on the basis that the OFR requirement essentially duplicated the requirement that the Directors' Report include a Business Review that had been introduced at the same time by s. 234ZZB of the Companies Act 1985.

[94] *Guidance on the OFR*, p. 6.

We might see provisions requiring reports such as the OFR as meta-regulatory because they implicitly require management or directors to collect information about the possibility of breach of CSR obligations (as a risk to reputation and performance).[95] The meta-regulatory hope is that, having collected the information for the report, management will be encouraged to use it in decision-making and to implement systems to manage the risks they have identified, or at least they might be forced to do so by their shareholders.

However, the law requiring OFRs, as with other laws requiring CSR reporting, was purely process-oriented – it was not aimed at any values, it did not require the company to identify and commit to any values, and it gave no external representative of any values any right to participate in defining what values or targets are to be met.[96] Laws requiring CSR reporting may well be a useful, facilitative adjunct to more substantive regimes that do have clear policy values and do give 'stakeholders' rights, but on their own they can achieve no meta-regulation of the corporate conscience.

It is rather like the way the term 'compliance culture' is used in Division 12.3 of Australia's *Commonwealth Criminal Code Act* (1995). 'Corporate culture' is defined in that legislation to mean 'an attitude, policy, rule, course of conduct or practice existing within the body corporate generally or in the part of the body corporate in which the relevant activities take place'. The existence or not of a 'corporate culture' defined in this way can be relevant to the determination of the criminal liability of companies and directors under certain Australian Commonwealth laws. But this is only useful if there are other laws that the definition will apply to. Similarly, proposals to amend directors' duties to allow them to take into account obligations to stakeholders would be purely facilitative – allowing directors to use such information in decision-making and to spend money on ensuring compliance, assuming that they are motivated to do so by some other means. Companies will go through the form and will do as much or as little internally of any substance as they would have done anyway.

[95] The OFR might also include information about the company's corporate governance processes, but it is not required: see ibid., p. 7.

[96] See D. Owen, 'Corporate Social Reporting and Stakeholder Accountability: The Missing Link', *International Centre for Corporate Social Responsibility Research Paper Series* No. 32–2005 (Nottingham: Nottingham University Business School, 2005) ('[reporting] reform is viewed in isolation from any necessary institutional reform which may provide the means for stakeholders to hold company directors accountable for actions affecting their vital interests'). One might also object that these reforms generally suggest 'social and environmental issues are only of relevance when there are financial implications for the company' (at 23).

These proposals are too generic in the absence of sufficient meta-regulation aimed at specific values. Contrast Australia's affirmative action regime – a regulatory regime with little teeth which was based purely on requiring companies to report on their process for setting targets and implementing equal employment opportunity measures. Although the affirmative action regime required only reporting of progress and the only sanctions available were being named in Parliament, and possibly losing government contracts, the regime did have a clear set of substantive values (equal employment opportunity) and required companies to go through a clear process and set substantive targets, and was relatively successful in improving the proportion of women employed in companies that came under the regime.[97]

B. A good example: the Environment Protection Authority Victoria's environmental improvement plans[98]

The environmental improvement plan (EIP) requires site representatives to develop an internal compliance management system aimed at improving environmental performance, and monitoring and reporting on those improvements on a regular basis. It is likely to cover issues such as regulatory compliance, waste minimisation, environmental audit, elimination, reduction or control of environmental impacts and risks (for example, greenhouse emissions, offensive odours, reduction of water consumption, introduction of new technology and so on), and arrangements for dealing with accidents and spills. The Victorian Environment Protection Authority (EPA) allows industrial sites to volunteer for the EIP programme, often requires an EIP as a licence condition, as a condition of works approval for new developments and also has legislative power to direct a site to enter into an EIP.[99]

The EIP programme was first developed in response to ongoing conflict between the manufacturers at a large chemical complex in Altona and local residents over odours, air emissions and noise. Not only were the

---

[97] See V. Braithwaite, 'The Australian Government's Affirmative Action Legislation: Achieving Social Change through Human Resource Management', *Law and Policy* 15 (1993), 327.

[98] More details on this case study are available in Gunningham and Sinclair, *Leaders and Laggards*, pp. 157–88; Parker, *The Open Corporation*, pp. 226–7.

[99] Environment Protection Act 1970 (Vic), s. 31C; EPA Victoria, *Guidelines for the Preparation of Environment Improvement Plans* (June 2002, Publication 739). Note that the 2002 *Guidelines* state that community involvement is not necessary for all types of EIPs. The discussion in the text, however, concerns only those EIPs where community participation was required.

site's neighbours unhappy, but the conflict meant it was difficult for the manufacturers to get approval to make any changes to their plants, as community members used the planning approval process to object to all proposed changes. In the late 1980s, the EPA hired a 'community liaison officer' (a social worker) to help set up a community consultation process in which site representatives, local community members (including those who had complained regularly) and local council representatives could meet together and agree an action plan for resolving problems. The success of this process led to the EPA's development of the EIP programme in the early 1990s.

The EIP process required representatives of site management to meet intensively with a Community Liaison Council (CLC) – local community members and local government representatives – which had to be consulted on every aspect of the development of an EIP from target-setting to implementation. Clear targets for performance had to be set as part of this consultative process, and the whole EIP (including the targets) generally became part of the site's licence to carry on its activities from the EPA. This process could take up to twelve months with regular meetings of the CLC and site management over that period. After agreeing the EIP, site representatives had to continue to meet regularly with the CLC and report on the site's implementation of systems and performance on the targets it set for itself. The site's activities also remained subject to local government planning approval and other legal controls (including the possibility of enforcement action for breach of the law or the site's licence) in the normal way. EIPs were not seen as a replacement for the normal application and enforcement of the law.

Gunningham and Sinclair published an in-depth evaluation of the programme in 2002 which concluded that 'as a form of process-based regulation, EIPs frequently generated greater environmental commitment within the enterprise' but 'over and above such process-based changes (and in contrast to initiatives such as ISO 14001 and Responsible Care), the EIP also requires ... [that] enterprises committing to an EIP must meet specified performance targets within a specified time-period (for example, they may commit to upgrade equipment to meet objectives under the plan, or to meet specified emission or waste reduction targets)'.[100] They cite interviews suggesting that entering into an EIP meant that companies incorporated community concerns at an early stage of the planning process for new developments, rather than fighting about them with local residents later on.[101] The EPA itself saw the EIPs as a way to improve how

[100] Gunningham and Sinclair, *Leaders and Laggards*, p. 170.   [101] *ibid.*, p. 169.

the companies conducted their businesses generally and communicated with their local communities.[102]

The EIP programme was therefore meta-regulatory and process-oriented. Companies that entered into an EIP had to go through a process of consultation and reporting with the CLC which was mainly focused on internal management issues. But the EIP was not a process-based sham. The companies' legal obligations were reasonably well-known and enforceable. The process itself required them to set clear 'beyond compliance' targets for environmental improvement outcomes for themselves, and made it clear that they would be held accountable for them – by having to face the CLC to report on their performance, and by making the EIP a licence condition.

This type of meta-regulation worked because community representatives were given a right to participate in the EIP process, and their right to participate in that process was backed up by the fact that they had clear rights at general law to object to developments or actions that impacted on the local environment, and the fact that the EPA was acting as broker for the whole consultation and negotiation process. Conflict was not swept under the carpet. Where the programme worked, conflict was brought into the open and dealt with in the CLC meetings – the EPA's community liaison officer reported that the first few meetings of the CLC were often quite heated as conflicting views and values were expressed. Indeed, according to Gunningham and Sinclair's evaluation, the process seemed to work best where conflict was greater and therefore community members' motivation to participate higher. The commitment of the EPA to providing officers to make sure that local community members who vociferously complained about companies' environmental impacts were included in community consultation processes and to guide the CLC through the early stages of negotiating an EIP was clearly key to making this meta-regulatory initiative successful.

V. Conclusion

'Meta-regulation' is a useful way of conceptualising what legal accountability for CSR ought to, and could, look like. As we have seen, it is relatively easy to find examples of partial, or attempted, meta-regulation. It is not so easy to find examples of regulation of CSR that fully meet the normative

---

[102] Environment Protection Authority, *25 Years of Making a Difference* (Melbourne, Victoria: Environment Protection Authority, 1996), p. 13.

criteria for meta-regulation that I have set out here. The argument of this chapter is that legal accountability for CSR must be aimed at making business enterprises put themselves through a CSR process aimed at CSR outcomes. The outcomes must themselves be accountable applications of substantive values to specific situations; and the process must be one that opens up management to external values, stakeholders and regulatory influences, not closes it down. In other words, legal accountability for CSR must amount to meta-regulation – an approach to legal regulation in which the *internal* 'corporate conscience' is *externally* regulated.

If by 'corporate social responsibility' is meant something voluntary and discretionary that businesses on their own can 'take responsibility' for, then the idea of legal accountability for CSR does not make any sense. Indeed, on its own, the whole notion of CSR makes sense only within the context of more substantive discussions of regulatory and social policy which tell us for *what* corporations must take responsibility. Mechanisms for nudging companies towards CSR indirectly (for example, tax incentives or government procurement policies aimed at encouraging CSR) or in a way that is aimed at CSR generically without setting specific substantive standards or goals (such as the United Kingom's repealed OFR requirement) are likely to fail badly unless they are adequately buttressed by specific regulatory regimes which specify social policy goals, and identify and give rights to stakeholders to participate in or contest corporate decisions. These regulatory regimes need not take the form of traditional, hierarchical legal regulation promulgated by nation states. 'Meta-regulating' law might include international networks of governance, more traditional state-based regulatory enforcement activity, and traditional law that authorises, empowers, co-opts or recognises the regulatory influence of industry, professional or civil society bodies to set and enforce standards for CSR processes and outcomes.[103] That type of regime generally only comes about through considerable struggle and conflict.

---

[103] Compare Gunningham and Grabosky, *Smart Regulation*, pp. 93–134.

Part III
Practice, Problems and Potential

[10]

THE *SANGAM* OF FOREIGN INVESTMENT, MULTINATIONAL CORPORATIONS AND HUMAN RIGHTS: AN INDIAN PERSPECTIVE FOR A DEVELOPING ASIA[†]

SURYA **DEVA**[*]

The *sangam* (confluence) of foreign investment, multinational corporations (MNCs) and human rights raises new challenges for the developing countries in Asia. Though development is the underlying current behind this *sangam*, there is a fundamental tension in how the three streams intermingle. For example, the trend of investment-driven development often compels developing countries to allure foreign investment by MNCs, even if it brings negative effects on human rights realisation and development of the majority. A "race to the bottom" for securing foreign investment amongst developing countries further reduces their bargaining position vis-à-vis MNCs. Taking India as an example of developing countries of Asia, this article explores the individual and collective strategies that developing countries could employ to exercise a control over the *flow* and *direction* of foreign investment. It argues that developing countries should realise their place in an interdependent world, be guided by an approach of "diversified integration", rely on human rights norms, and foster alliances with civil society organs in order to control the flow and direction of foreign investment.

I. INTRODUCTION

This article proposes to uncover the rainbow created by the *sangam* (confluence) of foreign investment,[1] multinational corporations ('MNCs')[2] and human rights in

---

[†] This article is a revised version of a paper presented at the Inaugural ASLI Conference on "The Role of Law in a Developing Asia", organised by the Asian Law Institute, Faculty of Law, National University of Singapore, Singapore, on 27-28 May 2004.

[*] B.A. (Hons.), LL.B., LL.M. (Delhi), Ph.D. Candidate, Faculty of Law, The University of Sydney, Australia. Formerly Assistant Professor, National Law Institute University, Bhopal, India; Lecturer, Faculty of Law, University of Delhi, India. I would like to thank Dr. Fleur Johns, Rosemary Lyster, Professor Mahendra P. Singh, Zhong Zhuang, and Swati Deva for their useful comments on an earlier draft of this article. This article also benefited from discussions I had with Professor Antony Anghie and the participants at the ASLI Conference. I thank them too.

[1] "Foreign investment" is taken to cover both foreign direct investment ('FDI') and portfolio investment. See Robert Pritchard, "The Contemporary Challenges of Economic Development" in Robert Pritchard, ed., *Economic Development, Foreign Investment and the Law* (London: Kluwer Law International, 1996) at 1, 3. But see, for the distinction between FDI and portfolio investment, M. Sornarajah, *The International Law on Foreign Investment* (Cambridge: Cambridge University Press, 1994) at 4-6.

[2] Despite the difference in terminology of MNCs and transnational corporations ('TNCs'), 'MNCs' has been used throughout this article to encompass both the entities. See generally David C. Korten, *When Corporations Rule the World* (West Hartford, Connecticut: Kumarian Press, 1995) at 125; Peter Muchlinski, *Multinational Enterprises and the Law* (Oxford: Blackwell Publishers, 1995) at 12-15; Cynthia D. Wallace, *Legal Control of the Multinational Enterprise* (Hague: Martinus Nijhoff, 1982) at 10-12.

306   *Singapore Journal of Legal Studies*   [2004]

Asia.[3] Let me begin with a brief description of the "actual" *sangam* in India, and why
I label the intersection of foreign investment, MNCs and human rights as a *sangam*,
albeit a "global" one. *Sangam* is the name given to a place where three rivers—Ganga,
Yamuna and Saraswati—meet at Allahabad.[4] Notably, whereas Ganga (*dhaval* or
whitish in colour and a symbol of purity) and Yamuna (*syamal* or grayish in colour)
are visible, Saraswati is a mythical or invisible river. How does this actual *sangam*
and its three streams resonate with the three straits of the global *sangam*—foreign
investment, MNCs and human rights—collectively as well as individually? I offer
two explanations for this simile. First, the three streams of actual *sangam* could
arguably be compared to the three variables of the global *sangam*. The human rights
are like Ganga; the language of human rights has become so powerful that it is used
to purify, justify or legitimise anything from putting trade restrictions to invading a
country.[5] The foreign investment, on the other hand, could be compared to Yamuna
in that the effects of foreign investment on host countries might be described more
appropriately in terms of gray rather than being totally white or black. Lastly, it is
fitting to see MNCs in terms of Saraswati, that is, invisible[6] but very real, important
and powerful entities.[7]

Second, the intersection of foreign investment, MNCs and human rights share a
common theme of development, though the patterns of such intersection might differ
from region to region. "Development", taken in its wider sense, is the underlying
current behind this global *sangam* of foreign investment, MNCs and human rights.
Foreign investment is about development, whether of the investors or of the place of
investment or of both. Again, the rise in the number, area of operation and influence of

---

[3]   Being conscious of vast literature on what human rights mean for Asia, I take human rights to mean all
      internationally recognised civil, political, social, economic, and cultural rights. Despite assuming an
      element of universality, I believe that culture plays an important role in contextualising, operationalising
      and realising human rights. See Robert McCorquodale & Richard Fairbrother, "Globalisation and
      Human Rights" (1999) 21 Human Rights Quarterly 735 at 741-2. See also Wright who demonstrates
      how local cultural differences might be used to promote human rights, and a failure to recognise such
      differences might in fact result in subverting human rights: Shelley Wright, *International Human Rights,
      Decolonisation and Globalisation: Becoming Human* (London: Routledge, 2001) at 88-93, 111, 213-4.
[4]   Allahabad (also known as Prayag) is one of the most sacred Hindu pilgrimages in India.
[5]   "Far from being a defence of the individual against the state, humans rights has become a standard
      part of the justification for the external use of force by the state against other states and individuals."
      David Kennedy, "The International Human Rights Movement: Part of the Problem?" (2002) 15 Harvard
      Human Rights Journal 99 at 119, and generally.
[6]   MNCs are invisible not only because I consider corporations to be a legal fiction but also because they
      could disappear totally and then be reborn in newer forms. This is besides the fact that the principles
      of separate personality and limited liability allow corporate actors to operate (and also hide if needed)
      behind a veil. See Harry Glasbeek, *Wealth by Stealth: Corporate Crime, Corporate Law, and the
      Perversion of Democracy* (Toronto: Between the Lines, 2002) at 6-14.
[7]   A 2003 survey shows that there are now 72 MNCs in the list of 100 largest economic entities.
      Paul Sheehan, "A Rising Force in Capital and Culture" *Sydney Morning Herald* (3-4 January 2004)
      at 21. See also Murray Dobbin, *The Myth of the Good Corporate Citizen: Democracy under the
      Rule of Big Business* (Toronto: Stoddart, 1998) at 85-121; Noreena Hertz, *The Silent Takeover:
      Global Capitalism and the Death of Democracy* (London: William Heinemann, 2001) at 6-8; Erin
      Elizabeth Macek, "Scratching the Corporate Back: Why Corporations have no Incentive to Define
      Human Rights" (2002) 11 Minnesota Journal of Global Trade 101 at 103-04; and Sarah Anderson
      & John Cavanagh, *Top 200: The Rise of Global Corporate Power*, online: Global Policy Forum
      <http://www.globalpolicy.org/socecon/tncs/top200.htm>.

Sing. J.L.S.   *The Sangam of Foreign Investment, Multinational Corporations and Human Rights*   307

MNCs is directly linked to their never-ending desire for growth. Similarly, there is a close relationship between human rights and development in that they are considered complementary to each other.[8]

Despite the fact that all the three straits of the global *sangam* share a common theme of development, their interrelation creates a fundamental tension, which is not too difficult to notice.[9] The root of this tension lies in a battle for the primacy or supremacy of developmental interests of concerned participants. Let us have a look at the sample of how this tension plays out. From the perspective of the foreign investor(s), foreign investment (by MNCs or otherwise) is primarily about earning maximum returns and creating or capturing markets[10] including by eliminating and distorting competition, and could have both positive and negative impact on the realisation of human rights. But the host countries of foreign investment do have different objectives in mind when seeking foreign investment. MNCs, which are prime vehicles of globalisation[11] and foreign investment,[12] do have the potential to promote as well as abridge human rights, including through investment.[13] Human rights, on the other hand, are increasingly becoming such a powerful weapon that

---

[8]   See, for example, Amartya Sen, *Development as Freedom* (New York: Oxford University Press, 1999). Some of the issues related to human rights and development are also dealt with in a special issue of the Australian Journal of Human Rights: vol. 4:2 (1998). Compare Rajagopal who points out the tension between human rights and development: "How come human rights discourse comes to terms with the fact that *it is the process of bringing development that has caused serious human-rights violations* among the deprived sections of Third World peoples?" Balakrishnan Rajagopal, *International Law from Below: Development, Social Movements and Third World Resistance* (Cambridge: Cambridge University Press, 2003) at 202 [emphasis in original]. He further highlights the problems associated with "developmentalisation of human rights". *Ibid.* at 216-30.

[9]   For example, how many corporations (and also their stockholders) will be ready to invest not for return but for the promotion of human rights, say, in feeding malnourished children or distributing free medicines to AIDS patients?

[10] "The dominant motivation for most FDI decisions is to pursue a market for goods or service." Pritchard, *supra* note 1 at 5.

[11] "Globalisation is powerfully driven by international corporations." Joseph E. Stiglitz, *Globalisation and its Discontents* (New York: W. W. Norton & Co., 2002) at 10. Spar and Yoffie also suggest this: "[C]ross-border activities of multinational firms are an integral piece—perhaps *the* integral piece—of globalisation." Debora Spar & David Yoffie, "Multinational Enterprises and the Prospects for Justice" (1999) 52 Journal of International Affairs 557. In this article, "globalisation" signifies a phenomenon of liberalisation of economies through privatisation, shifting of power from state to private actors, and removal of national barriers with reference to market, capital, services, governance, *etc.*

[12] Sornarajah, *supra* note 1 at 1, 6, 22, 50-53. Tolentino also examines in detail the emergence and evolution of MNCs (from the perspective of outward FDI) in resource-abundant countries, resource-scare large countries and resource-scare small countries. Paz Estrella Tolentino, *Multinational Corporations: Emergence and Evolution* (London: Routledge, 2000). See also Halina Ward, "Securing Transnational Corporate Accountability through National Courts: Implications and Policy Options" (2001) 24 Hastings International and Comparative Law Review 451 at 452; Macek, *supra* note 7 at 103.

[13] See Stephen Bottomley, "Corporations and Human Rights" in Stephen Bottomley & David Kinley, eds., *Commercial Law and Human Rights* (Aldershot: Ashgate/Dartmouth, 2002) at 47-68. See also Stiglitz, *supra* note 11 at 67-73; William H. Meyer, "Human Rights and MNCs: Theory Versus Quantitative Analysis" (1996) 18 Human Rights Quarterly 368; William H. Meyer, "Activism and Research on TNCs" in Jedrzej G. Frynas & Scott Pegg, eds., *Transnational Corporations and Human Rights* (New York: Palgrave Macmillan, 2003) at 33-52. Compare Jackie Smith, Melissa Bolyard & Anna Ippolito, "Human Rights and the Global Economy: A Response to Meyer" (1999) 21 Human Rights Quarterly 207.

308   *Singapore Journal of Legal Studies*   [2004]

everyone wants to have them in one's armoury.[14] For example, MNCs not only invoke human rights as a shield against government regulation[15] but also see them as a business tool that could help in achieving higher profit and/or giving an edge over competitors.[16] On the contrary, human rights activists look towards human rights as salvation against the "profit only" onslaught of MNCs.

In the light of above brief mapping of a fundamental tension between foreign investment by MNCs and human rights, I intend to investigate two separate but inter-related issues. First, this article seeks to examine the negative effects of foreign investment by MNCs on human rights and development, especially in developing countries. Second, given that the flow of foreign investment is critical to development[17] (especially of developing countries),[18] I am interested in exploring the individual and/or collective strategies that developing countries could, if at all, employ to exercise a control over the *flow* and *direction* of such investment. It is necessary to ponder these questions because not only Asia—the home of several developing/under-developed countries—require foreign investment to realise human rights and accomplish developmental goals, but also because Asia "forms a critical part of the growth strategies" of MNCs.[19] Besides being one of the most rapidly liberalising host regions for foreign investment,[20] Asia offers one of the world's largest consumers' markets, one of the cheapest labour forces, and generally lax (or less stringent) legal regimes regarding issues such as labour, environment, health and safety, consumer protection, competition, and unfair trade practices.[21]

---

[14] "Ours is the age of rights. Human rights is the idea of our time, the only political-moral idea that has received universal acceptance." Louis Henkin, *The Age of Rights* (New York: Columbia University Press, 1990) at ix. Rajagopal also refers to "the emergence of a new political culture of legitimacy in the form of human rights." Rajagopal, *supra* note 8 at 135. Compare Kennedy, *supra* note 5.

[15] See Michael K. Addo, "The Corporation as a Victim of Human rights Violations" in Michael K. Addo, ed., *Human Rights Standards and the Responsibility of Transnational Corporations* (Hague: Kluwer Law International, 1999) at 190 [*Human Rights Standards*]. See also *Autronic A.G. v. Switzerland* 12 (1990) E.H.R.R. 485.

[16] Simon Williams, "How Principles Benefit the Bottom Line: The Experience of the Co-operative Bank" in *Human Rights Standards, ibid.* at 63-8; John Harrison *et al.*, *Ethics for Australian Business* (Frenchs Forest: Prentice Hall - Sprint Print, 2001) at 1-9. See also 'CSR Facts and Figures', online: CSR Europe <http://www.csreurope.org/aboutus/CSRfactsandfigures_page397.aspx>.

[17] It can be said that the view one holds regarding the relation of foreign investment and development is determined largely by the theoretical position one takes. See Sherif H. Seid, *Global Regulation of Foreign Direct Investment* (Aldershot: Ashgate, 2002) at 9-30, 104-10; Sornarajah, *supra* note 1 at 38-50; Muchlinski, *supra* note 2 at 93-101. See also Theodore H. Moran, "Multinational Corporations and Developing Countries: An Analytical Overview" in Theodore H. Moran, ed., *Multinational Corporations: The Political Economy of Foreign Direct Investment* (Massachusetts: Lexington Books, 1985) at 3 [*Multinational Corporations*].

[18] "Developing states make up the great majority of the world's states, but they hold only a small fraction of international capital and must therefore depend on various external sources of capital for their development." Glen Kelley, "Multilateral Investment Treaties: A Balanced Approach to Multinational Corporations" (2001) 39 Columbia Journal of Transnational Law 483 at 497.

[19] Linda Y. C. Lim, "Prospects for Foreign Investment in Asia", speech delivered at the 10th Annual Corporate Conference, Manila, 26 February 1999, online: Asia Society <http://www.asiasociety.org/speeches/lim/html>.

[20] UNCTAD, *World Investment Report (2003)—FDI Policies for Development: National and International Perspectives* (New York: UN, 2003), Overview at 11 [*World Investment Report*].

[21] See Sornarajah, *supra* note 1 at 17-8.

But before we proceed further, few caveats about the scope of this endeavour. First, while I intend to examine the negative impacts of foreign investment on human rights and development, I am not suggesting that foreign investment has no positive effects. In fact, positive effects of foreign investment are underlying justifications for my second inquiry; the need to explore "controlling strategies" only arises because under the current global order foreign investment is essential but fraught with many avoidable adverse consequences. Second, though foreign investment could also flow from other sources other than MNCs,[22] presently I am concerned with foreign investment made by MNCs only. Third, my inquiry is limited to the perspective of developing countries of Asia (represented by India).[23] There is, however, a more profound reason for this limited treatment: in most of the cases it is the developing countries which face this difficult choice of creating an atmosphere conducive to foreign investment and also ensuring that such a scenario does not adversely affect the realisation of human rights and/or national developmental goals.[24] Fourth, I rely upon the case studies of Bhopal, Enron and Unocal to illustrate my arguments, in view of my greater familiarity with them. But again, this choice serves a purpose by demonstrating that human rights violations, as a result of investment/operation by MNCs, could occur in both democratic and non-democratic countries.

II. FOREIGN INVESTMENT AND HUMAN RIGHTS/DEVELOPMENT: LOOKING AT THE OTHER SIDE OF THE COIN?

Foreign investment does have, and could have, a positive impact on the realisation of human rights as well as development.[25] Though I do not intend, or need, to deny that, presently I am interested in exploring the other side of the coin, namely, the negative impacts of foreign investment by MNCs on human rights and development.[26] In this process, this article raises some fundamental questions regarding the relationship of foreign investment by MNCs and human rights/development. For example, even if we assume—as some would argue—that foreign investment promotes human rights, what are those human rights (and of whom) that get promoted? Similarly, given

---

[22] Foreign investment, for example, could also flow from developed countries and international financial institutions. See McCorquodale & Fairbrother, *supra* note 3 at 743.

[23] Two factors, among others, make India representative for my purpose. First, it ranked 28th in the world's top 30 FDI recipients in 2002. Second, none of India's MNCs figure in the list of top 25 non-financial TNCs from developing economies, ranked by foreign assets in 2001. *World Investment Report 2003*, *supra* note 20 at 4 and 6, respectively.

[24] See UNCTAD, *World Investment Report 1999: Foreign Direct Investment and the Challenge of Development* (New York: UN, 1999) Overview at 15: "The largest 10 home countries accounted for four-fifth of global FDI outflows." [*World Investment Report 1999*]. Besides, about 90 per cent of the top 100 MNCs, which are prime source of foreign investment, are from the European Union, Japan and the U.S.; *ibid.* at 2.

[25] Lance Compa, "Exceptions and Conditions: The Multilateral Agreement on Investment and International Labor Rights: A Failed Connection" (1998) 31 Cornell International Law Journal 683 at 684 and *supra* notes 13 and 17.

[26] See, for example, World Rainforest Movement, "Burma: Human Rights Abuses Linked to Foreign Investment in 'Development'", online: World Rainforest Movement <http://www.wrm.org.uy/bulletin/39/Burma.html>. See also generally Joel Bakan, *The Corporation: The Pathological Pursuit of Profit and Power* (London: Constable, 2004); and Glasbeek, *supra* note 6.

310 *Singapore Journal of Legal Studies* [2004]

that foreign investment leads to economic development, how is such "development" conceptualised? More importantly, whose development are we referring to, and at what cost?

A. *Negative Effects on Human Rights*

Foreign investment by MNCs adversely affects human rights realisation in several ways. Some of these are worthy of a brief treatment here. First, in view of the fact that the majority of foreign investment in developing countries is in the manufacturing sector and not in developing infrastructure or providing basic services,[27] such investment hardly contributes towards the promotion of basic human rights, *e.g.*, the right to food, water, shelter, education, or health.[28] The result is that people in villages may have access to Pepsi and Coke but not to safe drinking water. Moreover, it is probable, on the contrary, that the condition of basic human rights might worsen if governments in developing countries start withdrawing the resources allocated to providing these services without ensuring that foreign investment fills the vacuum created by them.[29] This is not to ignore the fact that the entry or level of foreign investment by MNCs in basic services remains a contentious issue;[30] general public in developing countries do not trust *foreign* corporations more than their *local* politicians or corporations.

Second, the way in which foreign investment affects tribal and cultural rights is another area of serious concern. There are reasons to believe that the policies of general or accumulative development[31] (might) impinge upon the vital rights of the disadvantaged sections of society,[32] including tribal people.[33] Displacement of tribal populations and lack of adequate rehabilitation due to construction of large

---

[27] See *World Investment Report 1999*, *supra* note 24, figure I.13.

[28] "There is little or no investment in primary health care, safe drinking water, and basic education." McCorquodale & Fairbrother, *supra* note 3 at 743.

[29] For example, in India the percentage of gross domestic product ('GDP') allocated for health has dropped from 1.4 per cent in 1991-92 to 0.9 per cent in 2001-02. Siddharth Narrain, "Health, for a Price", *Frontline*, Vol. 21, Issue 5, (28 February-12 March 2004), online: Frontline <http://www.frontlineonnet.com/fl2105/stories/20040312008112900.htm>. What is, however, encouraging that the government has recently imposed a two per cent "education cess" on all taxes in order to generate resources for funding education.

[30] Notably, the Human Resources Development Minister of India, in a recent interview, has indicated that the foreign investment in "elementary education" will be welcome, under a policy yet to be formulated. "Foreign Investment Welcome in Elementary Education: Arjun Singh" *The Hindu* (25 June 2004), online: The Hindu <http://www.thehindu.com/2004/06/25/stories/2004062502701200.htm>.

[31] "If you are to suffer, you should suffer in the interest of the country." Jawaharlal Nehru, speaking to villagers who were to be displaced by the Hirakund Dam (1948), as quoted by Arundhati Roy, "The Greater Common Good", *Frontline*, Vol. 16, Issue 11 (May 22-June 04 1999), online: Frontline <http://www.frontlineonnet.com/fl1611/16110040.htm>.

[32] In the context of public resistance to the construction of Narmada dam, Rajagopal writes: "Narmada [became] a symbolic struggle that raised basic questions about India's political and economic structure and *the place of most vulnerable persons within them*." Rajagopal, *supra* note at 124 [emphasis added].

[33] See Suprio Dasgupta, "Tribal Rights in Free Market Economy" in Parmanand Singh, ed., *Legal Dimensions of Market Economy* (New Delhi: Faculty of Law, University of Delhi, 1997) at 113 [*Legal Dimensions of Market Economy*]; McCorquodale & Faibrother, *supra* note 3 at 762.

dams,[34] resulting in severance of their ties with their past, history and culture[35] is a very good example of this.[36] The Narmada dam project in India has illustrated this point clearly.[37] Besides, the facts that corporations—offshoots of foreign investment as well—are not bound by affirmative action provisions of the Indian Constitution[38] and that they tend to exploit the disadvantaged position of women,[39] are also matters of deep constitutional anxiety.[40]

Third, though transfer of technology and know-how is an important and alluring facet of foreign investment, it is a contentious issue[41] and could also prove counter productive for the technology importing developing countries. The transfer of old, outdated, dangerous, untested, inappropriate or capital intensive technology to developing countries directly comes in conflict with various human rights.[42] The Bhopal gas disaster demonstrates how the use of an old and inferior technology in

---

[34]   Roy points out that "[a] huge percentage of the displaced are tribal people (57.6 per cent in the case of the Sardar Sarovar Dam)." Roy, *supra* note 31. See also Upendra Baxi, "What Happens Next is up to You: Human Rights at Risk in Dams and Development" (2001) 16 American University International Law Review 1507 at 1509-10; Erin K. MacDonald, "Playing by the Rules: The World Bank's Failure to Adhere to Policy in the Funding of Large-Scale Hydropower Projects" (2001) 31 Environmental Law 1011 at 1030-9; and Thomas R. Berger, "The World Bank's Independent Review of India's Sardar Sarovar Projects" (1993) 9 American University Journal of International Law and Policy 33 at 35, 41.

[35]   "Indigenous populations and tribal peoples whose interests policy makers do not take into consideration endure particularly egregious suffering. Dams often destroy not only their lands but also their sacred sites, and may even threaten the survival of certain indigenous groups." Sarah C. Aird, "China's Three Gorges: The Impact of Dam Construction on Emerging Human Rights" (2001) 8 Human Rights Brief 24 at 25.

[36]   Not to forget several other human rights implications that arise due to displacement, *e.g.*, housing, livelihood, employment. In view of huge human rights cost of large dams, Baxi wants us "to consider a call for an international moratorium on the construction of large dams until there is an installation of participatory policy-making processes." Baxi, *supra* note 34 at 527.

[37]   "Narmada had become a symbol of a highly destructive development model and the 'test case' of the [World] Bank's willingness and capacity to address the environmental and social impacts of its projects." Lori Udall, "The International Narmada Campaign: A Case Study of Sustained Advocacy" in William F Fisher, ed., *Toward Sustainable Development? Struggling over India's Narmada River* (New York: M. E. Sharpe, 1995) at 202, as cited by Rajagopal, *supra* note 14 at 124 and generally 122-6. See also Roy, *supra* note 31; and the Indian Supreme Court's judgment on the issue: *Narmada Bachao Andolan v. Union of India* (2000) 10 S.C.C. 664.

[38]   Only "state", as defined in article 12 of the Constitution and interpreted by judiciary, is bound by the affirmative action provisions, *e.g.*, articles 15(4) and 16(4)/(4A)/(4B), and it does not cover corporations unconnected with the state. See Mahendra P. Singh, ed., *Shukla's Constitution of India*, 10th ed. (Lucknow: Eastern Book Co., 2001) at 21-6; and generally Surya Deva, "Concept of 'State' in the Era of Liberalisation and Withering State—An Analysis" in Dr. D. S. Prakasa Rao, ed., *Constitutional Jurisprudence and Environmental Justice: A Festschrift Volume in the Honour of Professor A Lakshminath* (Visakhapatnam: Pratyusha Publishing Ltd., 2002) at 175.

[39]   The disadvantages to women prevail in diverse areas, including hiring and firing, wages, promotion, maternity benefits, and sexual advertising.

[40]   The issue of reservation of jobs in the private sector is a matter of current debate at national level in India. In this context, the Prime Minister Mr. Manmohan Singh recently observed: "Nobody can prevent an idea, whose time has come…those opposing the move will not be able to do so once a national policy is put in place." Kalpana Sharma, "Manmohan for Voluntary Quota in Industry" *The Hindu* (6 October 2004), online: The Hindu <http://www.hindu.com/2004/10/07/stories/2004100709300100.htm>.

[41]   Muchlinski examines the conflicting interests of technology-exporting (mostly developed) and technology-importing (mostly developing) countries. Muchlinski, *supra* note 2 at 427-44.

[42]   See Seid, *supra* note 17 at 12-4; McCorquodale & Fairbrother, *supra* note 3 at 744-5; Sornarajah, *supra* note 1 at 39-40; Robert J. Fowler, "International Environmental Standards For Transnational Corporations" (1995) 25 Environmental Law 1 at 8-10. See, on emerging human rights concerns of

312 *Singapore Journal of Legal Studies* [2004]

a hazardous activity[43] could violate human rights of several thousand people of a developing country.[44] One should also not forget that on many occasions it is the people of developing countries—who are easy targets due to poverty, lesser awareness and lax or no legal regime governing experimentation on humans—that bear the burnt of untested and potentially dangerous technologies.[45]

Technology could, however, influence the realisation of human rights on another level. Though technology has the potential to shape the nature of human rights,[46] it is possible that only certain sections of society get the benefit of the "technology-added dimension" of human rights because technologies generally have an inbuilt *dissemination bias*.[47] The uneven spread of internet—also known as the "digital divide"—is a good example of this trend. As the access to internet is limited to certain people, those who were disadvantaged are further disadvantaged; only "haves" could exploit technologies to their advantage and not the "haves not".[48] For example, farmers—who have limited or no access to traditional means (newspapers/radio/TV) to get information, say, about weather or prices of their crops—are hardly benefited from the internet revolution. And it is really doubtful if any MNC would come forward to fill in this gap!

Fourth, foreign investment by MNCs has the potential to drive out local and small industries of developing countries,[49] resulting in dislocation and displacement of people for livelihood. Most of the times, even such dislocation or displacement does not ensure an alternative means of livelihood because there is no compatibility

---

new technologies, Dinah Shelton, "Challenges to the Future of Civil and Political Rights" (1998) 55 Washington and Lee Law Review 669 at 674-81.

[43] See Jamie Cassels, "Outlaws: Multinational Corporations and Catastrophic Law" (2000/2001) 31 Cumberland Law Review 311 at 317; Sornarajah, *supra* note 1 at 47.

[44] See Cassels, *ibid.* at 316-7. See also Lapierre & Moro who draw a powerful socio-economic sketch of the use of inferior/unproven technology—from the Bhopal gas plant (UCC/UCIL) to recent genetically modified crops (Monsanto). Dominique Lapierre & Javier Moro, *It Was Five Past Midnight in Bhopal* (New Delhi: Full Circle Publishing, 2001).

[45] Drug trials provide a very good example of this. See Joe Ford & George Tomossy, "Clinical Trials in Developing Countries: The Plaintiff's Challenge" 2004 (1) Law, Social Justice and Global Development Journal, online: <http://elj.warwick.ac.uk/global/issue/2004-1/fordtomossy.html>; R. Krishanakumar, "Ethics on Trial", *Frontline*, Vol. 18, Issue 16 (4-17 August 2001), online: Frontline <http://www.flonnet.com/fl1816/18161230.htm>; "Fast Growing Business: Unethical Clinical Trials in India", online: Alliance for Human Research Protection <http://www.ahrp.org/infomail/04/07/27.html>.

[46] Balkin, for example, explains how the right to freedom of speech changes in the digital age. Jack M. Balkin, "How Rights Change: Freedom of Speech in the Digital Age" (2004) 26 Sydney Law Review 5.

[47] By "dissemination bias" I mean that the use of technology is dependant on certain key inputs—*e.g.*, electricity or telephone lines—which are not as easily available everywhere. The result is that the benefits of technology might be concentrated amongst some people. Arguably, the dissemination bias could also be result of other non-technological factors such as lack of political will. For example, The World Health Report 2003 demonstrates how technology could help in curing diseases in one part of the world but not in the other. World Health Organisation, *The World Health Report 2003: Shaping the Future* (Geneva: WHO, 2003).

[48] The Indian government though is aware of this gap and is proposing to take remedial action. The government has accepted the report of the "Working Group on Information Technology (IT) for Masses" and has launched the National IT Mission to oversee the implementation of this report: online: Government of India, Department of Information Technology <http://www.mit.gov.in/E-rural/index.asp> <http://www.mit.gov.in/E-rural/nitm.asp>.

[49] This phenomenon is known as "crowding out". *World Investment Report 1999*, *supra* note 24 at 37-8. See also *World Investment Report 2003*, *supra* note 20 at 104-5.

between the training and experience these dislocated possess and the jobs which are on offer in market. Lack of any adequate social security schemes in developing countries makes the position of these venerable sections of society worse.

Fifth, foreign investment could also have a negative bearing on labour rights. Even those countries—like India—that protect labour rights through constitutional provisions and other laws[50] tend to apply different rules regarding the protection of such rights in special export zones.[51] Besides, even outside such special zones, there are real possibilities that civil and political rights could be curtailed, especially when their exercise appears to interfere with expected returns on foreign investment.[52]

Sixth, the business policies adopted by MNCs to get quick return over their investment[53] pose a threat for human rights generally. MNCs engage in provocative (and also obscene) advertising in order to mould consumers' choices, even to the detriment of their health and safety;[54] promote consumerism to create market;[55] change peoples' social-cultural habits;[56] show scant respect to environment;[57] and remain non-committal to the philosophy of sustainable development. All these essentially result in slow but often irreversible adverse consequences for the realisation of human rights.

Besides some of the specific situations mentioned above, foreign investment in developing countries influences the realisation of human rights on a general policy level as well. Given the fact many developing countries compete for their share of foreign investment, this often leads to a "race to the bottom" regarding human rights, including environmental and labour standards;[58] developing countries are often left

---

[50] *Constitution of India 1950*, articles 23 and 24. See also the *Workmen's Compensation Act 1923*; the *Trade Unions Act 1926*; the *Payment of Wages Act 1936*; the *Industrial Disputes Act 1947*; the *Minimum Wages Act 1948*; the *Maternity Benefit Act 1961*; the *Child Labour (Prohibition and Regulation) Act 1986*.

[51] See Usha Ramanathan, "Business and Human Rights—The India Paper", I.E.L.R.C. Working Paper 2001-02, online: International Environmental Law Research Centre <http://www.ielrc.org/content/w0102.pdf>. See also Seid, *supra* note 17 at 126-7.

[52] See, for example, the impact of the activities of Enron in India and Unocal in Myanmar. See *infra* note 90.

[53] "In a globalised economy, the patience of investors to obtain returns on their investment is considerably reduced." McCorquodale & Fairbrother, *supra* note 3 at 745.

[54] Balmurli Natrajan, "Legitimating Globalisation: Culture and its Uses" (2002) 12 Transnational Law and Contemporary Problems 127 at 127-30; Ashish Kothari, "Environment and the New Economic Policies: 1991-96" in *Legal Dimensions of Market Economy*, *supra* note 33 at 57, 63. See also Glasbeek, *supra* note 6 at 94-103.

[55] See McCorquodale & Fairbrother, *supra* note 3 at 735.

[56] In retrospect, one may ask why plastic bags were promoted in the past as an alternative to paper or cloth bags. Similarly, doubts could be raised about the appropriateness of promoting the culture of "night shopping", "shopping malls", "sending greeting cards on ever-increasing days", and "weekends" in developing societies. See, on how MNCs influence social and cultural traits of people, Krishna Kumar, ed., *Transnational Enterprises: Their Impact on Third World Societies and Culture* (Boulder, Colorado: Westview Press, 1980).

[57] See, for example, the environmental damage caused by Shell in Nigeria. Joshua P. Eaton, "The Nigerian Tragedy, Environmental Regulation of Transnational Corporations, and the Human Right to a Healthy Environment" (1997) 15 Boston University International Law Journal 261 at 264-71. See also Fowler, *supra* note 42 at 8-18; Martin A. Geer, "Foreigners in their Own Land: Cultural Land and Transnational Corporations—Emergent International Rights and Wrongs" (1998) 38 Virginia Journal of International Law 331.

[58] Seid, *supra* note 17 at 120; Macek, *supra* note 7 at 104; Clare Duffield, "Multinational Corporations and Workers' Rights" in Stuart Rees & Shelley Wright, eds., *Human Rights and Corporate*

314   *Singapore Journal of Legal Studies*   [2004]

with no choice but to either lower their human rights standards or not enforce them.[59] As a "race to the bottom" is in the interest of MNCs,[60] it will not be unreasonable to assume that they, armed with a lollypop of foreign investment, often initiate such race by pressing the panic button during negotiations for investment deals.

B. *Negative Effects on Development*

Though it is widely argued and believed that foreign investment leads to economic development, this should not be accepted as a universal truth in all cases. McCorquodale and Fairbrother offer three reasons which question the above assumption: "the type of investment, the basis of investment decisions, and the type of economic growth."[61] Furthermore, we should ask more fundamental questions about development: what do we mean by development; about whose development are we talking; and what should be the acceptable cost of such development?[62] Below is a brief attempt to grapple with these questions.

1. *What do we mean by development?*

At a time when "development" is identified with industralisation, westernisation and economic growth,[63] it seems that the true meaning of development is lost.[64] Development ought to be associated with humans,[65] and not merely with the possession

---

Responsibility—A Dialogue (Sydney: Pluto Press, 2000) 191 at 194; Mahmood Monshipouri, Claude E. Welch, Jr. & Evan T. Kennedy, "Multinational Corporations and the Ethics of Global Responsibility: Problems and Possibilities" (2003) 25 Human Rights Quarterly 965 at 973; Fowler, *supra* note 42 at 16-8. See, for when such races occur and do not occur, Spar & Yoffie, *supra* note 11. Compare Kevin Banks, "Globalisation and Labour Standards: A Second Look at the Evidence" (2004) 29 Queen's Law Journal 533, who do not find a uniform race to the bottom.

59   "Economic globalisation may undermine national and international human rights protections as states make an effort to remain competitive and to entice investment. The 'race to the bottom' is a threat, as countries are pressured to relax their standards for the treatment of workers, denying collective bargaining, minimum wages, and, in some cases, the right to be free from forced labor." Shelton, *supra* note 42 at 684. Compa demonstrates how even "not lowering standards" provision in the Multilateral Agreement on Investment and other provisions in the OECD Guidelines may not be able to protect labour rights. Compa, *supra* note 25 at 688-91.

60   "Multinational corporations have the option of deliberately taking advantage of lower environmental or social standards or weak systems of governance in developing countries." Ward, *supra* note 12 at 452-3.

61   McCorquodale & Fairbrother, *supra* note 3 at 743.

62   Incidentally, Rajagopal also frames these questions in somewhat similar terms, though in the context of opposing views of developing and developed countries: "[D]evelopment of what, of whom, and at whose expense?" Rajagopal, *supra* note 8 at 220.

63   Hilary Charlesworth, "The Public/Private Distinction and the Right to Development in International Law" (1992) 12 Australian Yearbook of International Law 190 at 196-7, as quoted by McCorquodale & Fairbrother, *supra* note 3 at 750.

64   For example, Sen argues: "Development can be seen ... as a process of expanding the real freedoms that people enjoy. Focusing on human freedoms contrasts with the narrower views of development, such as identifying development with the growth of gross national product, or with the rise in person incomes, or with industralisation, or with technological advance, or with social moderanisation." Sen, *supra* note 8 at 3.

65   Sub-Commission on the Promotion and Protection of Human Rights, 54th Session, Agenda Item 4, *Report of the High Commissioner on Liberalisation of Trade in Services and Human Rights*, E/CN.4/Sub.2/2003/9 (25 June 2002) at para. 8.

of material goods[66] or accumulated growth.[67] For example, the ranking of India on the Human Development Index (HDI)—which takes into account factors other than economic prosperity—is on the decline despite the big claims of economic development made in the last few years:[68] India's ranking slipped to 127th in 2003 from 124th in 2002 and 115th in 2001.[69] It also seems that liberalisation of the Indian economy since the early 1990s and consequent flow of foreign investment into India had no significant impact on the value of HDI.[70]

Besides, two more factors should be central to the idea of development: sustainability and equitability. Development has to be such which could be sustained for the time to come.[71] Present generations could hardly make a rightful self-proclamation of development when such development comes at the cost of causing unreasonable consumption or irreparable loss of natural resources, which the past had left for the present to be preserved for the future.[72] Similarly, it has to be ensured that the opportunities for development are not limited to certain sections of society only (or certain countries if we talk about the world society).[73] Such exclusions will not only be unjust but will also invite historical analogies of colonial exploitation.

If we apply the above developmental parameters, it is doubtful if foreign investment is achieving development in this sense. There is ample evidence to suggest that the agenda currently promoted by the *sources* of foreign investment is resulting in

---

[66] Pritchard, for example, seems to suggest this when he argues that the policy of an open competitive market economy is going to advance the living standards of people. Pritchard, *supra* note 1 at 1-2. *Contra* Rajagopal who argues that designations such as "development", "developed", "advanced" and "backward" are influenced by the Western model of development which is based on the level of mass consumption. Rajagopal, *supra* note 8 at 91.

[67] An aggregate growth does not truly and necessarily reflect an improvement/development in the lives of *all* the people. Stiglitz, *supra* note 11 at 79; David Kinley, "Human Rights, Globalisation and the Rule of Law: Friends, Foes or Family?" (2002-03) 7 U.C.L.A. Journal of International Law and Foreign Affairs 239 at 255. See also generally James Petras & Henry Veltmeyer, *Globalisation Unmasked: Imperialism in the 21ˢᵗ Century* (Halifax, Nova Scotia: Fernwood Publishing, 2001) at 122-27. But see Brian Griffiths, "The Challenge of Global Capitalism: A Christian Perspective" in Dunning, ed., *infra* note 76, 159 at 169-70.

[68] The recent Human Development Report 2004, however, indicates that there is no further decline in India's ranking in 2004 as compared to 2003. UNDP, *Human Development Report 2004* (New York: UNDP, 2004) at 141.

[69] See the various Human Development Reports, online: Human Development Reports <http://hdr.undp.org/reports/default.cfm>. Ward also notes that "in a number of poor but oil-rich developing countries, UNDP Human Development Index ranking have fallen as oil revenues have increased." Ward, *supra* note 12 at 453.

[70] The value was as follows: 0.416 (1975); 0.443 (1980); 0.481 (1985); 0.519 (1990); 0.553 (1995); and 0.590 (2001). UNDP, *Human Development Report 2003* (New York: Oxford University Press, 2003) at 243.

[71] This is so because "infinite growth with a finite pool of resources is impossible". Richard Welford *et al.*, *Hijacking Environmentalism: Corporate Responses to Sustainable Development* (London: Earthscan Publications Ltd., 1997) at x. [*Hijacking Environmentalism*]. See also Rajagopal who refers to the "limits to growth" theory advanced by the Club of Rome in 1972. Rajagopal, *supra* note 8 at 113.

[72] Rajagopal highlights a critical contradiction "between the logic of economic growth, which is based on infinite economic exploitation of both labour and resources, and the logic of environment, which is premised on inherent limits to growth." Rajagopal, *supra* note 8 at 116. He, however, also cautions that the "language of sustainability" has made little progress to resolve this contradiction; *ibid.*

[73] Agamben highlights this politics of exclusion and inclusion in terms of the "*People*" (a whole, integral body politic) and the "*people*" (a subset consisting of needy and excluded). Giorgio Agamben, "What is a People?" in Giorgio Agamben (translated by Vincenzo Binetti & Cesare Casarino), *Means without Ends: Notes on Politics* (Minneapolis: University of Minnesota Press, 2000) at 29-36.

316 *Singapore Journal of Legal Studies* [2004]

lopsided, inequitable and unsustainable development.[74] In sum, neither developed countries nor the MNCs based therein are doing enough for the development of the *whole* "one community".[75]

2. *Whose development are we talking about, and at what cost?*

Whose development do we refer to when we talk about foreign investment-driven development? Is it the development of everyone, of the privileged few, or of the most disadvantaged? It is important, in my view, that the developmental benefits of foreign investment *reach first to those who need it most*. In fact, foreign investment fails in achieving its objective of bringing development if it creates or strengthens existing inequalities of wealth and opportunities.[76]

The recent government-run "India Shining" blitz[77] illustrates this very clearly. India is definitely shining: the economy is booming; the foreign exchange reserves are at an all time high; inflation is in control; poverty has declined; the information technology (IT) sector is leading the way. But this show campaign hides and mystifies what is not shining and who are not shining—the voiceless poor populace living in villages, slums and remote tribal areas: "Most of the India Shining claims are true. As long as we are talking about 10 per cent of the population ... The fastest growing sector in India Shining is not IT or software, textiles or automobiles. It is inequality."[78] The message is, therefore, clear: *when it is declared that foreign investment brings development, the reference seems to be to the development of not all but only of those who (and whose development) matter.* Consequently, the development indicators do not even take cognizance of suicides by farmers under debt trap,[79] or death of

---

74 Rubin, for example, suggests that "[o]ne source of [public interest] concerns is that a corporation may be perceived as not conferring benefits or costs equally on all regions of even a single country." Seymour J. Rubin, "Transnational Corporations and International Codes of Conduct: A Study of the Relationship between International Legal Cooperation and Economic Development" (1995) 10 American University Journal of International Law and Policy 1275 at 1279.

75 See generally Peter Singer, *One World: The Ethics of Globalisation* (Melbourne: Text Publishing Co., 2002) at 165-213. See also the recent report of the ILO which urges: "Obtaining a fair globalisation is a collective responsibility of many actors .... Those with the greatest power to make things better also have the greatest responsibility at every level ..." World Commission on the Social Dimension of Globalisation, I.L.O., *A Fair Globalisation: Creating Opportunities for All* (Geneva: ILO, 2004) at 1 [*A Fair Globalisation*].

76 Whether globalisation, which is the driving force behind foreign investment, increases or decreases poverty as well as economic disparity is a hotly debated and contested issue. See Petras & Veltmeyer, *supra* note 67 at 20-2; Stiglitz, *supra* note 11 at 4-10, 24-5, 86; Hertz, *supra* note 7, 8, 41-51; John H. Dunning, "The Moral Imperatives of Global Capitalism: An Overview" in John H. Dunning, ed., *The Moral Challenges of Global Capitalism* (Oxford: Oxford University Press, 2003) 11 at 18; Dinah Shelton, "Protecting Human Rights in a Globalised World" (2002) 25 Boston College International and Comparative Law Review 273 at 278-9.

77 Just before the 2004 general election for the 14th Lok Sabha, the outgoing BJP-led National Democratic Alliance government spent millions of rupees in projecting India's shining economy through all possible means of communication.

78 P. Sainath, "The Feel Good Factory", *Frontline*, Vol. 21, Issue 5 (28 February-12 March 2004), online: Frontline <http://www.frontlineonnet.com/fl2105/stories/20040312007800400.htm>. See also the other reports related to the cover story, "Is India Shining?", *Frontline*, Vol. 21, Issue 5 (28 February-12 March 2004), online: Frontline <http://www.frontlineonnet.com/fl2105/fl210500.htm>.

79 S. Nagesh Kumar, "Suicides by Andhra Pradesh Farmers Continue" *The Hindu* (10 June 2004), online: The Hindu <http://www.hindu.com/2004/06/10/stories/2004061002121200.htm>. See also W. Chandrakanth, "Farmers Reeling under Free Market Forces" *The Hindu* (11 June 2004), online: The Hindu <http://www.hindu.com/2004/06/11/ stories/2004061102101200.htm>.

thousands of malnourished tribal children,[80] because these people are not considered part of the development process.[81]

Concerns also arise not only about the unreasonable cost of development but also regarding the bearers of such cost inherent in foreign investment by MNCs. Care should be taken that the *future* of future generations is not mortgaged for achieving avoidable development of today.[82] Similarly, the cost of development should be spread out equitably as opposed to be borne out by selective few disadvantaged.[83] After all, why is it taken for granted that it is the tribals, farmers, small handicraftsmen and similar ignored voices who must bear the cost for "overall" societal development, as if they are lesser human than those who dress in designer clothes, dine in costly cutlery, live in palace-like "cottages" and roam in fancy cars.

In view of the above brief analysis, it is reasonable to argue that even if the claims of foreign investment-driven development are true, they present a distorted picture. Not only the meaning of true development is overshadowed, but also forgotten are the people excluded from the race for development[84] and the cost of such development. Development based on a model which designs developmental goals as per the needs of already well off, or excludes some from the focus of development, or places the cost of development on those shoulders that cannot bear it, is not only unfair but also amount to unjust enrichment. Arguably, we need to deconstruct such a model of development.

C. *What Lessons Could We Learn from Bhopal, Enron and Unocal?*

As mentioned before, it might be helpful to refer to three case studies—two of which relate to India and the third to Myanmar—that illustrate the chemistry of *sangam* explored in this article. I begin with Bhopal, probably the most catastrophic industrial tragedy, first. The establishment, operation of chemical plant at Bhopal was a typical response of an MNC, Union Carbide Corporation (UCC), to Indian government's

---

[80] S. Balakrishnan, "9,000 Kids Starve to Death in Shining India" *The Times of India* (5 July 2004), online: The Times of India <http://timesofindia.indiatimes.com/articleshow/766306.cms>.

[81] "In the process of carrying out projects they claim advance development goals, policy makers regularly ignore the needs of the most marginalized in society–minorities, indigenous and tribal peoples, peasants, and women–often worsening their situations. Development in this context betters the situation for a select few, while worsening the situation for many others." Aird, *supra* note 35 at 25.

[82] Welford argues that the "dominant corporate culture which believes that natural resources are there for taking and that environmental and social problems will be resolved through growth, scientific advancement, technology transfer..., free trade and the odd charitable hand-out" must be changed. Richard Welford, "Introduction: What are we Doing to the World?" in Welford *et al.*, *Hijacking Environmentalism*, *supra* note 71, 3 at 7.

[83] See generally McCorquodale & Fairbrother, *supra* note 3 at 743-4. Rajagopal characterizes it as "violence of development". Rajagopal, *supra* note 8 at 202.

[84] A recent report highlights the pervasive unemployment, especially among the youth and the educated, in South Asian countries despite an integrated development agenda being pursued at the international level. It blames South Asian governments, multilateral organisations and the governments of developed countries for this situation. Mahbub Ul Haq Human Development Centre, *Human Development in South Asia 2003: The Employment Challenge* (Karachi: Oxford University Press, 2004). Interestingly, this is despite the fact that a World Bank study has found a notable poverty reduction in South Asia: "Notable Poverty Reduction" *The Hindu* (31 July 2004), online: The Hindu <http://www.thehindu.com/2004/07/31/stories/2004073113211200.htm>.

desire "to modernise and become self-sufficient in food production".[85] UCC, which owned and operated the plant through its Indian subsidiary, Union Carbide India Ltd., applied inferior technology, sidelined safety measures in order to save on running cost and exploited the absence (or lax enforcement) of laws dealing with health, safety and environment. The result, on the night of 2-3 December 1984, of all this was what is called the "industrial Hiroshima", killing several thousands and exposing lakhs of people to a deadly cocktail of poisonous gases. After a long ordeal in the courts, both in the U.S. and in India, victims could get monetary compensation, but not justice.[86] Several proceedings are still pending in different Indian and U.S. courts in quest of justice.[87] Though it is not possible to even mention the saga of victims' miseries, both on account of the gas tragedy and the legal battle that ensued, it will be pertinent to note what is most relevant for the present purpose. With a view not to send a wrong signal to prospective foreign investors, the government of India not only did not press vigorously for the extradition of Warren Anderson, the ex-CEO of UCC,[88] but also applied to an Indian court, which was hearing a criminal case against him, to dilute the charge from "culpable homicide not amounting to murder" to "death by rash or negligent act", the latter being a less serious offence.[89]

Enron is another relatively recent example of human rights abuses caused by foreign investment. Dabhol Power Project (commonly known as Enron Project), initiated in the middle of 1992 by Enron Corporation, was the first major litmus test of the Indian government policy to allow foreign investment in power and electricity sector. But the project remained in controversy from the very inception due to various reasons such as corruption, lack of transparency and competitive bidding, and the high cost of electricity. When people protested against the project, the state government machinery muzzled such protests including through arbitrary arrests, beating, and harassment of protest movement leaders. What was, however, critical was that Enron

---

[85]   Cassels, *supra* note 43 at 316.

[86]   In accordance with a settlement agreement, reached with government of India and approved by the Indian Supreme Court, the UCC agreed to pay US$470 million to the government "for the *benefit of all victims* of the Bhopal gas disaster ... *and not as fines, penalties, or punitive damage.*" *Union Carbide Corp. v. Union of India* A.I.R. 1990 S.C. 273 at 275 [emphasis added]. It is important to note that recently the Indian Supreme Court directed the government to distribute *pro rata* the remaining amount of Rs. 1503 crore amongst the victims. It is estimated that every victim or his/her kith and kin will be getting about Rs. 26,000—after almost two decades of the tragedy. J. Venkatesan, "Court Orders Relief to Bhopal Gas Victims" (20 July 2004), online: The Hindu <http://www.hindu.com/2004/07/20/stories/2004072008760100.htm>.

[87]   A criminal case is pending against the UCC/UCIL and its employees, including Warren Anderson, the Chief Executive Officer of UCC, in a district court of Bhopal. Similarly, the proceedings under the *Alien Tort Claims Act* 28 U.S.C. § 1350 (2004) are continuing in the U.S. courts. See *Sajida Bano v. Union Carbide Corporation* 99 Civ. 11329 (JFK), 2000 U.S. Dist. LEXIS 12326; *Sajida Bano v. Union Carbide Corporation* 273 F.3d 120, 2001 U.S. App. LEXIS 24488 (2d Cir. N.Y. 2001); *Sajida Bano v. Union Carbide Corporation* 99 Civ. 11329 (JFK), 2003 U.S. Dist. LEXIS 4097; *Sajida Bano v. Union Carbide Corporation* 361 F.3d 696, 2004 U.S. App. LEXIS 5003 (2d Cir. N.Y. 2004).

[88]   See the opinion of the Attorney General on the extradition of Anderson at online: Union Carbide Corporation <http://www.bhopal.com/opinion.htm>. The US government has rejected the Indian government's plea for the extradition of Anderson, "U.S. rejects request for Anderson's extradition", *The Hindu* (21 July 2004), online: The Hindu <http://www.hindu.com/2004/07/21/stories/2004072111711100.htm>.

[89]   The court has, however, rejected this request, online: CorpWatch <http://www.corpwatch.org/article.phd?id=3729>.

Sing. J.L.S. *The Sangam of Foreign Investment, Multinational Corporations and Human Rights* 319

Corporation provided resources to aid and fund these state operations.[90] Enron is, thus, an example of how even a democratic state could take the side of a foreign investor MNC against its own people, whose human rights it is obliged to protect constitutionally.

Finally, let us refresh our memories of Unocal's operations in Myanmar (earlier Burma) vis-à-vis human rights. In 1993, Unocal, a California based oil company, entered into a joint venture with the State Law and Order Restoration Council (SLORC) and Myanmar Ministry for Oil and Gas Enterprises regarding oil and gas exploration in the Yadana gas field.[91] Whereas Unocal undertook to make the largest investment in the project,[92] the SLORC assumed the responsibility of clearing the land along the pipeline's path and providing labour, material and security.[93] This business partnership resulted in serious human rights violations—from forced dislocation to torture, forced labour, murder and rape.[94] As the Burmese government institutions were closely linked with the project, there was no hope of getting any redress at the municipal level. Victims' search for justice for human rights abuses outside the municipal framework continues as the trial of several cases under the *Alien Tort Claims Act* has offered mixed hopes but no concrete relief or positive results as yet.[95]

On the basis of above examination of the case studies of Bhopal, Enron and Unocal, one could say that they are instructive in at least three respects. First, foreign investment by MNCs could result in violation of all types of human rights—from civil and political to social, economic and cultural. Second, there are no strong reasons to believe that governments will be able to perform successfully their role of human rights guardians. Past experiences show that states, especially developing ones, may act in connivance with (or under pressure of) MNCs, or may consider behaving as a "good host" to foreign investment higher on their priority list than the protection of human rights. Third, contrary to a popular belief, foreign investment by MNCs could result in human rights violations in democratic and non-democratic settings alike; Bhopal and Enron demonstrate that democracy and a liberal, human rights enriched Constitution are no fool proof guarantee against corporate human rights abuses.

---

[90] The report of Human Rights Watch documents in detail this complicity. Human Rights Watch, *The Enron Corporation: Corporate Complicity in Human Rights Violations* (1999), online: Human Rights Watch <http://www.hrw.org/reports/1999/enron/>. See also Kelley, *supra* note 18 at 511-2.

[91] See David I. Becker, "A Call for the Codification of the Unocal Doctrine" (1998) 32 Cornell International Law Journal 183 at 186; John C. Anderson, "Respecting Human Rights: Multinational Corporations Strike Out" (2000) 2 University of Pennsylvania Journal of Labour and Employment Law 463 at 464.

[92] Becker, *ibid.* at 186.

[93] Anderson, *supra* note 91 at 464.

[94] Kelley, *supra* note 18 at 508-9.

[95] See a catena of cases: *Doe v. Unocal* 963 F. Supp. 880 (C.D. Cal., 1997); *Doe v. Unocal* 27 F. Supp. 2d. 1174 (C.D. Cal., 1998); *Doe v. Unocal* 67 F. Supp. 2d. 1140 (C.D. Cal., 1999); *Doe v. Unocal* 110 F. Supp. 2d. 1294 (C.D. Cal., 2000); *Doe v. Unocal* 248 F. 3d. 915 (9th Circuit Court of Appeal, 2001); *John Doe I v. Unocal* 2002 U.S. App. LEXIS 19263 (9th Cir. Cal., 2002); *Doe v. Unocal* 2003 U.S. App. LEXIS 2716 (9th Cir. Cal., 2003). See also Becker, *supra* note 91; Anderson, *supra* note 91; John Cheverie, "United States Court Finds Unocal may be Liable for Aiding and Abetting Human Rights Abuses in Burma" (2002) 10 Human Rights Brief 6.

320   *Singapore Journal of Legal Studies*   [2004]

III. FOREIGN INVESTMENT AND DEVELOPING COUNTRIES: TO ALLOW OR NOT TO ALLOW?

Though the previous section examined the negative impact of foreign investment by MNCs on human rights and development in developing countries, I am also interested in exploring the strategies that developing countries could employ to exercise a reasonable level of control on the *flow* and *direction* of foreign investment.

Regarding the entry and continuance of foreign investment, states, especially developing ones, face a Hobson's choice: should they allow foreign investment by MNCs or refuse it, considering that it might have a negative impact on human rights as well as local developmental issues and raise questions of states' autonomy or sovereignty?[96] Or is there a middle path available,[97] that is, developing countries could negotiate the terms and conditions of foreign investment to their advantage? Could collective bargaining help in improving the bargaining position of developing countries? Furthermore, what role could human rights and civil society organs play in ensuring that host countries are able to exert greater control over the flow and direction of foreign investment?

It should also be noted that the changing ideology about the role of the state poses another problem: states are now expected to act and regulate primarily (if not solely) to support and secure private sector activities and private property, including the intellectual property rights.[98] This runs counter to the conventional role regarding the protection and promotion of human rights assigned to states.[99]

A. *"Is It All about Bargaining?"*

The core issues related to foreign investment—which country gets *how much* foreign investment *from where* and on *what terms*—are the subject matter of bargaining and negotiations between potential investors and countries seeking foreign investment.[100] In other words, who controls the flow and direction of foreign investment depends essentially on the relative bargaining power of the parties involved in negotiation.[101] The stand of concerned parties is guided by "risks"—risks *to* and *of* foreign investment[102]—and "returns"—both to the investor and the investment host.

---

[96] See *Trends in International Investment Agreements, infra* note 102 at 87-88.

[97] Sornarajah, *supra* note 1 at 45-50.

[98] Pritchard, for example, argues: "A market economy needs a legal system to define and protect the rights of the private sector against encroachment by government, to remove special privileges accorded to state-owned enterprises and to reduce risk and transaction costs between private parties." Pritchard, *supra* note 1 at 2. See also Douglas Webb, "Legal System Reform and Private Sector Development in Developing Countries" in Pritchard, ed., *supra* note 1 at 45-6.

[99] "A strong and vigorous state is not only seen as a prerequisite to the protection of civil and political rights ... it is also seen as essential to protect economic and social rights." Rajagopal, *supra* note 8 at 191.

[100] "The relationship between the host state and a [multinational enterprise] will be the outcome of a bargaining process between them." Muchlinski, *supra* note 2 at 104.

[101] See Muchlinski, *ibid.*

[102] "The principal measures against which investors seek protection are expropriations, nationalisations and other major cases of deprivation of property and infringement of property rights of investors." UNCTAD, *Trends in International Investment Agreements: An Overview* (New York: U.N., 1999) at 76 [*Trends in International Investment Agreements*]. See also Pritchard, *supra* note 1 at 2.

The relative strength of MNCs and states has another role to play: whereas developed countries and the MNCs based therein promote an ideology conducive to foreign investment,[103] developing countries put more emphasis on developing regimes or strategies which ensure that foreign investment by MNCs works primarily for local development.[104] For example, one major reason why the final draft of the UN Code of Conduct on Transnational Corporations, proposed in 1990 by the United Nations Commission on Transnational Corporations, failed to materalise was because of the conflicting objectives of developed and developing countries: developed countries emphasised the need for including MNCs' rights in the Code whereas developing countries considered inclusion of responsibilities more important.[105]

B. *Relative Bargaining Position of MNCs and Developing Countries*

Under international law, states have an unlimited, absolute right to decide whether to allow foreign investment within their territory, and if so, then from whom, in which areas and on what terms.[106] It is also suggested by the proponents of bargaining theory that developing countries could, in fact, have stronger position,[107] and that the bargaining power of host states have increased on account of the emergence of many MNCs operating within the same industry.[108] Furthermore, that one should not overemphasise factors such as low wages, presence of raw materials, lax environmental measures, etc. present in developing countries as foreign investment is not solely determined by these factors.[109]

It seems however, that the actual position regarding the bargaining position of developing countries vis-à-vis MNCs is totally different. Undoubtedly, all states in principle can regulate foreign investment by MNCs by employing various techniques

---

[103] "Recent policy initiatives at the international level concerning TNCs focus instead on developing guidelines to facilitate FDI, with the principal issues being the development of standards for fair and equitable treatment, national treatment, and most favored nation treatment." Fowler, *supra* note 42 at 3. See also Seid, *supra* note 17 at 69-97.

[104] See generally Seid, *supra* note 17 at 99-118. Seid though concludes that developing countries have no "common strategy on how to tackle the issue of global investment rules." *Ibid.* at 116.

[105] *Draft of the U.N. Code of Conduct on Transnational Corporations*, U.N.E.S.C.O.R., 45th Session, U.N. Doc. E/1990/94 (1990). See generally Kwamena Acquaah, *International Regulation of Transnational Corporations: The New Reality* (New York: Praeger, 1986) at 108-20; Muchlinski, *supra* note 2 at 592-7.

[106] Each state has the right "to regulate and exercise authority over foreign investment within its national jurisdiction in accordance with its laws and regulations and in conformity with its national objectives and priorities." U.N. General Assembly Resolution 3281 (XXIX) (1974): *Charter of Economic Rights and Duties of States*, Article 2(2)(a). Article 2(2)(b) further provides that each state has a right "to regulate and supervise the activities of transnational corporations within its national jurisdiction and take measures to ensure that such activities comply with its laws, rules and regulations and conform with its economic and social policies." See also the U.N. General Assembly Resolution 1803 (XVII) (1962): *Permanent Sovereignty over Natural Resources*.

[107] See Muchlinski, *supra* note 2 at 105-6, referring to the position taken by Professor Moran. See also Joseph M. Grieco, "Between Dependency and Autonomy: India's Experience with the International Computer Industry" in *Multinational Corporations*, *supra* note 17 at 55.

[108] Sornarajah, *supra* note 1 at 18. In fact, Moran goes one step further and argues: "Third World countries will have to play an active role in *stimulating* rivalries within the international corporate sectors in which they are seeking investment." *Multinational Corporations*, *supra* note 17 at 13 [emphasis in original].

[109] See Pritchard, *supra* note 1 at 5.

322   *Singapore Journal of Legal Studies*   [2004]

at the entry and/or post-entry stage.[110] Even so, it would be misleading, in my view, to suggest that the bargaining position of developing countries is equal or higher to that of MNCs.[111] This is more so because on an "international political level, the relative cohesion of the third world [has] decreased considerably."[112] MNCs also set in motion a "race to the bottom" to exert more leverage during investment negotiations; it is doubtful if developing countries are capable of setting their investment priorities in the face of competition between countries for investment dollars.[113] Besides, there are reasons to believe that states may, in fact, be ready to forego their regulatory power over the activities of MNCs in favour of short-term economic gains.[114]

In sum, it is a challenge for developing countries to create an atmosphere conducive to foreign investment and at the same time ensure that doing so does not work, directly or indirectly, against their local needs[115] or the realisation of human rights.[116]

C. *Regulating the Flow and Direction of Foreign Investment: How to Bargain with MNCs?*

It is generally agreed that the countries that are host to foreign investment should regulate the flow and direction of such investment, in order to ensure that it serves their specific needs. There is, however, lesser consensus on how to exert the required control, which strategies to adopt and at what stage(s). States have entered into varied kinds of agreements—from bilateral to multilateral and regional[117]—to deal with the issue of foreign investment.[118] Despite the fact that bilateral investment agreements are on the rise since the 1990s[119] and seems to be the favoured strategy currently,[120] it is likely that states might move more towards multilateral or global agreements, especially under the umbrella of WTO in future.[121] This may happen

---

[110] See Muchlinski, *supra* note 17 at 172-203; Sornarajah, *supra* note 1 at 83-114.

[111] See, for example, *Trends in International Investment Agreements*, *supra* note 102 at 29. The study also suggests further the strategies that could be adopted to protect the special developmental needs of developing countries. *Ibid.* at 88-92.

[112] *Ibid.* at 30.

[113] For example, could India prioritise its investment needs? In other words, could it seek investment, as a matter of priority, in primary health and roads rather than in soft drinks, mineral water and potato chips industries? See also S. S. Singh & Suresh Mishra, "State and Market: A Constitutional Analysis" in *Legal Dimensions of Market Economy*, *supra* note 33, 13 at 15.

[114] See Acquaah, *supra* note 105 at 66; Steven R. Ratner, "Corporation and Human Rights: A Theory of Legal Responsibility" (2001) 111 Yale Law Journal 443 at 462; Robert McCorquodale, "Human Rights and Global Business" in Bottomley & Kinley, eds., *supra* note 13, 89 at 97-8. See also Beth Stephens, "The Amorality of Profit: Transnational Corporations and Human Rights" (2002) 20 Berkeley Journal of International Law 45 at 57-8; Muchlinski, *supra* note 2 at 104-7.

[115] See UNCTAD, *World Investment Report (2003)*, *supra* note 20 at 18-9.

[116] Dependency theorists argue that FDI does not help the home countries, which are developing or under-developed on many occasions. See Seid, *supra* note 17 at 17-23. FDI also raises concerns about state sovereignty, especially from developing countries. Seid, *ibid.* at 102-04.

[117] For example, the arrangements at the level of EU, NAFTA, ASEAN and OECD. See UNCTAD, *Trends in International Investment Agreements*, *supra* note 102 at 42-4; Seid, *supra* note 17 at 55-7.

[118] See, for a list of main instruments entered between 1948 and 1999, UNCTAD, *Trends in International Investment Agreements*, *supra* note 102 at 94-103.

[119] *Trends in International Investment Agreements*, *supra* note 102 at 33, and also at 44-7.

[120] See *World Investment Report 2003*, *supra* note 20 at 12.

[121] Currently, a Working Group on Trade and Investment is deliberating upon this issue. A special reference may be made to para. 22 of the Doha Ministerial Declaration, WT/MIN(01)/DEC/1

in spite of present disagreements amongst states, and opposition to the inclusion of investment within the WTO-fold.[122] It also seems that a departure from bilateral to multilateral treaties may suit the interest of developing countries,[123] provided they are able to act with a collective wisdom.

I argue, however, that developing countries—in order to exert control over the flow and direction of foreign investment by MNCs—should adopt an approach of "diversified integration", rely upon human rights jurisprudence, and try to develop synergy with NGOs, media, consumer and environmental groups, and public-spirited lawyers and academics.

1. *Developing Asian countries and the approach of "diversified integration"*

It is critical to the development of (Asian) developing countries that they not only attract foreign investment but also exercise control over the *flow* and *direction* of such investment. An accomplishment of these twin objectives requires effective individual as well as collective strategies. There is, however, a dichotomy between the adoption of individual and collective strategies: though acting individually is beneficial as it allows every country to choose and decide what is best for its specific developmental goals, it undermines the bargaining position of developing countries vis-à-vis MNCs. On the other hand, though collectivity strengthens the bargaining power of developing countries, it makes accommodation of diversified developmental goals more difficult.

There is, therefore, a need to mix the positives of both individual and collective strategies. I advocate for the approach of "diversified integration" as such a mixture. The approach assumes that developing countries could enhance their bargaining power, as well as position vis-à-vis MNCs, if they act collectively. At the same time it also recognises the existence of diversified developmental goals and the necessity for adopting flexible policies. The Asian developing countries should, therefore, act and bargain collectively as far as possible—both inside and outside the WTO—not only for attracting foreign investment but also for controlling its flow and direction.

But how could developing countries act collectively, especially when they have different (and sometimes conflicting) investment needs and usually remain eager to

---

(adopted on 14 November 2001) online: World Trade Organisation <http://www.wto.org/english/thewto_e/minist_e/min01_e/mindecl_e.htm#tradeinvestment>, which is instructive of the future framework: "Any framework should reflect in a balanced manner the interests of home and host countries, and take due account of the development policies and objectives of host governments as well as their right to regulate in the public interest. The special development, trade and financial needs of developing and least-developed countries should be taken into account as an integral part of any framework, which should enable members to undertake obligations and commitments commensurate with their individual needs and circumstances."

[122] In fact, the investment—one of the Singapore Issues—has been dropped from the current Doha Round of negotiations in a recent General Council's decision. *Draft General Council Decision of 31 July 2004*, WT/GC/W/535, para. g, online: World Trade Organisation <http://www.wto.org/english/tratop_e/dda_e/ddadraft_31jul04_e.pdf>. See generally Seid, *supra* note 17 at 153-9.

[123] "The problem with the bilateral approach is that Third World and industrialised states are unequal political and economic partners. ... may have significant implications for Third World states." Gloria L. Sandrino, "The NAFTA Investment Chapter and Foreign Direct Investment in Mexico: A Third World Perspective" (1994) 27 Vanderbilt Journal of Transnational Law 259 at 325.

324 *Singapore Journal of Legal Studies* [2004]

allure foreign investment by offering various types of incentives to MNCs?[124] The task is undoubtedly ambitious and difficult but not unprecedented or impossible to achieve, for international agreements on various issues and involving not merely developing countries but a mixture of developed, developing and least-developed ones are being reached.[125] As a first step towards attaining the above goal, the developing countries of Asia may constitute a working group to find out both common and diverse interests that they would like to accomplish through foreign investment by MNCs. Once that is done, it is possible to negotiate a regional investment agreement by applying different principles to common interests and diverse interests.

As far as the common interests are concerned, developing countries may agree on the principle of "non-lowering of standards", namely, that no country will offer incentives or lower the standards beyond the agreed level. Spar and Yoffie suggest that this is possible:

> Rather than directly competing for multinational investment, countries can sometimes agree to common standards for the treatment of multinationals and protocols for taxation. Rather than using wages differentials to compete in the trading arena, national governments can negotiate agreements that regulate their trade and promote more just outcomes.[126]

On the other hand, regarding diverse interests, developing countries should adopt the principle of reciprocity, that is, instead of competing for investment amongst them, countries should support each other's individual investment needs. Such a mutual cooperation, though difficult to achieve and sustain, would undoubtedly benefit all developing countries.[127]

It is hoped that if developing countries try to institutionalise the approach of diversified integration, they might be able to translate the "race to the bottom" into the "race to the top". In other words, instead of developing countries being forced to offering incentives or lower their standards, MNCs will offer incentives to get an approval for investment.

2. *Whether human rights could work as a regulating factor?*

I am of the view that the power of the language of human rights could and should be utilised to harness the process of foreign investment by MNCs.[128] Despite cultural apprehensions against the universality of human rights, they could still be used as a starting point of finding commonality amongst the developing countries of Asia.[129]

---

[124] Despite the inherent costs, offering incentives often becomes a compulsion for developing countries as they find themselves part of various "bidding wars". *World Investment Report 2003, supra* note 20 at 124, and generally 123-8.

[125] See Spar & Yoffie, *supra* note 11 at 572.

[126] *Ibid.* at 563.

[127] "[S]tates have a clear incentive to cooperate around common norms of governance. ... All parties are better off if they cooperate." *Ibid.* at 571-2.

[128] Rajagopal though highlights the risks involved for the Third World in relying entirely on human rights discourse, due to its colonial connection, for resistance and emancipation for the oppressed social majorities. Rajagopal, *supra* note 8 at 171-232.

[129] I suggest two guiding tools here. First, to begin with, we could probably start with more basic and non-controversial human rights such as food, health, shelter, clothing, and education. Second, universality

Culture, and cultural diversity, should be used to promote human rights and not to derogate them.[130] In view of wider acceptability of human rights in Western developed countries, the home of a majority of MNCs,[131] it may be relatively more difficult for MNCs to blatantly ignore human rights while negotiating/making investment decisions. This will also ensure that foreign investment is also made in basic services such as education, health care, food and water.

There is another dimension of this argument. It seems that even from the perspective of MNCs, investment in fulfilling basic needs or developing infrastructure in developing countries is a business compulsion for developed countries and/or MNCs based therein.[132] After all, it is in their interest that more and more people are educated, so that they could be allured by the language of advertising; that people receive (good) health care, so that they survive to consume the products manufactured by MNCs; that people earn reasonable wages, so that they retain the potential to buy products (even non-essential ones); that means of transport develop as well as spread to remote areas, so that goods could target a much larger audience; that people have roof over their head (even if that happens on account of debt), so that they have some space for storing leisure items.

Conversely, if the foreign investment by MNCs is not *seen*[133] by the general public in developing countries as making a positive difference to their life, it might result in a "backlash" both against MNCs and the foreign investment made by them.[134] Arguably, if this happens, it will harm the interests of both MNCs and the host countries of investment. Therefore, it is in the interest of all concerned parties that the "trumping"[135] power of human rights jurisprudence is used to ensure that foreign investment by MNCs not only not violate basic human rights but also contribute to sustainable as well as egalitarian development.

3. *Could NGOs et al. help states in asserting control over the flow and direction of foreign investment?*

Finally, developing countries should also pay attention to develop synergies with those NGOs, media, consumer and environmental groups, labour organisations,[136]

---

does not remain an unruly horse if we draw a distinction between "aspirational" and "operational" standards of human rights. See Surya Deva, "Human Rights Violations by Multinational Corporations and International Law: Where from Here?" (2003) 19 Connecticut Journal of International Law 1 at 41.

[130] See Wright, *supra* note 3. Grace also argues that "differences and diversity are also aspects of human rights", and that despite differences, commonalities could be found. Damian Grace, "Business Ethics and Human Rights" (1998) 4 Australian Journal of Human Rights 59, online: Australian Journal of Human Rights <http://www.austlii.edu.au/au/journals/AJHR/1998/4.html>.

[131] See Fowler, *supra* note 42 at 6-7.

[132] A recent report of the UN Commission on Private Sector and Development also urges private sector to contribute towards alleviating poverty. Commission on Private Sector and Development, *Unleashing Entrepreneurship: Making Business Work for the Poor* (2004), online: Commission on Private Sector and Development <http://www.undp.org/cpsd/fullreport.pdf>.

[133] In my view, it is essential that foreign investment not only contributes but is also seen as contributing to the promotion of human rights and the realisation of developmental goals.

[134] "There is evidence that a general backlash may develop among the populace of developing states against foreign direct investment." Kelley, *supra* note 18 at 502.

[135] See Jack Donnelly, *Universal Human Rights: In Theory and Practice* (Ithaca : Cornell University Press, 1989) at 8, citing Ronald Dworkin, *Taking Rights Seriously* (London: Duckworth, 1977) at xi, 90.

[136] See, for the role played by such groups in regulation of foreign investment, Seid, *supra* note 17 at 185-9.

326   *Singapore Journal of Legal Studies*   [2004]

and public-spirited lawyers and academics (NGOs *et al.*) who share a common objective with them,[137] namely, that foreign investment does not remain *foreign* to the realisation of human rights. As these non-state actors operate outside the formal state structure and do not rely upon mere legal means to resist what ought to be resisted, they are often capable of achieving what even states cannot accomplish. Because of this unique position, NGOs *et al.*—acting alone or in co-operation and coordination with developing countries—offer some hope to ensure that foreign investment by MNCs does not work for the development of MNCs alone or of certain sections of a country where the investment is made.

In my view, the networking with NGOs *et al.* is important for a number of reasons. First, the support of NGOs *et al.*,[138] which are already playing a key role in promoting human rights globally,[139] will provide a cushion to states against MNCs' possible backlash and threat of withdrawal. Second, the reliance on civil society organisations will be especially helpful when a state is not fully committed to the realisation of human rights or is acting in connivance with MNCs.[140] Third, on certain occasions NGOs *et al.* could prove far more effective in checking human rights abuses by MNCs as, unlike states, they do not suffer from territorial limitations. In view of the IT revolution, NGOs *et al.* could put pressure on MNCs even in their home states or wherever they operate. Fourth, fostering a bond between developing countries and NGOs *et al.* will also increase the bargaining position, at international forums or otherwise, of developing countries vis-à-vis developed countries and MNCs based therein, as international law as well as the international institutions are already taking cognisance of their resistance.[141]

IV. CONCLUSION

This article has tried to uncover the rainbow created by the *sangam* of foreign investment, MNCs and human rights in a developing Asia. The dynamics of the rainbow are explored by taking India as an indicator of developing countries and with the help of the case studies of Bhopal, Enron and Unocal. On the basis of this exploration, I have drawn three conclusions out of which the first two are descriptive whereas the third one is prescriptive in nature. First, it is argued that foreign investment by MNCs, or otherwise, do have and could have detrimental consequences for the

---

[137] See generally Julie Fisher, *Non governments: NGOs and the Political Development of the Third World* (West-Hartford: Kumarian Press, 1998).

[138] NGOs' dependence on donations and the polarisation of media in certain corporate hands are nevertheless matters of some concern, especially if seen from the perspective of developing countries. See Upendra Baxi, *The Future of Human Rights* (New Delhi: Oxford University Press, 2002) at 121-5. For a Marxist critique of the role played by NGOs, see Petras & Veltmeyer, *supra* note 67 at 128-38. See Dionne Bunsha, "Media Becoming Propaganda Vehicle for Corporates" *The Hindu* (19 January 2004), online: The Hindu <http://www.thehindu.com/2004/01/19/stories/2004011902161200.htm>; and also generally Hertz, *supra* note 7 at 133-41.

[139] See John Braithwaite & Peter Drahos, *Global Business Regulation* (Cambridge: Cambridge University Press, 2000) at 497-501; Monshipouri *et al.*, *supra* note 58 at 986-9; Scott Pegg, "An Emerging Market for the New Millennium: Transnational Corporations and Human Rights" in Fynas & Pegg, eds., *supra* note 13 at 23-4; OECD, *Foreign Direct Investment, Development and Corporate Responsibility* (Paris: OECD, 1999) at 14-5. Baxi also explores various techniques such as of reportage, lobbying, global direct action, *etc.* employed to ensure that human rights survive in market economy. Baxi, *ibid.* at 127-8.

[140] See Deva, *supra* note 129 at 2, 49.

[141] See generally Rajagopal, *supra* note 8.

realisation of human rights and developmental objectives, especially in developing countries. This is not to suggest though that foreign investment and MNCs do not have the "potential" to make a positive contribution towards the fulfillment of human rights and development generally. However, whether developing countries are able to exploit this potential of foreign investment or not depends upon the extent to which they could exercise control over the *flow* and *direction* of such investment.

Second, who has an upper hand in controlling the flow and direction of foreign investment depends, to a great extent, on the relative bargaining power of involved actors, namely, MNCs (and their external power centres) vis-à-vis developing countries. I have asserted that the bargaining power of most of the developing countries is considerably less than that of MNCs and their representative organisation, including international financial institutions. The bargaining position of developing countries is further adversely affected by a "race to the bottom" as in many cases such countries compete among themselves to obtain their share of the cake. Given so, it is suggested that developing countries are usually unable or incapable to derive optimal benefits out of foreign investment by MNCs. One could also treat it as a "deficit of capability" on the part of developing countries.

Third, developing countries could enhance their bargaining power, and consequently their position, qua MNCs if they realise their place in an interdependent world and act collectively, as far as possible. *Self-realisation* and *collective bargaining* are, thus, proposed as the two tools that might be employed by developing countries.[142] Developing countries first need to realise their place in an increasingly interdependent (not dependent) world; developed countries and MNCs based therein need developing countries as much as developing countries need them.[143] Further, developing countries could strengthen their position as well as bargaining power vis-à-vis MNCs if they act collectively. An approach of "diversified integration" is suggested to foster a relationship of collectivity while at the same time taking care of specific individual needs of developing countries. It was also emphasised that developing countries should invoke the language of human rights and also foster alliances with NGOs, media, and other socially conscious civil society organs to exercise a control over the flow and direction of foreign investment.

But it remains an open question whether developing countries will understand this and act accordingly, or will allow their exploitation, as they did historically, in newer (and often disguised) forms. Conversely, despite the fact that "the struggle for a fair globalisation will only grow in the future",[144] it remains uncertain whether developed countries and/or MNCs based therein will appreciate, and act[145] on the words of Chinese philosopher Mozi: "What is the way of universal love and mutual benefit? It is to regard other people's countries as one's own."[146]

---

[142] The dividends that have resulted on developing countries adopting a collective stand at the WTO negotiations demonstrate the efficacy of these tools.

[143] See "Developing Nations Emerge Stronger: World Bank" *The Times of India* (19 April 2004), online: The Times of India <http://timesofindia.indiatimes.com/articleshow/626380.cms>.

[144] *A Fair Globalisation*, *supra* note 75 at 3.

[145] Notably, recently certain rich countries and the World Bank/International Monetary Fund have indicated to provide a debt relief to world's poorest countries. Elizabeth Becker, "US Backs $55bn Debt Relief Deal for Poor Nations" *Sydney Morning Herald* (2-3 October 2004) at 42.

[146] W. T. Chan, *A Source Book in Chinese Philosophy* (Princeton: Princeton University Press, 1963) at 213, as quoted by Singer, *supra* note 75 at 214.

[11]

The UN Human Rights Norms for Corporations: The Private Implications of Public International Law

David Kinley* and Rachel Chambers**

Abstract

Though many years in the making, the UN Human Rights Norms for Corporations only registered on the radars of most states, corporations and civil society organisations in August 2003 when they began to move up the ladder of the United Nation's policy-making processes. Since then they have been subject to intense, and sometimes intemperate, debate, scrutiny and controversy. A particular legal feature of the deliberations has been the focus on the closely related questions of the legal standing of the Norms in their present format (namely, an imperfect draft, and therefore, of no direct legal force), and what they might become (possibly—though not likely soon—a treaty that speaks to corporations but binds states). A potent mix of distrust and suspicion, vested interests, politics and economics has given rise to a great deal of grand-standing

*Professor, Chair in Human Rights Law, University of Sydney, Australia (davidk@law.usyd.edu.au).
**Barrister, Cloisters Chambers, London (rch@cloisters.com). Research for this article was enabled through a three-year Linkage Grant from the Australian Research Council for a project researching human rights and multinational corporations. For details and the outcome of the project, see Castan Centre for Human Rights Law, 'Multinational Corporations and Human Rights' (Projects) available at: http://www.law.monash.edu.au/castancentre/projects/mchr/. Themes in, and earlier versions of, the article were aired at a US Congressional Human Rights Caucus hearing in November 2004; at a session on the Norms at the Business for Social Responsibility Conference in New York, November 2004; and at a number of Human Rights and Global Economy graduate seminars at Monash University and Sydney University Law Schools and at Washington College of Law, American University in 2004 and 2005. In addition to the two anonymous referees of the article and the editorial board of the Human Rights Law Review, the authors would like especially to thank Chris Avery, Eric Biel, Scott Jerbi, Sarah Joseph, Richard Meeran, Justine Nolan, John Ruggie, John Sherman, Sune Skadegard Thorsen and Natalie Zerial for their insightful constructive criticisms, comments and suggestions, and also the last-named for her peerless editorial and research assistance.

448 *HRLR* **6** (2006), 447–497

and cant concerning these questions and how they might be answered. In this article, the authors explore the history of the Norms and the form and content of the debate that surrounds them, in their attempt to disentangle the legal from the rest. That said, the article also focuses on the real politicking of the circumstances in which the Norms now find themselves and it seeks to offer some guidance as to where the Norms—or at least their substance, if not their form—might go from here.

1. Introduction

That leaves business having to blow the whistle on something that aims to subject firms to criticism and liability for abusing human rights. It is quite wrong to suggest that firms are generally involved in widespread abuse of human rights—where is the evidence?

John Cridland, Deputy Director-General of the Confederation of British Industries (CBI).[1]

We have been down this path many times in the UN, and it is both sad and undeniable that the anti-business agenda pursued by many in this organization over the years has held back the economic and social advancement of developing countries.

US Government Statement, 20 April 2005.[2]

Both of these statements were made in respect of the UN Norms on the Responsibilities of Transnational Corporations and Other Business Enterprises with Regard to Human Rights ('Norms').[3]

In the opening months of 2004, the prospect of an international regulatory framework under which companies might be subject to criticism or, worse, actually held liable for abusing human rights, sent shockwaves through business communities in Europe, the United States and the rest of the world. Particularly objectionable was the idea that companies might be liable for the ill deeds of

---

1   Letter to government trade and foreign affairs ministers, as quoted in Gow, 'CBI cries foul over UN human rights code', *Guardian*, 8 March 2004.
2   Available at the website of the US Government Delegation to the 61st Session of the UNCHR: http://www.humanrights-usa.net/2005/0420Item17TNC.htm. The purpose of the statement was to explain the Administration's decision to vote against the Commission on Human Rights Resolution 2005/69 requesting the Secretary-General appoint a Special Representative on the issue of human rights and transnational corporations (on which see infra n. 51). The only other state to vote against the resolution on similar grounds was Australia. South Africa also voted against the Resolution, but did so on the ground that it did not go far enough in promoting the importance of the issue. 49 states voted in favour of the Resolution. The Resolution was co-sponsored by 38 states: 30 from Europe, 4 from South America, as well as Canada, Ethiopia, India and Nigeria.
3   Norms on the Responsibilities of Transnational Corporations and Other Business Enterprises with Regard to Human Rights, 26 August 2003, E/CN.4/Sub.2/2003/12/Rev.2 ('Norms').

their suppliers, joint venture partners and other groups, including governments, from whose activities they benefited.[4] Whilst expressly acknowledging the undoubted capacity of corporations 'to foster economic well-being, development, technological improvement and wealth',[5] the essential focus of the Norms and the movement behind them has been on addressing the equal and opposite capacity of corporations 'to cause harmful impacts on the human rights and lives of individuals through their core business practices and operations, including employment practices, environmental policies, relationships with suppliers and consumers, interactions with Governments and other activities'.[6] This 'negative' focus has been prompted by the apparently increasing instance, and certainly visibility, of such examples of human rights abuse as sweatshop labour in the footwear and apparel industries; environmental, health and cultural degradation in the extractive industries; and personal integrity and freedoms abuses by security forces guarding infrastructure, factories and other installations of corporations in various fields of enterprise.

In response to the promulgation of the Norms, business leaders were quick to reiterate and highlight both the benefits that corporate enterprise bring to all societies, and their voluntary efforts to regulate the few instances where corporations are responsible for bad business practices and human rights abuses. It was on these bases that business leaders mounted critiques, not only of the Norms document itself, but also of any expansion of the concept of corporate liability for human rights responsibilities that went beyond the current model of self-regulation through codes of conduct, social responsibility policies and the like.

The corporate lobby made some headway. When the Norms came before the UN Commission on Human Rights, at its 60th Session in 2004, they encountered a frosty reception from member states already primed with the concerns of the corporate sector. The Norms were then effectively put on hold by the Commission, and, at its 61st session in 2005, the Commission recommended that the UN Secretary-General appoint a Special Representative (SRSG) to review the whole matter of corporations and human rights. That recommendation was duly acted upon, and an appointment was made in July 2005.[7]

---

4   Gow, supra n. 1, states: 'Among the CBI's particular concerns are proposals to make firms legally accountable for the actions of others, including suppliers, users of their products—and governments.' The article goes on to quote one of Mr Cridland's aides.' "You can imagine a demonstration in a difficult part of the world against a company's product that prompts a violent government response and protesters get killed".... "The company would be seen as complicit." '

5   Preamble, Norms.

6   Ibid. For a comprehensive and regularly updated catalogue of types, instances and trends in human rights abuses by corporations, see the 'Business and Human Rights Resource Centre' website available at: http://www.business-humanrights.org/Categories/Issues/Abuses.

7   See infra n. 52 and accompanying text.

450   *HRLR* **6** (2006), 447–497

The SRSG published an Interim Report in February 2006,[8] which dealt in part with the Norms, ultimately concluding that they should be abandoned rather than pursued. In this article we critically analyse this finding, together with the many other views, both complementary and contradictory, as to the worth and future of the Norms.

Integral to the aforementioned focus of the Norms on the abuses of corporate power is the particular concern over the activities of transnational corporations (TNCs)—that is, those corporate entities that undertake a significant proportion of their business in countries outside the state in which they are domiciled. In the face of the quantum and continued expansion of corporate power, as well as the persistent revelations of corporate human rights abuses, particularly in developing countries,[9] an important element of the project to curtail human rights abuses by companies will be missing without a common, enforceable set of international standards to which transnational corporations are required to adhere, whether through domestic law or directly under international law. This is a gap that the Norms seek, in part, to fill. The fundamental question addressed in this article is whether the Norms are the right vehicle through which to develop a framework for corporate accountability for human rights abuses at the international level. We will argue that the Norms do have this potential and ought to be supported as a viable first step in the establishment of an international legal framework through which companies can be held accountable for any human rights abuses they inflict, or in which they are complicit. It is in this respect that such an instrument of public international law can and will have private implications.

Following this introduction (Part 1), the article is divided into four parts. In Part 2, we describe what the Norms are and where they have come from. We also consider some of the peculiar and more controversial features of the Norms. In Part 3, we examine the arguments for and against the Norms, and discuss some of the recommendations that have been made for their amendment and improvement. In Part 4, we address in detail the legal implications of the Norms, both at the international and domestic law level, as well exploring

---

8   Interim Report of the Secretary-General's Special Representative on the Issue of Human Rights and Transnational Corporations and Other Business Enterprises, 22 February 2006, E/CN.4/2006/97 ('Interim Report'). The SRSG's Final Report is due mid-2007 at the end of his two-year tenure.

9   Weissbrodt and Kruger suggest that a number of human rights abuses by corporations 'disproportionately affect developing countries . . . and other vulnerable groups', Weissbrodt and Kruger, 'Current Developments: Norms on the Responsibilities of Transnational Corporations and Other Business Enterprises With Regard to Human Rights', (2003) 97 *American Journal of International Law* 901 at 901. For ongoing documentation of human rights abuses by corporations in developing countries, see Human Rights Watch, 'Business and Human Rights', available at: http://www.hrw.org/doc/?t=corporations, which includes their reports on child labour in Ecuador, war crimes and gold mining in the Congo and the violations associated with oil companies in Sudan and Nigeria. Amnesty International has similarly documented violations in this area, see Amnesty International, 'Economic Globalization and Human Rights', available at: http://web.amnesty.org/pages/ec-index-eng.

how the connections between these two legal spheres will impact on the implementation and efficacy of the Norms and the standards contained therein. In Part 5, we draw out our conclusions, underscoring the importance of what the Norms have achieved and what we see as their continuing relevance and value.

2. The Norms

A. Basic Provisions

The Norms and their accompanying Commentary[10] were compiled and drafted by the UN Sub-Commission on the Promotion and Protection of Human Rights as a statement of the human rights obligations of transnational corporations.[11] Based on key international human rights instruments, the Norms attempt to take up the human rights obligations most relevant to companies and apply them directly to TNCs and other business enterprises, within their respective spheres of activity and influence. That said, the Norms make clear that states retain primary, overarching responsibility for human rights protection. The rights covered by the Norms are, broadly, equality of opportunity and non-discriminatory treatment; the right to security of persons; labour rights; respect for national sovereignty and human rights, including prevention of bribery and corruption; consumer protection; economic, social and cultural rights; and environmental protection.[12]

B. Particularities

In most respects, the Norms follow a standard international law format: they are presently in draft form; accompanied by an explanatory commentary; comprise relatively broad principles presented as open-ended provisions, whose precise implementation in practice will vary according to circumstances; directed at states (though not solely so); and are the product of an international

---

10 Commentary on the Norms on the Responsibilities of Transnational Corporations and Other Business Enterprises with Regard to Human Rights, 26 August 2003, E/CN.4/Sub.2/2003/38/Rev.2 ('Commentary').

11 The term 'transnational corporation' is defined in para. 20, Norms, as 'an economic entity operating in more than one country or a cluster of economic entities operating in two or more countries—whatever their legal form, whether in their home country or country of activity, and whether taken individually or collectively'. The reference to TNCs in this article is adopted purely as a form of representation used in the Norms and within UN circles. This article does not address the different definitions of the term transnational enterprise or of other terms such as multinational corporation and multinational enterprise.

12 See paras 2–14, Norms.

452   *HRLR* **6** (2006), 447–497

law-making organ (the United Nations). However, they also possess a number of particular features. We will be analysing these features in detail throughout this article, but we here provide a brief outline of each as a departure point for the discussion.

(i) Duty-bearers

The Norms use the duty-bearer (i.e. corporations) as their central organising theme. This is unusual among human rights instruments which are typically centred on particular sets of human rights (e.g. civil and political; or economic, social and cultural), or rights holders (e.g. refugees; prisoners; women; racial groups; children or migrant workers) or types of rights violation (e.g. torture, genocide or war crimes). Drawing on the premise that corporations can and do violate international human rights standards, the Norms first identify corporations as duty-bearers and then ask what rights might, could or should corporations be expected to respect and protect. It is the very idea of an international instrument apparently speaking directly to non-state entities, as well as to states, which has caused consternation in some quarters.

(ii) 'Sphere of influence'

The notion of a state or corporation's 'sphere of influence', and the use of this notion to demarcate respective spheres of responsibility, although familiar to those in the corporate social responsibility movement, is not found in other human rights instruments. Its definition and application—especially its legal connotations—have been the subject of heated debate and some confusion.[13]

(iii) Enforcement mechanisms

The Norms are framed in mandatory terms, backed up by mechanisms for implementation and enforcement. Such terms are commonplace in relation to state obligations found in human rights treaties, such as the International Covenant on Civil and Political Rights,[14] but the Norms seek to extend implementation and enforcement obligations to non-state entities and provide novel mechanisms for ensuring that these obligations are met. The general provisions

---

13   See para. 52(e), Report of the United Nations High Commissioner on Human Rights on the responsibilities of transnational corporations and related business enterprises with regard to human rights, 15 February 2005, E/CN.4/2005/91.

14   1966, 999 UNTS 171.

of implementation require TNCs and other business enterprises to adopt, disseminate and implement internal operational rules in compliance with the Norms and also to incorporate the Norms in contracts with other parties.[15] There are provisions for the internal and external monitoring and verification of companies' application of the Norms, including the use of either a new or an existing UN monitoring mechanism.[16] In addition, states are called upon to establish and reinforce a legal framework for ensuring that the Norms are implemented,[17] although the wording of the relevant paragraph ('should' rather than 'shall') suggests that this is not an obligatory or normative provision. The monitoring and verification is backed up by a reparation provision, which obliges companies to provide prompt, effective and adequate reparations to those affected by a company's failure to comply with the Norms.[18]

(iv) Moving outside traditional human rights law

While many of the rights contained within the Norms are found in the Universal Declaration of Human Rights[19] and/or are part of customary international law, there are some provisions which are at the outer boundary of what are normally accepted as human rights. By way of example, rights associated with consumer protection, the environment and corruption are covered by different areas of law,

---

15   Para. 15, Norms provides that:

> As an initial step towards implementing these Norms, each transnational corporation or other business enterprise shall adopt, disseminate and implement internal rules of operation in compliance with the Norms. Further, they shall periodically report on and take other measures fully to implement the Norms and to provide at least for the prompt implementation of the protections set forth in the Norms. Each transnational corporation or other business enterprise shall apply and incorporate these Norms in their contracts or other arrangements and dealings with contractors, subcontractors, suppliers, licensees, distributors, or natural or other legal persons that enter into any agreement with the transnational corporation or business enterprise in order to ensure respect for and implementation of the Norms.

For a good overview of the scope of the enforcement mechanisms for the Norms, see Lucke, 'States' and Private Actors' Obligations Under International Human Rights Law and the Draft UN Norms', in Cottier, Pauwelyn and Bürgi (eds), *Human Rights And International Trade* (Oxford: Oxford University Press, 2005) 148 at 159–60.

16   Para. 16, Norms.

17   Para. 17, Norms.

18   Para. 18, Norms. Campagna notes that the duty of reparation has been a standard duty of international law since Grotius, and that 'prompt, effective and adequate reparation' is the standard owed by a host government which violates the property rights of a US corporation. See Campagna, 'United Nations Norms on the Responsibilities of Transnational Corporations and Other Business Enterprises With Regard to Human Rights: The International Community Asserts Binding Law on the Global Rule Makers', (2004) 37 *John Marshall Law Review* 1205 at 1251–2.

19   GA Res. 217A (III), 10 December 1948, A/810 at 71.

454   *HRLR* **6** (2006), 447–497

and some would argue that their presence in a human rights instrument is duplicative.[20]

While the Norms were originally drafted as a code of conduct for TNCs, and they still retain that focus, the net they cast is intentionally wider. Whereas other existing codes[21] carefully define the transnational nature of the corporations whose conduct they seek to regulate and are limited in their application to TNCs only, the Norms are also directed at 'other business enterprises', a catch-all phrase covering businesses that have relations with TNCs, or which have impacts that are not entirely local, or, more specifically, ones which undertake activities that involve violations of the right to security.[22] Thus a TNC's suppliers, joint venture partners and others with whom it does business are not exempt from the Norms' provisions.[23] A component of this new approach is that the Norms introduce the notion of liability for complicity in serious human rights abuses. The primary obligations in the Norms are that TNCs and other business enterprises promote, secure the fulfilment of, respect, ensure respect of and protect human rights;[24] although, paragraph 3 of the Norms, which covers the right to security of persons, goes further by prohibiting TNCs from engaging in or benefiting from certain serious human

20   The question is what value is gained by including these rights in a human rights instrument when provisions already exist in respect of each: national tort law for consumer protection, national and international environmental law and laws on bribery and corruption. The answer may be that given the inadequacy of national protection in many states, and the interrelation between the enjoyment of these rights and 'mainstream' human rights, TNCs should be held to clear international standards with respect to these rights.

21   For example: the OECD Guidelines and the ILO Tripartite Declaration, see infra n. 31 and n. 32, respectively.

22   The term 'other business enterprise' is defined in para. 21, Norms as including

> any business entity, regardless of the international or domestic nature of its activities, including a transnational corporation, contractor, subcontractor, supplier, licensee or distributor; the corporate, partnership, or other legal form used to establish the business entity; and the nature of the ownership of the entity. These Norms shall be presumed to apply, as a matter of practice, if the business enterprise has any relation with a transnational corporation, the impact of its activities is not entirely local, or the activities involve violations of the right to security as indicated in paragraphs 3 and 4.

23   The importance of this is noted in Deva, 'UN's Human Rights Norms for Transnational Corporations and Other Business Enterprises: An Imperfect Step in the Right Direction?', (2004) 10 *ILSA Journal of International and Comparative Law* 493 at 500–1. In many situations the apparent violator is not a TNC but its subsidiaries, contractors or suppliers.

24   Para. 1, Norms provides that: 'Within their respective spheres of activity and influence, transnational corporations and other business enterprises have the obligation to promote, secure the fulfilment of, respect, ensure respect of and protect human rights recognized in international as well as national law, including the rights and interests of indigenous peoples and other vulnerable groups.' Para. 1(b), Commentary states that: 'Transnational corporations and other business enterprises shall have the responsibility to use due diligence in ensuring that their activities do not contribute directly or indirectly to human abuses, and that they do not directly or indirectly benefit from abuses of which they were aware or ought to have been aware.'

rights abuses.[25] The difficult question of the nature of liability for complicity (beneficial or otherwise) in the wrongdoings of a third party is outside the scope of this article.[26] While the enforcement provisions provide that TNCs should include the Norms in contracts with suppliers and other business partners, thus establishing contractual liability within a company's supply chain,[27] the depth (or length) of liability for paragraph 3 violations further up or down the supply chain is not detailed (for example, what if the supplier to the TNC's supplier commits grave human rights abuses?). It is clear that a 'belt and braces' approach has been taken, in which other entities that do business with TNCs are themselves required to adhere to the standards in the Norms, and, in addition, TNCs have a responsibility to ensure this adherence.[28] However, a less clear and comprehensive approach is provided in terms of a TNC's liability for the actions of third parties, which is the real issue given that this is where the power and leverage of TNCs generally lies.

C. The Position of the Norms in Relation to Other Initiatives[29]

The Norms are not the first attempt by the United Nations to create international standards applicable to corporate entities. In the 1970s, at the instigation of developing nations, a Centre for Transnational Corporations was established in the United Nations, and codes were drafted which were completed in 1983 and 1990. The codes focussed on the need for foreign investors to obey host country law, follow host country economic policies and avoid interference with host countries' domestic affairs.[30] However, with the end of the Cold War and the growth of the free trade and investment movement, the emphasis began to shift away from the demands of host countries to their need to attract foreign companies

---

25   Para. 3, Norms provides that: 'Transnational corporations and other business enterprises shall not engage in nor benefit from war crimes, crimes against humanity, genocide, torture, forced disappearance, forced or compulsory labour, hostage-taking, extrajudicial, summary or arbitrary executions, other violations of humanitarian law and other international crimes against the human person as defined by international law, in particular human rights and humanitarian law.'

26   It is noted in para. 52(e), Report of the United Nations High Commissioner on Human Rights, supra n. 13, that 'complicity' is one of the concepts which would benefit from further clarification and research. For more on complicity see infra n. 90–2 and accompanying text.

27   Para. 15, Norms provides that: 'Each transnational corporation or other business enterprise shall apply and incorporate these Norms in their contracts or other arrangements and dealings with contractors, subcontractors, suppliers, licensees, distributors, or natural or other legal persons that enter into any agreement with the transnational corporation or business enterprise in order to ensure respect for and implementation of the Norms.'

28   What Upendra Baxi characterises as the 'network conception of corporate governance and business conduct'. See Baxi, 'Market Fundamentalisms: Business Ethics at the Altar of Human Rights', (2005) 5 *Human Rights Law Review* 1 at 6 *et seq.*

29   For a useful compendium of such codes and associated materials, see Leipziger, *The Corporate Responsibility Code Book* (Sheffield: Greenleaf Publishing, 2003).

30   Ratner, 'Corporations and Human Rights: A Theory of Legal Responsibility', (2001) 111 *Yale Law Journal* 443 at 457.

456　　*HRLR* **6** (2006), 447–497

and thus to deregulation. The Draft UN Code was abandoned in 1990 and, with certain limited exceptions, this left a vacuum in terms of international initiatives regulating the behaviour of TNCs. The exceptions include the Organisation for Economic Cooperation and Development's (OECD) Guidelines for Multinational Enterprises ('OECD Guidelines')[31] and the International Labour Organisation's (ILO) Tripartite Declaration of Principles concerning Multinational Enterprises ('ILO Tripartite Declaration').[32] So far, these initiatives, along with various industry and regional codes,[33] have been unable to hold companies to account for human rights abuses, principally due to their lack of an effective enforcement mechanism.[34]

D. Origins, Compilation and Drafting of the Norms

The Norms started life in the Sub-Commission on the Promotion and Protection of Human Rights (the Sub-Commission),[35] a body created by the UN Economic and Social Council (ECOSOC) in 1947 as a think-tank for the UN Human Rights Commission ('Commission'). The Sub-Commission's membership constitutes 26 independent experts who are nominated by their countries, with the remit to study cases of human rights violations, examine obstacles to human rights protection and develop new international standards.[36]

31　OECD Guidelines for Multinational Enterprises (Revision 2000), available at: http://www.oecd.org/dataoecd/56/36/1922428.pdf. The Guidelines are not legally binding and apply only to TNCs from members of the OECD plus a few other states.

32　Tripartite Declaration of Principles concerning Multinational Enterprises and Social Policy: Declaration adopted by the Governing Body of the ILO, November 1977, available at: http://www.ilo.org/public/english/employment/multi/. The Principles are internationally agreed but are only on the subject of labour rights, and the process by which they are interpreted is little utilised. Governments must request interpretation, and only if they fail to do so may workers and employers' associations make requests.

33　For example, the Equator Principles, July 2006, available at: http://www.equator-principles.com/principles.shtml (to which many leading financial institutions are party); the US/UK Voluntary Principles on Security and Human Rights, 20 December 2000, available at: http://www.state.gov/g/drl/rls/2931.htm; the European Parliament Resolution on EU Standards for European Enterprises Operating in Developing Countries: Towards a European Code of Conduct, A4-0508/98, 15 January 1999, [1999] OJ C 104/180; and the Fair Wear Codes (Australia) available at: http://fairwear.org.au/engine.php?SID=1000013. For a comprehensive list of these codes see Castan Centre for Human Rights Law, 'Multinational Corporations and Human Rights', available at: http://www.law.monash.edu.au/castancentre/projects/mchr/.

34　Including, and in particular, the UN Global Compact, information on which is available at: http://www.unglobalcompact.org/. Companies commit to adhere to 10 Principles as part of their membership. There is no enforcement mechanism. The Global Compact is a forum for dialogue, and for exchanging experiences and best practice rather than a means of holding companies to account for human rights violations. See infra Part 3 B ('The Need for the Norms?') of this article, where the Global Compact is addressed in relation to the Norms.

35　Originally called the Sub-Commission on Prevention of Discrimination and Protection of Minorities; the name was changed in 1999.

36　UNCHR Res. E/1371, The Prevention of Discrimination and the Protection of Minorities, Report of the Fifth Session of the Commission on Human Rights, 1949, E/CN.4/350 at para. 13(A).

In the 1990s, concern began to mount that against the background of liberalisation of trade rules and increased foreign direct investment in developing nations, some TNCs were violating human rights with impunity.[37] To address this concern a sessional working group was formed within the Sub-Commission to examine the working methods and activities of TNCs.[38] The working group was formed in 1998, initially for a three-year period;[39] its study was based on various background documents including a study on the connection between TNCs and human rights.[40] Consultation meetings were held,[41] and at each of the annual meetings of the Sub-Commission between 1998 and 2003 the working group's findings and outputs were debated, and comments from non-governmental observers were taken. After five years of developing, critiquing and refining the various instruments that the working group had produced, the final version of the Norms was adopted unanimously by the Sub-Commission in August 2003[42] and submitted, along with several recommendations for further action, to the Commission.

The Commission considered the Norms for the first time on 20 April 2004. In the lead up to this debate they had become a controversial subject facing vocal opposition from business groups such as the International Chamber of

37 Certain high profile cases gained wide publicity in the 1990s. For example, Shell was accused of grave human rights violations in the Niger Delta and similar charges were laid against BP in Colombia. It was also during the 1990s that the Bhopal case came to court following the disaster at the Union Carbide plant in 1984.

38 The power to form a working group is found in Rule 21, Rules of Procedure of the Functional Commissions of the Economic and Social Council (a fully amended version is available at: http://www.unhchr.ch/html/menu2/2/rules.htm). This rule allows ECOSOC to set up such committees or working groups as are deemed necessary and refer to them any questions on its agenda for study and report. See also the Guidelines for the application by the Sub-Commission of the rules of procedure of the functional commissions of ECOSOC and other decisions and practices relating thereto, annexed to Sub-Com. Dec. 1999/114, Methods of Work of the Sub-Commission, 16 August 1999, E/CN.4/Sub.2/Dec/1999/114.

39 The working group was established by the Sub-Commission in Sub-Com. Res. 1998/8, The Relationship Between the Enjoyment of Economic, Social and Cultural Rights and the Right to Development, and the Working Methods and Activities of Transnational Corporations, 20 August 1998, E/CN.4/Sub.2/Res/1998/8. In 2001, its mandate was extended for a further three years, see Sub-Com. Res. 2001/3, The Effects of the Working Methods and Activities of Transnational Corporations on the Enjoyment of Human Rights, 15 August 2001, E/CN.4/Sub.2/Res/2001/3.

40 Principles Relating to the Human Rights Conduct of Companies: Working paper prepared by Mr David Weissbrodt, 25 May 2000, E/CN.4/Sub.2/2000/WG.2/WP.1.

41 The meetings were held in 2000, 2001 and 2002. Representatives of TNCs, non-governmental and inter-governmental organisations and other interested parties were invited. See infra Part 3 A ('The Manner of their Making') for more on this.

42 Sub-Com. Res. 2003/16, Responsibilities of Transnational Corporations and Other Business Enterprises With Regard to Human Rights, 13 August 2003, E/CN.4/Sub.2/RES/2003/16.

458   *HRLR* **6** (2006), 447–497

Commerce (ICC) and the International Organisation of Employers (IOE).[43] These business alliances lobbied national governments, including those of the United States, the United Kingdom and Australia, with the message that the Commission should make a clear statement disapproving the Norms. In support of this standpoint, various arguments, both legal and non-legal, were tendered in a joint statement put out on behalf of the ICC and IOE.[44] In Part 3 of this article, we will address some of the arguments put forward in the ICC/IOE document and other sources of criticism.

A number of non-governmental organisations (NGOs), academics and human rights advocates from around the world took various opposing positions to that of the business alliances, lobbying national governments and making submissions directly to the Commission in support of the Norms. Their campaign culminated in a 194-strong joint oral statement of NGOs delivered to the Commission at its 60th Session,[45] which concluded by asking that the Commission, governments and business be given more time to study the Norms and urging the Commission not to take any action at the 60th Session that might prematurely undermine the Norms. The specific legal arguments put forward by the business alliances were largely not addressed in this statement.

At the 60th Session, a decision brokered and formally requested by the UK Government[46] was adopted by consensus.[47] The decision asked the Office of the High Commissioner for Human Rights (OHCHR) to consult with all relevant stakeholders[48] and compile a report setting out the scope and legal status of all existing initiatives and standards on business responsibilities with regard to human rights, including the Norms. While thanking the Sub-Commission for

---

43   Other examples of criticism of the Norms include that of the British CBI, supra n. 1; and Baker, 'Raising the Heat on Business over Human Rights', *Ethical Corporation*, 18 August 2003, available at: http://www.globalpolicy.org/globaliz/law/intllaw/2003/0818unregprob. htm. See also the comments of Thomas Niles, President of the US Council for International Business, interviewed with David Weissbrodt in 'UN Norms on Responsibility of Transnational Corporations', *Newshour: BBC World Service*, 13 August 2003; and Niles' letter to the Financial Times, 'UN code no help to companies', *Financial Times*, 17 December 2003.

44   IOE and ICC, 'Joint views of the IOE and ICC on the draft "Norms on the responsibilities of transnational corporations and other business enterprises with regard to human rights"', March 2004, available at: http://www.reports-and-materials.org/IOE-ICC-views-UN-norms-March-2004.doc. See also Thomas Niles interview, 13 August 2003, ibid.

45   Human Rights Council of Australia et al., 'Statement of support for the *UN Human Rights Norms for Business*', delivered at the 60th Session of the Commission on Human Rights 15 March – 23 April 2004, Geneva, available at: http://www.escr-net.org/EngGeneral/unnorms2.asp.

46   The decision was formally requested by the United Kingdom on behalf of Australia, Belgium, the Czech Republic, Ethiopia, Ghana, Hungary, Ireland, Japan, Mexico, Norway, South Africa and Sweden.

47   UNCHR Dec. 2004/116, Responsibilities of Transnational Corporations and Related Business Enterprises with Regard to Human Rights, 20 April 2004, E/CN.4/Dec/2004/116.

48   The decision requests that the OHCHR consult with 'all the relevant stakeholders' in compiling the report, including, *inter alia*, states, TNCs, employers' and employees' associations, treaty monitoring bodies and NGOs.

its work in preparing the draft Norms, and confirming the importance of the issues they address, the decision clarified that the draft proposal has no legal standing,[49] and—crucially—that the Sub-Commission should not perform any monitoring function regarding the Norms, as it had laid the ground work to do in paragraph 16.

E. The Current Status of the Norms

Following wide-ranging consultation and a two-day workshop on the Norms in October 2004 attended by representatives from corporate, labour and human rights organisations, a comprehensive report covering all sides of the debate was published by the OHCHR in February 2005. The report recommended that the subject of business and human rights remain on the Commission's agenda and that the 'draft Norms' be maintained amongst existing initiatives and standards, with a view to their further consideration.[50] However, the polarised debate regarding the Norms continued at the Commission in 2005, with certain countries, most notably the United States and Australia, adopting the approach advocated by the corporate lobby that there should be no binding human rights standards for TNCs at the international level and that the Norms should be buried. Notwithstanding such opposition, a resolution was finally adopted[51] which recognised that transnational corporations and other business enterprises can contribute to the enjoyment of human rights and which requested the aforementioned appointment by the UN Secretary-General of a Special Representative (the SRSG) on the issue of human rights and business. That appointment—of Professor John Ruggie of the Kennedy School of Government at Harvard University—was duly made on 27 July 2005 with the following mandate:[52]

(i) to identify and clarify standards of corporate responsibility and accountability for TNCs and other business enterprises with regard to human rights;[53]

---

49   Supra n. 47 at para (c). For further discussion see infra Part 4 on the 'Legal Implications of the Norms', particularly Part 4 B ('International Legal Implications of the Norms') and Part 4 C ('Questions of the Legal Status of the Norms').

50   Para. 52(d), Report of the United Nations High Commissioner for Human Rights, supra n. 13.

51   UNCHR Res. 2005/69, Human Rights and Transnational Corporations and Other Business Enterprises, 20 April 2005, E/CN.4/RES/2005/69. The United States and Australia voted against the Resolution. South Africa also voted against because the Resolution was not strong enough.

52   The mandate is precisely as recommended by the Commission in Res. 2004/116, supra n. 47.

53   It was noted that the Resolution was 'intentionally left ambiguous as to whether this covered existing or new standards', Chatham House, 'Human rights and transnational corporations: the way forward', a summary of discussion at the International Law Programme Discussion Group at Chatham House on 7 June 2005, is available at: http://www.chathamhouse.org.uk/pdf/research/il/ILP070605.doc.

460   *HRLR* **6** (2006), 447–497

(ii) to elaborate on the role of states in effectively regulating and adjudicating the role of TNCs and other business enterprises with regard to human rights, including through international cooperation;

(iii) to research and clarify the implications for TNCs and other business enterprises of concepts such as 'complicity' and 'sphere of influence';

(iv) to develop materials and methodologies for undertaking human rights impact assessments of the activities of TNCs and other business enterprises; and

(v) to compile a compendium of best practices of states and TNCs and other business enterprises.

The Norms were not mentioned in the Resolution but this omission may be explained by the aforementioned position taken by the United States and the attempts by other nations to reach a consensus in light of this. Certainly it was unavoidable that the Norms would be very much part of the SRSG's process and as such the initial view of the supporters of the Norms was that this would be a positive step in the consultative, dialogic and recommendatory role that it was anticipated the SRSG would take.[54] The SRSG's Interim Report of February 2006 expressly addressed the Norms debates precisely '[b]ecause those debates continue to shadow the mandate [of the SRSG]'.[55] In his preparation of the Interim Report, the SRSG was conspicuously inclusive and transparent, and sought to consult across the whole range of corporate, human rights and other stakeholder sectors (albeit thus far mainly in the West).[56] The Interim Report acknowledges that the Norms 'contain useful elements', namely: 'the summary of rights that may be affected by business, positively and negatively and the collation of source documents from international human rights instruments as well as voluntary initiatives . . .'.[57] However, it is the endeavour to have the Norms reach beyond such benign achievements that the SRSG has problems with; that is, in the particular respect to their form, if not necessarily their content. He regards as fatal, the well-ventilated twin criticisms that, first, the Norms supposedly purport, by implication, to invent a new avenue of international law that speaks directly to corporations; and second, they ill-define the resulting obligations that fall, respectively, on states and corporations. These criticisms are fatal because

> the flaws of the Norms make that effort a distraction rather than a basis for moving the Special Representative's mandate forward. Indeed, in the Special Representative's view, the divisive debate over the Norms

---

54   See website recently established by the Business and Human Rights Resource Centre, available at: www.business-humanrights.org, for materials posted by the Special Representative.
55   Para. 55, Interim Report.
56   Paras 3–6, ibid. Although at the time of writing regional consultations in the South are being held in Johannesburg, South Africa, 26–27 March 2006; and Bangkok, Thailand, 26–27 June 2006.
57   Para. 57, ibid.

obscures rather than illuminates promising areas of consensus and cooperation among business, civil society, governments and international institutions with respect for human rights.[58]

As our canvassing of both the arguments for and against the Norms, in Part 3, illustrates, the Norms are hardly flawless (they are, after all, avowedly in draft form), and they have certainly excited debate and controversy. But in our view, far from seeing these characteristics as sufficient cause to kill off the project, we see them as fertile ground for future growth. To disband a project, the aim of which is to investigate the legal dimensions (both international and, impliedly, domestic) of the human rights responsibilities of corporations, largely because that investigation has revealed divisions and distractions, seems to both expect too much of such an enterprise (can any alternative really promise any less controversy?) and undervalue what the Norms have achieved thus far. We consider the SRSG's forthright dismissal of the Norms in their current form to be a backward, rather than forward, step.

The fact is that the Norms—notwithstanding their work-in-progress status within the UN human rights machinery—have, in certain respects, taken on a life of their own outside the United Nations. Thus, despite the refusal of the Commission to endorse any form of monitoring function, one group of companies have already put their names forward to 'road-test' the Norms in their operations.[59] Certain human rights NGOs are working with these and other companies in efforts to promote the incorporation of the Norms into normal business practice and to encourage the use of the Norms as one set of standards against which companies might measure their performance.[60] NGOs are also using the Norms when lobbying governments on what they should be doing to monitor and control the activities of companies within their jurisdiction; and lawyers are beginning to look at how the Norms may be used in the course of

---

58   Para. 69, ibid.

59   That is, under the auspices of the Business Leaders Initiative on Human Rights (BLIHR), which comprises: ABB, Barclays, Body Shop International, Gap Inc., Hewlett-Packard, MTV Networks Europe, National Grid Transco, Novartis Foundation for Sustainable Development, Novo Nordisk and Statoil. See the BLIHR website, available at: http://www.blihr.org/; and the Business and Human Rights Seminar website, available at: http://www.bhrseminar.org/. The 'road-testing' of the Norms is explicitly not a controlled study exercise. Rather, it is an attempt to incorporate the Norms and their standards into the real world operations of the participant companies. For instance, Barclays, Novartis, National Grid Transco, Hewlett-Packard and MTV are trying to identify their respective 'spheres of influence'; Body Shop International is using the Norms in its annual reporting; and ABB is using the Norms in a risk management context to develop a checklist on human rights. See Miller, infra n. 173.

60   An example of a report criticising the actions of a TNC on the basis of the Norms is the Amnesty International report on Internet censorship in China: Amnesty International, 'People's Republic of China: Controls tighten as Internet activism grows', 28 January 2004, ASA 17/001/2004. Amnesty criticises various technology companies, including Microsoft, for providing technology used to censor and control the use of the internet. See also Mathiason, 'Microsoft in human rights row', *The Observer*, 1 February 2004.

462   *HRLR* **6** (2006), 447–497

running a business and also in litigation.[61] These are undoubtedly important developments in the movement towards greater corporate accountability in the area of human rights.

Whether and how these developments would survive any abandonment of the Norms in their present form—and especially should they be abandoned as abruptly as is being suggested—is a moot point. However, in view of the fact that their substantive content has, and always will be, more important than the format in which they are expressed, we maintain that the underlying sentiment of the Norms (that corporations be held responsible for the human rights violations they commit or cause to be committed) and certain key substantive features (the subordination of corporate responsibility to state responsibility and the assignment of only those human rights obligations proximate to a corporation's business) will retain their current, derivative legal presence in, and central significance to, the wider debate on corporate social responsibility.

3. Arguments For and Against the Norms

The arguments for and against the Norms were discussed during the aforementioned consultation process undertaken by the OHCHR in late 2004.[62] For the first time, representatives of business, NGOs and academia met under the auspices of the United Nations to air their views on the subject. The debate over the Norms, then and now, revolves around the intertwined matters of the process of their development, their substantive content, and the nature of the implementation and enforcement procedures they seek to put in place.

A. The Manner of their Making

In terms of their provenance, it has been argued that the manner in which the Norms were compiled and drafted was not transparent or sufficiently consultative and was not a legitimate exercise of the Sub-Commission's and/or the sessional working group's power. Questions surrounding the procedural legitimacy of the Norms' development are now largely historical, as the Commission has already twice considered the Norms and taken a view on the

---

61   See, for example, McCarthy, 'Business and Human Rights: What Do the New UN Norms Mean for the Business Lawyer', (2003) 28 *International Legal Practitioner* 73, which suggests, for example, that business lawyers should be using the Norms as a checklist of issues which should be monitored by business. See also Kinley, 'Lawyers, Corporations and International Human Rights Law', (2004) 25 *Company Lawyer* 298 at 301–2; Ward, 'The Interface Between Globalisation, Corporate Responsibility, and the Legal Profession', (2004) 1 *University of St Thomas Law Journal* 813; and Meeran, 'Multinational Litigation as a Weapon in Protecting Economic and Social Rights', in Squires, Langford and Thiele (eds), *The Road to A Remedy: Current Issues in Litigation of Economic, Social and Cultural Rights* (Sydney: University of New South Wales Press, 2006) 183.

62   See supra n. 48 and accompanying text.

process by which they came about. The Commission, in its 2004 decision, did appear to rap the Sub-Commission over the knuckles for its over-zealousness in drafting the Norms,[63] which, it notes, were not requested by the Commission in the first place.[64] That said, such an admonition does not derogate from the legitimacy of the Norms themselves and, in any case, the rules of the Sub-Commission clearly entitle it to request the sessional working groups to compile and draft instruments such as the Norms.[65]

The working papers and drafts that were created and developed by the sessional working group were available online[66] and circulated among interest groups including TNCs, business alliances, trade unions and NGOs. Public meetings[67] and focussed seminars[68] were held in Geneva. Much of the drafting

---

63 The Australian Chair of 60th Session of the UN Commission of Human Rights, Mike Smith, described the 2004 decision as having 'firm words' for the Sub-Commission: notes of discussion following his address to the Castan Centre for Human Rights Law, Monash University, Melbourne, Australia, 'The UN Commission on Human Rights & Australia', 2 September 2004 [on file with author (Rachel Chambers)]. A full text of Mike Smith's address is available at: http://www.law.monash.edu.au/castancentre/events/2004/smith-paper.html.

64 UNCHR Dec. 2004/116, supra n. 47 at para. (c).

65 The sessional working group, as established by and reporting to the Sub-Commission, was acting under the authority of Sub-Com. Res. 1998/8, supra n. 39, which empowered it *inter alia* to 'make recommendations and proposals relating to the methods of work and activities of transnational corporations in order to ensure that such methods and activities are in keeping with the economic and social objectives of the countries in which they operate, and to promote the enjoyment of economic, social and cultural rights and the right to development, as well as of civil and political rights' (para. 4(d)). When the working group's mandate was extended for a further three years through the adoption of Sub-Com. Res. 2001/3, supra n. 39, para. 4 of the relevant resolution provided more detail of the working party's expected output:

> (*b*) Compile a list of the various relevant instruments and norms concerning human rights and international cooperation that are applicable to transnational corporations; (*c*) Contribute to the drafting of relevant norms concerning human rights and transnational corporations and other economic units whose activities have an impact on human rights; (*d*) Analyse the possibility of establishing a monitoring mechanism in order to apply sanctions and obtain compensation for infringements committed and damage caused by transnational corporations, and contribute to the drafting of binding norms for that purpose;

> It is, therefore, clear that the working group did act within its mandate in compiling and drafting the Norms and in proposing methods of enforcement of the Norms. While it is correct that the Norms were not requested by the Commission (see UNCHR Dec. 2004/116, supra n. 47 at para. (c)) this misses the point that the Norms were legitimately requested by the Sub-Commission, as it is entitled to do under the ECOSOC rules and its own guidelines.

66 The Norms working papers (and other documents on business and human rights, trade and investment and globalisation) are available at: http://www.ohchr.org/english/issues/globalization/documents.htm.

67 The meetings took place in August 2000, 2001 and 2002. For details of the meetings, see Report of the Sessional Working Group on the Working Methods and Activities of Transnational Corporations on its Second Session, 28 August 2000, E/CN.4/Sub.2/2000/12; Report of the Sessional Working Group on the Working Methods and Activities of Transnational Corporations on its Third Session, 14 August 2001, E/CN.4/Sub.2/2001/9; and Report of the Sessional Working Group on the Working Methods and Activities of Transnational Corporations on its Fourth Session, 15 August 2002, E/CN.4/Sub.2/2002/13.

68 The seminars took place in March 2001 and 2003.

464   *HRLR* **6** (2006), 447–497

of the Norms took place in March 2001 at a seminar attended by the ILO, ECOSOC, trade unions and other interest groups. Some of the Norms' detractors were invited to this meeting but did not attend.[69] All comments tendered to the Sub-Commission as part of the consultation and drafting process were taken into account by the working group,[70] including those tendered by states (as they had been encouraged to do so),[71] even though there was some subsequent criticism that not enough was done to consult with states at the drafting stage.[72] It is, therefore, difficult to criticise the sessional working party's processes as lacking in transparency or insufficiently consultative.

The following discussion outlines and critiques the principal arguments put forward by business alliances and other critics of the Norms.[73]

B. The Need for the Norms?

Various reasons have been put forward to support the view that there is no need for the Norms, including that they duplicate what is out there already; that they do not fit in with existing initiatives—particularly the UN Global Compact, and that their 'one size fits all' approach is inappropriate. Undeniably, the Norms do set out in a single authoritative statement all of the international human rights law applicable to companies. This is a unique endeavour, differing from the OECD Guidelines, the ILO Tripartite Declaration and other such initiatives in that it attempts to detail each duty and obligation under the umbrella of human rights and thus to provide a broader-based indicative check-list for companies to follow. While at first glance there may appear to be a lack of fit between the Norms and the UN Global Compact, and confusion may arise from the fact that there are two UN initiatives in the same area, closer examination reveals this disjuncture to be more apparent than real. The Global Compact is

---

69   For example, the ICC: notes taken from public seminar with David Weissbrodt (Sub-Commission Working Group member and an architect of the Norms), hosted by the Castan Centre for Human Rights Law, Monash University Melbourne, and Holding Redlich Lawyers, Melbourne, 'Business and Human Rights', 30 April 2004 [notes on file with author (Rachel Chambers)].

70   At the Working Group meeting on 8 March 2003. See Weissbrodt and Kruger, supra n. 9 at 906.

71   As Weissbrodt and Kruger, supra n. 9 at 905, note (the former being a member of the working group and the principal drafter of the Norms), 'Resolution 2002/8 of the Sub-Commission asked that the Norms and Commentary be disseminated as widely as possible, so as to encourage governments [etc] to submit suggestions, observations, or recommendations.'

72   This was the view formed by Ambassador Mike Smith, the Australian Permanent Representative to the United Nations in Geneva, after he chaired (on behalf of Australia) the 60th session of the Commission on Human Rights in 2004, during which the Norms were first formally considered by states' representatives. See notes of discussion, supra n. 63.

73   Arguments were raised in submissions to the Commission, submissions to the OHCHR and during the consultation (see supra n. 48 for consultation details). Examples of arguments which will not be addressed in this article include: that the Norms are too negative about business (only the preamble has something good to say about business) and that the word 'norm' is legal jargon. See the Joint Views of the IOE and ICC, supra n. 44 at 10–1.

a voluntary initiative designed to encourage companies to address human rights, labour rights and environmental and corruption concerns, and to share their experiences in implementing the Global Compact principles. Though not without its critics,[74] this is a different approach altogether to that of the Norms—many of the projects and case studies put forward by members of the Global Compact[75] go over and above the minimum standard of human rights accountability laid out in the Norms. A number of these projects are unrelated to the companies' core business and as such are add-ons in the area of corporate social responsibility—for example, an Eastern European bread and cake business has included public health messages concerning HIV/AIDS on the packaging of its baked goods.[76] The human rights principles contained in the Global Compact are very broadly stated, and the standards for participants are not fleshed out in any detail.[77] They, therefore, lack the depth and precision provided in the Norms. For this reason Amnesty International has urged the Global Compact office to indicate formally that the Norms could be viewed as an authoritative guide to the first two principles of the Global Compact,[78] although so far it has declined to do so. However, there has been (tentative) support from the Global Compact office for the Norms,[79] which, at the very least, indicates their understanding that the two initiatives complement rather than contradict or duplicate each other.

The 'one size fits all' argument holds that the Norms are an imprecise tool for guiding or regulating the activities of companies, since different industries and sectors' activities impact on different human rights. This argument is flawed because human rights, by their very nature, are universal rather than bespoke.

---

74   See, generally, Murphy, 'Taking Multinational Codes of Conduct to the Next Level', (2005) 43 *Columbia Journal of Transnational Law* 389 at 413; and, more specifically, the concerns voiced by Amnesty International and Human Rights First, who were both original NGO signatories to the Global Compact, 'Statement by NGO Participants in the Global Compact Summit', (June–July 2004) 1 *Civil Society Observer*, available at: http://www.un-ngls.org/cso/cso3/statement.html.

75   Case studies available from the United Nations Global Compact Office, 'How to Participate: Guidance Documents', available at: http://www.unglobalcompact.org/HowToParticipate/guidance.documents/.

76   United Nations Development Programme (Bulgaria), 'Corporate social responsibility in action in Bulgaria: Pain d'Or', details of which are available at: http://www.undp.bg/en/gc.csr.in.action.php. It was noted by an NGO participant at the OHCHR consultation that 'voluntary initiatives under the current corporate social responsibility model had virtues, but were not a substitute for other enforceable approaches', OHCHR Report, supra n. 13.

77   Though for various accounts of how they might be pursued in practice, see The Global Compact Office and the OHCHR, *Embedding Human Rights Principles in Business Practice* (2004), available at: http://www.unglobalcompact.org/Issues/human.rights/index.html.

78   Amnesty International, 'The UN Human Rights Norms for Business: Towards Legal Accountability', IOR 42/002/2004, 18 January 2004 at 14–5.

79   See the quotation from the Global Compact office reproduced in Amnesty International, ibid. at 14. Also there has been collaboration between the Global Compact office and the OHCHR in hosting consultations and meetings concerning business and human rights and use of the Norms in the lead up to their joint publication, supra n. 77. See also Wynhoven, 'Introduction', in The Global Compact Office and the OHCHR, supra n. 77 at 11–2.

466   HRLR **6** (2006), 447–497

As basic minimum standards they are universally applicable and, although their relevance to each industry and sector varies,[80] they remain constant and indivisible.[81] Companies already impose their own codes of conduct on their thousands of suppliers, without differentiating between the industries of each supplier,[82] demonstrating their own version of universal application in this regard. However, the company codes imposed on suppliers are likely to be tailored to the industry of the purchasing company, and this may be very different to that of the supplier (for example, a footwear company will have suppliers from the paper and cardboard industry for boxes). In effect, the application of the Norms for each business would be tailored in much the same way, while the overall Norms framework would reinforce the essential and underlying universality of human rights. A holistic approach covering those human rights most relevant to commercial enterprise is, therefore, to be preferred and this is what the Norms seek to do.

C. Precision and Practicability

When considering complaints that the Norms are vague in respect of the duties they impose, the concepts they apply and in their enforcement mechanisms, one must not forget that the Norms are not, nor can they be compared with, domestic legislation. Typically of an international instrument, the Norms provide a framework designed to be used for national or international regulation. Assuming the former approach is preferred in any resulting instrument, it will be incumbent on states to articulate the specifics. In this way, the Norms are not different from any other instruments of international human rights law. The fact that they are open-ended is not only unexceptional, it is also necessary to achieve international consensus on the subject and to enable all parties to relate to the initiative.[83] In the fields of environmental protection and labour rights,

---

80   For example, Article 10, International Covenant on Civil and Political Rights (the rights of detained persons to humane treatment) is likely to be impacted by the activities of security and prison service companies.

81   At a consultation held by the OHCHR and the Global Compact Office '. . .several participants warned against classifying rights in terms of being fundamental or not as this could threaten the principle of the indivisibility of human rights'. OHCHR and the Global Compact Office, 'Consultation on Business and Human Rights: Summary of Discussions', 22 October 2004, at 6, available at: http://www.unglobalcompact.org/Issues/human_rights/business. human_rights_summary_report.pdf.

82   Thorsen and Meisling (Lawhouse.dk), 'Advice: Unfold Human Rights', Submitted for ISBEE Conference in Melbourne, 15–17 July 2004, available at: http://www.lawhouse.dk/?ID=261.

83   To argue that such 'vagueness' is fatal to the legitimacy and potential legality of the Norms—as does the advice tended to the CBI by Maurice Mendelson QC—is fundamentally to misrepresent the history and nature of public international law, especially international human rights law. See Mendelson, 'In the matter of the draft "Norms on the responsibilities of transnational corporations and other business enterprises with regard to human rights": Opinion of Professor Emeritus Maurice Mendelson QC', 4 April 2004, at para. 29, available as 'Report I' to CBI's stakeholder submission to the Report of the High Commissioner for Human Rights, available at: http://www.ohchr.org/english/issues/globalization/business/contributions.htm.

for example, states are already subject to a whole raft of international regulations, and it is their duty to take the principles from these regulations and work them into domestic legislation containing standards and concepts that are clear to all. Alternatively, should the international community come to support an international system of implementation and enforcement, then these duties would fall upon whichever international body is tasked with, or created, to implement and enforce the Norms.

Among the complaints relating to the Norms' vagueness, the most significant concern is the extent to which they apportion duties and responsibilities between states and TNCs. Beyond their provision for the state to bear primary responsibility for implementation of the Norms,[84] the Norms provide for the imposition of contemporaneous and complementary human rights responsibilities on corporations within their 'spheres of activity and influence'. The reasoning behind this second provision is two-fold: first, it is designed to bolster the potential for better human rights protection where the state's responsibilities are less than fully met; and second, even where a state is adequately fulfilling its responsibilities under the Norms, its jurisdictional reach may still be less than the reach of the TNCs in respect of whose activities there are human rights concerns. This explains the need for transnational regulations that go beyond states and seek to address corporations directly, and that have the potential to pierce the corporate veil, where necessary to trace liability back to the parent company. In the present environment, there is no incentive for states to fill the various gaps in corporate accountability that exist at the level of domestic laws (in both developed and developing states, though most especially the latter) and exploitation of these legal loopholes remain within easy reach of those TNCs minded to do so.[85]

In practice, the dividing of responsibility between the state and the TNC most often occurs when a government fails in its human rights duties. Joint responsibility can apply in such situations to both the government and the TNC, within their respective spheres of activity and influence.[86] The Norms do not purport definitively to establish binding legal obligations

---

84   As reflected in the concerns raised by the SRSG in his Interim Report. For further discussion, see infra n. 136 and accompanying text.

85   On the use, abuse and decline of *forum non conveniens* in this context, see Ward, 'Legal Issues in Corporate Citizenship', International Institute for Environment and Development, February 2003 at 12–5, available at: http://www.iied.org/pubs/pdf/full/16000IIED.pdf.

86   In this respect, see the International Law Commission's (ILC) express recognition of circumstances where state responsibility under international law can stretch to encompass the wrong-doings of non-state entities in Chapter II (especially Article 5) of the ILC's Draft Articles on the Responsibility of States for Internationally Wrongful Acts, A/56/10 (2001); and Crawford, Peel and Olleson, 'The ILC's Articles on Responsibility of States for Internationally Wrongful Acts: Completion of the Second Reading', (2001) 12 *European Journal of International Law* 963.

468   *HRLR* **6** (2006), 447–497

(although they do not rule out such an eventuality); still less do they purport to replace state responsibility with corporate responsibility to protect human rights. Rather, they establish that companies should not be able to hide behind governments that are failing to implement human rights, and deny any responsibility whatsoever for human rights violations in which they are involved or complicit.

The Norms also cover the situation where a state not only fails to uphold its citizens' human rights, but is itself the perpetrator of human rights violations. When this occurs, companies that work in concert with the state may find that they are complicit in the state's wrongdoing. The seminal case of *Doe v Unocal*[87] illustrates this point very well. Unocal and its business partner Total constructed a pipeline from Burma through to neighbouring Thailand. Burmese troops from the infamous military junta of the State Peace and Development Council were engaged by Unocal to provide security and build infrastructure for the project. These troops were accused of committing egregious human rights abuses including forced labour, rape, torture and summary execution in the course of their security and building activities under the project. In the ensuing case before the US Court of Appeals for the Ninth Circuit, the court ruled that Unocal could be held responsible under the Alien Torts Claims Act (ATCA) for aiding and abetting the Burmese government. There was no evidence of active participation or cooperation by the company in the government's wrongdoing, but its knowledge of the violations was sufficient for it to be complicit in the government's actions.[88] In December 2004, Unocal agreed to settle the claim for an unspecified sum, which included payment of compensation to the plaintiffs as well as funds to enable them and their representatives to develop programmes to improve living conditions in the area of the pipeline.[89]

The ATCA case law provides useful insight into how the concept of complicity might develop.[90] When a company benefits from human rights abuses committed by a third party, it is unlikely that this alone will attract ACTA liability. But as seen in *Unocal*, US courts have borrowed the concept of aiding and abetting from international criminal law in order to define what level of involvement in the wrongdoing results in complicity.[91]

---

87   395 F.3d 932 (2002).
88   Kinley and Tadaki, 'From Talk to Walk: The Emergence of Human Rights Responsibilities for Corporations at International Law', (2004) 44 *Virginia Journal of International Law* 931 at 980.
89   For further details on the case and the settlement, see EarthRights International, 'Doe v Unocal Case History', 30 January 2006, available at: http://www.earthrights.org/index.php?option=com.content&task=view&id=189&Itemid=25.
90   See further, Chambers, 'The Unocal Settlement: Implications for the Developing Law on Corporate Complicity in Human Rights Abuses', (2005) 13 *Human Rights Brief* 14.
91   Chambers, ibid. at 16, discussing *Presbyterian Church of Sudan v Talisman Energy, Inc* 244 F. Supp. 2d 289 (S.D.N.Y. 2003), in which the New York district court accepted that reference to international criminal law is appropriate when seeking to determine whether a corporation has aided and abetted a state in its commission of such acts as genocide and war crimes.

Similar reasoning could apply with respect to the Norms. Aiding and abetting or accomplice liability should require intentional participation in the wrongdoing, but not necessarily any intention to do harm. Rather, knowledge of foreseeable harmful effects should be sufficient to incur liability.[92] Thus, it should be made clear that if a company is warned of past or current abuses committed by a government or another entity, and if it nonetheless continues to take part in a venture that encompasses activities where the abuses are taking place, it should be liable for the wrongdoing as an accomplice.

TNCs (as well as other business enterprises linked to their operations) are singled out by the Norms because of their unique mobility, power and their transnational nature. The Norms attempt to address the width of TNCs' influence and power by using the notion of a company's 'sphere of activity and influence' to demarcate the scope of their responsibility. The delineation of responsibility in the specific terms of the 'sphere of activity' of the business is also used in the Global Compact.[93] Similarly, while the OECD Guidelines do not refer to a 'sphere of activity' *per se*, they do provide that TNCs should 'respect the human rights of those affected by their activities'. The phrase 'sphere of activity and influence' is not defined in the Norms. However, it might be reasonably assumed to encompass such actors as workers, consumers and members of the host community as well as the environment in which the company operates. The addition of the word 'influence' (not present in either the Global Compact or the OECD Guidelines) apportions responsibility where the company has some degree of influence, even if the human rights violations are at the periphery of the company's area of activity. This is noted by Justine Nolan, who cites the *maquiladoras* in Tijuana as an example of companies that could bring their influence to bear in the provision of potable water for the local population, despite the fact that their core

---

92 See Clapham and Jerbi, 'Categories of Corporate Complicity in Human Rights Abuses', (2001) 24 *Hastings International and Comparative Law Review* 339; and Ramasastry, 'Corporate Complicity: From Nuremberg to Rangoon an Examination of Forced Labour Cases and their Impact on the Liability of Multinational Corporations', (2002) 20 *Berkeley Journal of International Law* 106 at 143–4.

93 Principle 1, UN Global Compact, supra n. 34, states: 'Business is asked to support and respect the protection of international human rights within their sphere of influence'. No definition of 'sphere of influence' is given in the 'Guide to the Global Compact: A Practical Understanding of the Vision and Nine Principles', available at: http://www.uneptie.org/outreach/compact/docs/gcguide.pdf.

470　　*HRLR* **6** (2006), 447–497

business does not include potable water provision.[94] Using the OECD terminology, the people of Tijuana were affected by the activities of the *maquiladoras*
in that their potable water supplies were reduced. These companies, therefore,
have a duty to respect the right to clean water of the host community.

In another representation of the question, Frankental and House show
diagrammatically, through a series of concentric rings, the sphere of influence
of a company with respect to human rights. At the centre are its core operations,
followed by business partners, host communities and finally advocacy
and policy dialogue.[95] Legal liability is most likely to arise, if at all, within the
innermost circles. If the company violates human rights directly or indirectly
in its core operations, then it should be held legally accountable. The next
circle, business partners, opens up the difficult issue of supply chain liability.
Companies are urged to include the Norms in contracts and agreements,[96]
so that suppliers will be in breach of contract if they commit human rights
violations. TNCs must use due diligence to ensure that they do not benefit from
abuses that they were, or ought to have been, aware of.[97] Thus the Norms seek,
through states, to require that TNCs monitor the activities of their supply
chains to ensure compliance.[98] TNCs would be legally liable for the actions of
business partners only if they were found to be complicit in the wrongdoing.
This concept, from paragraph 3 of the Norms, applies with respect to government or other third party human rights abuses in the host community, and
makes TNCs accountable for benefits received as a result of serious human
rights abuses by third parties. Certainly, liability for complicity needs to be
fleshed out further if the Norms, or some derivative instrument, are to become
legally enforceable. And this will require addressing such thorny questions
as what constitutes a 'benefit' and what level of involvement or knowledge

---

94　Nolan, Background Research Paper (2003) [on file with authors], points out that the opera-
　　tions of a number of *maquiladoras* located in the region of Tijuana in Mexico have contrib-
　　uted to a scarcity of potable water. While none of the companies had *de facto* control of
　　potable water, their cumulative impact was to reduce severely water supplies. This poses
　　the question of whether they should be individually accountable for the water situation or
　　whether the state, which controls the number of *maquiladoras* in the area, is responsible. The
　　maquiladoras are able to influence the situation and have played a part in creating the
　　problem. They share responsibility, therefore, with the local authority. For a general study
　　of the role and impact of *maquiladoras*, see Reygadas, 'Corporate Responsibility and Social
　　Capital: The Nexus Dilemma in Mexican Maquiladoras', in Sullivan (ed.), *Business and Human
　　Rights* (Sheffield: Greenleaf, 2003) 207.
95　Frankental and House, *Human Rights—Is it Any of Your Business?* (Amnesty International
　　and the Prince of Wales International Business Leaders Forum, 2000).
96　Para. 15, Norms.
97　Para. 1(b), Commentary states: 'transnational corporations and other business enterprises
　　shall have the responsibility to use due diligence in ensuring that their activities do not
　　contribute directly or indirectly to human abuses, and that they do not directly or indirectly
　　benefit from abuses of which they were aware or ought to have been aware'.
98　See further, the SA8000—a social accounting standard which allows companies to imple-
　　ment and assess standards within the supply chain. For more information see Social
　　Accountability International, available at: www.sa-intl.org.

(e.g. subjective or objective) on the part of the company is required. Professor Ruggie, therefore, is clearly correct when he points out that there currently is no legal definition of the whole or any part of the notion of a corporation's 'sphere of activity and influence', either in the Norms or elsewhere in international law, and that defining its terms is crucial to any endeavour that seeks to make corporations liable for human rights abuses within their respective spheres.[99] However, it is our view that he should not be looking to the Norms to provide such a definition in the first place. As we consistently maintain throughout this article, this is the sort of task that will be derived from the Norms, to be addressed either in domestic regulation or some future international legal instrument, or possibly both. Indeed, the very debates that we are now having about what constitutes 'an activity' within a sphere of activity and influence and what liabilities should flow there-from, are precisely the sort of exploratory interactions one would expect to accompany any future domestic or international laws on the matter.

Thus, for example, in respect of Frankental and House's outer ring, it may be asked whether a company's sphere should stretch as far as government relations, where it potentially has influence through advocacy and policy dialogue.[100] This is not an area for legal liability. While such dialogue would not be beyond the capacity of most TNCs, to require companies to intrude in this way in respect of human rights issues would necessarily be seen as challenging state sovereignty. However, pushes in this direction have already occurred,[101] and there are also instances where precisely this sort of corporate influence has been brought to bear on governments.[102] The inherent circularity of the notion that the corporate responsibilities arising out of the Norms will accrue when and so far as the issue in question falls within the corporation's 'sphere of activity and influence', should not necessarily be seen as problematic.[103] It simply reduces the matter to

99 Para. 67, Interim Report.
100 See Frankental and House, supra n. 95.
101 For instance the US/UK Voluntary Principles on Security and Human Rights, supra n. 33, provide that: 'companies should support efforts by governments, civil society and multilateral institutions to provide human rights training and education for public security as well as their efforts to strengthen state institutions to ensure accountability and respect for human rights'; and further 'where companies operating in the same region have common concerns, they should consider collectively raising those concerns with the host and home government'.
102 See, for example, the argument made by the UK oil company, Premier Oil, which claimed that on account of the relationship it had established with the military government in Burma through its commercial interests there, it had been able to use its leverage 'to promote respect for international law' primarily through a series of human rights workshops that it sponsored for members of the Burmese government and military. See the section on Premier Oil in Ethical Corporation, *The Business and Human Rights Management Report: A Study of Eight Companies and Their Approaches to Human Rights Policy and Management System Development* (Ethical Corporation, November 2004) at 56–64.
103 See questions posed by Ratner, supra n. 30 at 510, in this respect. Ratner implies that he sees the ties between influence and responsibility as being somewhat amorphous in that they are not fixed but move with the given human right.

an evidentiary question; although it is yet to be determined upon whom the onus of proof should fall to show either the existence or the non-existence of influence and of the responsibility that follows it.

D. Coverage

Certain commentators[104] have attacked the Norms for the way in which they, supposedly, artificially stretch the definition of human rights by including *inter alia* labour rights, rights against corruption, consumer protection and environmental rights.[105] Such reasoning is clearly wrong in respect of labour rights, which overlap with international human rights in respect of not only their conceptual bases—both labour and human rights are based on notions of individual rights to equality, liberty and fairness—but also their form, since labour rights are expressly included as human rights in the International Covenant on Economic, Social and Cultural Rights (ICESCR).[106] On the other hand, while the Norms' proposed obligations in respect of consumer protection are not traditional human rights law, their infringement could certainly amount to violations of human rights if this results in personal injury or death.[107] Likewise, the Norms' anti-corruption obligations are not drawn directly from international human rights law. Although, here again, their infringement could have the effect of denying populations economic, social and cultural rights where national resources are squandered for the benefit of a privileged few leaving the country unable to fund social services for the poor or disadvantaged. There is room to argue over questions of categorisation, but in so doing there is a danger of losing sight of the importance of these matters—whatever their precise label—to states, communities and corporations alike.

The inclusion of the collective rights to development and to a healthy environment presents problems as to the identification both of rights holders and duty bearers. These two rights are nonetheless appropriately included in the Norms as both are expressly recognised in international law and are intimately connected to corporate enterprise. The right to a healthy environment is an integral part of the right to health under Article 12 of the ICESCR,[108] and the right to development is proclaimed 'an inalienable human right by virtue of which every human person and all peoples are entitled to participate in, contribute to and enjoy economic, social, cultural and political development,

104   See IOC/IOE submission, supra n. 44 at 25; and Mendelson, supra n. 83 at para. 11.
105   Paras 23, 13 and 14, Norms, respectively.
106   1966, 993 UNTS 3. Specifically, Articles 6, 7 and 8, ICESCR.
107   Muchlinski, 'The Development of Human Rights Responsibilities for Multinational Enterprises', in Sullivan (ed.), supra n. 94, 43.
108   And additionally, in Principle 1, Rio Declaration on Environment and Development, Annex I to the Report of the United Nations Conference on Environment and Development, 12 August 1992, A/CONF.151/26 (Vol I).

in which all human rights and fundamental freedoms can be fully realised'.[109] What is more, as states and business are rightly keen to point out, the activities of corporations can and do bear directly and beneficially on development and environmental issues by, crucially, raising standards of living.[110] But, equally, their activities can and do impact detrimentally on these areas—especially through environmental degradation which can infringe such rights as the right to food, health, shelter and security of person—a fact that corporations are less keen to advertise.[111] Certainly, in respect of protection of the environment, corporations have for a long time been regulated by legislative codes, and there is also emerging regulation in respect of corporate activities that affect development rights.[112] The bottom line is that both the negative and positive aspects of the impact of business on economic development and the

109   See Article 1, GA Res. 41/128, Declaration on the Right to Development, 4 December 1986, A/41/53. See also Part I para. 10, Vienna Declaration and Programme of Action, 12 July 1993, A/CONF.157/23. Furthermore, there is now strong argument to suggest that there is an intimate relationship between the UN's Millennium Development Goals and international human rights laws more generally: see Alston, 'Ships Passing in the Night: The Current State of the Human Rights and Development Debate Seen Through the Lens of the Millennium Development Goals', (2005) 27 *Human Rights Quarterly* 755.

110   See, for example, the statement of the US Government, supra n. 2; and the US Council for International Business declaration in its submissions to the OHCHR Inquiry that 'private enterprise is unmatched in its ability to assemble people, capital and innovation to create meaningful jobs and profitably produce goods and services that meet the needs and requirements of the world's peoples', para. 2, US Council for International Business, 'Submission to the High Commissioner for Human Rights for the report on "Responsibilities of transnational corporations and related business entities with regard to human rights"', available at: http://www.ohchr.org/english/issues/globalization/business/docs/uscouncil.pdf. See also, generally, UN Commission on the Private Sector and Development, 'Report to the Secretary General of the United Nations: Unleashing Entrepreneurship: Making Business Work for the Poor', United Nations Development Program, 1 March 2004, available at: http://www.undp.org/cpsd/documents/report/english/fullreport.pdf.

111   Some of the most extreme examples of environmental and human rights violations by companies have occurred in the oil rich Niger Delta, beginning with Shell last century; see Amnesty International, 'Nigeria: Ten years on: Injustice and violence haunt the oil Delta', AFR 44/022/2005, 3 November 2005. However, violations by corporations are not limited to developing countries. In December 2005 DuPont was fined $16.5million for not disclosing that a toxic chemical was used in the manufacture of Teflon; see Montgomery, 'DuPont fined $16.5million by the EPA', *Delaware Online*, 15 December 2005, available at: http://www.delawareonline.com/apps/pbcs.dll/article?AID=/20051215/NEWS/512150347/1006.

   Corporations are increasingly indirectly responsible for human rights violations due to financing roles, and this was recognised in December 2005, when Action Aid, Amnesty International, Friends of the Earth, New Economics Foundation and several other NGOs published 'A Big Deal? Corporate Social Responsibility and the Finance Sector in Europe', December 2005, available at: http://www.corporate-accountability.org/docs/Big-Deal.Report.12-2005.pdf, discussing the impact of the finance sector on environmental and social rights.

112   See, for example, the International Finance Corporation's (IFC) Safeguard Policies cum Performance Standards (for example on Forestry, International Waterways, Indigenous People, etc.), available at: http://ifcln1.ifc.org/ifcext/enviro.nsf/Content/Safeguardpolicies; and the Equator Principles, supra n. 33, that cover the social (and environmental) impacts of development project financing.

474   *HRLR* **6** (2006), 447–497

environment need to be recognised. However, to do so properly, a balance must be struck between protecting the individual rights associated with these issues, while at the same time not stifling the enterprise of business that benefits communities at large.[113]

In any event, it does not appear that business alliances are against these rights *per se*. Rather their criticism appears to be that social, economic and cultural rights (including environmental rights and the right to development), as laid out in the Norms, are too vague and this leaves businesses vulnerable to arbitrary criticism. However, this approach seems to deflect attention away from the undeniable fact that it is in the area of economic, social and cultural rights that the activities of TNCs are most likely to have a direct impact,[114] covering, as they do, the rights to access to adequate health care, housing, education, working conditions, fair pay, trade union membership and non-discrimination.[115] The criticism might be valid if the standards in these areas were intended to be precise in form and substance, but the fact is that such standards are, as argued above, necessarily imprecise. In the event, therefore, of claims that corporations are accused of infringing human rights, the burden of proof will necessarily be shared between those who make the claims to support their assertions, and the corporations themselves to show how, on the contrary, their actions are human rights-compliant. As noted earlier, it is the nature of international human rights law to provide a framework for standards in a particular area, which states then implement and enforce by fleshing out the standards in detailed domestic legislation. The nature of duties imposed upon states by international human rights law with respect to economic, social and cultural rights are different from those imposed with respect to civil and political rights. While the state must work towards accomplishment of the former, it should already be in a position to address and remedy the latter.[116] However, the nature of economic, social and cultural

113   This is the essential message of the UN Commission on the Private Sector and Development's 2004 report, supra n. 110.
114   In this respect, Kinley and Tadaki, supra n. 88 at 962–93, argue, that these sorts of 'self-reflexive' duties on corporations (not to interfere with the enjoyment of human rights on which a company's activities have direct impact) are of a higher order than the more distant, 'third party' duties placed on corporations (such as those regarding a right to fair trial, rights to political participation and freedom from arbitrary arrest), which obliges the corporations merely to act so as to prevent others from breaching human rights.
115   As protected by ICESCR.
116   Article 2, ICESCR obligates each State Party to take steps 'to the maximum of its available resources' with a view to the progressive achievement of the rights set out in the Covenant. The state's role with respect to the right to development is also programmatic: the Declaration on the Right to Development, supra n. 109, requires states to formulate national development policies (Article 2(3)) and to take all necessary measures for the realisation of the right to development (Article 8(1)). This can be contrasted with Article 2, ICCPR which requires states to takes steps necessary for the implementation of the rights contained in the Covenant. However, in reality, the achievement of the rights set out in both Covenants is progressive rather than immediate: e.g. a right to fair trial cannot be achieved overnight if the country is poor and the courts or the judiciary are under-developed.

rights does not prevent them from being legally binding and subject to checks such as other rights. The duty to uphold economic, social and cultural rights is contained in a legally binding covenant[117] and interpreted by the Committee on Economic, Social and Cultural Rights (CESCR) in its General Comments and through periodic country reports. On the other hand, the progressive nature of the duty does translate into allowing some latitude to states as long as they act in good faith in trying to raise the standards,[118] illustrated in part by the fact that there is presently no individual petition procedure under the ICESCR as there is for civil and political rights.[119] Many of the types of rights which fall under the mantle of economic, social, cultural and environmental rights are already pro-tected in the corporate context through labour, occupational health and safety and environmental protection law, and have long been accepted as part of the domestic legal landscape of Western countries in particular.[120]

The Norms themselves provide that TNCs shall respect economic, social and cultural rights (including the rights to development and protection of the environment) and to 'contribute to their realisation'.[121] This is a less onerous obligation than, for example, those required of states by the ICESCR. Contribution to the realisation of these rights would be limited to those people who fall within a company's sphere of activity and influence, perhaps extending only to the rights of the workforce (which coincides with other obligations, such as the requirement set out in paragraph 8 that remuneration is sufficient to ensure an adequate standard of living for workers and their families) and the immediate communities in which they operate. It is noted that although these are the people who would usually fall within the company's sphere of activity and influence, the boundaries of that sphere

---

117   ICESCR to which 152 states are party.
118   CESCR General Comment No. 3, The Nature of States Parties Obligations (Article 2, para. 1), 14 December 1990, E/1991/23 Annex III; 1-1 IHRR 6 (1994). See also the Maastricht Guidelines on Violations of Economic, Social and Cultural Rights 1997, (1998) 20 *Human Rights Quarterly* 691.
119   However, see the ongoing discussions of and proposals for an Optional Protocol to the ICESCR. The Open-ended Working Group on an Option Protocol had its third session at the 62nd session of the Commission on Human Rights (6–17 February 2006). The Working Group's documents are available on the OHCHR website: Commission on Human Rights 62nd Session: Open-ended Working Group to consider options regarding the elaboration of an Optional Protocol to the International Covenant on Economic, Social and Cultural Rights, available at: http://www.ohchr.org/english/issues/escr/group3.htm.
120   See Kinley, 'International Human Rights as Legally Binding or Merely Relevant', in Bottomley and Kinley (eds), *Commercial Law and Human Rights* (Aldershot: Ashgate Dartmouth, 2002) 25.
121   This is the phrase used in para. 12, Norms. In para. 1, the phrase 'secure the fulfilment of . . . human rights' is used, and according to para. 1(a), Commentary, all other provisions in the Norms should be read in the light of this paragraph. What this means in practice is unclear. The obligation in para. 12 is less onerous than that contained in para. 1. It is submitted that 'contribute to the realisation of' is the correct obligation with respect to the rights contained in para. 12 and that the Commentary should clarify this position.

476　*HRLR* **6** (2006), 447–497

are not pre-determined and will almost certainly vary from corporation to corporation and situation to situation.[122]

The Norms further propose that TNCs and other business enterprises be required to conduct their activities in a manner contributing to the wider goal of sustainable development.[123] While, in this regard, there have been several significant declarations on the right to a healthy environment,[124] there has been no relevant General Assembly declaration and there is no international legal definition of 'sustainable development'. However, in the 20 years since the term was first coined by the World Commission on Environment and Development (WCED), the concept it represents has become known and understood.[125] It is not only a buzzword in the context of business development, but is also used in respect of community development in the wider context. In order to conduct business in a manner that contributes to sustainable development, a company will need to engage in complex balancing exercises to evaluate the strength of competing rights such as the economic development needs of the country versus the environmental, social and other consequences of a proposed development. Inherent in such a balancing process is the fact that there will be no 'correct' answers, rather a penumbra of what might be described as reasonable responses to the situation. This balancing process should not expose companies to unfair criticism: it should provide a framework for decision-making that allows companies a reasonable margin of discretion in what they decide. Companies which undertake this balancing exercise diligently and in good faith will have fulfilled their obligations under the Norms.

E. Enforcement

Human rights laws, both domestic and international, generally require balancing between the interests of the state and the rights of the individual,[126]

122　Thus, some TNCs will have a role that goes beyond merely abstaining from interference with these rights, if, for example, a TNC has assumed *de facto* control of a region in which it operates or of the resources of that region.

123　Para. 14, Norms provides that 'as well as human rights, public health and safety, bioethics and the precautionary principle, and shall generally conduct their activities in a matter contributing to the wider goal of sustainable development'.

124　The Stockholm Declaration on the Human Environment, 16 June 1972, A/CONF.48/14/REV.1, linked human rights and the environment: 'Both aspects of man's environment, the natural and the man-made, are essential to his well-being and to the enjoyment of basic human rights—even the right to life itself'. Its successor, the Rio Declaration on the Environment and Development, supra n. 108, contains a more definitive right: 'Human beings are at the centre of concerns for sustainable development. They are entitled to a healthy and productive life in harmony with nature' (Principle 1).

125　The World Commission on Environment and Development (WCED) defined the principle to mean: 'development that meets the needs of the present without compromising the ability of future generations to meet their own needs', in WCED, *Our Common Future* (Oxford: Oxford University Press, 1987) at 43.

126　Ratner, supra n. 30 at 513.

and this holds true in respect of TNCs. A company's responsibilities must turn on a balancing of the individual right at issue with the company's interests and other legal rights,[127] using concepts such as proportionality and reasonableness to determine whether the ends justify the means. For example, a state that prevents a citizen from criticising the actions of a company will normally be infringing that citizen's right to freedom of expression.[128] However, if that citizen works for the company in question, it is not likely that the company would be infringing that citizen's rights by preventing them from criticising the company in correspondence with a competitor.[129] Such balancing is not a novel concept— all human rights treaties are replete with qualifications that at all times require balancing. One example is the right to freedom of thought, conscience and religion.[130] A person's right to practise their religion must be balanced against the rights of others, including the right of non-discrimination, which may be breached if that religion vilifies other religions or groups in society.[131] Thus the balancing exercises inherent in many of the rights laid out in the Norms are not new to international law. Rather, international human rights law is new to corporations and their legal advisers, and its processes are, for the moment, somewhat alien.[132]

A key element of corporate criticism of the Norms is an apparent fear that their implementation and enforcement will be arbitrary, or at least

---

127   See infra n. 132.
128   An exception is when the criticism amounts to defamation and is therefore actionable in the courts.
129   As pointed out by Kinley and Tadaki, supra n. 88 at 968. See also the example given by Ratner, supra n. 30 at 514, of a TNC breaking into a person's home to tap telephones or intercept mail under suspicion of theft of company property. It is likely that in such a case the TNC would violate the right against arbitrary interference with privacy, family, home or correspondence, but it is less likely to be violating employees' human rights by screening their work email for inappropriate or illegal use.
130   Article 18, ICCPR.
131   See, for example, *Peterson v Hewlett-Packard Co.* 358 F.3d 599 (2004), in which an employee pasted quotations from biblical scriptures in a prominent position in the office where he worked, in response to a diversity poster campaign which highlighted that members of the Hewlett–Packard workforce are homosexual. Apparently, he hoped that his gay and lesbian co-workers would read the passages, repent and be saved. Company management requested that he take down the quotations, as they were a violation of the company's policy prohibiting harassment. When he refused to do so he was dismissed. He then brought an action claiming Hewlett–Packard engaged in differential treatment by terminating him because of his religious views, and that it failed to accommodate his religious beliefs. His case was unsuccessful. The court found that the company was not required to accommodate his religious beliefs in such a way that would result in discrimination against his co-workers.
132   Mendelson, supra n. 83 at para. 19, makes this point, but his view is that balancing exercises are 'best left to the political process and to governments' and that it is not for TNCs to make these judgments. This view does not take into account that TNCs routinely engage in these balancing exercises in the course of carrying out their business, and while states set the parameters (e.g. when freedom of speech must be curtailed in order to prevent racial vilification) TNCs have their own decisions to make within their spheres of activity and influence which require the same careful balancing.

478 *HRLR* **6** (2006), 447–497

unpredictable, due to the imprecise nature of the duties they contain. Implementation of the Norms by states will inevitably involve undertaking the balancing exercise described earlier, in order to determine the validity of competing and, at times, imprecise human rights claims as well as legitimate corporate interests. This is not different from the process undertaken by the state in incorporating any international legal obligation into domestic law. In order for corporations to comply with the standards set by the Norms, they will be required to undertake a comparable exercise, through establishing appropriate processes within the company to identify and attach value to the rights in question and, crucially, to calibrate the nature and extent of their responsibilities to protect those rights. Any disputes that do occur will be resolved through determining whether a careful, good-faith balancing exercise has been conducted and whether the company's decisions fall within the range of reasonable responses or its margin of discretion. This type of balancing exercise is an ever-present feature of courts when they adjudicate on vague standards or competing rights, and it does not result in arbitrary decisions.[133]

Outside of formal enforcement mechanisms, the business alliances fear that the Norms will be used as the basis of criticism in campaigns, by NGOs or other political actors, aimed at vilifying TNCs. This vilification, it is argued, will breach the rights of TNCs and the business people who work for them, to keep and protect their reputation and, therefore, make a living. However, the fact is that the Norms are, on their own, hardly likely to generate unfair criticism of corporations—that can and will happen regardless of the Norms. Rather, they introduce some form of universal standard, which might control less principled and reasoned criticism. The commercial rights to reputation and pursuit of legitimate business aims will be protected by the laws of defamation and libel for untruths and by well-established curial intolerance of vexatious or unwarranted law suits (potentially with costs awarded to penalise vexatious plaintiffs). In broader terms, the public can, and will, make reasonable judgments about corporate behaviour and about whether criticism, from whatever quarter, is fair and legitimate. The reality is that companies will need to accept some level of engagement in public debate and, perhaps, greater transparency will be necessary.[134]

---

133 Consider, for example, the use in tort of 'the reasonable man' or the notion of 'reasonable foreseeablity', or the balancing of legal protections to privacy on the one hand, and the demands of free speech and/or criminal law on the other.

134 The Business and Human Rights Resource Centre, supra n. 54, gives corporate and other subscribers the opportunity to learn of, and respond to, public criticism through an alert service. This service informs TNCs of criticisms in the international press, and then publishes the TNC's response, if any is given.

4. The Legal Implications of the Norms

A. *Non-State Parties Under International Law*

As international rules directed at TNCs, the Norms engage in the growing recognition of non-state parties in international law.[135] A battle cry of the anti-Norms lobby has been that states are the only subjects of international law and that the Norms fly in the face of this legal orthodoxy by attempting to regulate the behaviour of TNCs from an international standpoint. However, this view ignores developments over the last 60 years or so that have seen non-state parties grow in their roles and responsibilities on the global stage, albeit usually mediated through the direct international responsibilities of states' parties.[136] As Nicola Jägers reminds us, legal personality is not a static concept: it is flexible and can be conferred and then later withdrawn.[137] The complexity lies in that there is no central body that determines whether an entity has international legal personality. It is only through the behaviour of the principal actors, states, that we can establish which entities have legal personality.[138]

The behaviour of states in respect of TNCs indicates, at the very least, an emerging recognition of their legal personality. States have applied the international rules prohibiting genocide, slavery and torture to bar such conduct by individuals, including companies, as well as by governments.[139] These rules and others have been applied by international tribunals against corporations, most notably at the Nuremberg Tribunals, which found

---

135   Ratner, supra n. 30 at 476, states that 'the orthodoxy now accepts that non-state entities may enjoy forms of international personality'.

136   On which, see Higgins, *Problems and Process: International Law and How We Use It* (Oxford: Clarendon Press; New York: Oxford University Press, 1994) at 49–50; Chirwa, 'The Doctrine of State Responsibility as a Potential Means of Holding Private Actors Accountable for Human Rights', (2004) 5 *Melbourne Journal of International Law* 1; and, generally, Clapham, *Human Rights Obligations of Non-State Actors* (Oxford: Oxford University Press, 2006).

137   Jägers, 'The Legal Status of the Multinational Corporation Under International Law', in Addo (ed.), *Human Rights Standards and the Responsibility of Transnational Corporations* (The Hague/Boston: Kluwer,1999) 262.

138   The state behaviour that is required, according to the International Court of Justice, is the conferral of both rights and responsibilities on non-state entities. See *Reparation for Injuries Suffered in Service of the United Nations*, Advisory Opinion, ICJ Reports 1949, 174 at 178–9.

139   States have applied international rules prohibiting genocide, slavery and torture to bar such conduct by individuals and legal persons (including companies) as well as by government officials.

480　*HRLR* **6** (2006), 447–497

that employees and directors of the I.G. Farben Corporation had violated international law[140] through the company's role in the Holocaust.[141] Beth Stephens points to international treaties that specifically refer to corporate crimes, including the Apartheid Convention,[142] and treaties governing corruption and bribery, hazardous wastes and other environmental violations as examples of duties borne by companies under international law. The fact that there may be few or no enforcement mechanisms for these norms does not negate their legal status. These treaties imposing duties on corporations are complemented by treaties bestowing rights upon them— for instance, rights regarding access to dispute settlement mechanisms (e.g. under the North American Free Trade Agreement).[143] Thus, it can be seen that companies, according to the widely accepted qualifying criteria, have at least some form of legal personality in public international law.[144] This is not exactly the same type of personality as that of states, but this does not negate its existence.

The phrase 'privatising human rights' is often used by critics of the Norms to characterise their view that somehow implementation of the Norms will let states 'off the hook' in respect of their role in upholding human rights shifting the responsibility for protection and promotion of human rights onto the private sector. Thus, for example, in their joint submission to the OHCHR inquiry on the Norms, the IOE and the ICC declared that the privatisation of human rights 'leaves the real duty-bearer—the state—out of the picture, by shifting the human rights duties to civil society and 'placing the entire burden on private

---

140　Stephens, ibid. at 76 and 77.

141　Ramasastry, supra n. 92 at 106: 'In 1947, twenty-three employees of I.G. Farben were indicted for plunder, slavery, and complicity in aggression and mass murder [in the case of *U.S. v Krauch et al*, 'The I.G. Farben Case' 10 *Law Reports of Trials of War Criminals* 1]. I.G. Farben was a major German chemical and pharmaceutical manufacturer. The defendants in the Farben case were prosecuted for "acting through the instrumentality of Farben" in the commission of their crimes. Five of the Farben directors were held criminally liable for the use of slave labour. This was the first time that a court attempted to impose liability on a group of persons who were collectively in charge of a company'.

142　International Convention on the Suppression and Punishment of the Crime of Apartheid 1973, 1015 UNTS 243.

143　The North American Free Trade Agreement Between the Government of Canada, the Government of Mexico and the Government of the United States, 17 December 1992, (1993) 32 *International Legal Materials* 368 (entered into force 1 January 1994) (NAFTA). NAFTA's infamous 'Chapter Eleven' provisions enable corporations to sue governments for various violations of the NAFTA. Mexico, Canada and the United States have all been forced to defend claims. For an overview of NAFTA Chapter 11 litigation, and a history of similar clauses see Alvarez and Park, 'The New Face of Investment Arbitration: NAFTA Chapter 11', (2003) 28 *Yale Journal of International Law* 365.

144　Kinley, 'Corporate Responsibility and International Human Rights Law', in Mullerat (ed.), *Corporate Social Responsibility, The Corporate Governance of the 21st Century* (The Hague: Kluwer Law and International Bar Association, 2005) 205 at 205–7.

business persons'.[145] The UK Foreign and Commonwealth Office has raised the same concern.[146]

These apprehensions are misplaced. Notwithstanding the above discussion regarding the increasing prominence of non-state actors in international law, the fact is that international law still overwhelmingly speaks directly to states and imposes legal obligations directly upon them. Certainly, those obligations may entail domestic regulation of the actions of non-state actors within their jurisdiction, but that is not the same as placing those non-state actors under a direct international legal obligation.[147] It is very much in this sense that the Norms proclaim that states will retain primary responsibility for the protection of human rights.[148] In any event, no matter what the level of direct or indirect legal effects that the Norms may have on corporations, it does not follow that from the expansion of sites of responsibility comes a corresponding reduction of a state's liability in respect of human rights protection and promotion.[149] Rather, the human rights burden is increased and to some extent differently composed, as the duty to discharge that burden is shared across the different entities.[150] In any event, paragraph 19 of the Norms confirms that nothing in the document shall be construed as diminishing the human rights obligations of states. This is a view consistent with the case law of supervisory bodies of the principal UN human rights treaties. These treaty bodies have found that privatising a state's functions—for example, the provision of drinking water—does not absolve the state from its responsibility to ensure respect for human rights.[151]

---

145 Joint views of the IOE and ICC, supra n. 44 at paras 2, 4 and 32.

146 In his CBI Advice, Mendelson, supra n. 83 at para. 21, quotes the Parliamentary Under-Secretary of the FCO, Bill Rammell MP, replying to a Parliamentary question by stating that 'according human rights responsibilities to private business enterprises in international law could be used by certain states to avoid their own obligations and to distract from human rights abuses by states'.

147 The direct imposition on individuals of responsibilities for war crimes and crimes against humanity under the Rome Statute of the International Criminal Court is the exception that proves this rule in international law.

148 Preamble, Norms states: '*Recognizing* that even though States have the primary responsibility to promote, secure the fulfilment of, respect, ensure respect of and protect human rights, transnational corporations and other business enterprises, as organs of society, are also responsible for promoting and securing the human rights set forth in the Universal Declaration of Human Rights . . .'.

149 Kinley, supra n. 144 at 207–8.

150 Ibid.

151 Kamminga, 'Corporate Obligations under International Law', Stakeholder submissions to the report of the High Commissioner for Human Rights on the Responsibilities of Transnational Corporations and related Business Enterprises with regard to Human Rights, Paper presented at the 71st Conference of the International Law Association, plenary session on Corporate Social Responsibility and International Law, Berlin, 17 August 2004, at 5, available at: http://www.ohchr.org/english/issues/globalization/business/docs/kamminga.doc.

482 *HRLR* **6** (2006), 447–497

B. *International Legal Implications of the Norms*

In their present form as a compendium of human rights principles relating to TNCs and other business enterprises, the Norms have no immediate ramifications in international law. The Sub-Commission, which compiled the Norms, is not able to enact new international law: such law can only be created through international agreement in the form of a treaty, or through the development of customary international law. At present there is no treaty that incorporates the Norms; nor is there evidence of any state practice supporting such a development in customary international law.

The Norms are not therefore, 'instant international law',[152] although some have mistakenly believed them to be so.[153] The Commission itself expressly stated, in its 2004 decision, that the Norms, in their present form (i.e. merely a draft proposal), have no binding legal effect.[154] The most that can be said regarding the Norms' legal status, is that any existing international law (as it applies to states)[155] that has been codified in sections of the Norms obviously retains its force as international law and is unchanged by its re-statement in certain paragraphs of the Norms. These paragraphs may be described as having a 'declaratory effect'.[156] They merely reinforce rights contained in either customary international law or treaties. While there remains dispute as to whether the Universal Declaration of Human Rights and even possibly

---

152 The expression is quoted by Baade, 'The Legal Effects of Codes of Conduct for Multinational Enterprises', in Horn (ed.), *Legal Problems of Codes of Conduct for Multinational Enterprises* (Deventer/Boston: Kluwer, 1980) 3 at 13, footnote 52; and is taken from Cheng, 'United Nations Resolutions on Outer Space: 'Instant' International Customary Law', (1965) 5 *Indian Journal of International Law* 23.

153 By both supporters and detractors of the Norms, as well as those who might at some future point be called upon to arbitrate disputes concerning the Norms. See Mendelson, supra n. 83 at paras 7–10.

154 See supra n. 49 and accompanying text.

155 The SRSG's concern that the Norms cannot 'restate' something that at present does not exist—namely, directly binding obligations on corporations (as opposed to states) under international human rights law—would indeed be valid were it *clearly* the case and intention (see Interim Report at para. 60), but, in reality, such concern is borne of the corporate lobby's over-eager interpretation of the (admittedly) indefinite terms of the Norms, rather than unimpeachable and immovable fact.

156 Brownlie describes three categories of situation in which informal prescriptions such as the Norms can have legal effect, one being when such instruments are declaratory of existing human rights standards: Brownlie, 'Legal Effect of Codes of Conduct for MNEs: Commentary', in Horn (ed.), supra n. 152, 40.

the two International Covenants are, in part or in their entirety, customary international law,[157] it is clear that certain principles contained within them do amount to customary international law and are thus binding on all states.[158] Furthermore, these and other named instruments cited in the Norms remain binding on their states parties and, therefore, are part of international law as it applies to those states.[159] The question of whether international law can impose obligations on individuals (or companies) as well as states is addressed above.[160] At the very least it is clear that obligations, such as those in paragraph 3 of the Norms, which prohibit TNCs and other business enterprises from engaging in or benefiting from egregious human rights abuses, including war crimes and genocide, are already binding on individuals as well as states and as such are re-statements of existing obligations or paragraphs of 'declaratory effect'.[161]

C. *Questions of the Legal Status of the Norms*

It is a fact, therefore, that most provisions of the Norms do not represent international law (instant or otherwise), and that they would not become so even if they had been adopted by the Commission, or the Human Rights Council that has replaced it.[162] However, this does not prevent them from 'hardening' into

157 Simma and Alston, 'The Sources of Human Rights Law: Custom, Jus Cogens and General Principles', (1988–89) 12 *Australian Year Book of International Law* 82, argue that it is only valid to describe a rule as customary international law when state practice and *opinio juris* have had a chance to establish themselves solidly in an initial, formative stage (it is not sufficient for the rule to be universally proclaimed). Hannum, 'The Status of the Universal Declaration of Human Rights in National and International Law', (1995–96) 25 *Georgia Journal of International and Comparative Law* 287 at 317–39, concludes that although there is insufficient international support to find that the entire Universal Declaration of Human Rights constitutes binding customary international law, there would seem to be little argument that today many provisions of the Declaration do reflect customary international law.

158 For example, the prohibition against torture under Article 5, Universal Declaration of Human Rights and Article 7, ICCPR.

159 Examples of named instruments cited in the Norms include the Convention on the Prevention and Punishment of the Crime of Genocide 1948, 78 UNTS 277; the Convention against Torture and Other Cruel, Inhuman or Degrading Treatment or Punishment 1984, 1465 UNTS 85; the Slavery Convention 1926, 60 LNTS 253; the Supplementary Convention on the Abolition of Slavery, the Slave Trade, and Institutions and Practices Similar to Slavery 1956, 266 UNTS 3; and the International Convention on the Elimination of All Forms of Racial Discrimination 1966, 660 UNTS 195.

160 See supra Part 4 A ('Non-State Parties under International Law').

161 Despite the fact that some paragraphs of the Norms re-state existing international human rights law as it is applicable to companies, there is, at present, little by way of international enforcement mechanisms to ensure that companies comply with international human rights obligations. See Stephens, supra n. 139 at 76: 'International tribunals have applied human rights and humanitarian norms to corporations from the time of the Nuremberg Trials', but at 77 she notes a 'reluctance' to apply international criminal law to corporations in the mid-20th century. Note also the quotation from Louis Henkin that Stephens quotes at 77.

162 See UN Press Release, 'General Assembly Establishes New Human Rights Council By Vote Of 170 In Favour To 4 Against, With 3 Abstentions', 15 March 2006, available at: http://www.un.org/News/.

484   *HRLR* **6** (2006), 447–497

'international custom, as evidence of a general practice accepted as law',[163] if state practice moves accordingly. In order for custom to develop, states would have to participate in the implementation of the Norms, through whatever mechanism for enforcement is created, with the necessary legal intention that enforcement is required under international law.[164] Baade makes this point in his discussion of the legal effects of codes of conduct,[165] as an example of a method by which initially non-binding codes can, over time, become legally binding, whether through international custom or adoption in domestic law, or both. Baade was writing in the late 1970s when the original version of the OECD Guidelines[166] and the ILO Tripartite Declaration[167] had recently been launched. It is apparent from reading Horn, who builds on Baade's thesis,[168] that there was an expectation that the OECD Guidelines, for example, would take on a more binding character as their implementation procedure was utilised, and conflicts were settled with due regard to their rules. It is certainly open to question whether, with respect to the OECD Guidelines, any such development has in fact taken place.[169] However, this does not preclude such a process occurring with the Norms, which are different in many important respects to the OECD Guidelines. Unlike the Guidelines, the Norms are legally framed. Also, they are the product of a broad-based international treaty-making body, which specialises in human rights. The Guidelines, in contrast, were developed by a small group of nations joined together to progress economic development and cooperation goals.

Brownlie adds a further category to Baade's methods by which informal prescriptions can become legally binding.[170] He describes the catalytic effects of

---

163 Article 38(1)(b), Statute of the International Court of Justice 1945, 1976 YBUN 1052.
164 Muchlinski, supra n. 107 at 47: 'the Working Group has recognised that, given the uncertainties around the precise legal status of companies and other non-state actors, some form of "soft law" exercise is a necessary starting point. This has been the normal pattern of operation in relation to the adoption of other binding human rights instruments. Hence, in the absence of state opinion to the contrary (perhaps an unlikely eventuality), some transition from 'soft' to 'hard' law is more likely to occur, with the Draft Norms as the first step in the process'.
165 Baade, supra n. 152 at 13.
166 See supra n. 31.
167 See supra n. 32.
168 Horn, 'Codes of Conduct for MNEs and Transnational Lex Mercatoria: An International Process of Learning and Law Making', in Horn (ed.), supra n. 152, 45 at 52.
169 Although the OECD Guidelines, supra n. 31, have been utilised and interpreted by the OECD's Committee on International Investment and Multinational Enterprises (CIIME) and the National Contact Points (NCPs), there is no method for enforcement of decisions made by these bodies and so the rules have little impact on the behaviour of specific companies or the state members of the OECD. For a description of the enforcement mechanisms for the Guidelines see International Council on Human Rights Policy, *Beyond Voluntarism: Human Rights and the Developing International Legal Obligations of Companies* (Versoix, Switzerland: International Council on Human Rights Policy, 2002) at 99–102, available at: http://www.international-council.org/paper_files/107_p.01.pdf. For a critique of whether the implementation of the OECD Guidelines' constitutes their becoming custom, see Kinley and Tadaki, supra n. 88.
170 Brownlie, supra n. 156 at 41.

normative statements, which, although lacking in legal status, can nonetheless be picked up by states—and other bodies that are able to take part in the orthodox international law-making process—and be 're-stated' in the practice of such bodies. Thus informal prescriptions are given legal significance by the actions of authoritative decision-makers, without necessarily hardening into a general principle of international law. An example Brownlie gives is the Truman Declaration of 1945 on the continental shelf, which had no legal status whatsoever when made, but had a 'Pied Piper effect' in that it was re-stated in practice by states and thus given legal significance. This process would enable the Norms to obtain a limited degree of legal authority in a relatively short time span. However, the debate about whether the Universal Declaration of Human Rights has crystallised into customary international law is illustrative of the imprecise and protracted nature of this process.[171] The catalytic process described by Brownlie could occur if the Norms were followed in practice by states or corporations, or both. A *de facto* implementation of the Norms is being undertaken under the auspices of the Business Leaders Initiative on Human Rights (BLIHR). As mentioned earlier, the member corporations of BLIHR are 'road-testing' the Norms over the period 2004–2006.[172] Due to the variety of corporations involved over a wide range of industry sectors (including finance, energy, manufacturing and more), each company is testing the Norms in a way that fits their own operations. This diversity of practice means that the road test may be of limited value in providing clear precedent in respect of the Norms, but it does illustrate that the Norms are amenable to being followed in business practice.[173]

Another means by which codes and other non-binding instruments may acquire legal authority is if they are used as a means of interpreting existing treaty law. Baade cites the European Union employment law case of *Hertz*[174] to illustrate how non-binding codes are used as tools of interpretation and gap-filling in existing treaty law. In *Hertz*, the provision to be interpreted was the principle of free movement of workers in the Treaty establishing the European Community[175] (EC Treaty). The company, Hertz, was accused of importing labour to Denmark in order to break a strike, which is prohibited by the ILO Tripartite Declaration, but which the EC Treaty made no provision in respect of. Hertz sought to rely on the free movement provisions of the EC

---

171   For example some rights from the Universal Declaration of Human Rights which are argued to have 'hardened' into customary international law, such as the right to freedom from torture, may have done so regardless of their inclusion in the Declaration. It is not clear at all that their inclusion in the Declaration is instrumental to their becoming customary international law.

172   As mentioned earlier, the member corporations of BLIHR have been 'road-testing' the Norms since 2004.

173   Millar, 'An Overview of the BLIHR "Road-testing" of the Norms', in *BLIHR Report 2: Work in Progress* (London, December 2004) at 15, available at: http://www.blihr.org/Pdfs/BLIHR%20Report%202004.pdf.

174   [1976] OJ C 293/12.

175   [2002] OJ C 325.

486   *HRLR* **6** (2006), 447–497

Treaty to defend its actions. The Council of the European Communities, in an opinion requested by Denmark, interpreted the free movement provisions as being of use in the positive sense of enabling workers to travel and work throughout the EC rather than as a defence in trade disputes such as this. The opinion concluded by citing the ILO Tripartite Declaration and stating its substance. In a similar fashion, the Norms could develop an indirectly binding character if, and in so far as, international forums use them as an aid to interpretation of existing international law.[176] Alternatively, it has been suggested that the various UN human rights treaty bodies might require accounts from states of how they are ensuring that corporations within their jurisdiction are complying with the international human rights obligations that the state itself has signed up to.[177] If such a situation arises, one might reasonably expect the treaty bodies to refer to the Norms as an appropriate standard against which to measure the behaviour of corporations and the efficacy of their regulation by the state.[178]

In respect of the indirect means of making the Norms binding, there is another, unorthodox, avenue that states might take. It has been argued that, if a state makes a declaration of commitment (or unilateral action) to a non-binding code, such as the Norms, that declaration can give rise to legal obligations on the part of the state not to go back on the declaration; a type of estoppel is formed to prevent this.[179] Thus, if states commit to the Norms through

---

176   Human rights treaties are increasingly viewed as 'living instruments' (see, for example, *Loizidou v Turkey (Preliminary Objections)* A 310 (1995); (1995) 20 EHRR 99 at para. 71) and the use of other treaties and even informal documentation such as draft instruments as interpretative aids is not uncommon (for example, the European Court of Human Rights has referred to ILO Conventions in a number of cases, including *Van Der Mussele v Belgium* A 70 (1983); (1984) 6 EHRR 163 at para. 32; and the Inter-American Court of Human Rights has relied on the Draft UN Declaration on the Rights of Indigenous Peoples: see, for example, the Concurring Opinion of Judge Sergio García Ramírez in *Mayagna (Sumo) Awas Tingni Community v Nicaragua* (2001) IACtHR Series C 79; 10 IHRR 758 (2003) at para. 8).

177   Typically, international human rights treaties require states to ensure to all within their jurisdiction, the protection afforded by the rights in the relevant treaty; see, for example, Article 2(1), ICCPR and Article 2(1), ICESCR. The Human Rights Committee has stressed that obligations placed on states to ensure Covenant rights 'will only be fully discharged if individuals are protected by the State, not just against violations of Covenant rights by its agents, but also against acts committed by private persons or entities that would impair the enjoyment of Covenant rights in so far as they are amenable to application between private persons or entities'. HRC General Comment No. 31, The Nature of the General Legal Obligations Imposed on States Parties to the Covenant, 26 May 2004, CCPR/C/21/Rev.1/Add.13; 11 IHRR 905 (2004). The Committee for Economic, Social and Cultural Rights (CESCR) routinely stresses the responsibilities of corporations in their General Comments, for example in: CESCR General Comment No. 12, The Right to Adequate Food (Article 11), 12 May 1999, E/C.12/1999/5; 6 IHRR 902 (1999) at paras 20 and 27; and CESCR General Comment No. 14, The Right to the Highest Attainable Standard of Health (Article 12), 11 August 2000, E/C.12/2000/4; 8 IHRR 1 (2001) at paras 42 and 55.

178   See Nolan, 'With Power Comes Responsibility: Human Rights and Corporate Accountability', (2005) 28 *University of New South Wales Law Journal* 581 at 607.

179   Baade, supra n. 152 at 17–9 citing the *Nuclear Tests Case (Australia v France)*, Merits, Judgment, ICJ Reports 1974, 253.

a formal declaration, intending to be bound to that declaration, an obligation to implement and enforce the Norms would be legally effective as such for those states.[180] This is very much a defensive mechanism that might be utilised in the long term to hold states to their commitments to the Norms. There have been no such commitments to date.

Finally, aside from the somewhat distant prospect of the Norms (or some derivative document) becoming a treaty, it is conceivable that the Norms might be adopted by the United Nations as a declaration, resolution or some other strictly non-binding instrument. Any one of these outcomes would significantly increase the Norm's potential to develop into positive law. Michael Bothe has analysed the factors that indicate the authority of a non-binding instrument and its potential to create legal obligations. His view is that the circumstances that have led to the adoption of an instrument, and the degree of agreement upon which it is based, are both significant.[181] Also important is the form of the instrument (whether a declaration or a resolution); the content of the instrument; the political rank of the organ adopting the instrument; and the implementation procedures contained in the instrument. Thus, the Norms are more likely to take on a binding character if they are adopted by the UN General Assembly, with a broad support base from different governments. The creation of an effective implementation procedure would also be crucial, as this would provide proof to TNCs and states that compliance is expected. It would further provide a means of exerting pressure to secure compliance.[182] But this is some way down the track. What is clear at the present time is that there are no immediate international legal implications of the Norms beyond their re-statement of existing law in certain paragraphs. There are various ways in which the legal importance of the Norms might develop, extending from the hardening of the Norms into law through the creation of an international convention including an enforcement mechanism like the International Criminal Court,[183] to a development into 'soft law' through the adoption

---

180 Brownlie, supra n. 156 at 40 does not agree with Baade's characterisation of legally binding unilateral acts because he refutes that one can discover acquiescence by states in the face of a whole set of legal principles such as the Norms. His view is that the reaction of the state in the *Nuclear Tests Case* was to a very specific setting and specific obligations on particular occasions in respect of particular subjects.

181 Bothe, 'Legal and Non-Legal Norms—A Meaningful Distinction in International Relations?', (1980) 11 *New York International Law Journal* 65 at 78.

182 In this respect, see Nolan's insistence that there must be 'credible procedures for their [the Norms] monitoring and verification' and her overview of the 'multiplicity of possible approaches' by which this could be achieved, supra n. 178 at 606 *et seq.*

183 See Muchlinski, supra n. 107 at 50. He sounds a note of caution about a 'hard law' approach—even hard law agreements, in provisions concerning controversial social issues, have been put into very general, and probably meaningless, hortatory language, simply to show that something has been done, where there is little intention to see these provisions have any real legal effect.

488   *HRLR* **6** (2006), 447–497

of the Norms by states or other international law-creating bodies and their re-statement in state practice (Brownlie's 'catalytic effect'[184]) or their use in interpretation of international treaties.

D. Domestic Legal Implications of the Norms

It is at the domestic level that international law, including international human rights law, finds its most effective expression of legal effect. And so it would be with the Norms, in so far as they are and might further be implemented within a national human rights framework.[185] This fits with the traditional model of implementation of international human rights law, in which the front line of implementation and enforcement is to be found in domestic legislatures, executives and courts; international apparatus are nearly always secondary to these municipal organs.[186] However, even as a non-binding international code, the Norms might still have domestic impact. It is argued in this respect that since codes or other non-binding 'solemn high-level endorsements of preferred courses of conduct'[187] can become a source of binding international obligations for states, states will rely on and utilise such codes to fill in gaps in the relevant law and practice at the domestic level. Thereby, 'the Code may become a springboard for legally creative action by national courts and other agencies'.[188] In the same vein, others have cited the less specific example of how principles from the Universal Declaration of Human Rights were picked up by domestic courts and applied as international law despite the Declaration's 'designedly non-binding status'.[189] The Norms could similarly shape legal and policy thinking at the state level, or otherwise be utilised in domestic courts, despite their status as

184   Supra n. 156.
185   The Norms do not contain any jurisdictional provisions or 'home state control'. Para. 17, Norms addresses state implementation, providing: 'States should establish and reinforce the necessary legal and administrative framework for ensuring that the Norms and other relevant national and international laws are implemented by transnational corporations and other business enterprises.'
186   For discussions of this international/domestic law nexus generally, see Cassese, *International Law*, 2nd edn (Oxford: Oxford University Press, 2005) at 213–37; and in respect of human rights specifically, see Donnelly, *Universal Human Rights in Theory and Practice*, 2nd edn (Ithaca: Cornell University Press, 2003) at Chapter 2, particularly 34–7.
187   Baade, supra n. 152 at 29.
188   Ibid., quoting the UN Commission on Transnational Corporations: Certain Modalities for Implementation of a Code of Conduct in Relation to its Possible Legal Nature, 22 December 1978, E/C.10/AC.2/9. Baade also (at 29–32) cites the German case of *Nigerian Cultural Property* BGHZ 59 (1972), as an example of the use of internationally accepted standards of public policy (here a UNESCO recommendation and a treaty to which West Germany (as it was then) was not party) for the purposes of domestic adjudication of a transnational dispute.
189   Brownlie, supra n. 156 at 42. See also, in an Australian High Court case, Kirby J's invocation of the Universal Declaration of Human Rights in his discussion on the 'interpretive principle' in his dissenting judgment in *Newcrest Mining (WA) Ltd v Commonwealth* (1997) 190 *Commonwealth Law Reports* 513.

an informal statement of non-binding international law. Although, at present, the latter effect is likely only in situations where the state already has relevant legislative provisions relating to the same matters covered by the Norms, the former effect may have greater potential.[190]

Use could also be made of the Norms in private law suits without their prior adoption as a convention or other legally binding instrument. For example, an action in contract could be brought against a company where adherence to the standards contained within the Norms is a term of a contract to which the company is a party, and the company fails to comply with one or more of the Norms. Such an action could also be brought on grounds of misrepresentation, or false or misleading conduct, if a company holds out that it is complying with the Norms and this turns out to be false.[191] An action for misrepresentation could be brought by any party, including a consumer who has purchased from the company in reliance upon the assertion of compliance with the Norms.[192] Finally, negligence actions might be brought in which the tortious standard of care is based upon the Norms. Thus, it could be alleged that failure to comply with the Norms is evidence that the company in question is not meeting accepted standards of conduct—including in respect of corporate disclosure[193]—and that the company is, therefore, not exercising reasonable care or diligence in conformity with generally accepted standards.[194]

190   See, for example, discussion in Kinley and Tadaki, supra n. 88 at 958–60; and Murphy's more general advancement of his 'carrot and stick' middle way of bringing 'government more actively back into the process of promoting good corporate conduct, but would do so by both reinforcing the value and benefits of the voluntary codes to MNCs [carrots] and holding MNCs to the codes to which they have subscribed [sticks]', in Murphy, 'Taking Multinational Codes of Conduct to the Next Level', (2005) 43 *Columbia Journal of Transnational Law* 389 at 423 *et seq.*

191   The prospect of such litigation, however faint, appears to have been of sufficient concern to some signatory corporations to the Global Compact to have prompted the Global Compact secretariat to have taken the extraordinary step of issuing an 'indemnity letter' to those of its concerned clients stating, in effect, that their agreement to abide by the principles contained in the Global Compact constitutes no legal expectation that they would necessarily do so. Georg Kell, Executive Head of the Global Compact, revealed this much in an 'in conversation' session at the Business for Social Responsibility Annual Conference, New York, 11 November 2004 [notes on file with author].

192   For an example of such litigation see *Marc Kasky v Nike* 27 Cal 4th 939 (2002) and the US Supreme Court decision dismissing a writ of certiorari, *Nike v Marc Kasky* 123 S.Ct 2554 (2003). For a discussion of the Australian position and in particular the impact of sections 52, 53 and 75AZC of the Trade Practices Act 1974 (Commonwealth) which prohibit misleading and deceptive conduct on the part of companies, see Spencer, 'Talking about Social Responsibility: Liability for Misleading and Deceptive Statements in Corporate Codes of Conduct', (2003) 29 *Monash University Law Review* 297.

193   See Nolan's, supra n. 178 at 609–10, assessment of case law and various domestic legislative initiatives in respect of disclosure and reporting requirements relating to human rights matters.

194   Muchlinski, supra n. 107 at 51.

490   *HRLR* **6** (2006), 447–497

One method of encouraging the development of the Norms as legal standards is by incorporating them into procurement procedures. Governments could lead by example through buying goods and services from Norm-certified companies.[195] The Norms would then become a term in all government procurement contracts, thus enabling them to be domestically enforced if the companies supplying governments are found to be in breach.[196] Alternatively, regulatory authorities,[197] or ethical investment indexing bodies,[198] might adopt the Norms as part of their mandatory reporting requirements. For example, socially responsible investment (SRI) performance criteria in the area of human rights could be based on the Norms. In this way, companies subject to the regulation or participating in the ethical investment index would be required to report on human rights issues as laid out in the Norms and would be subject to legal sanction if they misstated their compliance. Thus the Norms would take on a legally binding character despite their current informal status.

E. *Legal Framework Rather Than Voluntary Initiative*

One of the most outspoken detractors of the Norms, the Vice-President of Shell, Robin Aram, while speaking on behalf of the ICC, made the following statement

---

195   Government departments/local authorities commonly adhere to voluntary/external standards in their procurement policies. See, for example, San Francisco's 'Sweat Shop Free Ordinance' on procurement implemented in 2005, details of which are available at: http://www.sfgov.org/site/mayor.index.asp?id=32792.

196   It is not uncommon that government procurement contract regulations require compliance with broad human rights standards. See, for example, provision 26 of the Canadian Human Rights Code, RSO 1990, Chapter H19, regarding discrimination in employment under government contracts; and Section 1120.2570, 'Equal Employment Opportunity: Affirmative Action' of the Illinois Administrative Code, Title 44: Government and Procurement Contracts, Subtitle B: Supplemental Procurement Rules, Chapter XIV: Comptroller, Part 1120 Standard Procurement, available at: http://www.ilga.gov/commission/jcar/admincode/044/04401120sections.html.

197   Kinley and Tadaki, supra n. 88 at 956–8, discuss some of the legislative and regulatory authorities that have adopted mandatory reporting requirements on social and/or environmental issues. See also Nolan, supra n. 178 at 608 (in particular, the discussion in footnote 129 and accompanying text).

198   For example:
(i) the Dow Jones Sustainability Indexes, launched in 1999, available at: http://www.sustainability-indexes.com/default.html;
(ii) the Ethibel Sustainability Index, available at: http://www.ethibel.be/subs.e/4.index/main.html;
(iii) the FTSE4Good Index Series, available at: http://www.ftse.com/ftse4good/index.jsp; and
(iv) the Johannesburg Stock Exchange's Socially Responsible Investment Index, available at: http://www.jse.co.za/sri/index.htm.

in an interview: 'The problem is the legalistic form that has been used in drafting the Norms... We [the ICC] didn't like the look of it. It contained too many *whereases*.'[199] This negative perception of the Norms may well be the crux of the matter. As we have noted throughout this article, business alliances have advanced a number of substantial and procedural criticisms of the Norms. Some of these, such as the apparent novelty of such a venture in international law, the imprecision of some of the language used and the concerns over divisions of responsibility, are, at least on their face understandable and even appealing, but none stand up to analysis. It is evident that a multi-faceted attack was used to obscure the true message, which is, quite simply, that business alliances, in the main, do not want TNCs to be held legally accountable for the human rights abuses that they may inflict or are complicit in, and that the Norms are seen as a first step towards such regulation.[200] The question of whether TNCs should be made legally accountable for their human rights violations can be answered in part by looking at the effectiveness of voluntary initiatives in this area. Corporate codes of conduct and policies addressing human rights have proliferated in recent years,[201] but so far these have been unable to stem the flow of human rights violations by TNCs.[202] For a number of reasons, such initiatives are weak in terms of the protection they give. Often authored by the companies themselves, these codes and policies regularly involve careful picking and choosing of the rights to be included. Internal codes only bind those corporations which adopt and implement them, which are by no means all TNCs,[203] thus leaving an un-level playing field in which

199   SustainAbility, 'In the Hot Seat: Robin Aram, Vice President of External Relations, Policy and Social Responsibility, Shell', 24 February 2005, available at: http://www.sustainability. com/network/business-leader.asp?id=219. In point of fact, the term is not used anywhere in the Norms!

200   Their concern is to avoid the construction of the type of regulatory regime that allows for an 'escalation to punishment'. Braithwaite, 'Rewards and Regulation', (2002) 29 *Journal of Law and Society* 12 at 21, sees such punitary enforcement mechanisms as providing the only real 'incentives for the rational actor' (that is the market-conscious corporation) to actually comply with the system's provisions.

201   See Murphy, supra n. 190 at 413–20; and Kinley and Tadaki, supra n. 88 at 953–62. For a more comprehensive compilation see Jägers, supra n. 137.

202   Growing corporate spheres of influence have led to even more areas in which corporations are impinging on rights. New areas such as internet censorship have come to the forefront, such as when internet provider Yahoo! came under attack for giving the Chinese Government details of internet activists and journalists, see Amnesty International, 'Yahoo's data contributes to arrests in China: free Shi Tao from prison in China!', ASA 17/003/2006, 31 January 2006. In relation to resources, while oil remains a critical area, another growing area of concern is water, with Coca-Cola at the centre of debate on sustainability and community access, as well as being the subject of ongoing criticism regarding its relationship with workers and unions, particularly in Columbia, see Srivastava, 'Coca-Cola and Water—An Unsustainable Relationship', India Resource Centre, 8 March 2006, available at: http://www.indiaresource.org/campaigns/coke/2006/ cokewwf.html.

203   Joseph, 'The Human Rights Accountability of MNEs', in Kamminga and Zia-Zarifi (eds), *Liability of Multinational Corporations Under International Law* (The Hague: Kluwer Law International, 2000) 75 at 82–3.

492   *HRLR* **6** (2006), 447–497

companies that stick out their necks and do the right thing are penalised.[204] This highlights two issues: first, that infringements are often the result of the actions of rogue corporations or those with little or no reputation to protect; and second, the challenge of determining how far we ought to make TNCs at or near the top of the supply chain responsible for the actions of those further down it. Thus far, broad-based legislative proposals aimed at levelling this playing field at the national level have failed to be translated into law.[205]

Perhaps most significantly, it is strongly argued that such voluntary measures will be ineffective, and thereby lose their legitimacy, unless there are enforcement and reparations provisions put in place, and such schemes are independently monitored.[206] Currently, this is seldom the case, and consequently, companies may either pay lip service to human rights, using codes as mere public relations exercises, or they may follow a code until such time as serious profits are at stake, at which point human rights considerations are pushed aside.[207] Therefore, self-regulation cannot be relied on as the primary means for ensuring respect of basic human rights by TNCs, if only because of its necessary reliance on an 'internal' frame of reference rather than, as Christine Parker trenchantly argues for, a system of external legal enforcement built on social (i.e. non-corporate) values and expectations.[208] Indeed, it is precisely this sort of thinking in the broader field of corporate governance that prompted consideration of extending the type of regulation of financial probity as represented by such legislation as the Sarbanes-Oxley Act in the United States,[209] to cover corporate social responsibilities,[210] and the 2004 amendments to the US Sentencing Guidelines requiring Boards of Directors not only to abide by the law, but further to cultivate an 'organizational culture that

---

204   For example, British Petroleum (BP) Plc in line with its internal codes and policies published details of the bribes that it gave to the authorities in Angola. The authorities responded by throwing BP out of Angola, thus allowing other less scrupulous oil companies to take over the business.

205   See McBeth, 'A Look at Corporate Code of Conduct Legislation', (2004) 33 *Common Law Review* 222.

206   For accounts of a number of these arguments see Murphy, supra n. 190 at 420–32.

207   See McCarthy, supra n. 61.

208   Parker, 'Meta-Regulation: Legal Accountability for Corporate Social Responsibility', in McBarnett, Voiculescu and Campbell (eds), *The New Corporate Accountability: Corporate Social Responsibility and the Law* (Cambridge: Cambridge University Press, forthcoming).

209   Sarbanes-Oxley Act (2002) Pub. L. No. 107–204.

210   See, for example, in the United Kingdom, s.173(1)(d), Companies Bill 2006, which, within the general duty of directors to act in ways that 'promote the success of the company', obliges directors to have regard to 'the impact of the company's operations on the community and the environment'. In Australia, see the discussion paper produced by the Australian Government's Corporations and Market Advisory Committee (CAMAC) into the question of amending the current scope of directors' duties under the Australian Corporations Act 2001 (Commonwealth) to require directors to consider the interests of stakeholders other than shareholders when making corporate decisions. See CAMAC, 'Corporate Social Responsibility Discussion Paper', November 2005 available at: www.camac.org.au, along with further updates of the inquiry. See also, Nolan, supra n. 178 at 610 (at footnote 141 and accompanying text).

encourages ethical conduct'[211]—an initiative which John Sherman argues has prompted US courts to interpret the fiduciary duties of directors to encompass taking due heed of the interests of stakeholders beyond merely those of the shareholders.[212]

Considering the imposition of fundamental, international legal obligations on such non-state actors as individuals[213] and armed oppression groups,[214] it would be anomalous for companies to remain almost wholly outside the ambit of international law. This is particularly striking when one considers the enormous economic power that TNCs wield and the often considerable size of their social footprint. The growing importance of companies in the face of increased 'contracting out' of state functions attaches particular urgency to the need to scrutinise corporate activities and to punish corporate wrongs.[215]

5. Conclusion

Despite their imperfections, it cannot be overlooked that the Norms already represent a big leap forward in the setting of human rights standards for TNCs at the levels of both international and domestic law. Their traits of being universal, broad-based and authoritative set them apart from all other initiatives

---

211 Available at: http://www.ussc.gov/2005guid/8b2..htm.
212 See Sherman, 'Human Rights Implications of the 2004 Amendments to the US Sentencing Guidelines for Organizational Defendants', Draft Position Paper prepared for the International Commission of Jurists Expert Legal Panel on Corporate Complicity in International Crimes, available at: http://www.icj.org/news.php3?id.article=3910&lang=en.
213 For example, in respect of the crimes listed in Articles 6, 7 and 8, Rome Statute of the International Criminal Court 1998, 2187 UNTS 90.
214 In this respect, Article 1(1), Additional Protocol II to the Geneva Conventions relating to the Protection of Victims of Non-International Armed Conflicts 1977, 1125 UNTS 609, expressly binds 'other [ie non-state] organized armed groups'.
215 An example of a traditional function of the state now taken over by corporations is that of interrogating prisoners of war: this has been demonstrated in Iraq where companies such as Titan Corporation and CACI International have been accused of torture and unlawful killing of Iraqi prisoners at Abu Ghraib prison (Iraq) in the case of *Sami Abbas Al Rawi et al. v Titan Corp.*, S.D. Cal., No. 04 CV 1143R (NLS), complaint filed 9 June 2004, available at: http://www.mirkflem.pwp.blueyonder.co.uk/pdf/alrawititan60904cmp.pdf. See also a complaint lodged in 2005 with the Australian National Contact Point (NCP) under the OECD Guidelines for Multinational Enterprises by a number of human rights NGOs against Global Solutions Limited, a corporation that has been contracted by the Australian Government to administer a number of detention centres across Australia. The complaint alleges that the corporation has been complicit in a series of human rights violations including detention without trial or judicial review, detention of children in circumstances other than as a last resort, and physical and psychological abuses of detainees. See 'Statement by Australian National Contact Point: GSL Australia Specific Instance', 6 April 2006, available at: http://www.oecd.org/dataoecd/28/2/36453400.pdf.

494   HRLR **6** (2006), 447–497

and this, in itself, has an inherent value. The SRSG has an important role in ensuring that this is not lost, either by throwing the baby (of inherent value) out with the (politically compromised) bathwater, or by overlooking what little derivative legal status the Norms have already. With respect to this latter concern, the SRSG, for example, cannot ignore the legal force of the Norms where they re-state what is already international human rights law in respect of states, and by derivation, what have become domestic legal human rights obligations in respect of corporations. As a 'work in progress', moving through the UN human rights machinery (albeit haltingly and at the lower end of the UN hierarchy), the Norms in their entirety gain a certain status, best described as soft law, and the newly minted Human Rights Council will be in a position to preserve this.

Evidently, the Commission, that the Human Rights Council has replaced, took the view that what was needed was further deliberation, discussion and debate in respect of the whole question of the relationship between human rights and corporations, and, especially, whether there ought to be some sort of supranational regulatory regime established to police it. In response to this, we pose a series of questions. First, can a company infringe the human rights of individuals? It is clear that this is not only possible, but is an all too frequent reality, albeit systematically perpetrated by a small minority of corporations, or inadvertently or carelessly by many more.[216] Second, should there be a set of international human rights standards by which the conduct of corporations can be judged?[217] Or, in the alternative, should companies be adhering to the laws of the home or host states in which they locate themselves and setting their own standards where lacunae in those state laws exist? In our view, the answer to each of these questions is 'yes'. Not only would such an initiative generally enhance the international framework for the protection and promotion of human rights, more specifically it would prompt and assist states to develop and strengthen their own domestic laws that govern corporate conduct relating especially to labour and workplace rights, rights to privacy and security of person, and environmental, health, education and housing standards within their respective jurisdictions. Moreover, these enhancements at the levels of international and domestic law would surely push individual corporations and peak industry bodies to bolster their own voluntary standards in the area of human rights compliance. If these inter-connected outcomes are to be realised, the task in front of those who want to build upon, rather than dismantle, the Norms is to overcome the fact that companies have set their faces against the Norms because of the enforcement mechanisms contained therein, despite these mechanisms being putative at best, and there

---

216   See, supra Part 3 A ('Non-State Parties under International Law').
217   Or as stated in the Report of the United Nations High Commissioner, supra n. 13 at 16, under 'Outstanding Issues': is there a need for a UN statement of universal standards setting out the responsibilities of business entities with regard to human rights?

being a strong argument that the establishment of clear and explicit standards on human rights is very much in their interest.[218]

Flowing from the above, the final question is the key: is there any point in setting out standards without any means of enforcing them? This article has shown that there is some point. Soft law standards can be used in a number of ways to effect hard law outcomes. Even fully fledged public international law is by its very nature often difficult to enforce, but this does not detract from its legal and political importance. That said, something more is needed to ensure that the standards are not simply ignored as toothless tigers. Over 20 years ago, Norbert Horn identified the discrepancy between the transnational reach of TNCs' business activities and the territorial limits of national legal and administrative control over the economy, as constituting the classic problem raised by TNCs.[219] That dilemma remains true today. This problem is exacerbated in the area of human rights by the fact that many states are unwilling to regulate TNCs within their jurisdiction or beyond. There are many reasons why a mechanism which seeks to fix liability on TNCs through domestic regulation alone will fail, including the fact that sometimes states are in connivance with the very TNCs that are encroaching on human rights guarantees. States are also notoriously inconsistent, or at any rate self-serving,[220] in their respect for and enforcement of international human rights, which thereby calls into question the efficacy of any approach that relies solely on states to enforce human rights obligations on TNCs.[221]

The most practical and effective method of ensuring that standards are enforced is, in light of the current state of international human rights law, a treaty that speaks to states and obliges them to regulate the conduct of TNCs in relation to human rights in their own jurisdictions.[222] Ultimately and ideally, therefore, we are looking for a mature instrument of public international law to emerge, after appropriate modification and amendment, from the presently neophyte Norms. In that way, when standards are not enforced in

---

218   Corporations are very adept at handling compliance frameworks in respect of matters such as product specification and financial accountability and incorporating them within their strategic and operational planning. Likewise compliance with human rights obligations could and would inform corporate decision making, and therefore, be aided by the establishment of universally agreed, relatively clear transnational standards.

219   Horn, supra n. 168 at 50.

220   On this particular point, see Chapter 4 in Goldsmith and Posner, *The Limits of International Law* (Oxford: Oxford University Press, 2005) especially at 119–26.

221   Deva, 'Human Rights Violations by Multinational Corporations and International Law: Where from Here?', (2003–04) 19 *Connecticut Journal of International Law* 1.

222   As the UN High Commissioner for Human Rights was reported to have 'stressed in her statements that even though states retain the primary responsibility for ensuring the protection of human rights under the human rights treaties, there is a new awareness that such responsibility entails ensuring that companies operating from or within their jurisdiction must not undermine existing human rights obligations or the international rule of law'. See Weissbrodt and Parker, Report of the Seminar to Discuss UN Human Rights Guidelines for Companies, 29–31 March 2001, E/CN.4/Sub.2/2001/WG.2/WP.1/Add.3 at paras 11–2.

496   *HRLR* **6** (2006), 447–497

host states under existing domestic laws, victims might be able to seek redress in the home state. It would be reasonable to expect, furthermore, that the establishment of an international regime would increase both the instance and range of a state's definition of what constitutes a home state, a definition wide enough to encompass the countries in which TNCs locate significant assets, as well as their headquarters. Thereby, victims might be able to look to a number of different national jurisdictions so that, if the home state has not signed up to the treaty, redress could be sought in another state which was a signatory. And indeed, there appears to be a pattern of wider acceptance by domestic courts, in countries such as the United Kingdom and Australia, that jurisdictional hurdles should not prevent claims being heard. The European case of *Owusu v Jackson*[223] spelt the end of *forum non conveniens* in England and Wales, while in Australia a claimant-friendly legal test for *forum non conveniens* has been in place for some time.[224] These developments, furthermore, at least allow these common law countries to sit more comfortably alongside civil code states where there is an absence of any such jurisdictional barrier.[225]

One immediate way forward is to focus on persuading the SRSG that an international legal document of this type needs to be drawn up, and that the Norms, or something like them, can and should be used as a basis for such an initiative. In that way, the task as identified by the Special Representative himself will be advanced—namely, that we must address the 'core challenge of business and human rights, [which] lies in devising instruments of corporate and public governance to contain and reduce the tendencies' of corporations to 'run afoul of [their] own corporate principles or community expectations of responsible corporate behaviour'.[226]

And yet, the *Realpolitik* which constitutes the background to any international law route is the slow and tortuous process of treaty-creation. Presumably partly in recognition of this difficulty, the Norms contain other interim and parallel enforcement measures such as incorporation into internal operation rules and contracts with other parties. The current Norms document attempts to cover all bases; it is not the case that we necessarily need all of the forms of enforcement which it provides, but, until such time as we achieve the 'gold standard' set out previously (whereby the Norms are widely and effectively enforced through national courts), the Norms' piece-meal measures, such as incorporation into contracts and the like, fill the gap in the interim.

---

223   C-281/02, [2005] QB 801, ECJ.
224   See *BHP Billiton Ltd v Schultz* (2004) 2 DDCR 78; *Dagi v BHP* [1995] 1 VR 428; *Gutnick v Dow Jones and Company Inc* [2001] VSC 305; *Dow Jones and Company Inc v Gutnick* (2002) 194 ALR 433; and *Regie Nationale des Usines Renault SA v Zhang* (2002) 210 CLR 491.
225   The resort to pursuing corporations through litigation in civil jurisdictions is traditionally nothing like that found in common law jurisdictions. For an account of this and other features of the position in France, see Colonomos and Sanisto, 'Vive La France! French Multinationals and Human Rights', (2005) 27 *Human Rights Quarterly* 1307.
226   Interim Report at para. 23.

It seems then, that in the short term, the private law implications of the Norms will be fairly limited. The United States is the only jurisdiction in which—through ATCA—violations of international human rights law by corporations can be the subject of civil suits no matter where the violation occurs[227] (and there has not yet been a judgment against a defendant corporation under ATCA).[228] However, in the context of ATCA, the definition of international law is limited,[229] and in no way encompasses all the rights contained in the Norms. Greater private law implications require states to put the Norms on a full treaty footing, and then to sign up to the resultant instrument. The primary obstacle to this is the strength of the corporate lobby's opposition to, and criticism of, the Norms. This article has shown that many of the criticisms of the Norms fall away when the document is seen for what it really is: not a treaty, and not national law, but a draft set of standards that, in their present form, guide and suggest rather than compel.

By framing issues as standards and responsibilities—and purported legal standards and responsibilities at that—the Norms have promoted awareness, discussion and debate and have managed to flush out both extreme and compromised reactions to what are unarguably complicated and confronting questions. It is our view that far from contaminating the debate by exciting controversy, the Norms have helped to mark out the boundaries of debate. To dismiss them now as a distraction would be counterproductive in that the powerful arguments for something like them will certainly not disappear, and indeed, if anything, are likely to be heightened by the sense of having to make up lost ground. In any event, form aside, the Norms' subject matter of human rights is, by nature, not about unambiguous absolutes, but rather is about circumstantial interpretation and balancing of competing rights and interests. The Norms provide a starting point for the proclamation and protection of human rights standards, and as such are necessarily less than perfect. The fact that as a draft instrument of public international law the Norms have already provoked such interest and debate, while at the same time obtaining a level of derivative authority within private, domestic legal relations, represents an important first step in what will inevitably be a long journey.

---

227 Though courts in a number of civil code countries have the capacity to prosecute individuals and corporations through their exercise of universal jurisdiction for crimes against humanity and other egregious human rights violations. For a survey of European states whose courts have this capacity, see Breining-Kaufmann, '"The Legal Matrix of Human Rights and Trade Law" State Obligations versus Private Rights and Obligations', in Cottier, Pauwelyn and Bürgi (eds), supra n. 15, 95 at 120–2.

228 See Interim Report at para. 62.

229 In the case of *Sosa v Alvarez-Machain* 542 US 692 (2004) at 732, the US Supreme Court proclaimed that to qualify, the purported international law must be 'specific', 'obligatory' and 'universal'. For discussion of the implications of the case for corporations, see Vázquez, '*Sosa v Alvarez-Machain* and the Human Rights Claims against Corporations under the Alien Tort Statute', in Cottier, Pauwelyn and Bürgi (eds), supra n. 15, 137 at 137–47.

[12]

Engage, Embed, and Embellish: Theory Versus Practice in the Corporate Social Responsibility Movement

John M. Conley[*] and Cynthia A. Williams[**]

I. INTRODUCTION

One of the most striking developments in the business world over the last decade has been the emergence of a coherent and energetic "corporate social responsibility" (CSR) movement.[1] This Article reports the results of an empirical study of that movement. "CSR," as it is universally referred to, has as its theoretical base the notion that the responsibility of a corporation extends beyond the traditional Anglo-American objective of providing financial returns to its shareholders. Instead, CSR proponents have argued, the legitimate concerns of a corporation should include such broader objectives as sustainable growth, equitable employment practices, and long-term social and

* William Rand Kenan, Jr. Professor, University of North Carolina School of Law.
** Richard W. and Marie L. Corman Scholar, Professor of Law, University of Illinois College of Law.

    1. For an introduction to the CSR movement and its theoretical underpinnings, see Ruth V. Aguilera et al., *Putting the S Back in Corporate Social Responsibility: A Multi-Level Theory of Social Change in Organizations*, 31 ACAD. MGMT. REV. (forthcoming 2006), *available at* http://ssrn.com/abstract=820466; Ronen Shamir, *Between Self-Regulation and the Alien Tort Claims Act: On the Contested Concept of Corporate Social Responsibility*, 38 L. & SOC'Y REV. 635, 643-49 (2004); *cf.* Paul Hohnen, *Setting the Standard in Salvador*, ETHICAL CORP., Mar. 21, 2005, *available at* http://www.ethicalcorp.com/content.asp?ContentID=3570 (reporting on the debate over meaning of social responsibility).

environmental well-being.[2] Corporate managers, it is argued, should consider not only their shareholders in making their decisions but also a variety of "stakeholder" constituencies, including employees, residents of communities affected by their activities, governments, and organizations advocating for various social and environmental interests.

The CSR movement has manifested itself in a variety of ways. On the legal front, it has thus far had limited impact in this country. Although Enron and related disasters have led to legislation to make corporate conduct more transparent, the focus has been principally on financial issues.[3] In Europe and the United Kingdom, however, the CSR movement has been a major factor in moving corporate disclosure in the stakeholder direction. On the Continent, stakeholder interests have long enjoyed greater recognition than in the "Anglo-Saxon" corporate world,[4] as evidenced by the requirements in some European countries of labor representation on boards of directors and facility-level works council.[5] Building on this tradition of stakeholder thinking, several countries now require direct attention to stakeholder interests through highly detailed disclosure of social and environmental risks and impact.[6] Those countries with the most expansive disclosure regulations are the very countries where a stakeholder concept of the firm has been most dominant: France, Germany, the Netherlands, Belgium, Norway, Denmark, and Sweden.[7] At the European Union level, though progress has been uneven, the trend has been in the same general direction.[8] The EU's own gradual turn in the direction of mandatory disclosure is clearly based on the broader European penetration of the stakeholder concept.

The United Kingdom has become an especially interesting case as it pursues what we have elsewhere described as a "third way."[9] In some important respects, the United

---

2. *See* Brian R. Cheffins, *The Metamorphosis of "Germany Inc.": The Case of Executive Pay*, 49 AM. J. COMP. L. 497, 498-501 (2001) (providing an overview of the shareholder-stakeholder divide); Ben Schiller, *Stock Price Maximisation 'Drives' Corporate Irresponsibility*, ETHICAL CORP., June 8, 2005, *available at* http://www.ethicalcorp.com/content.asp?ContentID=3721 (attacking corporate managers' focus on short-term stock performance).

3. *See* Douglas M. Branson, *Corporate Governance "Reform" and the New Corporate Social Responsibility*, 62 U. PITT. L. REV. 605, 611-15 (2001).

4. For an introduction to the extensive literature on this topic, see Ruth V. Aguilera & Gregory Jackson, *The Cross-National Diversity of Corporate Governance: Dimensions and Determinants*, 28 ACAD. MGMT. REV. 447 (2003) (proposing a theory that explains the differences between the Continental European stakeholder model and the British and American shareholder model).

5. *See* Catherine Barnard et al., *"Fog in the Channel, Continent Isolated": Britain as a Model for EU Social and Economic Policy?*, 34 INDUS. REL. J. 461, 473 (2003) (describing the German situation).

6. We have described and analyzed these European developments in detail in Cynthia A. Williams & John M. Conley, *An Emerging Third Way? The Erosion of the Anglo-American Shareholder Value Construct*, 38 CORNELL INT'L L.J. 493 (2005). For general background on expanded social and environmental disclosure, see Cynthia A. Williams, *The Securities and Exchange Commission and Corporate Social Transparency*, 112 HARV. L. REV. 1197, 1273-99 (1999).

7. *See* Aguilera & Jackson, *supra* note 4, at 454-57.

8. For a review of these EU-level developments, see Williams & Conley, *supra* note 6, at 503-10. The Commission of the EU is due to issue a set of CSR proposals by the end of March 2006. The emphasis is expected to be on incentives for voluntary corporate action rather than new regulation. *See* Stephen Gardner, *European Commission and Corporate Responsibility—Favouring a Light Touch*, ETHICAL CORP: EUROPE, Mar. 15, 2006, *available at* http://www.ethicalcorp.com/content.asp?ContentID=4149.

9. Williams & Conley, *supra* note 6, at 510-22.

States and the UK continue to share corporate law values. These include broad-based, dispersed share ownership, in contrast to Europe and Japan, which feature ownership by families, dominant shareholders, or banks.[10] The United States and Britain both have well-developed securities markets[11] and depend on financial transparency, stock market valuations, and the market for corporate control to promote managerial accountability.[12]

In other respects, though, the UK is beginning to diverge from the American model in pursuit of a long-term "enlightened shareholder value" perspective that incorporates significant elements of European stakeholder theory. This divergence is driven in substantial part by institutional interests that can be loosely characterized as elements of the CSR movement.[13] These interests include the British government; institutional investors, particularly pension funds and insurance companies (which are increasingly concerned about climate change and other long-term environmental risks); and nongovernmental organizations (NGOs). The pressures that such institutions bring to bear have yet to be felt anywhere near as strongly in the United States.

Perhaps the best example of the growing—but not yet dominant—influence of CSR thinking in the UK is the ebb-and-flow process of developing a new code concerning the disclosure of environmental and social risk. On March 21, 2005, after an extensive public consultation process, the British government promulgated regulations that would have required 1290 British-based companies listed on the London Stock Exchange, the New York Stock Exchange (NYSE), or NASDAQ to publish an annual Operating and Financial Review and Directors Report (OFR).[14] The OFR, which was the culmination of a decade-long process of prestigious commissions examining corporate governance, would have required companies to identify and disclose material social and environmental risks.[15]

Then, in an unexpected policy reversal, the Blair government withdrew the OFR regulations in late November 2005.[16] According to Chancellor of the Exchequer Gordon Brown, the purpose of the reversal was to diminish the regulatory burden on British business and thereby soothe strained relations between the Labour government and the corporate sector.[17] Instead, the government's efforts "backfired spectacularly," eliciting a firestorm of criticism "from an unlikely alliance of business leaders, City investors, trade

---

10. *See* Rafael LaPorta et al., *Corporate Ownership Around the World*, 54 J. FIN. 471 (1999) (presenting empirical evidence illustrating the different corporate ownership patterns in various countries).

11. *Id.* at 491-511.

12. *See* Barnard et al., *supra* note 5, at 469-73 (discussing the efficiency of the corporate control market as an accountability mechanism).

13. For an analysis of these institutional pressures, see Ian Jones & Michael Pollitt, *Understanding How Issues in Corporate Governance Develop: Cadbury Report to Higgs Review*, 12 CORP. GOVERNANCE 162 (2004).

14. The Companies Act 1985 (Operating and Financial Review and Directors' Report etc.) Regulations 2005, S.I. 2005/1011 (U.K.), *available at* http://www.opsi.gov.uk/si/si2005/20051011.htm.

15. *See* Jones & Pollitt, *supra* note 13, at 164.

16. *See* Jill Treanor & Mark Milner, *Brown Plan to Cut Red Tape for Business Provokes Chorus of Disapproval*, GUARDIAN UNLIMITED, Nov. 29, 2005, *available at* http://business.guardian.co.uk/story/0,,1653143,00.html (reporting on OFR withdrawal and describing immediate criticism from wide range of sources).

17. *See id.*; Larry Elliott & Ashley Seager, *Brown Pledges to Cut Red Tape in Drive to Woo Industry*, GUARDIAN UNLIMITED, Nov. 29, 2005, *available at* http://business.guardian.co.uk/story/0,,1652097,00.html (quoting Brown on desire to end "gold-plating" of regulations).

unions, and green activists."[18] Further twists and turns have ensued. In early February, after the environmental group Friends of the Earth threatened litigation, the government agreed to a "consultation" with interested parties that has since been extended.[19] Some observers now expect the OFR to be reinstated.[20]

Three elements of this story are especially revealing of the influence of stakeholder thinking in the UK. First, it is sufficiently advanced to have prompted the OFR process in the first place. Second, when the government reversed course, even the business interests that were the presumed beneficiaries of the withdrawal joined in criticizing it. And third, institutional investors have been especially prominent in demanding reinstatement.[21]

During the period when it was developing the OFR proposal, the British government was also taking steps to promote CSR consciousness among institutional investors. In both the United States and the UK, institutions comprise more than half of the equity market.[22] In the UK, however, pension funds and insurance companies, which are necessarily focused on the long term, are the dominant institutions. The United States' institutional sector, by contrast, is dominated by mutual funds, which may have a shorter-term outlook.[23] Investors with a longer-term perspective are more likely to see a company's social and environmental behavior as material to investment decisions. Building on this openness to unconventional and longer-term considerations, the British government has sponsored a series of "best practices" codes for institutional investors that urge, but do not yet require, that they "intervene" in the companies whose stock they own, by voting or otherwise, when doing so might enhance the value of the investment.[24] Several important institutional investor organizations have also adopted codes that call on members to demand increased corporate disclosure on both financial and CSR issues, and to engage in discussions with companies whose approach to CSR is problematic.[25]

Beyond these European legal developments, the influence of the CSR movement can also be seen in the voluntary behavior of corporations, particularly in the area of reporting. A significant number of global firms, both in the United States and abroad, go well beyond what is required in reporting publicly about social and environmental issues. Many of the world's largest companies have started to produce social, environmental, or sustainability reports, which integrate social, environmental, and financial information, in addition to their required financial reports. Between 1999 and 2002, the percentage of *Fortune* Global Top 250 companies that produced a separate social, environmental, or sustainability report increased from 35 to 45, and these figures compare to only 10% of

18. Treanor & Milner, *supra* note 16; *see* Mark Milner & Jill Treanor, *Big Investors May Insist on Good Governance Reviews*, GUARDIAN UNLIMITED, Nov. 29, 2005, *available at* http://business.guardian.co.uk/print/0,,5343896-108725,00.html.

19. *See* Paul Grant, *OFR Back on the Agenda After Government U-turn*, ACCOUNTANCY AGE, Feb. 2, 2006, *available at* http://www.accountancyage.com/accountancyage/news/2149618/ofr-back-agenda-government-u.

20. *See id.* (quoting Friends of the Earth legal advisor to the effect that "there was now a real opportunity for the OFR to be reinstated").

21. *See* Milner & Treanor, *supra* note 16.

22. *See* Williams & Conley, *supra* note 6, at 536-37.

23. *See id.* at 537.

24. *See id.* at 513-14, 539-40.

25. *See id.* at 542.

the Global 500 in 1993.[26] In 2002, 29% of these reports were independently verified, most often by accounting firms, versus 19% in 1999.[27] These statistics reflect worldwide trends that began in the early 1990s.[28] Moreover, these aggregate percentages may understate the significance of the reporting phenomenon, given much higher rates in some of the countries with the largest economies. Thus, 72% of the top 100 companies publish social reports in Japan, 49% of the top 100 publish in the UK, 36% publish in the United States, and between 30% and 40% publish in Northern Europe.[29]

Many of the same companies that are issuing social and environmental reports have also altered the way they interact with their stakeholders, especially the NGOs—the environmental, labor, human rights, and other issue-advocacy organizations that are often their most strident critics.[30] As a representative from a leading British scientific research organization put it in a recent interview, "multinational businesses have had to respond to a changing paradigm."[31] Instead of adversarial standoffs, one now often sees "engagement" and "partnerships" with NGOs that are helping corporations identify issues, produce and audit reports, conduct "dialogues" with diverse stakeholders throughout the world, and address specific problems.

A critical question is whether these developments will prove to be nothing more than trends in corporate *communication*. That is, do these activities reflect, or at least portend, an important shift in managers' perceptions of their social responsibilities, or are they simply efforts at public relations and reputation-building? Reasonable minds might differ about the substantive effects of this paradigm shift, but the forms of conducting multinational business have clearly changed over the last ten years.

The many participants in this changing paradigm comprise the contemporary CSR community. They include a new class of CSR professionals within for-profit companies; yet another new class of outsiders who consult with companies and audit their nonfinancial reports; and executives at pension funds, insurance companies, and other institutional investment organizations who believe in socially responsible investing. They also include like-minded independent investment managers to whom institutional portfolios may be entrusted; those who work for and on behalf of NGOs, from the largest and most visible (e.g., Greenpeace and the World Wildlife Federation) to the smallest local advocacy group; and government officials worldwide whose mandate covers social and environmental issues.

We have elsewhere dealt in great detail with the legal changes that the CSR movement has helped to bring about.[32] In this Article, we report on a companion empirical study of the movement in action that employs the methods of anthropology and

---

26. KPMG INT'L, INTERNATIONAL SURVEY OF CORPORATE SUSTAINABILITY REPORTING 2002 9 (2002), *available at* http://www.wimm.nl/publicaties/kpmg2002.pdf. The KPMG Sustainability Group has been doing international surveys of sustainability reporting for over a decade. It has time-series data describing this phenomenon, but it has changed its measurement database over that time, which is why we cannot compare the reporting rates among the Global 250 in 1993 to the reporting rates for the Global 250 in 2002.

27. *Id.* at 18.

28. The percentage of the top 100 companies in each of the 19 countries that produced social reports increased from 13 in 1993 to 23 in 2002. *Id.* at 12.

29. *Id.* at 14.

30. These interactions are described *infra* Part III.

31. Our interview attribution conventions are described *infra* note 49 and accompanying text.

32. Williams & Conley, *supra* note 6.

linguistics. Using the specific techniques of business ethnography,[33] we have, over the past two years, interviewed people involved in every aspect of CSR, attended CSR events as ethnographic observers, participated in "stakeholder dialogues,"[34] and performed linguistic analyses of corporate CSR reports.

The results of this research, which we believe are without precedent, are significant on many levels. Most obviously, our findings are valuable as a deep description of what the preeminent legal realist Karl Llewellyn called "law-stuff," a cataloguing of "the patterns according to which behavior actually occurs."[35] We compare the theory and practice of the CSR movement by addressing such questions as what these participants seek to accomplish, whether they are achieving those ends, and what the social consequences of their activities—both intended and inadvertent—may be. As lawmakers in this country are encouraged to emulate Europe in mandating, or at least encouraging, the corporate behaviors and transparency urged by CSR activists, they would be well advised to attend to those consequences.

On a more theoretical level, our findings also constitute an early case study of what has been called "the new governance."[36] According to new governance theory, the democratic state is in the midst of a shift to a "post-regulatory" model characterized by a weakening of top-down governmental regulation in favor of a diffusion of rights and responsibilities among governments, private companies, NGOs, and other interested parties. Power, in other words, is to be spread and shared. This is precisely what the CSR movement seems to be demanding and, up to a point, producing. But the critics of the new governance question the processes, or lack thereof, for selecting those who will share this diffused power, and ask how these people and institutions will be held accountable. These turn out to be questions that CSR protagonists are asking of themselves, with no consensus about the answers. In many respects, understanding the realities of CSR provides a unique opportunity to test new governance theory against practice.

In Part II of this Article we explain our empirical methods in more detail. In Part III we set out and analyze the results of our ethnographic interviews and observations. Part IV presents our analysis of the discourse of CSR reporting and considers its implications. Part V discusses new governance theory and assesses CSR practice as a test case. The conclusion in Part VI reviews both the promise and the dangers posed by governance using the CSR model. Our overriding concern is that the diffusion or power promised by both new governance and CSR theorists may amount to nothing more than the subtle reinforcement of existing power relationships.

II. THE METHOD OF BUSINESS ETHNOGRAPHY

We have approached these issues through a variation on anthropology's ethnographic method. Made famous by such public intellectuals as Margaret Meade, ethnography is "participant observation": in simplest terms, going to the place to be studied, "living with the natives," sharing their way of life, and observing their customs

---

33. Our research methods are described in Part II.
34. This term is defined *infra* Part III.B.2.
35. KARL LLEWELLYN & E.A. HOEBEL, THE CHEYENNE WAY 20-21 (1942).
36. *See infra* Part VI.

and rituals, all in an effort to see the world through their eyes.[37] For much of the history of the discipline, Western anthropologists have focused their attention on so-called traditional societies[38] in the non-Western parts of the world. Accordingly, anthropology's most-read books include such titles as Meade's *Coming of Age in Samoa;*[39] Bronislaw Malinowski's *Argonauts of the Western Pacific,*[40] which described the epic open ocean canoe voyages of the people of Melanesia; and E.E. Evans-Pritchard's *The Nuer,*[41] an account of life in a tribe of Sudanese pastoralists. As part of a multifaceted turn toward introspection, however, the current generation of anthropologists has devoted much more attention to the ethnographic study of their own societies.[42] As part of the same trend, anthropologists have also begun to examine the cultures of business and other contemporary institutions.[43] The anthropologist member of this team has, for example, conducted ethnographic studies of lawyers and witnesses in American criminal trials,[44] lay people trying to navigate the small claims court system in this country,[45] and institutional investment organizations.[46]

As we have applied it here, the method has involved participant observation of gatherings and activities of the CSR community as well as wide-ranging interviews of people within corporations, NGOs, investment funds, institutional investment organizations, and public relations firms and other consultancies.[47] In the course of their field projects, anthropologists have always devoted a significant amount of time to lengthy and qualitative interviews of members of the society they are studying. Working from a general and flexible topic outline, anthropologists prompt their interlocutors,

---

37. *See* CONRAD PHILLIP KOTTAK, CULTURAL ANTHROPOLOGY 11, 20, 34-40 (11th ed. 2006).

38. To an anthropologist, "traditional" implies a relatively small society, whose members know each other on a face-to-face basis, at a premodern stage of technical and economic development. *See generally* RAYMOND SCUPIN, CULTURAL ANTHROPOLOGY: A GLOBAL PERSPECTIVE 285-86 (4th ed. 2000) (discussing concepts of premodernism and traditionalism).

39. MARGARET MEAD, COMING OF AGE IN SAMOA (1928).

40. BRONISLAW MALINOWSKI, ARGONAUTS OF THE WESTERN PACIFIC (1922).

41. E.E. EVANS-PRITCHARD, THE NUER (1940).

42. *See* KOTTAK, *supra* note 37, at 39-40, 51-54. The trends toward introspection and the examination of one's own culture are epitomized by the title that one of the most famous 20th century anthropologists gave to a 1990s textbook: PAUL BOHANNAN, WE, THE ALIEN: AN INTRODUCTION TO CULTURAL ANTHROPOLOGY (1992). Parallel developments have included a major reevaluation of anthropology's received wisdom and a dramatic increase in the numbers of professional anthropologists who are members of societies previously studied by Westerners. For leading examples of these developments, see, respectively, JAMES CLIFFORD & GEORGE E. MARCUS, WRITING CULTURE: THE POETICS AND POLITICS OF ETHNOGRAPHY (1986); GANANATH OBEYESEKERE, THE APOTHEOSIS OF CAPTAIN COOK: EUROPEAN MYTHMAKING IN THE PACIFIC (1992).

43. *See, e.g.,* James Ferguson, *Seeing Like an Oil Company: Space, Security, and Global Capital in Neoliberal Africa,* 107 AM. ANTHROPOLOGIST 377 (2005); JAMES C. SCOTT, SEEING LIKE A STATE: HOW CERTAIN SCHEMES TO IMPROVE THE HUMAN CONDITION HAVE FAILED (1998) (both analyzing the interaction among states, corporations, NGOs, and other governance actors).

44. *E.g.,* JOHN M. CONLEY & WILLIAM M. O'BARR, JUST WORDS: LAW, LANGUAGE, & POWER (1998); John M. Conley et al., *The Power of Language: A Multi-Disciplinary Study of Language in the Courtroom,* 1978 DUKE L.J. 1375.

45. *E.g.,* JOHN M. CONLEY & WILLIAM M. O'BARR, RULES VERSUS RELATIONSHIPS: THE ETHNOGRAPHY OF LEGAL DISCOURSE (1990).

46. *E.g.,* WILLIAM M. O'BARR & JOHN M. CONLEY, FORTUNE & FOLLY: THE WEALTH AND POWER OF INSTITUTIONAL INVESTING (1992).

47. For a more detailed discussion of the ethnographic method and its use in business contexts, see *id.* at 1-10.

traditionally called "informants," to set the specific agenda, move from topic to topic as they see fit, give various topics such emphasis as they may choose, and comment freely on their cultural outlook and practices. The theory of the ethnographic interview is that, in addition to the substantive information that may be provided, the informant's selection of some topics, avoidance of others, and relative emphasis on particular subjects is itself an invaluable form of data. To enhance the value of these data even further, in recent years many anthropologists have engaged in highly detailed linguistic analyses of the precise ways in which informants choose to express themselves, in the belief that language and thought are inextricably intertwined.[48]

Our objective has been to investigate the meaning of "corporate social responsibility" to people in corporations and their various stakeholders, and the potential impact, within a company and beyond, of a firm's undertaking CSR initiatives. We are more than two and one-half years into this project, attending CSR events as ethnographic observers and interviewing people at various levels of the relevant organizations. We have attended seven major CSR conferences in the United States and Europe, watching, listening, and conducting follow-up interviews as CSR activists from the corporate and nonprofit sectors gather to debate issues, inform each other, and develop practical plans for action. We also participated in one month-long online conference. We have been involved in three "multi-stakeholder dialogues," two lasting a day or a day and a half, and one lasting six months. This latter dialogue among companies, NGOs, and labor unions included three days of in-person meetings and online communications in work groups between the face-to-face sessions. We have conducted 40 interviews of corporate CSR specialists, consultants, institutional investors, investment advisors and money managers, government officials, journalists who cover CSR, and representatives from a wide range of NGOs.[49] Finally, as we discuss in Part V, we have used the methods of discourse analysis to study CSR reports issued by two multinational corporations. Several significant themes have emerged.

III. THE PRACTICE OF CORPORATE SOCIAL RESPONSIBILITY

A. The Language and Culture of the Movement

A "CSR community" has clearly emerged both in the United States and Europe, constituting itself as a coherent cultural entity complete with rituals and language. This reality was vividly illustrated at the outset of the project. In November 2003, we attended

---

48. *See, e.g.*, CONLEY & O'BARR, *supra* note 45 (providing a linguistic analysis of narratives told by small claims court litigants); SUSAN F. HIRSCH, PRONOUNCING AND PERSEVERING: GENDER AND THE DISCOURSES OF DISPUTING IN AN AFRICAN ISLAMIC COURT (1998). For an introduction to the relationship between language and thought, see JOHN J. GUMPERZ & STEPHEN C. LEVINSON, RETHINKING LINGUISTIC RELATIVITY 1-18 (1996).

49. We were able to tape-record some of the interviews. For the remainder of the interviews and observations, we have relied on the analysis of our ethnographic notes. We did not promise anonymity in our interviews and our observations of CSR events were not carried out under any conditions. Nonetheless, in keeping with what we believe to be the spirit of the interviews, we do not name persons or organizations except where we were asking questions about a publication or public statement by that person or organization. In reporting on our observations of CSR events, we have identified speakers and organizations where the identification is material to our analysis.

the annual meeting of Business for Social Responsibility (BSR), an umbrella organization in the United States that brings together companies ranging from the *Fortune* 50 to local boutiques, CSR consultants, advocacy groups of many stripes, religious organizations, socially responsible investment advisors, journalists, and an eclectic mix of interested individuals.[50] The group, which numbered approximately 1000, gave rapturous welcomes to, and asked adulatory, softball questions of, such keynote speakers as celebrity CEOs Carly Fiorina, then of HP, and Mike Eskew of UPS, and the conservative-turned-liberal columnist and talking head Arianna Huffington. Three days of breakout sessions dealt with such topics as "North v. South: How CSR Standards Impact Economic Development," "Diversity and the Bottom Line," "Addressing the Impact of Your Core Product: Kraft and Obesity," "Case Studies in Effective Government Engagement," and "Embedding CSR."

We were repeatedly struck, indeed taken aback, by the behavioral homogeneity of so diverse a group. At the simplest level, the group *looked* homogeneous, with virtually everyone affecting a mellow-casual look (a grade less formal than corporate casual) that made the gathering look more like a Howard Dean rally than the high-powered business meeting that in many respects it was. The discourse was uniformly affirming, congratulatory, and therapeutic; *process, journey, dialogue* (as noun or verb), *facilitating, verified* (on one occasion combined into "facilitated and verified dialogue"), *embedding,* and *message* were recurrent terms and dominant themes. Regardless of whether the speaker was the "Vice-President for People and Culture" at a fashion boutique or a tobacco company scientist, we did not hear a single question that was even challenging, let alone hostile. From all available evidence, this was a gathering of believers, a movement in progress. Everyone was trying to do the right thing, and the major issue was continued self-improvement. Interviews of speakers and participants during breaks in the conference confirmed this impression; the language and demeanor were virtually identical to what we observed in the group sessions. Much of the talk focused on "us," presumably in reference to the CSR movement.

Despite its egalitarian tone, the movement clearly has its stars. At the BSR gathering, the CSR team from British American Tobacco (BAT) was at the top of the A-list, at least as judged by audience size and reaction. Their breakout session on "Stakeholder Engagement: Learning from Experience" was the subject of intense anticipation. The presentation, delivered by a strikingly diverse four-member panel brought from BAT's locations around the world, to the accompaniment of sophisticated PowerPoint slides, played to a packed room.[51] The question period featured universal praise for BAT's engagement of stakeholders ranging from European health authorities to South African office workers to Central American farmers. When the formal session concluded the audience crowded onto the stage to continue the discussion. Only the clearing of the room for the next session enabled the BAT people to extricate themselves and dash off to their next venue.

A somewhat different sense of the CSR movement emerged in February 2005, when

---

50. The meeting was held November 11-14, 2003, in Los Angeles.

51. The BAT group was led by its CSR head, an Englishman who had been a medical researcher in a prominent scientific institute. It included a Central American man, an Australian woman, and a white South African man.

we observed a conference sponsored by *Ethical Corporation* magazine entitled "Business/NGO Partnerships and Engagement: How To Make Sure Everyone Gets What They Want." Held at a hotel in London, it was considerably smaller than the BSR gathering, with about 200 attendees. Perhaps because of the British venue, it was also considerably more formal, with business suits the order of the day. Other aspects of the gathering exhibited both similarities and differences with the earlier American meeting.

The language was similar in many respects. Indeed, the two key words in the conference title, *partnerships* and *engagement*, had figured prominently in the discourse in Los Angeles. *Process* and *dialogue* were also recurrent words and themes. By contrast, however, the language of affirmation, congratulations, and therapy that was so prominent in Los Angeles was largely absent in London. This difference was probably attributable to the narrower purpose of the London meeting. Whereas the Los Angeles conference had been a big tent gathering of CSR enthusiasts, the London conference was focused on the nuts-and-bolts activity of organizing and managing partnerships in which an NGO advises and monitors a corporation in the area of the NGO's expertise—the environment, labor, human rights, etc.

This difference in purpose probably also accounted for a marked difference in tone between the two conferences. Every discussion we heard in Los Angeles was uniformly positive, but there was considerable tension in the air at the London sessions. Even when successful partners appeared on stage together to discuss and analyze their arrangements, each side took considerable care to preserve its separate identity. One especially striking pairing involved the executive director of Greenpeace UK and the CEO of the British power company npower.[52] Although the particular engagement involved the monitoring of an offshore windmill project, the Greenpeace representative anticipated skepticism about his organization's involvement with a company that also generates nuclear power. He repeatedly stressed that Greenpeace remains a "campaigning NGO," always ready to take "direct action" in support of its "fairly radical policy positions." Speaking preemptively, he acknowledged "the risk of selling out." Aggressive questions from the floor indicated that his concern was well placed.

Another session, entitled "When Agreements Do Not Work Out," produced a level of hostility that would have been unthinkable at the Los Angeles gathering. The featured speaker was a former CSR executive from Asia Pulp and Paper (APP), an Indonesian company that has been targeted by environmentalists for its alleged destruction of rainforests. He analyzed the company's failed environmental partnership with the World Wildlife Federation (WWF). In neutral tones, he discussed the "language barriers" that can arise between NGOs, which speak an "aspirational language," and companies, which must speak a "specific language of performance." The barrier becomes particularly daunting, he said, with respect to the definition of success or failure. He also discussed the inherent difficulties in developing a relationship with an NGO that may have its own stakeholders all over the world: "Who are you actually dealing with?"

During the question period, his remarks elicited an attack from a woman in the audience who worked for the WWF. She asserted that "APP kept on talking while they logged the rainforest," and contrasted APP's behavior with that of other companies with which WWF had engaged. The APP representative responded that "the differences

---

52. *See infra* notes 80-81 and accompanying text (further discussing the Greenpeace-npower partnership).

between companies on the ground are very small," and arise "on the basis of style of engagement." He concluded that he was "personally hurt by WWF's failure to make meetings and return calls."

These details reveal an important distinction between CSR engagement in theory and in practice. At the theoretical level, the CSR movement is a monolith of like-minded people who engage in uniformly positive rhetoric. When it comes time to practice the theory, however, as the London conference suggests, CSR practitioners are subject to the same pressures as business and political partners. The new governance is, after all, governance, with all its attendant complexities.

A final and striking point is that at conferences and in interviews we have observed a convergence of the speaking styles of the corporate and the nonprofit participants in the CSR movement. The corporate participants are entirely comfortable with the jargon of the NGO world, with its feel-good, therapeutic focus on process. But at the same time, NGO executives are now routinely talking about their respective "brands." Indeed, in one interview, a representative from a well-known environmental organization dismissed a somewhat rowdier competitor as "unbranded." NGO people also regularly discuss adapting the corporate concept of accountability to their own organizations, by seeking various kinds of "bottom lines" to apply to their activities. And even as NGOs function as stakeholders, they are beginning to acknowledge that they, too, have stakeholders who may have divergent views of the organization's mission.[53] The following Sections explore some of these substantive themes.

B. The Substance of CSR Discourse

1. Who Counts as a Stakeholder?

Beyond these issues of look and feel, the substance of the discourse at these and other conferences and in our interviews has also been revealing. In Los Angeles in 2003, for example, much discussion involved the organization of stakeholder dialogues: who participates, in what venues, and in what form. An obvious question is who counts as a stakeholder. As someone asked the BAT representatives in Los Angeles, "Who are the key players?" According to the head of a non-profit CSR research group, the stakeholder category should include everyone who is in some sense an "investor" in the corporation.[54] We would include employees, residents of communities where the company has a significant presence (or "footprint"), and the governments of affected locales. Our informants within corporations, even in the United States, almost always list employees, customers, and community residents as stakeholders.[55] To this list the Los Angeles and London conference participants added, uncritically, "civil society," which tends to be used synonymously with NGOs.[56]

---

53. As one of the BAT representatives succinctly put it during the Los Angeles conference: "stakeholders have stakeholders."

54. This person spoke at the 2005 BSR conference, held November 1-4, 2005, in Washington, D.C.

55. *See* Eric W. Orts, *Beyond Shareholders: Interpreting Corporate Constituency Statues*, 61 GEO. WASH. L. REV. 16 (1992) (analyzing the corporate law implications of expanding the corporation's constituency beyond its shareholders).

56. At one of the 2005 London conference panels, the research director of an educational NGO criticized

In all of our observations and interviews, we have heard surprisingly little analysis of how particular NGOs become stakeholders in particular companies. One obvious way is by campaigning against the company and then being approached to enter into a partnership, as in the Greenpeace-npower case just discussed. Others gain de facto stakeholder recognition from a company after campaigning against it, though they are not offered formal partnerships. We have heard of other instances in which companies invite NGOs into partnerships because of their visibility and apparent expertise on particular issues, such as rainforest protection, climate change, or labor rights. Neither in our observations nor our interviews (where we have posed the question directly), however, has anyone set out any explicit criteria for deciding who gets a seat at the stakeholder table. Instead, some have acknowledged that it depends largely on an NGO's ability to make noise. This reality tends to vindicate the concerns of new governance critics about the legitimacy and accountability of participants.[57]

2. What Is "Stakeholder Dialogue"?

Stakeholder dialogues are structured discussions among company participants, members of civil society, employees, community members, and advocacy groups. The specific goals of the dialogue vary depending on the company and the social issues it faces. In general, they have the goal of creating a forum and a format for two-way communication. Stakeholders provide information to the company about their views while the company has a context outside advertising or formal public relations to express its views about contested social issues. Engagement through stakeholder dialogue is treated as a great good throughout the CSR movement. NGOs and socially responsible investors demand it, and, at least in Europe and the United Kingdom, governments encourage it,[58] and may even delegate their regulatory roles to such dialogues.[59] Dialogue with non-shareholders is seen as the process through which the concerns of the powerless are heard.

But even as dialogue gives stakeholders a voice in corporate deliberations, it offers companies a way to control the way in which that voice is exercised. This point initially occurred to us during the BAT presentation at the 2003 BSR conference, when one of the company's representatives described the stakeholder dialogue as beginning with the "mapping and classification" of stakeholders. BAT speakers also talked of using consultants to select stakeholder participants by determining "who exactly the key players are"; extensive preparation in order to "systematize" the dialogue; achieving

---

this common usage, arguing that "civil society" includes both cause-oriented NGOs "and think tanks, church groups, and even the media."

57. *See infra* notes 176-79 and accompanying text.

58. *See supra* notes 24-25 and accompanying text.

59. One such "regulatory dialogue" involved the American and British governments convening stakeholders to establish voluntary principles for security arrangements to be used by the extractive industries (oil, gas, and mining). One participant in this dialogue told us that the UK government would host most of the meetings, but would do little more than bring industry, investors, and NGOs together, "give them a nice tea, and then tell them to go off to a conference room and figure the problem out, and report back when they had a solution." *See* Cynthia A. Williams, *Civil Society Initiatives and "Soft Law" in the Oil and Gas Industry*, 36 N.Y.U. J. INT'L L. & POL. 457, 477-82 (2004) (describing voluntary principles); Shamir, *supra* note 1, at 645 (discussing "soft law" solutions generally).

"consistency across regions" in order "to avoid sending different messages to different parts of the world"; and being careful to "provide stakeholders with clear parameters to show if the company was really doing what it had committed."[60]

The good news is that all of these approaches are perfectly rational, if not inevitable, steps in organizing a potentially chaotic conversation with a host of self-proclaimed stakeholders. But this might also be construed as the bad news. To organize is to discipline, to control, and to limit. As the social philosopher Michel Foucault and others have argued, becoming engaged with the state comes at a cost.[61] To be recognized by the apparatus of the state often means to acquiesce in, if not surrender to, its principles of classification and rules of engagement, to give up a part of one's autonomy.[62] These same principles may apply to the corporation, a creature of the state that, especially in the case of the large multinational company, mimics the state in many important respects.[63] Indeed, new governance theory recognizes the corporation as a partner of government in the post-regulatory paradigm.[64] From this perspective, what a company like BAT characterizes as the value-neutral "facilitation" of stakeholder dialogue can be seen as an exercise in control—control over who participates, how things get said, and consequently, if indirectly, what gets said. Although intent may be irrelevant to effects, this issue does bring into focus a question that remains central in evaluating CSR: what are the motivations of the companies that are participating?

3. How Serious Are the Participating Corporations?

Our interviews of corporate CSR specialists and their consultants are providing a window on the day-to-day world of CSR in practice. As might be expected, what we have heard is calmer, more reflective, and sometimes more cynical than what is said in the revival-like atmosphere of a large gathering. Nonetheless, the content is consistent. People think CSR is here to stay and is effecting a meaningful change in corporate

---

60. At the same time, BAT's CSR reports indicate that a number of key stakeholders, in particular members of health advocacy organizations, refuse to participate. *See infra* note 141 and accompanying text.

61. *See, e.g.*, MICHEL FOUCAULT, DISCIPLINE AND PUNISH: THE BIRTH OF THE PRISON 222 (Alan Sheridan trans., 2d ed. 1995) (1977).

> Historically, the process by which the bourgeoisie became in the course of the eighteenth century the politically dominant class was masked by the establishment of an explicit, coded and formally egalitarian juridical framework . . . . But the development and generalization of disciplinary mechanisms constituted the other, dark side of these processes. The general juridical form that guaranteed a system of rights that were egalitarian in principle was supported by these tiny, everyday, physical mechanisms, by all those systems of micro-power that are essentially nonegalitarian and asymmetrical that we call the disciplines. . . .

Id. For a general discussion of Foucault's point, see CONLEY & O'BARR, *supra* note 46, at 7-9.

62. For example, in an ethnographic study of working class Americans seeking redress from the legal system, the anthropologist Sally Engle Merry has documented the "paradox of legal entitlement." The use of the legal system empowers such people, but it can also result in the encroachment of the state on their privacy and autonomy; entitlement can lead to dependency. SALLY ENGLE MERRY, GETTING JUSTICE AND GETTING EVEN: LEGAL CONSCIOUSNESS AMONG WORKING-CLASS AMERICANS 172-82 (1990).

63. For an excellent discussion of the state-like features of global companies, see Dirk Matten & Andrew Crane, *Corporate Citizenship: Toward an Extended Theoretical Conceptualization*, 30 ACAD. MGMT. REV. 166 (2005).

64. *See infra* Part V. For an example of this new reality, see *supra* note 59.

behavior. Both corporate CSR specialists and consultants believe that the executives they work for take it seriously. It is widely believed that if a company adopts appropriate processes for talking with stakeholders and reporting its performance then salutary outcomes will ensue.

Interestingly, the jury of CSR insiders is still out on the economic benefits to be derived from good corporate citizenship. With the exception of those in the socially responsible investment business, we have not heard anyone make a robust claim that CSR can be shown to boost the traditional bottom line.[65] One corporate CSR specialist told us that his very large agricultural company had seen a measurable effect on reducing pesticide use, but the number he cited was orders of magnitude short of materiality. Other people within companies have discussed positive effects on employee recruitment and retention as well as customer loyalty, but, surprisingly to us, most have made no serious efforts to quantify these perceived benefits. Nonetheless, everyone with whom we have spoken believes that CSR will prove itself to be economically efficient, at least in the negative sense of heading off such things as labor unrest, customer defections, costly environmental problems, and, importantly, government interventions.[66] As far as consumers are concerned, however, every person we have heard or interviewed has agreed with the proposition that they (except for an affluent niche) will not pay more for responsibly-produced products. According to a "sustainable product" development expert who spoke at the 2005 BSR conference, "[i]n many cases the green story is a non-starter."[67]

Against this background of general corporate optimism, our field work has also suggested a number of cautionary notes. An initial observation is that the very existence of a coherent CSR movement may invite insincerity. A company could learn the culturally appropriate behaviors and participate in the CSR discourse without significantly changing their real world behavior. In this view, CSR participation is little more than a show of voluntary reform intended to head off government mandates, preempt NGO attacks, and succor favor with the minority of CSR-conscious consumers. One proponent of this view has described corporate participants in CSR as "struggling to structure it around voluntary self-regulation and to position themselves as authoritative

---

65. *See generally* Poulomi Mrinai, *What Case for the Business Case*, ETHICAL CORP., June 3, 2005, *available at* http://www.ethicalcorp.com/content.asp?ContentID=3718. There is now a meta-analysis of 52 prior studies, comprising 33,878 observations, that finds a positive relationship between a company's social performance and its financial performance. *See* Marc Orlitzky et al., *Corporate Social and Financial Performance: A Meta-Analysis*, 24 ORG. STUD. 403 (2003). The point is that CSR insiders, including those within companies, seem not to have taken the trouble to quantify the benefits of their CSR initiatives, notwithstanding their presumed interest in measuring return on investment.

66. For two recent examples of potential bottom line effects, see Press Release, Ethical Corp., Study Reveals Corporate Social Responsibility a Major Factor in Overseas Investment and Purchasing (Jan. 20, 2004), *available at* http://www.cswire.com/article/cgi/2410.html (reporting a study by a CSR consulting firm that suggests that multinationals take CSR issues into account in selecting suppliers and business partners), and Press Release, World Econ. Forum, Why Global Citizenship Matters for Shareholders: A Survey of CEOs (Jan. 8, 2004), *available at* http://www.cswire.com/article.cgi/2377.html (indicating that 70% of CEOs believe that mainstream investors will factor CSR into their investment decisions). For a review of the argument that CSR may be a threat to economic growth, see *A Matter of Priorities for Europe*, ETHICAL CORP., Feb. 24, 2005, at 9, *available at* http://www.ethicalcorp.com/content_print.asp?ContentID=3500.

67. *See supra* note 54. The same person later asked, however, whether companies have "really started to market green."

players within it."[68]

The response to this concern is that since reporting is a fundamental tenet of CSR a corporate *poseur* would not escape detection for long. The counter-response, however, is that the bulk of what is reported is itself process; indeed, the substance of CSR seems to be process. Despite a great deal of talk about emerging CSR "metrics," the things that command attention among those we have observed and interviewed are, as we noted above, such intangibles as dialogue, the embedding of CSR "in the corporate DNA," and embarking on journeys. We have heard corporate CSR people ask, "What should we be doing to *demonstrate* we're a socially responsible company?" Others have spoken of the need "to avoid sending different *messages* to different parts of the world" and, perhaps most tellingly, have characterized themselves as "stewards of our *reputation*." If one considers this reality against the background of an active and growing CSR communication industry,[69] then at least some skepticism is warranted.

In fact, some CSR insiders have expressed a concern that *others* may be "gaming the system," as a corporate CSR manager put it to us. This individual, who is particularly knowledgeable about labor practices in China, worried aloud about the difficulty of translating stakeholder dialogue into lasting improvements in the workplace. He noted that a socially responsible American buyer of Chinese goods might listen to its worker-stakeholders, impose a code of conduct on its suppliers, get their promised compliance, and even engage a third-party CSR auditor to perform monthly inspections, only to hear through back channels that the suppliers were reverting to business as usual the other 353 days of the year. Remarkably, the week after our informant had discussed this problem in the abstract, the *New York Times* reported the very same behavior in the Chinese toy industry.[70] If Chinese manufacturers can learn and manipulate the rules of CSR discourse with such evident facility, then there may be reason to wonder if others, closer to home, are doing similar things.

Similar skepticism emerged as we participated in an online conference during the last week of January and first week of February 2004. Sponsored by the World Bank, it was titled "E-conference on the Possibilities and Challenges of Corporate Social Responsibility Among Small and Medium Enterprises."[71] Although no conference roster

---

68. Shamir, *supra* note 1, at 655. A participant in the 2005 BSR conference described the objective as seeking "a credit for early action against future regulation."

69. Subscribers to the various electronic CSR news and reporting services (as we are) receive regular invitations to conferences on CSR public relations, communications, and reputation management. One of the most useful of these services, London-based CSRWire Weekly Alerts, regularly carries this legend: "Your company has a story to tell that sets it apart—CSRWire delivers it. Contact us at sales.csrwire.com for information on how CSRWire can work for you." *See generally* Ian Davis, *The Biggest Contract*, ECONOMIST, May 26, 2005, *available at* http://www.economist.com/PrinterFriendly.cfm?Story_ID=4008642 (stating that companies "need to articulate a business's social contribution and define its ultimate purpose in a way that has more subtlety than the 'business is business' worldview and is less defensive than most current CSR approaches").

70. Joseph Kahn, *Ruse in Toyland: Chinese Workers' Hidden Woe*, N.Y. TIMES, Dec. 7, 2003, at A1.

71. The World Bank has not issued any post-conference report. Although we participated without any understandings concerning confidentiality, we see no reason to identify participants or their organizations when quoting their remarks. Hard copies of all quoted remarks are on file with the authors. We copy-edited the kinds of minor typographical errors that are common in rapid-fire e-mail correspondence. We used brackets to mark instances in which we added or changed a word that had obviously been omitted or mistyped. We have not marked corrections to punctuation.

was distributed, the postings suggested that a majority of participants came from the public and nonprofit sectors with substantial representation of the underdeveloped world.

As evidenced by its frequent citation, the conference seemed strongly influenced by a report that had just been issued on January 21, 2004 by Christian Aid, a respected British relief agency. The report, *Behind the Mask: The Real Face of Corporate Social Responsibility*,[72] is a scathing indictment of the CSR movement in general and several companies in particular, including British American Tobacco, Shell, and Coca-Cola. Christian Aid defines CSR as "a catch-all term increasingly used by businesses, which encompasses the voluntary codes, principles, and initiatives companies adopt in their general desire to confine corporate responsibility to self-regulation."[73] It characterizes the whole movement as a disingenuous public relations exercise:

> Corporate enthusiasm for CSR is not driven primarily by a desire to improve the lot of the communities in which companies work . . . . [R]ather, companies are concerned with their own reputations, with the potential damage of public campaigns directed against them, and overwhelmingly, with the desire—and the imperative—to secure ever-greater profits.[74]

Noting the emergence of what we characterized above as the CSR community, the report observes that London "is now awash with PR consultants, social auditors, firms providing verification or 'assurance' for companies' social and environmental reports, and bespoke investment analysts, all vying for business."[75]

Several of the participants in the World Bank conference made direct reference to the Christian Aid report, or to an article in *The Economist* that described it.[76] A representative of a for-profit CSR consultancy took a shot at the messenger—"*The Economist* is very much against CSR, so anything they write on it should be taken with a very large pinch of salt"—and defended the multinationals that are prominent in the CSR movement—"Those companies who are brave enough to engage with CSR, to do something and put their heads above the parapet will get shot at—this is an early price of engagement." Others retorted quickly and strongly. For example, an American of uncertain affiliation criticized "overly optimistic reports by many leading companies." He argued that

---

72. CHRISTIAN AID, BEHIND THE MASK: THE REAL FACE OF CORPORATE SOCIAL RESPONSIBILITY (2004), *available at* http://www.christianaid.org.uk/indepth/0401csr/csr_behindthemask.pdf.

73. *Id.* at 5.

74. *Id.*

75. *Id.* at 8. The report specifically accuses Shell of making false promises of responsible behavior in Nigeria, and Coca-Cola of depleting village wells in India. *Id.* at 2, 22-33, 44-49. In a chapter called "Hooked on Tobacco," BAT is attacked for allegedly jeopardizing farmers' health in Kenya. CHRISTIAN AID, *supra* note 72, at 34-43. Referring to BAT's much-praised stakeholder dialogue, Christian Aid criticizes BAT for imposing "rules in which participants are unable to reveal discussions to outsiders" and for "the lack of NGO and campaigning-group participants." *Id.* at 12; *see also* Jeff Collin & Anna Gilmore, *Corporate (Anti)Social (Ir)Responsibility: Transnational Tobacco Companies and the Attempted Subversion of Global Health Policy*, 2 GLOBAL SOC. POL'Y 354 (2002) (criticizing tobacco companies for using CSR initiatives to undercut global treaties on smoking and health).

76. *Two-faced Capitalism*, ECONOMIST, Jan. 22, 2004, *available at* http://www.economist.com/PrinterFriendly.cfm?Story_ID=2369912. A later issue of *The Economist* featured a much-discussed series of articles that took a generally skeptical view of the CSR movement. *The Good Company*, ECONOMIST, Jan. 20, 2005.

[r]ather than dismissing this with "a large grain of salt," because it is reported by *The Economist*, we should embrace and discuss the point being reported that corporations and their suppliers have to raise [their] equitable social standard globally through enforcement of their own or face the inevitable calls . . . .

Numerous other correspondents, especially those from the underdeveloped world, took up Christian Aid's point about the primacy of economics. Echoing the comments quoted above about labor practices in China, they emphasized how unrealistic CSR may seem to small and medium enterprises (SMEs) trying to establish themselves in multinational supply networks. A comment by a representative of a Nigerian NGO was both pointed and poignant: the "challenge of being [a] socially responsible SME is not valid when their possibilities of existence [are] close to zero." A person from another African NGO said that "here in Nigeria, SMEs are currently locked up with big issues on funding and how to secure loans for themselves . . . so any mention of CSR is strange to a good [number] of them."

The postings by a person describing himself as "a CSR practitioner responsible for ethical supply chain management" in a British retail company were especially interesting because of the breadth of his perspective. Speaking of his company's suppliers, he confirmed that "most SMEs, particularly in the developing world, are under severe pressure on cost/price, leaving little money, time or empathy for CSR." In addition, "many workers state that the most important CSR issue FOR THEM is the fair payment of wages . . . . A shiny new factory with great health and safety but miserable wages is still a miserable factory." Ultimately, "a race to the bottom in pricing may result in a lack of pick-up amongst SMEs or CSR or, worse, a race to the bottom in labour standards."

Confirming his own observations, on several issues the correspondent quoted "one friend who owns a factory." First, "the 'business case' for CSR in SMEs is weak. Unfortunately CSR leads to significantly higher profits much more often in textbooks than it does in reality." At best, "there can be 'fringe' business benefits of higher staff morale, better attendance, easier recruitment, better staff retention, etc.," but "the actual contribution of these factors to the bottom line is limited in an SME context." And in a harsh comment on the CSR community that Christian Aid had mocked, the factory owner was reported to have said, "I was convinced by a consultant/customer/business association of the business benefits of CSR, but it doesn't work!"

These comments by informants within small and medium-sized entities indicate the importance of large corporations in "driving" CSR through the global supply chain. Yet those responsible for CSR in large corporations are typically not management heavyweights. The people holding this portfolio whom we have interviewed vary in age and tenure with the company. Some have come from public relations, some from personnel, some from safety, some from operations, and some were hired as CSR specialists. None, however, seems to have come from a background of management participation at a strategic level.

Without exception, our sources stress the dependency of CSR on "senior management buy-in." As the head of an independent CSR research firm described it, CSR "needs to get assigned to the boring guy with a green eye shade;" CSR people "need to speak the language of the operating committee." Some CSR specialists tell stories of CEOs starting a CSR program on their own initiative, whereas others talk of top executives being persuaded by others. In all cases, though, carrying through on CSR is described as a "top-down" proposition, and those who carry the CSR banner for very large companies tend not to be very near the top. While this state of affairs may not threaten the CSR movement, it is grounds for concern about the capacity of CSR programs to survive executive turnover, especially of the involuntary sort. To be fair, the uniform response to this concern among the mid-level flag bearers is that CSR has become an imperative that any future management will be forced to respect.

A final and related point about corporate commitment involves the nature and scale of CSR projects. Two phrases that have recurred throughout our observations and interviews are *scale-up* and *core businesses*. The former is usually heard in a discussion of a particular CSR demonstration project, such as the Greenpeace-npower wind power partnership, or a water purification project launched in India by a British water company.[77] The obvious point is that companies must "scale-up" their CSR efforts to have more than a token impact. This often leads to a mention of the second point: that companies typically focus on CSR in niche activities, not "core businesses." At the 2005 London conference, for example, a Kraft representative who spoke about fair trade for the company's coffee suppliers was reminded by questioners from the floor that this initiative represented only a tiny piece of Kraft's food-buying activities.[78] There is, our evidence suggests, much skepticism in the CSR world about how much impact dialogue, embedding, and buying-in have had on large-scale corporate behavior.[79]

4. What is the Attitude of the NGOs?

There is evidence from our observations and interviews that even as NGOs develop a more corporate style, their substantive outlook and behavior grow more corporate as well. At the recent London conference, SustainAbility's research and advocacy director observed that the nature of NGOs' power is changing. Traditionally, he said, NGOs sought and exercised power "through confrontation." Now, however, they are "controlling the agenda and defining the choices that are available" to companies facing CSR pressure. NGOs are "no longer just gadflies," he continued, but are "part of the system." NGO officials acknowledge this, but at the same time worry about the effect on their "brands." As noted above, the Greenpeace UK executive director, analyzing his

---

77. This project, which involved a partnership between RWE Thames Water and Care International, was the subject of a panel at the 2005 London conference.

78. Compare these comments at the 2005 London conference with a panel at the 2003 Los Angeles conference on "Addressing the Impact of Your Core Product: Kraft and Obesity."

79. There are some widely discussed CSR success stories, and the question of what success looks like will be a subject of our future research. British Petroleum is one frequently cited example, although a complex one given the nature of the company's business. *See, e.g.,* Lisa Roner, *BP's Safety Commitment: Hot Air or the Real Deal?,* ETHICAL CORP., Apr. 10, 2005, *available at* http://www.ethicalcorp.com/content-print.asp?ContentID=3638 (critique of BP's safety and environmental performance). Another is the fruit company Chiquita, where we have already conducted some interviews. The elements of success at Chiquita appear to include living wages and other labor advances, sound environmental practices, and control over the supply chain. A critical factor in achieving success may be the development of multiple pro-CSR forces acting within the company, including strong unions and a board that seeks and receives independent reports on the company's CSR performance, spurred on by effective outside pressure groups such as the Rainforest Action Network. For a laudatory account of Chiquita, see J. GARY TAYLOR & PATRICIA J. SCHARLIN, SMART ALLIANCE: HOW A GLOBAL CORPORATION AND ENVIRONMENTAL ACTIVISTS TRANSFORMED A TARNISHED BRAND (2004).

relationship with npower, went to great lengths to stress that his organization is still a "campaigning NGO."[80] But he recognized that once Greenpeace allows itself to be used for corporate marketing, "We're at risk of selling out."[81] Greenpeace and other environmental organizations repeatedly stress the need to avoid complicity in the "greenwashing" of corporate environmental malfeasance.

Another piece of evidence of the NGOs' adoption of corporate language and behaviors is a growing concern with accountability. For example, a plenary panel at the 2005 London conference was devoted to "NGO accountability . . . What's being done to create greater transparency?" Transparency is not just a business buzzword, of course, but has long been the pivotal concept in financial reporting. One speaker, from the educational NGO One World Trust, carried the linguistic merger so far as to say that accountability must be "embedded" *in the NGO, from the top down*—a statement we have heard from and about dozens of corporations. There was also general agreement that as NGOs demand that corporations account to their broad stakeholder base, the NGOs must do the same.

But the same discussion also illuminated a number of significant differences between NGO and corporate accountability. An anonymous questioner from the floor argued that NGOs must be wary of demands for accountability, since they are sometimes a pretext for efforts to defang aggressive NGOs and limit their ability to act. Another made the related point that pro-plaintiff libel laws in the UK have already tipped the accountability balance too far in favor of companies, while yet another pointed out that NGOs are inherently accountable to those upon whose financial largess they depend.

All of the members of the panel appeared to accept the basic premise of accountability, but they too pointed to a number of distinctions between the corporate and NGO versions. The representative of One World Trust made the point that, whereas NGOs are spread out across cultures, accountability is an Anglo-Saxon word and concept: "*Accountability* doesn't translate into almost any other language." He asked what accountability could mean in the case of NGOs, arguing that "it's not legitimacy, not democracy, nor transparency." A panelist from Christian Aid acknowledged that "NGOs like Christian Aid are not as accountable as they should be." He pointed out, however, that a company can make money and thus succeed even if its investment is bad for the community, but an NGO fails and dooms itself to extinction by doing the same thing. He also decried NGOs that engage in "horrible company-style CSR presentations." The only corporate comment during the session, from a BAT representative, took a completely different tack, suggesting that the issue was "not accountability, but contestability," meaning that NGOs should present their positions in the form of testable and refutable scientific positions.[82]

On this issue as well, then, the CSR movement is grappling with one of the

---

80. *See supra* Part III.A.

81. npower advertises this project as "npower Juice . . . clean, green electricity . . . developed through a partnership between npower and Greenpeace." *See* npower, About Juice, http://www.npower.com/At_home/Juice-clean_and_green/About_Juice.html (last visited Apr. 5, 2006).

82. The comments quoted in the text appear not to have been directed to NGOs' financial accountability. That issue, too, has recently become front page news. *See, e.g.*, Michael M. Phillips, *Big Charities Pursue Certification to Quell Fears of Funding Abuses*, WALL ST. J., Mar. 9, 2005, at A1.

fundamental dilemmas identified by the critics of the new governance paradigm.[83] If devolved governance is to have legitimacy, then so must the participants. This legitimacy, the critics argue, must relate both to selection and to conduct going forward. In the case of CSR, our research indicates, those whose legitimacy is at issue recognize the problem but are far from any consensus on its resolution.

5. The Role of Government

An irony of the CSR movement is that even as governments devolve power onto private actors, those same actors express great concern about the role of government. This concern focuses on two levels of government. First, NGO representatives have repeatedly told us that multinational corporations take social responsibility seriously only when pressured by their home governments—the United States, the UK, and the EU. Many NGOs have emphasized the significance of the British government's activity in fostering enhanced social and environmental responsibility.[84] Again with reference to the British case, they point out that mandating particular behaviors is not always necessary; requiring disclosure and then exerting public pressure in favor of the adoption of best practices codes can be as or more effective.[85] Nonetheless, in our observations and interviews, there has been unanimity that the CSR movement will stall without government involvement. Not surprisingly, these comments often conclude with criticism of the American government's inactivity.[86]

At the other end of the government spectrum, there is also great concern about the potential of the CSR movement to inhibit the growth of strong local government in places where corporations are "engaged" with NGOs. In some instances, circumventing a corrupt local government is the very purpose of the corporate-NGO partnership. But even where the local government (particularly at the regional or village level) is doing its honest best, the partnership's economic and political muscle may make it appear irrelevant. When this happens, a number of our informants have warned, local good government advocates may simply give up. The effects of this are particularly pernicious when the specific work of the partnership (in one example given, insuring that an influx of workers to build a plant did not disrupt local life) is done, the foreigners have largely withdrawn, and the locals are, once again, left to fend for themselves. Far from being strengthened by the activities of the corporate-NGO partnership, local institutions will have atrophied, leaving the community less prepared than ever to deal with the challenges of globalization.[87]

---

83. *See infra* notes 176-79 and accompanying text.

84. *See supra* notes 23-25 and accompanying text.

85. *See supra* notes 9-25 and accompanying text.

86. There is a dissenting view. In an interview in 2004, one of the most prominent Dutch scholars of CSR argued to us that the United States was far ahead of Europe in promoting "green" corporate behavior. When we expressed surprise at this flouting of the conventional wisdom, she responded, "It's the lawsuits." Without the threat of litigation, European-style government cajoling was, in her view, meaningless.

87. Perhaps tellingly, we have seen no representatives of affected local governments making presentations at any conference. The closest voice we heard was that of a Nigerian employee of Shell who, poignantly and effectively, reaffirmed the points made in the text in a comment from the floor during an environmental panel at the London conference. For an anthropologist's perspective on the relationships among states, corporations, and NGOs, see Ferguson, *supra* note 43.

C. The Investor Perspective

We have been repeatedly told that the critical impetus toward corporate social responsibility will come from large institutional investors, particularly pension funds. Individual investors, however large their portfolios, are deemed uninterested and therefore irrelevant. CSR enthusiasts hope, however, that those who direct institutional investment will construe the promotion of CSR as part of their fiduciary duty and either limit their investing to responsible companies or take an active role in the governance of the companies they buy so as to demand socially and environmentally responsible behavior. Encouraging this kind of institutional investor activism is a critical part of the British government's CSR initiative.[88]

Our interviews have revealed, however, that the institutional investor outlook is complex. It is true that there is a growing voluntary movement in favor of socially responsible investing. Some mutual funds with strong track records are successfully selling the proposition that social and environmental responsibility is good for business, and offer portfolios limited to companies that pass their particular screens.[89] TIAA-CREF, the huge pension fund to which most American college professors belong, has long offered participants in its defined contribution plans the option to invest their money in socially responsible funds.[90]

Offering a voluntary option to beneficiaries who control their own accounts is straightforward. Defined benefit pension plans[91] present a far more difficult case.[92] Because the plan promises to fund benefits at a particular level, beneficiaries who agitate for socially responsible investing, or any particular investment strategy, are playing with house money, not their own.[93] Our interviews suggest that the defined benefit community (pension fund trustees and managers, and their advisors) has divided itself into three camps. All three start from the premise that the law requires trustees and those who work under them to act solely in the best interests of their beneficiaries. At one end of the spectrum are those who believe that those best interests include a just and environmentally sustainable world.[94] Thus, they argue, trustees are not only permitted

---

88. *See supra* notes 22-25 and accompanying text.

89. For examples of such funds and descriptions of their performances, see KLD Research & Analytics Homepage, http://www.kld.com (last visited Apr. 5, 2006), and Domini Social Investments Homepage, http://www.domini.com (last visited Apr. 5, 2006).

90. *See* TIAA-CREF Homepage, http://www.tiaa-cref.org (follow "Social Choice" hyperlink) (last visited Apr. 5, 2006). In a defined contribution plan, the participant and the employer both make regular contributions in the participant's name over the course of his or her working life. The pension that the participant actually receives is entirely dependent upon the market performance of the investments. *See* O'BARR & CONLEY, *supra* note 46, at 21.

91. In a defined benefit plan, the employer promises a particular level of pension payments and then invests assets in an effort to fund the future payouts it will be obligated to make. *See* O'BARR & CONLEY, *supra* note 46, at 21.

92. Pension plans as a whole are critical targets for CSR activists because they comprise about one-third of the institutional investment market in both the U.S. and the UK. *See* Williams & Conley, *supra* note 6, at 537, 547.

93. This is how the problem was described to us by an SRI specialist at a large British educational pension fund.

94. The closest thing to an authoritative statement in U.S. law of a pension fiduciary's proper approach to social and environmental risk is a pair of Department of Labor Interpretive Bulletins. Regrettably, they do little to clarify the issue. Interpretive Bulletin 94-1 relates to "economically targeted investments," defined as

but even required to take CSR into account when making investment decisions and, most importantly, in exercising their governance authority as shareholders. The latter activities include voting proxies, occasionally filing resolutions, and "engaging" (another use of that term) with corporate management to promote CSR. One high-level executive at a British company that manages investments for many pension funds told us that she thinks it is her obligation to "lead" those funds toward a socially responsible investing philosophy.

At the other end are those who characterize themselves as "mainstream" pension fund managers. Their perspective is almost 180 degrees opposite. An executive for another British company that also manages assets for a large number of pension funds described CSR investor activism as a fringe movement. He said that his clients express no interest in it and that it is his responsibility to make money for those clients—not to advocate for his own social or political views.

The tension between these two approaches was strikingly evident in an interview with a British consultant who practices both mainstream and socially responsible investing at the same time. One facet of his professional life involves advising "ultra high net worth individuals" for a mainstream investment company. These people, he reports, are interested only in financial returns. But he also is a prominent member of several nonprofit CSR think tanks, including one organized by British business interests. In that capacity, he has helped to compile an "engagement index": a list of companies, half of which are located in the developing world, that provide good returns for investors and whose CSR performance will be monitored according to a set of "engagement principles." Our source's group "licenses" the list to institutional investment managers, who then invest in some or all of the companies and also agree to pay a small portion of their returns to a group of "engagement professionals" who monitor the companies'

"investments selected for the economic benefits they create apart from their investment return to the employee benefit plan." Interpretive Bulletin Relating to the Fiduciary Standard under ERISA in Considering Economically Targeted Investments, 29 C.F.R. § 2509.94-1 (2004). It is generally viewed as directed at such things as a union plan investing in worker neighborhoods, and concludes that such an investment "will not be prudent if it would be expected to provide a plan with a lower rate of return than available alternative investments with commensurate degrees of risk." *Id.*; *see also* Stewart J. Schwab & Randall S. Thomas, *Realigning Corporate Governance: Shareholder Activism by Labor Unions*, 96 MICH. L. REV. 1018, 1079 (1998) (noting the controversy over whether the Interpretive Bulletin allows pension fund managers to consider other values beyond shareholder wealth maximization). Interpretive Bulletin 94-2 identifies the voting of proxies as a fiduciary duty and requires that, in voting proxies, "the responsible fiduciary consider those factors that may affect the value of the plan's investment and not subordinate the interests of the participants and beneficiaries in their retirement income to unrelated objectives." Interpretive Bulletin Relating to Written Statements of Investment Policy, Including Proxy Voting Policy or Guidelines, 29 C.F.R. § 2509.94-2(1) (2004). It also recognizes that shareholder activism

> intended to monitor or influence the management of corporations in which the plan owns stock is consistent with a fiduciary's obligations under ERISA where the responsible fiduciary concludes that there is a reasonable expectation that such monitoring or communication with management . . . is likely to enhance the value of the plan's investment . . . .

Id.; *see also* O'BARR & CONLEY, *supra* note 46, at 229-32 (discussing the influence of fund managers in shaping the corporate governance debate under Interpretive Bulletin 94-2). Curiously, during the British debate over the proper role of institutional fiduciaries, the weakly worded Interpretive Bulletins were hailed as a strong endorsement of stakeholder activism. In the United States, however, they are sometimes seen as more of an impediment than a mandate. *See* Williams & Conley, *supra* note 6, at 539 n.257.

behavior and interact with management as appropriate. Significantly, the listed companies are chosen because of their investment value and are not dropped on the basis of their substantive CSR performance. The source contrasted this approach with the more common practice of "filtering,"[95] which involves refusing to invest in companies that fail to pass some CSR test. He described the index approach as still in its formative stages, with three licensees thus far.

A middle ground may well be the wave of the future. In our interviews, this position was represented by an executive at a large defined benefit pension plan in the UK. He agreed with his "mainstream" counterparts that his sole legal duty is to manage investments in the best financial interests of his beneficiaries. But, he continued, successful risk management is a critical component of corporate success. Since social or environmental irresponsibility can, in his judgment, create material financial risk for a company, it is his job to screen investments for such risks and, once invested in a company, to advocate forcefully with management to minimize those risks going forward. He acknowledged that his behavior is similar to that of the "leadership" proponent, but he was careful to point out that it is motivated by a very different theory that is entirely consistent with the traditional financial view of fiduciary responsibility.

A final point is that even those institutional investors who are philosophically inclined to value CSR struggle with the question of *how* to value it. A fundamental problem is that, despite the proliferation of CSR reports, the information is rarely presented in a way that is meaningful to investment people. At the 2005 BSR conference in Washington, a well-attended panel debated the question, "Is Wall Street Paying Attention?" A Dutch banker observed that "equity analysts are not well-placed to assess the information and, especially, the legitimacy of the people providing it." A Goldman Sachs analyst said that "we try to put numbers on [environmental performance] or other analysts won't take it seriously"; nonetheless, it still "needs to be integrated into balance sheets." A representative from the World Economic Forum captured the problem succinctly when he asked, rhetorically and somewhat plaintively, "[h]ow do you mainstream CSR?"

IV. ANALYZING THE DISCOURSE OF CSR REPORTING

Similar themes can be seen in the written CSR reports that increasing numbers of global companies now publish.[96] These reports are typically glossy and elaborate documents that resemble annual reports to shareholders in their professional production values. Various sorts of specialists are presumably involved in their preparation. However, they are entirely voluntary, neither their existence nor their format being dictated by governments.[97] Thus, they reflect the considered choices that companies make about how to discuss corporate social responsibility, and their style and content are

---

95. This source and others have associated filtering with American socially responsible investment practices.

96. *See supra* notes 26-29 and accompanying text.

97. Although several European governments now require the disclosure of social and environmental risks that are financially material, *see supra* notes 6-15 and accompanying text, these wide-ranging CSR reports are voluntary. As noted above, some critics, like Christian Aid, characterize them as an effort to preempt mandatory reporting. *See supra* notes 72-75 and accompanying text.

especially revealing for this reason.

Sharon Livesey, a lawyer and business communication scholar, has recently initiated the critical linguistic analysis of corporate CSR reports. We have also begun work of our own in this area, and we describe some of our results below.[98] Livesey has analyzed the discourse[99] employed in the 1998 CSR reports of Royal Dutch/Shell Group and Body Shop International, PLC.[100] Her method involves the identification and categorization of "salient themes, metaphors, modes of expression, and argument structures."[101] She, too, draws on Foucault's theoretical perspective, emphasizing his belief that "meaning is not fixed; rather, it must be constantly reproduced and reconstituted."[102] CSR discourse represents such a reconstitution, "the emergence of a new, unstable discursive order, which joins the heterogeneous elements of the distinct domains of economics, environmentalism, and social justice."[103] From the Foucaltian perspective, power can be both a cause and an effect of control over this emergent discourse.[104]

Examining the Shell report, Livesey looks specifically at the concept of the "triple bottom line" (economical, social, and environmental performance).[105] She attributes the concept to the British environmental activist-turned sustainability consultant Steven Elkington, whom Shell hired as a consultant and whose writing is incorporated into the report. (Livesey calls developments such as the use of communication consultants the "institutionalization" of CSR discourse.)[106] The use of the triple bottom line has two somewhat contradictory effects. On the one hand, it "softens" traditional business discourse by importing "values of environment and social welfare," and introducing language such as "social value added," "environmental value added," and "natural and social capital." Consequently, "'[w]ealth creation,' the fundamental objective of the economic paradigm, [is] transformed into 'sustainable value creation.'"[107] Simultaneously, however, the discourse of the triple bottom line "hardens" the inherently imprecise discourse of social and environmental justice. "[T]his metaphor and methodology constructed sustainable development as a measurable outcome to be

---

98. *See infra* notes 114-159 and accompanying text.

99. For a description of discourse analysis, see CONLEY & O'BARR, *supra* note 45, at 2-19.

100. Sharon M. Livesey, *The Discourse of the Middle Ground: Citizen Shell Commits to Sustainable Development*, 15 MGMT. COMM. Q. 313 (2002); Sharon M. Livesey & Kate Kearins, *Transparent and Caring Corporations? A Study of Sustainability Reports by The Body Shop and Royal Dutch/Shell*, 15 ORG. & ENV'T 233 (2002). Shell's move to CSR reporting followed a strong international reaction against its plan in 1995 to dispose of the North Sea oil platform Brent Spar, and the Nigerian government's execution that same year of nine activists who opposed Shell's oil business. Shell has also been accused of leading a campaign against the United Nations' proposed Norms on Business and Human Rights. *See* CORP. EUR. OBSERVATORY, SHELL LEADS INTERNATIONAL BUSINESS CAMPAIGN AGAINST UN HUMAN RIGHTS NORMS (Mar. 2004), http://www.corporateeurope.org/norms.pdf.

101. Livesey, *supra* note 100, at 321.

102. *Id.* at 319.

103. *Id.*

104. *Id.; see also* CONLEY & O'BARR, *supra* note 45, at 7-8; LISA LITOSSELITI & JANE SUNDERLAND, GENDER IDENTITY AND DISCOURSE ANALYSIS 18-22 (2002).

105. Livesey, *supra* note 100, at 329-30. Shell refused to adopt the triple bottom line literally, but made a functionally equivalent commitment.

106. *See* Livesey & Kearins, *supra* note 100, at 246.

107. Livesey, *supra* note 100, at 329-30.

objectively determined."[108] As a result, Shell was able to present itself as sensitive and scientific, caring without being sentimental, and equally attentive to the straightforward financial demands of shareholders and the inchoate desires of the loosely defined stakeholder class. Above all, Shell imposed discipline on the potentially messy CSR discourse, preserving as taken for granted "certain fundamental values of economic and management models, such as consumerism, growth, and efficiency."[109]

Livesey emphasizes the same contradiction in her comparative analysis of the reports from Shell and The Body Shop. On the one hand, both companies employed "the discourse of care," "bolster[ing] their claims of transparency with the assertion that they were companies who 'cared.'"[110] In response to criticisms that their CSR reporting was therefore imprecise and unscientific, "these corporate reporters asked that—for the time being—they be judged by a seemingly more generous set of criteria, those of human feeling and trust, and that they be given credit for doing reports in the first place."[111] But even as they asked for trust as a substitute for evidence, both companies made strategic use of the ostensible objectivity of adherence to "expert" standards. They recognized that in an impersonal world "standardization is key to making results transparent, and professional verification of report content and processes by outside experts replaces personal witnessing."[112] Of particular value is quantification, "a fundamentally social technology that provides 'a way of organizing commercial and bureacratic life.'"[113] Shell and The Body Shop thus have it both ways, cloaking their "soft" and subjective appeals for trust in the "hard" rhetorical forms of the rigorous domains of accounting and science.

We have also begun our own program of analyzing the discourse of CSR reports. Our first two subjects have been the 2003 reports issued by ExxonMobil and British American Tobacco.[114] We chose ExxonMobil to provide a sector comparison to Livesey's Shell analysis and because ExxonMobil entered the CSR era as perhaps the world's greatest environmental villain following the Exxon Valdez oil spill in 1989. We selected BAT to complement our previous analysis of the public discourse strategies employed by its CSR team,[115] and because of the particular difficulties faced by a tobacco company seeking to be socially responsible.[116] Our analyses are consistent with Livesey's findings, and reveal some additional themes.

From the very beginning, the short, succinct, and glossy ExxonMobil report blends the social and the economic, the soft and the hard, the rhetoric of care and the rhetoric of

---

108. *Id.* at 330.

109. *Id.*

110. Livesey & Kearins, *supra* note 100, at 251.

111. *Id.* Livesey & Kearins' use of "the discourse of care" is strongly evocative of Carol Gilligan's now-classic liberal feminist formulation of "the ethic of care." CAROL GILLIGAN, IN A DIFFERENT VOICE: PSYCHOLOGICAL THEORY AND WOMEN'S DEVELOPMENT 62-63 (1982).

112. Livesey & Kearins, *supra* note 100, at 251.

113. *Id.* at 249 (citation omitted).

114. EXXONMOBIL, CORPORATE CITIZENSHIP REPORT (May 2003) *available at* http://www.exxonmobil.com/corporate/files/corporate/CorporateCitizenship2002.pdf; BRIT. AM. TOBACCO, SOCIAL REPORT 2004/05, *available at* http://www.bat.com/socialreport.

115. *See supra* note 51 and accompanying text.

116. BAT's dilemma was reflected in a recent interview with a representative of a British scientific research institute that is advising BAT on managing its land around the world. He said, "We wish BAT didn't exist. But it does, and it's a steward of the land. So we help them."

analysis. The single-page introductory letter from Chairman and CEO Lee R. Raymond states as the company's goal the creation of "sustainable shareholder value."[117] This simple yet powerful phrasing merges the traditionally narrow economic vision of corporate fiduciary responsibility with the loosely defined notion of sustainability, with all of its connotations of broader social and environmental responsibility.[118] But the next two paragraphs redefine social responsibility in primarily economic terms, and disclaim the ability to exert substantial influence in the non-economic sphere:

> However, we cannot be all things to all people . . . . [O]ur primary responsibility to society is to do our job well—providing the world with abundant, affordable energy in a safe, reliable and environmentally responsible manner.

> Many other forces—cultural, political and environmental—have an impact on society that is greater than ours.[119]

The chairman then reiterates this Adam Smith-like conception of social good by stating, "[O]ur activities and those of others in private industry deliver economic benefits and help advance worthwhile societal goals," and backs up the assertion by citing the "value to consumers" of the company's products, the billions it invests in research, the billions more it pays in taxes and royalties, the still more billions it spends on goods and services, the dividends it pays to its shareholders, and the employment opportunities it offers.[120] Only then does the letter allow for the possibility of "other" forms of social contributions, and that in a backhanded way: "Although these economic contributions form the core of the social benefits that ExxonMobil delivers, there are many other ways we contribute."[121] Finally, the chairman states that even ExxonMobil's "wider involvement in society" will be governed by hard analysis, the "rigorously applied management systems" that mark its core endeavors: "Our approach to corporate citizenship reflects our scale and the disciplined approach we take to all aspects of our business."[122]

The remainder of the 41-page report is a detailed playing-out of these themes. The illustrations, which are found on every page, are a striking combination of colorful graphs and charts and photographs of children, tigers, and ExxonMobil employees of every race and many nationalities. In the text, disciplined management and analysis are repeatedly described as the keys to ExxonMobil's social accountability. The Operations Integrity Management System (OIMS) is the critical "framework for meeting [ExxonMobil's] commitments to the highest operational standards of safety, health and environmental protection"; under this system, "[a] broad range of factors is analyzed, including economic, environmental and social."[123] In the environmental sphere, OIMS is

---

117. EXXONMOBIL, *supra* note 114, at 1.
118. As Livesey points out, "Sustainable development is a complex notion that seeks to reconcile the goals of economic development and ecological wellbeing." Livesey, *supra* note 100, at 315. She further characterizes it as "a contested terrain" and "a source of confusion." *Id.* at 315-16.
119. EXXONMOBIL, *supra* note 114, at 1.
120. *Id.*
121. *Id.*
122. *Id.*
123. EXXONMOBIL, *supra* note 114 at 3; *see also id.* at 17 (listing the key components of the OIMS).

augmented by Environmental Business Planning,[124] which helps the company "to prevent incidents."[125] Quantitative "performance indicators" are used to track environmental progress.[126] ExxonMobil brings a new and literal salience to the notion of micro-management, employing "'molecule management' to yield high-value products while improving energy efficiency and lowering emissions."[127] Even the air is systematized, with emissions being "most effectively managed at the point of discharge."[128]

The section headed Engagement with Communities begins with a restatement of the chairman's assertions about the financial contributions ExxonMobil makes through taxes, wages, the purchase of goods and services, and other forms of distributions.[129] Here, too, systematic management is emphasized. Each major project is said to begin with an Environmental and Social Impact Assessment, which identifies risks, specifies mitigation plans, and "forms the basis for ongoing monitoring of the environmental and social performance of the project."[130] So also with security, which is the subject of "Integrated Security Management,"[131] and "workforce development and diversity," which "requires leadership, action plans, accountability, stewardship and constancy of purpose over the long term."[132]

Greenhouse gases and climate change are the subject of a more complex and ambiguous rhetoric. The discussion begins with a qualified acknowledgment of the problem: "We recognize that the risk of climate change and its potential impacts on society and ecosystems may prove to be significant."[133] The essence of the response is consistent with the rest of the report: "to take sensible, economic actions now to improve efficiency and reduce future global emissions."[134] But the application of the management-based logic seen elsewhere is complicated by the absence of appropriate discourse structures, there being "currently no commonly accepted methodology for accounting for greenhouse gas emissions."[135] One of the few appeals to hard fact in these sections of the report is the statement that it is really someone else's problem: "[D]eveloping countries represent only 25 percent of the global economy and yet produce almost 50 percent of the world's carbon dioxide (or carbon) emissions," and are likely to account for 80% of the carbon increase in the next 20 years.[136]

The BAT document is very different in appearance. It is a dense sprawling report,

---

124. *Id.* at 12.
125. *Id.* at 13.
126. *Id.*
127. EXXONMOBIL, *supra* note 114, at 14.
128. *Id.* at 16.
129. *Id.* at 24.
130. *Id.* at 25.
131. *Id.* at 28-29.
132. EXXONMOBIL, *supra* note 114, at 32.
133. *Id.* at 9.
134. *Id.*
135. *Id.* at 15. With the Kyoto Protocol coming into effect, which limits greenhouse gases, this statement may not be entirely accurate. It may be technically correct that there is no "commonly accepted methodology" to account for greenhouse gas emissions because the United States is not part of Kyoto and has no such accounting system, but Western European and Japanese companies and Japan do account for emissions, and are rapidly developing markets in unused greenhouse gas allowances.
136. *Id.* at 9.

with 158 pages of compact text and few illustrations. Its content is entirely consistent with what we heard from BAT's CSR team,[137] and exhibits both similarities to and differences from the approach taken by ExxonMobil. In his single-page introduction, BAT chairman Martin Broughton stresses, in a highlighted sidebar that accompanies his photograph, as ExxonMobil does, the primacy of economics as a motivation for CSR: "Corporate social responsibility is integral to our approach to the management of our businesses globally and to building long term shareholder value."[138]

Elsewhere on the same page, however, the discourse of traditional financial management yields to the alternative soft discourses of communication and feelings. For example, whereas the sentence just quoted is the only reference to shareholders in the chairman's letter, there are eight mentions of the open-ended, contested category of "stakeholders."[139] There is repeated emphasis on the goal of dialogue with these undefined stakeholders—"stimulating discussions, as stakeholders share their views, concerns, criticisms and indeed some praise."[140] This communicative process can evoke emotional responses, as when the chairman acknowledges that "[i]t is disappointing that we still encounter reluctance amongst the tobacco control and public health communities to engage in dialogue."[141] Nonetheless, BAT's "doors remain open" to "stakeholders in these groups" as BAT strives to show by action that they "mean it." Presumably, any representative of these interests who chooses to join the dialogue thereby becomes a stakeholder, which further highlights the indeterminacy of that category.

Significantly, the chairman's letter devotes two full paragraphs to what Livesey terms the "institutionalization" of CSR discourse.[142] The first paragraph describes the commendations that the company has received from major CSR reporting players such as the Dow Jones Sustainability Index and the UK Business in the Environment Index. Then, after "sincerely" thanking the stakeholders for their contributions, the chairman goes on to thank the Institute of Business Ethics and Market & Opinion Research International (MORI) for facilitating much of the dialogue, and Bureau Veritas for verification and assurance of BAT's compliance with the AA1000 Assurance Standard.[143] The message is clear that BAT endeavors to talk to everyone, and also talks about this talk to the most widely recognized monitors of CSR discourse.

A major objective of all this talk is "embedding CSR principles," a concept that BAT's CSR team mentioned repeatedly in their public presentation. Despite its significance to the BAT report, it, like "stakeholder," is nowhere defined. It was clear in

---

137. *See supra* Parts III.B.1-2.

138. BRIT. AM. TOBACCO, *supra* note 114, at 3.

139. *See supra* Part III.B.1. For a discussion of the legal difficulties inherent in defining the stakeholder category, see Orts, *supra* note 55.

140. BRIT. AM. TOBACCO, *supra* note 114, at 3.

141. *Id.*

142. Livesey & Kearins, *supra* note 100, at 246.

143. The named organizations are among the most prominent independent groups that conduct CSR dialogues, monitor CSR activities, and audit CSR reports. The AA1000 Assurance Standard, promulgated by the British NGO AccountAbility, is a set of "guiding principles" for auditing ("assuring") CSR reports—a CSR version of Generally Accepted Accounting Principles. *See* AccountAbility, AA1000 Assurance Standard, http://www.accountability.org.uk/aa1000/?pageid=52 (last visited Apr. 5, 2006). The BAT report elsewhere makes repeated references to the Global Reporting Initiative, another set of sustainability reporting standards. *See* Global Reporting Initiative, http://www.globalreporting.org/ (last visited Apr. 5, 2006).

the public presentation that it refers to making CSR a norm that is taken for granted by everyone in the company. Embedding has become such a prominent feature of CSR discourse that its meaning is apparently now taken for granted.

The concluding paragraph of the chairman's letter is significant in two respects. First, it emphasizes that the process of communication is at the core of BAT's view of CSR: "I believe that our reporting and our Statement of Business Principles demonstrate that we continue to address difficult issues facing our business, including those around our products." Note the absence of any reference in this peroration to substantive achievements; instead, the chairman's concluding claim is that by *reporting* and making a *statement* BAT *demonstrates* that it is *addressing* difficult issues. Process rules; the message is the message. Second, the chairman makes a striking concession to the power of stakeholders by stating that BAT's performance "is for our stakeholders to judge."[144] It would be extraordinary if the chairman were delegating to a largely self-appointed constituency the power to judge the substance of the company's performance. But in fact all that is being put up for judgment is BAT's performance as a communicator, which prompts the suspicion that the objective of the whole exercise is simply to keep everyone talking in a forum that BAT controls.

The body of the report pursues the chairman's themes at great length. It begins with a 12-page description of BAT's CSR process, including a summary of its independent standards compliance assurance and a "stakeholder global issues map."[145] There follows a statement of BAT's three "business principles"—mutual benefit, responsible product stewardship, and good corporate conduct—each of which is then broken down into several "core beliefs."[146] Next comes an 11-page explication of the Framework for Corporate Social Responsibility, which is itself an elaboration of the three business principles and the core beliefs.[147] The three determinations that structure the framework are "where we should take the lead," "where we should work together with others," and "where others should take the lead."[148] This section is followed by a 22-page report on the past year's UK stakeholder dialogue, which "focused on the development of the Framework for Corporate Social Responsibility, based on the Statement of Business Principles . . . facilitated by Stewart Lewis, a Director of MORI and assisted by the Director of the Institute of Business Ethics . . . [and] monitored and evaluated by Bureau Veritas."[149] This section quotes numerous statements by participating stakeholders. True to the chairman's letter, there is a mixture of praise (e.g., "it's good to see your use of AA1000"), concern (e.g., "[i]f they do everything that they say, they're not going to sell tobacco"), and criticism (e.g., "[t]his is about the appearance of virtue, rather than actual virtue").[150]

---

144. BRIT. AM. TOBACCO, *supra* note 114, at 3.

145. *Id.* at 5-16.

146. *Id.* at 17-20. The core beliefs include: (1) "We believe in engaging constructively with our stakeholders"; (2) "We believe in the provision of accurate, clear health messages about the risks of tobacco consumption"; and (3) "We believe the tobacco industry should have a voice in the formation of government policies affecting it." *Id.* at 18.

147. *Id.* at 21-31.

148. BRIT. AM. TOBACCO, *supra* note 114, at 21.

149. *Id.* at 32.

150. *Id.* at 36.

The final 60% of the report deals with such specific areas of performance as supplier responsibility (making sure that BAT's suppliers live up to its standards),[151] environmental management,[152] labor practices,[153] and human rights.[154] Whereas everything up to this point has consisted of talk about talk, these sections blend the discourses of talk and action. Considerable attention is devoted to communications, participation in dialogue based programs, and awards bestowed by various CSR institutions,[155] but there are also references to things that BAT has *done*. A section on occupational health and safety[156] illustrates the point. It discusses a survey, as well as such communicative acts as "encourag[ing]" affiliated companies to take various steps. But the company also reports "providing condoms," "trac[ing] and test[ing]" the contacts of TB patients, "offer[ing] a cheap method for disinfecting water," and "issu[ing] nets impregnated with insecticide."[157]

It is not our purpose in this analysis to challenge ExxonMobil or BAT's good faith or performance or the accuracy of any of their assertions. We agree with Livesey that CSR data "allow stakeholders to call corporate actors to account" and that the new discourse of social responsibility has coincided with an "emerging practice of sustainability."[158] Our point, rather, is that by preempting the CSR reporting issue, corporations have gained a significant form of power: the power to define and frame. ExxonMobil has exercised this power to define social responsibility in economic terms, and to frame the appropriate response in terms of management, discipline, and control. Significantly, while ExxonMobil emphasizes "engagement with communities" in assessing the environmental and social impact of its projects,[159] its report makes no mention of open-ended and all-inclusive conversations. In particular, there is no invitation to interested constituencies to define themselves as stakeholders and join the dialogue. This is a discourse of action, not talk. Those who would contest the company's approach must do so on its terms or risk being dismissed as irrelevant.

In sharp contrast, BAT's report frames CSR in terms of a communication process. Any self-identified stakeholder can apparently claim a seat at the table, and no comment

---

151. *Id.* at 87.

152. *Id.* at 95.

153. BRIT. AM. TOBACCO, *supra* note 114, at 109.

154. *Id.* at 121.

155. To take but one example, two pages on biodiversity and conservation mention a "Biodiversity Week [at a BAT factory] to raise awareness," "discussing forming a Business and Biodiversity Forum," a "presentation at the IUCN Centre," and an "exhibition" that was "featured in the World Conservation Union Stand" at the 2002 "Summit on Sustainable Development." *Id.* at 106-07.

156. *Id.* at 117-21.

157. *Id.* at 119. The particular actions are explained as part of a Significant Indigenous Disease programme directed at diseases that "cause suffering to employees, their families and their communities and can cause long term financial problems in the developing world." BRIT. AM. TOBACCO, *supra* note 114, at 117.

158. Livesey, *supra* note 100, at 341.

159. EXXONMOBIL, *supra* note 114, at 24-25.

For example, in Chad and Cameroon, during the planning of an oil-development and pipeline project, the company conducted the largest consultation ever undertaken in Africa and perhaps the world. The consultation included more than 1,000 public meetings in 300 villages . . . . As a result of these discussions, the pipeline was rerouted to avoid settlements, important hunting areas and environmentally sensitive habitats.

Id. at 25.

is a priori irrelevant. Indeed, BAT grants to stakeholders the right to pass judgment on its CSR performance. BAT thus appears to cede to stakeholders the very control that is the hallmark of ExxonMobil's discourse. But perhaps BAT exerts a subtler yet more effective form of control. Whereas ExxonMobil purports to control the content and substance of CSR, BAT effectively defines CSR as being without substance. If a company's responsibility to society is defined in terms of communication, then what better form of control than to manage the forum in which that communication takes place—to own the table, as it were? By choosing a hard discourse of economics, management, and science, ExxonMobil rules out many forms of criticism, but still sets itself up for fact-based attack. BAT, however, can plausibly reply to any charge of failure of communication with more communication. While its open-ended discourse invites criticism in any form and from any source, it binds the company to nothing more than listening.

V. THE CSR MOVEMENT AS AN EXPERIMENT IN THE NEW GOVERNANCE

The CSR movement can also be interpreted as an ongoing experiment in what has been called "new governance" or "the new governing paradigm."[160] New governance theory is complex, its terminology and taxonomies contested, and its theoretical framework still inchoate.[161] A core element in virtually all formulations, however, is the idea of the "post-regulatory state." According to Colin Scott, the prior concept of the "regulatory state" was developed "to contrast a distinctive and emergent form of governance from the practices and institutions of the welfare state."[162] Whereas the welfare state was characterized by reliance on "instruments of public ownership, direct state provision of benefits and services, [and] integration of policy making and operational functions," the regulatory state involves "the separation of operational from regulatory activities in some policy areas (sometimes linked to privatization), a trend towards separating purchasers and providers of public services (through policies of contracting out and market testing) and towards separation of operational from policy tasks within government departments and the creation of executive agencies."[163] The welfare state, in other words, was characterized by direct state intervention. The regulatory state still exerts top-down "command and control" authority,[164] but exercises its power in more diffuse ways. The essence of the post-regulatory state, captured in the linguistic shift from *government* to *governance*, is the further diffusion of regulatory power among networks of state and non-state actors that transcend national boundaries.[165] The hallmarks of the post-regulatory state include the possibility of "regulatory governance functioning in a manner not dependent on state law or in which state law is not central" and "a loosening of the sharp distinction between states and

---

160. Colin Scott, *Regulation in the Age of Governance: The Rise of the Post-Regulatory State* 5 (Austl. Nat'l Univ., Nat'l Europe Centre Paper No. 100, 2003), *available at* http://www.anu.edu.au/NEC/scott1.pdf.

161. For a cogent summary of the emerging theoretical themes, see *id.*

162. *Id.* at 4.

163. *Id.*

164. Anne-Marie Slaughter, *Global Government Networks, Global Information Agencies, and Disaggregated Democracy*, 24 MICH. J. INT'L L. 1041, 1059 (2003).

165. *See id.*

markets and between the public and the private."[166]

Anne-Marie Slaughter has emphasized the prominence of networks in the post-regulatory "pluralist mix of global governance mechanisms."[167] These include many forms of "transgovernmental networks" defined as interactions among sub-units of governments that are not closely controlled by their respective legislatures or executives.[168] They may arise as a matter of conscious planning or spontaneously, when an agency "would reach out on its own account to its foreign counterparts" in an effort to address a common problem.[169] Importantly, "transgovernmental networks can be folded into larger 'mixed networks' of governmental and private actors."[170] In one view, these networks become mere "talking shops" where information is collected and disseminated but no real power is exercised.[171] Slaughter argues, however, that this view is short-sighted because it misses "a key dimension of the exercise of power in the Information Age."[172] Her general point is that information can be power: by virtue of their ability to "generate compilations of best practices, codes of conduct, and templates for everything," the networks' "dissemination of information has played a far greater role in triggering policy convergence in various issue areas than more deliberate and coercive attempts."[173]

The CSR movement can be usefully seen as nascent governance by just such a global information network. A variety of actors have come together to disseminate information and to use that process to influence conduct. Just as Slaughter describes, these actors "generate compilations of best practices, codes of conduct, and templates for everything."[174] In the case of the UK and some other EU countries, governmental actors have participated, with the precise effect of "triggering policy convergence."[175] The fact that CSR has yet to become part of American regulatory policy may be a reflection less of differing ideologies than of the fact that network governance is far better developed within the EU than in this country. In fact, it has been widely argued that such governance, sometimes labeled "comitology," is the very essence of the EU.[176]

The new governance has its strident critics. The most pervasive critique concerns democratic accountability. Simply put, the argument is that as the nodes of decisionmaking become more numerous, less well defined, and harder to locate, they stray dangerously far away from the people and institutions that are under direct electoral control. Network governance proponents argue that the process ultimately enhances democracy. Some applaud the "de-politicization" of decisionmaking[177] that ensues when the traditional linear and law-centered system of control is displaced by a pluralistic and

---

166. Scott, *supra* note 160, at 2-3; *see also* Shamir, *supra* note 1, at 645 (discussing the "soft law" approach).

167. Slaughter, *supra* note 164, at 1044.

168. *Id.* at 1045.

169. *Id.* at 1056.

170. *Id.* at 1057.

171. *Id.*

172. Slaughter, *supra* note 164, at 1057.

173. *Id.*

174. *Id.*

175. *Id.*

176. *See id.* at 1058-62 (reviewing comitology scholarship).

177. Slaughter, *supra* note 164, at 1068.

decentered "deliberative" process.[178] The result, it is argued, will be "much better outcomes for the society as a whole, reflecting the supposed choices of a hypothetical median voter."[179] A different kind of support for the new governance comes from what Slaughter terms the theory of "horizontal democracy."[180] Its starting point is "the empirical fact of mushrooming 'private governance regimes' in which individuals, groups, and corporate entities in domestic and transnational society generate the rules, norms, and principles they are prepared to live by."[181] Correlatively, the function of the state is viewed as "not to regulate directly, but rather to manage these processes by facilitating problem solving and information pooling."[182] Thus, the argument goes, even as it appears to cede political power to unelected governmental and private actors, the post-regulatory state actually promotes democracy by domesticating this irresistible tide of self-help.

The critical response to these arguments goes well beyond the basic point of attenuated electoral control. Some contend that disaggregated democracy[183] is "fatally flawed by the inevitably elitist identity of the participants in these networks, their corresponding biases in making vitally important public decisions and their unawareness of these biases, and the impossibility of creating equal access to these networks without destroying the very conditions that make them work as deliberative bodies."[184] Another worry is that capture of the regulatory process by the regulated becomes an even greater danger when the state backs away from its traditional role of intervening to balance inequalities.[185] If it is "*economic* power which ground[s] the capacity of non-state actors to govern or coerce,"[186] there is no reason to believe that those actors' motive or opportunity would diminish in a post-regulatory environment. Moreover, those in the Foucaultian tradition argue that power has always been exercised by "disparate practices and technologies" that do not derive explicitly from law and the state.[187] Consequently, one might conclude, new governance is likely to become a particularly effective servant of old power relations.

Once again, the CSR movement may be a revealing test of these theories in action. The sociologist Ronen Shamir has characterized "the field of CSR as one conceptual space where various regulatory/disciplinary regimes are pursued and negotiated among a host of players."[188] In the United States, the government directly regulates some of the

---

178. *See id.* at 1068-69 (reviewing "vertical democracy" argument); Scott, *supra* note 160, at 7-10 (discussing theories of "autopoeisis" and "governmentality").

179. Slaughter, *supra* note 164, at 1068.

180. *Id.* at 1071-72.

181. *Id.* at 1072.

182. *Id.* at 1072-73; *see* Scott, *supra* note 160, at 9 (emphasizing the "modest role of law in steering or proceduralizing those activities over which control is sought").

183. Slaughter, *supra* note 164, at 1069.

184. *Id.* at 1070.

185. *See* Scott, *supra* note 160, at 9.

186. *Id.* at 10 (emphasis in original).

187. *See id.* (applying Foucault's analysis of power to theory of "governmentality").

188. Shamir, *supra* note 1, at 659. Consistent with new governance theory, Shamir concludes:

> [The contemporary] notion of corporate governance signifies a decisive move in the direction of abandoning traditional "command and control" state regulatory schemes in favor of "responsive regulation", which is supposed to facilitate—yet not enforce and dictate—self-regulation

specific corporate behaviors, particularly in the environmental and safety areas, that comprise the category "social responsibility,"[189] but it has thus far left the larger field entirely to emerging networks of private actors. Even in the UK, where the national government has threatened to take an overt, top-down regulatory role, what would be regulated is disclosure, not behavior; behavior would be determined through a private discourse in which markets would presumably have the ultimate say.[190] In the above-quoted language of the new governance, the British government would be "facilitating problem solving and information pooling."[191]

Most of the elements that the new governance critics fear are also at least latent in the CSR movement. Elites are everywhere. Participating global corporations are the apotheosis of economic elitism, while some stakeholder actors can be seen as representing various cultural and information elites. No one has been elected, of course; with the exception of such obvious participants as employees and residents of company towns, the class of private stakeholders is self-appointed and limited only by an aspirant's ability to get heard. Capture seems to be a clear and present danger, with the target corporations both managing the stakeholder dialogue and using its very existence to deflect demands for old-style government intervention. And finally, as we have argued above,[192] Foucault himself could not have conjured a better example of the exercise of power through subtle and distributed disciplinary practices.

The practical significance of the theoretical disputes surrounding the new governance is reflected vividly in a report recently issued by SustainAbility, a British consultancy that is one of the most prominent and respected players in the CSR movement.[193] The report came about when the UN Global Compact, a voluntary CSR standards initiative, "asked SustainAbility to evaluate the extent to which CSR initiatives are helping drive the transition to more sustainable forms of development."[194] SustainAbility then interviewed CSR leaders from business, government, and civil society; conducted a public opinion poll; reviewed corporate best practices; and conducted several case studies.[195]

SustainAbility situates the report squarely within the discourse of the new

---

programs and "compliance-oriented" regulation, which is to be carried out through corporate consent and voluntary organizational processes of reflexive learning.
Id. at 660.

189. *See, e.g.*, Robert A. Kagan et al., *Explaining Corporate Environmental Performance: How Does Regulation Matter?*, 37 L. & SOC'Y REV. 51 (2003) (demonstrating interaction of government regulation and pressures from private actors in determining corporate environmental behavior); Peter J. May, *Compliance Motivations: Affirmative and Negative Bases*, 38 L. & SOC'Y REV. 41 (2004) (analyzing complex motivations of homebuilders to comply with codes); *cf.* Cary Coglianese & David Lazer, *Management-Based Regulation: Prescribing Private Management to Achieve Public Goals*, 37 L. & SOC'Y REV. 691 (2003) (arguing for shift to regulatory regime that "directs regulated organizations to engage in a planning process that aims toward the achievement of public goals, offering firms a flexibility in how they achieve public goals").

190. This is, of course, exactly how traditional capital market regulation works, suggesting that the new governance may not be so new after all.

191. *See supra* note 182 and accompanying text.

192. *See supra* notes 61 & 187 and accompanying text.

193. SUSTAINABILITY, GEARING UP: FROM CORPORATE RESPONSIBILITY TO GOOD GOVERNANCE AND SCALABLE SOLUTIONS (2004), *available at* http://www.sustainability.com/publications/gearing-up.asp.

194. *Id.* at 2.

195. *Id.*

governance by defining "'governance' to refer to mechanisms, processes and institutions which set the 'rules of the game' for societies at the domestic or global levels."[196] The report expressly acknowledges the reality of the post-regulatory state: "Governments are a fundamental component of governance, but increasingly non-state actors from business and civil society are seen to play key roles."[197] As with the new governance generally, the specific phenomenon of CSR has come about "as a pragmatic response where governance has failed or been weak."[198] The report finds in the evolution of CSR almost all of the pros and cons that have been put forward in the new governance literature. On the plus side, for example, is the "good news" that "many [CSR] initiatives are evolving in the right direction, with a growing variety of companies acknowledging a wider range of stakeholders and acting on an increasing number of key issues."[199] These positive developments are the product of a "type of governance shift" that might not have been possible "twenty, ten or even five years ago."[200] This governance shift is seen in turn as enabled by "a maturation in the types of relationships that are feasible."[201] This process of maturation has many elements, all of which are recognizable as key pieces of the new governance paradigm:

> Internationally, we are seeing a growing focus on "ethical" or "responsible" globalization . . . . Citizens in many developing countries are achieving greater rights and recognizing greater responsibilities. Although trust in both business and government often remains low, the potential for collaboration clearly exists. Internationally, NGOs . . . are actively increasing their capacity to work with business in forging solutions to key sustainable development challenges.

> This does not suggest that dissent has ceased to exist—which is neither likely nor desirable. However, collaborative relationships . . . are increasingly becoming an alternative and complementary model . . . . [T]hey demonstrate shifting relationships between government, business and civil society and an opportunity for more constructive joint working.[202]

The dangers seen by new governance critics are equally real. The self-interested presence of business is both essential and problematic. Since global corporations are economic enterprises backed by vast economic power, there is both incentive and opportunity to manipulate CSR. The core problem is that "the business case for getting in front of the corporate pack remains weak."[203] SustainAbility characterizes the problem as a species of prisoners' dilemma: "Collectively, society would benefit from solutions, but there is little or no incentive for any single actor to take the first move and risk bearing all the costs alone. Indeed the individual incentive is to do nothing and hope to 'free ride,' benefiting from the actions of others."[204]

---

196. *Id.* at 4.
197. *Id.*
198. SUSTAINABILITY, *supra* note 193, at 17.
199. *Id.* at 2.
200. *Id.* at 18.
201. *Id.*
202. *Id.*
203. SUSTAINABILITY, *supra* note 193, at 3.
204. *Id.* at 13.

Instead of leading, many companies use their power to structure and dominate a CSR discourse that devolves into little more than a public relations exercise—a post-regulatory version of regulatory capture.[205] SustainAbility sees evidence of precisely this problem in the current state of affairs, in that "most [CSR] initiatives still sit at a distance from the company's core business activities, disengaged from long-term strategy."[206] The future will test the strength of the new governance paradigm, in particular, whether CSR stakeholders will be able "to ensure that voluntary initiatives do not serve as camouflage or alibis for participants."[207]

Finally, SustainAbility cautions against being too quick to dispense with the traditional role of government. The report argues that "stronger government policies in these areas are necessary and perhaps inevitable."[208] SustainAbility acknowledges that government intervention gives rise to two sets of concerns: (1) too much government control over business, and (2) too much corporate influence over government. Ultimately, the report concludes, "the challenge is not to get companies to take on the responsibilities of governments but to help to insure governments fulfill their own responsibilities."[209] Although the report does not mention the recent legal developments in the UK, they would seem to be an apt illustration of what SustainAbility has in mind.

From theory to practice, the new governance paradigm provides an excellent account of the CSR movement. The inadequacy of traditional regulation at the national level has provided the stimulus for the collection of actions that comprise the movement. As the model predicts, the result to date has been a template that blurs traditional public/private and state/market boundaries and introduces new categories of actors into the regulatory process. On the ground, our ethnographic findings and SustainAbility's observations confirm that the strengths and weaknesses attributed to new governance are all present in abundance, with ultimate success or failure still in the balance.

VI. CONCLUSION

Our ethnographic and linguistic research has amply confirmed the existence, vitality, and relative coherence of the corporate social responsibility movement. Governments, corporations, and their stakeholder critics take it seriously at the rhetorical level. At the level of action, governments outside the United States increasingly promote its primary objectives: the identification, planning, and disclosure of corporate responses to social and environmental problems. Companies themselves have begun to go well beyond the modest legal requirements that have so far been imposed. Disclosure is now a widespread practice, as is "engagement" with a wide range of stakeholders. This includes everything from talk to the implementation of specific environmental and social projects to the solicitation of independent CSR audits. Among NGOs, observing, critiquing, and sometimes participating in these engagement activities has become a core activity. Some investors, especially publicly funded institutions, are also taking notice, either by subjecting their share purchases to CSR filters or by requiring their trustees and managers

---

205. *Id.* at 19.
206. *Id.* at 2.
207. *Id.* at 3.
208. SUSTAINABILITY, *supra* note 193, at 3.
209. *Id.*

to engage (that ubiquitous word again) the management of portfolio companies on CSR issues. All of this activity has generated a new industry of CSR support, featuring consultants, facilitators, auditors, and communications specialists.

One view of these developments is that the "progressives" are winning. Even if governments are not mandating that corporations clean up their behavior, both literally and figuratively, at least governments are forcing disclosure of the instances when they do not. As is assumed in the financial world, transparency will presumably beget substantive changes for the better. Moreover, according to the optimistic view, companies are hiring people with CSR sensibilities and taking them seriously as they "embed" social and environmental principles in their respective corporate cultures. At the same time, corporations are cooperating with NGOs and other stakeholders rather than treating them as nuisances to be ignored or silenced.

Our empirical research is casting doubt both on the conclusion that the CSR movement is actually succeeding and on the ultimate desirability of that success. With respect to the first issue, there is reason to be skeptical of corporate motives. We have heard many expressions of concern that companies' CSR activities rarely encompass their "core" activities, as well about the need to "scale-up" social and environmental activities from the demonstration project level. Moreover, our linguistic analyses suggest that companies are treating both stakeholder dialogue and CSR reporting as opportunities to shape and control the debate over their conduct—and bringing sophisticated communication strategies to bear in doing so. Rather than redressing the power imbalance between corporations and civil society, these processes may be reinforcing it in subtle but effective ways.

Even if the optimistic view is correct and CSR is indeed carrying the day, there are attendant costs, both actual and potential. One obvious problem, acknowledged by the protagonists, is the effect on NGOs as they evolve from gadflies into corporate partners. NGOs are already beginning to talk like corporations, with their discussions of "branding" and "accountability." As their representatives readily admit, these habits of language may presage adverse changes at the level of thought and action as well. They worry constantly about capture and co-optation, about becoming accomplices to "greenwashing." They find it hard to resist the logic when corporations demand the same kind of accountability that NGOs demand of them. But the NGOs realize that their social utility lies in being independent, aggressive, and sometimes hyperbolic—in other words, in not always being accountable. They see the very real possibility that the demand for accountability, so eminently reasonable on the surface, may be a Trojan horse, disguising an effort to domesticate, bureaucratize, and ultimately neuter the most stridently effective among them.

Finally, if the CSR movement is indeed ascendant, then we are in the midst of an experiment in the new governance whose consequences are difficult to gauge. As new governance theorists have suggested, CSR shifts the emphasis from traditional government regulation of corporate conduct to the promotion of disclosure by corporations and their engagement with civil society. The world of CSR is, precisely as predicted by new governance theory, a complex communication network among public and private actors. Critically, the latter—NGOs, for example—bear much more responsibility for shaping outcomes than they did in the old regulatory state.

Equally evident, however, are the risks predicted by new governance critics. Who chose the private actors that are central to the process? Some, such as employees and local residents, are consensus candidates. But others—the "partnering" NGOs, or those who are recognized as tribunes of various interests—seem to have chosen themselves. As befits a communication network, they have leveraged themselves into a place at the table by their ability to communicate, with the public as well as their corporate targets. This is not to say that they are inappropriate or ineffective tribunes, but merely that they have come by their positions by a process that has none of the hallmarks of liberal democracy. Above all, the CSR world is a profoundly paternalistic one. Powerless people are occasionally seen in the dialogue process, but at the sufferance of corporations. Otherwise, they must be spoken for by their unelected representatives.

The discussion of selection brings us inevitably back to accountability. Representatives who are not chosen by their constituents cannot be removed by them either. One manifestation of this problem is the widely-expressed concern that corporate-NGO partnerships may be preempting the development of strong local governments. The essence of this concern is that the entities that have appointed themselves to speak for local interests have displaced the very institutions that would be most likely to call them to account. We have heard the response that corporations and NGOs are subject to discipline by their respective customers and contributors. But we have repeatedly been told that customers will not pay for CSR, and in any event both customers and contributors are far removed from the locales where accountability issues are most salient.

So CSR remains a work in progress. At its best, it promises a corporate decisionmaking process in which managers think and talk openly about social and environmental issues and then tell the world what they did and why. At its worst, it is nothing more than an elaborate public relations charade in which companies perform certain prescribed rituals but continue to do business as usual. But it may be even worse than business as usual, as the effect of the rituals may be to co-opt critics, mislead consumers, and preempt regulation. Only ongoing empirical scrutiny of the CSR movement will tell. At this relatively early point in that process, our research leaves us still hopeful, but increasingly skeptical.

[13]

SEPARATING MYTH FROM REALITY ABOUT CORPORATE RESPONSIBILITY LITIGATION

Harold Hongju Koh*

ABSTRACT

In recent months, commentators, corporations and the Bush Administration have joined forces to attack human rights and environmental litigation against corporate defendants under the Alien Tort Statute. This article argues that this attack rests on four myths: that United States courts cannot hold private corporations civilly liable for torts in violation of international law; that there is a flood of such cases that would impose liability on corporations simply for doing business in a difficult country; that statutory amendment or doctrinal reversal is necessary to stem this flood of litigation; and that domestic litigation is in any event a bad way to promote higher corporate standards. This article debunks each of the myths, explaining why in fact the sky is not falling, and why radical solutions are not needed to solve non-problems.

INTRODUCTION

Gary Clyde Hufbauer and Nicholas K. Mitrokostas have authored an article in this Journal that summarizes their recent report, vividly entitled *Awakening Monster: The Alien Tort Statute of 1789.*[1] That article and report follow a brief recently filed in the U.S. Court of Appeals for the Ninth Circuit by the Bush Administration in *Doe v Unocal*, which argues that litigation under the Alien

---

* Gerard C. and Bernice Latrobe Smith Professor of International Law and Dean Designate, Yale Law School, PO Box 208215 New Haven, CT, USA 06520-8215, Harold.koh@yale.edu. The author has served as Assistant Secretary of State for Democracy, Human Rights and Labor, 1998–2001 and as counsel and co-counsel for plaintiffs and amici in several cases brought under the Alien Tort Statute. This article derives from Harold Hongju Koh, *Wrong on Rights*, 18 July 2003, available at http://yaleglobal.yale.edu/display.article?id=2121 and presentations given on 4 July 2003 in the Hague at a panel on Corporate Responsibility of the American Society of International Law and the Netherlands Society of International Law (forthcoming in the Proceedings of that conference) and on 9 September 2003 to the Asia Society in New York.

[1] Gary Clyde Hufbauer and Nicholas K. Mitrokostas, 'International Implications of the Alien Tort Statute', 7(2) JIEL (2004) 245–62 [hereinafter Hufbauer and Mitrokostas], summarizing Gary Clyde Hufbauer and Nicholas K. Mitrokostas, *Awakening Monster: The Alien Tort Statute of 1789* (Washington, DC: Institute for International Economics, 2003).

Tort Statute (ATS)[2] against corporate defendants threatens US foreign policy, endangers corporations, will discourage trade and foreign investment in dozens of developing countries, and will undermine the war against terrorism.[3] 'Unless the [Alien Tort Statute] is limited by the Supreme Court or Congress,' these authors breathlessly assert, 'millions of impoverished people may be denied an opportunity to participate in the global market.'[4]

These developments underscore just how much overreaction and hysteria have developed regarding corporate responsibility litigation in US courts for environmental injury and human rights abuse under the Alien Tort Statute. I come to this subject wearing three hats: as a professor of international law, as a human rights litigator who has been involved in a number of these cases, and as a policymaker who helped develop US policy toward corporate responsibility in human rights during the Clinton Administration. Each of these perspectives tells me that we need to separate the reality from four major myths about corporate responsibility litigation under the Alien Tort Statute.

MYTH I: DOMESTIC COURTS CANNOT HOLD PRIVATE CORPORATIONS CIVILLY LIABLE FOR TORTS IN VIOLATIONS OF INTERNATIONAL LAW

Some commentators argue that only states and individuals, not corporations, can be held directly liable under international law.[5] But in fact, many treaties and international instruments do impose substantive duties upon corporations. The International Labor Organization (ILO) Tripartite Declaration, for example, obliges corporations not to interfere with employees' rights to form unions and not to use child or slave labor.[6] Nuclear treaties, such as the Paris Convention,[7] and oil spill treaties hold shipowners and operators of nuclear facilities liable for damage or loss of life to persons and property from private

---

[2] 28 U.S.C. § 1350 (2000); see also Act of September 24, 1789, ch. 20, 9(b), 1 Stat. 73, 77. I personally prefer the term Alien Tort Claims Act (ATCA).

[3] *Doe I et al.* v *Unocal Corporation et al,* Brief for the United States of America as *amicus curiae,* (9th Cir. 8 May 2003), 00-56603, 00-56628, argued en banc 17 June 2003.

[4] Hufbauer and Mitrokostas, above n 1, at 247. See also Robert Bork, *Coercing Virtue: The Worldwide Rule of Judges* (Washington, DC: AEI Press, 2003) at 27 ('The modern expansion of the Alien Tort Claims Act is judicial activism – indeed, moral presumption – at its highest pitch.').

[5] See Pieter H. F. Bekker, Provisional Report on 'Corporate Aiding and Abetting and Conspiracy Liability under International Law', given on 4 July 2003 in the Hague at a panel on Corporate Responsibility of the American Society of International Law and the Netherlands Society of International Law (forthcoming in the Proceedings of that conference) (unpublished manuscript on file with author).

[6] See Declaration Adopted by the Governing Body of the International Labour Organization at its 204th Session (November 1977), at 10, 16, 37, 41, available at http://www.ilo.org/public/english/standards/norm/sources/mne.htm .

[7] Paris Convention on Third Party Liability in the Field of Nuclear Energy, done 29 July 1960, 956 U.N.T.S. 251.

nuclear accidents or oil spills.[8] Hazardous waste conventions, such as those concluded at Basel, impose strict liability on corporate generators of hazardous waste.[9] The OECD Anti-Bribery Convention effectively holds corporations liable for bribery.[10] So how can it be that corporations can be held responsible under international law for their complicity in oil spills, but not for their complicity in genocide? How can corporations be held liable under European law for anticompetitive behavior, but not for slavery?

The commonsense fact remains that if states and individuals can be held liable under international law, then so too should corporations, for the simple reason that both states and individuals *act through* corporations. Given that reality, what legal sense would it make to let states and individuals immunize themselves from liability for gross violations through the mere artifice of corporate formation?

If corporations have rights under international law, by parity of reasoning, they must have duties as well. As history and precedent make clear, corporations can be held liable in two ways, particularly when they are involved in *jus cogens* violations.[11] First, corporations can be held liable as agents of the state committing what Andrew Clapham calls 'complicity offenses', namely, acting under color of state law or in concert with state actors.[12] Second, it has always been true that private actors, including corporations, can be held liable under international law if they commit certain 'transnational offenses' – namely, heinous offenses that can be committed by either a public or a private entity. For example, if a corporation committed piracy or slave trading or fostered an attack on an ambassador, it would be

---

[8] See, e.g., the International Convention on Civil Liability for Oil Pollution Damage, done 29 November 1969, 26 U.S.T. 765, 973 U.N.T.S. 3; the Brussels Convention Relating to Civil Liability in the Field of Maritime Carriage of Nuclear Material, done 17 December 1971, 974 U.N.T.S. 255; the Convention on Civil Liability for Oil Pollution Damage Resulting from Exploration for and Exploitation of Seabed Mineral Resources, done 17 December 1976, 16 I.L.M. 1450. The 1969 Brussels Convention states: 'The owner of a ship at the time of an accident, or where the incident consists of a series of occurrences at the time of the first such occurrence, *shall be liable* for any pollution damage caused by oil which has escaped or been discharged from the ship as a result of the incident.' 1969 Convention, above, at 5 (emphasis added).

[9] Basel Convention on the Control of Transboundary Movements of Hazardous Wastes and Their Disposal, done 22 March 1989, arts. 4(3), 9(5), 1673 U.N.T.S. 57, 132, 137, see also ibid art. 2(14), 1673 U.N.T.S. at 130 ('"Person" means any natural or legal person.').

[10] See Convention on Combating Bribery of Foreign Public Officials in International Business Transactions, 17 December 1997, [hereinafter OECD Anti-Bribery Convention] at art. 3, available at http://www.oecd.org/document/21/0,2340,en_2649_34855_2017813_1_1_1_1,00.html ('The bribery of a foreign public official shall be punishable by effective, proportionate and dissuasive criminal penalties. The range of penalties shall be comparable to that applicable to the bribery of the Party's own public officials and shall, in the case of natural persons, include deprivation of liberty sufficient to enable effective mutual legal assistance and extradition.')

[11] For an excellent review, from which many of the examples in this section derive, see Steven R. Ratner, 'Corporations and Human Rights: a Theory of Legal Responsibility', 111 Yale L.J. (2001) 443.

[12] Andrew Clapham, 'On Complicity', in M. M. Henzelin and R. Roth (eds), *Le droit pénal à l'épreuve de l'internationalisation* (Paris: LGDJ, Genève: Georg, Bruxelles: Brulant, 2002) 241–75.

considered *hostes humani generis* (enemies of all mankind) even if it acted in a purely private capacity. Even Judge Bork acknowledged this point in his concurring opinion in *Tel-Oren v Libyan Arab Republic*.[13] Indeed, it was on this basis that the Nuremberg Tribunal held private German industrialists – Flick, I.G. Farben and Krupp – criminally liable for their support of and participation in the Holocaust, finding that the Nuremberg Charter permitted prosecution of a private group or organization and stating that the action of the company and its representatives 'under these circumstances cannot be differentiated from acts of plunder or pillage committed by officers … or … officials of the Third Reich'.[14] Moreover, under Article 4 of the Genocide Convention, a private corporation can commit or aid and abet in genocide, for example, by producing lethal toxic gas for use in a concentration camp.[15] The same goes for Common Article 3 of the Geneva Conventions, which binds all parties to an armed conflict, including those who may be non-state actors.[16]

There is no serious argument that corporations cannot have specific intent to commit crimes. After all, under many US federal laws, such as the antitrust statutes[17] or the Racketeer Influenced Corrupt Organizations (RICO) statutes,[18] corporations have long been held criminally liable for their specific intent to commit a crime.

Nor does it make sense to argue that international law may impose criminal liability on corporations, but not civil liability. Congress passed two statutes –

[13] 726 F.2d 774, 798, 813–14 (D.C. Cir. 1984) (Bork, J., concurring) ('What kinds of alien tort actions, then, might the Congress of 1789 have meant to bring into federal courts? According to Blackstone, a writer certainly familiar to colonial lawyers, 'the principal offences against the law of nations, animadverted on as such by the municipal laws of England, [were] of three kinds; 1. Violation of safe-conducts; 2. Infringement of the rights of ambassadors; and 3. Piracy. … One might suppose that these were the kinds of offenses for which Congress wished to provide tort jurisdiction for suits by aliens in order to avoid conflicts with other nations.') (citations omitted). See also ibid at 794–95 (Edwards, J., concurring) (there are a 'handful of crimes', including slave trading, 'to which the law of nations attributes *individual liability*' (emphasis added), such that state action is not required for ATS liability).

[14] *United States v Krauch*, 8 CCL No. 10 Trials, at 1081, 1140 (1952) (U.S. Mil. Trib. VI 1948). In three cases decided by American courts sitting in occupied Germany under Control Council Law No. 10 – *United States v Flick, United States v Krauch* (the *I.G. Farben* case), and *United States v Krupp* – leading German industrialists were prosecuted for crimes against peace (i.e., initiating World War II), war crimes, and crimes against humanity. See *1 Trials of War Criminals before the Nuremberg Military Tribunals*, at xvi (photo. reprint 1998), vols 6–9 (1950–1953) (1949). These trials led to convictions of the industrialists not only for slave labor, but also, in the case of *Flick*, for financial contributions to the SS.

[15] Convention on the Prevention and Punishment of the Crime of Genocide, 78 U.N.T.S. 277, entered into force 9 December 1948, art. IV ('Persons committing genocide or any of the other acts enumerated in article III shall be punished, whether they are constitutionally responsible rulers, public officials or private individuals'). Cf. 'The Zyklon B Case: Trial of Bruno Tesch and Two Others', *1 Law Reports of Trials of War Criminals* (1997) at 93 (Brit. Mil. Ct. 1946) (holding individuals liable for producing and supplying lethal gas to a concentration camp).

[16] Geneva Conventions Relative to the Laws of War, Common Art. 3, 6 U.S.T. 3316, 3318, 75 U.N.T.S. 135, 136.

[17] 50 U.S.C. §§ 1–2 (2003).

[18] 18 U.S.C. §§ 1961 et seq., (2003).

the Alien Tort Statute and the Torture Victim Protection Act (TVPA) – precisely to provide civil remedies for international law violations.[19] These statutes constitute a form of domestic legislative internalization of an international norm. Finally, even if for some reason international law did not impose civil liability directly, there is nothing to prevent domestic law (e.g. the ATS) from supplementing international criminal law remedies with civil remedies arising out of domestic law.[20] Indeed, in *Kadic v Karadzic* and its progeny, the Second Circuit and other Circuits have held that the ATS provides domestic civil remedies against non-state actors who violate international law.[21]

Moreover, corporations are surely liable not just for direct, transnational offenses – which can be committed by private or public actors – but also for their indirect offenses in complicity with gross human rights abuses. Thus, like any aider and abetter, corporations can be held liable for the small class of cases that arise out of a claim of violation of obligatory, definable, and universal norms of international law (direct offenses) as well as for their complicity in a public actor's violation of international law. Indeed, it was precisely the theory of the recent Holocaust Assets deal that private companies, banks, and officials were part of a common plan or conspiracy to commit war crimes or crimes against humanity.[22]

To constitute a 'complicity offense', the corporate conduct must meet a very high threshold. As the International Criminal Tribunal for the Former Yugoslavia (ICTY) specified in the *Tadic* case, the assistance must be direct and substantial,[23] and as the Tribunal noted in the *Furundzija* case in

---

[19] 28 U.S.C. § 1350 & 1350a.

[20] See, e.g., *Restatement (Third) of the Foreign Relations Law of the United States* § 404, comment b (1987) ('international law does not preclude the application of non-criminal law on [the] basis [of universal interests], for example, by providing a remedy in tort or restitution for victims of piracy.')

[21] 70 F. 3d 232, 239 (2d Cir. 1995) ('certain acts violate the law of nations whether undertaken by those acting under the auspices of a state or only as private individuals'). See also *Doe v Unocal*, 2003 WL 31063976, at *31 (9th Cir. 18 September 2002) ('Thus, under *Kadic*, even crimes like rape, torture, and summary execution, which by themselves require state action for ATCA liability to attach, do *not* require state action when committed in furtherance of other crimes like slave trading, genocide or war crimes, which by themselves do not require state action for ATCA liability to attach. We agree with this view and apply it below to Plaintiffs' various ATCA claims').

[22] See generally Stuart E. Eizenstat, *Imperfect Justice: Looted Assets, Slave Labor, and the Unfinished Business of World War II* (Public Affairs, 2003) (describing evolution of Holocaust Assets Deal).

[22] See *Prosecutor v Tadic*, Case No. IT-94-I-T, para. 674 (Int'l Crim. Trib. for Former Yugoslavia Trial Chamber II, 7 May 1997), http://www.un.org/icty/tadic/trialc2/judgement/ index.htm:

[23] The most relevant sources for such a determination are the Nuremberg war crimes trials, which resulted in several convictions for complicitous conduct. While the judgments generally failed to discuss in detail the criteria upon which guilt was determined, a clear pattern does emerge upon an examination of the relevant cases. First, there is a requirement of intent, which involves awareness of the act of participation coupled with a conscious decision to participate by planning, instigating, ordering, committing, or otherwise aiding and abetting in the commission of a crime. Second, the prosecution must prove that there was participation in that the conduct of the accused contributed to the commission of the illegal act.

December 1998, the corporate conduct must constitute 'practical assistance, encouragement, or moral support which has a substantial effect on the perpetration of a crime'[24]

The International Law Commission's rules of state responsibility suggest that complicity constitutes provision of 'aid or assistance to another . . . facilitating the commission of the wrongful act by the latter'.[25] Similarly, Art. 7(1) of the ICTY statute[26] and Article 25 of the International Criminal Court treaty hold private citizens criminally liable for committing crimes jointly with or through another person.[27] So all of this would appear to rebut the first myth: that private corporations cannot be held liable in the first place for their direct human rights violations or their acts in complicity with state human rights violations.

MYTH 2: THERE IS A FLOOD OF ATS LITIGATION IN US COURTS THAT WOULD IMPOSE LIABILITY ON A CORPORATION SIMPLY FOR ITS PRESENCE IN A COUNTRY WHERE BAD THINGS HAPPEN[28]

First, and most obviously, there is no flood of cases. Hufbauer and Mitrokostas count 'more than a dozen current cases' against corporate defendants under the ATS.[29] Given the 215 years of the ATS's history, more than a dozen cases does not constitute a flood. Of these, only three or four have survived a motion to dismiss, and only one, the *Unocal* case, is even past the stage of a summary judgment motion.[30] As Hufbauer and Mitrokostas concede, '[s]ome cases have been dismissed, and so far no suit against a corporate defendant has been adjudicated in the plaintiffs' favor.'[31] Under

---

[24] See *Prosecutor v Furundzija*, Case No. IT-95-17/1 'Lasva Valley', (Int'l Crim. Trib. for Former Yugoslavia Trial Chamber II) (10 December 1998) (ICFTY Chamber), available at http://www.un.org/icty/furundzija/trialc2/judgement/index.htm para 249 ('the legal ingredients of aiding and abetting in international criminal law . . . consists of practical assistance, encouragement, or moral support which has a substantial effect on the perpetration of the crime').

[25] James Crawford, International Law Commission, 'Second Report on State Responsibility' UN Doc. A/CN.4/498/Add.1, 1 April 1999, at para 159.

[26] Statute of the International Tribunal for the Prosecution of Persons Responsible for Serious Violations of International Humanitarian Law Committed in the Territory of the Former Yugoslavia Since 1991, UN Doc. S/RES/827, art. 7(1) ('A person who planned, instigated, ordered, committed, or otherwise aided and abetted in the planning, preparation or execution of a crime [under this Statute] shall be individually responsible for the crime.')

[27] Rome Statute of the International Criminal Court, U.N. Doc. A/CONF.183/9, 39 ILM 999 (1998), adopted 17 July 1998, art. 25(3) ('a person shall be criminally responsible . . . if that person . . . aids, abets, or otherwise assists in its commission or attempted commission.').

[28] As Pieter Bekker puts it: plantiffs are using the liberal provisions of the Federal Rules of Civil Procedure to sue private companies 'based simply on their participation in the global economic system' Bekker, above n 5, at 1.

[29] Hufbauer and Mitrokostas, International Implications, above n 1, at 246.

[30] The cases to date are summarized in the appendices to Hufbauer and Mitrokostas, Awakening Monster, above n 1.

[31] Hufbauer and Mitrokostas, 'International Implications', above n 1, at 253.

current law, the reason why seems clear. There are currently very high, multiple barriers to recovery under the ATS. To be actionable, the acts committed by a private corporation:

(a) Must be brought in a proper forum with personal jurisdiction and venue;

(b) Must not be barred by statute of limitations;

(c) Must state a claim upon which relief can be granted, which means alleging either a transnational offense that either a state or private individual could commit, for example, a violation of an obligatory, definable, and universal norm of international law, or an act of actionable complicity in violation of international law in the *Furundzija* sense of practical assistance, encouragement, or moral support which has a substantial effect on the perpetration of a state crime; and

(d) The claim must be proven, not just pleaded, and the plaintiff has a significant burden of proving the link between cause and effect.

Understandably, these are hard standards to prove. What all this means is that the plaintiff needs to show much, much more than simply that the multinational enterprise has chosen to invest in a 'troublesome country'. Small wonder, then that since 1993, there have been more than 20 ATS cases against private corporations, but the courts have dismissed most of these cases for lack of subject matter jurisdiction, *forum non conveniens* and the like.

Hufbauer and Mitrokostas paint a doomsday scenario of economic loss and devastation, '[c]onservatively ... calculate[ing] that $55 billion of U.S. FDI could be deterred by ATS suits'.[32] But their number-crunching only proves the saying, 'When you cannot measure what is important, you make important that which you can measure.' What is important here is the likelihood that a frivolous lawsuit will succeed. The two authors rest their entire numerical analysis on 'mights' and 'coulds'. '[T]he Chinese plaintiffs *might* allege that multinational corporations ("MNCs") violated international law. ... The complaint *might* claim actual damages of $6 billion and punitive damages of $20 billion. To minimize their potential liability, the defendant corporation *could* settle for an intermediate amount, such as $10 billion.'[33]

But of course, the sky might also fall in tomorrow. As Chicken Little learned, just because it *might* happen, does not mean that sky-falling is a likely scenario, particularly when prudent federal judges are properly managing their dockets. Indeed, the authors admit, '[t]o be sure, no *decided* ATS cases can be cited to confirm that the nightmare scenario we have just sketched will come to pass',[34] for the simple reason that no judge has let a frivolous case go

---

[32] See Hufbauer and Mitrokostas, 'International Implications', above n 1, at 256.

[33] See Hufbauer and Mitrokostas, 'International Implications', above n 1, at 246 (emphasis added).

[34] Ibid at 2 (emphasis in original).

to judgment. At this writing, no court has rendered any final judgment against any US company under the ATS, and no US corporation has yet paid any ATS damages. Hyperbole notwithstanding, it is hard to see where the litigation 'crisis' is, when no corporate defendant has yet paid an ATS plaintiff a penny.

MYTH 3: TO LIMIT THE FLOOD OF ALIEN TORT CLAIMS ACT LITIGATION, WE NEED TO EITHER AMEND THE STATUTE OR REPEAL IT, OR REJECT THE LINE OF ATS CASES STARTING WITH *FILARTIGA*

At this writing, two 'fixes' are being discussed to address this 'crisis'. The first is legislative reform: amendment of the ATS or its repeal. But again, these suggestions bring to mind an adage: 'If it ain't broke, don't fix it.' Given the relative paucity of litigation, legislative reform would be a massive over-reaction. As I suggested more than a decade ago, if frivolous ATS suits are brought, why address them through jurisdictional overkill? The best way to deal with them is for judges to continue to manage their dockets wisely and to dismiss insubstantial suits by applying ordinary rules of jurisdiction, pleading, and proof and invoking the sanctions provisions of Federal Rule of Civil Procedure 11 if necessary to prevent frivolous suits.[35]

An even more radical approach has been taken by the Bush Administration in the *Unocal* case,[36] the *Exxon Mobil* case,[37] and most recently, *Sosa v Alvarez-Machain*[38] (to be decided this year by the Supreme Court), in each of which it has filed *amicus curiae* briefs essentially urging the overruling of the entire line of Alien Tort Statute litigation since *Filartiga v Pena-Irala*. In the lawsuit involving Unocal, the lower courts initially ruled that the case could proceed, and the full appeals court reheard the case in June 2003 with its decision likely early in 2004.

---

[35] Harold Hongju Koh, 'Transnational Public Law Litigation', 100 Yale L.J. (1991) 2347, 2382–94.

[36] The *Unocal* case was brought in California federal court by Burmese citizens, who alleged that a California corporation, Unocal, had aided and abetted the Burmese military junta's use of forced labor and other human rights abuses during the construction of a gas pipeline. The Clinton Administration had vociferously condemned Burmese human rights abuses, which included the brutal arrest of Burma's rightful leader, Nobel Peace Prizewinner Aung San Suu Kyi, and the killing and imprisonment of many of her supporters. The Burmese plaintiffs filed their suit under the ATS, citing precedents from seven different federal circuits over the last two decades which have upheld the rights of victims of human rights abuse residing in the US to seek recovery from such perpetrators as torturers from Paraguay, officials of Castro's government, state sponsors of terrorism like Iran, former Philippine president Ferdinand Marcos and indicted Bosnian Serb war criminal Radovan Karadzic.

[37] Brief *Amicus Curiae* of the United States in *Doe v Exxon Mobil Corp.*, Civ. No. 01-1357 (LFO) (D.C.D.C. 2002) (suit alleging corporate complicity in human rights abuses in Aceh).

[38] Brief *Amicus Curiae* of the United States Supporting Petitioner in *Sosa v Alvarez-Machain*, No. 03-339 (U.S. S. Ct. 2004), available at http://sdshh.com/Alvarez/SOSA_DTP_BR%20(03-339).pdf. For the lower court opinion in this case, see 331 F.3d 604 (2003), cert. granted, 72 U.S.L.W. 3248 (1 December 2003).

The Bush Administration's Justice Department under John Ashcroft faced four choices. First, in landmark briefs filed in the New York federal courts in 1980 and 1995, the Carter and Clinton Administrations had supported the foreign plaintiffs' right to sue gross violators under the ATS. Thus, the Bush Administration, like prior administrations, could have simply maintained the position of its predecessors and supported the plaintiffs, citing the need to maintain a consistent governmental interpretation of an unchanging statute. Second, it could have supported the defendants on case-specific grounds; or third, it could have taken a neutral position (as it did, for example, in *Lawrence v Texas*,[39] the Supreme Court's recent Texas sodomy case). Instead the Administration chose a fourth, radical option, urging a position that would wipe out nearly 25 years of appellate precedent. The Administration dramatically changed the US government's interpretation of the 200-year-old statute. Opposing victims of the Burmese military junta, the government's brief insisted that victims of gross abuse cannot sue any foreign defendants under the ATS for fundamental violations of international human rights norms. Even if the victims could prove that defendants shared responsibility for the abuses, the government argued, no ATS recovery should be available because the claimed abuses occurred outside of the United States and a ruling against the corporation would endanger American interests in the war on terror.[40]

The Bush Administration's approach is singularly misguided. In the first place, there has been no congressional change in the wording of either the Alien Tort Statute (ATS) or the Torture Victim Protection Act (TVPA), and thus, no apparent legal reason why the United States should suddenly depart from the positions of the Carter and Clinton Administrations supporting the use of US courts for *Filartiga*-type recovery under these two statutes. In addition, the Department's position violates a long line of established legal precedent. In 1795, only seven years after the ATS first became law, the then-Attorney General opined that 'there can be no doubt' that the law affords aliens injured by torts committed in violation of the law of nations 'a remedy by a civil suit in the courts of the United States'.[41] In the Torture Victim

---

[39] 123 S. Ct. 2472 (2003).

[40] Similarly, in *Doe v Exxon Mobil*, which is currently pending before Judge Oberdorfer in the U.S. District Court for the District of Columbia, the Legal Adviser of the State Department filed another *amicus* brief, as well as an affidavit asserting that adjudication of an ATS lawsuit against a US corporation operating in Aceh, Indonesia, would 'risk a potentially serious adverse impact on significant interests of the United States, including interests related directly to the ongoing struggle against international terrorism. Letter of 29 July 2002 written to Judge Louis F. Oberdorfer by William H. Taft IV, The Legal Adviser of the Department of State, in *Doe v Exxon Mobil Corp.*, Civ. No. 01-1357 (LFO) (DCDC 2002). But see Affidavit of Harold Hongju Koh in *Doe v Exxon Mobil Corp.*, Civ. No. 01-1357 (LFO) (DCDC 2002) (challenging those assertions).

[41] See 1 Op. Att'y Gen. 57, 58 (1795) ('there can be no doubt' that the victims 'have a remedy' under the ATS for a civil claims despite its foreign origin). See also 26 Op. Att'y Gen. 250, 253 (1907) ('I repeat that the statute thus provide a forum and a right of action.').

272 *Journal of International Economic Law (JIEL) 7(2)*

Protection Act of 1992, Congress reaffirmed the ATS by enacting a modern statute along the same lines.[42] The federal courts of appeals have since unanimously held that corporations can be sued under the Alien Tort Statute so long as it can be proved that they knowingly committed or collaborated in the commission of crimes against humanity.[43]

Moreover, as a matter of human rights policy, the Administration's position toward the ATS and TVPA is perverse in five ways. First, it would virtually repeal these laws, without congressional participation, by granting immunity to all human rights abusers, whether official or corporate, so long as they commit their violations abroad. Second, contrary to the Administration's claims, this approach does not help, but rather undermines, the war against terrorism, for it would immunize from suit not just corporate defendants, but also Fidel Castro, Kim Jong Il, Saddam Hussein, or any state sponsor of terrorism. Third, if under this theory 'private enterprises' such as corporations cannot be held liable for gross human rights abuse overseas, then how can Al Qaeda, terrorist groups like Hizbollah and Hamas, or any other private terrorist organization be held so liable? Fourth, a California state judge has recently ruled that the *Unocal* case could be heard in state court if necessary, thus making the government's assault on federal jurisdiction sufficient only to shift venue, not to remove these cases from United States court altogether.[44] Fifth and finally, if fully adopted, the Administration's position would perversely push similar lawsuits against US companies into foreign courts, where they would lack the protections of US law. Surely, it is a strange way to fight a war against terrorism to deprive victims of terrorism of a well-tested tool of accountability.

MYTH 4: DOMESTIC LITIGATION IS A BAD WAY TO PROMOTE HIGHER CORPORATE STANDARDS IN HUMAN RIGHTS AND THE ENVIRONMENT

My answer: litigation is not a bad way, but neither should it be the only way to promote higher corporate standards with respect to the environment and human rights. One can imagine a host of other ways to promote the same outcome, for example: the voluntarism exemplified by British Petroleum's 2002 human rights code of conduct to govern its operations abroad; domestic

---

[42] According to the House Report, '[t]he TVPA would establish an unambiguous and modern basis for a cause of action that has been successfully maintained under an existing law, section 1350 of the Judiciary Act of 1789 ... ' H.R. Rep. No. 367, 102d Cong., 1st Sess., pt. 1 (1991). Significantly, the House Report referred to *Filartiga* with approval, affirmed the importance of ATS, and indicated that it 'should not be replaced'. Id. See also S. Rep. No. 249, 102d Cong., 1st Sess. (1991) (virtually identical language in Senate report).

[43] See generally *Presbyterian Church of Sudan v Talisman Energy, Inc.*, 244 F. Supp. 2d 289 (S.D.N.Y. 2003) (reviewing cases).

[44] 'Judge rules Unocal can be tried in US for alleged Myanmar rights abuses', available at story.news.yahoo.com/news?tmpl=story&cid=1519&e=18&u=/afp/us_myanmar_unocal.

legal regulation; promulgation of industry codes of conduct, and the creation of private-public regimes.

With respect to the last, there are many recent efforts worth examining. During the Clinton Administration, for example, Undersecretary of State Stuart Eizenstat helped to negotiate a private-public deal in which foreign corporations that had profited from the Holocaust paid survivors billions of dollars in compensation for their losses.[45] In 1994, the White House announced Model Business Principles for corporations seeking to maintain high human rights standards, and many leading corporations have subscribed to both the Global Sullivan Principles and UN Secretary-General Kofi Annan's Global Compact. In 2000, several major oil companies and then-Secretary of State Madeleine Albright announced a code of conduct – which had been negotiated under the auspices of the United States and United Kingdom governments – to regulate human rights abuses for security forces in the extractive industries.[46]

But the most promising avenue, in my opinion, is neither statute nor judicial doctrine, but rather, treaty. Corporations do not need immunity from ATS suits so much as they need a safe harbor: certainty that conduct in which they self-consciously and thoughtfully engage will not automatically expose them to domestic human rights lawsuits. The United States and British Governments have been seeking to develop common standards to clarify when a corporation illegally aids and abets official human rights abuse, and work has been proceeding to draft an international convention on the subject under OECD auspices. What we need most now is not judicial repeal of the ATS, but international legislative developments: draft norms of responsibility for transnational corporations and other business enterprises with regard to rights. Indeed, at this writing, the Working Group of the Subcommission on Human Rights has made the most promising efforts to develop such norms.[47]

I have long argued in favor of a transnational legal process approach whereby techniques of process are used to internalize into transnational actors – here, multinational corporations – standards of right and wrong behavior.[48]

[45] See generally Stuart E. Eizenstat, *Imperfect Justice: Looted Assets, Slave Labor, and the Unfinished Business of World War II* (Public Affairs, 2003).

[46] See US Department of State, Bureau of Democracy, Human Rights and Labor, Voluntary Principles on Security and Human Rights (released 20 December 2000), available at http://www.state.gov/www/ global/human_rights/001220_fsdrl_principles.html. For a summary of these principles, see Sean D. Murphy, 'Voluntary Human Rights Principles for Extractive and Energy Companies', 95 Am. J. Int'l L. (2001) 636.

[47] See Andre Noellkaemper, 'Translating Principles of Public International Law into Principles of Corporate Liability' (2003), given on 4 July 2003 in the Hague at a panel on Corporate Responsibility of the American Society of International Law and the Netherlands Society of International Law (forthcoming in the Proceedings of that conference) (unpublished manuscript on file with author).

274 *Journal of International Economic Law (JIEL) 7(2)*

Precisely such an approach has been applied for the past quarter century with regard to bribery. In 1977, following the Lockheed scandal, Congress passed a Foreign Corrupt Practices Act, which imposed certain standards on US corporations through domestic civil and criminal legislation. Then, as now, alarmists claimed that the chance of liability would cost US corporations billions and slash foreign direct investment. But the fact that US corporations were subjected to these legal constraints soon made them advocates for an OECD Bribery Convention, which is now functioning and becoming internalized into the law of the member nations. With luck, the same strategy that has been applied to counter corporate bribery practices can be applied to counter corporate complicity in human rights abuses.

In conclusion, let me say that the characterization by the Bush Administration, certain commentators, and corporate defendants of Alien Tort Statute litigation as an 'awakening monster' is wrong, as a matter of both law and policy. It credits four myths over reality, and marks a gross overreaction to a litigation trend that the US courts are in fact properly managing with existing judicial tools. Furthermore, as a policy matter, efforts to repeal or reform the ATS undermine meaningful efforts to promote corporate responsibility abroad. These efforts would be far better approached by international treaty drafting aimed at providing safe harbors for responsible corporations and clarifying what does or does not constitute actionable complicity in human rights abuse.

In sum, corporate counsel have nothing to fear but fear itself. If you are sued frivolously under ATS, don't panic, litigate. But if you genuinely care about corporate responsibility, you should put your efforts into developing these kinds of standards and encouraging responsible companies to meet them, not attacking a venerable law that has been used for more than two decades to call terrorists and human rights abusers to account.

---

[48] For elaboration of this argument, see Harold Hongju Koh, 'Bringing International Law Home', 35 Hous. L. Rev. (1998) 623; Harold Hongju Koh, 'Why Do Nations Obey International Law?', 106 Yale L.J. (1997) 2599; Harold Hongju Koh, 'How Is International Human Rights Law Enforced?', 74 Ind. L.J. (1999) 1397.

[14]

THE INTERFACE BETWEEN GLOBALISATION, CORPORATE RESPONSIBILITY, AND THE LEGAL PROFESSION

HALINA WARD[1]

I. INTRODUCTION

This paper considers the consequences of addressing legal ethics through the lenses both of globalisation and of corporate responsibility. The interface between globalisation, corporate social responsibility (CSR), and legal ethics is important for a number of reasons. First, just as law and legal processes tend to have been underplayed in the contemporary corporate social responsibility agenda (notwithstanding their significance to it), so too has the role of lawyers. Second, both globalisation and corporate social responsibility form part of the context in which lawyers work. Lawyers are also distinct actors in both agendas. Yet whilst the consequences of globalisation for legal ethics are receiving increasing attention,[2] the consequences of the contemporary corporate social responsibility agenda for legal ethics have received almost none. This paper maps out the links; introduces some dilemmas at the intersection of legal ethics and corporate social responsibility; and provides pointers towards future efforts to integrate the two.

II. LINKS BETWEEN GLOBALISATION AND CORPORATE SOCIAL RESPONSIBILITY

A. Corporate Social Responsibility

There is no consensus on the meaning of the terms 'corporate social responsibility', 'corporate responsibility' (CR—increasingly the preferred

1. LL.B., LL.M., solicitor (non-practising). Halina Ward is director of the programme on Corporate Responsibility for Environment and Development (CRED) at the International Institute for Environment and Development in London.
2. *See* Andrew Boon & John Flood, *Globalization of Professional Ethics? The Significance of Lawyers' International Codes of Conduct*, 2 Leg. Ethics 29 (1999) (discussing attempts to establish international codes of ethics by bodies such as the International Bar Association).

term in the U.K. at least), or 'corporate citizenship.'[3] At heart, all definitions aim to drive forward understanding on the role of businesses as part of society—rather than somehow separate from it. The CR agenda is potentially both wider and deeper than the 'business ethics' agenda. The overall focus lies with the goal of maximising the positive contributions that businesses make to societal goals such as environmental protection, social justice, or maintenance of respect for human rights.

Commentators remain divided on the extent to which efforts to minimise the negative impacts that business activity can have on society belong within the corporate responsibility agenda, or whether they should instead be considered within a distinct 'corporate accountability' agenda. In this paper, the starting point is the broad view, namely that CSR or CR are at heart both about maximising the positive impacts or contributions of business activity to society, and minimising the negatives. The issues that lie within the agenda are encapsulated within the notion of 'sustainable development' and its focus on balancing economic, social, and environmental considerations.[4] Indeed, CSR or CR in this broad sense may be understood as synonymous with the 'business and sustainable development' agenda.

B. *Globalisation*

The term 'globalisation' has been used in many different ways. At the highest level of generalization, it is sometimes taken to be synonymous with 'interconnectedness' or even 'capitalism.'[5] At its simplest, the key components can be understood as trade and investment liberalisation (associated with deregulation and privatisation)—collectively referred to as 'economic globalisation'—and the technological advances that transform communications.

The results of these processes of economic and technological globalisation have included significant shifts in the balance of public and private sector responsibilities around the world; governments finding that pressures to attract and sustain business investments make it difficult to implement new laws or regulations with negative competitive impacts; and increasing gaps between rich and poor people in some parts of the world.

---

3. *See e.g.* The Corporate Citizen, *Defining Corporate Citizenship,* http://www.uschamber. com/ccc/news/2004/aug-sep/0409letter.htm (Aug./Sept. 2004); International Institute for Sustainable Development, *Issue Briefing Note: Perceptions and Definitions of Social Responsibility,* http://www.iied.org/cred/pubs.html (May 2004).

4. *See* World Commission on Environment and Development, *Our Common Future* 8 (Oxford U. Press 1988) (classic working definition of sustainable development, defined as development that "meets the needs of the present without compromising the ability of future generations to meet their own needs").

5. *See e.g. Economic Focus: Anti-Liberalism Old and New,* The Economist 92 (October 21, 2000). Capitalism would perhaps be better introduced as the "driving idea" of globalisation, as in Thomas Friedman's iconic and accessible work. *See* Thomas L. Friedman, *The Lexus and the Olive Tree* 8 (Farrar, Straus & Giroux 2000).

Globalisation of communication in turn has facilitated transnational organisation of civil society groups and organisations, making it easier to scrutinize business or government practices around the world. Today, when transnational businesses choose to adopt different environmental or social standards in their home countries than those that they apply in other countries, their activities and impacts are increasingly judged against the benchmark of home country standards.

C. Links between Corporate Social Responsibility and Globalisation

The contemporary corporate social responsibility agenda emerged alongside the great debate of the 1990s over the nature and consequences of globalisation in all its forms. Alongside continued advocacy of trade and investment liberalisation, powerful evidence also began to emerge of circumstances in which the core strategies of economic globalisation had been associated with impoverishment and marginalisation of poor people and damage to the environment.

Who was to blame for these negative impacts? The dogma that accompanied trade and investment liberalisation, privatisation, and deregulation by multilateral institutions and governments in the countries of the Organisation for Economic Cooperation and Development (OECD) throughout the 1990s was that the potential benefits of market liberalisation would be realised *if* the right policies and practices were in place at the national level to distribute the benefits in ways that furthered social and environmental progress and equitable human development.[6] From this starting point, any negative consequences that flowed from liberalisation were not the primary fault of liberalisation *per se*, but of weak, or corrupt, or ineffective government policy. Policy prescriptions included capacity-building, institutional strengthening, and eradication of bribery and corruption.

At the same time, critics began to ask whether business lobbying behind the scenes might be preventing governments from adopting the right policies. Concern over the negative impacts of economic globalisation began increasingly to focus on the role of business—particularly big businesses—in lobbying governments to adopt investment-friendly policies without placing any matching emphasis on the need to develop and maintain strong environmental and social institutions, or to sustain the respect for human rights that could facilitate overall improvements in quality of life and progress towards sustainable development. Indeed, concern began to be raised that the economic power of big business, when expressed as political power, lay behind a 'race to the bottom' among some host countries, in which maintenance of low environmental or social standards, or in some

---

6. *See e.g.* General Agreement on Tariffs and Trade (GATT), Secretariat, *Trade and the Environment*, ch. 2 in *International Trade 1990-91*, vol. 1, available at http://www.ciesin.org/docs/008-082/008-082.html (Feb. 3, 1992).

cases even a lowering of standards could be applied as a strategy to attract foreign direct investment.[7]

If sustainable development could flow from economic globalisation when supported by appropriate policies and institutions at the domestic level, a number of strategies for responding to the potential mismatches might be deployed. One strategy might be to halt the processes of economic liberalisation—whether at the national, regional, or sectoral level—until such time as the right policies were in place, whilst investing simultaneously in building strong environmental, social, and human rights-based public sector institutions at the domestic level, and strengthening the political and institutional clout of environmental and social institutions at the international level. This approach can be seen for example in the advocacy of some civil society groups around the World Trade Organization (WTO) agenda.[8]

A second strategy might involve dismantling the current international economic architecture, rebuilding it so as to ensure that environmental, social, and human rights-based considerations became integrated directly within its institutions.[9] A third approach—reflected in the mainstream corporate social responsibility agenda—is to focus on the role that market actors—specifically businesses—can play *independently* of public sector actors to ensure that economic globalisation is supportive of social and environmental progress. It is this approach that is reflected in the mainstream CSR agenda.

No single initiative exemplifies the links between globalisation and corporate responsibility more clearly than the United Nations Global Compact,[10] launched at the personal initiative of UN Secretary-General Kofi Annan to a community of international business leaders at the Davos World Economic Forum in 1999. There, Secretary-General Annan called for a new compact of shared values and principles between the United Nations and the business community to give a human face to the global market. "Globalization is a fact of life," he began.

> But I believe we have underestimated its fragility. The problem is this. The spread of markets outpaces the ability of societies and their political systems to adjust to them, let alone to guide the course they take. History teaches us that such an imbalance be-

---

7. *See generally* Lyuba Zarsky, *Havens, Halos and Spaghetti: Untangling the Evidence about Foreign Direct Investment and the Environment*, in *Conference on Foreign Direct Investment and the Environment* (OECD 1999).

8. *See generally* Friends of the Earth International, http://www.foei.org/publications/cancun/index.html.

9. *See e.g.* Colin Hines, *Localisation: A Global Manifesto* (Earthscan 2000).

10. *See What Is the Global Compact?*, http://www.unglobalcompact.org; *select* About The GC (accessed July 26, 2004).

tween the economic, social and political realms can never be sustained for very long.[11]

Whilst the links between the globalisation agenda and the contemporary corporate social responsibility agenda are undeniable, it might be argued today, given the increasing preoccupation with the war on terrorism and international security concerns, that making those links is no longer helpful in guiding business behaviour. Certainly, in the new political climate after the attacks of September 11, 2001, academic discussion on the relevance of globalisation as an organising concept for understanding relations across national boundaries appears to have subsided. Yet as Kofi Annan noted at the World Economic Forum meeting in Davos in January 2004,

> [i]n just a few short years, the prevailing atmosphere has shifted from belief in the near-inevitability of globalization to deep uncertainty about the very survival of our global order. This is a challenge for the United Nations.[12]

But it obliges the business community, too, to ask how it can help put things right. The corporate social responsibility agenda is as relevant in today's political environment as it was in the 1990s. And it is potentially just as relevant a response to the negative impacts of the contemporary political environment as to the negative impacts of economic globalisation.

III. GLOBALISATION AND THE LEGAL PROFESSION

Law firms, and the legal profession, are also actors in the processes of economic globalisation.[13] Business lawyers help to generate the laws, the legally binding obligations, and the institutional architecture that underpin trade and investment liberalisation and privatisation. As one lawyer writes, exchange of capital and technology transfers are "legally intensive."[14] With 'internationalisation' of business transactions, businesses and their advisers turn to the best suited jurisdictions for the deals that they have in mind.

---

11. Press Release, Kofi Annan, *Secretary-General Proposes Global Compact on Human Rights, Labour, Environment*, http://www.un.org/News/Press/docs/1999/19990201.sgsm6881. html (Feb. 1, 1999). Later that same year, at the World Trade Organization's Seattle Ministerial Conference, demonstrators dubbed 'anti-globalisation' protestors took to the streets to air a variety of concerns over the impacts of further trade and investment liberalisation. The conference ended without meeting its aim of launching a new round of trade talks. *See* Halina Ward, *Trade Trouble*, The World Today 24-25 (Jan. 2000).

12. Kofi Annan, Address, *Special Address by Kofi Annan* (World Economic Forum, Jan. 23, 2004), available at http://www.weforum.org/site/homepublic.nsf/Content/Special+Address+Kofi+ Annan.

13. *See generally* Special Issue, 23 Intl. Bus. Law. 509 (1995) [hereinafter *Intl. Bus. Law. Special Issue*] (a special issue on globalisation of the legal profession); Special Issue, 34 Vand. J. Transnatl. L. 897 (2001) [hereinafter *Vand. J. Special Issue*]; *e.g.* Steven Mark, *Harmonization or Homogenization? The Globalization of Law and Legal Ethics – An Australian Viewpoint*, in *id.*

14. John Crawford, *Why Do Law Firms Seek to Practise Globally?* in *Intl. Bus. Law. Special Issue, supra* n. 13, at 536.

818   *UNIVERSITY OF ST. THOMAS LAW JOURNAL*   [Vol. 1:2

Forum-shopping (or 'regulatory arbitrage') between different jurisdictions is common, with the legal profession in key practice areas acting as promoters of the dominance, or superiority, of their particular jurisdiction or mix of jurisdictions.[15] As businesses, international law firms stand to benefit from investment liberalisation[16] that helps them to establish new presences in other countries or to establish multinational partnerships.

Globalisation of legal businesses is at work in the intensified practise of public international law (for example, the law related to the WTO or the law of the 'home' jurisdiction in other countries); in the retraining of 'home' jurisdiction lawyers to practice the law of the local jurisdiction; in the hiring of local lawyers; or simply through engagement in commercial practice in one of a number of areas that are quintessentially 'international' in scope, such as international arbitration, intellectual property, or global project financing.[17] As professionals, increasing numbers of lawyers find themselves working in different jurisdictions to those where they trained, whether because they have followed existing client demand,[18] anticipated client demand in relation to underexploited jurisdictions,[19] or physically followed the establishment of new intergovernmental organisations or international treaty secretariats.

Together, these factors generate new influences for the evolution of commercial law—and new ethical challenges. As a new generation of 'globalised' lawyers spends long periods of time working away from their home country jurisdictions, some have pointed to "worrisome consequences for . . . their sense of obligation to adhere to professional rules and stan-

---

15. *See e.g.* Robert Briner, *Globalisation of the Lawyer*, in *Intl. Bus. Law. Special Issue, supra* n. 13, at 521, 522 ("One has also heard the opinion that many international contracts are governed either by English or New York law and that it is therefore essential but also sufficient to know these laws. . . . [I]t would seem to me that . . . this is mainly a public relations campaign by English and New York lawyers which is not borne out by the facts."); *cf.* William B. Matteson, *Building an International Practice*, in *Intl. Bus. Law. Special Issue, supra* n. 13, at 516, 518 (referring to a Fin. Times article which notes that the city of London still has 65-75% of Eurobond and international equity offerings).

16. *See generally* Laurel S. Terry, *GATS' Applicability to Transnational Lawyering and its Potential Impact on U.S. State Regulation of Lawyers*, in *Vand. J. Special Issue, supra* n. 13, at 989.

17. Matteson, *supra* n. 15, at 517-18. Public interest legal practices are also globalising, including through strategies that include networks and informal alliances and establishment of offices away from 'home countries.' *See e.g.* Interamerican Association for Environmental Defense, *About AIDA*, http://www.aida-americas.org/aida.php?page=about (accessed Oct. 26, 2004) (combination of network/membership coupled with a 'home' office in California); Environmental Law Alliance Worldwide, *About E-LAW*, http://www.elaw.org/about/ (accessed Oct. 26, 2004) (a multidisciplinary network of public interest attorneys, scientists and other advocates); EarthRights International, *About ERI*, http://www.earthrights.org/about.shtml (accessed Oct. 26, 2004) (offices in Washington and Thailand, with strategies combining litigation and campaign work).

18. John Flood, *The Globalising World*, in *Intl. Bus. Law. Special Issue, supra* n. 13, at 509, 511.

19. China or, following lifting of U.S. sanctions, Vietnam are examples. *See* Simon Ip, *International Strategies Adopted by Firms in the Asia Pacific Region*, in *Intl. Bus. Law. Special Issue, supra* n. 13, at 542-43.

dards."[20] One increasingly frequent response is likely to be the development of transnational or even universal standards of professional responsibility.[21]

Notwithstanding the major trend to globalisation of legal businesses and the practice of commercial law, it is striking that law understood through the lenses of government legislation and regulation has not 'globalised' overall at the same pace as the economy, business or communications. Institutions have struggled to catch up with the pace of change in the economy. There have been some significant developments: the establishment of an International Criminal Court; the development of a near-global intellectual property regime in the form of the WTO Agreement on Trade-Related Aspects of Intellectual Property Rights;[22] and the continuing evolution of multilateral frameworks for addressing environmental issues such as climate change. But the world is still very far from having achieved a system of 'global governance' through formal intergovernmental process.

The nature and sources of the norms that lawyers work with have also shifted with globalisation. New forms of 'soft' regulation generated by market actors acting in concert are burgeoning. Codes of conduct, labelling and certification schemes, and negotiated agreements are but a few of the body of instruments now in place to manage environmental and social issues. As normative instruments, these are also entering the lawyer's toolbox and forming an increasingly important part of business regulation.[23] Mapping and understanding networks of various kinds has become a key to

---

20. Deflev F. Vagts, *The Impact of Globalization on the Legal Profession*, in *The Internationalization of the Practice of Law* 31, 35 (Jens Drolshammer & Michael Pfeifer eds., Kluwer Law International 2001). *But cf.* Robert Briner, *Globalisation of the Lawyer*, in *Intl. Bus. Law. Special Issue, supra* n. 13, at 522 (who writes "I do not think that any particular ethical training is necessary for so-called international lawyers as opposed to other lawyers who are more domestically oriented").

21. *See e.g.* the materials cited in Christopher Whelan, *Ethics Beyond the Horizon: Why Regulate the Global Practice of Law?*, in *Vand. J. Special Issue, supra* n. 13, at 931, 943-45 (which explores whether global self-regulation of the legal profession is desirable). The author concludes that global rules of professional responsibility based on core values will add value to private clients, but add little to the public interest. Whelan links the cultural dimensions of globalisation—which include exporting of English law—to the potential for the globalisation or export of a perception of the lawyer's role as entrepreneur, whose highest duty is to please clients.

22. Uruguay Round Agreement, *Final Act Embodying the Results of the Uruguay Round of Multilateral Trade Negotiations* Annex 1C (Apr. 15, 1994), available at http://www.wto.org/english/docs_e/legal_e/03-fa_e.htm.

23. *See* John Braithwaite & Peter Drahos, *Global Business Regulation* (Cambridge U. Press 2000). In this seminal book, Drahos and Braithwaite argue that globalisation of business regulation has taken place through a messy process involving a web of actors—state and non-state—exerting influence at a variety of levels, and building 'global regulation' through a variety of tools and norms in a process of competing principles and models in which no single set of actors emerges as dominant. Drahos and Braithwaite's insights invite attention to non-legally-binding forms of regulation, to non-state actors, and to patterns of behaviour that are likely to prove strategically influential in the competition among norms and mechanisms. Their insights alone can be understood as a justification for lawyers to understand the 'voluntary instruments' of the corporate social responsibility agenda—though, as I argue below, there are risks in their doing so, both for other actors, and indeed for progress in the agenda as a whole.

unlocking an understanding both of commercial imperatives and of global governance more widely.[24]

As the economic pressures of globalisation have driven processes of deregulation around the world, so too globalisation has brought into sharp focus the complexities of social and environmental management in an increasingly interconnected world.[25] Chief among the remaining challenges is the task of making governable the activities and impacts of actors who organise their activities above and beyond the borders of territorial sovereignty.[26] Businesses are among these actors.

IV. The Case for Bringing Law into the Corporate Social Responsibility Agenda

The corporate social responsibility agenda is often associated with a definitional dogma that is clearly reflected in a July 2002 Commission Communication—that corporate social responsibility is "a concept whereby companies integrate social and environmental concerns in their business operations and in their interaction with their stakeholders *on a voluntary basis.*"[27] The Communication goes on: "Despite the wide spectrum of approaches to CSR, there is large consensus on its main features [including that] CSR is behaviour by businesses over and above legal requirements, voluntarily adopted because businesses deem it to be in their long-term interest."[28]

There is a richness in the voluntary CSR agenda's emphasis on partnerships, on joint decision-making, and on voluntary discussion as a means

---

24. This applies to government networks at different levels as much as multi-stakeholder networks or single-actor networks of different kinds. *See* Anne-Marie Slaughter, *A New World Order* (Princeton U. Press 2004).

25. Indeed, at one point this led George Ball, formerly a U.S. under-secretary of state and U.N. representative, to make a radical proposal for 'denationalization' of transnational corporations [TNCs]. He argued that a supranational citizenship for TNCs should be provided by treaty, since, in his view, the pragmatic policy followed by TNCs of obeying local laws in each country where they operate would not resolve the "inherent conflict of interest between corporate managements that operate in the world economy and governments whose points of view are confined to the narrow national scene." Sol Picciotto, *Rights, Responsibilities and Regulation of International Business*, 42 Colum. J. Transnatl. L. 131, 133-34 (2003) (citing George W. Ball, *Cosmocorp: The Importance of Being Stateless*, 2 Colum. J. World Bus. 25, 28-29 (1967)).

26. In Mary Robinson's words, "[n]ow, in many areas, power has shifted from the public to the private, from national governments to multinational corporations and international organisations. This has resulted in a gap in accountability for human rights protection and an absence of transparency and broad public participation in critical policy decisions." Mary Robinson, Speech, *Human Rights, Development and Business – An Introduction* (Basel, Switzerland, Nov. 27, 2003), available at http://www.novartisfoundation.com/en/articles/human/symposium_human_rights/speeches/speech_robinson.htm.

27. Commission of the European Communities, *Communication from the Commission Concerning Corporate Social Responsibility: A Business Contribution to Sustainable Development* 3, http://europa.eu.int/comm/employment_social/soc-dial/csr/csr2002_en.pdf (July 2, 2002) (emphasis added).

28. *Id.* at 5.

to take forward collective understanding on improving business practices. Voluntary initiatives have the potential to express a crystallisation in emerging values more quickly and more flexibly than law is able. Indeed, there is much that lawyers can learn for their own practices from some of the values that underline approaches that have been adopted within the voluntary CSR agenda—particularly the values of transparency, partnership, and consensus-building dialogue, and consideration of the interests of all business stakeholders.

But it would be wrong to conclude from the definitional dogma that lawyers have little role to play in corporate social responsibility. Many lawyers themselves practise in firms—businesses—that are themselves potentially addressed by the corporate social responsibility agenda. And the dogma itself is unhelpful. Law needs to be recognised to have a more expansive role than that allowed within the 'voluntary only' definition of corporate social responsibility.

There are many reasons for adopting an approach to CSR that allows consideration of law. For present purposes it is sufficient simply to point to a few of them.

First, by focusing on a particular set of *tools* for addressing business responsibilities—those that are 'voluntary'—the 'voluntary only' definition of CSR focuses on responses to managing business impacts rather than the impacts themselves.

Second, the voluntary approach has a tendency to disconnect CSR from key issues of power that have informed much of the discourse about economic globalisation, taking for granted the institutions and laws associated with economic globalisation. To the extent that the 'voluntary' CSR agenda speaks directly to the economic globalisation agenda, it tends to do so by inviting further liberalisation or removal of regulatory burdens—such as discriminatory implementation of domestic tax laws in respect to large foreign investors[29]—so that competitive enterprise and effective economic globalisation are more effectively supported. From a response to the downsides of economic globalisation, corporate social responsibility then becomes a tool for furthering and strengthening the very starting points that have generated a status quo that corporate social responsibility is designed to change.

Third, the voluntary only definition of CSR tends to be associated with a focus on encouraging 'best practice' and innovation among businesses. It does little to contribute to the much-needed discussion on how the worst and most exploitative forms of business behaviour could be eradicated from the global economy.

---

29. For example, the business grouping 'Private Investors for Africa' has as one of its core themes the development of 'sustainable taxation models.' *See* Private Investors for Africa, *EMS Development Roundtable*, http://europa.eu.int/comm/enterprise/csr/documents/20030317/csrdevpiapps.pdf (Mar. 17, 2003).

Fourth, the business coverage of voluntary approaches to CSR is limited. A voluntary approach to CSR cannot hope directly to address all businesses, since market-based drivers of responsible business behaviour that take the form of consumer demand, or investor pressure, or campaign activity by non-governmental organisations, cannot reach all businesses in the same way.

Fifth, law and litigation are bringing new light to the CSR agenda in a variety of cases that test the boundaries of business responsibility. These cases—many of them transnational in scope—test the application of existing legal principles, such as civil liability, to some of the most difficult areas of the CSR agenda. One example involves investments by transnational corporations in host countries, such as Myanmar, the Niger Delta, or Sudan, associated with human rights abuses, violent conflict, or oppressive regimes.

Sixth, the voluntary tools of corporate social responsibility operate in a legal context. Once a code of conduct is adopted in a supply chain contract, it acquires legal status as a matter of contract. As mentioned above, the range of norms for business regulation—with which lawyers work—increasingly encompasses voluntary instruments such as labelling schemes or codes of conduct. The laws of defamation, misleading advertising, competition policy, and negligence already frame the voluntary CSR agenda.

Seventh, the voluntary CSR agenda is itself giving rise to new laws and legislation—particularly in the corporate governance arena and in relation to company reporting on environmental and social issues.[30]

Eighth, law and litigation have the potential to shape business reputations as responsible—or irresponsible—players and drive improvements in business practices or in engagement with external stakeholders.

Ninth, in many parts of the world, the notion of responsible business behaviour remains inextricably linked to the challenges of ensuring that businesses meet minimum legal requirements for environmental or labour protection, fair competition or corporate governance. Even-handed implementation and enforcement of minimum standards around the world is an essential precondition for creating a level playing field in which businesses can seek additional marketplace benefits by distinguishing themselves through voluntary action.

Once it is accepted that law forms an important tool of CSR, it becomes clear that the legal profession must play a part. Lawyers and the legal profession remain key guardians at the gateway to justice through the law. It is lawyers who remain principally responsible as agents for upholding the rights of citizens in the face of business transgressions, or for enforcing minimum baseline requirements of acceptable business behaviour

---

30. *See e.g.* the French example cited in Halina Ward, *Legal Issues in Corporate Citizenship* 4, http://www.iied.org/docs/cred/legalissues_corporate.pdf (Feb. 2003).

from a legal perspective. The legal profession is a lynchpin of the foundations of CSR. For all these reasons, it makes sense to adopt an approach to CSR in which law, litigation, and lawyers are accorded a significant place. Some of the issues that this raises for lawyers, and the profession as a whole, are outlined in the next section.

V. APPLYING CORPORATE SOCIAL RESPONSIBILITY TO LAW FIRMS AS BUSINESSES

Many law firms are themselves businesses. This fact is also an entry point for the argument that lawyers—and the legal profession—need to play a role in CSR.

When the CSR agenda is understood as a framework for minimising negative impacts of business activities whilst maximising their positive contribution, it calls for companies to pay attention to three core areas: managing the potential impacts—positive and negative—of core business operations including supply chain-related issues; social investment in the wider community; and enhancing the positive engagement of business in public policy processes.[31]

Applying this breakdown to lawyers and law firms might lead to a view of lawyers and the 'for-profit' legal profession essentially as 'corporates'—as business actors in their own right, and therefore audiences for and subjects of the corporate responsibility agenda.[32]

Lawyers are different from businesses driven by the need to maximise shareholder returns in some important ways. Businesses can only do what their constitutions allow them to do—which in most cases requires them to focus on shareholder returns. The consequence is that there needs to be a clear 'business case' for environmentally or socially responsible action. That 'business case' may result from the operation of a number of distinct drivers, including regulation, consumer demand, NGO pressure, or the need to attract and retain the best possible employees.

In contrast, lawyers can be understood as learned professionals pursuing a calling. The nature of the lawyer's function in society—however narrowly construed—is such that it is possible, indeed desirable, to make a case for the profession to maximise its contribution to CSR not simply on

---

31. Jane Nelson, *Building Competitiveness and Communities: How World Class Companies Are Creating Shareholder Value and Societal Value*, Prince of Wales Bus. Leaders Forum 30-79 (1998) (copy on file with author).

32. *See* Neil Hamilton, *Applying Business Ethics to the Law Firm*, Minn. Law. 2 (Dec. 16, 2002). This refers to Harris and Gallup polls indicating that the (presumably U.S.) public perceives the legal profession's public standing, honesty and ethics as 'virtually indistinguishable' from those of business. Professor Hamilton suggests that it is the competitive pressures of the marketplace that drive lawyers to see themselves as a business like any other, not a profession constraining self-interest in the service of justice. The piece seeks to apply key themes from the Minnesota Principles, http://www.cebcglobal.org/Publications/Principles/MN_PRIN.htm, to the practise of law as a business.

the individual business interests of law firms or their lawyers, but on the basis of the collective functions and roles exercised by the profession, and its overall calling.

Viewing law firms as businesses would indicate that law firms should consider taking action in three main areas. First, firms should address the direct impacts of their core business activities with a view to enhancing the positive contribution that the profession makes to sustainable development. Second, they should consider social investment in the wider community. Third, law firms should consider their role in public policy processes of relevance to their core competencies or areas of influence. Each area is considered briefly in turn below.

A. *Lawyers and Core Business*

Two examples offer insights into the range of approaches that lawyers may choose to adopt in addressing CSR issues associated with their core business activities. The first is from South Africa, a country where a major plank in the national corporate responsibility agenda is black economic empowerment. This affects law firms both as businesses—since the legal profession itself lies within the ambit of legislation and notions of best practice on black economic empowerment—and as advisers, since law firms are involved in advising on financing mechanisms and corporate structuring to facilitate black economic empowerment—such as through the establishment of financial instruments to facilitate black ownership. In the third quarter of 2003, the South African magazine *Black Business Quarterly* carried three articles featuring the work of a number of South African commercial law firms in furthering the black economic empowerment agenda. It highlighted both the role of law firms as professional advisers on implementation of black economic empowerment within clients, and the strategies adopted by the individual firms for addressing their own internal black economic empowerment issues.[33]

A second approach is for lawyers to consider acquiring CSR advisory capacity in ways that help to maximise the potential positive contribution of business to sustainable development. For example, the website literature of the U.S. law firm Foley Hoag announces that:

> We help savvy business leaders limit their companies' risk by incorporating internationally recognized standards into their strategic planning, crisis response strategies, and relationships with stakeholders.[34] We help our clients succeed by providing them

---

33. *Black Economic Empowerment: The Professional Services Experience*, 4 Black Bus. Q. 46 (2003); Ellora Ghosh, *Synergistic Rainmakers, Working Together, Aligned in the Same Direction, Must Be Stronger than One or Two Larger-than-Life Individuals*, 4 Black Bus. Q. 49 (2003); *BEE Drives the Economy*, 4 Black Bus. Q. 52 (2003).

34. Foley Hoag LLP, *Corporate Social Responsibility: Practice Description*, http://www.foleyhoag.com/practice.asp?pID=000320864101 (accessed Oct. 28, 2004).

with the information by which they can adopt risk-controlling, strategic business practices. Benefits of our advice include the reduction of threats to corporate reputation, the reduction of risks associated with the uncertainties of globalization, enhanced brand image, increased customer and employee loyalty and retention, and improved relationships with external stakeholders and public opinion leaders.[35]

B. Lawyers and Social Investment

Like other businesses, lawyers could also consider developing social investment programmes to contribute to the progressive development of the communities in which they are based. This is familiar territory for many lawyers. For example, there are rules of professional conduct that exhort lawyers to carry out pro bono work.[36] But the potential contributions are wider than this. For example London based City law firm Linklaters has adopted a global community investment programme covering legal pro bono work, staff volunteering and charitable donations.[37] And the Swedish commercial law firm Vinge has established a programme to complement the Swedish Confederation of Industry's initiative on diversity for economic growth, working with five schools with the aim of inspiring young people with 'immigrant backgrounds' to attend law school.[38]

C. Lawyers as Advocates for Social Progress

Businesses of all kinds, including law firms, are generally comfortable with the idea that lobbying public policy makers to uphold their commercial interests is an acceptable activity. Yet in those areas where broader public goods are at stake—such as in relation to environmental protection, social justice and poverty reduction, education, and upholding human rights, businesses are often reluctant to play a transparent public advocacy or lobbying role. In fact, business lobbying often undermines efforts to strengthen social or environmental protection.[39]

Viewed through the lens of the economic globalisation agenda this points attention to an uncomfortable dilemma: that whilst business lobbying helps to generate the trade and investment rules that underpin inequity in

---

35. Foley Hoag LLP, *Corporate Social Responsibility: Description*, http://www.foleyhoag. com/overview.asp?pID=000320864101 (accessed Oct. 28, 2004).

36. *See e.g.* Patrick R. Burns, *Pro Bono: It's Good and It's Good for You!*, http://www. courts.state.mn.us/lprb/fc99/fc041999.html (Apr. 19, 1999) (reprinted from Minn. Law.).

37. *See* Linklaters, *Who Cares?*, http://www.linklaters.com/pdfs/community/brochure.pdf? navigationid=222 (accessed Oct. 28, 2004).

38. *See* Press Release, Vinge, *Vinge Launches Diversity Project*, http://www.vinge.se/ templates/en/about/ShowNews.asp?a=132 (May 13, 2002).

39. Halina Ward & Bernice Lee, *Corporate Responsibility and the Future of the International Trade and Investment Agendas*, 1 IIED Persps. on Corp. Resp. for Env. & Dev. (Oct. 2003), available at http://www.iied.org/cred/pubs.html.

the impacts of economic globalisation, it is those same businesses who are invited to help to put a 'human face' on the global economy through the adoption of cutting-edge voluntary corporate responsibility practices.

Lawyers could play a positive advocacy role in public policy processes that touch on the sphere of influence of the legal profession. Far from advocating for the narrow interests of those that they represent, a social responsibility perspective might call for even business lawyers to advocate change in the law in those areas where it fails to ensure that business and sustainable development are mutually supportive.

The potential implications of lawyers adopting a social responsibility perspective are far reaching. For example, at its most contentious, this basis for social responsibility could call for business lawyers to think more carefully about the circumstances in which key principles of company law generate incentives to carry on business in ways that fail to maximise contributions to sustainable development.[40] For example, directors' fiduciary duties are owed principally to the company—usually defined as the shareholders present and future.[41] Consequently, the judgment of directors in areas of social or environmental responsibility is potentially vulnerable to challenge by shareholders where a clear 'business case' for socially or environmentally responsible action does not exist. The business case may be market-based—for example, as a result of the reputational considerations that flow from campaign pressure from non-governmental organisations; or the potential to recognise opportunities to innovate in the production of environmentally or socially progressive goods and services—or it can be provided by regulation or legislation.

Lawyers are also among the key actors in the maintenance of the principle of limited liability; a principle that can work to allow companies to externalise environmental and social costs through risk management strategies that include the establishment of undercapitalised subsidiaries charged with carrying out riskier parts of companies' operations. Activist lawyers sensitive to the issues at stake within the corporate social responsibility agenda might seek to expose and challenge some of the potential negative consequences that principles of company law can have for people or the environment.[42]

---

40. This idea is reflected in the so-called 'stakeholder' debate in the field of company law, which posits that directors should owe duties not only to the company but also to a range of external 'stakeholders.' For recent discussion in the U.K. context (ultimately rejected), *see e.g.* Company Law Review Steering Group, *Modern Company Law for a Competitive Economy: The Strategic Framework* ch. 5.1 (Feb. 1999), available at http://www.dti.gov.uk/cld/comlawfw/.

41. *See e.g.* John H. Farrar & Brenda Hannigan, *Farrar's Company Law* 381-82 (4th ed., Butterworths 1998).

42. This is by no means to suggest that the principle of limited liability should be abandoned. Rather, there needs to be a more reflective discussion on the social and environmental costs associated with the maintenance of the principle of limited liability, and the circumstances in which alternative bases for liability—including corporate group liability—might have a role in allocating responsibility for 'worst case' environmental disasters or human rights abuses.

VI. WHAT KIND OF LAWYERS DOES THE CORPORATE SOCIAL RESPONSIBILITY AGENDA NEED?

We need law firmly in the corporate social responsibility agenda. But what kind of lawyers do we need? As this paper has already shown, the CSR agenda itself points to a number of characteristics of the 'CSR-friendly' lawyer, including:

- absorbing the relevance of the 'voluntary' tools of CSR for their work;
- being equipped to maximise the positive contribution of their work to society—recognising that that task necessarily involves a number of delicate balancing acts—whilst minimising negatives;
- a willingness to act as advocates for social justice and environmental protection, within their spheres of influence.

The role of lawyers in society is also the domain of legal ethics. And both legal ethics and principles of professional conduct potentially have a significant role to play in aligning the work of the legal profession with the goals of CSR.

Already, the basic starting points for addressing the interface between CSR and the legal profession outlined above go further than the so-called 'standard conception' of legal ethics, according to which lawyers' ethics are based on two principles, namely:

1. The Principle of Neutrality: the lawyer may (and if no other lawyer is willing to represent a client *must*) represent people who wish to employ the lawyer's services regardless of the lawyer's opinion of the justice of the cause. In so doing however, the lawyer is absolved of any moral responsibility for acts done in the name of the client, and

2. The Principle of Partisanship: the lawyer is permitted and required to do everything to further the client's interests provided only that it is neither technically illegal nor a clear breach of a rule of conduct. The principle holds even when it clearly thwarts the aims of the substantive law.[43]

Happily, alternative conceptions of legal ethics go further than addressing simply the roles and responsibilities of lawyers in relation to the provision of legal services and address also the social context in which lawyers work, and arrangements for the delivery of legal services.[44] Drawing the sphere of legal ethics more widely in this way allows it to encompass concerns for access to justice, societal aspirations for law—as it relates to legal practice—and the social responsibilities of lawyers.

Taking this broader starting point for understanding the realm of legal ethics, the management of legal ethics focuses on the challenges inherent in arriving at a balancing act between two broad principles. The first is the

---

43. Richard O'Dair, *Legal Ethics: Text and Materials* 134 (Butterworths 2001).
44. *See generally id.* at 134-86.

principle of duty to the client that is often expressed as a duty to act in the best interests of the client, or to act zealously in the interests of the client, within the limits allowed by law. The second is reflected in the notion that the lawyer owes a wider duty to ensure that his or her practice reflects a commitment to the proper administration of justice and, indeed, to the institution of law.

Linking law to the CSR agenda brings with it an imperative to align notions of CSR with legal practice. But does maximising the legal profession's contribution to CSR call for changes in the principal vehicle for expressing legal ethics—namely rules of professional conduct? One way to address this issue is to look to those areas where there are potential tensions. It is beyond the scope of the paper to make detailed suggestions for changes in rules of professional conduct. But the remainder of this paper considers a range of areas where the intersection of CSR and the legal profession pose professional dilemmas that could usefully be addressed as issues of professional ethics. The focus throughout lies with two kinds of lawyers: lawyers working in private commercial practice and 'public interest' lawyers.[45]

VII. Is There a Fundamental Clash of Cultures between the Practices of Commercial Law and CSR Respectively?

Those corporate lawyers who have so far engaged directly with the CSR agenda generally stress the potential benefits to their clients of engaging them in new CSR advisory roles. For example, two lawyers with Baker and Mackenzie, James Cameron and Sunwinder Mann, see "increasing convergence in what corporate lawyers and corporate citizenship teams are advising their clients."[46] They argue that, in the U.K. context, the enactment of the Human Rights Act—which incorporates the European Convention on Human Rights into U.K. Law—has created a legal culture in which "corporations can no longer ignore human rights issues in the running of their business." Cameron and Mann argue that:

> [T]he business lawyer has never advised his or her clients in a vacuum. Most, if not all, commercial clients expect their lawyers not only to advise on the legal position, but also to provide practi-

---

45. Public interest lawyers, whose practices are sometimes referred to as 'cause lawyering,' are those who commit themselves through their pursuit of legal practice to furthering social justice or a vision of a 'good' society. *See generally Cause Lawyering: Political Commitments and Professional Responsibilities* (Austin Sarat &' Stuart Scheingold eds., Oxford U. Press 1998). Three core strategies deployed by public interest law firms have been identified as access to justice, law reform and political empowerment. *See* Thomas Hitchens & Jonathan Klaaren, *Public Interest Law Around the World: An NAACP-LDF Symposium Report* 4 (Julius L. Chambers et al. eds., Colum. Hum. Rights L. Rev. 1992).

46. James Cameron & Sunwinder Mann, Presentation, *Corporate Law and Corporate Responsibility—Meeting of the Minds or Miles Apart?* (The Royal Inst. of Intl. Affairs Conf. on Leg. Dimensions of Corp. Resp., Nov. 23, 2001) (copy on file with Royal Inst. of Intl. Affairs).

cal advise on the commercial impact of a legal course of action they may choose to pursue. The litigation lawyer may advise his client not to pursue a contractual claim despite a strong legal claim. . . . The intellectual property lawyer may advise his multinational pharmaceutical client not to act against a third world country manufacturing cheap generic drugs in order to help fight disease even if this amounts to a violation of the client's patent rights.[47] The construction or property lawyer may advise his client not to develop a site in case this would have an adverse effect on either the environment or in case this would involve numerous people being displaced from their homes. The employment lawyer may advise his corporate client to settle a claim brought by an employee for sexual or racial harassment so that litigation and adverse publicity may be avoided . . . There is one fundamental reason why the business lawyer has already been providing practical commercial advice in addition to traditional legal advice – to guarantee the protection and integrity of the client's most valuable asset, its brand name and reputation.[48]

Nonetheless, non-lawyer practitioners of corporate social responsibility—particularly those with connection to jurisdictions in the United States—are sometimes prone to the view that lawyers hinder, rather than help, progress in the CSR agenda. In a 2001 presentation,[49] the late David Husselbee, who at the time was Global Director of Social and Environmental Affairs with Adidas-Salomon AG, pointed to some of the tensions between the overall characteristics of CSR, as distinct from legal approaches.

CSR	Legal
Responsibility	Liability
Transparency	Confidentiality
Building Bridges	Cautious Defensiveness

The optimistic view—that a 'good' lawyer will aim for integration between legal and reputational risk management—is not always borne out in practice. The legal profession has not played as much of a positive role in the CSR agenda as it might. A number of examples, highlighted in the following section, indicate that efforts to revisit the balance between core tenets of professional ethics could help to achieve a shift to a more positive contribution.

---

47. An example of precisely the opposite happening concerns litigation in South Africa by a large number of pharmaceutical companies over the constitutionality of provisions in the 1997 Medicines and Related Substance Control Amendment Act "on the grounds that they were in breach" of intellectual property law. "The legislation formed a key part of South Africa's response to the AID[S] pandemic, though its coverage was not limited to HIV/AIDS treatment drugs." The action was eventually withdrawn. Ward, *supra* n. 30, at 22-23.

48. Cameron & Mann, *supra* n. 46.

49. *See* Ward, *supra* n. 30, at 27.

VIII. Lawyers Chilling Voluntary Approaches to Corporate Social Responsibility

There are a number of ways in which lawyers and legal advice can undermine or exert a 'chilling effect' on voluntary approaches designed to respond to contemporary demands for corporate social responsibility. Four specific examples follow.

A. *The United Nations Global Compact*

Many critics of the Global Compact have focused on its voluntary, non-binding, nature—arguing that it does little to prevent 'bluewash'[50] and that company support for the ten Global Compact principles[51] should, at a minimum, be linked to third party processes to monitor company compliance with the principles. By way of contrast, there have also been anecdotal suggestions that levels of participation by U.S.-based companies in the U.N. Global Compact may have been held back as a result of advice from U.S. lawyers worried that claims of adherence to the Compact's nine principles—three labour, three environmental, and three human rights—could generate risks of litigation.[52] Indeed, there appears to be a concern within the U.N. to educate business lawyers to ensure that they are supportive of the efforts reflected in the U.N. Global Compact.

In January 2004, the U.N.'s legal counsel and Under-Secretary-General for Legal Affairs, Mr. Hans Corell, appealed to business lawyers at the 2004 Midwinter Council Meeting of the American Bar Assocation's Section of Business Law:

> You may ask: what is the role of corporate counsel in relation to the Compact? Let me take human rights as a point of departure even if the argument could be made equally for labour and the environment. Lawyers have a special responsibility in society. It is of particular importance that they are familiar with the international obligations that their country has undertaken at the international level, i.e. vis-à-vis other states, and contribute to the fulfilment of such obligations.

---

50. This is defined by CorpWatch as referring to "corporations that wrap themselves in the blue flag of the United Nations in order to associate themselves with UN themes of human rights, labor rights and environmental protection." CorpWatch, *Greenwash Fact Sheet*, "Other Forms of Greenwash," http://www.corpwatch.org/article.php?id=242 (Mar. 22, 2001).

51. The Global Compact was initially based on nine principles. A tenth principle addressing corruption was added in 2004. *See* United Nations, *The Ten Principles*, http://www.unglobalcompact.org/content/AboutTheGC/TheNinePrinciples/thenine.htm (accessed Oct. 26, 2004).

52. Though this has not prevented a handful of law firms from participating, such as Allens Arthur Robinson; Amaro, Stuber e Advogados Associados S/C; Bufete Jurídico Sapena Soler Borras; Bunag Kapunan Migallos & Perez; and Roco Kapunan Migallos Perez & Luna Law Offices. One, a leading Australian commercial law firm, Allens Arthur Robinson, has submitted an example of what it is doing to implement the Global Compact Principles within its own firm to the Compact Secretariat. E-mail from Ursula Wynhoven, Global Compact Secretariat (Feb. 26, 2004) (on file with author).

You will of course counter and maintain that your main responsibility is to your client. This is correct, but the two responsibilities may not necessarily be in conflict with each other. On the contrary! The matters that the Compact focuses on are often given prominent attention in the media and public discussion. Ultimately, companies will be assessed by public opinion, and as we know the agenda for the debate is here often set by non-governmental organizations. It is therefore important that companies that are proactive in this field also act in their own interest.[53]

Mr. Corell stressed the voluntary nature of the Compact and his belief that companies would not be held accountable if they failed to meet the standards of the Compact. The Global Compact Secretariat itself stresses that participation in the Compact does not bring legal consequences. A 'common questions' document prepared by the Secretariat emphasises that:

Support for the Global Compact initiative does not call for an expression of intent to legally bind the company or to create a duty towards third parties.

As the initial step for participation by a company in the Global Compact initiative, a company has to send a letter to the UN Secretary-General, signed by the Chief Executive Officer and possibly endorsed by the board, expressing support for the principles of the Global Compact. The statement is an aspirational commitment rather than a commitment "to comply with the principles" or to "meet the objectives." The large number of letters from companies, including leading US companies, that the Secretary-General has received, shows that corporations have fully understood and internalized this concept.

While participating companies are expected to publicly advocate the Global Compact and its principles in company press releases or speeches, they are not required to comment on their specific actions with regard to the Global Compact principles in these public communications. Thus, such statements do not raise issues of legal liability regarding the company's compliance with the principles it has publicly endorsed – as is the case in current judicial review.

Companies are only expected to describe the ways in which they are supporting the Global Compact and its nine principles in their annual reports or similar corporate reports, i.e. documents whose accuracy is mandated by law. Thus, a company will not be subject to a greater risk of liability by including a description of the corporate practices related to the Global Compact principles.

---

53. Hans Corell, Speech, *The Business Lawyer and International Law: Reflections on the Lawyer's Role with Respect to Teaching of International Law, the Global Compact and International Trade Law* (Santa Barbara, Cal., Jan. 17, 2004), available at http://www.unglobalcompact.org/irj/servlet/prt/portal/prtroot/com.sapportals.km.docs/ungc_html_content/NewsDocs/Corell.pdf.

> During three years of operation of the Global Compact, there has not been any indication that participating companies have been exposed to a greater risk of liability.[54]

More recently, the Global Compact Secretariat has worked directly with the American Bar Association to develop a model letter that U.S. based companies can use to sign on to the Global Compact.[55]

B. *Legalisation of the OECD Guidelines for Multinational Enterprises*

The principal inter-governmentally agreed instrument for securing corporate accountability through a non-legally binding mechanism is the OECD Guidelines for Multinational Enterprises.[56] The Guidelines were initially agreed in 1976, with negotiations on the most recent revisions to the Guidelines concluded in 2000. They contain voluntary principles and standards for responsible business conduct, including human rights, labour, environment, and taxation.

The OECD Guidelines do not directly bind enterprises, but their force for businesses lies in the political agreement of the OECD member countries, together with an additional group of eight[57] non-OECD countries that have indicated their intention to adhere to them; to establish 'National Contact Points' (NCPs) to make the Guidelines known; to disseminate them; to respond to enquiries about the Guidelines; and to report annually to the OECD's Committee on Investment and Multinational Enterprises (CIME) on its activities.[58] Importantly, NCPs are also charged with contributing

> to the resolution of issues that arise relating to implementation of the Guidelines in specific instances. The NCP will offer a forum for discussion and assist the business community, employee organisations and other parties concerned to deal with the issues raised in an efficient and timely manner and in accordance with applicable law.[59]

---

54. *Common Questions Regarding the Global Compact* (on file with author).

55. *See* Press Release, United Nations, *ABA Business Section Approves Letter for U.S. Firms*, http://www.unglobalcompact.org; *select* News & Events (Mar. 25, 2004) (noting that "[t]he leadership of the ABA Business Law Section expressed their hope that the letter, with its emphasis on the voluntary nature of the Global Compact, will allay legal-oriented concerns to U.S. corporations joining the Global Compact").

56. Organisation for Economic Co-operation and Development, *The OECD Guidelines for Multinational Enterprises: Revision 2000*, http://www.oecd.org/dataoecd/56/36/1922428.pdf (2000).

57. *See* Organisation for Economic Co-operation and Development, *The OECD Guidelines for Multinational Enterprises: A Key Corporate Responsibility Instrument*, http://www.oecd.org/dataoecd/52/38/2958609.pdf (June 2003) (for a general introduction).

58. Organisation for Economic Co-operation and Development, *Decision on the OECD Guidelines for Multinational Enterprises*, http://www.oecd.org/document/39/0,2340,en_2649_34889_1933095_1_1_1_1,00.html (July 19, 2000).

59. *Id.* at 5.

Already, there are indications that law and lawyers are contributing to delays in the resolution of issues raised with NCPs. Documenting specific instances with any degree of rigour is impossible, since the Procedural Guidelines provide expressly for "confidentiality of proceedings"[60] whilst an NCP is engaged in providing good offices where it considers that the issues raised merit further examination. Though the Procedural Guidelines do not have force of law for parties raising issues with an NCP, the relevant provision is clearly directed to the parties[61] and complainants appear generally to have complied with the spirit of this norm.

There are real risks that the effectiveness of the Guidelines, and their potential positive contribution to the corporate social responsibility agenda as a whole, could be held back by a process of 'creeping legalisation'. Examples include:

- When companies whose activities are the subject of complaints to the NCPs seek legal advice on the application of the Guidelines to the instant at issue, holding back speedy resolution of the substantive issues underlying complaints to NCPs may occur.
- When lawyers acting for companies whose activities or operations are the subject of a complaint place a major burden of proof on complainants or on NCPs by putting forward large volumes of paperwork to refute claimants' assertions—in a level of detail that complainants cannot refute without a major investment of resources—and, potentially, legal advice.
- When lawyers acting for companies whose operations are the subject of a complaint NCPs raise arguments that information held by a third party, and that might be relevant to the resolution of a complaint, should not be released since it is potentially relevant to ongoing litigation.
- Any 'creeping legalisation' of the Guidelines by businesses and their legal advisers may act to strengthen the hand of non-governmental organisations who have rejected a 'voluntary only' CSR agenda in favour of work to strengthen corporate accountability—including by campaigning for a new corporate accountability convention. As the Clean Clothes Campaign argues, "[a]lthough [the] guidelines are very weak it is hard to ignore them, because whenever there's an attempt to push for legislation that would hold companies accountable for labor conditions almost every government refers to the OECD guidelines and procedures."[62]

---

60. *Id.* at ¶¶ 4(a), 5.

61. "At the conclusion of the procedures, if the parties involved have not agreed on a resolution of the issues raised, they are free to communicate about and discuss these issues." *Id.*

62. Clean Clothes Campaign, *Complaining at the OECD*, http://www.cleanclothes.org/legal/oecd.htm (accessed Oct. 25. 2004).

C. *Litigation that Holds Back Voluntary Corporate Environmental and Social Reporting*

Litigation in California against the sports goods and apparel company Nike has threatened to chill take-up of voluntary corporate environmental and social reporting. In *Nike, Inc. v. Kasky*,[63] California resident and environmental activist Marc Kasky challenged a variety of statements made by Nike over a period beginning in 1996, a time when the company was under sustained attack from a variety of individuals and NGOs over labour practices in its supply chain. Nike responded to these attacks through a variety of communications ranging from press releases to letters addressed to university presidents. In essence, these communications said that Nike products were manufactured throughout the world in accordance with a strict code of conduct, and that they were free from sweated labour.

California consumer protection legislation, recognising the limited resources available to public attorneys-general, enables any California resident, whether she or he has suffered damage or not, to bring an action as a 'private attorney general.' Mr. Kasky claimed, in this capacity, that a number of Nike's statements were false or deceptive, and that, consequently, as false advertising they were not covered by the U.S. Constitution's First Amendment enshrining freedom of speech. Nike cited the U.S. Constitution's First Amendment protection. Initially, the San Francisco Superior Court and the California Court of Appeals dismissed the action, agreeing with Nike that the company's statements were indeed protected by the First Amendment. But in May 2002, the California Supreme Court ruled by a majority of 4-3 against dismissing the action on First Amendment grounds.[64] Key to the court's ruling was its determination that Nike's statements amounted to "commercial speech," because they were directed by a commercial speaker to a commercial audience (consumers of Nike products), making representations of fact about Nike's business operations "for the purpose of promoting sales of its products."[65]

Commercial speech is not subject to the same level of protection as 'political speech' under the First Amendment, and U.S. legislatures are free to prohibit commercial speech that is false or misleading. The consequence is that Nike's statements made in efforts to defend their Asian business practices—in the specific contexts in which they were made—were subject to California's laws on unfair competition and false advertising in the usual way. That, in turn, means that Nike will have breached unfair competition

---

63. *See generally* 539 U.S. 654 (2003); Goldstein & Howe, P.C., http://www.goldsteinhowe. com/; *select* Go to the Filings in Nike v. Kasky (accessed Oct. 26, 2004).

64. *Kasky v. Nike, Inc.*, 119 Cal. Rptr. 2d 296 (Cal. 2002).

65. *Id.* at 300-01.

law if members of the public are likely to have been deceived by its statements.[66]

Nike indicated that as a result of the California Supreme Court judgment, it had decided "to restrict severely all of its communications on social issues that could reach California consumers, including speech in national and international media."[67] It cancelled release of its annual corporate responsibility report, decided not to pursue a listing in the Dow Jones Sustainability Index, and refused "dozens of invitations . . . to speak on corporate responsibility issues."[68]

Yet, it is far from clear that the tests applied by the California Supreme Court would *necessarily* apply to voluntary company reports or speeches in the same way as Nike's factual statements. The long-term reputational benefits that are among the principal drivers of voluntary company reporting may not be held to have the same nexus with 'promoting sales' as the kinds of defensive factual statements that are at stake in the *Kasky* case.

Business lawyers were quick to point to the risks inherent in company reporting. For example, two analysts with DLA Upstream argued, before the case reached an out of court settlement (which is considered further below), that "[i]f Nike loses, [*Nike, Inc. v. Kasky*] it could mean the end of voluntary CSR reports as they currently exist as they could prove too great a potential liability."[69]

In contrast, very little press coverage of the *Nike* case placed the litigation within the broader context of the corporate responsibility agenda and the public interest in clear and truthful corporate communications.[70] Public perceptions of the 'public interest' surrounding the case, in other words, are likely to have been influenced by press coverage that appears at first blush to have been heavily influenced by Nike's own publicity.

There were substantial risks that if Nike's 'chilling effect' arguments took hold, the case could have an adverse effect on developments in the field of corporate social responsibility overall. In other words, Mr. Kasky's action had the potential to hold back the corporate responsibility agenda

---

66. Cal. Bus. & Prof. § 17200 (1997). Nike appealed and in January 2003 the U.S. Supreme Court announced that it would review the California Supreme Court's judgment. In an opinion issued in June 2003, the Court dismissed a writ of certiorari on the basis that it lacked jurisdiction, in part because no final judgment had yet been issued by a California court. *Nike, Inc. v. Kasky*, 539 U.S. 654 (2003).

67. *Nike, Inc.*, 539 U.S. at 682 (Kennedy, J., dissenting).

68. *Id.*

69. Stuart Thomson & Sam Hinton-Smith, *U.K. Takes Step Towards CSR Reporting*, Ins. Day (July 23, 2003), available at http://www.stuartthomson.co.uk/articles/csr/.

70. My unscientific reading of the press coverage of the California Supreme Court decision would certainly appear to support the analysis of the U.S. NGO, ReclaimDemocracy, *Major Newspapers Publishing Editorials on Nike v. Kasky*, http://www.reclaimdemocracy.org/nike/ nike _v_kasky_editorial_record.html (accessed Dec. 6, 2004).

when coupled with scaremongering publicity about its chilling effect, and lack of clarity over the territorial reach of the California legislation.[71]

In the litigious U.S., the discovery that companies can be sued—by people who have not suffered damage—over the statements that they make about their social or environmental practices in defence of NGO attacks is bound to set alarm bells ringing; but the case has not gone to trial. No court has ruled directly on how California law actually applies to the facts at issue—only on the extent to which Nike's statements are protected by the First Amendment. And California legislators remain free, as one commentator has suggested, to establish a clear 'safe haven' where right-minded corporate communications can remain free from the threat of litigation.[72]

D. Tactical Use of Legal Arguments Holding Back Progress

A final example of the potential chilling effect of legal advice on the corporate social responsibility agenda concerns the suggestion made by a major U.S. oil company that mandatory transparency over payments made by companies in the extractive sectors could open it to a risk of litigation under the Alien Tort Claims Act.[73] There have been reports that concerns about liability under the Alien Tort Claims Act were cited by ExxonMobil in June 2003 to secure a change in emphasis in the U.K. government-led Extractive Industries Transparency Initiative, from "a compact that would be formally endorsed by companies and governments to a vague set of principles with no bite."[74]

IX. JOINING UP LITIGATION AND CORPORATE COMMUNICATIONS

With globalisation, the challenges of legal risk management have become broader, both substantively and geographically. As one in-house counsel writes:

---

71. Now that it has been unleashed, the issues raised are unlikely to disappear. Litigation has already begun in the broadly comparable "happy cows" case in which the animal welfare NGO People for the Ethical Treatment of Animals has brought an action against San Francisco based Milk Advisory Board over adverts showing cartoon cows with the caption "Great cheese comes from happy cows. Happy cows come from California." Center for Individual Freedom, *Boo-Hoo, Moo-Moo*, http://www.cfif.org/htdocs/legal_issues/legal_updates/other_noteworthy_cases/happy_cows_campaign.htm (Dec. 19, 2002).

72. Elliot Schrage, *A New Model for Social Auditing*, Fin. Times (May 27, 2002), available at http://www.cfr.org/pub5083/elliot_schrage/a_new_model_for_social_auditing.php. For a collection of press articles, see http://www.cleanclothes.org/companies/nike02-05-02.htm (accessed Aug. 23, 2004).

73. "The Extractive Industries Transparency Initiative was announced by UK Prime Minister Tony Blair at the World Summit on Sustainable Development in Johannesburg, September 2002. Its aim is to increase transparency over payments by companies to governments and government-linked entities, as well as transparency over revenues by those host country governments." Department for International Development, *News*, "The Extractive Industries Transparency Initiative," http://www2.dfid.gov.uk/news/files/extractiveindustries.asp (accessed Oct. 25, 2004).

74. E-mail from Gavin Hayman, Global Witness (Feb. 27, 2004) (on file with author).

The 'fire-fighting' lawyer, hidden away in the legal department waiting for assignments from the business people, is a thing of the past. The new-style lawyer is more integrated in the decision making process and more proactive, has a broader perspective of the business strategies and is generally more informed.[75]

Corporate social responsibility forms an important part of the business landscape for this new-style lawyer. That insight has direct consequences for the management of litigation in cases with strong associations with the corporate social responsibility agenda. There is a strong case to be made for a defendant company's legal advisers to develop tailored litigation strategies – so that the company's approach to CSR is demonstrated to be congruent with its approach to litigation.

The body of transnational legal claims against parent companies of multinational corporate groups, in relation to environmental or human rights impacts in developing countries, offer useful case studies for both legal advisers and potential defendant companies. For example, in U.S. litigation against Unocal over its alleged links to human rights abuses by government forces in Myanmar, the company chose to adopt an aggressively defensive external relations strategy. Alongside policy commitments to respect human rights the company issued a series of statements rejecting the allegations, whilst casting doubt on the motives of the claimants' lawyers. In a variety of statements[76] the company asserted that:

> The claims made in the Cristobal Bonifaz law firm press release concerning human rights abuses on the Yadana natural gas project in Myanmar (Burma) in which Unocal holds a financial interest are false, irresponsible and frivolous.[77]
>
> We are confident that no human rights abuses have occurred in the construction or operation of the pipeline. In fact, the company has met with the government on a number of occasions to express our concerns about reports of human rights abuses by the Burmese armed forces. We are absolutely convinced that the presence of Unocal and other companies who follow high ethical standards and modern business practices can have a positive impact on the economic and political life of the people of Myanmar.[78]

---

75. Markus U. Diethelm, *Globalization and the Future of the International Practice of Law from a General Counsel's Perspective of a Multinational Enterprise – A Navigator of Management and Steward of the 'Future of Law'?* in *The Internationalization of the Practice of Law* 75, 79 (Jens Drolshammer & Michael Pfeifer eds., Kluwer L. Intl. 2001).

76. *See generally* Unocal, *The Yadana Project in Myanmar,* http://www.unocal.com/myanmar/ (accessed Oct. 24, 2004).

77. Unocal, *Unocal Statement in Response to Press Release from Law Offices of Cristobal Bonifaz,* http://www.unocal.com/uclnews/96htm/090396b.htm (Sept. 3, 1996). A settlement of the claim "in principle" was announced in December 2004.

78. Unocal, *Unocal Actions Not on Trial in California Case; Company Expects to Be Vindicated of 'Vicarious Liability' Charges,* http://www.unocal.com/uclnews/2002news/061202.htm (June 12, 2002).

Unocal's statements sit uneasily against court findings during the course of the litigation. For example, the Ninth Circuit Court of Appeals judgment of September 18, 2002 in *Doe v. Unocal*[79] included the following passages:

> [T]he evidence . . . suggest[s] that Unocal knew that forced labor was being utilized and that the Joint Venturers benefitted from the practice.[80]
> [T]he evidence . . . supports the conclusion that Unocal gave practical assistance to the Myanmar Military in subjecting Plaintiffs to forced labor.[81]
>
> Unocal knew or should reasonably have known that its conduct – including the payments and the instructions where to provide security and build infrastructure – would assist or encourage the Myanmar Military to subject Plaintiffs to forced labor.[82]

The CSR agenda calls for lawyers to have sufficient understanding of the agenda to be able to play a role in preventing these kinds of mismatches. The balancing act is not an easy one. Whilst transparency is a key theme in the corporate social responsibility agenda, factual statements that prove false could, in circumstances, open companies to the prospect of litigation. Yet, silence is an uneasy option from a CSR perspective. Companies whose lawyers are well-attuned to the nuances of the CSR agenda can help their clients to find a middle way—for example through the provision of factual statements about the litigation, and comments on the underlying principles—in this case those concerning the boundaries of company and state responsibility and liability respectively.

X. Transnational Corporate Accountability Litigation: Implications for Public Interest Lawyers

It is not only practitioners in commercial law firms who face professional dilemmas when defending clients in transnational litigation. Alongside the 'for-profit' commercial law firms, there is another body of lawyers whose work and ethical positions are directly relevant to the corporate accountability and responsibility agendas. This is the body of lawyers who work within 'public interest'[83] law firms. Their role in the emerging body of transnational litigation against parent companies of multinational corporate groups also raises a number of ethical dilemmas.

Plaintiffs in many U.S. Alien Tort Claims Act actions have been represented not by commercial law firms, but by public interest lawyers based

---

79. *Doe v. Unocal Corp.*, 2002 WL 31063976 (9th Cir. Sept. 18, 2002).
80. *Id.* at 14212 (quoting *Doe v. Unocal Corp.*, 110 F. Supp. 2d 1294, 1310 (C.D. Cal. 2000)).
81. *Doe v. Unocal*, 2002 WL 31063976 at 14221.
82. *Id.* at 14227.
83. See discussion of public interest law, *supra* n. 45.

with non-governmental organisations including for example the Center for Constitutional Rights,[84] EarthRights International,[85] and the International Labor Rights Fund.[86] Many of these organisations, with the financial support of large foundations, use the law and courts in both home and host countries to pursue environmental or social justice.

Public interest lawyers may be convinced that litigation offers a powerful way to secure improvements in multinational corporate performance, or that in the absence of a comprehensive multilaterally agreed framework for corporate accountability in 'worst case' circumstances it is important to make the most of the scope for corporate accountability that is offered by existing legal principles. There may also be a hope that adverse publicity and falling share prices that result from such litigation may shame companies into better practice.

NGOs have often campaigned alongside individual legal actions. NGOs or trade unions based in host countries may also work with plaintiffs' lawyers to gather evidence, identify potential plaintiffs, or support community-based groups or individuals involved in 'foreign direct liability' claims. One example is offered by the U.S.-headquartered Center for Economic and Social Rights (CESR), whose aim is to promote social justice through human rights.[87] CESR's Latin America programme, which works to challenge development projects in the Amazon "for lack of accountability and community participation," has been involved in litigation against Texaco under the Alien Tort Claims Act.[88]

XI. PUBLIC INTEREST LAWYERS, PRIVATE RIGHTS AND COMMUNITY IMPACTS

Transnational personal injury claims against parent companies of multinational corporate groups in relation to impacts in developing countries offer sharp insights into a range of professional ethical dilemmas facing public interest lawyers acting for clients drawn from historically poor or marginalized communities in middle and low income countries.

English litigation against Cape PLC, at one time among the world's largest asbestos mining companies, is a case in point.[89] The Cape litigation ultimately involved over 7,500 South African citizens suffering from asbestosis and mesothelioma. The claimants, who were former workers at Cape's South African asbestos mining subsidiaries or members of commu-

---

84. Center for Constitutional Rights, http://www.ccr-ny.org/v2/home.asp.

85. EarthRights International, http://www.earthrights.org/.

86. International Labor Rights Fund, http://www.laborrights.org/home.html.

87. Center for Economic and Social Rights, http://cesr.org/.

88. *See generally* Centro de Derechos Económicos y Sociales, http://www.cdes.org.ec/quehemos.htm.

89. *See generally* Halina Ward, *Towards a New Convention on Corporate Accountability? Some Lessons from the Thor Chemicals and Cape PLC Cases,* in *Yearbook of International Environmental Law* 105 (Oxford U. Press 2001).

nities around its former mining sites, brought a series of actions seeking damages from the parent company. Since 1989, Cape had had no presence in South Africa, and indeed it no longer carries on asbestos mining operations.

Initially, in 1997, the London based law firm Leigh, Day & Co. issued two writs in London on behalf of five claimants funded through the public funds under the so-called 'legal aid' system. They argued that Cape's South African operations were in fact controlled by Cape in London, and that the parent company knew that its operations risked the health of workers and people in the surrounding communities. Cape argued, under the *forum non conveniens* principle,[90] that the action should have been brought in South Africa and that it would be willing to make itself available to be sued there. For three years, the claimants fought to bring their action in England. It was July 2000 before the House of Lords agreed that they were right to do so. The delay was due to legal arguments over the proper application of the *forum non conveniens* principle. Initially, the Court of Appeal refused to rule in favour of South Africa as the proper legal forum. After this ruling, in 1999, further writs were issued by two English law firms. The claimants now totalled more than 1,500. Once more, Cape argued that the cases were more appropriately brought in South Africa.[91] This time, the Court determined that South Africa was the proper forum. The case progressed to the House of Lords on the issue of *forum non conveniens*. By the time the House of Lords gave its judgment in favour of the claimants, there were over 3,000 claimants. More than 100 had died since initiating their actions. After protracted settlement negotiations, Cape finally agreed to a £7.5 million settlement in March 2003.[92]

Leigh, Day & Co. established offices near to the communities from which its clients were drawn, working in association with two South African law firms. A second English law firm, John Pickering & Co., acted for a smaller number of the claimants—though nonetheless more than 2,000 of

---

90. The *forum non conveniens* principle, which is widely applied, with some variations, in common law jurisdiction, essentially allows a court to refuse to hear a case where there is some other available legal forum "in which the case may be tried more suitably for the interests of all the parties and for the ends of justice." *Spiliada Mar. Corp. v. Cansulex Ltd.*, [1987] AC 460 (H.L. 1986).

91. Cape's lawyers also made an ethical argument. They argued that Leigh, Day & Co. had known all along that a group action would follow on from the initial action by five claimants, and that its approach to the first two actions had been structured as a tactic to make it easier for the English courts to accept jurisdiction. Leigh, Day & Co. were forced to seek legal representation for themselves as Cape argued that their behaviour amounted to an abuse of the process of the court. In the event, the Court of Appeal was critical of Leigh Day's conduct, but stopped short of judging it an abuse of process.

92. *See* Press Release, Coombs, Pickering and Partners, *End of Struggle for Cape Asbestos Victims*, http://www.minesandcommunities.org/Action/press124.htm (Mar. 13, 2003). An earlier settlement of £21 million had been reached, but Cape failed to make the first payment within the specified time frame and the litigation was revived, leading to the eventual £7.5 million settlement.

an eventual total of some 7,500 clients. Pickering had considerable experience with asbestos litigation in the U.K. It teamed up with a Johannesburg based personal injury firm with small bases in two communities. The litigation attracted considerable media attention, both domestically and internationally. Both firms established links with affected communities at the local level, and both attracted clients through community meetings and printed media. Local radio stations were also used to broadcast information about community meetings around the cases.

The way in which plaintiffs' lawyers discharge their duties to the clients is critically important in setting, and restraining, expectations. In the Cape case many people who suffered from asbestos-related diseases were unable to join the litigation; for example, because they did not work for Cape over the period in question, or because they could not prove their employment history. The exigencies of legal evidence do not always match the ways in which local people order their lives. Law is often unable to take into account the broad social and political background to disputes when determining which facts are legally relevant. In impoverished communities, expectations of the arrival of large sums of money can also attract fraudsters, who are free to attend community meetings to learn about progress with cases and plan ways to rob successful claimants of their compensation.

In South Africa, the situation is further complicated by the legacy of the system of migrant labour in the mining industries. Without considerable outreach work, settlement would be unlikely to reach unidentified foreign migrant workers who worked at Cape's sites and then returned home to the labour-sending areas outside South Africa. The 'hidden' victims remain hidden, unaddressed by the requirements of legal professional ethics.

Even a successful case could not necessarily bring improvements to the quality of life of the vast majority of residents in former asbestos-mining communities. The claimants' lawyers do not have any formal professional ethical responsibilities to the communities from which their clients are drawn, only to those clients themselves. Any creative out of court agreement to provide for environmental remediation in a personal injury action, or for building broader community-based social infrastructure, could only be concluded with the agreement of all the claimants. Ethically, such agreement would demand complete consensus to the extent that it reduced total sums available to compensate claimants in respect of their individual injuries.

Cases like the Cape case offer opportunities for lawyers to work in collaboration with local campaigning organisations and donor agencies or even businesses. Effective collaboration could maximise the impact of the litigation and the publicity that it attracts so as to bring benefits to communities as a whole. As a matter of ethics—if not formal professional ethics—lawyers should seek to maximise the opportunities for bringing community-level benefits in partnership with other organisations, including local trade union representatives. Indeed, lawyers engaged by Leigh, Day & Co. engaged in a variety of fundraising initiatives for projects around the communities that their clients are drawn from—in one example to raise money for a lung function machine.

XII. THE CHALLENGES OF TRANSCULTURAL LITIGATION

Lawyers committed to absorbing the relevance of the corporate responsibility agenda into their work would do well to seek to apply insights from the CSR agenda's focus on partnerships in circumstances where they are advising or acting for clients in transcultural human rights, labour or personal injury litigation.[93] The Cape case was not only transnational, but also transcultural in nature. One of the central themes of the CSR agenda concerns processes for stakeholder engagement. Often the focus lies with provision of advice to companies seeking to engage with local communities—sometimes in remote regions where the public sector has little effective reach. Much of the literature and advice that has been developed on stakeholder engagement comes from the distinct sub-theme of 'partnership' among different stakeholders—particularly partnership between businesses and other actors.[94]

Michael Anderson's account of the Bhopal litigation raises the central issue for public interest lawyers succinctly:

> [D]isadvantaged or injured parties may be active participants in the legal process, or they may remain alienated, disempowered "victims" at the mercy of an ambivalent altruism. . . . [I]s the traditional client-lawyer relationship adequate to represent the broader interests which are the real subject-matter of public interest litigation?[95]

A key benchmark of 'responsible' behaviour by lawyers in a North-South transcultural context might thus relate to the extent to which genuine

---

93. *See e.g. Putting Partnerships to Work: Strategic Alliances for Development between Government, the Private Sector and Civil Society* (Michael Warner & Rory Sullivan eds., Greenleaf Publg. 2004).

94. *See e.g.* Jane Nelson, *Business as Partners in Development: Creating Wealth for Countries, Companies and Communities* (Prince of Wales Bus. Leaders Forum 1996); Building Partnerships for Development, *Press Office*, http://www.bpd-naturalresources.org (accessed Aug. 31, 2004); Building Partnerships for Development, *Water and Sanitation Resource Centre*, http://www.bpd-waterandsanitation.org/english/resource.asp (accessed Aug. 31, 2004); University of Cambridge, *Programme for Industry's Postgraduate Certificate in Cross-Sector Partnership*, http://www.cpi.cam.ac.uk/pccp/ (accessed Aug. 31, 2004) (curriculum); AccountAbility, *AA1000 Series*, http://www.accountability.org.uk/aa1000/default.asp (accessed Nov. 3, 2004) (standard for stakeholder engagement developed by U.K. based non-governmental organisation).

95. Michael Anderson, *Public Interest Perspectives on the Bhopal Case: Tort, Crime or Violation of Human Rights?*, in *Public Interest Perspectives in Environmental Law* 153, 154 (David Robinson & John Dunkley eds., Wiley Chancery 1995).

partnerships are developed with local lawyers, and the quality of engagement with clients.

Public interest lawyer Emily Yozell's account of litigation in the U.S. against Standard Fruit by workers at its Costa Rican banana plantations and their families is a further illustration of the case management challenges for plaintiff lawyers in transcultural litigation.[96] Her analysis can in some respects be usefully understood as a rare contribution, from within the legal profession, to the development of the broader 'partnerships' and 'stakeholder engagement' theme of the corporate responsibility agenda as it relates to core business impacts.[97] There is clearly a difference between the relationship that lawyers have with their clients and the relationship between, say, a mining company and local communities. But, understanding Ms. Yozell's piece in this way incidentally serves as a challenge to the corporate responsibility agenda; to broaden the focus of the 'stakeholder engagement' and 'partnerships' themes of that agenda to allow the application of best practice principles in these areas; and to value chain relationships including buyer-supplier relations.

Ms. Yozell draws insights from the *Castro Alvaro* case, which centred on Costa Rican banana workers hired by Standard Fruit. The workers were required to handle dibromochloropropane (DBCP), a pesticide used to kill nematodes in the roots of the banana plants. DBCP can cause sterility in men when used without proper protective measures. Food-related use of DBCP had been banned in the U.S. since the 1970s after U.S. agricultural plant workers had launched an—ultimately successful—action against the Occidental Chemical Company's agricultural products division. The supplier companies, Dow and Shell, continued to export DBCP overseas to Standard Fruit for use in its Costa Rican plantations for two years after the United States Environmental Protection Agency banned food-related use of the chemical.[98] In Costa Rica, Standard Fruit continued to use the product. Thousands of Costa Rican workers were using the chemical with no protection at all.

The workers, and wives living with their husbands' sterility, were referred to a Texan law firm which duly filed a product liability and negligence suit in state courts in Texas, Florida, and California against Dow, Shell and, later, Standard Fruit. The defendants shifted the cases to federal courts and invoked the principle of *forum non conveniens*—that the case

---

96. Emily Yozell, *The* Castro Alfaro *Case: Convenience and Justice – Lessons for Lawyers in Transcultural Litigation*, in *Human Rights, Labour Rights and International Trade* 273 (Lance A. Compa & Stephen F. Diamond eds., U. of Pa. Press 1996).

97. *See* Jem Bendell, *Growing Pain? A Case Study of a Business-NGO Alliance to Improve the Social and Environmental Impacts of Banana Production* (May 1999) (copy on file with author) (for a case study of a business-NGO partnership directly relevant to corporate responsibility issues in the Costa Rican banana industry).

98. It seems that Standard Fruit had threatened legal action for breach of contract if they failed to do so—a factor which raises substantial issues of legal ethics in its own right.

should have been brought in Costa Rica, not the U.S. At that time, the maximum sum recoverable under Costa Rican law was $1,500. The *forum non conveniens* arguments were ultimately rejected, and in 1992, an outline settlement agreement was reached among the U.S. attorneys for presentation to local lawyers and the plaintiffs.

As Ms. Yozell points out, "[t]he concept of negotiating about one's rights, like the concept of plea bargaining, is utterly foreign to the Costa Rican legal system, and to the culture of the plaintiffs."[99] The cultural challenges that are relevant to case management include differing perceptions of the passing of time; culturally specific constructions of psychological damage; cultural perceptions of sterility; and the incongruity of monetary compensation for the injuries at issue. In cases where plaintiffs' lawyers are acting on a contingency basis the pressure to cut corners in addressing these challenges may be magnified by the lawyers' need to reach a settlement. As Ms. Yozell points out, "[i]t is easier to write a formula for failure than a formula for success in these cases. The formula for failure is simple. Think first world or 'North;' assume your values, experiences, culture, and legal system are (a) universal and (b) best."[100]

XIII. Lawyers Supporting Unethical Business Practices

In September 2003, the keynote address at the opening ceremony of the International Bar Association's annual conference in San Francisco was given by the chief prosecutor of the newly established International Criminal Court. In his speech, Luis Moreno-Ocampo called on business lawyers to assist in bringing perpetrators of international crimes to account. He highlighted atrocities in the Congo and noted that businesses in 25 countries, including the U.K. and the U.S., stood accused of helping to finance activities of the perpetrators of these crimes through the illegal trade of arms and natural resources, as well as money laundering. "There is a network of lawyers out there able to give information on these countries and to give information to their clients," he was reported as saying. Coverage of the speech in the legal press suggested that it served the incidental effect of bringing home to his audience that "some of the illegal business activities he referred to are likely to have been facilitated by lawyers."[101]

A narrow view of professional ethics in relation to the lawyer's role in business would fail to speak directly to these concerns. As a commentary on SEC activities to implement Section 307 of the Sarbanes-Oxley Act notes:

---

99. Yozell, *supra* n. 96, at 278.

100. *Id.* at 283.

101. John Malpas, *If You're Going to San Francisco*, Legal Week (Sept. 18-24, 2003), available at http://www.legalweek.net.

There are, essentially, two models of the lawyer's role in business, the Trusted Counselor model and the Legal Enabler model. . . . Counselors act as officers of the court whose job is to prevent clients from falling into crime. When their advice goes unheeded, they withdraw in protest. On rare occasions, they even blow the whistle. The Legal Enabler model, by contrast, is what the average corporate lawyer follows to make a living at the law. Legal Enablers pass no judgment on corporate acts and take no position on the wisdom of business decisions. Instead, they provide morally neutral risk analysis. Their stock in trade is not legal judgment; it is legal rationalization.[102]

The CSR agenda demands Trusted Counselors with a strong sense of their broader societal responsibilities.

Recent discussion in the U.S. on the interplay between legal ethics and corporate responsibility has been heavily dominated by the debate on the implications of the 2002 Public Accounting Reform and Investor Protection Act[103] (Sarbanes-Oxley). Sarbanes-Oxley reflected a formal response to the corporate governance issues associated with the collapse of the Enron Corporation.[104] The Act implicated lawyers and legal ethics in a number of ways, but most directly through section 307, which requires the SEC to adopt rules of professional conduct for lawyers "appearing and practicing" before it on behalf of an issuer of securities.[105] It appears that these rules will preempt conflicting state level rules of ethics.[106]

The SEC's Part 205 regulations, effective from August 5, 2003,[107] now incorporate mandatory 'up the ladder reporting'—namely, reporting on

---

102. *It's About Time: Corporate Responsibility Law Finally Makes Lawyers More Accountable*, http://www.upenn.edu/researchatpenn/article.php?379&bus (Aug. 14, 2002) [hereinafter *It's About Time*].

103. H.R. 3763, 107th Cong. (July 30, 2002) [hereinafter *Sarbanes-Oxley*].

104. *See* Special Issue, *Corporate Transparency, Accountability and Governance*, J. of Corp. Citizenship (Winter 2002) (a series of articles that address these issues in terms of their nexus with the corporate citizenship agenda).

105. *Sarbanes-Oxley, supra* n. 103, at § 307. It states

Not later than 180 days after the date of enactment of this Act, the Commission shall issue rules, in the public interest and for the protection of investors, setting forth minimum standards of professional conduct for attorneys appearing and practicing before the Commission in any way in the representation of issuers, including a rule —

(1) requiring an attorney to report evidence of a material violation of securities law or breach of fiduciary duty or similar violation by the company or any agent thereof, to the chief legal counsel or the chief executive officer of the company (or the equivalent thereof); and

(2) if the counsel or officer does not appropriately respond to the evidence (adopting, as necessary, appropriate remedial measures or sanctions with respect to the violation), requiring the attorney to report the evidence to the audit committee of the board of directors of the issuer or to another committee of the board of directors comprised solely of directors not employed directly or indirectly by the issuer, or to the board of directors.

106. *See e.g.* LegalEthics.com, *The Intersection of Ethics and the Law*, 08/04/03: An interesting exchange between the Washington State Bar and the SEC, http://legalethics.com (accessed Oct. 26, 2004).

107. 17 C.F.R. § 205 (2003).

actual or potential transgressions to individuals or functions 'higher up' the organisational hierarchy—in circumstances where a lawyer falling within the scope of the provisions "becomes aware of evidence of a material violation" of securities law, breach of fiduciary duty, or similar violation by the issuer or any of its representatives or agents.[108] However, they stop short of requiring immediate direct reporting to the board, incorporating instead a graduated approach.

The SEC postponed providing a rule on 'noisy withdrawal' to outline instead the circumstances in which a legal adviser not receiving a satisfactory response to a 'material violation' should withdraw from acting in defined circumstances; notify the SEC of the withdrawal and disaffirm relevant documents. The rules do, however, permit an attorney to disclose confidential information (relating to the disclosure) to the SEC in certain limited defined circumstances.[109]

Section 307, and the SEC's rules have generated hot debate within the legal profession—both in the U.S. and abroad. Concerns were raised about potential conflicts of interests inherent in the SEC delivering rules to 'regulate the advocate of one's adversary;' tensions between the SEC rules and existing rules of professional conduct; the balance to be drawn between the interests of investors and the interests of issuers;[110] and the impact of the rules on the relationship between lawyers and their clients more widely. Yet one commentator asks, "[w]hy is the legal profession so worried? Because the new law pricks at the heart of a system under which lawyers have always escaped accountability in business cases."[111]

A proactive approach from the community of business lawyers to the promotion of responsible business behaviour as an integral part of legal professional practice could help to enhance the profession's reputation post-Enron at the same time as reflecting a vision of professional ethics that understands the business lawyer's role in its wider social context.

XIV. NEGOTIATED SETTLEMENTS: PRIVATE CLIENTS OR PUBLIC INTEREST?

The post-Enron debate on professional ethics in the U.S. points to a deep underlying dilemma: where the interests of private clients are at odds with the public interest, however defined, how should lawyers act? The private/public interest dilemma for professional ethics has been a particular focus of attention for legal ethics commentators when lawyers negotiate

---

108. 17 C.F.R. § 205.3 (2003).

109. Memo., O'Melveny & Myers L.L.P., *SEC Adopts Rules to Implement Standards of Professional Conduct for Attorneys under Section 307 of the Sarbanes-Oxley Act*, http://www.omm.com/webdata/content/publications/sec_rules.pdf (Feb. 24, 2003).

110. *See* Richard Hall, *Section 307: The Slippery Slope?*, The European Law. (Dec. 2002/Jan. 2003) (example of discussion in the context of the EU).

111. *See It's About Time, supra* n. 102.

resolutions of disputes away from the public stamp of court oversight. As Lax and Sebenius point out, "[i]t is often easy to solve the negotiation problem for those in the room at the expense of those who are not."[112]

Alongside litigation strategies that serve to reveal deficiencies in existing legal principles in the light of contemporary concerns for corporate social responsibility and accountability, a new body of lawyers is now seeking to integrate an understanding of the corporate social responsibility agenda into out of court settlements. Their actions raise new issues about the strained relationship between the values reflected in law and dispute resolution through the courts, and those associated with the corporate social responsibility agenda.

A. *Saipan*

In 1999, three separate lawsuits were filed in California state and federal courts and in a U.S. federal court on the West Pacific island of Saipan against a number of U.S. clothes retailers and against garment contractors based in Saipan.[113] Saipan is generally exempt from U.S. immigration and minimum wage laws. The legal actions were brought by NGOs and a class of some 30,000 foreign textile workers, most of whom had been brought from China and the Philippines by apparel companies to work in their factories in Saipan. Some workers were forced to pay recruitment fees in their home countries. These fees effectively tied people to their employers in Saipan to pay back the debt.

A first legal action alleged breaches of California state law on unfair business practices on the basis that the defendant companies had falsely advertised their goods as sweatshop free, and aided and abetted violations by their contractors in Saipan of laws against involuntary servitude, as well as other misleading labelling and advertising practices.

A second action was based on federal laws: the Alien Tort Claims Act, the Anti-Peonage Act, which prohibits use of forced labour, and RICO—the Racketeer Influenced and Corrupt Organizations Act. To state a claim, plaintiffs must allege unlawful conduct of an enterprise through a pattern of racketeering activity violating specified "predicate acts," which include involuntary servitude and indentured labour. RICO broadly defines "enterprise" to include "any union or group of individuals associated, in fact, although not a legal entity."[114] The plaintiffs alleged that the defendants' behaviour amounted to a pattern of racketeering activity, which exists when a person commits or aids and abets two or more specified acts that have

---

112. David A. Lax & James K. Sebenius, *Three Ethical Issues in Negotiation*, 2 Negot. J. 363, 368 (1986).

113. *See generally* Sweatshop Watch.org, http://www.sweatshopwatch.org.

114. 18 U.S.C.A. §§ 1961 et seq. (2003) (RICO).

sufficient continuity and relationship so as to pose a threat of continued criminal activity.

The substantive legal principles at stake in the case have not been tested, since settlement talks began early in the action. By March 2002, agreements had been reached with a total of 19 mainland retailers. And in September 2002, settlements on different and more stringent terms were reached with a further seven U.S. retailers and 23 Saipan based manufacturers. The settlements, billed as worth $20 million in total, received court approval in April 2003, without admission of liability.[115] Alongside agreement on back pay, damages, recruitment fees, and prohibitions on future violations of relevant laws, the settlements are innovative in providing for strict monitoring of conditions in the factories and living quarters, and for incorporating a comprehensive new Saipan Code of Conduct which governs working and living conditions.[116] The provisions of the settlement agreements are far more creative than any adjudicated resolution of the case could have been.

Yet it appears that legal ratification of the settlement may eventually have hampered its potential directly to benefit workers. According to one insider,[117] when some of the defendant companies went bankrupt or failed to sign the agreement, the budget for implementing its monitoring programme was reduced. But the monitoring requirements under the agreement did not change. Changes could not be made without the agreement of all parties, something that nobody was prepared to countenance. As a result, some potential monitoring bodies including the preferred choice of the plaintiffs withdrew, leaving those that remained promising only to do one-day audits with none of the followup inspections and checking of remediation that had marked out the agreement as something special.[118]

B. *Nike, Inc. v. Kasky*

A second example of an out of court settlement with strong connections to the CSR agenda arises out of the *Nike, Inc. v. Kasky* case. In September 2003, the parties announced that they had arrived at an out of court

---

115. Jenny Strasburg, *Saipan Lawsuit Terms OKd: Garment Workers to Get $20 Million*, http://www.sweatshopwatch.org/headlines/2003/chronsaipan.html (Apr. 25, 2003).

116. This of course raises the issue of whether, as a matter of professional ethics, lawyers should negotiate settlements that are not faithful to the values reflected in the legal principles that would be at stake were the case to be resolved through the courts. *Cf.* Owen M. Fiss, Student Author, *Against Settlement*, 93 Yale L.J. 1073, 1085 (1983-84) (arguing that "when parties settle, society gets less than what appears, and for a price it does not know it is paying").

117. E-mail from Michael Blowfield (Mar. 1, 2004) (on file with author).

118. One company, Levi Strauss, continued to fight the case, which was voluntarily dismissed in January 2004 alongside a negotiated out of court settlement. SweatshopWatch.org, *Levi's Lawsuit Dropped/Saipan Workers' Case Dismissed in Victory for Clothier*, http://www.sweatshop watch.org/headlines/2004/levis_suit_jan04.html (Jan. 8, 2004).

settlement.[119] In a joint announcement, the two parties "mutually agreed that investments designed to strengthen workplace monitoring and factory worker programs are more desirable than prolonged litigation."[120] As part of the settlement, Nike agreed to make additional workplace-related program investments totalling $1.5 million. Nike's contribution will go to the Washington, D.C. based Fair Labor Association (FLA) for program operations and worker development programs in three specific areas:

- Increased training and local capacity building to improve the quality of independent monitoring in manufacturing countries;
- Worker development programs focused on education and economic opportunity; and
- Multi-stakeholder collaboration to advance a common global standard to measure and report on corporate responsibility performance among companies.

Though Mr. Kasky brought his action as a 'private attorney general,' the settlement agreement does not appear to be publicly available. The agreement has been criticised on a number of counts, including Nike's existing interest in the Fair Labor Association and the impact of Nike's FLA funding for collaboration to 'advance a common global standard' on efforts to develop globally applicable reporting standards elsewhere. As the general counsel of Domini Social Investments has argued,

> I have concerns about the money going to the FLA, as Nike was a founding member, and my understanding is that they have a significant influence over the FLA's agenda. . . . Part of the FLA money will go toward working on some generally acceptable reporting format on labor issues, which is good in some ways, but the GRI [Global Reporting Initiative] is already out there. . . . I would have preferred to see the money go to GRI to strengthen its labor component. . . . It would be a shame to divert resources and energy from GRI—I would encourage FLA to work with GRI on this.[121]

The settlement does not appear to take the logical—though hard-to-draft—potentially 'win-win' step of requiring Nike to advocate for mandatory reporting standards that could help to define the acceptable boundaries of corporate communications and level the playing field among companies.[122]

---

119. Press Release, Nikebiz, *Nike, Inc. and Kasky Announce Settlement of* Kasky v. Nike *First Amendment Case*, http://www.stanford.edu/~wacziarg/downclass/Nike_press_release.pdf (Sept. 12, 2003).

120. *Id.*; Kasky v. Nike, Inc. *Settled*, http://reclaimdemocracy.org/nike/nike_settles_lawsuit.html (Sept. 12, 2003) (critiquing the settlement agreement).

121. SocialFunds.com, *The Implications of the Nike and Kasky Settlement on CSR Reporting*, http://www.socialfunds.com/news/article.cgi/article1222.html (Sept. 18, 2003) (critique of the settlement agreement).

122. This argument would likely be countered in similar terms to the suggestion that Nike has an interest in seeing the SEC adopt mandatory reporting standards for listed companies, namely,

Two ethical issues arise out of the Nike out of court settlement:

Whether either party ought to have had an ethical obligation to pursue litigation so as to establish a precedent in an area that lacks legal clarity and has the potential to hold back progress in the wider corporate responsibility agenda.

Whether, in precedent-setting litigation with wide public policy implications where the expression of public values through the law is incomplete and unclear, a higher ethical standard should apply, so that a 'private attorney general' should have an obligation to engage in some form of consultation or engagement on the potential impact and implications of an out of court settlement. It seems that there is no publicly available information on how the settlement was arrived at, nor who was involved. Indeed, the parties may well have been bound by the terms of the settlement not to discuss it. The result, in a private attorney general action, is the perverse one that, to use Fiss's words, "when parties settle, society gets less than what appears, and for a price it does not know it is paying."[123]

C. Thor Chemicals

A final example of the interface between professional ethics, negotiated settlements and corporate social responsibility raises the following question: Can legal ethics be expected to provide a stop-gap in those circumstances where failures in statutory drafting open the space for out of court settlements that take effect at the expense of unrepresented third party interests?

In the *Thor Chemicals* case, two separate actions were brought by workers at the site of the South African facility of this small English multinational corporation.[124] The site carried on mercury-related operations, which were said to have resulted in the deaths or injuries of a number of workers there. There was evidence to suggest that the company had intensified its mercury-related operations in South Africa shortly after its mercury-related processes in England had attracted criticism from the English health and safety regulator, the Health and Safety Executive. Workers at the parent company's plant in Margate had been found to have unacceptably high levels of mercury in their urine. Two separate legal actions brought in England by workers at the South African subsidiary were eventually settled out of court for a total of £1.3 million.

A third action was brought in England in February 1998 against the parent company, Thor Chemicals Holdings (TCH), by a further group of twenty-one workers at the South African site. Again, a *forum non con-*

"it's impossible for us to hypothesize in such general terms as to whether or not we'd embrace the current legislative proposals, however vague they might be, without having given them further scrutiny." *Id.*

123. Fiss, *supra* n. 116, at 1085.

124. *See generally* Ward, *supra* n. 89, at 113-122.

veniens argument was rejected.[125] By now, the Thor Chemicals Group had completed a demerger, the effect of which was that by March 1997 all but three subsidiaries of TCH had been transferred to a new parent company. TCH was left with just three companies, of which only the South African subsidiary was still trading. As a result of the 1997 demerger, "TCH was deliberately isolated from the resources of the majority of companies within the group to the tune of a sum in excess of £20,000,000."[126]

The Insolvency Act 1986[127] makes provision for challenges by victims of transactions at an undervalue.[128] In such circumstances, the court may make "such order as it sees fit" for protecting the interests of persons who are victims of the transaction if the court is satisfied that it was entered into by him for the purposes of putting assets beyond the reach of a person who is making, or may at some time make, a claim against him, or otherwise prejudicing the interest of such a person in relation to the claim which he is making or may make. Section 424(2) expressly provides that an application brought by a victim is to be treated as if it were made on behalf of every victim of the transaction. However, neither section specifies how this critically important provision is to be reflected in the responsibilities of claimants—who may in some cases be funded by public monies to bring their claim.

In September 2000, on an interlocutory application under Section 423 of the Insolvency Act 1986, the English Court of Appeal took the view that the demerger may well have been motivated by a desire to put the group's assets beyond the reach of future claimants after the first two actions had settled.[129] The Court of Appeal ordered Thor Chemical Holdings to disclose documents relating to the restructuring and to pay £400,000 into court—effectively a payment on account of a possible future damages award—if it wanted to continue to defend the action.[130] In October, this third action settled out of court for a total sum of £240,000.[131]

Though the claimants in this case were able to create pressure for an out of court settlement by casting doubt on the motives for the group's demerger, South African officials seeking to deal with the remaining mercury wastes were forced to work with its legacy. The Court of Appeal case resulted in orders to disclose documents and for Thor Chemical Holdings to make a payment into court. The court's order itself did not reveal any arguments designed to identify the potential class of victims, nor any effort to

---

125. This argument had already been rejected in the earlier two cases.

126. *Sithole & Others v. Thor Chems.* [2000] C.L.Y. 316 (Q.B.).

127. Insolvency Act, 1986, c. 45 (Eng.).

128. Defined as "a person who is, or is capable of being, prejudiced by" a relevant transaction. *Id.*

129. *Sithole* [2000] C.L.Y. 316.

130. Greg Dropkin, *UK Judges Block Thor Chemicals Manoeuvre*, http://www.labournet.net/world/0010/thor1.html (Feb. 10, 2000).

131. *See generally* Ward, *supra* n. 89, at 105-43.

take account of the interests of victims other than those who appeared before it. There are still several tons of mercury-containing wastes at the South African site. Environmental legislation in South Africa allows public authorities to oversee a clean-up of the site and then claim back the cost; but the South African government faces the prospect of being unable to recover its costs since the South African subsidiary has very limited assets.

Neither the South African subsidiary nor its parent company—itself renamed Guernica Holdings—have shown inclination to accept responsibility for paying the full costs of remediating the site.[132] At worst, the South African government would themselves need to bring a separate legal action in England. Quite apart from considerations of time limits for bringing such a claim, efforts to trace monies from the demerger would likely, some seven years on, face considerable obstacles. The problem is this: neither the judges in the Court of Appeal case nor the legal representatives of the parties to the action were required to adduce evidence of other potential claimants—even though it was arguably clear at the time to the Court of Appeal that the South African government was a potential claimant. What was perhaps ethically right for the legal advisers in the context of interlocutory proceedings, funded in part by public monies contributed to frustrating the possibility of a remedy for an unrepresented potential victim—the South African government. The out of court settlement exacerbated the effect of this initial gap.

One immediate argument might be that the claimants should have an ethical duty to refrain from settling out of court—or perhaps notifying the remaining class of victims of the potential claim so that they could seek to revive the proceedings. In this case, the basis for a duty to do just this can be found in the relevant legislation itself. The solicitor's duty as an officer of the Supreme Court could be argued to extend to a duty not to frustrate the public interest behind the legislation—to ensure that the class of victims have a remedy—by settling out of court at a point when a potential remedy has clearly become available. However, this formulation of the specific circumstances of the *Thor* case is clearly open to argument since it is not clear that a claim—let alone a claim in England—by the South African government would have fallen within the definition of "a person who . . . may at some time make[,] a claim" when the facts were viewed at the time of the demerger.[133]

As John Murray, Alan Scott Rau, and Edward Sherman eloquently ask, "[t]he structure of dispute resolution processes in society should provide

---

132. In August 2004, however, a contribution towards the costs of the clean-up was announced.

133. Insolvency Act, 1986, c. 45 (Eng.).

adequate protection for the public interest. But given the role of private negotiation, does it?"[134]

XV. CORPORATE SOCIAL RESPONSIBILITY AND THE LEGAL PROFESSION: RESPONSES TO DATE AND OUTSTANDING CHALLENGES

The examples of intersections between corporate social responsibility and legal ethics that have been given in this paper raise three central ethical dilemmas again and again. The first concerns the age-old dilemma of the proper balance to be drawn between lawyers' duties to their clients—to act in their clients' best interests—and their duty to serve the interests of society at large. The second concerns the question of the extent to which generally held ethical principles, or the ethic of collegiality among lawyers, indicate a principle of 'voluntary restraint,' so that lawyers should refrain from bringing legal actions that are likely to frustrate efforts elsewhere within the legal profession to drive forward progressive developments in law. The third, itself a subset of the first dilemma, concerns commercial lawyers more specifically: To what extent do commercial lawyers have an ethical or a professional duty to consider the broad societal context in which their clients operate? To what extent is it a lawyer's ethical, if not professional, duty to give advice that maximises the potential for corporate social responsibility strategies and management practices to be sustained?

With few exceptions, the legal profession has not been quick to recognise that there are circumstances in which an understanding of the corporate social responsibility agenda generates powerful calls for commercial lawyers *not* to act, or to act in *different ways* in some of the areas that have long been established as falling within their direct sphere of activity.

---

134. John S. Murray et al., *Processes of Dispute Resolution: The Role of Lawyers* 212 (Foundation Press 1989). They argue that under current codes of ethics, the lawyer has a duty to provide all relevant information to the client, especially information on 'the public interest.' But the client has the final decision. In the *Thor* cases, the clear solution (to continue with the section 423 claim to a conclusion) is balanced by the duty to the Legal Aid Board (which was funding the claimant's case) and the duty to clients who were pursuing a remedy that appeared the best chance to obtain meaningful compensation and who could not necessarily be expected to weigh 'the public interest' above their own emotional and financial needs to secure speedy redress. The question then is the extent to which a 'public interest' based duty in these circumstances should be given priority—particularly the risk thereby simply of creating a route for underscoring the financial interests of lawyers on all sides in prolonging the case. *Cf.* Stephen B. Goldberg et al., *Dispute Resolution: Negotiation, Mediation, and Other Processes* (2d ed., Little, Brown & Co. 1992) (for the balance that has been struck for mediators in the Colorado Council of Mediation Organizations Code of Professional Conduct [1982], paragraph 5 of which argues that "the mediation process, may include a responsibility of the mediator to assert the interest of the public or other unrepresented parties in order that a particular dispute be settled, that costs or damages be alleviated, and that normal life be resumed. Mediators should question agreements that are not in the interests of the public or other unrepresented parties whose interests and needs should be and are not being considered. Mediators should question whether other parties' interests or the parties themselves should be present at negotiations. It is understood, however, that the mediator does not regulate or control any of the content of a negotiated agreement.").

The report of the American Bar Assocation's Task Force on Corporate Responsibility[135] sets out a concept of the corporate lawyer as a promoter of corporate compliance with law. In their words, "[t]he competition to acquire and keep client business, or the desire to advance within the corporate executive structure, may induce lawyers to seek to please the corporate officials with whom they deal rather than to focus on the long-term interest of their client, the corporation."[136] Yet, though the Task Force argues that lawyers who provide legal advice to corporate clients most effectively "fulfill that duty of independent professional judgment by gaining a thorough understanding of the client's objectives, so that they can most readily identify means to achieve those objectives that comply with applicable law,"[137] they do not seize the opportunity offered by their terms of reference to go further and comment on the potential role of lawyers in promoting the highest possible standards in relation to the company's responsibilities to society at large through the corporate social responsibility agenda. To the extent that lawyers are simply facilitators or 'enablers,' "trained to use rules as a means to facilitate an end,"[138] they do not have direct professional responsibilities for setting the goals of societal aspirations. They are backroom players.

Discussion on CSR and the legal profession in Europe scarcely goes further. In a guide on CSR and the legal profession aimed at European business lawyers,[139] the Council of the Bars and Law Societies of the European Union (CCBE) CSR Discussion Group points to an emerging body of legislation and litigation related to the corporate responsibility agenda. It argues that:

> Responsibility for advising on CSR issues has not always been seen as falling to the legal profession. The CCBE believes that this should change. Law is the codification of basic human values. The goal of CSR is to implement these values in corporations, thus CSR develops and functions in a legal framework. There is no other professional who both has such ready access to EU boardrooms, and enjoys legal privilege. As a result, advising on CSR issues should become an everyday matter for corporate lawyers.[140]

---

135. ABA, *Report of the American Bar Association Task Force on Corporate Responsibility* (ABA 2003), available at http://www.ccbe.org/doc/En/guidelines_csr_en.pdf.

136. *Id.* at 14-15.

137. *Id.* at 24.

138. Amanda Perry, *Lawyers in Urban Development: Providing a Means to an End?*, http://elj.warwick.ac.uk/global/issue/2001-2/perry.html (accessed Nov. 8, 2004).

139. CCBE (CSR Discussion Group), *Corporate Social Responsibility and the Role of the Legal Profession: A Guide for European Lawyers Advising on Corporate Social Responsibility Issues* (Sept. 2003), available at http://www.ccbe.org/doc/En/guidelines_csr_en.pdf [hereinafter *CCBE Guide*].

140. *CCBE Guide*, *supra* n. 139, at 8.

The Guide's starting points are a) that the role that lawyers play in applying law—which it says represents a codification of basic human values—equips them well to the task of advising on CSR issues; b) that there may be strong reasons to keep such advice private; and c) that the business lawyer's access to boardrooms is itself a strong reason for lawyers to advise on CSR issues. This third argument depends for its impact and potential contribution critically on the model of corporate social responsibility that is reflected through that access. The second argument—essentially that legal privilege is a distinctive selling point for lawyers to advise on CSR—runs the risk of perpetuating, rather than resolving, the tension between the corporate social responsibility agenda's emphasis on transparency and openness and the inclination of many business lawyers to celebrate confidentiality. And the first argument is also open to question. In fast-moving agendas such as CSR, it is reasonable to suggest that human values are often expressed and evolve more quickly than law is able to catch up. In any event, the role of business lawyers is frequently held to be the essentially passive one of *applying* values already expressed in law—rather than playing a key role in ensuring that emerging values are supported by the application of law. The Guide lends credence to the notion that the *practice* of law has no impact on ability to realise the values that are reflected in *laws*. Furthermore, much of the most heated discussion within the CSR agenda concerns the content of 'CSR values systems.' The agenda is far from having achieved consensus.[141]

The CCBE Guide adds a note of fear. It reminds business lawyers that, when acting as members of, or secretaries to, boards of directors, they need to recognise that negligence may well result in losses of a considerable size for the involved company.[142]

Worryingly, the CCBE Guide does not incorporate any reflection on the potential implications of the corporate social responsibility agenda for legal practice in those areas where tensions may arise. And it includes no reference to any ethical dilemmas that may become apparent when seeking to insert CSR considerations into the practice of law—or vice versa. The Guide assumes that today's professional conduct tools remain adequate for the new and wide-ranging business opportunities that it sketches out. In other words, it does little to ensure that the contribution of the profession to the progressive development of the CSR agenda is a positive one.

Clearly, given the nature of the challenges to professional conduct and ethics that have been outlined in this paper, much remains to be addressed and analysed if the positive contribution of the legal profession to CSR is to be maximised. For example, there is as yet no data on the extent to which

---

141. For example, there is no consensus on the value of differential protection or support for small enterprise or the informal sector in low-income countries.

142. *CCBE Guide, supra* n. 139, at 8.

the kinds of CSR issues outlined in this paper are being picked up by law firms *and* passed on to business clients. Assuming that integration of CSR into legal practice is not yet happening in any systematic way, why not? And if things are to change in this respect, where will the decisive drive come from—the arena of public opinion, pressure groups, government law/regulation, or from clients themselves?

The inside front cover of the December 2002/January 2003 issue of the *European Lawyer* magazine included a full page advertisement by the international commercial law firm Eversheds. Headed, "Ethical Lawyers for an Unpredictable World," the text ran:

> The relationship you have with your lawyers is based on trust. But could you trust lawyers who are willing to:
> offer advice that's based on what you want to hear rather than what you should be hearing?
>
> We think the answer is no. That's why Eversheds is guided by strict ethical guidelines. We won't work for inappropriate clients. We have the ability to say 'no' when necessary. And we provide objectivity in all the advice we give. You can trust Eversheds.[143]

Could Eversheds' advert offer an indication of a way forward? For a community of in-house lawyers, public interest lawyers, and business lawyers to begin to map out a voluntary code of ethics that makes a clear statement that "these are the kinds of lawyers that we are; here is how we view our role in relation to the CSR agenda; here is how we will strive to fulfil it in the context of the advice that we offer. You might not always agree with us, but this is what we'll try to do." Minneapolis is the home both of the Minnesota Principles[144] and a faith-based law school. Might this be a good place to start?

---

143. Eversheds, *Ethical Lawyers for an Unpredictable World*, The European Law, inside cover (Dec. 2002/Jan. 2003) (advertisement).

144. Center for Ethical Business Cultures, *The Minnesota Principles: Toward an Ethical Basis for Global Business*, http://www.cebcglobal.org/Publications/Principles/MN_PR125IN.htm (accessed Oct. 17, 2004).

Name Index